W9-CEY-654

C. Merle Johnson, PhD
William K. Redmon, PhD
Thomas C. Mawhinney, PhD
Editors

Handbook
of Organizational Performance
Behavior Analysis
and Management

Pre-publication
REVIEWS,
COMMENTARIES,
EVALUATIONS . . .

"The *Handbook of Organizational Performance: Behavior Analysis and Management* provides a solid foundation upon which academics, scholars, and practitioners can build. Of particular importance to behavior analysis is the inclusion of chapters on basic operant learning principles in the context of a book on organizational performance. Chapters acknowledging industrial/organizational psychology movements outside behavior analysis, and how behavioral science can be reconciled with and complement these movements, outline ingredients essential for an integrated theory of organizational behavior management. If it is our mission to increase the acceptability of behavior analysis in the general population, the chapters in this book provide a nice starting point. The field of organizational behavior management has long needed such a compilation of writings."

Thomas E. Boyce, PhD
Assistant Professor,
Department of Psychology,
University of Nevada,
Reno

More pre-publication
REVIEWS, COMMENTARIES, EVALUATIONS . . .

"**U**pon receipt of the review copy of this handbook, I immediately revised the reading list of my graduate-level organizational behavior management (OBM) course to include most of the chapters presented. This handbook will be required reading for my students for many years to come. And it should be required reading for any OBM professional.

The chapters presented in this handbook advance the science and practice of OBM substantially, with clear connections to basic research, theoretical issues, and organizational applications written by the top researchers and practitioners in our field.

The crossover of OBM models to traditional industrial organizational psychology issues is apparent in this handbook."

Timothy D. Ludwig, PhD
Director, Industrial/Organizational Graduate Program;
Associate Professor,
Department of Psychology,
Appalachian State University,
Boone, North Carolina

"**A** wonderful cornucopia of knowledge demonstrating the contribution of applied behavior analysis to organizations and businesses. The powerful behaviorally oriented procedures and in-depth illustrations will help the neophyte as well as the seasoned professional to broaden and deepen their knowledge of the field.

The contributing authors provide detailed information that can help individuals and organizations achieve higher levels of effectiveness. The *Handbook of Organizational Performance* is a must-read for students, teachers, and practitioners involved in behavior analysis and management. Business, governmental, and not-for-profit organizations will benefit from the research and teachings in this handbook."

Paul L. Brown, PhD
Adjunct Professor of Psychology,
State University of New York
at New Paltz

"**T**he *Handbook of Organizational Performance* is a very welcome addition to the field of performance management, and long overdue. It is the definitive consolidated sourcebook for both the science and practice of performance management.

The handbook is divided into three main parts: Foundations, Applications, and Professional and Theoretical Issues. The chapters included in the Foundations section provide a sophisticated treatment of the cohesive principles that underlie the *science* of management. In addition, the chapters in this section present the tools for the objective assessment and evaluation of management inverventions—tools that enable organizations to continually improve their management practices and hence, their market status.

The applications section reflects the competitive edge that science-based practice offers organizations. The chapters represent a cogent blend of research and practice, supplemented by reviews of the demonstrated effectiveness of a behavior analytic approach to specific areas such as training, safety, sales, and leadership. In short, the chapters present practical solutions to practical problems.

Part III, Professional and Theoretical Issues, consists of a diverse mix of articles that address marketing, ethics, theoretical extensions, organizational development, and organizational culture.

The editors have achieved their stated purpose: the readings are indeed 'interesting, provocative, and useful.' This book is an important resource for anyone who is serious about organizational performance."

Alyce M. Dickinson, PhD
*Professor and Director,
Industrial-Organizational
Psychology Program,
Western Michigan University,
Kalamazoo*

The Haworth Press, Inc.

Handbook
of Organizational Performance
Behavior Analysis and Management

THE HAWORTH PRESS
Organizational Behavior Analysis and Management

Thomas C. Mawhinney
Senior Editor

Handbook of Organizational Performance: Behavior Analysis and Management edited by C. Merle Johnson, William K. Redmon, and Thomas C. Mawhinney

Handbook
of Organizational Performance
Behavior Analysis
and Management

C. Merle Johnson, PhD
William K. Redmon, PhD
Thomas C. Mawhinney, PhD
Editors

The Haworth Press®
New York • London • Oxford

The Haworth Press, Inc., 10 Alice Street, Binghamton, NY 13904-1580

Library of Congress Cataloging-in-Publication Data

Handbook of organizational performance : behavior analysis and management / C. Merle Johnson, William K. Redmon, Thomas C. Mawhinney, editors.
    p.   cm.
    Includes bibliographical references and index.
    ISBN 0-7890-1086-0 (hard : alk. paper)—ISBN 0-7890-1087-9 (soft : alk. paper)
    1. Organizational behavior. 2. Personnel management. I. Johnson, C. Merle. II. Redmon, William K. III. Mawhinney, Thomas C.

HD58.7.H364 2000
658.3—dc21   00-040768

CONTENTS

ABOUT THE EDITORS

C. Merle Johnson, PhD, is Professor of Psychology at Central Michigan University. Carl teaches courses in organizational behavior management, behavioral medicine, behavior therapy, and learning. He is a member of the Association for Behavior Analysis (ABA), Society for Developmental and Behavioral Pediatrics, Organizational Behavior Management Network of ABA, and the Behavior Analysis Association of Michigan. He has served as both co-editor (1982-1984) and associate editor (1980-1982, 1985-1990) for the *Family Practice Research Journal* and associate editor (1983-1986) for *Education and Treatment of Children.* His published articles appear in *Pediatrics, Journal of Developmental and Behavioral Pediatrics, Family Practice Research Journal, Journal of Organizational Behavior Management, Academy of Management Review, Behavioral Assessment,* and *The Psychological Record.*

William K. Redmon, PhD, is Vice President of Knowledge and Practice Areas for the Continuous Learning Group, Inc., a behavioral consulting firm that serves Fortune 500 companies worldwide. Bill has consulted with numerous organizations in the private and public sectors to help refine their strategic directions and develop supporting performance systems. He has worked with companies in telecommunications, engineering and construction, petroleum and chemicals, and other industries to design and implement large-scale behavior change and leadership programs to impact bottom-line business results. Prior to joining CLG, Bill was Professor of Industrial/Organizational Psychology and designed and taught graduate courses in behavioral systems analysis, organizational change, metrics, and strategic planning. Bill is a Fellow of the American Psychological Association (Division 25) and a long-standing member of the American Psychological Association, Association for Behavior Analysis (ABA), and the Organizational Behavior Management Network of ABA. He served as associate editor of the *Journal of*

Organizational Behavior Management from 1986 to 1993. His published works have appeared in the *Journal of Organizational Behavior Management, Journal of Applied Behavior Analysis*, and as chapters in numerous edited books.

Thomas C. Mawhinney, PhD, is Professor of Organizational Behavior and Management in the College of Business Administration at the University of Detroit Mercy. He is co-editor of the *Journal of Organizational Behavior Management* (having served as editor from 1985 to 1998), Fellow of the American Psychological Association (Division 25), and a long-standing member of the Academy of Management, the American Psychological Association, the Association for Behavior Analysis (ABA), Decision Sciences Institute, the Florida Association for Behavior Analysis, the Organizational Behavior Management Network of ABA, the Society for Human Resource Management, and the American Compensation Association (Worldatwork). His empirical and theoretical works concerning behavior analysis applied in work organizations and relations between behavior analysis and other fields have been published in *Academy of Management Review, Journal of Applied Behavior Analysis, Journal of Applied Psychology, Journal of the Experimental Analysis of Behavior, Journal of Management, Journal of Organizational Behavior Management, Organizational Behavior and Human Decision Processes* (formerly *OB&HP*), *Performance Improvement Quarterly,* and *Psychological Reports.*

Note: As editors, we are donating all royalties from the book to the Organizational Behavior Management Network, a special interest group of the Association for Behavior Analysis, International (ABA). This will be used to promote student research or other learning activities that the OBMNetwork sanctions.

CONTRIBUTORS

Terry A. Beehr, PhD, is Professor of the PhD Program in Industrial/Organizational Psychology at Central Michigan University, Mount Pleasant, Michigan.

Howard C. Berthold Jr., PhD, is Chair of the Psychology Department at Lycoming College, Williamsport, Pennsylvania.

Diane Braatz, PhD, is a consultant for Training Strategies Incorporated, Kalamazoo, Michigan.

Leslie Wilk Braksick, PhD, is the Co-Founder, President, and Chief Executive Office for the Continuous Learning Group, Inc., headquartered in Pittsburgh, Pennsylvania (www.clg-online.com).

William W. Casey, PhD, is President of Executive Leadership Group, Inc., Elizabeth, Colorado (www.ExecutiveLeadershipGroup.com).

Phillip K. Duncan, PhD, is Professor of Psychology and Assistant Department Chair at West Chester University, West Chester, Pennsylvania.

James L. Eubanks, PhD, is Professor of Psychology at Central Washington University, Ellensburg, Washington.

Paul Fadil is Associate Professor of Management, Valdosta State University, Valdosta, Georgia.

E. Scott Geller, PhD, is Senior Partner at Safety Performance Solutions, Inc., Blacksburg, Virginia and Professor of Psychology at Virginia Polytechnic Institute and State University, Blacksburg, Virginia.

Papia Ghosh, MA, is a student in Computer Science at Central Michigan University, Mount Pleasant, Michigan.

Sonia M. Goltz, PhD, is Associate Professor of Organizational Behavior at the School of Business and Economics, Michigan Technological University, Houghton, Michigan.

Donald A. Hantula, PhD, is Associate Professor and Director of the graduate division of Social and Organizational Psychology, Temple University, Philadelphia, Pennsylvania.

Todd C. Harris, PhD, is a graduate of Organizational Psychology from the University of Connecticut and is a management consultant at the

Continuous Learning Group, Inc., Coraopolis, Pennsylvania (www.clg-online.com).

Steve M. Jex, PhD, is Associate Professor and Director of Graduate Training in Industrial/Organizational Psychology at the University of Wisconsin Oshkosh, Oshkosh, Wisconsin.

Judith L. Komaki, PhD, is Professor of Psychology at Baruch College, The City University of New York, New York.

Fred Luthans, PhD, is George Holmes Professor of Management in the College of Business Administration, University of Nebraska-Lincoln, Lincoln, Nebraska.

Mark J. Martinko, PhD, is President of Performance Associates and Professor of Management, College of Business Administration, Florida State University, Tallahassee, Florida.

Matthew A. Mason, PhD, is a licensed clinical psychologist and Director of Research and Quality at Pressley Ridge Schools, Pittsburgh, Pennsylvania.

Kathleen Blake McCann, PhD, is Assistant Vice President of Risk Services in Human Resources Development at Liberty Mutual Insurance Group, Boston, Massachusetts.

Michelle Reynard Minnich is Training and Performance Consultant, Lucent Technologies, Allentown, Pennsylvania.

Richard Perlow, PhD, was Associate Professor of Psychology, Clemson University, Clemson, South Carolina when writing his chapter. He is now in the Department of Business Administration, I. H. Asper School of Business, University of Manitoba, Winnipeg, Manitoba.

Alan Poling, PhD, is Professor of Psychology at Western Michigan University, Kalamazoo, Michigan.

Julie M. Smith, PhD, is the Co-Founder and Vice President of the Continuous Learning Group, Inc., headquartered in Pittsburgh, Pennsylvania (www.clg-online.com).

Dee Tinley Smoot, PhD, is Senior Behavioral Safety Consultant at Aubrey Daniels & Associates, International, Atlanta, Georgia and Adjunct Professor at West Chester University, West Chester, Pennsylvania.

Beth Sulzer-Azaroff, PhD, is Principal of The Browns Group, Inc. and Professor Emeritus at the University of Massachusetts, Amherst, Massachusetts.

Robert Waldersee, PhD, is Professor and Director of the Center for Organizational Change, Queensland University of Technology, Australia.

Foreword

The formal use of behavior analysis in business goes back only about thirty-five years. I was fortunate to have been one of the first to make extensive use of this technology in business.

My first application was with the staff of a mental retardation unit. The focus was on training severely retarded, multihandicapped, nonambulatory, bedfast patients. The performance management program was simple. S&H Green Stamps gave us 50,000 stamps; we set up a token system and awarded stamps to staff based on the acquisition of self-help skills by the residents. The program was extremely successful. Twenty-one of twenty-six residents, previously thought to be untrainable, made significant progress in caring for themselves. Backed by this success, we started reinforcement systems for the staff on all the hospital units. Later I set up similar systems for a vocational rehabilitation center in Atlanta and a facility in North Carolina.

In 1967, I created my first pure business application when a friend asked for help with pharmaceutical salespeople; my second with jewelry sales reps. These experiences led me to leave clinical work and to form a company specializing in behavior analysis in business and industry.

My first major business project, in 1970, involved a textile company in South Carolina. My associates and I trained 600 supervisors in the basics of applied behavior analysis. Absenteeism and turnover were the targets. This project was so successful that very quickly we had similar projects with all the major textile firms in the southern United States.

In those days, interventions were simplistic. The training we delivered relied heavily on our experience in hospital and mental retardation settings. Even though we had no business experience and no business training, the power of the technology was such that we generated amazing results. Thirty-day personnel turnover was routinely cut in half within ninety days of the intervention. Productivity and quality were often improved by 20 percent or more in a matter of weeks.

These first consulting interventions consisted of twenty hours of training and then follow-up with supervisors on the mill floor for up to six months. Upper management was usually only informed about what was being done and what was being accomplished. At most, they received an executive briefing of a couple of hours.

Most of our applications involved feedback on some result and tangible and social rewards for improvement. Coffee and doughnuts were standard fare for celebrations.

In the early 1970s, it was an unusual executive who was able to see the bottom-line advantages of this "positive management." Roger Milliken, chairman and president of Milliken and Co., was such an executive. When he first heard about behavior management, as I called it then, and saw the results in the first plant to use it, he said he wanted it in his entire operation—all sixty-five plants. Not all of his managers were as far-seeing as he was.

He sent me to talk to the general manager of his carpet division to plan the start of a behavior management program. I knew before the meeting that he was not happy to have a "psychologist" come and meddle in his business. He made me wait for over an hour and a half. When he finally came into the conference room, he plopped down at the end of the table, pointed his finger in my direction, and said in a gruff voice, "Can you help me make carpet?" I responded rather timidly, "Yes, sir." But he didn't believe me. Not for a minute. In his mind, the only thing he could expect from some "positive motivation" training program, in which supervisors and managers would go around smiling and waving and patting people on the back, was the ruination of the business.

This was not an uncommon attitude in the late 1960s and early 1970s. Business was good. There was more demand than supply and customers were willing to accept almost any level of quality in order to keep their factories running. "Get it out at all costs" was the credo in business. The costs of inefficiency and poor quality were simply passed on to the customer. The impact of human behavior on the business was not considered an important part of the success equation. People were often viewed as a necessary problem, on a par with environmental problems and other governmental rules and regulations. They were something you had to deal with, not something of central importance.

Times changed overnight. The economy slowed. Competition intensified. Customers now would accept only quality goods and services. Enter Deming.

In my opinion, W. Edwards Deming has done more to establish the field of behavior analysis as a force in management than any other person in business to date. He focused managers on data and the necessity of controlling the variance in business processes. Although Deming did not seem to understand the role of behavior in maintaining processes within control limits and in reducing variance in the process, his system will inevitably require an understanding and control of the variance caused by the behavior of the employees operating within the business system. In the final analysis, the methodology will lead management to see behavior as the only way to control and narrow variance in any business process.

You will notice in this book that several names are given to the application of behavior analysis in business—organizational behavior management (OBM), performance management, and behavior analysis. In my clinical work I used the then-popular term, behavior modification, to describe my work there. About the time I started to work in industry, however, a popular movie was released, *A Clockwork Orange.* In the movie, aversive techniques were used to control behavior. The techniques were referred to as "behavior modification." There were other occasions in the popular press when the term was used in a negative context.

Since the term had negative connotations, I decided to call the business applications of behavior analysis "behavior management," and I named the first company Behavioral Systems, Inc. While I thought this was a great name, I soon discovered that customers did not understand that behavior, as they used the word, had any place in business. I often heard, "Our people behave all right; they just don't want to work."

Therefore, in 1978 I changed the term to performance management because I thought that even if managers did not understand what it was, they might think they should find out about it. In fact, the name has done that. Today when you see those terms, they all relate to the same behavior analysis technology and research base.

Today, the word "behavior" is appearing more and more in training and management literature. Although this is recognition at some level that things change in business only when people change what they do, careful examination of most of this literature shows an imprecise understanding of what behavior really is and little or no understanding of how to change it.

Early applications of behavior analysis in industry were used to solve problems such as absenteeism, turnover, and morale. Today's applications are beginning to focus more on the systemwide use of the technology. Business is now asking people to behave in ways that contribute to the business; to ask them to be innovative, to take responsibility for the quality of their own work, and to manage themselves as members of a team. I have begun to use the phrase "enabling technology" to describe what behavior analysis can do for an organization trying to incorporate the management of behavior into their overall improvement efforts. That is, it is a way to make all of an organization's systems and programs work and produce better results.

This book gives you a broad-based understanding of behavior analysis, its foundations, and its applications to business problems over a wide range of corporate activities. Some important professional and theoretical issues are also raised as they relate to the broad-scale use of the technology.

I have made the prediction that the executive that does not know this technology will not survive and, more important, will put his or her company at financial risk. Needless to say, I think it is imperative for every manager and executive to know and apply this technology in their business. If they do I am convinced that not only will their business thrive and be a better place to work, but that the world will be a better place to live.

Aubrey C. Daniels, PhD
Chairman and CEO
Aubrey Daniels & Associates, Inc.
Tucker, Georgia

Acknowledgments

This volume developed as a replacement for two trailblazing edited books, *Industrial Behavior Modification* by O'Brien, Dickinson, and Rosow (Wiley, 1982), and *Handbook of Organizational Behavior Management* by Frederiksen (Pergamon, 1982). Unfortunately, both of these texts are now out of print. As the twenty-first century begins, the authors in this volume have updated the research and practice of performance management to reflect how organizational behavior management principles and applications may be used in the next millennium. We hope you find the readings interesting, provocative, and useful for your own work.

We would like to thank a number of people who made this text possible. Rich O'Brien, Alyce Dickinson, and Lee Frederiksen were inspirations, and we used their excellent texts as models for developing this volume. Mary Grace Luke was instrumental in starting the project. Beth Sulzer-Azaroff was terrific in keeping the project on track and was very supportive in developing the study guide and objectives that accompany this book. Bill Palmer of The Haworth Press supported both the text and the series that has been spawned with this volume.

This project took a long time to complete. Thus, a quote from Jonas Salk, inventor of the polio vaccine, seems appropriate. "There are no failures, just some people who quit too soon." We never gave up on completing this project and hope you find this volume worth the efforts it took to finish it.

The contributors to this book deserve most of the credit for its content, and as editors, we owe them a great deal. All of them worked hard and some waited a long time for their manuscripts to be published as chapters while others added work late in the game under great time pressure. We wish to express our gratitude for their efforts.

Finally, we are dedicated to the dissemination of behavior analysis and management to professionals, researchers, and especially students. Therefore, as editors we have elected to donate all royalties to the Organizational Behavior Management Network of the Association for Behavior Analysis to be used for student research or other projects that the OBMNetwork deems appropriate.

PART I:
FOUNDATIONS

Chapter 1

Introduction to Organizational Performance: Behavior Analysis and Management

C. Merle Johnson
Thomas C. Mawhinney
William K. Redmon

Behaviorism is a philosophy of science that rests on the assumption that a science of behavior is possible. Whether any one of the various psychologies that currently exist should be called the "scientific psychology" or the "science of behavior" is the subject of an ongoing debate. "For better or worse, the science of behavior [in the opinion of behaviorists] has come to be called *behavior analysis* [emphasis in the original]" (Baum, 1994, p. 3). The *Journal of the Experimental Analysis of Behavior* was founded in 1958 and its objective is publishing basic research in the behavior analytic tradition. In 1968 the *Journal of Applied Behavior Analysis* was founded with the objective of publishing research that focuses on applications of basic principles of behavior analysis to solve problems in ways that improve human society. And in 1977, the *Journal of Organizational Behavior Management* was founded, and its objective is extending the application of the principles of behavior analysis to improve individual, group, and organizational productivity and safety and the quality of work life among all organizational members. The evolution of behavior analysis in terms of its major contributors, organizations, and publications from 1870 to the mid-1980s is graphically depicted in *Concepts and Principles of Behavior Analysis* (Michael, 1993, p. 21). In this rendition of the history of behavior analysis, the community of researchers, scholars, and practitioners involved with publication of the *Journal of Organizational Behavior Management* are depicted as members of the behavior analytic community.

Links between early behavior analysts (i.e., B. F. Skinner) and traditional management movements (e.g., the human relations school) are graphically depicted from about 1900 to the mid-1980s in *Organizational Behavior Modification and Beyond* (Luthans and Kreitner, 1985, p. 37). This rendition of the history of organizational behavior modification (O.B. Mod.) differs from the history of behavior analysis in two important ways. First, it explicitly admits to being influenced by the works of Lewin and Tolman, in addition to Skinner, and most recently by the works of Bandura, who is depicted as the most proximate source of influence on O.B. Mod. Second, it recognizes the line of influences on O.B. Mod. from the following movements, listed from temporally most distant to most recent: scientific management, Hawthorne studies, human relations movement, McGregor's Theory X and Y, and organizational behavior. In addition, by recognizing the influences of Lewin and Tolman and what is called "cognitive behaviorism," O.B. Mod. is de facto linked with industrial/organizational (I/O) psychology. As might be expected, given these somewhat differing renderings of historical foundations that underpin organizational behavior management (OBM), exactly what OBM is depends in large measure on who is providing the characterization. At the same time, there is considerably more common ground among various contributors to the field than grounds that might be in dispute. This historical backdrop should help readers understand why OBM cannot be described by reference to a single source even though behavior analysis as the behaviorists' science of behavior can be recognized as the fundamental scientific discipline from which the discipline we call OBM has evolved.

Research concerning the efficacy of principles of behavior analysis applied to improve performance in business, industry, and other organizational settings has been called organizational behavior management (Prue, Frederiksen, and Bacon, 1978), organizational behavior modification (Luthans and Kreitner, 1975, 1985), industrial behavior modification (I.B. Mod.) (O'Brien, Dickinson, and Rosow, 1982), and performance management (PM) (Daniels, 1989, 2000). Aldis (1961), in his groundbreaking article, "Of Pigeons and Men," may have been the first to suggest that the principles of behavior analysis be systematically applied to manage behavior in organizations. The systematic analysis and management of work-related behavior and its relationship with environmental antecedents and consequences had already appeared in Frederick Taylor's (1911) scientific management and James Lincoln's (1951) methods of incentive management. They might, therefore, be considered precursors of organizational behavior management, although neither specifically reflects any influence on their methods arising directly from scientific behavior analyses of operant and respondent behavior.

Early work in performance management was characterized by simple applications modeled from laboratory research results in the experimental analysis of behavior and applied behavior analysis to various organizational settings (Mawhinney, 1975). Others have noted that this approach to applied organizational research is an amalgamation of the fields of organizational behavior (OB) and behavior modification (B. Mod.). This probably accounts for the use of titles such as O. B. Mod. (Luthans and Kreitner, 1975, 1985) as well as I. B. Mod. (O'Brien, Dickinson, and Rosow, 1982) as alternative ways of naming the field we now call organizational behavior management (Frederiksen, 1982). The name that is most generic and least reflective of its roots in behaviorism is performance management (Daniels, 1989, 2000). From this vantage point, O. B. Mod. and I. B. Mod. both exhibit relatively strong linkages with behavior analysis. These linkages appear in both their theoretical foundations and methods recommended for validating effects of behavior based interventions aimed at changing individual, group, and organizational performance.

As noted previously, in 1977 a major step occurred in the development of OBM. That was the year Aubrey Daniels, author of the foreword of this volume, founded the *Journal of Organizational Behavior Management (JOBM)* while employed at Behavioral Systems, Inc. in Atlanta, Georgia. The journal developed over the next decade under the editorships of Brandon Hall and Lee Frederiksen. Recently it has continued to prosper under the editorship of Tom Mawhinney and the publisher of this text, The Haworth Press, Inc.

Meanwhile, members of the organizational behavior management community expanded their sphere of influence by creating their own magazine, *Performance Management.* They also made inroads into the more established journals by publishing featured articles in the *Academy of Management Journal, Academy of Management Review, The Behavior Analyst, Journal of Applied Behavior Analysis, Journal of Applied Psychology, Organizational Behavior and Human Decision Processes,* and *Personnel Psychology.*

The field has evolved over the past twenty-five years in ways that currently make it more than the limited application of behavioral principles in the private sector and public nonprofit settings. Some of this is due to parallel developments in the experimental analysis of behavior, applied behavior analysis, behavioral economics, and verbal behavior. Other developments have occurred within the field of OBM per se.

As noted above, early work in this area was characterized by simple applications of principles of the experimental analysis of behavior in various organizational settings. More often than not, the host organizations were private for-profit businesses and industries. Systematic demonstrations of contingency management and the effects of various schedules of reinforcement in the workplace provide early examples of research in this tradition (Yukl and Latham, 1975).

Several techniques shared by management and more traditional areas in industrial/organizational psychology, such as feedback and goal setting, emerged as core themes in the OBM literature (At Emery Air Freight, 1973). Elaboration on these themes occurred as more complex contingencies evolved and the long-term efficacy of OBM procedures was demonstrated (O'Hara, Johnson, and Beehr, 1985).

As the field matured, cross-pollination with other disciplines occurred. This cross-pollination was evident when OBM began to incorporate elements of systems analysis, organization development, organizational culture, safety research, statistical process control, financial management, and marketing. Marketing, as it relates to OBM, is a particularly interesting area. This is due to the history of one of the first behaviorists, J. B. Watson (Skinner, 1959). After leaving Johns Hopkins University in 1920, Watson worked in an advertising agency in New York. He assured the success of his second career on Madison Avenue by utilizing the newly discovered Pavlovian classical conditioning procedures to increase sales of consumer goods, such as Maxwell House coffee and Johnson's Baby Powder, to American consumers (Myers, 1998; Wood and Wood, 1999).

In a process analogous to the one responsible for the formation of behavioral medicine (Schwartz and Weiss, 1978), OBM emerged as a field of study distinguishable from other applied psychological sciences in the 1970s. In 1978, a variety of books and journals were annotated in the *Journal of Organizational Behavior Management* (Prue, Frederiksen, and Bacon, 1978). For better or worse, reviews of the field published in *JOBM* in more recent times have focused exclusively on the contents of *JOBM* (Balcazar et al., 1989; Nolan, Jarema, and Austin, 1999). But the sort of narrowing of the field's focus implied by reviews focused exclusively on *JOBM* is to be expected.

The diversity of topics addressed from a behavior analytic vantage point and published in *JOBM* has, if anything, increased through the years. The idea that organizations are processing systems with feedback loops from customers or clients back to managers in organizations first conceptualized and graphically depicted in Brethower's (1972) conception of a total performance system (TPS) has been elaborated into an ecological framework by Rummler and Brache (1995); and, de facto, both of these systems approaches to OBM have been related to behavior analytic conceptions of organizational culture (Mawhinney, 1992a; Redmon and Mason, Chapter 17, this volume). After briefly reviewing what might be called legacy concepts or themes, we shall provide brief sketches of emerging concepts and themes in the OBM literature.

RECURRING THEMES
IN OBM RESEARCH LITERATURE

Some themes are so fundamentally ubiquitous that they appear repeatedly throughout this book, whether formally developed or not. Goal setting and feedback are two such themes.

Goal Setting and Feedback

Goal setting and feedback are concepts and associated procedures so often used in the context of organizational behavior management that a discussion of their definitions probably seems passe. As a review and critical discussion of these concepts by Duncan and Bruwelheide (1986) clearly reveals, however, nothing could be further from the truth. Ford (1980) characterized feedback as a "cumbersome and disorganized aggregation of procedures and methods" (p. 183). This viewpoint was echoed by Peterson (1982), who criticized feedback as "professional slang." The OBM conceptions of both goal setting and feedback have been considerably sharpened since Ford and Peterson made their observations. Organizing this literature in a matrix that relates dimensions of feedback with behavioral functions (e.g., stimulus control and reinforcement) that Duncan and Bruwelheide (1986) introduced more than a decade ago remains useful to this day. We present their matrix after briefly reviewing evolution of goal setting and feedback concepts as they are used in OBM.

In an article aptly titled "A Behavioral Analysis of Goal Setting," Fellner and Sulzer-Azaroff (1984) present a succinct analysis of goal setting and feedback in Skinner's (1969) tradition of rule-governed behavior:

> A goal is a stimulus that precedes behavior. When the antecedent goal reliably accompanies a reinforced response it acquires "discriminative control," increasing the probability it will cue the individual to repeat the behavior. Also, attainment of a goal can function as a reinforcing stimulus. For example, if meeting the goal is paired frequently with a positive consequence or removal of a negative consequence, the goal can function as a conditioned reinforcing stimulus. (pp. 34-35)

According to this conception of goal setting and its relations to behavior, a goal statement can function as "both a discriminative stimulus, and a conditioned reinforcer" (Fellner and Sulzer-Azaroff, 1984, p. 35).

Huber (1986) extended the OBM analysis of goals by recognizing that goal setting can and often is a response (dependent variable) evoked by discriminative stimuli that occur in the form of contingency-specifying statements (CSS). CSSs can occur as independent variables, such as the introduction of pay-for-performance incentive systems. Examples of CSSs that can evoke goal setting include the following: (a) announcement of a contingency, (b) an incentive statement, (c) goal-setting statements made by others (e.g., managers and supervisors), and (d) normative information that implies contingencies between performance levels and consequences. Although it may seem obvious in hindsight, Huber makes it clear that CSSs that specify the type and amount of some consequence are more likely to be effective than those that do not. She includes an important caveat. If a goal in the form of a CSS specifies a level of task effort that is great relative to the amount of consequence to be garnered contingent on achieving the goal level specified, it is entirely possible that the goal statement will have no impact on performance.

Malott (1992) introduced a thoroughly OBM-related theory of rule-governed behavior and recognized that some rules are de facto goals or evoke goal statements. Malott adopted Skinner's (1969) definition of a rule as a verbal description of a behavioral contingency or CSS. Malott draws a distinction between two classes of contingencies that OBM researchers have pointed to when attempting to explain why interventions aimed at improving performance have and have not worked in formal organizations. One class he called the *direct-acting contingency*, which is "a contingency for which the [immediate] outcome of the response reinforces or punishes that response" (p. 46). Direct-acting contingencies are isomorphic with those used to shape behavior of participants in laboratory studies involving reinforcement contingencies. Most contingencies in work settings, according to Malott, are not of this type. Rather, they belong to the second class of contingencies he calls *indirect-acting contingencies* or *rule-governed analogs to reinforcement*. They include contingencies within which consequences that function as "real" reinforcers are delayed too long to directly function as reinforcers. However, CSSs that describe easy-to-follow rules (e.g., goals) can convert some of these indirect-acting contingencies into direct-acting contingencies in accordance with Malott's (1992) two-factor theory of rule-governed behavior. In response to the question "How do rules govern behavior?" Malott (1992) answers with the following theoretical account of a rule statement and rule following in the context of a person facing a performance deadline:

> . . . this overall analysis suggests direct-acting escape contingencies control our rule-governed behavior, even when the rule describes an indirect-acting contingency. For example, working to avoid looking bad as a consequence of failing to meet the deadline involves an indirect-acting contingency, because the outcome is delayed from the behavior of finishing the preparations; and the delay means the outcome is not part of a direct-acting avoidance contingency that would reinforce those final preparations. But all operant control may require direct-acting contingencies; so I have theorized that the most likely direct-acting contingency is an escape contingency based on the learned aversive condition resulting from stating the rule combined with noncompliance. (For an alternative analysis, see Schlinger and Blakely, 1987.) (p. 55)

Baum (1994) opens his analysis of rules and rule-governed behavior by answering the question "What is rule-governed behavior?" "To say that behavior is 'governed' by a rule is to say that it is under stimulus control by the rule and that the rule is a certain type of discriminative stimulus—a verbal discriminative stimulus" (p. 130). According to Baum (1994), "Rule-governed behavior always involves two contingencies: a long-term, *ultimate contingency*—the reason for the rule in the first place—and a short-term or *proximate contingency* of reinforcement for following the rule." Baum's proximate and ultimate contingencies refer to virtually the same environmental contingencies as do Malott's (1992) direct-acting and indirect-acting contingencies, respectively. Baum recognizes that proximate contingencies that support rule following may be temporary.

For example, a child's parent may directly instruct the child to wear shoes when going outdoors, and the parent immediately praises the child for compliance. The parent does this because he or she has set a goal of protecting the child from the consequences of the ultimate contingency for those who fail to follow the rule of wearing shoes outdoors, i.e., cuts, bruises, and perhaps disease. Once the ultimate contingency occurs, there may be no evidence of a history of learning to follow the rule. The ultimate contingency takes over, as it were. In sunny climates, for example, children may be taught to wear hats and sunscreen when outdoors and do so without being told once their behavior is under control of the ultimate contingency, sunny days. Later in life, however, those who work indoors and do not often venture outdoors may then make contact with the ultimate contingency in the form of an unexpected sunburn. Moreover, the potential delayed consequence of skin cancer becomes another indirect-acting or ultimate contingency. Note how those who have encountered such direct-acting or proximate contingencies advocate this rule for themselves and for others. Similar contingencies exist for safety behaviors such as wearing safety belts in cars or employee safety behaviors in organizational settings (Sulzer-Azaroff, McCann, and Harris, Chapter 10 and Geller, Chapter 11, this volume). Encounters with the ultimate contingency may occasion their restating rules learned from parents and the posting of reminders to help them follow those "forgotten" but still important rules.

Although these accounts of what is called rule-controlled behavior exhibit considerable face validity among behaviorists, they do not seem to handle numerous real-life instances in which a contingency-specifying statement is made at one point in time and action in conformity with the rule or goal implied by the CSS must occur after a considerable amount of elapsed time. Consider, for example, a memo delivered on Monday that announces an important meeting scheduled away from one's work site earlier than the usual work time on Wednesday. To make it to this meeting on time one must be prepared to awake earlier than usual on Wednesday, but not on Tuesday, and drive to a less familiar location and find the meeting room on time. If Malott and Baum are correct, and we believe they are, then the chain of behavior resulting in an on-time arrival at the meeting must include respectively direct-acting and proximate contingencies or reinforcement. Perhaps the person verbally restates the appointment date, time, and place periodically until it is time to prepare for the meeting. Not likely. Perhaps the person responds to the ultimate rule implied by the ultimate contingency, i.e., "Plan ahead and be on time." More likely. But, what controls making the plans, and when and how does making plans get started? The alternative analysis of rule-governed behavior by Blakely and Schlinger (1987) and Schlinger and Blakely (1987), to which Malott (1992) referred, has been interpreted by Agnew and Redmon (1992) for use in OBM contexts. And this alternative may handle such complexities better than traditional accounts of rules as discriminative stimuli.

In agreement with other behavior analysts, Agnew and Redmon (1992) use Skinner's (1969) definition of a rule as a verbal description of a behavioral contingency or contingency-specifying statement. However, Agnew and Redmon (1992) contend that arguments by Schlinger and Blakely (1987) against the classification of rules as discriminative stimuli are convincing. For this reason, among others, the alternative definition provided by Schlinger and Blakely (1987) should be adopted for describing OBM research and practice. In the hypothetical situation described above the person is not likely to receive the memo, state the rule "I must be on time to this meeting," then go to his or her auto, start it, drive to the meeting site, and wait there until the meeting time arrives. The memo is more likely to function as a discriminative stimulus for stating a rule such as, "I must take steps to ensure that I arrive at this meeting on time." That statement might then evoke making a note on one's personal and business calendar or personal digital assistant (PDA) and then making a special mark on a wall calendar at home. The appointment either in the PDA or on the wall calendar will eventually function as a discriminative stimulus, but not on Tuesday morning. More likely, on Tuesday night the wall calendar note will function as a discriminative stimulus that evokes setting one's alarm an hour earlier than usual and, perhaps, drawing a map of the route to the off-site meeting location and so on until one arrives at the meeting on time.

What was the effect of the initial CSS in this example? It enacted a complex chain of interactions among behavior and environmental contingencies by altering the functions of once-neutral environmental stimuli the person encountered between receipt of the memo and arrival at the meeting. In addition to the obvious operant behaviors involved in this lengthy chain, the person might also experience increased respondent behavior, called "stress" or "anxiety," as the meeting drew closer in time. "According to this position, rules influence behavior by changing the function of other stimuli; and it is those other stimuli, whose function has been altered, that directly control the behavior" (Agnew and Redmon, 1992, p. 68). This analysis of rules suggests that they should be defined as "function-altering, contingency-specifying stimuli and that the term be used exclusively for such stimuli" (p. 69).

Much confusion regarding how and why interventions involving goal setting and feedback fail or succeed in producing behavior change can be cleared up, we believe, by adopting Schlinger and Blakely's (1987) account regarding how rules effect behavior change. Attempting to clear up the confusion within the context of field interventions, however, is likely to prove a daunting task. Results of a recent review of the feedback intervention literature using methods of meta-analysis and theory building (Kluger and DeNisi, 1996) offer little hope for understanding how feedback works to improve performance, when it does, from a behavior analytic vantage point using behavior analytic terms and concepts. Nevertheless, the review of feedback interventions by Kluger and DeNisi (1996) did corroborate results of the Balcazar, Hopkins, and Suarez (1986) review of feedback intervention that found inconsistent effects of feedback interventions on task performance. In addition, the Kluger and DeNisi (1996) review may suggest to behavior analysts some classes of task context, task performance, and individual reinforcement history variables that might prove worthy of behavior analysts' attention when they begin to critically and systematically analyze feedback intervention components and processes. A replication of the Balcazar, Hopkins, and Suarez (1986) review by Alvero, Bucklin, and Austin (in press) found that after yet another decade of research, feedback interventions do not uniformly improve performance dimensions they are targeted to improve. At the moment we cannot fill in all the relations among dimensions of feedback interventions as they relate to specific empirical results regarding their behavioral functions as recommended by Duncan and Bruwelheide (1986). Nevertheless, we think it is important to present a slightly altered version of their matrix, which presented possible relations among dimensions of feedback interventions that might precipitate performance improvements via the behavioral functions they listed. Our adaptation appears in Table 1.1.

Our adaptation of the Duncan and Bruwelheide (1986) matrix differs in at least one important way. It explicitly recognizes that a dimension of feedback might include goals and standards that initially function as establishing operations (EOs). For example, the first occasion of feedback in some cases is an announcement with related empirical evidence indicating that current performance levels are too low relative to some standard, e.g., performance of a competing organization, the consequences of which cannot bode well for the group. Antecedent contingency-specifying stimuli (statements) of this sort can have function-altering effects on existing sources of feedback that had heretofore been ineffective. That they had been ineffective would be evident in that these sources of information had not been functioning as reinforcement prior to the announcement, but their function changed from neutral to reinforcing following the announcement. From the normative vantage point of OBM, of course, we should strive to create and maintain organizational systems that obviate the need to rely on the creation of such negative reinforcement contingencies. The fact that they do occur, however, cannot be denied (Malott, 1992). But that is all the more reason for directing efforts at their elimination (Daniels, 2000) by more and more competent use of positive methods of organizational behavior and performance management.

The most recent review of the feedback literature from an OBM vantage point (Alvero, Bucklin, and Austin, in press) yielded results that support the following general conclusions: (a) feedback, across a host of interventions, still does not yield consistently positive effects on performance; and (b) the most consistent desired effects on performance occur

TABLE 1.1. Matrix Relating Possible Behavioral Functions of Feedback and Known Dimensions of Feedback

	FUNCTION			
	Consequence		Antecedent	
	Reinforcement	Punishment	S^D	EO
DIMENSION			Rule(s)	

As antecedent event(s)
  goal/standard-setting event(s)
    fixed individual/group
    individual relative to
      self/group
    group relative to
      itself/other group(s)
  model(s)
  status				

Source of consequent events
  "self"-monitor
  other monitor
    Individual
    Group
      Credibility
      Power				

Mode of Transmission
  oral
  written
  graphic
  tabular				

Message relative to antecedents
  sign
  accuracy
  specificity
  amount/length
  frequency
  timing/delay				

Source: Adapted from Duncan and Bruwelheide (1986).

when feedback is used with other procedures and it is delivered at the group level. Nevertheless, feedback is most often delivered in the absence of other procedures by supervisors, and directed at individuals relative to individual performance levels.

In spite of the call for critical experimental analyses of feedback in the 1980s (e.g., Duncan and Bruwelheide, 1986), progress seems to be limited to the conceptual clarification of its relationship with other concepts such as the EO (Agnew and Redmon, 1992). If members of our culture presume that most effects of feedback drive from its relationship to a process of differential reinforcement, there will be little "motivation" to explore the precise ways in which various dimensions of feedback contribute to or detract from desired effects on performance. But, according to a recent meta-analysis in the I/O psychology tradition, an appreciable number of feedback interventions actually produce decrements in performance. Unless such decrements never occur in OBM-related interventions, it behooves us to increase our knowledge and hone our skills based on that knowledge in ways that ensure first and foremost that we "do no harm."

SPC and Quality Management

Another recurring theme in the literature of OBM is quality as it has been developed in terms of statistical process control (SPC) and total quality management (TQM) and interpreted with respect to performance improvement initiatives in the OBM tradition (Mawhinney, 1986, 1992b; Redmon and Dickinson, 1987). Organizational behavior management is rooted in the philosophical and experimental traditions of behavior analysis and its close relative, applied behavior analysis. Thus, it should come as no surprise to learn that Deming's (1982) emphasis on the control of a system's variation is very much a part of what is emphasized by applied researchers working in the traditions of OBM (Mawhinney, 1986). Neither should anyone be surprised to learn that differences exist between the targeted locus of what is to be controlled by the methods of SPC and TQM compared to behavior analysis and OBM (Redmon and Dickinson, 1987). Critical comparisons of similarities and differences between the traditions of SPC/TQM and OBM (Brethower and Wittkopp, 1987; Gilbert, 1978; Luthans and Kreitner, 1975, 1985; Luthans and Thompson, 1987; Malott and Garcia, 1987; Redmon and Dickinson, 1987) set the stage for achieving synergies based on integrating the best elements of the two paradigms.

In the past, SPC/TQM traditions tended to underestimate the impact of performance consequences (all performance-contingent rewards and competing and conflicting reward contingencies) on quality performance while OBM traditions tended to neglect social validity of interventions, with social validity defined with respect to ultimate consumer satisfaction. Although the American quality movement is by no means dead, at least some experts are now willing to admit that due to numerous fad-related characteristics "failed attempts at implementing quality practices are commonplace" (Cole, 1995, p. 3). Even the term TQM is recognized as faddish (Cole, 1995) and some proponents of the paradigm now refer to it simply as Total Quality or TQ (e.g., Evans and Dean, 2000). Evidence from OBM-based research suggests that at least one reason SPC methods may not become effective practice on the shop floor (and higher up) is that consequences of using the methods properly, if they occur at all, are too delayed in time to reinforce the practices involved in using the methods. (For a discussion of this with specific reference to work by Henry and Redmon (1990) see Malott (1992).) Using a multiple baseline design, Henry and Redmon (1990) evaluated the impact of relatively immediate performance-contingent feedback on percent SPC task completions (across six tasks) among three machine operators. The good news was that the very complex array of behavior associated with completing the six tasks was clearly improved by the provision of relatively immediate feedback. At the same time, however, quality of outputs from the three machine operators did not change across conditions of the study for reasons discussed by Henry and Redmon (1990). Thus, economic consequences of the intervention could not have been positively changed by the intervention.

One of the most direct measures of service quality is customer satisfaction with service assessment, which can be problematic in many service organizations. Nevertheless, Brown and Sulzer-Azaroff (1994) devised an inexpensive means of assessing customer satisfaction with service provided by three tellers in a bank. Before each observation session tellers were provided with colored poker chips that they dispensed to customers when providing services, inviting the customers to place them in a collection box in the lobby. On their way out of the teller area customers passed the collection box, with five slots labeled from very satisfied to unsatisfied. The sign on the box invited them to describe the service just received by placing their chip in one of the slots. A feedback procedure was used, which effectively increased teller rates of smiling, greeting, and making eye contact with customers. Results of computing Spearman rank order correlations revealed that only one of the tellers' behaviors was reliably correlated with customer ratings of service satisfaction, which was greeting. Whether improved customer satisfaction with service had an impact on financial outcomes for the bank was not determined, but a link between teller behavior and customer-rated service satisfaction was established for one behavior.

It seems evident that OBM has the tools for analyzing and improving quality performance in both goods and service organization settings. But more research aimed at demonstrating effectiveness of OBM methods of operationalizing quality performance systems is required to make our case.

The current "mini fad" within the TQ movement is teams and team-based quality performance. Fortunately, the concept of environmental contingencies that effectively regulates behavior of individuals can be used to reinforce dimensions of group or team behavior, as basic research regarding dyadic interactions has clearly shown (Rao and Mawhinney, 1991).

In addition, the behavior analytic and OBM approach to the concept of organizational culture promises to provide the means of demystifying popular notions about organizational culture as some sort of relatively intangible elements of organizational life. And this orientation will apply equally to answering questions regarding practices in quality performance cultures that make a difference in quality result and those that do not. Proponents of practices that define a quality performance culture now contend that the improved competitiveness enjoyed by quality driving cultures will require more and more organizational cultures to adopt quality practices as a matter of ensuring their survival. Behavior analysis provides members of the OBM culture with some powerful analytic tools not only for gaining an understanding of relations between practices in organizations and their survival-related consequences (Mawhinney, 1992a), but also providing guidelines for changing practices in ways that provide an organization with some degree of protection against decline in an age of ever-increasing quality-based competition for markets (Redmon and Agnew, 1991) and public funding (Redmon and Wilk, 1991).

Behavioral Economics

Another topic that has recently emerged blends behavior analysis with economic concepts (Hursh, 1980), and this field is known as behavioral economics (Hursh, 1984). Traditional research in the experimental analysis of behavior typically employed animals kept at 80 or 85 percent free feeding weight to ensure that food was reinforcing. After daily sessions, food-deprived rats or pigeons were fed to maintain body weight. Other research kept animals in chambers continuously so that they earned all their food in what Hursh termed a "closed economy." Divergent results between the first "open economies" and findings in closed economies may explain some inconsistent findings in basic research. Animals seem to respond differently when all their food is earned in the chamber. Economic concepts such as demand for these reinforcers are relevant. Demand for food is inelastic; that is, animals respond at high rates to keep supplies available. Demand for other reinforcers are elastic because consumption will decrease when increasing amounts of responding are required. Moreover, in open economies demand tends to be elastic for all reinforcers because substitutable sources are provided after sessions.

This has obvious implications for OBM research. Rarely would participants be confined in a closed economy by being restricted to an organizational setting that provided the only source of reinforcement, and the various alternative sources of reinforcement, outside the organizational setting, can have major effects on performance. Critical differences in design as well as findings between basic research on schedules of reinforcement in the experimental analysis of behavior and OBM have been noted elsewhere (Dickinson and Poling, 1996; Hantula, Chapter 5 of this volume). Behavioral economics provides additional contextual factors to consider that may influence topics such as choice and the viability of the matching law (Baum, 1973; Herrnstein, 1970; Hursh, 1980). Differences in behavior between open and closed economies may be related to different survival strategies (Zeiler, 1999). Although economic survival rather than biological survival is meaningful for research on organizational performance, consideration of alternative sources of reinforcement such as money earned both in and outside the work setting under investigation seems critical. This can have major implications for work on pay for performance (Abernathy, 1996; Duncan and Smoot, Chapter 9 this volume), especially when individuals have choices in employment. As basic and OBM research continue, the utility of applying economic concepts to these fields remains viable, but clearly in its infancy.

Variation and Selection

Finally, Skinner (1987) described how variation and selection of behavior occurs at three levels simultaneously:

> . . . human behavior is the joint product of (1) the contingencies of survival responsible for the natural selection of the species and (2) the contingencies of reinforcement responsible for the repertoires acquired by its members, including (3) the special contingencies maintained by an evolved social environment . . . three levels of variation and selection has its own discipline—the first, biology; the second, psychology; and the third, anthropology. (p. 55)

We propose that variation and selection occur in organizational settings in a similar manner. The first substitutes organizations for species. Adaptive organizations survive and flourish, as evidenced during the agrarian, industrial, and information revolutions that have occurred in recent centuries. Organizations that have not evolved with changing contingencies for survival either merge or undergo extinction as evidenced recently in the automotive industry (Mawhinney, 1992a) as well as the computer and information technology fields. The second, behavior, occurs as Skinner described except that we are limiting our discussion to organizational settings. Obvious reinforcement and punishment contingencies exist in all organizations and behavior adapts to the various contingencies within these contexts. The third is how organizational cultures select and shape practices within organizational settings (Redmon and Mason, Chapter 17, this volume) and that this process involves leader behavior within organizations (Mawhinney, Chapter 7 this volume). This last level includes verbal behavior, policy and other work rules, attire, and countless other workplace behaviors and practices. Although not commonly accepted until recently, evolutionary psychology has been applied to interventions in organizational settings supporting a variation and selection analysis (Colarelli, 1998).

CONCLUSION

The contents of this book concern the theoretical and practical implications of analyzing behavior based on the causal mode of selection by consequences (or variation and selection). This causal mode effectively explains behavior of individual persons, cultural practices among groups of persons, and the performance of formally organized groups of persons in complex organizational cultures. The remaining chapters in this book provide insights not only into the causes of performance at the individual and group levels and how such performances support ultimate organizational performance, but also concerning how to analyze and take actions to improve performance at all three levels. Although people do create rules that help them better manage individual, group, and formal organization levels of performance, the ultimate measure of success is to be found in the *consequences* of following such rules.

REFERENCES

Abernathy, W. B. (1996). *The sin of wages: Where the conventional pay system has led us and how to find a way out.* Memphis, TN: PerfSys Press.

Agnew, J. L. and Redmon, W. K. (1992). Contingency specifying stimuli: The role of "rules" in organizational behavior management. *Journal of Organizational Behavior Management, 12*(2), 67-75.

Aldis, O. (1961). Of pigeons and men. *Harvard Business Review,* 39 (July-August), 59-63.

Alvero, A. M., Bucklin, B. R., and Austin, J. (in press) *Journal of Organizational Behavior Management.*

At Emery Air Freight: Positive Reinforcement Boosts Performance (1973). *Organizational Dynamics, 1*(3), 41-50.

Balcazar, F., Hopkins, B. L., and Suarez, Y. (1986). A critical, objective review of performance feedback. *Journal of Organizational Behavior Management, 7*(3/4), 65-89.

Balcazar, F., Shupert, M., Daniels, A. C., Mawhinney, T. C., and Hopkins, B. L. (1989). An objective review and analysis of ten years of publication in the *Journal of Organizational Behavior Management. Journal of Organizational Behavior Management, 10*(1), 7-37.

Baum, W. M. (1973). The correlation-based law of effect. *Journal of the Experimental Analysis of Behavior, 20*(1), 137-153.

Baum, W. M. (1994). *Understanding behaviorism: Science, behavior, and culture.* New York: HarperCollins.

Blakely, E. and Schlinger, H. (1987). Rules: Function-altering contingency-specifying stimuli. *The Behavior Analyst, 10*(2), 183-187.

Brethower, D. M. (1972). *Behavior analysis in business and industry: A total performance system.* Kalamazoo, MI: Behaviordelia, Inc.

Brethower, D. M. and Wittkopp, C. J. (1987). Performance engineering: SPC and the total performance system. *Journal of Organizational Behavior Management, 9*(1), 83-103.

Brown, C. S. and Sulzer-Azaroff, B. (1994). An assessment of the relationship between customer satisfaction and service friendliness. *Journal of Organizational Behavior Management, 14*(2), 55-75.

Colarelli, S. M. (1998). Psychological interventions in organizations: An evolutionary perspective. *American Psychologist, 53*(9), 1044-1056.

Cole, R. E. (Ed.). (1995). *The death and life of the American quality movement.* New York: Oxford University Press.

Daniels, A. C. (1989). *Performance management: Improving quality productivity through positive reinforcement* (Third edition). Tucker, GA: Performance Management Publications.

Daniels, A. C. (2000). *Bringing out the best in people* (Second edition). New York: McGraw-Hill.

Deming, W. E. (1982). *Quality, productivity and competitive position.* Cambridge, MA: Center for Advanced Engineering Study, MIT.

Dickinson, A. M. and Poling, A. (1996). Schedules of monetary reinforcement in organizational behavior management. *Journal of Organizational Behavior Management, 16*(1), 71-91.

Duncan, P. K. and Bruwelheide, L. R. (1986). Feedback: Use and possible behavioral functions. *Journal of Organizational Behavior Management, 7*(3/4), 91-114.

Evans, J. R. and Dean, J. W. (2000). *Total quality: Management, organization and strategy* (Second edition). Cincinnati, OH: South-Western College Publishing.

Fellner, D. J. and Sulzer-Azaroff, B. (1984). A behavioral analysis of goal setting. *Journal of Organizational Behavior Management, 6*(1), 33-51.

Ford, J. E. (1980). A classification system for feedback systems. *Journal of Organizational Behavior Management, 2*(3), 183-191.

Frederiksen, L. W. (Ed.). (1982). *Handbook of organizational behavior management.* New York: Wiley.

Gilbert, T. F. (1978). *Human competence: Engineering worthy performance.* New York: McGraw-Hill.

Henry, G. O. and Redmon, W. K. (1990). The effects of performance feedback on the implementation of a statistical process control (SPC) program. *Journal of Organizational Behavior Management, 11*(2), 23-46.

Herrnstein, R. J. (1970). On the law of effect. *Journal of the Experimental Analysis of Behavior, 13*, 243-266.

Huber, V. L. (1986). The interplay of goals and promises of pay-for-performance on individual and group performance: An operant interpretation. *Journal of Organizational Behavior Management, 7*(3/4), 45-64.

Hursh, S. R. (1980). Economic concepts for the analysis of behavior. *Journal of the Experimental Analysis of Behavior, 34*(2), 219-238.

Hursh, S. R. (1984). Behavioral economics. *Journal of the Experimental Analysis of Behavior, 42*(3), 435-452.

Kluger, A. N. and DeNisi, A. (1996). The effects of feedback interventions on performance: A historical review, a meta-analysis, and a preliminary feedback intervention theory. *Psychological Bulletin, 119*(2), 254-284.

Lincoln, J. F. (1951). *Incentive management: A new approach to human relationships in industry and business.* Cleveland, OH: Lincoln Electric Co.

Luthans, F. and Kreitner, R. (1975). *Organizational behavior modification.* Glenview, IL: Scott, Foresman.

Luthans, F. and Kreitner, R. (1985). *Organizational behavior modification and beyond: An operant and social learning approach* (Second edition). Glenview, IL: Scott, Foresman.

Luthans, F. and Thompson, K. R. (1987).Theory D and O.B. Mod.: Synergistic or opposite approaches to performance management? *Journal of Organizational Behavior Management, 9*(1), 105-124.

Malott, R. W. (1992). A theory of rule-governed behavior and organizational behavior management. *Journal of Organizational Behavior Management, 12*(2), 45-65.

Malott, R. W. and Garcia, E. M. (1987). A goal-directed model for the design of human performance systems. *Journal of Organizational Behavior Management, 9*(1), 125-159.

Mawhinney, T. C. (1975). Operant terms and concepts in the description of individual work behavior: Some problems of interpretation, application and evaluation. *Journal of Applied Psychology, 60,* 704-712.

Mawhinney, T. C. (1986). OBM, SPC, and Theory D: A brief introduction. *Journal of Organizational Behavior Management, 8*(1), 89-105.

Mawhinney, T. C. (Ed.), (1992a). Organizational culture, rule-governed behavior and organizational behavior management [Special issue]. *Journal of Organizational Behavior Management, 12*(2).

Mawhinney, T. C. (1992b). Total quality management and organizational behavior management: An integration for continual improvement. *Journal of Applied Behavior Analysis, 25,* 525-543.

Michael, J. L. (1993). *Concepts and principles of behavior analysis.* Kalamazoo, MI: Association for Behavior Analysis.

Myers, D. G. (1998). *Psychology* (Fifth edition). New York: Worth.

Nolan, T. V., Jarema, K. A., and Austin, J. (1999). An objective review of the *Journal of Organizational Behavior Management*: 1987-1997. *Journal of Organizational Behavior Management, 19*(3), 83-114.

O'Brien, R. M., Dickinson, A. M., and Rosow, M. P. (Eds.). (1982). *Industrial behavior modification: A management handbook.* New York: Pergamon Press.

O'Hara, K., Johnson, C. M., and Beehr, T. A. (1985). Organizational behavior management in the private sector: A review of empirical research and recommendations for further investigation. *Academy of Management Review, 10*(4), 848-864.

Peterson, N. (1982). Feedback is not a new principle of behavior. *The Behavior Analyst, 5*(1), 101-102.

Prue, D. M., Frederiksen, L. W., and Bacon, A. (1978). Organizational behavior management: An annotated bibliography, *Journal of Organizational Behavior Management, 1*(4), 216-257.

Rao, R. K. and Mawhinney, T. C. (1991). Superior-subordinate dyads: Dependence of leader effectiveness on mutual reinforcement. *Journal of the Experimental Analysis of Behavior, 56,* 105-118.

Redmon, W. K. and Agnew, J. L. (1991). Organizational behavioral analysis in the United States: The private sector. In P. A. Lamal (Ed.), *Behavior analysis of societies and cultural practices* (pp. 125-139). Washington, DC: Hemisphere.

Redmon, W. K. and Dickinson, A. M. (1987). A comparative analysis of statistical process control, theory D, and behavior analytic approaches to quality control. *Journal of Organizational Behavior Management, 9*(1), 47-65.

Redmon, W. K. and Wilk, L. A. (1991). Organizational behavioral analysis in the United States: Public sector organizations. In P. A. Lamal (Ed.), *Behavior analysis of societies and cultural practices* (pp. 107-123). Washington, DC: Hemisphere.

Rummler, G. A. and Brache, A. P. (1995). *Improving performance: How to manage the white space on the organization chart* (Second edition). San Francisco: Jossey-Bass.

Schlinger, H. and Blakely, E. (1987). Function altering effects of contingency specifying stimuli. *The Behavior Analyst, 10*(1), 41-45.

Schwartz, G. E. and Weiss, S. M. (1978). Behavioral medicine revisited: An amended definition. *Journal of Behavioral Medicine, 1,* 249-251.

Scott, W. E., Jr., and Podsakoff, P. M. (1985). *Behavioral principles in the practice of management.* New York: Wiley.

Skinner, B. F. (1959). John Broadus Watson, behaviorist. *Science, 129,* 197-198.

Skinner, B. F. (1969). *Contingencies of reinforcement: A theoretical analysis.* New York: Appleton-Century-Crofts.

Skinner, B. F. (1987). *Upon further reflection.* Englewood Cliffs, NJ: Prentice-Hall.

Taylor, F. W. (1911). *The principles of scientific management.* New York: Harper and Row.

Vollmer, T. R. and Iwata, B. A. (1991). Establishing operations and reinforcement effects. *Journal of Applied Behavior Analysis, 24,* 279-291.

Wood, S. E. and Wood, E. G. (1999). *The world of psychology* (Third edition). Needham Heights, MA: Allyn and Bacon.

Yukl, G. and Latham, G. (1975). Consequences of reinforcement schedules and incentive magnitude for employee performance: Problems encountered in an industrial setting. *Journal of Applied Psychology, 60,* 294-298.

Zeiler, M. (1999). Reversed schedule effects in closed and open economies. *Journal of the Experimental Analysis of Behavior, 71,* 171-186.

Chapter 2

Principles of Learning: Respondent and Operant Conditioning and Human Behavior

Alan Poling
Diane Braatz

In essence, organizational behavior management involves changing what people do by giving them new experiences. What people do constitutes behavior, and *learning* refers to relatively permanent changes in behavior due to experience. Through controlled research and careful theorizing, behavior analysts have attained a reasonable understanding of learning and the variables that affect it. The purpose of this chapter is to overview learning principles that are relevant to organizational behavior management. These principles are considered from the perspective of radical behaviorism, the psychological paradigm originated by the late B. F. Skinner (e.g., 1938, 1953, 1957, 1969, 1974, 1987).

Learning can be accomplished through respondent or operant conditioning. Pavlov's salivating dogs provide the classic example of respondent conditioning, whereas Skinner's lever-pressing rats exemplify operant conditioning. Because humans are verbal organisms, salivating dogs and lever-pressing rats do not provide models that are fully adequate for understanding human behavior. Nevertheless, the learning principles that control simple responses in nonverbal organisms are relevant to, and in fact ultimately determine, the majority of human behavior, however complex. For this reason, rudimentary principles of respondent and operant

---

This chapter was written at the University of Waikato, while the senior author was on sabbatical leave from Western Michigan University.

conditioning will be covered initially, followed by a discussion of the role that language plays in human behavior.

RESPONDENT CONDITIONING

Pavlov (e.g., 1927) demonstrated that dogs could be taught to salivate upon presentation of a tone that normally did not control salivation. Three steps were involved in this basic demonstration. First, Pavlov presented the tone alone to verify that it did not elicit salivation. The second step was to present the tone just before giving food on many occasions. Finally, the tone was again presented alone. Each dog salivated. The tone, previously neutral with respect to salivation, had by virtue of being paired with food acquired the ability to elicit salivation. This is *respondent* (also termed Pavlovian, or classical) *conditioning.*

Respondent conditioning depends upon the temporal pairing of stimuli, which are defined environmental events. Procedurally, *respondent conditioning* involves presenting a conditional stimulus (CS) shortly before an unconditional stimulus (US). *Unconditional stimuli,* like the food presented to Pavlov's dogs, elicit a response in the absence of any special training. The response elicited by the US, salivation in the dogs, is termed an *unconditional response* (UR), and the relation between the US and the UR constitutes an *unconditioned reflex.*

A *conditional stimulus* is behaviorally neutral prior to conditioning, but elicits a *conditional response* (CR) after conditioning. The tone when first presented to Pavlov's dogs failed to elicit salivation, but after repeated pairings the tone CS elicited salivation as a CR. Respondent conditioning has occurred when a CS reliably elicits a CR. The relation between the CS and CR is a conditioned reflex, and conditioned reflexes are the stimulus-response (S-R) units acquired through respondent conditioning. For them to appear, the CS must be predictive of the US. This means that the CS precedes the US in time, and the probability of the US occurring must be higher immediately after CS presentation than at any other time. It is not essential that all US presentations follow the CS, nor that all CS presentations are followed by the US. What is essential is that the CS and US are correlated in time, so that the probability of the US occurring is greatest after the CS occurs. This constitutes a predictive relation between the CS and the US, which is the necessary condition for respondent conditioning (Rescorla and Wagner, 1972). As a rule, the speed and the strength of respondent conditioning is directly related to the predictive value of the CS relative to the US.

After a given stimulus is established as a CS, it can be paired with a neutral stimulus to establish that stimulus as a CS. This procedure, known as second-order conditioning, characteristically does not engender robust learning.

It is common, but incorrect, to assume that the relation between a US and UR, or between a CS and CR, is invariant. Although the US elicits the UR, this does not mean that every US presentation is followed by a UR of fixed form and magnitude. Several variables influence unconditioned reflexes. Among them are the intensity of the US and the frequency of its presentation. If, for instance, a lawn mower is started just outside your living room window, it initially elicits the complex of reactions encompassed by the term "startle response." But if the mower is started and stopped repeatedly throughout the day, *habituation* occurs and your reaction to the noise weakens and perhaps fades entirely.

Similarly, the relation between a CS and a CR is not fixed, but is influenced by environmental variables. For example, the CS continues to elicit the CR only so long as the CS-US pairing is at least occasionally maintained. If the pairing is broken, either by presenting the CS without the US or by presenting the two stimuli independent of each other (i.e., in uncorrelated fashion), the CR weakens and eventually ceases to occur. *Respondent extinction* is the term applied to the cessation of responding due to presentation of a CS not paired with a US.

Stimuli that are similar to a CS along some physical dimension frequently elicit the same CRs, even though these stimuli have never been paired with a US. This phenomenon is termed *respondent stimulus generalization.* In general, the greater the physical similarity between a novel stimulus and a CS, the greater the likelihood that the novel stimulus will elicit a response similar to the CR. Unconditional stimuli, and conditional stimuli that are paired with them, often produce what is commonly termed emotional behavior. For example, a worker who receives an electrical shock while operating a drill is likely to curse and fling the tool, to exhibit activation of the sympathetic branch of the autonomic nervous system (resulting in increased heart rate, blood pressure, and general arousal), and to avoid using the tool on subsequent occasions. If such unpleasant events regularly occur in the workplace, the person may become chronically anxious and fearful. Anxious and fearful workers are apt to be unhappy and unproductive.

Respondent conditioning can produce responses that are significant in the workplace, but do not involve emotional behavior. A scenario described by Catania (1992, p. 189) makes this clear. Catania's scenario involves a person who has just switched from a soft drink that contains sugar to a sugar-free drink. The release of insulin is a UR elicited by the US of sugar in the gut. Sugar in the gut is reliably preceded by the taste of the sweetened drink, which eventually is established as a CS that controls insulin release as a CR. The unsweetened drink, which tastes similar to the sugared one, also elicits insulin release. But there is no forthcoming sugar for the insulin to act upon. If blood sugar levels are low to begin with, hypoglycemia, with attendant feelings of weakness and shakiness and deterioration of on-the-job performance, may result.

Respondent conditioning does not produce new behavior; it only brings reflexive behavior under the control of new stimuli. For this reason, procedures based primarily on respondent conditioning are rarely used in organizations. Nonetheless, stimuli that elicit behavior play a critically important role within and outside organizations. These unconditional stimuli, and conditional stimuli that are paired with them, often produce what is commonly termed emotional behavior. Such behavior can have important consequences in the workplace.

If for instance, an executive delivers only "good news" (e.g., pay bonuses, praise) to employees, leaving the bearing of "bad news" (e.g., layoff notices, criticism) to an underling, the approach of the executive is apt to be a source of joy for workers, whereas the approach of the underling is a source of discomfort. Moreover, interactions with the executive will be established as a desired event that employees will work to produce (i.e., as a conditioned positive reinforcer), whereas interactions with the underling will be established as an undesired event that employees will work to avoid (i.e., as a conditioned negative reinforcer). Here, the capacity of particular people to function as stimuli in operant relations (see below) is established by correlating their presence with the presence of other objects or events (stimuli), which is the essence of respondent conditioning.

OPERANT CONDITIONING

Skinner (e.g., 1938) demonstrated that hungry rats confined in small chambers could easily be trained to depress levers located on the chambers' walls when such responses produced food. If lever presses produced food when a tone was present, but not when it was absent, most lever pressing came to be confined to periods when the tone was present. This example demonstrates the three-term contingency that describes stimulus-response-stimulus relations in time. The three-term contingency is central to operant conditioning and often is summarized by the mnemonic A-B-C: antecedent stimulus (A)—operant behavior (B)—consequence (C). *Oper-*

ant behavior is behavior that is primarily controlled by its consequences, that is, by the changes in the environment that it produces. Those consequences determine the likelihood of the behavior recurring. Because they are correlated with particular response-consequence relations, antecedent stimuli also come to influence the future probability of responding.

In our example, the probability of a lever press occurring is greater when the tone (antecedent stimulus) is present than when it is absent because, historically, lever pressing (operant behavior) produced food (a particular kind of consequence) when the tone was present, but not when it was absent. This is operant conditioning.

Of course, not all consequences have a behavioral function. When a consequence does affect behavior, the future likelihood of occurrence of the response under similar circumstances can increase (as did the rat's lever pressing), or it can decrease. The term reinforcement is used to refer to the former relation, whereas punishment (discussed later) is used to describe the latter. *Reinforcement* is an operant conditioning process (or procedure) in which behavior is strengthened by its consequences. The response-strengthening effects of reinforcement typically involve an increase in the future rate (number of responses per unit time) of occurrence of the response, although other changes in behavior (e.g., a decrease in response latency or an increase in response magnitude) may also be indicative of a reinforcement effect. It is important to recognize that reinforcement always strengthens the operant response class, although this process may weaken, strengthen, or have no effect on other behaviors. An operant response class includes all behavior, regardless of topography (form), that produces the same effect on the environment. For instance, a server at a Mexican restaurant may be praised by a supervisor for greeting customers politely, serving chips promptly, and taking orders accurately. If each of these responses produces the same outcome, that is, equivalent praise, then they are members of the same operant response class.

Reinforcers can involve adding something to the environment (e.g., presenting money, increasing the volume of a stereo), or taking something away (e.g., ceasing to yell or complain, reducing the volume of a stereo). The former are *positive reinforcers;* the latter are *negative reinforcers.* A common misconception is that negative reinforcers inevitably, and perhaps by definition, terminate an aversive state. For instance, many people consider heroin a negative reinforcer when it is administered to a physically dependent person undergoing withdrawal. The rationale here is that the drug terminates the aversive state of withdrawal; hence it is a negative reinforcer. This has some initial appeal, but by the same logic, food, water, and sexual activity are negative reinforcers because they terminate aversive states of hunger, thirst, and desire. These states are not directly observable and their importance to the reinforcing effects of the objects and events in question is moot. If the distinction between positive and negative reinforcers is to be preserved, and there is debate as to the usefulness of this practice (e.g., Michael, 1975), it is important to make the distinction on the basis of the changes in the environment caused by a stimulus (adding something or taking something away), not in terms of subjective states.

More useful, perhaps, than the distinction between positive and negative reinforcers is the distinction between unconditioned (or primary) and conditioned (or secondary) reinforcers. The former are objects and events that do not depend upon a particular learning history for their reinforcing function. The latter are objects and events that gain their ability to strengthen behavior through learning, usually by being correlated with established reinforcers. Examples of unconditioned positive reinforcers are food and water, which, given appropriate deprivation, strengthen the behaviors that acquire them in almost all humans. Unconditioned negative reinforcers, which organisms will *escape* (respond to terminate), or *avoid* (respond to prevent contact with) include high-intensity stimulation in most modalities (e.g., loud sounds, bright lights, intense cold or heat).

The stimuli that serve as conditioned reinforcers differ across people because people differ in their learning histories. In a given culture, however, some conditioned reinforcers are widely effective. These objects and events are paired with many other reinforcers, which establish them as *generalized conditioned reinforcers*, of which money and praise are fine examples. Giving an adult American a dollar bill for each frown would dramatically increase frowning, but the same operation would not affect frowning by a baby. This difference reflects the fact that adults, but not babies, have a long history in which dollar bills have been exchanged for various reinforcers. Generalized conditioned reinforcers, like all conditioned reinforcers, acquire their response-strengthening properties from their correlation with primary reinforcers (or other established conditioned reinforcers). When this correlation ceases, the reinforcing capacity is lost. People do not work long for currency that is totally devalued, or for praise not backed up by other significant events.

Some theoreticians have argued that it is the opportunity to engage in a particular behavior that a stimulus affords, not the stimulus itself, that is reinforcing. For example, food allows eating, and it is the eating, not the food, that is important. Be that as it may, it is apparent that the opportunity to engage in a particular behavior per se can function as a positive reinforcer. This function is codified in the *Premack principle* (Premack, 1959): For any two behaviors that occur with different probabilities, the opportunity to engage in the higher probability behavior will reinforce the lower probability behavior. Conversely, forcing an organism to engage in the lower probability behavior contingent on the higher probability behavior will punish the higher probability behavior. Consider two behaviors that a professor might perform: grading student projects and writing articles. When allowed to do either, much time is spent in writing, little in grading. Arranging conditions so that the professor must grade (the lower probability behavior) before writing (the higher probability behavior) is likely to increase grading.

The basic disequilibrium analysis of learned performance provided by Premack (1959, 1965, 1971) has been extended by other researchers. In an important extension, Allison and Timberlake proposed a response-deprivation model, which states that the opportunity to engage in an activity serves as a positive reinforcer so long as access to the activity is restricted so that it cannot occur at its baseline rate in the absence of the operant response (e.g., Allison and Timberlake, 1975; Timberlake and Allison, 1974). Timberlake (1980, 1984) promulgated a behavioral-regulation analysis of learned performance that emphasizes the importance of behavioral setpoints in determining whether access to an activity is reinforcing. Further coverage of these models is beyond our scope. As Schwartz (1989) noted, "Refinements of Premack's theory in recent years have changed it substantially in form, though not in spirit" (p. 172). The Premack principle remains useful for scheduling activities as reinforcers in organizational settings. Konarski, Johnson, Crowell, and Whitman (1981) compare the Premack principle with the response-deprivation hypothesis and make useful suggestions for determining whether access to particular activities will be reinforcing.

Even though the reinforcing effectiveness of an unconditioned reinforcer does not depend upon a particular learning history, that effectiveness is variable. Michael (1982) has proposed the term *establishing operation* (EO) as a general label for operations that (1) increase (or decrease) the effectiveness of a particular reinforcer and (2) increase (or decrease) the likelihood of occurrence of behavior that has in the past been followed by that reinforcer. As an example of an establishing operation, consider food deprivation. If we have just eaten, food is not a very effective reinforcer, and we do not engage in behaviors that have produced food in the past. In this case, satiation is evident. Satiation refers to a momentary reduction in the reinforcing efficacy of a stimulus as a result of repeated presentations. It is common with most unconditioned positive reinforcers (e.g., food, water, sex), but characteristically does not occur with negative reinforcers, or with conditioned reinforcers alone. If, however, the unconditioned positive reinforcer paired with a conditioned reinforcer is presented often enough, satiation may be evident with both the unconditioned and the conditioned reinforcer. Satiation rarely occurs with generalized conditioned reinforcers such as money and praise.

If a response is no longer followed by a reinforcer, the response eventually stops occurring. Cessation of responding due to a response occurring without reinforcement is known as *operant extinction*. The same term is also used to refer to the procedure of failing to reinforce an established operant. As an example of operant extinction, consider what happens when someone tries to operate a photocopying machine that is out of order. The manuscript is positioned, buttons are pushed, and nothing happens. More presses. Eventually, pressing ceases. But the waning of responsiveness is not necessarily smooth. In fact, rate of responding often goes up on initial exposure to extinction, a phenomenon known as *extinction-induced* bursting. Emotional responding and an increase in the variability of behavior are also characteristic results of extinction. The person whose manuscript is not copied after an initial press of the "Start" button is likely to press repeatedly (extinction-induced bursting), curse (an emotional response), and press other buttons, open doors, and behave in other unusual ways (increased variability of responding).

Reinforcers need not follow every occurrence of a behavior to determine the rate and pattern of its occurrence; intermittently occurring reinforcers can strengthen responding. In organizations, few behaviors are always reinforced. It is fair to say that intermittent reinforcement is ubiquitous in the working world. The term *schedule of reinforcement* is used to describe the rules used to present reinforcing stimuli. Schedules of reinforcement have been extensively studied using nonhuman subjects in laboratory settings. Under these conditions, the schedule under which behavior is maintained is an exceptionally powerful determinant of the rate and temporal patterning of responding, choice, and resistance to extinction (e.g., Zeiler, 1977). Schedules of reinforcement also influence human behavior, although as discussed later verbal behavior may override the effects of direct exposure to the contingencies that constitute a particular schedule.

In organizations, it is often difficult to specify the schedule under which a particular operant of importance is maintained, or to manipulate that schedule if it can be isolated. Despite these potential difficulties, several simulations and field studies have improved worker productivity by manipulating the schedule of monetary reward. Studies in this area have been reviewed by Ayllon and Kolko (1982), Latham and Huber (1992), and Hantula (Chapter 5, this volume). These reviews indicate that schedule manipulations based on extrapolations from laboratory findings with non-humans sometimes improve workers' output. For instance, Latham and Dossett (1978) demonstrated that experienced trappers caught more mountain beavers when a variable-ratio 4 (VR 4) schedule was arranged than when a fixed-ration 1 (FR 1, also called continuous reinforcement) schedule was in effect. Under the VR 4 schedule, a trapper received $4 contingent on (a) catching a beaver, and (b) correctly specifying the color of one of four marbles prior to drawing it from a bag held by their supervisor. Under the FR 1 schedule, a trapper received $1 for each beaver caught. Twenty-three percent more beavers were caught when the VR 4 schedule was in effect, and the average total cost of catching a single beaver was appreciably lower ($12.86) under this schedule as compared to the FR 1 ($16.75). Similar results were observed four years later in a follow-up study (Saari and Latham, 1982). These findings generally parallel results with nonhumans, in which short VR schedules characteristically engender more responding that FR 1 schedules (e.g., Lewis, 1963).

Although reinforcement schedules can be powerful determinants of behavior, Latham and Huber (1992) emphasize that it is difficult to apply basic research findings on schedule-controlled responding to the solution of organizational problems. Many uncontrollable variables (e.g., learning history, competing schedules) influence how humans will respond under a given schedule, and there are practical limits as to the schedule manipulations that are tenable in a given situation (e.g., contracts specify pay schedules). Further discussion of these issues is beyond our scope; Latham and Huber (1992) and Hantula (Chapter 5 of this volume) provide detailed consideration of field applications of schedule manipulations.

When the schedule in effect for one operant in an organizational setting is altered, not only that behavior but other operants are likely to be affected. This occurs because human behavior usually is maintained under concurrent schedules. *Concurrent schedules* occur when two or more sources of reinforcement are available for two or more incompatible responses. Under these conditions, we make choices. Consider the people with whom workers in a four-person office interact during breaks. Perhaps Sam spends 60 percent of his time interacting with Sarah and 30 percent interacting with Joe. Robin, in contrast, spends little time interacting with Sarah and much time interacting with Joe. Why? There are several possibilities. It is conceivable that, by virtue of their histories, the objects and events that function as reinforcers differ for Sam and Robin. Sarah may talk enthusiastically about politics, which reinforces Sam's listening, but not Robin's. Another possibility is that Joe arranges different schedules for Robin and Sam. Perhaps he rarely says a kind (and reinforcing) word to

Sam, but is richly supportive of (i.e., frequently reinforces) most of what Robin says and does. Assume that the latter is the case, and it is pointed out to Joe by his supervisor. Joe consequently attempts to become more supportive of Sam. If he succeeds, what is likely to happen? Clearly, the dynamics of the group, at least in the sense of the amount of time particular dyads interact, are going to change. Although they are complex and difficult to tease apart even with close observation, operant relations control most of what is done in organizations. The precision with which this control can be understood is moot, but it is worth noting that some authors have proposed that the matching law, which describes mathematically the relation between behavioral outputs and reinforcement inputs, may be relevant to how behavior is allocated in organizations. For example, Redmon and Lockwood (1986) considered the general importance of the matching law for understanding behavior in organizations and Mawhinney and Gowen (1991) examined how the matching law may explain adoption rates and differing levels of effectiveness among gainsharing programs.

These articles are significant for three reasons. First, they introduce an important basic research concept, matching, to readers who may well be unfamiliar with it. Second, they use that concept in attempting to account for important human behaviors in the workplace. Third, they suggest several areas for future research. It will be interesting to see whether the matching law, which arose from basic laboratory research with non-humans, actually proves useful in organizational behavior management.

Response-Independent Reinforcement

In some cases, operant relations simply involve temporal contiguity between a response and a stimulus: The response does not cause the stimulus to occur, but the two are nonetheless juxtaposed in time in the sequence response-stimulus, and this juxtaposition strengthens the behavior. A mechanic who, for unknown reasons, says "Turn, damn ya" while attempting to loosen a bolt is likely to repeat the statement on similar occasions in the future if the bolt comes loose just after the command, even though there is no mechanism through which the verbal statement could affect the bolt. Reinforcement of this type has been termed superstitious, adventitious, or response-independent and is undoubtedly involved in the control of some human behaviors. But responses maintained only by superstitious reinforcement are apt to vary in form over time and are rarely robust. Therefore, mechanisms other than superstitious reinforcement are apt to be responsible for the maintenance of enduring human behaviors. For instance, superstitious reinforcement does not provide an adequate account of the behavior of the weekend athlete who wears the same pair of "lucky" socks throughout the season.

Stimulus Control

A good example of stimulus control is answering the telephone. People answer it when it rings, not when it is silent. They do so because they have learned that answering the phone pays off (with a conversation that is valuable in some sense) after a ring, but not at other times. Technically, the telephone's ringing has been established as a discriminative stimulus for answering the phone.

A discriminative stimulus (S^D) evokes a response because in the past that kind of response has been more successful in the presence of that stimulus than in its absence. Discriminative stimuli come to control a particular type of behavior by being present when that behavior is reinforced. Stimuli present when a particular type of behavior is not successful (i.e., is not reinforced) can also influence responding. The term S^{delta} (S^Δ) is used to designate such stimuli. An S^Δ is a stimulus that (1) fails to evoke a particular type of behavior (2) because in the past, that type of behavior was extinguished in its presence. Such stimuli often have inhibitory properties; that is, they decrease the likelihood that the response in question will occur, although this effect can be difficult to demonstrate.

When behavior differs in the presence and absence of a particular stimulus, stimulus control is evident. In the extreme case, the response always occurs in the presence of one stimulus, and never occurs in the presence of any other stimulus. This almost never happens, because stimulus generalization occurs with discriminative stimuli, as well as with conditional stimuli. Therefore, stimuli that are physically similar to an S^D along some dimension also control the operant controlled by the established S^D. For example, an executive may answer the phone on his or her desk when the phone on the receptionist's desk, located nearby, rings. As a rule, the greater the similarity between another stimulus and an S^D, the greater the likelihood that the former stimulus will control the response in question. Appropriate training can establish desired degrees of stimulus control. For instance, botanists learn to differentiate (e.g., verbally label) many plants that are not differentiated by laypeople. They do so because of a history in which particular responses (e.g., that is a white pine, that is a red pine) are reinforced only in the presence of particular stimuli (white pines, red pines). Although not all white pines are precisely alike, they share sufficient characteristics to be readily differentiated from red pines so long as the differentiation is supported by reinforcement contingencies.

Much formal education and on-the-job training entails establishing specialized stimulus control over the repertoires of students and trainees. Through appropriate training, stimulus control can be extended to multiple stimulus dimensions, as when a mason accepts as well laid bricks that are plumb, level, and on bond. Conditional discriminations can also be trained. In a conditional discrimination, no single stimulus is correlated with reinforcement of a particular response. Instead, the response is reinforced (and subsequently occurs) in the presence of one stimulus only if one or more other stimuli are also present. A worker on an assembly line who places a nut on a shaft only if a washer is in place is performing a conditional discrimination.

Functionally Equivalent Stimuli

Stimuli that control the same operant response class are *functionally equivalent* even if they are unlike physically. For instance, someone might say "that's a computer" when presented with the printed word "Macintosh," a picture of an IBM personal computer, or a Cray machine. Stimuli can be established as functionally equivalent in several ways. Obviously, each member of a set of functionally equivalent stimuli can come to control the same operant response class through systematic training in which each stimulus is established as an S^D. Through stimulus generalization, control by members of this set will also extend to other, physically similar stimuli.

More noteworthy are those situations in which novel, untrained stimuli act as members of a functional class even though they do not closely resemble any member of that class (for discussion of this phenomenon, see Sidman, 1986). This is often demonstrated under a matching-to-sample procedure,[1] where stimulus A is established as equivalent to stimulus B (A = B) and stimulus B is established as equivalent to stimulus C (B = C). Then, without further training, testing reveals that stimulus A is equivalent to stimulus C (A = C); this is an untrained equivalence relation. For instance, a person learning about behavioral principles may be taught that "unconditional stimulus" is equivalent to "a stimulus that reflexively elicits an unconditional response." This same person may be separately taught that "unconditional stimulus" is equivalent to the abbreviation "US." When subsequently asked to define US, the response "a stimulus that reflexively elicits an unconditional response" is likely to occur, although it was not formally established under the control of the stimulus "US."

Verbal mediation plays an important part in establishing functionally equivalent stimuli: By naming an object or event, it can be imbued with the stimulus properties of other, like-named stimuli. If, for instance, a new employee is introduced by the foreman as "a trainee," other workers initially are apt to treat that person as they have learned to treat other trainees. Of course, a given object or event can enter into many equivalence relations simultaneously. Assume that the foreman further describes the new employee as "a hell of a basketball player." This information probably would not substantially alter everyday behaviors in the workplace, but it would increase substantially the odds of the trainee's being invited to play on the company team.

Response Acquisition

Unlike respondent conditioning, operant conditioning can create new behavior. One way in which this occurs is through the reinforcement of successive approximations, or shaping. *Shaping* is a procedure whereby a given operant response is achieved by the reinforcement of successively closer approximations to that response. Initially, the response in the existing behavioral repertoire closest to the desired response is reinforced on a few occasions. After this, a new criterion for reinforcement is adopted. This new criterion demands a response more similar in topography to the desired response than the previously reinforced behavior. The process of gradually shifting the criterion for reinforcement continues until the desired response is attained.

Shaping is a potent device for producing new responses. Consider an apprentice carpenter learning to drive nails with a hammer. Initially, the device is likely to be held close to the head and swung gently, with weak rap-a-tap-tap strokes. Experienced carpenters are likely to provide little verbal encouragement (i.e., reinforcement) for such maneuvers. Very soon, their praise will be dependent on longer, more forceful strokes, with the hammer held at handle's end. Differential success in driving nails, too, will help to shape correct strokes. Certain response topographies (forms) are more successful in meeting environmental demands than are others, and when this occurs a kind of "automatic shaping" can be manifested. Unfortunately, exposure to environmental contingencies alone often produces patterns of responding that are partially, but not optimally, effective. Athletes, for instance, often learn bad habits when self-taught.

In part to prevent this form from occurring, people are often given instructions for performing the desired response, or the desired response is simply demonstrated (modeled) for them. (Modeling is considered later, in the section on self-generated rules.) Prompting, too, is commonly used to produce appropriate responding in organizations. In prompting, stimuli that are intended to exercise immediate control over some segment of the desired response are provided when the behavior fails to occur. A journeyman carpenter observing an apprentice holding a hammer too near the head might, for instance, say "don't choke up" or move the apprentice's hand to the proper location. These actions would constitute verbal and physical prompts. Of course, the apprentice's response to these prompts is operant behavior in its own right, as is the prompting.

Response chaining is another procedure commonly used to develop new behaviors in laboratory settings. Response chaining also is frequently used to develop new behavior patterns in young and mentally deficient people, although it is used less frequently with adults in the workplace. In response chaining, a sequence of behaviors must be emitted before an unconditioned reinforcer is delivered. Only the final response is followed by an unconditioned reinforcer; prior responses in the sequence simply produce a stimulus change (which probably is a conditioned reinforcer for the behavior just completed, and a discriminative stimulus for the next behavior in the sequence) and provide an opportunity for subsequent responses to occur. Walking to and purchasing candy from a vending machine is an example of response chaining. A sequence of many different responses is involved, but only the final act produces food in the mouth, which is the reinforcer that ultimately maintains behavior.

Although response chaining provides a mechanism for maintaining long sequences of behavior with relatively few unconditioned reinforcers, one must not inappropriately apply chaining analyses to sequences of work-related behaviors. A person who works all week, receives a paycheck on Friday, buys groceries, and finally eats them may appear to be engaging in a chain of responses, but this analysis is far-fetched at best. The activities that occur each week are not fixed and discrete units followed by clear stimulus changes, and the unconditioned reinforcer (food) is not available only when the week is done. The paycheck and the food it provides certainly affect the worker's activities through the week, but not as the penultimate and ultimate reinforcers in a response chain.

In some situations, patterns of responding that resemble response chains but do not end with primary reinforcement are evident in humans. Consider a person operating a computer under conditions in which a printed document is reinforcing but can be obtained only through a series of keystrokes, each of which changes what appears on the screen. The printed document, which terminates the series of keystrokes, is a conditioned reinforcer. Thus, this series of responses does not constitute a response chain as defined above. However, the other defining features of a response chain are evident.

Punishment and Aversive Control

Stimuli sometimes weaken the response classes that they follow. The term punishment is used to describe relations of this kind. *Punishment* is an operant conditioning process (or procedure) in which behavior is weakened by its consequences. Punishment is defined in exactly the same way as reinforcement, with one critical difference: Punishment always weakens behavior, whereas reinforcement always strengthens it. Although punishment typically is unpleasant, subjective effects are irrelevant in determining whether a particular operation constitutes punishment.

Like reinforcers, punishers can be unconditioned or conditioned, depending on whether their response-suppressing actions depend on a special learning history. Intense stimuli in any modality (e.g., loud sounds, bright lights, high temperatures) are likely to function as unconditioned punishers; such stimuli can produce physical damage, and there is obvious benefit in not repeating behaviors that produce them. *Conditioned punishers* acquire their ability to control behavior through being paired with established punishers, and continue to have this effect only so long as the pairing is maintained.

Several criticisms have been raised about the use of punishment with humans. One is that punishment only diminishes someone's repertoire; it adds no behaviors of value. A second is that the effects of punishment often are weak and short-lived. A third is that punishment is unpleasant. A fourth is that strong punishers usually generate powerful, and negative, emotional reactions. A fifth is that individuals exposed to punishment are apt to escape or avoid the situation in which punishment occurs and to be aggressive, often toward the person who delivers punishment. A sixth is that punishment is especially coercive. A seventh is that punitive environments produce obstacles to the flow of valid information in work settings.

These criticisms are not without substance. Nonetheless, as Arvey and Ivanevich (1980) have emphasized, punishment often occurs and must be considered in attempts to explain behavior in organizations. Consider a situation in which Person A and Person B are interacting socially. Person A normally uses a racial epithet quite often. Each time this occurs, Person B breaks eye contact and briefly looks downward. If this operation reduces the frequency with which Person A uses the derogatory term, it is a punishment procedure, albeit a subtle one. Even if it is neither planned nor acknowledged, punishment plays a role in the behavior of people in organizations. This is natural: adapting to one's environment requires failing to repeat responses with adverse consequences, as well as repeating responses with beneficial consequences. Punishment produces the former outcome, reinforcement the latter.

There is some precedent for lumping together under the rubric of "aversive control" procedures that involve negative reinforcement (i.e., escape and avoidance contingencies) and those that involve punishment. There is little to recommend this practice. Stimuli that an individual will respond to escape or avoid in one situation do not necessarily suppress (i.e., punish) responding when delivered dependent on a response in another situation. Moreover, the primary behavioral effects of negative reinforcement and punishment are opposite in direction, and the behavioral "side effects" of these operations, if any, do not necessarily overlap. For instance, the subjective state of a person who has successfully emitted an escape response might accurately be termed "relieved," while that of a person who has just received punishment might be closer to "chagrined." It is, however, true that people exposed to escape, avoidance, or punishment contingencies are likely to describe the whole business as "unpleasant" or "aversive," but this is a poor basis for grouping them together.

The Importance of Basic Operant Principles

It is beyond the scope of this chapter to consider adequately the variables that influence operant responding, even in the absence of verbal behavior. Table 2.1 briefly describes nine such variables, including some mentioned previously. All of the variables listed in Table 2.1 are of potential importance in organizations, for they influence how, and even if, a given person performs a particular task.

The basic principles of operant conditioning are relatively simple once mastered, and it is easy to see examples of these principles operating in organizations. But it is practically impossible to provide a meaningful explanation of organizational behavior management in terms of basic operant conditioning principles alone, for three reasons. First, adults have a rich and complicated history of behavior-environment interactions. Because of this history, a given stimulus usually has more than one behavioral function, and these functions change across time or situations. Second, a given behavior typically is multiply controlled, which means that many variables interact to determine whether the behavior occurs in a given situation. Important human behaviors often cannot be accounted for in terms of a simple A-B-C analysis. Third, and importantly, verbal behavior plays a crucial role in determining human activities. Verbal behavior is complex operant behavior and its understanding requires an analysis that goes beyond the unaugmented rat-in-a-Skinner-box model.

TABLE 2.1. Variables That Influence Operant Behavior in Verbal and Non-verbal Individuals*

1. Schedule of reinforcement: The schedule under which a response is maintained influences the rate and temporal pattern of operant behavior, choice, and resistance to extinction.**

2. Magnitude of reinforcement: Within limits, reinforcers that are larger in a physical sense have larger behavioral effects.

3. Delay of reinforcement: The longer the delay between a response and its consequence, the weaker the effects of that consequence.

4. Concurrent response options: The amount of time and effort that an individual spends in engaging in a particular operant is determined, in part, by the relative payoff of other responses that are possible in the situation.

5. Establishing operations: Altering the degree of deprivation relevant to a particular reinforcer, and related operations, influences the likelihood of occurrence of behaviors maintained by that reinforcer.

6. Learning history: An individual's history determines, in part, the reinforcing effectiveness of particular stimuli. It also influences the pattern of responding maintained under a given schedule of reinforcement, resistance to extinction, and choice.

7. Antecedent (i.e., discriminative) stimuli: Most operants are stimulus-controlled. The likelihood of such an operant occurring is determined, in part, by the degree to which the current circumstances resemble prior circumstances in which that operant was successful in producing reinforcement.

8. Response topography: The physical form of a response influences how easily that response is acquired, as well as its absolute rate of occurrence under given conditions.

9. Physiological perturbations: Variables that alter an individual's physiological status, including drugs and disease, often also alter operant behavior.

---

* These variables are considered in the context of reinforcement; they also influence the response-suppressive effects of punishment.

** The schedule of reinforcement actually specifies the delay of reinforcement, magnitude of reinforcement, response topography, and antecedent stimuli. These variables are considered separately in order to emphasize their effects.

VERBAL BEHAVIOR

Language, which comprises speaking, listening, reading, signing, and writing, sets humans apart from other animals. From the perspective of radical behaviorism, language neither exists apart from behavior nor represents ideas, concepts, or thoughts. Instead, it is simply a special class of operant behavior. To emphasize this, Skinner (1957) used the term verbal behavior to refer to what is commonly called language. The unique and defining aspect of *verbal behavior* is that it is reinforced through the mediation of other persons who are trained (although usually not formally) to reinforce such behavior (Skinner, 1957). Verbal behavior is like nonverbal operant behavior in that it is acquired as a result of its effects on the environment. Verbal behavior differs from nonverbal operant behavior primarily in that its effects on the environment are indirect; they are mediated by other people. For example, a bricklayer who runs out of mortar can get it by going to the mortar box and fetching a bucket, or by shouting to the mason's helper, "More mud." In the latter case, reinforcement (procurement of mortar) is mediated through the actions of another person. Therefore, verbal behavior is involved. The importance of such behavior in organizations is obvious. People constantly talk to one another and to themselves, and their words have powerful effects.

Making sense of how this occurs requires some method for classifying different kinds of verbal responses. Like all operant behavior, verbal behavior can be classified according to (a) the antecedent variables that evoke it, and (b) its consequences. On this basis, Skinner (1957) described five basic units of verbal behavior. Their characteristics are outlined in Table 2.2.

In Skinner's scheme, a given word can have many different functions, depending on the circumstances in which it occurs. Moreover, the function of an utterance is its "meaning." Suppose someone says "strike." What does it mean? The answer depends on the variables responsible for its emission, that is, on why it was spoken. If it is directed to an apprentice by a farrier making horseshoes, "strike" is a mand—it specifies an action on the part of the listener. If the farrier is passing by a picket line, "strike" is probably a tact—it describes a feature of the environment (i.e., people on strike). If it is in response to the question, "In baseball, if a pitch is not a ball, what is it?" then "strike" is an intraverbal. The "meaning" of the response "strike" cannot be discerned by its form or by the way it sounds. Instead, its meaning depends on why the speaker said it.

Any verbal response, whether a single word or a combination of words (e.g., a sentence or paragraph), usually has multiple functions and is under the control of more than one antecedent stimulus. This means that verbal behavior is not simply a linear sequence of stimuli and responses. For

TABLE 2.2. Characteristics and Examples (in Parentheses) of Basic Verbal
Operants

Response Type	Evoked by*	Usual Reinforcer
Mand (Speaker says, "A cheeseburger, please")	Motivational variable (Lack of cheeseburger)	Unconditioned or conditioned (Listener provides a cheeseburger)
Tact (Speaker says, "That is the Imagewriter ribbon")	Physical characteristics of an object or event (Appearance of the ribbon)	Conditioned (Listener says, "That's good to know")
Intraverbal (Speaker says, "How are you?")	Spoken stimulus (Approaching person says, "Good morning")	Conditioned (Listener smiles and says, "I'm fine")
Textual (Speaker says, "arbitrage")	Written stimulus (The word "arbitrage" is written on a blackboard)	Conditioned (Listener says, "Right")
Echoic (Speaker, a baby, says, "Ma-Ma")	Spoken stimulus (The baby's mother says, "Ma-Ma")	Conditioned (Listener says, "Good girl")

* Because verbal behavior involves the activity of a listener, the presence of such a person characteristically plays a role in the evocation of all verbal operants. But the same person can play the role of listener and speaker, which enables verbal behavior to occur when a person is alone.

example, a carpenter's response "it fits fine" to a co-worker's question, "How's that angle?" is determined not only by the characteristics of the joint in question (tact) but also by the co-worker's request for information (mand). Moreover, the carpenter's response is partly influenced by past interactions with the co-worker, for instance, the kind of joinery that person described as a "fine fit." Verbal behavior is audience-controlled behavior; what we say is determined, in a large part, by the people around us and our past experiences with them. For example, consider how sales-peoples' conversations differ when they are talking to customers, supervisors, and one another.

RULE-GOVERNED BEHAVIOR

Contingency-shaped behavior, exemplified by the lever pressing of Skinner's rats, is directly controlled by its consequences. The term contingency-shaped behavior emphasizes the importance of relations among stimuli and responses (i.e., contingencies) in controlling behavior. Unlike the behavior of other organisms, human behavior can be rule-governed, as well as contingency shaped (Hayes, 1989; Skinner, 1969). *Rule-governed behavior* is controlled by descriptions of contingencies. Those descriptions are termed rules (or instructions).

There is debate as to how rules affect behavior. Several authors have suggested that rules have an S^D function (e.g., Catania, 1984; Hayes et al., 1986). There is no doubt that, given an appropriate history, verbal behavior can serve as an S^D. Though important, such a function requires no special analysis.

The novel aspect of rules is that they are *contingency-specifying stimuli* that alter behavior by changing the function of other stimuli (Blakely and Schlinger, 1987; Schlinger and Blakely, 1987). Schlinger and Blakely (1987) provide thorough discussion and examples of the function-altering effects of rules. In the context of operant conditioning, rules may alter (a) the reinforcing function of stimuli, (b) the punishing function of stimuli, (c) the evocative function of establishing operations, and (d) the evocative function of discriminative stimuli. Rules also are capable of altering the control of behavior by stimuli in respondent arrangements.

As an example of the function-altering effects of rules, let us return to the farrier, who addresses the apprentice as the latter prepares to fabricate shoes independently for the first time. The farrier says, "Pump the bellows on the forge until the iron bar turns the color of straw; you can work it then. If it turns yellow, it's too hot and soft." This simple instruction is likely to render a straw-colored bar positively reinforcing, red and yellow bars something to avoid (i.e., negatively reinforcing). But it may not. Simply voicing a rule certainly does not ensure that it will be followed. Whether or not a person follows a particular rule is influenced by prior experiences with respect to the rule giver and the accuracy of similar rules provided in the past. People learn through operant conditioning to follow rules, or to refrain from following them.

The control of behavior by rules is significant in organizations because it provides for very rapid behavior change, and enables people to behave effectively without direct exposure to harmful or unpleasant outcomes. Rules also can increase the effectiveness of consequences that are too delayed to affect behavior directly. Although behavior controlled by the description of a given contingency (rule) does not necessarily closely resemble behavior controlled by actual exposure to that contingency, when rules provide an accurate description of actual contingencies, behaviors appropriate to those contingencies often emerge rapidly and are maintained (e.g., Baron, Kaufman, and Stauber, 1969; Weiner, 1970). But when rules are inconsistent with actual contingencies, behavior that does not meet environmental demands often emerges, and sensitivity to the actual consequences of responding is diminished (e.g., Buskist, Bennett, and Miller, 1981; Matthews, et al., 1977; Hayes et al., 1986).

Rules can be provided by others or formulated by the individual whose behavior they are to control. Self-generated rules play a significant role in observation learning, in which one behaves in a manner consistent with the actions of another person who was viewed at an earlier point in time. When a systematic attempt is made to generate behavior through observation learning, the procedure is termed modeling. Observation learning, which is considered further by other authors (Baer and Deguchi, 1985; Kymissis and Poulson, 1990), begins early in childhood, when reinforcement is provided for responses that mimic a model's actions as soon as they occur (e.g., parent waves bye-bye, baby waves bye-bye, baby gets cuddled). This operation establishes generalized imitation as operant behavior. Over time, stimulus control is established over imitative responding and self-generated rules come to play an important role in observation learning: The observer describes to himself or herself the contingencies in effect for the model and, if subsequently exposed to a situation similar to that in which a model's behavior produced a positive outcome, behaves in a manner consistent with those contingencies (i.e., as did the model). Modeling is most effective when antecedents and consequences of the model's operant responses, as well as the topography of those responses, are clearly evident.

The multitude of businesspeople who "dress for success" each working day provides a prime example of people following rules that allow them to resemble, in the case literally, successful individuals. As Tokyo's sea of blue suits emphasizes, people in organizations constantly generate and follow rules. Interventions that directly alter contingencies of reinforcement (or punishment), and therefore are intended to alter contingency-shaped responding, are apt also to affect rule-governed behavior. Delayed feedback, for instance, probably has little direct effect on the behaviors about which feedback is provided. More likely, it leads to the generation of rules that alter the function of the behaviors or products of behavior about which feedback is given, and this leads to behavior change. To illustrate, assume that an automobile salesperson meets with a supervisor on Friday afternoon and is criticized for failing several times through the week to get the telephone numbers of potential buyers, but is praised for having done so on rare occasions. This feedback is too delayed to affect salesperson-shopper relations directly. But it may cause the salesperson to generate a rule, something to the effect that: Every day at work (antecedent stimulus), I'll get the phone number of everyone who stops in (response), and then the boss will be happy (i.e., subsequently will praise and won't criticize). This rule renders the telephone number of potential customers reinforcing, and increases the likelihood of behaviors that have produced telephone numbers in the past.

Even though behavior analysts generally recognize the importance of rule-governed behavior, the vast majority of basic and applied studies have emphasized contingency-shaped responding. There is no generally accepted theoretical analysis of rule-governed behavior, and the various models proposed (including the one offered here) are hard to test. Moreover, strategies for systematically altering rule-governed behavior are essentially lacking. Hayes (1989) provides a good summary of the current status of research and theorizing in the general area, and Agnew and Redmon (1992) specifically consider the significance of rule-governed behavior for organizational behavior management. Clearly, although a good start has been made, there is work to be done.

CONCLUDING COMMENTS

Radical behaviorists are convinced that operant conditioning is primarily responsible for the complex repertoires that are evident in most adult humans. The classes of variables that affect operant behavior can be specified with some confidence, and it is possible to offer at least a plausible account of how these variables interact to produce elaborate sequences of responding, including such protypically "cognitive" activities as "thinking," "insight," and "problem solving" (e.g., Epstein, 1986; Epstein, Kirshnit, Lanza, and Rubin, 1984; Skinner, 1974).

It is also possible to isolate and manipulate variables that improve performance under a wide range of organizational settings. Consider, for example, the role of money in controlling employee activities. Although many other variables are important in determining precisely how workers behave, the money they receive for work performed is an especially important determinant. Despite individual differences in employee histories and current circumstances that create individual differences in their sensitivity to a given incentive system, most employees increase productivity when it pays off in terms of dollars earned. Hence, generally useful monetary incentive programs can be arranged in a variety of organizational settings (see Fritsch and Dickinson, 1990).

With very few exceptions, interventions in organizational behavior management are crude in the sense that they involve the manipulation of powerful and generally effective variables. Precisely why these variables are effective is seldom perfectly clear. As a case in point, performance feedback could in principle alter behavior by acting as a reinforcing, punishing, or discriminative stimulus, by serving as an establishing operation, or, as discussed previously, by fostering rule-governed behavior (c.f., Duncan and Bruwelheide, 1985/86; Peterson, 1982). The mechanism through which a particular feedback procedure affects behavior in a given person is rarely specifiable. But, regardless of mechanism, feedback procedures have repeatedly proven effective in producing desired changes in many (although not all) studies (e.g., Balcazar et al., 1985/86). This is true because, despite the uniqueness of every human being, most people have histories and current environments that are enough alike to render their behavior similarly sensitive to the kinds of arrangements termed feedback. Selection is partially responsible for this similarity: Intentionally or not, members of organizations are selected on the basis of shared repertoires, and probable susceptibility to behavioral control by the kinds of contingencies the organization arranges. Moreover, to remain part of an organization, an employee characteristically must respond in the desired fashion to behavior-change procedures implemented. The salesperson whose sales fall in the face of an incentive program that increases everyone else's sales will not be a salesperson for long.

The fact that behavior can sometimes be changed substantially without fine-grained analysis of the variables controlling behavior prior to an intervention, or of the behavioral mechanisms through which that intervention works, should not create false confidence for those intending to work in organizations. When contingencies have been arranged with little understanding of the variables that actually control behavior, as has often been the case in both the private and public sectors in the United States, it is not terribly difficult for a behavioral technician to make reasonable suggestions for improvement. But, as organizations faced with increasingly stringent competition necessarily become better at arranging contingencies that engender behaviors relevant to their survival, more subtle skills will be required to solve those problems that do arise. In the future, behavior analysts will be called upon to fine-tune, not jump-start, behavior in organizations.

Sophisticated behavior analytic skills will be demanded as the United States moves increasingly toward providing training for unskilled youth, older workers shifting positions, and managers and others performing complex and variable tasks (Goldstein and Gilliam, 1990; U.S. Congress, 1990). Specifying precisely what repertoires these people need to succeed and devising procedures for assessing, developing, and maintaining these repertoires requires exquisite understanding of behavior and its controlling variables. Radical behaviorists have that understanding; they should not miss this opportunity to use it.

NOTE

1. In matching-to-sample, during each trial one of a number of stimuli is initially presented alone, as a sample. After this occurs, two or more comparison stimuli are presented and a response to one of them, the correct comparison, is reinforced. The comparison stimulus designated as correct depends on the sample stimulus. In, for example, establishing stimulus A as equivalent to stimulus B and B as equivalent to C, B would be the correct comparison when A was the sample, and C would be the correct comparison when B was the sample.

REFERENCES

Agnew, J. L. and Redmon, W. K. (1992). Contingency specifying stimuli: The role of "rules" in organizational behavior management. *Journal of Organizational Behavior Management, 12*(2), 67-76.

Allison, J., and Timberlake, W. (1975). Response deprivation and instrumental performance in the controlled-amount paradigm. *Learning and Motivation, 6,* 112-142.

Arvey, R. D. and Ivanevich, J. M. (1980). Punishment in organizations: A review, propositions, and research suggestions. *Academy of Management Review, 5,* 123-132.

Ayllon, T. and Kolko, D. J. (1982). Productivity and schedules of reinforcement in business and industry. In R. M. O'Brien, A. M. Dickinson, and M. Rosow (Eds.), *Industrial behavior modification: A learning-based approach to business management* (pp. 35-50). New York: Pergamon.

Baer, D. M. and Deguchi, H. (1985). Generalized imitation from a radical-behavioral viewpoint. In S. Reiss and R. R. Bootzin (Eds.), *Theoretical issues in behavior therapy* (pp. 179-217). Orlando, FL: Academic Press.

Balcazar, F., Hopkins, B. L., and Suarez, Y. (1985/86). A critical, objective review of performance feedback. *Journal of Organizational Behavior Management, 7*(3/4), 65-89.

Baron, A., Kaufman, A., and Stauber, K. A. (1969). Effect of instructions and reinforcement feedback on human operant behavior maintained by fixed-interval reinforcement. *Journal of the Experimental Analysis of Behavior, 12,* 701-712.

Blakely, E. and Schlinger, H. (1987). Rules: Function-altering contingency-specifying stimuli. *The Behavior Analyst, 10,* 183-187.

Buskist, W. F., Bennett, R. H., and Miller, H. L., Jr. (1981). Effects of instructional constraints on human fixed-interval performance. *Journal of the Experimental Analysis of Behavior, 35,* 217-225.

Catania, A. C. (1984). *Learning.* (Second edition). Englewood Cliffs, NJ: Prentice-Hall.

Catania, A. C. (1992). *Learning.* (Third edition). Englewood Cliffs, NJ: Prentice-Hall.

Duncan, P. K. and Bruwelheide, L. R. (1985/86). Feedback: Use and possible behavioral functions. *Journal of Organizational Behavior Management, 7*(3/4), 91-114.

Epstein, R. (1986). Simulation research in the analysis of behavior. In A. Poling and R. W. Fuqua (Eds.), *Research methods in applied behavior analysis: Issues and advances* (pp. 127-155). New York: Plenum Press.

Epstein, R., Kirshnit, C., Lanza, R. P., and Rubin, L. (1984). "Insight" in the pigeon: Antecedents and determinants of intelligent performance. *Nature, 308,* 61-62.

Frisch, C. J. and Dickinson, A. M. (1990). Work productivity as a function of the percentage of monetary incentives to base pay. *Journal of Organizational Behavior Management, 11,* 13-33.

Goldstein, I. L. and Gilliam, P. (1990). Training system issues in the year 2000. *American Psychologist, 45,* 134-143.

Hayes, S. C. (1989). *Rule-governed behavior: Cognition, contingencies, and instructional control* (pp. 153-190). New York: Plenum Press.

Hayes, S. C., Brownstein, A. J., Zettle, R. D., Rosenfarb, I., and Korn, Z. (1986). Rule-governed behavior and sensitivity to changing consequences of responding. *Journal of the Experimental Analysis of Behavior, 45,* 237-256.

Konarski, E. A. Jr., Johnson, M. R., Crowell, C. R., and Whitman, T. L. (1981). An alternative approach to reinforcement for applied researchers: Response deprivation. *Behavior Therapy, 12,* 653-666.

Kymissis, E. and Poulson, C. L. (1990). The history of imitation in learning theory: The language acquisition process. *Journal of the Experimental Analysis of Behavior, 54,* 113-127.

Latham, G. P. and Dossett, D. L. (1978). Designing incentive plans for unionized employees: A comparison of continuous and variable-ratio reinforcement *Personnel Psychology, 31,* 47-61.

Latham, G. P. and Huber, V. L. (1992). Schedules of reinforcement: Lessons from the past and issues for the future. *Journal of Organizational Behavior Management, 12*(1), 125-149.

Lewis, D. J. (1963). *Scientific principles of psychology.* Englewood Cliffs, NJ: Prentice-Hall.

Matthews, B. A., Shimoff, E., Catania, A. C., and Sagvolden, T. (1977). Uninstructed human responding: Sensitivity to ratio and interval contingencies. *Journal of the Experimental Analysis of Behavior, 27,* 453-467.

Mawhinney, T. C. and Gowen, C. R., III. (1991). Gainsharing and the law of effect as the matching law: A theoretical framework. *Journal of Organizational Behavior Management, 11*(2), 61-75.

Michael, J. L. (1975). Positive and negative reinforcement, a distinction that is no longer necessary; or a better way to talk about bad things. *Behaviorism, 3,* 149-155.

Michael, J. L. (1982). Distinguishing between discriminative and motivational functions of stimuli. *Journal of the Experimental Analysis of Behavior, 37,* 149-155.

Pavlov, I. P. (1927). *Conditioned reflexes* (C. V. Anrep, trans.). Oxford, England: Clarendon.

Peterson, N. (1982). Feedback is not a new principle of behavior. *The Behavior Analyst, 5,* 101-102.

Premack, D. (1959). Toward empirical laws. Part 1: Positive reinforcement. *Psychological Review, 66,* 219-233.

Premack, D. (1965). Reinforcement theory. In D. Levine (Ed.), *Nebraska Symposium on Motivation* (Vol. 13, pp. 123-180). Lincoln: University of Nebraska Press.

Premack, D. (1971). Catching up with common sense or two sides of a generalization: Reinforcement and punishment. In R. Glaser (Ed.), *The nature of reinforcement* (pp. 121-150). New York: Academic Press.

Redmon, W. K. and Lockwood, K. (1986). The matching law and organizational behavior. *Journal of Organizational Behavior Management, 8*(1), 57-72.

Rescorla, R. A. and Wagner, A. R. (1972). A theory of Pavlovian conditioning: Variations in the effectiveness of reinforcement and nonreinforcement. In A. H. Black and W. F. Prokasy (Eds.), *Classical conditioning II* (pp. 64-99). New York: Appleton-Century-Crofts.

Saari, L. M. and Latham, G. P. (1982). Employee reactions to continuous and variable ratio reinforcement schedules involving monetary incentive. *Journal of Applied Psychology, 67,* 506-509.

Schlinger, H. and Blakely, E. (1987). Function-altering effects of contingency-specifying stimuli. *The Behavior Analyst, 10,* 41-45.

Schwartz, B. (1989). *Psychology of learning and behavior.* New York: Norton.

Sidman, M. (1986). Functional analysis of emergent verbal classes. In T. Thompson and M. D. Zeiler (Eds.), *Analysis and integration of behavioral units* (pp. 213-245). Hillsdale, NJ: Erlbaum.

Skinner, B. F. (1938). *The behavior of organisms.* New York: Appleton-Century-Crofts.

Skinner B. F. (1953). *Science and human behavior.* New York: Macmillan.

Skinner, B. F. (1957). *Verbal behavior.* Englewood Cliffs, NJ: Prentice-Hall.

Skinner, B. F. (1969). *Contingencies of reinforcement.* New York: Meredith.

Skinner, B. F. (1974). *About behaviorism.* New York: Knopf.

Skinner, B. F. (1987). *Upon further reflection.* Englewood Cliffs, NJ: Prentice-Hall.

Timberlake, W. (1980). A molar equilibrium theory of learned performance. In G. H. Bower (Ed.), *The psychology of learning and motivation* (Vol. 14, pp. 1-58). New York: Academic Press.

Timberlake, W. (1984). Behavioral regulation and learned performance: Some misapprehensions and disagreements. *Journal of the Experimental Analysis of Behavior, 41,* 355-375.

Timberlake, W. and Allison, J. (1974). Response deprivation: An empirical approach to instrumental performance. *Psychological Review, 81,* 146-164.

U.S. Congress, Office of Technology Assessment. (1990). *Worker training: Competing in the new international economy,* OTA-ITE-457. Washington, DC: U.S. Government Printing Office.

Weiner, H. (1970). Instructional control of human operant responding during extinction following fixed-ratio conditioning. *Journal of the Experimental Analysis of Behavior, 13,* 391-394.

Zeiler, M. (1977). Schedules of reinforcement: The controlling variables. In W. K. Honig and J. E. R. Staddon (Eds.), *Handbook of operant behavior* (pp. 201-232). Englewood Cliffs, NJ: Prentice-Hall.

Chapter 3

Developing Performance Appraisals: Criteria for What and How Performance Is Measured

Judith L. Komaki
Michelle Reynard Minnich

Despite the lip service paid to the fair definition and accurate appraisal of target behaviors, these two steps are often glossed over when setting up motivational programs. Yet, both the industrial/organization (I/O) and applied behavior analysis (ABA) communities emphasize the importance of what and how performance is measured. In I/O psychology, *performance appraisal* is one of five major areas (Campbell, 1990; Cardy and Dobbins, 1994; Dunnette, 1963; James, 1973; Latham, Skarlicki, Irvine, and Siegel, 1993; Latham and Latham, 2000; Murphy and Cleveland, 1995; Shaw, Schneier, Beatty, and Baird, 1995; Smither, 1998). I/O psychologists constantly grapple with their failure to develop decent indices of performance, what they refer to as the "criterion problem" (Blum and Naylor, 1968). Steers, Porter, and Bigley (1996) admit that even in "the best-designed reward systems . . . , the evaluation or appraisal of performance [is] perhaps the most basic concern" (p. 500). ABA researchers agree that the way in which targets are defined and measured profoundly influence the ultimate goal of enhancing desired performance (Bellack and Hersen, 1988; Ciminero, Calhoun, and Adams, 1986; Goldfried and Kent, 1972; Johnston and Pennypacker, 1993). Weist, Ollendick, and Finney (1991) frown on such dubious practices as basing definitions on expediency and choosing erroneous or irrelevant indices. Foster and Cone (1986) question whether the expectations of the raters will bias the results.

These criticisms continue, however. This faultfinding is not restricted to academics. Employees complain as well. Some have successfully sought compensation in court, affirming their charges that raters were influenced

51

by irrelevant characteristics such as their race, gender, or age rather than employees' sustained performance on the job (Ashe and McRae, 1985; Cascio and Bernardin, 1981; Feild and Holley, 1982; Werner and Bolino, 1997). Two major problems have been identified with traditional performance appraisal systems: the vague way in which performance is defined and the bias of the raters. An analysis of law court cases since 1973 indicated that "in six of ten cases decided against the organization, the plaintiffs were able to show that subjective standards had been applied unevenly to minority and majority employees" (Barrett and Kernan, 1987, p. 501).

This chapter begins by illustrating some prevalent problems. To do this, we draw upon articles in the research and professional literature, as well as court cases. Although the examples presented here take place in work settings, they can be found in virtually any applied setting. To counteract these criticisms, five criteria for appraisal systems are proposed, referred to as the SURF and C (Komaki, 1998a). Examples are from diverse settings with different work groups doing a variety of jobs.

PROBLEMS WITH WHAT TO APPRAISE

One of the major problems is the substance, or content, of what is measured, whether it be employees' personality traits (e.g., cooperation, dependability), the outcomes of the work (e.g., the number of injuries per million hours worked, the accuracy of preventive maintenance checklists), or the work behaviors themselves (e.g., providing customer service, being safe).

When Judgments of Performance Are Based on Aspects of the Job That Do Not Adequately Represent the Job

What is measured does not always reflect what is critical to the job or include all of the many essential aspects of the job. For example, a sales agent at a California carrier was dismayed to find that an important aspect of her job—providing quality service—was apparently disregarded in appraising her performance (Bravo, 1991). One day the agent received a call from a distraught customer whose relative had died. The agent not only made a complicated set of arrangements, booking flights from one remote area to another, but also managed to keep the customer calm. Later, she was appalled when her supervisor reprimanded her for spending too much time on the call. Evidently, she was judged on the amount of time she had spent with one customer, and she had exceeded the prescribed amount. While efficiency was, no doubt, an integral aspect of the job, another vital aspect—the quality of the service—was downplayed. Thus, she questioned whether her supervisor's appraisal took into consideration both of these important aspects of her job.

This same concern about *substance* surfaces in the complaints aired about the Internal Revenue Service (Rosenbaum, 1998, p. A15). A major criticism was its heavy emphasis on "production quotas" to the detriment of the taxpayer ("After Critical Inquiry," 1992, p. A18). A consultant notes that "in a numbers-driven organization, . . . if they say, 'You've got to collect X amount of dollars. . . , well, all of a sudden the taxpayer becomes subordinate to that goal' " (p. A18). If IRS agents are judged primarily in terms of the amount of revenue they bring in and the high "producers" are promoted, then other aspects of the job, such as following prescribed regulations and properly justifying tax assessments, will fall by the wayside. Although perhaps inadvertently, those who "take advantage of taxpayers" (p. A18) may be reinforced.

Questions have also been raised about what is being monitored electronically (Griffith, 1993; Schrage, 1992). The aspects of the job that are typically assessed are those things that are amenable to being counted; for example, the number of keystrokes, the length of phone calls, and "down" time. Because of the ease of obtaining information on these factors, more and more organizations (department stores, airlines, insurance agencies, and telephone companies) are using them to appraise their employees. Unfortunately, other critical aspects, such as the accuracy of the information entered, may be neglected. Assessments of insurance clerks, for example, are typically made on the quantity of claim forms processed, regardless of accuracy. In each of these examples, the issue is the substance of the appraisal and whether it adequately reflects what employees do; whether the critical aspects are included and the noncritical excluded.

When Judgments of Performance Are Based on Aspects of the Job That Persons Cannot Sufficiently Influence

Another content-related issue concerns the control that employees can realistically exert over the indices of their performance.

A woman's mother, who had suffered a serious heart attack, lay dying in a hospital in need of an operation that no doctor would perform (Byer, 1992). The cardiologist believed that the woman's mother would die within a few days if the operation was not performed, but the surgeons whom the family contacted either refused to operate or wanted to wait a week.

Why did the surgeons refuse to operate? In this case, the surgery was too risky and the surgeons contacted had too many black marks on their names. One doctor who spoke frankly with the woman and her family was quoted as saying, "Don't you think that the chief of surgery would love to do this operation? . . . He's a great surgeon but he's taken too many high-risk cases lately . . ." (Byer, 1992, p. A23). At that time (it has since changed), the New York State Department of Health judged surgeons solely by what is known as a "surgical scorecard": a record of the number of patient deaths (Altman, 1992). What the scorecards failed to reflect, however, was the complexity of the operation and the patient's health condition before surgery. Patients may die not because of the physician's skill in performing the surgery, but because of these "uncontrollable factors." Hence, to judge surgeons' competence solely on the basis of fatalities would not fairly reflect their performance in the operating room.

A similar control issue is raised in relation to an index sometimes used to reflect employee performance—stock prices. Although some economists would argue that the best measure of a company's performance (and by inference, the employees in the company) is the stock price (e.g., Baker, Gibbons, and Murphy, 1994), stock prices reflect many factors over which employees can exert relatively little control. A memorable illustration of this can be seen in a graph depicting stock prices for United Airlines from January through September 1990 (Berg, 1990). The carrier's stock price tumbled dramatically in July from $160 to less than $100 per share. If one assumes that stock prices reflect employee performance, then by inference one would have to conclude that their performance had plummeted at the same time. Astute observers of the airlines, however, attributed the precipitous drop in stock prices to a variety of uncontrollable factors: takeover bids confounded by the departure of three chief executives in four years, rising fuel prices, and a need to cut costs. Furthermore, countervailing evidence suggested that the employees' performance was actually on the upswing during the same period—the airline had improved its service, the number of times that the ground crews had mishandled baggage was down, and on-time arrivals and departures were up.

Relying on stock prices or surgical scorecards as the sole evaluation makes it more likely that the "uncontrollables" get overestimated and employees' performance is underestimated. Latham and colleagues (1993) refer to this problem as the omission of "the organizational context in which the appraisal process is embedded" (p. 122).

In summary, problems can occur with the substance of what is measured. When the appraisals are primarily based on indices over which employees can exert relatively little influence and when measures are incomplete, neglecting all of the critical aspects of the job, misleading estimates of employees' performance may be produced.

THE "HOW" ISSUES IN PERFORMANCE APPRAISAL

Besides these two content-oriented problems, another challenge concerns the way in which performance is measured: the relatively low (or nonexistent) levels of interrater reliability, the indirect methods used in evaluating performance, and the rarity of appraisals.

When Judgments of Performance Are Based on Information That Has Been Collected Semiannually or Annually

A common practice in many organizations is to evaluate employees once, or at most twice, a year. About one-third of a sample of about 700 survey respondents, who were exempt employees in a manufacturing organization, reported on an anonymous questionnaire that their performance was not even evaluated at least once a year (Landy, Barnes, and Murphy, 1978). (Note: Significantly enough, the frequency of appraisals was found to be one of the factors related to employee perceptions of the fairness and accuracy of their evaluations.)

In discussing the difficulties of appraising employees, one executive admitted: "Many of us have trouble rating for the entire year. If one of my people has a stellar three months prior to the review . . . you don't want to do anything that impedes that person's momentum and progress" (Longenecker, Sims, and Gioia, 1987, p. 188). The implication here is that employee ratings occur once a year and reflect performance over less than the entire year.

Because of a reliance on retrospective and rarely made accounts, questions are raised about the accuracy of the judgments in relation to performance.

When Performance Judgments Are Based on Information That Is Collected Indirectly

Many appraisals do not go directly to the source, but instead rely on secondhand information. For instance, a store manager evaluates supervisors by the letters received from distraught customers; a city manager judges the performance of the superintendent of the wastewater treatment plant by relying on the opinion of the assistant superintendent; a department chair judges the quality of professors' teaching by relying on student complaints. Among the problems with these secondary sources is that the information may be generated from biased sources, and hence sifted through a nonneutral filter. The assistant superintendent may aspire to the job of the superintendent. Customers and students who complain may not be representative.

Even when the sources are neutral, the fidelity of the information may suffer when it is not directly sampled. The case of a bond trader, Jett, at a Wall Street firm provides an involved but nonetheless realistic example of what happens when one relies on secondhand information (Nasar, 1994). To judge Jett's performance, his supervisor depended on the firm's accounting system. However, discrepancies turned up between what was recorded on the system as trades (and profit) and the trades that were actually consummated. This particular discrepancy turned out to be major, resulting in a $350 million inflation of Kidder's profits for the year. In discussing how such a discrepancy could have occurred, Jett's supervisor vehemently disagreed, pointing out that it was "unrealistic and irresponsible to suggest one person could personally supervise a dozen departments without relying on a firm's internal auditing system" (p. D 14). An analyst at another company pointed out that, even though Jett's supervisor didn't have responsibility for the auditing system, he did have "responsibility for independently verifying what's going on" (p. D 14). Another Wall Street manager agreed that it was critical for a general manger to be aware of what employees are doing with respect to their trading practices. "He should never have had to rely entirely on secondary sources" (p. D 14). Only when Jett's supervisor did an "initial look-see" did he uncover the loophole of trades that counted as trades even though they were never consummated.

When Judgments of Performance Are Based on Information That Is Not Confirmed by More Than One Rater

Rarely does more than one supervisor rate the performance of employees; a lone supervisor usually conducts the appraisal. Not surprisingly, few checks are made to determine if one supervisor would rate an employee the same way as another. That is often a problem. In a comprehensive and thoughtful analysis of observational measures, Foster and Cone (1986) express skepticism about having a single rater do an evaluation alone. They point to rater drift in which a rater's definitions shift over time, and rater bias in which a rater's beliefs and perceptions about who and what they are observing can taint their findings. For the latter, it has been shown that both conscious and inadvertent biases or distortions can creep in and reduce the accuracy of the information obtained. In a study comparing direct observations and self-ratings, biases were found even when college students estimated something as neutral as how often they interacted with given individuals in their dorm. The tendency was to discount interactions with persons with ". . . whom they were relatively low-frequency co-interactants, in favor of those with whom they were reciprocally high" (Hammer, 1985, p. 201). Discrepancies have even been found between the data recorded by managers themselves and their estimations of what they had done (Lewis and Dahl, 1976). The discrepancies were not necessarily random. Managers in another study were found to substantially overestimate some activities (e.g., the time spent on production) and underestimate others (e.g., personnel) (Burns, 1954), leading to biased estimates of performance.

Rater bias continues to be raised by employees as well: women at the Voice of America (Kilborn, 2000), Asian-American scientists at the Los Alamos weapon laboratory (Glanz, 2000) and African-American agents at the Federal Bureau of Investigation (Johnston, 1998). One court case involved Texaco's employment practices particulary regarding its performance appraisal system (*Roberts v. Texaco*, 1994). The class action suit filed on behalf of 1,400 minority employees asserted that Texaco systematically discriminates against minority employees in promotions. Besides generating front-page head-lines with taped conversations of Texaco executives disparaging African-American employees and identifying them as being "glued to the bottom of the bag" (Eichenwald, 1996, p. D4), the lawsuit characterized the company's performance appraisal system as "entirely arbitrary, and . . . used as a pretext for denying qualified minority employees promotions to which they are otherwise entitled" (*Roberts v. Texaco*, 1994, p. 9). As evidence, plaintiff Bari-Ellen Roberts pointed out that in Texaco's own Diversity Assessment Survey throughout the company, all groups—women and men, minority and majority—saw "criteria other than performance as being barriers to promotions, with most employees feeling that promotions are based on who you know, rather than performance" (p. 11).

Complicating matters is the fact that the traditional performance appraisal systems used in most any Fortune 1000 firm are faulty. Even the most well meaning raters would have difficulty rendering fair and accurate judgments, given the forms they are asked to fill out with few if any definitions of performance, the sparseness of their training, and, perhaps most important, the utter lack of follow-through to ensure that employees are rated irrespective of their gender, age, race, or sexual orientation on only what matters—their sustained record of performance on the job. Supervisors are typically asked to rate employees on a variety of generic dimensions such as quantity and quality of work, job or trade knowledge, ability to learn, cooperation, dependability, industry, and attendance. Generic dimensions are often used so that supervisors in a wide variety of departments can utilize preprinted forms to evaluate all of their employees. Problems have occurred with these generic dimensions, however. In another court case, for example, referred to as *James v. Stockham Valves and Fittings Co.* (1977), an employee named James brought a case against his employer, Stockham Valves and Fittings Co. James' contention was that the seven dimensions used to appraise him were so general as to be open to a wide variety of individual definitions, interpretations, and possible biases. For example, in assessing dependability, Supervisor A might think of it as the person being on the job every day, regardless of circumstances such as illness or bad weather, whereas Supervisor B might see it as being able to count on the person to do what he said he would do in a timely manner. This could lead to a situation in which James would be judged highly by Supervisor A and poorly by Supervisor B. The company could have countered by providing data showing that interrater reliability checks had been made between supervisors collecting data on the same employees and that agreements between the different raters were uniformly high. If such evidence had been presented, a case could have been made that the definitions were clear, the supervisors were trained, and that factors unrelated to performance did not bias the ratings employees were given.

Besides the lack of interrater reliability checks, the infrequency of the appraisals and the indirectness of the sampling were raised as methodological issues. As can be seen, both the method in which evaluations are made and the content of the appraisals have been problematic.

WHAT CAN BE DONE TO IMPROVE CONTENT AND METHOD?

Given the gamut of complaints that exist in relation to what and how to assess performance, we have surveyed the literature in I/O psychology that focuses on appraising employee performance. In some cases, we found that problems were satisfactorily resolved. At an air freight company (Doyle and Shapiro, 1980), it was found that numerous errors and delays occurred in tracking shipment counts: "it took from three to five months for feedback on sales to reach" sales representatives, and "it was often impossible to determine whether they or the salespeople on the other end should get credit for the sale" (p. 139). This lack of consistency in pinpointing who was responsible for closing the sale was identified as causing problems in motivating the sales personnel. In this case, the appraisal system was redesigned to ensure accurate and timely sales information. After this change, the three test offices "moved to among the top producers in their respective regions, increasing shipments an average of 34.7 percent" (p. 140).

Revisions to a measure of preventive maintenance (PM) were also successfully made in the U.S. Marines (Komaki, 1998a). During Year 1, a measure was developed including the time Marines utilized, and a program was introduced that included the exchange of time-off with pay. Data were collected for a year. Surprisingly, no changes were forthcoming. The failure forced Komaki (1998a) to see how she had fallen prey to expediency. Among the reasons for the failure was her choice of the target. Time utilization could be easily and reliably defined in four words—"manipulating tools or equipment." It entailed no specialized knowledge. Interrater reliability was obtained quickly. Unfortunately, it did not meet the criterion of being under workers' control. The marines complained that they could not utilize their time well if they could not control when they were sent to do the work. In Year 2, she redesigned the measure of PM so that it was primarily under the marines' control, thus meeting all of the SURF & C criteria. Even though the program was less potent, utilizing only feedback, significant improvements were found. Supervisory personnel rated the intervention as "very" to "extremely" effective. All parties agreed that they had a better idea of the maintenance effort. One unit supervisor remarked that the targets were "probably as objective as any evaluation could be" (p. 271).

Traditional Performance Appraisal Literature Is Primarily Descriptive

Disappointingly, the previous examples are rarities. Much of the literature does not go beyond a description of the different types of appraisals. One listing divides them into (1) "objective" indices such as production and sales data, as well as personnel information about absences, tardiness, promotions, tenure, and accidents; and (2) judgmental indices in which supervisors give their opinion of employee performance (DeVries et al., 1980). The latter includes: (1) global essays (a narrative about the worker's performance); (2) graphic rating scales ("rate this person on dependability where 1 = excellent and 5 = poor"); (3) ranking ("list employees in order in terms of dependability"), and four techniques combining various ways of producing the target behaviors and presenting the information to the rater; (4) the critical incident technique ("describe a situation in which employees were either very dependable or very undependable") (Flanagan, 1954); (5) mixed standard scales (Blanz and Ghiselli, 1972); (6) behaviorally anchored rating scales (Smith and Kendall, 1963); and (7) behavioral observation scales (Latham and Wexley, 1981). (For more detailed information, please refer to the citations.)

Occasionally, comparisons are made among the different types of appraisals. DeVries and colleagues (1980) evaluated the above types of appraisals according to various criteria: content validity (or job relatedness), criterion/construct validity, reliability, discriminability for selecting employees, usefulness for administrative decisions such as promotions, and feedback for motivational purposes—the focus of the present chapter. When feedback is the aim, behaviorally anchored rating scales (BARS) and the objective approach were judged to be the "strongest" (p. 50). Although these comparisons go beyond describing the types of appraisals, few studies have been conducted to determine whether one type of appraisal is superior to another (c.f., Gomez-Mejia, 1988).

Prescriptions Are Limited

The earliest research to focus on appraisals concerned the format, or layout, of graphic rating scales (Landy and Farr, 1980). Formats were varied with changes in the types of anchors, the position of the high end of the scale, the spatial orientation of the scale, the segmentation of the scale line, the numbering of scale levels, and the number of response categories. For example, when the research consistently showed that an excessive number of response categories had detrimental effects on reliability, no more than nine scale anchors were recommended.

Unfortunately, this format-oriented research is limited to rating scales. Moreover, many of the results were inconclusive. Though raters had preferences for some formats (e.g., physical arrangements of high and low anchors and numbering systems), Landy and Farr (1980) conclude that even when they were granted their preferences, the new formats had relatively little effect on the quality of the ratings.

Recently, attention has shifted to the raters themselves and the cognitive processes involved when appraising others. A variety of models have been proposed (e.g., DeNisi, 1996; Feldman, 1981; Ilgen and Feldman, 1983; Landy and Farr, 1980). All view the rater as an active collector of information, and all are based on a process whereby raters acquire, store, recall, and combine information to make judgments. The major difference among the models is that each focuses on a different part of the process. The

DeNisi (1996) model, for instance, concentrates on the information acquisition activities of the rater and also emphasizes the importance of information storage in memory. A basic assumption in this model is that the pattern in which information is acquired has a significant impact on later information processing. The authors postulate that the observation of behavior is affected by the rater's preconceived notions or impressions of the person he or she is rating, the purpose for which the appraisal is conducted, time pressures on the rater, and the nature of the rating instrument (including the different dimensions). Raters are not thought to use all information available to them, but rather to form global impressions of employees that obscure behavioral detail.

The primary recommendation that has come from this line of research is that raters should be trained, usually by learning the standards by which they are to judge performance or in the cognitive processes they go through in observing, encoding, storing, recalling, and integrating performance information (Borman, 1991). To make more accurate ratings, DeNisi, Cafferty, and Meglino (1984) suggest the use of diary keeping and familiarity with rating scales. These techniques are thought to reduce distortion by providing a way in which raters can structure and organize information to be stored in memory (to facilitate processing), and also to rely less upon memories of performance. If this is the case, then this recommendation would have direct implications for improving the inter-rater reliability of the raters. Even if raters could be trained until they are reliable, the training deals with only one methodological aspect of the process and does not address any of the content issues.

Few Specifics Related to Content

Although few investigators have touched upon the content and method problems identified earlier in this chapter, suggestions about the content of appraisals have not been entirely absent. Many of these discussions take place over the selection or hiring of employees. When hiring a worker, various tests (e.g., of cognitive ability or motor skills) are sometimes given to prospective employees to predict the person's performance on the job, referred to as the "criterion." Many problems have occurred when defining what constitutes an adequate assessment of a person's performance. To avoid this criterion problem (Blum and Naylor, 1968), many suggestions have been made. The traditional advice is to make sure that the criterion is valid and related to the job, and that it represents important aspects of the job, is free from contamination (or the influence of factors other than important aspects of the job), and is free from deficiency (or the incompleteness and omission of important aspects) (Smith, 1976).

Three problems exist, however, with this general guidance. One, many of the definitions are not clear. How relevant does a criterion need to be before it is "relevant"? Exactly what is considered "deficient"? Two, few, if any, constructive suggestions are made about what to measure. For example, as long as measurements of any of three basic categories of content (individual personality traits, behaviors, and outcomes/results) identified by DeVries and colleagues (1980) are part of a job, they are considered appropriate for use. If we take the case of IRS agents, several questions can be posed. Should agents be judged on outcomes/results—the amount of revenue they amass? Should other factors be included? If so, which ones? Furthermore, almost no mention is made of how the information is collected other than to highlight the importance of reliability.

In short, few recommendations have indicated how to constructively improve what is appraised in order to ensure that the target behaviors include critical aspects of the job and are responsive to workers' efforts. At the same time, relatively little research deals with how employees are evaluated. These issues are not addressed by the comparisons among the different types of performance. The models generated about the cognitive processes of raters and the research conducted on the graphic rating scale have implications for only one methodological issue, that of the reliability of the raters.

NEW CRITERIA FOR CRITERIA

SURF & C

In response to the concerns raised, five criteria (or standards) are recommended (Komaki, 1998a). These criteria, referred to by the mnemonic SURF & C, include:

S: the target being directly *sampled* rather than relying on filtered or secondary sources;

U: the target being primarily *under* the control of workers, responsive to their efforts, and minimally affected by extraneous factors;

R: independent observers consistently agreeing on their recordings and obtaining interrater *reliability* scores of 80 percent to (ideally) 90 percent or better during the formal data collection period;

F: the target being assessed *frequently* and on a regular reoccurring basis—at least twenty and ideally thirty times—during the period of the intervention; and

C: evidence indicating that the target is *critical* for the successful completion of the task. Data must be provided showing a significant relationship between the target and the intended outcome.

When two of the criteria—being under control (U) and being critical (C)—are met, the target is considered to be appropriate in content for appraising performance. To ensure the method used in obtaining the information is appropriate, the appraisal should meet the criteria of being directly sampled (S), passing the test of interrater reliability (R), and being frequently (F) assessed.

The term target is used here in the same sense as operational definition or criterion. It is not restricted to behaviors, but it can include the outcomes of these behaviors as well. Hence, making errors as well as the errors themselves could be considered targets.

Application

These SURF & C criteria are designed to provide standards for measuring behaviors needing improvement. As such, they are explicitly limited to these motivational situations. When the aim is performance improvement, however, they are highly recommended.

The SURF & C criteria lend themselves to providing consequences that are frequent, positive, and contingent, the hallmarks of a well-designed motivational program based on operant conditioning principles (Kazdin, 2000; Komaki, Coombs, Redding, and Schepman, 2000; Malott, Whaley, and Malott, 1997; Sulzer-Azaroff and Mayer, 1991). Furthermore, they reflect the operant model of effective supervision inspired by the theory (Komaki, 1998b). The *frequent* (F) assessment of targets is the foundation for providing consequences on a regularly reoccurring basis, as required in the frequency of reinforcement principle (Miller, 1997). The frequency criterion counters the common practice in organizations to appraise performance semiannually or annually. When targets are responsive to workers' efforts, workers are more apt to engage in the desired targets. The reliability of the assessments (R), and the frequent (F) and direct sampling (S) of the target, enhance obtaining more representative and accurate information. In turn, the higher quality information enhances the closeness of the relationship between behavior and consequences. Thus, the groundwork is laid for providing *contingent* consequences. The criteria of being critical (C) and under control (U) also lend themselves to providing *positive* consequences. Management is more likely to recognize workers for target behaviors tapping critical aspects of the task. Furthermore, the process of gathering evidence to identify which behaviors are critical aids in the specification of the desired behaviors. Ensuring that the target behaviors are responsive to workers' efforts and minimally affected by extraneous influences makes it more likely that workers will be motivated to improve and maintain their behavior.

Examples

To show how the criteria can be applied, examples are presented of different work groups doing a variety of jobs. Summarized in Table 3.1, the examples are drawn from four areas, identified as safety, service, human services and education, and professional/complex.

To set the context for each of the areas, we will briefly identify the research questions, subjects and settings, and some of the dependent variables or targets. A frequent aim of *safety* experiments is to improve workers' practices, with the ultimate aim of reducing accidents (Fellner and Sulzer-Azaroff, 1984; Hopkins, Conrad, and Smith, 1986; Komaki, Collins, and Penn, 1982; Ludwig and Geller, 1991; Reber and Wallin, 1983). The targets have consisted of various behaviors (e.g., wearing hard hats, ear protection, and goggles; working in areas with exhaust ventilation; spraying chemicals away from other workers; using seat belts and turn signals) and outcomes (e.g., housekeeping conditions or the status of materials in the organization). These studies took place in a paper mill, a plastic products manufacturing plant, and a pizzeria, with laborers, machine operators, and deliverers.

The second area deals with the *service* provided by bank tellers, foreign exchange clerks, and retail salespeople (Elizur, 1987; George, 1991; Komaki, Collins, and Temlock, 1987; Luthans, Paul, and Baker, 1981). Different aspects of service were assessed, including both functional—contact with customers (e.g., words of courtesy, smiling, approaching), service rendered (e.g., assessing customer's needs, relating merchandise to needs), merchandise handling (e.g., tagging, arranging, replenishing, or unpacking merchandise—and dysfunctional behaviors (e.g., socializing, standing idly, and leaving the work area).

In the third area, staff worked in various *human service* and *educational* organizations—an institution, a center for psychological services, and a pediatric clinic (Callahan and Redmon, 1987; Frederiksen et al., 1982; Ingham and Greer, 1992; Iwata et al., 1976; Johnson and Frederiksen, 1983). The dependent variables included patient care (e.g., dental care and patient contact), the rate and accuracy of teaching behaviors, being on or off the unit, use of time (e.g., number of patients seen), and recording the progress of patients (e.g., errors made on client charts).

TABLE 3.1. Examples of Appraisals Meeting One or More SURF & C Criteria

	S: Direct Sampling	U: Under Control	R: Reliability Between Observers	F: Data Collected Frequently	C: Critical Aspects of the Task
Safety	Checking of safe and unsafe behaviors of employees while operating a machine or conducting a task; also examining condition of materials and equipment in a paper mill (Fellner and Sulzer-Azaroff, 1984)	Driving practices of pizza deliverers; use of safety belts and turn signals (Ludwig and Geller, 1991) vs. accidents	Observers practiced before each day of observation until they achieved scores higher than 90 percent; if score dropped below 90 percent during formal observations, the observer had to be "requalified"; median agreements were 97 percent for behaviors and 94 percent for conditions (Hopkins, Conrad, and Smith, 1986)	Data were collected over four groups of workers 32, 30, 29, and 32 times during the first experimental condition and 77, 64, 50, and 39 times during the second (Komaki, Collins, and Penn, 1982)	Found that safety behaviors were associated with the reduction of injury rates; examined the relationships between an observational measure of safety behavior and both overall and lost-time injury rates collected over a 3-year period; correlations were $-.76$ ($p < .01$) and $-.65$ ($p < .05$), respectively (Reber and Wallin, 1983)
Service	Observations taken while standing in line between customers, during "high load" hours when many customers were waiting (Elizur, 1987)	Behaviors—words of courtesy, eye contact, and smiling—performed by employees of an Israel bank (Elizur, 1987) vs. transactions per hour	Interrater reliability (IRR) used when defining target customer service behaviors; in training observers who collected data while acting as shoppers; and during data collection, for 8 percent of the the formal observations—scores average 97.8 percent overall (Komaki, Collins, and Temloc, 1987)	Observations were made 18 times in the experimental group and 21 times in the control group during the intervention phase of the experiment (Luthans, Paul and Baker, 1981)	To see whether customer service behaviors made a difference in a salesperson's amount of sales, looked at the relationship between the two; a correlation of .20 ($p < .01$) was found (George,1991)
Human Services and Education	Examination of client charts in psychological services center for status, format, and signature errors, and errors of completeness (Frederiksen et al., 1982)	Staff behaviors: indirect and direct custodial work, stimulation, training, off-task, off-unit, and area supervision; also 3 types of resident treatment: dental care, out-of-bed, and soiled clothing (Iwata et al., 1976) vs. patient progress	IRR was used to train supervisor in data collection techniques. In study 1, agreement scores coding videotapes were 91 percent on average. In study 2, agreement between the supervisor and an observer coding videotapes was about 96 percent; the mean reliability score between the supervisor and the subjects recording their own data was 94 percent (Ingham and Greer, 1992)	Data on 3 variables were collected 28 times during the baseline period, 19 times during each of 2 intervention periods, 8 times during a return to baseline, and 13 times during a month-long follow-up period (Callahan and Redmon, 1987)	No improvement was found in the number of reality orientation questions answered by patients from a staff feedback intervention designed to increase contact with patients (Johnson and Frederiksen, 1983)

65

TABLE 3.1 *(continued)*

	S: Direct Sampling	U: Under Control	R: Reliability Between Observers	F: Data Collected Frequently	C: Critical Aspects of the Task
Profess- ional/ Complex	Videotaping and coding of community board meetings for 3 types of problem-solving behaviors: problem identification, generating solutions, and deciding upon an action to take (Briscoe, Hoffman, and Bailey, 1975)	Tasks done related to completion of master's theses: discussing one article per week; presenting new data each week; attending meeting with supervisor; keeping a log; reporting the number of hours worked on thesis activities; formally writing 750 new words or rewriting; editing; and preparing a research proposal (Dillon, Kent, and Malott, 1980) vs. acceptance of master's thesis	IRR was calculated on instructional and noninstructional behaviors during formal data collection; mean score for the baseline period was 96 percent; mean score for post-training period was 97 percent; range was from 84 to 100 percent (Maher, 1982)	Observations of two target behaviors took place in one group 21 to 23 times during the 35-week intervention period and 15 to 16 times during the 25-week intervention period (Komaki, 1998a)	A negative correlation was found between the targets and the ultimate criterion (in this case, the actual deficiencies in the equipment). In addition, a comparison of successful and unsuccessful weeks showed that it was necessary to detect deficiencies before appropriate action could be accomplished (Komaki, 1998a)

The fourth area—designated *professional/complex*—was exemplified by a community board, a barnstorming baseball team, resource room teachers, graduate students working on their theses, and Marine Corps personnel within a heavy artillery battalion (Briscoe, Hoffman, and Bailey, 1975; Dillon, Kent, and Malott, 1980; Heward, 1978; Komaki, 1998a; Maher, 1982). The behaviors assessed included problem solving, teaching and discussion, team members' overall contribution to the team's run production, thesis-completion activities, and the preventive maintenance of heavy equipment.

IDENTIFYING WHAT SHOULD BE APPRAISED

To specify what should be evaluated, the criteria of U and C should be applied.

Make Sure the Target Is Under (U) the Control of the Worker

The importance of making sure that behaviors are under the control of workers is well illustrated in the area of safety. A typical way of judging employees' safety practices is to look at the number of injuries that have occurred and then to infer that workers are performing unsafely when the injury rate is high. This assumption is not always warranted. Some injuries occur not because the worker has performed unsafely, but because of some extraneous factors (to that particular worker) such as the condition of the work environment and equipment. If coal miners have accidents after a roof caves in or a seat mechanism fails, it might not be appropriate to assume that their injuries were a function of unsafe acts on their part. When assessing how safely pizza deliverers drove, safety was defined not in terms of accidents occurring on the job, but in terms of driving practices—the use of safety belts and turn signals (Ludwig and Geller, 1991), each of which were under the control of the deliverers.

Along the same lines, behaviors representing service—words of courtesy, eye contact, and smiling—were chosen to represent the quality of customer service rendered in an Israeli bank (Elizur, 1987). The traditional measures, which include the number of transactions completed, customers' letters of commendation or complaint, and voluntary responses to customer surveys, are more likely to be affected by forces beyond the control of employees, such as customer traffic, the season of the year, the economic climate, the merchandise mix, and customer perceptions of service.

An assumption sometimes made in the human services field is that better performing staff have patients who make more progress. The problem with this inference is that the progress of patients is typically a function of many factors, only one of which is staff performance. Patients may improve in spite of the quality of the care they receive, for instance. At the same time, patients may decline in functioning for reasons having little to do with the quality of care. Hence, strictly patient-oriented appraisals are not recommended as the best (or sole) measure of job performance. Instead, the focus should be on performance that the staff can more readily control. Iwata and his colleagues (1976), for example, defined staff performance in terms of nine behaviors ranging from indirect and direct custodial work with residents to area supervision, each of which was minimally affected by extraneous factors.

The same case can be made for assessing students' progress in completing their theses and dissertations. Sometimes the lack of student progress may not be solely attributable to a lack of student effort, but rather to factors not wholly under their control. As every student who has attempted to complete a thesis will attest, difficulties often arise in trying to gain acceptance from a diverse set of committee members. To assess students' progress toward completion of their theses, an index was developed (Dillon, Kent, and Malott, 1980). From one to six major tasks were examined depending on the stage of the work: reading, reviewing, and discussing one article per week; presenting new data each week; attending a weekly half-hour meeting with supervisors; keeping a log of ideas, procedures, and changes gained from meetings, courses, and faculty; reporting the total number of hours worked on thesis-research activities; formally writing 750 new words or rewriting; editing; and preparing a research proposal. Each of the tasks was more or less under the student's control, and together they provided a more sensitive barometer of students' progress toward completing their theses.

As shown in Table 3.1, the indices under the control heading are more responsive to worker efforts than the measures that are typically used.

Empirically Verify the Critical (C) Aspects of the Task

The criteria of criticalness also should be applied when deciding what target behavior to assess. To do this, empirical verification of the relationship between the target and the ultimate criterion is required. When such a relationship exists, then and only then is the target behavior considered critical. Expert opinion, no matter how exalted, does not count as empirical evidence. Convening a corporate personnel manager, a store manager, and several highly ranked store associates to generate definitions of customer service (Komaki, Collins, and Temlock, 1987), for instance, would be considered only expert opinion and not as meeting the criterion of criticalness. The target behavior is judged as critical only when data are gathered on site about the target behavior and a relationship is found between the target behavior and the outcome of interest. To obtain such evidence, a Southwestern retailer gathered data on various customer service behaviors—as rated by superiors and the employees themselves—and sales, defined as sales per hour and standardized within departments. When a correlation of .20, p < .01, was found between the service behaviors and sales, these behaviors were thought to be critical.

Similar evidence was obtained in the area of safety. Although previous experimenters had designed observational measures of safety (e.g., Fellner and Sulzer-Azaroff, 1984; Hopkins, Conrad, and Smith, 1986; Komaki, Barwick, and Scott, 1978), they merely assumed that these measures were related to accidents. No attempt was made to collect similarly constructed observational data in a number of different departments and then examine the injury rates in these departments. Reber and Wallin (1983) took the commendable step of actually doing that. They assessed the relationship between an observational measure of safety (like that of Fellner and Sulzer-Azaroff, Hopkins, Conrad, and Smith, and Komaki, Barwick, and Scott) and both overall and lost-time injury rates over a three-year period. When correlations were obtained ranging from −.65 to −.76 between the safety behaviors and accidents, the observational measures of safety they were using as well as other similarly constructed measures were considered critical.

Confirming evidence of the target behavior was found in both of the previous examples. In some cases, confirmation is not obtained despite extensive data collection efforts. Johnson and Frederiksen (1983), for example, tried to obtain evidence that their target was critical. They defined the target behavior in their study as the total number of daily nursing staff contacts with patients in group sessions of a "reality orientation program." The intended outcome—improved patient orientation to person, place, and time—was measured by the number of correct patient responses to questions posed by staff members assessing orientation to person, place, time, and past and recent events. Both the target behavior and the outcome were assessed for twenty-two weeks, and periodic interrater reliability checks were performed during data collection to check for accuracy. An improvement was shown in the target behavior of staff contact, but no relationship was found between the target behavior and the intended outcome of patient orientation. Although the results were not confirmatory, the investigators were a step ahead of many in the field: They knew that they should abandon the target behaviors and search for alternatives.

How does one generate ideas about target behaviors? Our recommendation is to look for opposites. *Compare known extreme groups;* that is, contrast a group known to possess a certain characteristic with a group lacking it. In developing targets in a poultry processing plant, for example, neophyte and seasoned employees were compared while performing the same operation (Komaki, Collins, and Penn, 1982). The differences in timing and motion that distinguished between the groups were used as the safety targets. In a much more extensive effort, Crawley and colleagues (1982) observed the top-producing sales people "during four months for 1,000 hours, as they worked with actual customers in stores and in homes" (p. 187) to see what these top producers actually did. Using the same strategy, Johnson and Frederiksen (1983) compared staff that have been successful in improving patient orientation with staff who have not been successful. The identified differences between the two groups were used as the basis for a new set of target behaviors.

Another way of sparking ideas about new target behaviors is to make comparisons between *successful and unsuccessful situations*. Contrasts can be made between weeks judged by superiors to be successful and those judged to be unsuccessful. To generate a new target in the area of preventive maintenance, Komaki (1998a) went on site and observed what occurred when preventive maintenance was and was not done successfully. During the successful weeks, she found that deficiencies were detected in the equipment; when these deficiencies were identified, the marines could order replacement parts and continue the maintenance chain. In contrast, during the unsuccessful weeks, few deficiencies were detected or reported or both, therefore reducing the number of successful follow-throughs. In this way, the new target of detected deficiencies was generated. To verify the criticalness of the targets, the relationship between the targets and the ultimate criterion (in this case, the actual deficiencies in the equipment) was found to be positively correlated. As the targets improved, the actual deficiencies declined over time. These two pieces of evidence lent credence to the criticalness of the targets.

Of the five criteria of criticalness fewer examples exist in which this criterion can be illustrated. However, as shown in Table 3.1, a careful search of the literature unearthed at least one in each of the areas. In each case, no armchair opinions, no matter how expert or exalted, were taken as evidence. Data had to be gathered and the data had to show a significant relationship between the target behavior and the ultimate criterion.

Designating How Performance Should Be Appraised

To identify how the target behavior should be assessed, the criteria of S (direct sampling), R (interrater reliability), and F (frequent data collection) should be used.

Use the Test of Interrater Reliability (R)

A series of checks and balances are recommended, referred to as the test of interrater reliability (IRR). In this IRR test, two raters independently sample the work of an employee, using the same standards, and then check to see each time they agree or disagree. When the agreement score reaches 80 or 90 percent, then one has evidence that the appraisal actually reflects their performance.

This test helps ensure the clarity of definitions, the rigor of observer training, and the lack of bias in the formal data collection, and has been successfully used in a variety of cases, as shown in Table 3.1. Reliability was calculated during data collection in a study of a time management program for resource room teachers (Maher, 1982). The formula used for occurrence reliability (of the targeted behaviors) was the total number of agreements that behaviors had occurred divided by the sum of the agreements and disagreements. Scores averaged 96 percent for pretraining sessions and 97 percent for posttraining sessions (the range was 84 to 100 percent).

To ensure that observers in a safety experiment were trained adequately, they completed qualifying practice observations until they obtained agreement scores of at least 90 percent (Hopkins, Conrad, and Smith, 1986). Reliability checks were also conducted during formal data collection. The checks were randomly performed on 17 percent of the items. If observers' scores dropped below 90 percent, they needed to requalify before they could collect any more data. The median score reported for safety behaviors was 97 percent, with 94 percent reported for housekeeping conditions.

The test of interrater reliability was used at three points during the data collection process when assessing the ephemeral area of customer service (Komaki, Collins, and Temlock, 1987). First, it was used during the *development* of the measure as a benchmark to determine whether the definitions were clear and objectively defined. The definitions continued to be revised until the observers could reliably agree with one another on virtually all of the definitions. The observers frequently disagreed when they initially scored the quality of service provided. After the researchers made several abortive attempts to change the definition and to improve the reliability scores, the global "quality" item was dropped and a list of specific types of comment categories was added. Only then did the observers pass the tests of interrater reliability. Second, the test of interrater reliability was used in *training* the observers; observers were not considered to be trained until they obtained scores of at least 90 percent on three consecutive, representative occasions. Lastly, to ensure that customer service performance was being accurately measured, reliability was assessed during the formal data *collection* phase. The reliability percentage score was calculated as the number of agreements divided by the number of agreements plus disagreements. Interrater reliability was assessed during 8 percent of the formal observations. Overall, the average reliability was 97.8 percent.

Interrater reliability was calculated in two different ways in a two-phase study conducted in a mental health setting (Ingham and Greer, 1992). In the first part, the test was used to train the primary observer, or to "calibrate" the individual to a standard. This was necessary because the teachers, the subjects of the study, would not allow videotaping or more than one observer to collect data. Therefore, the supervisor, who was the primary observer, had to learn to be a reliable and accurate coder before the data were collected. To do this, she coded "previously validated videotapes" of the same types of teachers in a similar setting. Indices of agreement were calculated by dividing the number of agreements by the number of agreements plus disagreements. Percentages ranged from 85 to 97 percent, with a mean of 91 percent. In the second phase, conducted in the same setting one year later, data were collected via the supervisor, the teachers themselves, and videotape. A second observer coded the videotape, and interobserver agreement scores were calculated using the same formula. (Note: Ideally, the data in each of these two phases should be collected during a random and a less restricted set of observations.) Scores were calculated for each behavior measured. Scores between the supervisor and the observer ranged from 75 to 100 percent, with a mean of about 96 percent. The average percentage agreement between the supervisor and teachers was 94 percent, ranging between 85 and 100 percent.

Collect Data Frequently (F)

To meet the frequency criterion, information should be collected at least twenty to thirty times during the intervention period. This recommendation is based on: (a) theoretical considerations (Miller, 1997)—one of the most straightforward ways to increase the potency of an intervention is to increase its frequency; (b) statistical concerns regarding the representativeness of the information obtained (Cronbach et al., 1972) and the risks involved in drawing conclusions with too few data points in a time series (Gottman, 1981), with one statistician (R. Millsap, personal communication, April 10, 1997) stipulating that at least twenty to thirty data points are necessary to discern trends reliably; and (c) the reactions of target subjects. Employees who thought their evaluations were more fair and accurate identified their appraisals as being conducted more often (Landy, Barnes, and Murphy, 1978).

The assessment of safety practices during the forty-six-week period of one study was judged to meet the criterion of frequency (Komaki, Collins, and Penn, 1982). The field experiment consisted of four groups observed over two conditions. Across the four groups, thirty-two, thirty, twenty-nine, and thirty-two observations of behaviors were reported during the first experimental condition; seventy-seven, sixty-four, fifty, and thirty-nine were reported for the second condition.

During the experimental phase of another study, service behaviors during the intervention phase were reported on a graph eighteen times in the experimental group and twenty-one times in the control group (Luthans, Paul, and Baker, 1981).

Data on three variables—the amount of time a patient spent in the clinic, staff use of time, and patient satisfaction—were collected for approximately five months in a pediatric outpatient clinic (Callahan and Redmon, 1987). The baseline phase of one type of patient scheduling system consisted of twenty-eight data points, while two intervention phases of another type of scheduling system contained nineteen data points each. Data were also collected eight times in the return-to-baseline phase separating the interventions and thirteen times during a follow-up period.

In an experiment by Komaki (1998a) conducted in the Marine Corps to improve preventive maintenance of equipment, data were collected in one group on two target behaviors twenty-one to twenty-three times during the thirty-five-week intervention period, and in the other group fifteen to sixteen times during the twenty-five-week intervention period. This was an average data collection of .6 times per week. At the end of the intervention period, which occurred after a year-long experiment, it was determined if the intervention had been effective.

Directly Sample (S) the Target

Rather than secondhand and/or filtered reports, assessments should be firsthand. Workers should be appraised as they are doing the work, or the products of their work should be examined. To assess safety, for example, observers recorded the condition of materials and equipment or observed the safe and unsafe behaviors of employees while they were operating a machine or conducting a task (Fellner and Sulzer-Azaroff, 1984). Similarly, observers watched Israeli bank employees while standing in line between customers (Elizur, 1987). This was done during "high load" hours when many customers were waiting. Along the same line, client charts, a common product in the area of mental health, were sampled for errors (Frederiksen et al., 1982). In the professional/complex area, community board meetings were videotaped and then coded for target behaviors (Briscoe, Hoffman, and Bailey, 1975). An interesting and unique measure of performance for barnstorming baseball players also utilized direct sampling (Heward, 1978). The measure consisted of a numerical description of the individual's contribution to the team's run production. This was calculated by dividing the total number of times the player went to the plate into the total number of hits, runs, runs batted in, walks, sacrifices, and hits by a pitch that the player accumulated during times at bat.

In all of the previous examples, investigators showed how they had successfully applied one or more of the SURF & C criteria. In some cases, the researchers could make use of existing indices; Heward (1978) did this when he tallied individual baseball players' actions such as the number of times a player goes to the plate. In other cases, Briscoe, Hoffman, and Bailey (1975) had to get permission to set up videotaping equipment and then code the data to ensure that community board members' actions would be directly sampled.

By presenting examples occurring in ongoing work settings, we hope that readers will be better able to evaluate their current and planned appraisals. To return to one of the previous examples of the IRS: An audit of the agency substantiated claims that taxpayers were being treated shoddily (Rosenbaum, 1998). A major criticism was that the appraisals were primarily based on "statistical enforcement goals and not on the services they provided taxpayers" (p. A15). A proposed plan was to simply deemphasize the financial goals by "ending the practice or ranking . . . districts on the basis of how closely they met their goal of tax collections" (p. A15). Just because districts are no longer ranked, however, does not mean that employees will necessarily be judged on the judicious treatment of taxpayers. Another suggestion—to bolster the treatment of taxpayers by setting up "a board made up largely of private citizens . . . to make it easier for taxpayers to prevail in tax court" (p. A15)—is no substitute for a fair and accurate measure. Besides questions of content, such a board could not meet the frequency, reliability, or direct sampling criteria.

At the same time, we hope that these actual examples will help future investigators to better see how they too can enhance the appraisals in their own organizations and perhaps be inspired to initiate these efforts. The criteria can be beneficially applied to the problematic but unfortunately widespread rating scale used at both Texaco and Stockham Valves (Komaki, in preparation). To clarify the definitions of such vague dimensions as dependability and work quality, the test of interrater reliability could be profitably used in the development of a new performance appraisal form. When raters disagree with one another, for example, their disagreements should provoke discussions about how to change the definitions so that the disagreements diminish. After rewriting the definitions and obtaining improvements in the reliability scores, it should be clearer as to what constitutes performance, leading hopefully to more uniform evaluations on the next round. Similarly, the IRR test should be used, in the training of raters as a standard to show they are qualified, and during the formal data collection to show that the raters' standards are not shifting over time. Both of these will also enable the screening out of biased evaluators. Finally, the supervisors should collect data directly and frequently.

Likewise, the assessment of service, whether it be for airlines, hotels, or restaurants, could be improved by meeting the criterion of criticalness and seeking out empirical rationale such as that provided by Bitner, Booms, and Tetreault (1990). They collected hundreds of critical incidents, providing evidence from the customers' point of view of satisfactory service encounters. The incidents went beyond smiling and greeting to highlight the ways in which personnel handled failures and how they responded to customers with special needs. Based on criticality data like these, developers of appraisal instruments could empirically verify what matters to the customer in providing constitutes quality service.

In short, when developing and evaluating performance appraisals, the SURF & C criteria are highly recommended. The criteria of being under the workers' control (U) and critical to the task at hand (C) address the content of the target. The criteria of sampling directly (S), collecting information frequently (F), and conducting interrater reliability (R) checks identify how the appraisals should be done. Meeting all these criteria helps to minimize such perennial and pernicious problems as rater bias and to promote the fair and accurate appraisal of workers' performance on the job, the foundation for any effective and sustained improvement effort.

REFERENCES

After critical inquiry, I.R.S. turns to ethics expert. (1992). *The New York Times,* April 7, p. A18.

Altman, L. K. (1992). Surgical scorecards: Can doctors be rated just like ballplayers? *The New York Times,* January 14, p. C3.

Ashe, R. L. and McRae, G. S. (1985). Performance evaluations go to court in the 1980s. *Mercer Law Review, 36,* 887-905.

Baker, G., Gibbons, R., and Murphy, K. (1994). Subjective performance measures in optimal incentive contracts. *Quarterly Journal of Economics, 109,* 1125-1156.

Barrett, G. V. and Kernan, M. C. (1987). Performance appraisal and terminations: A review of court decisions since Brito v. Zia with implications for personnel practices. *Personnel Psychology, 40,* 489-503.

Bellack, A. S. and Hersen, M. (Eds.). (1988). *Behavioral assessment: A practical handbook* (Third edition). New York: Pergamon Press.

Berg, E. N. (1990). United thrives amid turmoil. *The New York Times,* October 2, p. C1.

Bitner, M. J., Booms, B. H., and Tetreault, M. S. (1990). The service encounter: diagnosing favorable and unfavorable incidents. *Journal of Marketing, 54,* 71-84.

Blanz, R. and Ghiselli, E. E. (1972). The mixed standard scale: A new rating system. *Journal of Applied Psychology, 63,* 677-688.

Blum, M. L. and Naylor, J. C. (1968). *Industrial psychology, its theoretical and social foundations* (Revised edition). New York: Harper & Row.

Borman, W. C. (1991). Job behavior, performance, and effectiveness. In M. Dunnette and L. Hough (Eds.), *Handbook of industrial and organizational psychology* (Vol. 2, pp. 271-326). Palo Alto, CA: Consulting Psychologists Press.

Bravo, E. (1991). Mistrust and manipulation: Electronic monitoring of the American workforce. *USA Today, 119* May, 46-48.

Briscoe, R. V., Hoffman, D. B., and Bailey, J. S. (1975). Behavioral community psychology: Training a community board to problem solve. *Journal of Applied Behavior Analysis, 8,* 157-168.

Burns, T. (1954). The directions of activity and communication in a departmental executive group. *Human Relations, 7,* 73-97.

Byer, M. J. (1992). Faint hearts. *The New York Times,* March 21, p. A23.

Callahan, N. M. and Redmon, W. K. (1987). Effects of problem-based scheduling on patient waiting and staff utilization of time in a pediatric clinic. *Journal of Applied Behavior Analysis, 20,* 193-199.

Campbell, J. P. (1990). Modeling the performance prediction problem in industrial and organizational psychology. In M. D. Dunnette and L. M. Hough (Eds.), *Handbook of industrial and organizational psychology* (pp. 687-732). Palo Alto, CA: Consulting Psychologists Press.

Cardy, R. L. and Dobbins, G. H. (1994). *Performance appraisal: Alternative perspectives.* Florence, KY: South Western.

Cascio, W. F. and Bernardin, H. J. (1981). Implications of performance appraisal litigation for personnel decisions. *Personnel Psychology, 34,* 211-226.

Ciminero, A. R., Calhoun, K. S., and Adams, H. E. (Eds.). (1986). *Handbook of behavioral assessment.* New York: Wiley-Interscience.

Crawley, W. J., Adler, B. S., O'Brien, R. M., and Duffy, E. M. (1982). Making salesman: Behavioral assessment and intervention. In R. M. O'Brien, A. M. Dickinson, and M. P. Rosow (Eds.), *Industrial behavior modification: A management handbook* (pp. 184-199). New York: Pergamon Press.

Cronbach, L. J., Gleser, G. C., Nanda, H., and Rajarathnam, N. (1972). *The dependability of behavioral measures.* New York: Wiley.

DeNisi, A. S. (1996). *A cognitive approach to performance appraisal: A program of research.* London: Routledge.

DeNisi, A. S., Cafferty, T. P., and Meglino, B. M. (1984). A cognitive view of the appraisal process: A model and research propositions. *Organizational Behavior and Human Performance, 33,* 360-396.

DeVries, D. L., Morrison, A. M., Shullman, S. L., and Gerlach, M. L. (1980). *Performance appraisal on the line.* Greensboro, NC: Center for Creative Leadership.

Dillon, M. J., Kent, H. M., and Malott, R. W. (1980). A supervisory system for accomplishing long-range projects: An application to master's thesis research. *Journal of Organizational Behavior Management, 2,* 213-227.

Doyle, S. X. and Shapiro, B. P. (1980). What counts most in motivating your sales force. *Harvard Business Review,* May-June, 133-140.

Dunnette, M. D. (1963). A note on the criterion. *Journal of Applied Psychology, 47,* 251-254.

Eichenwald, K. (1996). Texaco executives, on tape, discussed impeding a bias suit. *The New York Times,* November 4, pp. A1, D4.

Elizur, D. (1987). Effect of feedback on verbal and nonverbal courtesy in bank setting. *Applied Psychology: An International Review, 36,* 147-156.

Feild, H. S. and Holley, W. (1982). The relationship of performance appraisal system characteristics to verdicts in selected employee discrimination cases. *Academy of Management Journal, 25,* 392-406.

Feldman, J. M. (1981). Beyond attribution theory: Cognitive processes in performance appraisal. *Journal of Applied Psychology, 66,* 127-148.

Fellner, D. J. and Sulzer-Azaroff, B. (1984). Increasing industrial safety practices and conditions through posted feedback. *Journal of Safety and Research, 15,* 7-21.

Flanagan, J. C. (1954). The critical incident technique. *Psychological Bulletin, 51,* 327-355.

Foster, S. L. and Cone, J. D. (1986). Design and use of direct observation procedures. In A. R. Ciminero, K. S. Calhoun, and H. E. Adams (Eds.), *Handbook of behavioral assessment* (Second edition, pp. 253-324). New York: Wiley-Interscience.

Frederiksen, L. W., Richter, W. T., Johnson, R. P., and Solomon, L. J. (1982). Specificity of performance feedback in a professional service delivery setting. *Journal of Organizational Behavior Management, 3*(4), 41-53.

George, J. M. (1991). State or trait: Effects of positive mood on prosocial behaviors at work. *Journal of Applied Psychology, 76,* 299-307.

Glanz, J. (2000). Amid race profiling claims, Asian-Americans avoid labs. *The New York Times,* July 7, p. A1.

Goldfried, M. R. and Kent, R. N. (1972). Traditional versus behavioral personality assessment: A comparison of methodological and theoretical assumptions. *Psychological Bulletin, 77*(6), 409-420.

Gomez-Mejia, L. R. (1988). Evaluating employee performance: Does the appraisal instrument make a difference? *Journal of Organizational Behavior Management, 9*(2), 155-172.

Gottman, J. M. (1981). *Time series analysis: A comprehensive introduction for social scientists.* Cambridge, UK: Cambridge University Press.

Griffith, T. L. (1993). Teaching big brother to be a team player: Computer monitoring and quality. *Academy of Management Executive, 7,* 73-80.

Hammer, M. (1985). Implications of behavioral and cognitive reciprocity in social network data. *Social Networks, 7,* 189-201.

Heward, W. L. (1978). Operant conditioning of a .300 hitter? The effects of reinforcement on the offensive efficiency of a barnstorming baseball team. *Behavior Modification, 2,* 25-40.

Hopkins, B. L., Conrad, R. J., and Smith, M. J. (1986). Effective and reliable behavioral control technology. *American Industrial Hygiene Association Journal, 47*(12), 785-791.

Ilgen, D. R. and Feldman, J. M. (1983). Performance appraisal: A process focus. In L. Cummings and B. Staw (Eds.), *Research in organizational behavior* (Vol. 5, pp. 141-197). Greenwich, CT: JAI.

Ingham, P. and Greer, R. D. (1992). Changes in student and teacher responses in observed and generalized settings as a function of supervisor observations. *Journal of Applied Behavior Analysis, 25,* 153-164.

Iwata, B. A., Bailey, J. S., Brown, K. M., Foshee, T. J., and Alpern, M. (1976). A performance-based lottery to improve residential care and training by institutional staff. *Journal of Applied Behavior Analysis, 9,* 417-431.

James v. Stockham Valves and Fittings Co., 559 F.2d 310 (U.S. Ct. App. 5th Circuit 1977).

James, L. R. (1973). Criterion models and construct validity for criteria. *Psychological Bulletin, 80,* 75-83.

Johnson, R. P. and Frederiksen, L. W. (1983). Process vs. outcome feedback and goal setting in a human service organization. *Journal of Organizational Behavior Management, 5*(3/4), 37-56.

Johnston, D. (1998). Black F.B.I. agents renew bias complaint. *The New York Times,* October 15, p. A24.

Johnston, J. M. and Pennypacker, H. S. (1993). *Strategies and tactics of human behavioral research* (Second edition). Hillsdale, NJ: Lawrence Erlbaum.

Kazdin, A. E. (2000). *Behavior modification in applied settings* (Sixth edition). Belmont, CA: Wadsworth Thomson Learning.

Kilborn, P. T. (2000). For women in bias case, the wounds remain. *The New York Times,* March 24, p. A14.

Komaki, J. L. (1998a). When performance improvement is the goal: A new set of criteria for criteria. *Journal of Applied Behavior Analysis, 31*(2), 263-280.

Komaki, J. L. (1998b). *Leadership from an operant perspective.* London: Routledge.

Komaki, J. L. (in preparation). Daring to dream: How organizations can come closer to fulfilling Martin Luther King's (1963) dream. *Applied Psychology: International Review.*

Komaki, J. L., Barwick, K. D., and Scott, L. R. (1978). A behavioral approach to occupational safety: Pinpointing and reinforcing safe performance in a food manufacturing plant. *Journal of Applied Psychology, 63,* 434-445.

Komaki, J. L., Collins, R. L., and Penn, P. (1982). The role of performance antecedents and consequences in work motivation. *Journal of Applied Psychology, 67,* 334-340.

Komaki, J. L., Collins, R. L., and Temlock, S. (1987). An alternative performance measurement approach: Applied operant measurement in the service sector. *Applied Psychology: An International Review, 36,* 71-89.

Komaki, J. L., Coombs, T., Redding Jr., T. P., and Schepman, S. (2000). A rich and rigorous examination of applied behavior analysis research in the world of work. In C. L. Cooper and I. T. Robertson (Eds.), *International Review of Industrial and Organizaitonal Psychology.* Sussex, England: John Wiley.

Landy, F. J., Barnes, J. L., and Murphy, K. R. (1978). Correlates of perceived fairness and accuracy of performance evaluation. *Journal of Applied Psychology, 63,* 751-754.

Landy, F. J. and Farr, J. L. (1980). Performance rating. *Psychological Bulletin, 87,* 72-107.

Latham, G. P. and Latham, S. D. (2000). Overlooking theory and research in performance appraisal at one's peril: Much done, more to do. In C. Cooper and E. A. Locke (Eds.), *International Review of Industrial-Organizational Psychology.* Chichester, England: Wiley.

Latham, G. P., Skarlicki, D., Irvine, D., and Siegel, J. P. (1993). The increasing importance of performance appraisals to employee effectiveness in organizational settings in North America. In C. L. Cooper and I. T. Robertson (Eds.), *International review of industrial and organizational psychology* (Vol. 8, pp. 87-131). Chichester, NY: John Wiley & Sons.

Latham, G. P. and Wexley, K. N. (1981). *Increasing productivity through performance appraisal.* Reading, MA: Addison-Wesley Publication Co.

Lewis, D. R. and Dahl, T. (1976). Time management in higher education administration: A case study. *Higher Education, 5,* 49-66.

Longenecker, C. O., Sims, H. P., and Gioia, D. A. (1987). Behind the mask: The politics of employee appraisal. *The Academy of Management Executive, 1,* 183-193.

Ludwig, T. S. and Geller, E. S. (1991). Improving the driving practices of pizza deliverers: Response generalization and moderating effects of driving history. *Journal of Applied Behavior Analysis, 24,* 31-44.

Luthans, F., Paul, R., and Baker, D. (1981). An experimental analysis of the impact of contingent reinforcement on salespersons' performance behavior. *Journal of Applied Psychology, 3,* 314-323.

Maher, C. A. (1982). Improving teacher instructional behavior: Evaluation of a time management training program. *Journal of Organizational Behavior Management, 4*(3/4), 27-36.

Malott, R. W., Whaley, D. L., and Malott, M. E. (1997). *Elementary principles of behavior* (Third edition). NJ: Prentice-Hall.

Miller, L. K. (1997). *Principles of everyday behavior analysis* (Third edition). Pacific Grove, CA: Brooks/Cole.

Murphy, K. R. and Cleveland, J. (1995). *Understanding performance appraisal: Social, organizational, and goal-based perspectives.* Thousand Oaks, CA: Sage.

Nasar, S. (1994). Jett's supervisor at Kidder breaks silence. *The New York Times,* July 26, p. D1, D14.

Reber, R. A. and Wallin, J. A. (1983). Validation of a behavioral measure of occupational safety. *Journal of Organizational Behavior Management, 5*(2), 69-77.

Roberts v. Texaco, 94 Civ. 2015 (CLB, 1994).

Rosenbaum, D. E. (1998). Internal audit confirms abusive I.R.S. practices. *The New York Times,* January 14, p. A15.

Schrage, M. (1992). When technology heightens office tensions. *The New York Times,* October 5, p. A12.

Shaw, D. G., Schneier, C. E., Beatty, R. W., and Baird, L. S. (1995). *The performance measurement, management, and appraisal sourcebook.* Amherst, MA: Human Resource Development Press.

Smith, P. C. (1976). Behaviors, results, and organizational effectiveness: The problem of criteria. In M. Dunnette (Ed.), *Handbook of industrial and organizational psychology* (pp. 745-775). New York: John Wiley & Sons.

Smith, P. C. and Kendall L. M. (1963). Retranslation of expectations: An approach to the construction of unambiguous anchors for rating scales. *Journal of Applied Psychology, 47,* 149-155.

Smither, J. W. (Ed.). (1998). *Performance appraisal.* San Francisco: Jossey-Bass.

Steers, R. M., Porter, L. W. and Bigley, G. A. (1996). *Motivation and leadership at work.* New York: McGraw-Hill.

Sulzer-Azaroff, B. and Mayer, G. R. (1991). *Behavior analysis for lasting change.* Fort Worth: Holt, Rinehart and Winston.

Weist, M. D., Ollendick, T. H., and Finney, J. W. (1991). Toward the empirical validation of treatment targets in children. *Clinical Psychology Review, 11,* 515-538.

Werner, J. M. and Bolino, M. C. (1997). Explaining U.S. courts of appeals decisions involving performance appraisal: Accuracy, fairness, and evaluation. *Personnel Psychology, 50*(1), 1-24.

Chapter 4

Within-Group Research Designs: Going Beyond Program Evaluation Questions

Judith L. Komaki
Sonia M. Goltz

If you have no doubt of your premises or your power and want a certain result with all your heart, you naturally express your wishes in law and sweep away all opposition. . . . But when men have realized that time has upset many fighting faiths, they may come to believe even more than they believe the foundations of their own conduct that the ultimate good desired is better reached by free trade in ideas—that the best test of truth is the power of the thought to get itself accepted in the competition of the market.

> Oliver Wendell Holmes, Jr.
> arguing on the Supreme Court for freedom of expression
> (*Abrams v. United States,* 1919)

The pursuit of truth is not an easily traversed path; signposts are often nonexistent or at best confusing. Furthermore, the same destination can be reached in many different ways. Sometimes, "the best test of truth" (*Abrams v. United States,* 1919) takes a debate format where speakers present their views and individuals are polled. In other cases, "truth" is tested in a court of law where attorneys argue opposing positions and juries determine how well arguments are made. In still other contexts, "truth" is determined by the scientific method in which data are systematically collected to assess which explanation is most consistent with the evidence. Whether the decisions are based on the weight of scientific evidence, the deliberations of a jury, or the vote of one's peers, the ultimate goal is to make the best possible judgment.

Although not every issue can be addressed using the scientific method, a variety of questions can be answered this way (Staw, 1977). A spectrum of questions concerning social policy, for instance, has been addressed by bringing evidence to bear on the issues (e.g., Ashenfelter, 1987; Lalonde and Maynard, 1987; Passell, 1993; Wyatt, 2000). Among them are questions regarding the effectiveness of a program such as Head Start or treatment such as home health care or policies such as school vouchers, trends such as the immediacy of food-stamp effects, or the continuing levels of participation in inoculation programs by families with small children and lastly, comparisons among competing programs developed to solve social problems, such as the effectiveness of providing free sterilized needles to drug users versus the effectiveness of educating them about AIDS.

In this chapter, the questions that typically occur in applied settings are classified, and the designs used in conducting the research are presented. Emphasis is placed on the fit between research question and design.

SCIENTIFIC METHOD:
MATCHING RESEARCH QUESTIONS AND DESIGNS

In the scientific method, investigators specify the research objective or question and identify the formal plan for conducting the research or research design, and ensure a proper fit between the question and the design. The fit is critical. In a now-classic analysis of 605 research proposals submitted to the National Institutes of Health, Allen (1960) found that nearly one-third of the proposals were not approved because "the proposed tests, methods, or scientific procedures are unsuited to the stated objective" (p. 1533).

An Array of Research Questions

These questions can be categorized as concerning: (1) program evaluation, (2) trend assessment, or (3) comparisons among programs.

Program Evaluation

Questions, referred to as program evaluation questions, can be phrased in a variety of ways: Does the program work? Does it have an impact? The questions are alike in that the answers require the drawing of causal inferences about a particular program. In work environments—the focus of the present chapter—questions of the following type are raised: Does the incentive program make a difference? Are our clients better because we have implemented a particular program? Does this program result in improved service? In other words, have individuals acquired the desired responses as a result of a newly instituted program, and did the program have the desired effect on critical outcomes?

The program—sometimes referred to as the treatment, intervention, or independent variable—can vary. For example, it can consist of a wage subsidy, a training opportunity, or a reinforcement program. The treatment can also consist of a single component (e.g., providing goals) or a set of components (e.g., providing goals and feedback). Pritchard and his colleagues (1988) wanted to know, for example, if "giving group-based feedback with the productivity measurement system increase(s) productivity" (p. 341). In this case, the program involved providing group feedback and using a new performance appraisal system; the question was whether using group feedback with the productivity measurement system caused productivity to rise.

Trend Assessment

A second set of questions looks beyond the evaluation of programs and is concerned with trends in performance taking place over time. Some of these questions concern what happens after a program is introduced: Does it have an immediate impact? Is there a stepwise jump or do the effects take place gradually? Does the program slow down the rate of previous declines in performance or speed up the rate of previous increases? The maintenance of the program over time may also be of concern: Do the program's effects last? For how long do they last? For instance, Pritchard and colleagues (1988) were interested in whether "any treatment effects continue after the departure of a research team" (p. 341). Similarly, Fox, Hopkins, and Anger (1987) wanted to see whether safety interventions in two mining companies had long-term effects: "The interventions were maintained for several years, an unusually long period of time, and therefore provided an extended opportunity for examining efficacy" (p. 216).

Comparisons

A third set of questions involves comparisons between or among programs. Thus, two or more independent variables are always involved. For example: Is program B more effective than program C? Is program B better than programs C or D? Which results in better service, B or C? Does service improve more if B is implemented or if C is implemented? In these cases, one wants to know not only whether each of the programs works, but how well they each work when compared with the other. For example, Dickinson and Gillette (1993) titled their article: "A Comparison of the Effects of Two Individual Monetary Incentive Systems on Productivity: Piece-Rate Pay versus Base Pay Plus Incentives" (p. 3). The authors wanted to know not only whether piece-rate pay and base pay with incentives each improved productivity, but also which improved productivity more.

The three categories of research questions are listed in Table 4.1: (1) questions 1-4 concern program evaluation, (2) 5-6 concern trend assessment, and (3) 7-8 concern comparison. (Note: Questions 9-10 involving multiple treatments are discussed in a later section on alternatives to asking comparison questions.)

Families of Research Designs

Research designs can be divided into two families, the within- and the between-group designs. Both families are similar in that one can draw causal conclusions with confidence about the effect of programs. They differ from one another in four ways: (1) their manner of comparison— either within the group or between the group; (2) whether and how persons are assigned to groups—via random assignment or using intact groups; (3) how often data on the dependent variable are collected—once or repeatedly; and (4) the introduction of the treatment—to all or only some of the groups.

Within-Group Family

In the family of within-group designs—the focus of this chapter—comparisons are made within the group in question. For example, using the within-group reversal design, one contrasts what occurs during baseline (referred to as A) with what occurs after the program is introduced (B) and, most important, what happens after the program has been removed, called reversal to baseline (A). Hence, in this ABA design, comparisons are not made between groups receiving different treatments. Instead comparisons are made using a single group that receives the treatment by examining the behavior of group members across the baseline, treatment, and reversal phases. Thus, each group serves as its own control. This comparison of behavior across phases is possible, in part, due to the repeated or multiple observations that are made in all within-group designs.

TABLE 4.1. Research Questions Appropriately Addressed Using Within-Group and Between-Group Designs

Question	Design Appropriate? Within	Between
A. PROGRAM EVALUATION	+	+
1. Program: B vs. No B Is B effective relative to no other program?		
2. Program package $P^{1,2,3}$ vs. No P Is the program package (P) with all its components (1, 2, 3) effective relative to no package?		
3. Program components: $P^{1,2}$ vs. No P Is the program package with some of its components (1,2) effective relative to no package?		
B. TREND ASSESSMENT	+	?
4. Immediacy of Effect Does the treatment have an immediate effect? Does performance decline gradually or precipitously?		
5. Maintenance What happens over time? Do the improvements continue? For how long?		
C. COMPARISON	–	+
6. Between or Among Programs: B vs. C, B vs. C vs. D Is program B more effective than program C? Is program B more effective than program C or D?		
7. Between or Among Program Components: P^1 vs. $P^{1,2}$ vs. $P^{1,2,3}$ Is the partial package (P) with one of its components (1) more effective than the program package (P) with two of its components (1, 2) or three of its components (1, 2, 3)?		
D. OTHERS INVOLVING MULTIPLE TREATMENTS OR EXPERIMENTS	+	+
8. Facilitative: $P^{1+2} > P^1$ Does one component (P^2) add (>) to the effectiveness of the other component(s)?		
9. Sufficient Is one program or component adequate for an effect to occur?		

Note: + = yes, it would be possible to draw inferences with confidence using the designs described in Table 4.2. ? = usually not given the traditional pretest, posttest measurement, however, these designs do not preclude the use of repeated measurement. – = no, given the designs in Table 4.2.

To clarify how within-group designs differ from one another, the most prominent ones—the ABA, BAB, ABAB reversal and the multiple-baseline—are illustrated in Table 4.2. The features of the designs are represented by combining two symbol systems. One system comes from Campbell and Stanley's (1966) classic experimental design text. The other comes from texts about within-group designs (e.g., Hersen and Barlow, 1976; Barlow and Hersen, 1992; Kazdin, 1997). In the ABA design (designated as design 1P where P stands for program evaluation), the letter "A" in the diagram refers to baseline (before the treatment is introduced) and reversal phases (when the treatment is taken away or "reversed"), and "B" refers to the treatment. The letter "O" refers to an observation or measurement. "O's vertical to one another are simultaneous" and "the left-to-right dimension indicates the temporal order" (Campbell and Stanley, 1966, p. 61). To reflect that data are collected repeatedly during each of the phases, the Os are presented in sequences of four, e.g., O1O2O3O4. Thus, 1P indicates the following: After a baseline period during which time data were collected repeatedly, the treatment was introduced and repeated data collection continued. Subsequent to the treatment phase, the treatment was removed and data continued to be collected repeatedly.

Between-Group Family

Between-group designs, as their name suggests, make comparisons between groups. Unlike within-group designs that can use intact groups without compromising the quality of the conclusions drawn, it is essential to randomly assign subjects to groups in a between-group design. R indicates the random assignment to separate groups, as does the solid (rather than dashed) line separating the observation and treatment symbols for each group. For instance, in the pretest-posttest control group design (4P in Table 4.2), two groups are formed by randomly assigning subjects to one of two groups: the treatment and the control or no-treatment group. In this design, behavior is observed before and after the treatment, as designated by the Os.

DRAWING INFERENCES WITH CONFIDENCE

Depending on the question and the design, the quality of the conclusions drawn varies from high (permitting one to draw causal inferences with confidence) to medium (allowing one to draw conclusions but with severe restrictions or limited generalizability) to low (often not permitting one to draw causal inferences).

TABLE 4.2. Research Designs in Terms of Research Questions, Single or Multiple Treatments, and Quality of Conclusions That Can Be Drawn

---

Program (P) Evaluation Question: Single Treatment (B)

Designs Permitting Causal Inferences with Confidence

Within-group

1P. ABA or BAB reversal/interrupted time series with removed treatment[a]
$AO_1O_2O_3O_4BO_5O_6O_7O_8AO_9O_{10}O_{11}O_{12}$
or
$BO_1O_2O_3O_4AO_5O_6O_7O_8BO_9O_{10}O_{11}O_{12}$

(Figure 4.2, Welsh, Luthans, and Sommer, 1993; Figure 4.11, Hantula, Stillman, and Waranch, 1992)

2P. ABAB or ABABAB reversal/interrupted time series with multiple replications[b]
$AO_1O_2O_3O_4BO_5O_6O_7O_8AO_9O_{10}O_{11}O_{12}BO_{13}O_{14}O_{15}O_{16}$
or
$AO_1O_2O_3O_4BO_5O_6O_7O_8AO_9O_{10}O_{11}O_{12}BO_{13}O_{14}O_{15}O_{16}AO_{17}O_{18}O_{19}O_{20}BO_{21}O_{22}O_{23}O_{24}$

(Figure 4.1, Callahan and Redmon, 1987)

3P. Multiple-baseline/interrupted time series with switching replications[a]
$$\overline{AO_1O_2O_3O_4BO_5O_6O_7O_8O_9O_{10}O_{11}}$$
$AO_1O_2O_3O_4O_5O_6O_7BO_8O_9O_{10}O_{11}$

(Figure 4.3, Boudreau, Christian, and Thibadeau, 1993; Figure 4.4, George and Hopkins, 1989; Figure 4.5, Wilk and Redmon, 1990; Figure 4.6, Wittkop, Rowan, and Poling, 1990; Figure 4.7, Johnson and Masotti, 1990; Figure 4.8, Rogers et al., 1988; Figure 4.9, Fox, Hopkins, and Anger, 1987; Figure 4.10, Hopkins et al., 1986)

Between-group

4P. Pretest-posttest control group[b]
$$\underline{R\ O_1\ B\ O_2}$$
$R\ O_1\quad O_2$

5P. Posttest only control group[b]
$$\underline{R\ BO_1}$$
$R\quad O_1$

Designs That Often Do Not Permit Causal Inferences/Preexperimental[b]

6P. One-shot case study[a]/one-group posttest only[b]
BO_1

7P. One group pretest-posttest[ab]
O_1BO_2

8P. Posttest only with nonequivalent groups[b]
BO_1

O_1

TABLE 4.2 *(continued)*

Designs That Sometimes Permit Causal Inferences but with Severe Restrictions

9P. Pretest-posttest with nonequivalent groups/untreated control group design with pretest and posttest[b]

O_1BO_2

$O_1\ O_2$

(Siero et al., 1989)

10P. AB only/simple interrupted time series

$AO_1O_2O_3O_4BO_5O_6O_7O_8$

(Latham and Baldes, 1975)

11P. AB only with nonequivalent no-treatment control group[b]

$AO_1O_2O_3O_4BO_5O_6O_7O_8$

$AO_1O_2O_3O_4\ O_5O_6O_7O_8$

(Lawler and Hackman, 1969)

12P. ABC or ABCD

$AO_1O_2O_3O_4BO_5O_6O_7O_8O_9O_{10}O_{11}O_{12}$

or

$AO_1O_2O_3O_4BO_5O_6O_7O_8CO_9O_{10}O_{11}O_{12}DO_{13}O_{14}O_{15}O_{16}$

(Pritchard et al., 1988)

Trend (T) Assessment Question: Single Treatment (B)

Designs Permitting Causal Inferences with Confidence

1T. ABA or BAB reversal/interrupted time series with removed treatment[a]

(Figure 4.10, Hantula, Stillman, and Waranch, 1992)

2T. ABAB or ABABAB reversal/interrupted time series with multiple replications[b]

(Welsh, Miller, and Altus, 1994)

3T. Multiple-baseline/interrupted time series with switching replications[a]

(Figure 4.9, Fox, Hopkins, and Anger, 1987)

Designs That Sometimes Permit Causal Inferences but with Severe Restrictions

10T. AB only/simple interrupted time series[b]

11T. AB only with nonequivalent no-treatment control group[b]

Comparison Question: Multiple Treatments (B, C, D)

Designs Permitting Conclusions with Confidence

13C. Pretest-posttest

R O_1BO_2

R O_1CO_2

14C. Posttest only

R BO_1

R CO_1

Designs Permitting Conclusions but with Limited Generalizability

12C. ABC or ABCD (Anderson et al., 1988)

15C. ABABACABACAB or ABABCABACB

$AO_1O_2O_3O_4BO_5O_6O_7O_8AO_9O_{10}O_{11}O_{12}B_{13}O_{14}O_{15}O_{16}AO_{17}O_{18}O_{19}O_{20}$
$BO_{21}O_{22}O_{23}O_{24}AO_{25}O_{26}O_{27}O_{28}BO_{29}O_{30}O_{31}O_{32}AO_{33}O_{34}O_{35}O_{36}CO_{37}O_{38}$
$O_{39}O_{40}AO_{41}O_{42}O_{43}O_{44}BO_{45}O_{46}O_{47}O_{48}$

(Van Hauten and Nau, 1981)

16C. BCB or ABCB with a reversal

$BO_1O_2O_3O_4CO_5O_6O_7O_8BO_9O_{10}O_{11}O_{12}$

or

$AO_1O_2O_3O_4BO_5O_6O_7O_8CO_9O_{10}O_{11}O_{12}BO_{13}O_{14}O_{15}O_{16}$

(Dickinson and Gillette, 1993)

17C. ABC/ACB Counterbalanced[c]
$AO_1O_2O_3O_4BO_5O_6O_7O_8CO_9O_{10}O_{11}O_{12}$

$AO_1O_2O_3O_4CO_5O_6O_7O_8BO_9O_{10}O_{11}O_{12}$

or

$AO_1O_2O_3O_4OBO_5O_6O_7{}_8O_9O_{10}O_{11}O_{12}CO_{13}O_{14}O_{15}O_{16}\ O_{17}O_{18}O_{19}O_{20}$
$AO_1O_2O_3O_4\ O_5O_6O_7CO_8O_9O_{10}O_{11}O_{12}\ O_{13}O_{14}O_{15}O_{16}BO_{17}O_{18}O_{19}O_{20}$

(Fox and Sulzer-Azaroff, 1989)

Facilitative Question: Multiple Treatments (B, C)

Designs Permitting Conclusions with Confidence

18F. ABC multiple-baseline
$AO_1O_2O_3O_4BO_5O_6\quad O_7O_8CO_9O_{10}\quad {}_{11}O_{12}O_{13}O_{14}$

$AO_1O_2O_3O_4\ O_5O_6BO_7O_8\ O_9O_{10}CO_{11}O_{12}BO_{13}O_{14}$

(Calpin, Edelstein, and Redmon, 1988; Ducharme and Feldman, 1992)

TABLE 4.2 *(continued)*

19F. ABC with reversal to B
$AO_1O_2O_3O_4BO_5O_6O_7O_8CO_9O_{10}O_{11}O_{12}BO_{13}O_{14}O_{15}O_{16}$

(Figure 4.14, Goltz et al., 1989)

Sources: [a]Cook and Campbell (1979); [b]Campbell and Stanley (1966); [c]Neale and Liebert (1986); [d]Hersen and Barlow (1976).

Note: For research questions, P = Program evaluation question, T = Trend assessment, C = Comparison, F = Facilitative. For within-group design phases, A = Baseline: Before treatment/ intervention or reversal to preintervention, B = intervention, C = intervention other than B, D = intervention other than B or C. For between-group designs, R = groups randomly assigned with at least 30 in each group, solid line (____) = designates that subjects have been randomly assigned. Dotted line (_ _ _) = groups that are not randomly assigned. For both within- and between-group designs, O = observation; O_1 = 1st observation; O_x = number of observation.

Generally speaking, high-quality conclusions can be drawn about program evaluation questions using either within- or between-group designs. These designs are labeled as those "permitting causal inferences with confidence" in Table 4.2. Maintenance questions can be answered with confidence using within-group designs, whereas comparison questions are best answered using between-group designs.

Ruling Out Alternative Explanations

The quality of the conclusions made depends on how confidently one can rule out plausible alternative explanations or sources of internal invalidity (Campbell and Stanley, 1966). Let's say dramatic improvements in productivity—from 75 to 90 percent—were reported after a program was introduced. With results such as this, one might conclude the improvements were due to the program. "The possibility of false positive findings" (Cook and Campbell, 1979, p. 50) also exists, however. Perhaps a change in managers, the implementation of new technology, or a shift in the economy explains why productivity increased. Factors other than the program such as those above, which Campbell and Stanley (1966) refer to as history, need to be ruled out. Another alternative explanation is that workers could gain more practice or grow older—referred to as maturation— and this could explain why improvements occurred. Another alternative explanation is statistical regression. Perhaps the group was selected because the pretest scores showed everyone to be in the lowest quartile; the next measurement would probably be higher simply because the scores would regress toward the mean. These threats to internal validity or other plausible alternative hypotheses, as listed in Table 4.3, could explain the improvements.

How can one rule out these potential threats to internal validity? They can be ruled out by using an internally valid design such as a within-group (1-3P) or a between-group (4P) design. With a between-group design, the key is the random assignment of subjects to groups. Because each and every person has an equal and likely chance of being in one group or the other, the groups will be essentially equivalent prior to the treatment. That is, persons in the treatment group will be comparable to persons in the control group within known limits of sampling error. Then if improvements occur in the treatment group, and not in the control group, one can conclude with confidence that the program was responsible for the improvements. It is just as likely that persons in one group will experience a significant event (history) or become more practiced at a task (maturation) as it is that persons in the control group will be affected by these factors. Similarly, regression artifacts would be likely to appear in any series of repeated measurements in the treatment as well as in the control group.

Selecting a Research Design

Before selecting a research question, it is critical to determine what research design can be implemented. This determination is particularly important when doing applied research.

TABLE 4.3. Threats to Internal Validity

Threat	Definition	Example
History	Specific events occurring in addition to treatment	New supervisor Force reduction Job opportunities Getting married
Maturation	Processes within respondents operating as function of time	Gaining experience Getting more rest Becoming wiser
Statistical Regression	Operating where groups have been selected on the basis of extreme scores	Selecting lowest 10 percent for training

Source: Campbell and Stanley (1966).

When it is possible to randomly assign at least thirty subjects to each group, one can use a between-group design. All else being equal, between-group designs are the first choice because they can be used to answer both program evaluation and comparison questions. In addition, if data are collected repeatedly, rather than just once before and once after the introduction of the treatment, between-group designs can be used to assess trends such as the maintenance of effects.

Unfortunately, difficulties often arise in conducting randomized experiments. At least eight obstacles are listed by Cook and Campbell (1979). In work settings, one of the major drawbacks to randomly assigning employees to groups is that it is difficult to arrange. Assigning employees in quality control to work in the marketing department and vice versa and then giving workers in the newly reconstituted group a unique treatment can rarely be done outside of training situations. Groups in work settings have typically been formed according to the particular skills, experience, and knowledge that are required for the activities at hand, as found in the production, visual inspection, and final quality assurance inspection groups in the microelectronics plant serving as the setting for a study by Goltz and colleagues (1989).

WITHIN-GROUP DESIGNS

Fortunately, within-group designs are viable alternatives in that they do not require the random assignment of subjects to groups. The application of these designs in clinics and work settings has been described by researchers in the field of operant conditioning (Barlow and Hersen, 1992; Kazdin, 1997; Komaki, 1977, 1982; Komaki and Jensen, 1986). In this section, we present two of the most widely used within-group designs—the reversal and multiple-baseline designs—as well as the rationale underlying their use and examples demonstrating how they have been used in a variety of work settings.

Our discussion of these designs is structured by emphasizing the types of questions that can—and cannot—be answered with confidence, using these designs. Our experience has been that it is easy to learn the characteristics of within-group designs but quite another thing to understand when and how to use them. Hence, we present how within-group designs can be used to answer program evaluation and trend assessment questions. Also, in a rare departure from the typical presentation of research designs, we discuss variations of within-group designs that are not appropriate for answering these questions.

In another departure, we go beyond questions that arise when evaluating single treatments to those relatively unexplored questions of comparisons among multiple treatments. Within each section, we describe designs that have been improperly used, as well as ones that have been correctly used.

ANSWERING PROGRAM EVALUATION QUESTIONS USING WITHIN-GROUP DESIGNS

To illustrate how within-group designs can answer program evaluation questions, examples are presented of two of the most widely used designs—the reversal and multiple-baseline.

Using a Reversal Design

Examples

An ABAB reversal design was used to examine the effectiveness of a new scheduling method on reducing patient waiting time in a pediatric clinic (Callahan and Redmon, 1987). During the baseline phase of the study (referred to as A), baseline data were collected daily on the amount of time patients spent waiting when a time-based scheduling system (fifteen minutes regardless of problem type) was being used (see Figure 4.1). In the next phase (B), a new system was introduced in which appointments were allocated differing lengths of time depending on the problem. During the third phase (reversal to A), the clinic reverted to using the original time-based system. Finally, in the fourth phase, the problem-based system was reintroduced (B). The ABAB reversal design has also been used to evaluate an intervention designed to improve the setting up of banquets by hotel employees (LaFleur and Hyten, 1995). Other examples of the use of the reversal design include the evaluation of a staff management system in a housing cooperative, in which the intervention was introduced first using a BAB design (Johnson et al., 1991), and the evaluation of a contingent reinforcement program on salespersons' performance in a department store, in which an ABA design was used (Luthans, Paul, and Baker, 1981; Luthans, Paul, and Taylor, 1986).

Essential Characteristics

At the minimum, a reversal design must contain at least three phases, one of which has to be a reversal phase. An ABA reversal design includes

FIGURE 4.1. Example of Use of an ABAB Reversal Design to Assess Program Effectiveness

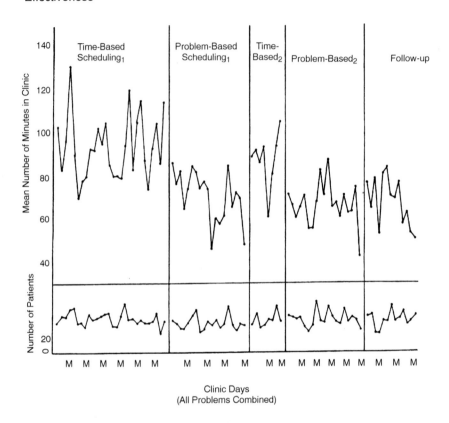

Clinic Days
(All Problems Combined)

Note: Mean number of minutes patients spent in a pediatric outpatient clinic per day. Implementation of a problem-based scheduling system was followed by decreased waiting time; waiting time increased after reversal to the previous system; and the reintroduction of the new scheduling system was again followed by decreased waiting time. From Callahan and Redmon (1987). Copyright 1987 by the Society for the Experimental Analysis of Behavior, Inc. Reprinted by permission.

the following: (1) baseline, during which performance is measured regularly over time before the introduction of the program (A); (2) intervention, during which the program is introduced and performance information continues to be collected regularly over time (B); and (3) reversal, during which the program introduced in the second phase is discontinued while performance data continues to be collected (A) (e.g., Kortik and O'Brien, 1996;

Luthans, Paul, and Baker, 1981; Luthans, Paul, and Taylor, 1986). Hence, this design is described as an ABA reversal design. However, the BAB reversal design would also include the essential reversal phase and start with the treatment (B), continue with the removal of the treatment (A), and end with the reintroduction of the treatment (B) (e.g., Johnson et al., 1991).

Ruling Out Alternative Explanations

One can say that performance improvements resulted from the intervention and not from other events if performance markedly improves when the intervention is in effect and worsens during its removal. For example, in the Callahan and Redmon (1987) study, the waiting time decreased from baseline levels when the intervention was in effect, increased to baseline levels when the treatment was discontinued, and then decreased again when the new system was reintroduced (see Figure 4.1). Hence, it was correctly concluded that the intervention was responsible for the improvements. As the authors stated, "Results of this study demonstrated that patient waiting time in a medical clinic can be reduced by manipulating environmental antecedents" (p. 7).

The reversal phase allows the authors to rule out alternative explanations (such as history). It is unlikely that another significant event within the organization would have occurred precisely with the introduction of the intervention and then later disappeared precisely with the removal of the intervention. It is also unlikely that results are attributable to practice effects since these changes could be expected to occur gradually, rather than rapidly when the intervention was introduced. Finally, it is unlikely that the change in performance resulted from the tendency of extreme scores to move toward the mean (regression toward the mean), since this could be expected to occur in any series of repeated measurements.[1]

The more times one can demonstrate that performance changes as the intervention is introduced and reversed, the more confident one can be that the changes were caused by the intervention rather than by other events. For example, an ABABAB reversal design was used to evaluate the effectiveness of an incentive program on tardiness; the program was introduced and withdrawn three times (Hermann et al., 1973). The fact that tardiness decreased when the incentive program was introduced and increased when the program was withdrawn was striking, particularly because the level of tardiness changed not once, not twice, but three times. Hence, the authors could conclude with assurance that the program, rather than some extraneous variable, was responsible for the improvements.

When Behavior Does Not Reverse

In the results of the studies presented thus far, performance improved each time the treatment was introduced and worsened each time the treatment was removed. That is, the behavior level reverted to baseline. When results such as these occur, they suggest that plausible alternative causes were not likely to have occurred just as the program was introduced and removed just as the reversal of behavior occurred. The conclusion that the program was responsible for the improvements naturally flows from such results, because the only remaining variables perfectly correlated with improvements and reversals of these improvements are the introduction and removal of the intervention.

When improvements or reversals are not forthcoming with the introduction or removal of the intervention, however, one cannot draw the same conclusions. For example, an ABA design was used to examine the effectiveness of an intervention consisting of praise and corrective feedback in a Russian textile mill (Welsh, Luthans, and Sommer, 1993). Although improvements occurred during the intervention, performance remained the same during the reversal (see Figure 4.2), so it was not possible to rule out alternative explanations to make a causal inference. Welsh, Luthans, and Sommer (1993) properly noted: "the absence of a true reversal weakens the arguments that the intervention was the whole 'cause' of increased (decreased) behavior frequencies" (p. 30). In this study, the ABA design was appropriate to answer the question. If performance had reversed, it would have been possible to rule out threats to internal validity and to draw conclusions about causality with confidence. In short, the authors did not obtain results, through no fault of theirs, that would allow them to confidently state that the intervention was the sole cause of the effect observed, even though the design they chose was appropriate.

As can be seen, the reversal design is one tool for assessing the effectiveness of a program when random assignment to groups is not feasible. It allows alternative explanations such as history to be ruled out in another way—by demonstrating that changes occur as predicted during the introduction and withdrawal of the treatment. However, for this to occur, the reversal phase must be present and performance must reverse during the reversal phase.

Using a Multiple-Baseline Design

Examples

Another design that can be used to answer program evaluation questions is the multiple-baseline design. It was used to assess a program

FIGURE 4.2. Illustration of the Use of a Reversal Design in Which Performance Did Not Reverse

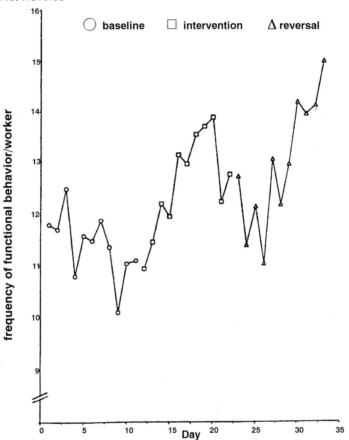

Note: The frequency of performance-related behaviors by workers in a Russian textile mill. After baseline, an intervention was applied that resulted in an increase in functional behaviors, which continued even during reversal to baseline conditions; thus, alternative explanations for performance improvements could not be ruled out. From Welsh, Luthans, and Sommer (1993). Copyright 1993 by The Haworth Press, Inc. Reprinted by permission.

designed to reduce unscheduled absences of staff at three homes (Boudreau, Christian, and Thibadeau, 1993). During the first phase of the study (A), unscheduled absences were measured at all three homes under the original absence-reporting policy, which required that absences be reported only to a clerical worker who arranged for substitute staff (see

Figure 4.3). In the second phase (B), the new absence-reporting policy, which required that absences also be reported to immediate supervisors, was introduced at different times to each of the group homes: in July at the first home, in October at the second home, and in December at the third home. Unscheduled absences continued to be measured at all three homes after the new policy was introduced.

Multiple-baseline designs have been employed to evaluate the effectiveness of a variety of programs. For instance, they have been used to assess the impact of an instruction-and-feedback package on the correct completion of civil forms by psychiatric personnel (Jones, Morris, and Barnard, 1986); a lottery-based group reinforcement program on reducing unscheduled sick leave by residential treatment workers (Brown and Redmon, 1990); a performance-contingent pay system on sales by waitstaff in family-style restaurants (George and Hopkins, 1989); a performance feedback program on the collection of quality control data by machine operators in a metal-part processing company (Henry and Redmon, 1990); and the graphing of product losses on reducing product thefts (Carter et al., 1988).

Essential Characteristics

One of the critical features of the multiple-baseline design is *concurrent baselines*—the collection of data repeatedly over time on two or more units of behavior. Using a multiple-baseline design across groups, Boudreau, Christian, and Thibadeau (1993) collected baseline data on three units (three homes). As will be described in more detail later, the units of behavior in a multiple-baseline design can also include different: (a) individuals, (b) behaviors, or (c) settings (for examples, see Figures 4.4 to 4.8).

The second characteristic of the multiple-baseline design is the use of *staggered interventions,* in which the intervention is introduced in a staggered or stepwise fashion across these units. In a multiple-baseline design across groups, for example, Boudreau, Christian, and Thibadeau (1993) first introduced the treatment to one home in July. When the desired change in performance occurred and the data were stable, the treatment was begun with the second home in October. Following a change in the second home, the treatment was introduced in the third home in December.

Different Types: By Person/Group, Setting, Behavior

The multiple-baseline design lends itself to a variety of situations in that data can be collected, as indicated earlier, across groups or individuals,

FIGURE 4.3. Illustration of the Use of a Multiple-Baseline Design to Evaluate Program Effectiveness

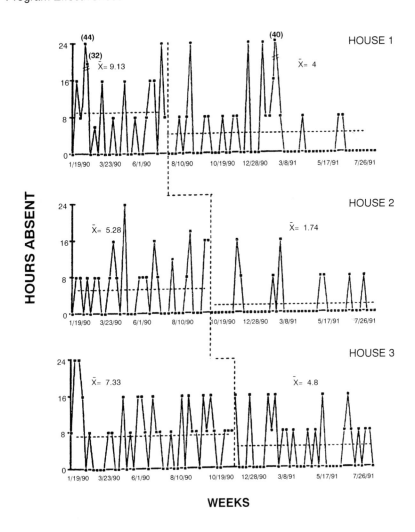

Note: Mean number of unscheduled hours absent per week among staff at a children's residential program. The invervention, a new system of reporting absences, was introduced in a staggered fashion to three group homes. $\bar{X}$ refers to the mean during each phase. From Boudreau, Christian, and Thibadeau (1993). Copyright 1993 by The Haworth Press, Inc. Reprinted by permission.

settings, or behaviors. Studies using a *multiple-baseline design across groups* have looked at groups, as in the previous study, consisting of workers in three group homes (Boudreau, Christian, and Thibadeau, 1993), workers in two mines (Fox, Hopkins, and Anger, 1987), and waitpersons in three restaurants (George and Hopkins, 1989). In the last of these studies, the effectiveness of performance-contingent pay on the dollar amount of food sold by servers was assessed by introducing the new pay system in a staggered manner to each of three restaurants (see Figure 4.4). Since the dollar amount of food sold increased after, and not before, the introduction of the new pay system in each restaurant, it was concluded that the performance changes were probably due to the new pay system.

The *multiple-baseline design across individuals* is similar to the one across groups except that data are collected on individuals. Examples of the use of this design include assessments of the effects of feedback on instructor performance (Arco, 1997) and on productivity in a university admissions department (Wilk and Redmon, 1990). In the latter study, effects of a daily goal-setting and feedback procedure on the number of tasks completed by each of three admissions processors were assessed (Wilk and Redmon, 1990). After baseline information had been collected, the intervention was introduced in a staggered fashion to each individual—first to processor 1, second to processor 2, and third to processor 3 (see Figure 4.5). Since the number of tasks completed increased only after, and not before, the intervention was introduced to each processor, it was concluded that observed performance changes were due to the new procedure.

With a *multiple-baseline design across settings,* more than one setting is included. For example, three different machines served as the settings in a study of the effectiveness of a feedback package in reducing machine setup time in an extrusion department of a rubber manufacturing company (Wittkop, Rowan, and Poling, 1990). After the collection of baseline information on machine setup time, feedback was provided at staggered intervals, using videotapes about setup time, on each of the machines (see Figure 4.6). If setup times on each machine decreased only after the videotaped feedback intervention was introduced for that particular machine, it would have been appropriate for the experimenters to conclude that the decreases in setup time were due to the program. (Note, however, in this particular study, setup time began to decline in two settings [machine 2 and machine 4] during the baseline phase for those settings when the intervention had begun in another setting [machine 1]. Therefore, other factors, such as history, may have been responsible for the improvements in setup time. Thus, these authors, like Welsh, Luthans, and Sommer [1993] chose an appropriate design, but did not obtain results that would

FIGURE 4.4. Example of a Multiple-Baseline Design Across Groups

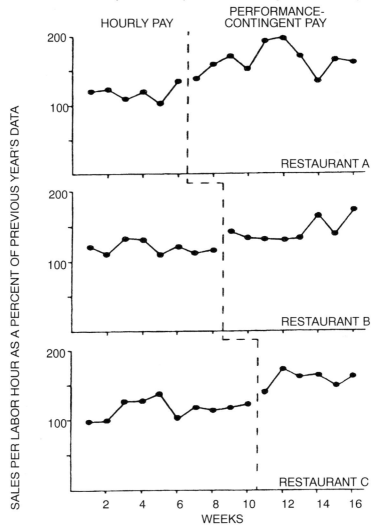

Note: Dollar sales per hour (as a percentage of dollar sales a year earlier) by waitpersons in three family-style restaurants. The intervention, a performance-contingent compensation system, was introduced in a staggered manner to waitpersons in the three separate restaurants. From George and Hopkins (1989). Copyright 1989 by the Society for the Experimental Analysis of Behavior, Inc. Reprinted by permission.

FIGURE 4.5. Example of a Multiple-Baseline Design Across Individuals

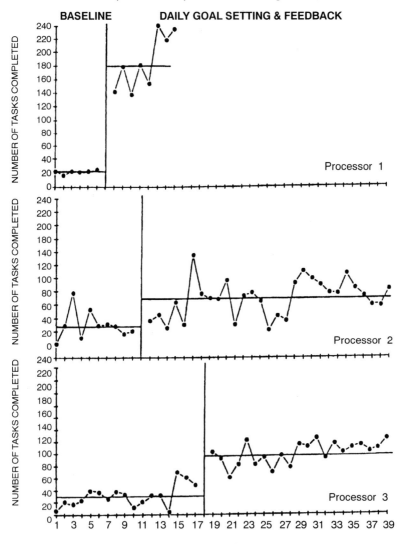

WEEKS

Note: Number of admissions processing tasks completed in a week by each of three employees. Mean number of tasks completed by each processor increased after a daily goal setting and feedback intervention was applied. From Wilk and Redmon (1990). Copyright 1990 by The Haworth Press, Inc. Reprinted by permission.

FIGURE 4.6. Example of a Multiple-Baseline Design Across Settings

Average Setup Time in Minutes

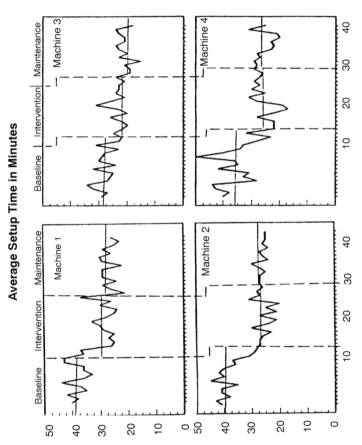

Note: Average weekly setup time for each of four machines in an extrusion department of a rubber manufacturing company. Setup time decreased for each machine following the application of a treatment package involving supervisory feedback on videotaped performance. From Wittkop, Rowan, and Poling (1990). Copyright 1991 by The Haworth Press, Inc. Reprinted by permission.

allow them to conclude that the intervention per se was responsible for the effects observed.)

It is also possible to examine whether an intervention, when applied to different behaviors of the same individuals or groups, is effective. In this case, a *multiple-baseline design across behaviors* is used (Christian and Poling, 1997). To evaluate the effect of training seminars in an automobile dealership, for instance, Brown (1980) suggests collecting data on the topics of three seminars—"the sales of sunroofs, power windows, and leather upholstery" (p. 14). In a restaurant, Johnson and Masotti (1990) actually did something similar, assessing the sale of cocktails, appetizers, and desserts. To examine whether the intervention (goalsetting, feedback, and reinforcement) increased performance, they first applied the intervention to the sale of cocktails, then to appetizers, and finally to desserts, as shown in Figure 4.7. Since sales of each of these three types of items increased only after, and not before, the introduction of the intervention to each behavior, it was concluded that the changes in performance were a function of the program.

Ruling Out Alternative Explanations

To assess whether the intervention is effective, one compares baseline and intervention conditions. If performance improves during, and not before, the intervention, and this result occurs each time the treatment is introduced, then one can conclude confidently that the experimental manipulation is responsible for the changes. The probabilities of events other than the intervention occurring at the same time and in the same order are relatively small. Although it is possible that an event other than the intervention might occur at time X for baseline A, it becomes less likely that the same event would occur at time Y for baseline B, even less likely that it would also occur at time Z for baseline C, and so on. This lends increasing support to the explanation that the intervention caused the changes.

Potential Pitfalls

A common mistake is altering the treatment. To be able to draw conclusions with confidence about a given intervention, it is critical that the intervention remain the same each time it is implemented. In all the preceding multiple-baseline designs (see Figures 4.3 to 4.7), the same intervention was introduced. In Figure 4.4, for example, the waitpersons in each of the three restaurants received the same intervention, performance-contingent pay. However, this rule was violated in a study assessing the

FIGURE 4.7. Example of a Multiple-Baseline Design Across Behaviors

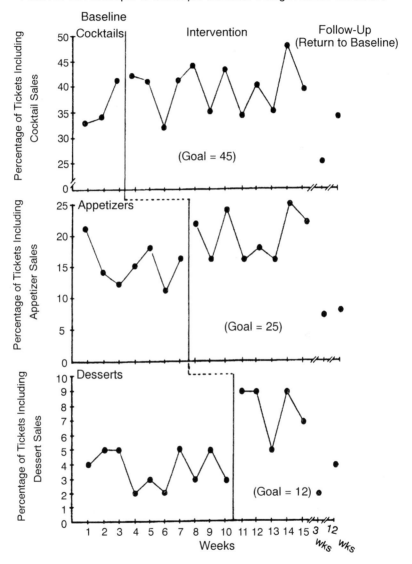

Note: Percentage of tickets including sales of three target items in a family-style restaurant. Increases in sales of each item occurred upon the introduction of the intervention, which was staggered across the behaviors of sales of cocktails, sales of appetizers, and sales of desserts. From Johnson and Masotti (1990). Copyright 1990 by The Haworth Press, Inc. Reprinted by permission.

effectiveness of an intervention to improve safety belt usage in state-owned vehicles in three agencies (Rogers et al., 1988). Two agencies received intervention B. The third agency received a different intervention C (see Figure 4.8). When performance improved following the staggered introduction of intervention B, the authors correctly concluded that it "resulted in substantial increases in safety belt use" (p. 267). However, when improvements were forthcoming after the introduction of intervention C, the authors erroneously concluded that it "also resulted in modest increases in safety belt use" (p. 267). To be able to draw conclusions with confidence about intervention C, it would have been necessary to introduce C in a staggered manner and for performance to improve in at least one other agency.

In summary, the multiple baseline design is internally valid and can be used when random assignment and the reversal of the treatment are not possible. The introduction of the treatment to two or more units of behavior at staggered points in time allows one to rule out alternative explanations. Thus, the within-group designs—ABA, BAB, ABAB, and ABA-BAB reversal and multiple-baseline across groups, individuals, settings, or behaviors—can all be used as alternatives to between-group designs to draw causal conclusions with confidence about program effectiveness.

Designs to Avoid

At this point, we present some designs that researchers commonly use inappropriately when evaluating program effectiveness. Our discussion will cover the conclusions that are and are not justifiable based on these designs.

Difficulties with Preexperimental Designs

The preexperimental designs—one-shot case study, one group pretest-posttest, and posttest-only with nonequivalent comparison group listed in Table 4.2 (6-8P)—often do not allow conclusions regarding causality to be confidently made. Hence, they are virtually never recommended to answer program evaluation questions.

Complications with Designs That Compare Nonequivalent Groups

Designs relying on making comparisons between groups but without randomly assigning subjects to groups—referred to as nonequivalent group designs (9P, 11P)—are also not recommended for assessing pro-

FIGURE 4.8. Example of a Modified Within-Group Design
Safety Belt Usage—Target Vehicles

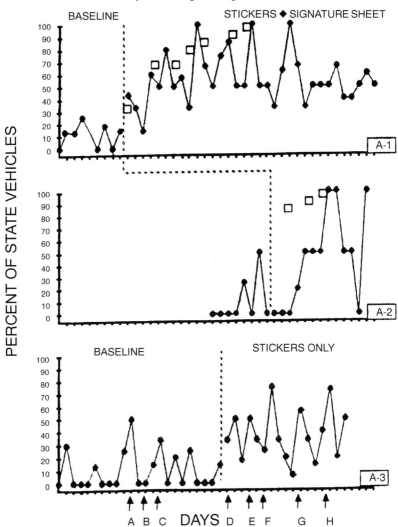

Note: Percentage of drivers of state-owned vehicles wearing safety belts. History effects have not been ruled out as a possible influence on the stickers-only effect; selection effects have not been ruled out as plausible explanations for the differential effects of the interventions. From Rogers et al. (1988). Copyright 1988 by the Society for the Experimental Analysis of Behavior, Inc. Reprinted by permission.

gram effectiveness. Because they sometimes permit causal influences, albeit with severe restrictions, they are considered superior to the preexperimental designs. The pitfalls of both the preexperimental and nonequivalent group designs have been amply described; hence, the reader is encouraged to consult Campbell and Stanley (1966) and Cook and Campbell (1979).

Problems with AB-Only Designs

The popular AB, ABC, and ABCD designs, like the nonequivalent control group design, are not recommended because of the severe restrictions on causal inferences that can be drawn from them. Because data are collected repeatedly over time within these designs, however, they too are preferable to the preexperimental designs. They are described in more detail here.

A study by Latham and Baldes (1975) illustrates the problematic AB design. In this study, the researchers were attempting to show the effectiveness of using specific moderately difficult goals. The aim was to motivate loggers to load trucks with logs close to, but not over, the trucks' maximum legal weights. Unfortunately, the design is what is called an AB design (10P in Table 4.2) in which A refers to the baseline phase and B refers to the treatment phase. In both phases, data are collected repeatedly as indicated by the multiple Os. In this study, managers asked workers to "do your best" in loading the trucks during baseline, whereas during the intervention, managers asked workers to load the trucks to weigh 94 percent of their maximum legal weight. Performance improvements appeared with the introduction of the goal-setting intervention in the study. However, without a reversal phase or the introduction of the treatment to other units in a staggered fashion, one cannot easily rule out other explanations for the improvements. For example, the increase in performance might have resulted from other events in the trucking operation that occurred simultaneously with the introduction of the intervention. Despite this problem, the authors erroneously concluded that "The immediate change in the slope and level of the performance curve supports the hypothesis that setting a specific hard goal versus a generalized goal of 'do your best' leads to a substantial increase in performance" (Latham and Baldes, 1975, p. 123).

Objections to ABC or ABCD Designs

Another popular design often inappropriately used is the ABC or ABCD design (12P in Table 4.2). With this design, two or more different interventions are introduced successively after an initial baseline period. For example, Pritchard and colleauges (1988) used an ABCD design to assess productivity improvements in a maintenance section of an Air Force base. Feedback was introduced (B) after a nine-month baseline period (A). Next, goal setting was added to the feedback (C). Finally, incentives (D) were added to the goal setting and feedback. The researchers wanted to know if "giving group-based feedback with the productivity measurement system increase(s) productivity" (p. 341). The problem with using an ABCD design to answer this program evaluation question is that it is not possible to rule out alternative hypotheses. Even Pritchard and colleagues (1988) acknowledged that "there could have been changes occurring in the larger organizations of which the five experimental units were a part that were causing general increases in productivity for all units" (p. 347).

As one can see, some designs, such as the AB, ABC, and ABCD designs, present problems when it comes to ruling out alternative explanations, whereas the reversal and multiple-baseline designs are well suited to answering program evaluation questions.

ASSESSING TRENDS OVER TIME USING WITHIN-GROUP DESIGNS

Within-group designs are uniquely suited to questions regarding trends over time because data are obtained frequently over extended periods of time. At least thirty observations per phase are recommended (Doan, 1992). This repeated measurement allows one to assess whether improvements occur immediately, whether they continue, and for how long they last. Multiple-baseline designs are more prevalent than reversal designs but either can be used.

Using a Multiple-Baseline Design

Determining Maintenance of Effects

Data were obtained every year for fifteen years (Fox, Hopkins, and Anger, 1987), allowing the authors to determine the long-term effects of an intervention in two mines. Using a multiple-baseline design as shown in Figure 4.9, awarding trading stamps reduced lost time from work-related injuries over an eleven-year period.

Assessing Immediacy of Effects

The repeated assessment of behavior over time also enables one to see how quickly the intervention works. Some of the effects were fairly immediate in a study designed to reduce workers' exposure to styrenes (Hopkins et al., 1986). Within one to two days after the intervention took place, at least five of the nine behaviors (e.g., placing the molds, closing the doors) improved, as shown in Figure 4.10. In contrast, for at least two of the behaviors (e.g., spraying the molds, using airflow), the effects were more

FIGURE 4.9. Illustration of Using a Multiple-Baseline Design to Examine the Maintenance of Effects

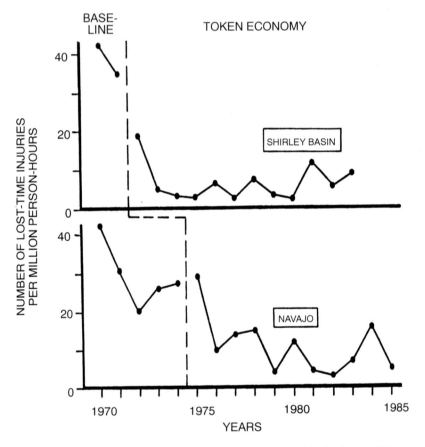

Note: Effects of a safety program on the rate of lost-time injuries in two different mines over several years. From Fox, Hopkins, and Anger (1987). Copyright 1987 by the Society for the Experimental Analysis of Behavior, Inc. Reprinted by permission.

FIGURE 4.10. Illustration of Using a Multiple-Baseline Design to Assess the Immediacy of Effects

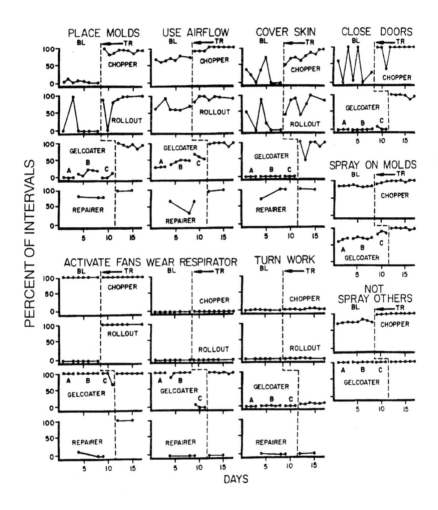

Note: Percentage of intervals during which plastics workers at a laboratory equipment plant performed each of nine safety behaviors. (BL = Baseline; TR = Training.) Intervention resulted in immediate effects for some behaviors, but not others. From Hopkins et al. (1986). Copyright 1986 by the Society for the Experimental Analysis of Behavior, Inc. Reprinted by permission.

gradual. By making frequent assessments, one can gauge the length of time the intervention might take to develop and hence avoid prematurely withdrawing an effect-producing intervention when its effects might not be immediately obvious.

Using a Reversal Design

Reversal designs can also be used to assess trends (Welsh, Miller, and Altus, 1994). For example, an ABA design was used, as shown in Figure 4.11, to determine whether the Great American Smokeout Day, a mass media campaign sponsored by the American Cancer Society, resulted in smoking reduction in an urban hospital (Hantula, Stillman, and Waranch, 1992). Smoking behavior was measured prior to the smokeout week (A), during the smokeout week (B), and for a period of two months subsequent to the smokeout week, when the mass media campaign had subsided (A). Since the number of smokers observed in the cafeteria declined during the smokeout week and resumed subsequent to the smokeout week, the authors concluded that the campaign decreased smoking while it was in effect. (Note: Since the number of nonsmokers observed declined during the smokeout week as well, an alternative explanation is that the campaign may have simply decreased the number of people frequenting the cafeteria.) Perhaps most important was the reversal that occurred when the campaign subsided, indicating that, if the campaign was indeed limited to the time of the mass media campaign.

As we have seen, within-group designs have been successfully used to assess the impact of programs over extended periods of time. Thus far, the emphasis has been on single treatments. The next section discusses studies having more than one treatment.

PROBLEMS USING WITHIN-GROUP DESIGNS TO ADDRESS COMPARISON QUESTIONS

Comparison questions are often asked by decision makers who must choose among various options: Should I choose program B or program C? Will goal-setting (B) be better than feedback (C)? Which results in better service, treatment B, C, or D?

To answer these comparison questions with confidence, we highly recommend using between-group designs such as the pretest-posttest (13C in Table 4.2) or the posttest only (14C) designs. To compare program B and program C, for instance, subjects would be randomly assigned to each of

FIGURE 4.11. Illustration of Use of a Reversal Design to Examine the Effectiveness of a Treatment Over Time

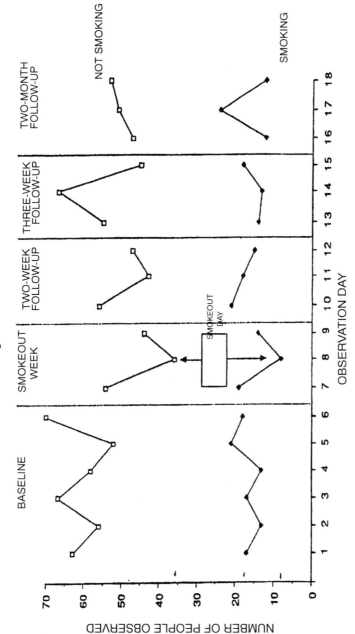

Note: Number of people observed smoking in the cafeteria of a hospital before, during, and after National Smokeout Week. Results suggest Smokeout Week decreased smoking only during that week and not later. From Hantula, Stillman, and Waranch (1992). Copyright 1992 by The Haworth Press, Inc. Reprinted by permission.

the groups, and program B would be introduced to one group and program C to the other group. If B is found to be superior, then one could recommend with assurance that it should be used rather than program C.

What options exist for comparing treatments when random assignment is not possible? Unfortunately, few, if any. In fact, virtually all of the designs that do not make use of random assignment are inappropriate. Contributing to the problem is the fact that the topic of multiple treatment is rarely discussed. In classic research methods texts, no examples of designs with two treatments are given (Campbell and Stanley, 1966; Cook and Campbell, 1979). In fact, only one symbol *(X)* designates the treatment in Campbell and Stanley's (1966) text; no symbol exists to designate a program other than "*X*."

Because of the popularity of the comparison question, however, investigators continue to ask the question. Regrettably, because of the difficulties of random assignment in work settings, the questions have not been successfully answered. A popular but inappropriate design is the pretest-posttest design with nonequivalent groups (9P). With this design, the groups consist of intact or nonequivalent groups in which subjects have not been randomly assigned. To compare program B and program C, for instance, the day shift would receive program B, the night shift program C. The problem with this design is that even though the pretest scores between the day and night shifts may not be significantly different from the posttest scores, extraneous factors cannot readily be ruled out because subjects have not been randomly assigned to the groups. If program B is shown to be superior to program C, other plausible alternative hypotheses (e.g., history, maturation, statistical regression) could explain the results. Hence, designs using nonequivalent or intact groups severely compromise the quality of the conclusions that can be drawn, and are not recommended.

Designs making comparisons within the group are also not advisable. These designs, referred to as variations of within-group designs—ABC or ABCD (12C), ABABACABACAB (15C), BCB with a reversal (16C), ABC/ACB counterbalanced (17C)—are problematic. Until now, however, the ground rules for using these designs have been either unclear or ambiguous. Hersen and Barlow (1976), for instance, suggest that some variations of within-group designs (e.g., the difficult-to-arrange multielement design) are appropriate in assessing the relative efficacy of different treatments.

In an effort to shed light on the topic, two sections are devoted to questions of multiple treatments. The next section focuses on variations of within-group designs and how they are often improperly used to answer comparison questions. Given the problems in arranging for randomized designs, the lack of discussion about multiple treatments in research methods texts, and the ambiguities within the within-group literature, it is not surprising that investigators have had problems when assessing multiple treatments.

The second section discusses alternative questions that can be answered, using variations of the within-group designs. For a succinct overview, refer to the sections on multiple treatments in Table 4.2. In the table, designs 12-17C and 18-19F have two or more treatments, with B, C, and D representing the different treatments. Designs 12-17C are concerned with comparison questions, while designs 18-19F deal with facilitative questions; designs 13C and 14C are between-group; the rest are variations on within-group designs. Like the preceding sections on single-treatment designs, the designs are grouped in terms of the quality of the conclusions that can be drawn, with the highest quality designs—those permitting conclusions with confidence—listed first.

Problems with ABC or ABCD Designs

A common design that includes repeated measures and multiple treatments is the ABC or ABCD design. Unfortunately, it does not allow one to answer comparison (12C) questions with confidence.

An ABCD design was used in comparing the effects of individual feedback, goal setting, and praise on hockey team members (Anderson et al., 1988). After baseline recording (A), publicly posted individual feedback (B) was introduced, then goal setting was introduced (C), and finally praise was added (D). Use of this design, according to the authors, "permitted a components analysis of the respective contributions of each treatment" (p. 88). Further, they erroneously declare:

> Although it was not possible to explore in a single study all of the possible combinations and permutations of intervention sequences that eventually will be needed to fully unravel the conditions that maximize the effectiveness of each, we nonetheless were able to operationally divorce feedback effects from the results of feedback-plus-goal setting, and the latter from a combination of feedback, goal setting, and praise effects. (p. 88)

Why one cannot do a component analysis and divorce the effects of one component from another can be seen after taking into account problems with multiple-treatment interference.

Multiple-Treatment Interference

The problem with the ABCD (12C) design and others like it (15-17) is that comparisons are made *within* the group and the group is exposed first to one treatment and then another opens up the possibility of multiple-treatment interference, which limits the generality of the results. In the example of the hockey team with an ABCD design in which the same players performed first on system B, then switched to system C, and then to system D, one system might have an impact on a subsequent one. Hence, the fact that the same individuals are exposed to more than one system or treatment may "interfere" and thus limit the conclusions that can be drawn about the impact of any single system. Since many questions concern the effectiveness of a single system when presented alone, the interference caused by the introduction of multiple treatments to the same group can be a major problem.

Two types of interference can be major threats to the generalizability of the findings. One type of interference, termed the *contrast effect*, results from juxtaposing treatments in such a way that individuals can contrast treatment B with treatments C and D and perhaps behave differently. It is possible that in the Anderson et al. (1988) investigation, for instance, that goal setting increased performance further only because subjects already had information about their performance level from the feedback introduced in phase B, and had the benefit of being able to contrast their goals with their previous performance. "Exposure to one manipulation or test may produce persistent consequences . . . that influence the subject's response to any subsequent manipulation" (Neale and Liebert, 1986, p. 175).

The second type of interference, called the *sequence effect*, results from introducing treatments in a particular order. In this case, first B was introduced, then C, and finally D. Factors contributing to sequence effects are many, and include practice and experience. When players are given the same treatments in the same order, it is likely that they "would improve as they became more familiar with the procedure, more comfortable with the . . . setting, and more practiced in the task" (Neale and Liebert, 1986, p. 176). For example, Anderson and colleagues (1988) found that feedback was associated with larger effects than were goal setting and praise, but they note the possibility of a sequence effect: "this may have been due to the temporal precedence of this treatment" (p. 92). Hence, using an ABC or an ABCD design may compromise the conclusions drawn because of limitations in the generalizability of the results. Thus, because of the possibility of multiple-treatment interference, ABC and ABCD designs are not recommended when asking comparison questions.

Difficulties with Variations of Reversal Designs

Attempts also have been erroneously made to address comparison questions using modifications of the reversal design.

Using ABABACABACAB Designs

To compare the effects on speeding of two programs, an extension of the reversal design—ABAB followed by ACA that in turn overlaps with another reversal component ABA that in turn overlaps with another reversal component ACA—was used (Van Houten and Nau, 1981). On two highways, the authors introduced the two programs, increased surveillance (B) and feedback posted on billboards (C), in a mixed order, e.g., ABABACABACAB (15C). After examining the results, the authors concluded that program C was substantially more effective than program B in reducing speeding.

The problem with this conclusion is that the conditions under which these findings are likely to recur are limited to situations in which drivers are exposed to both treatments. One cannot readily rule out multiple-treatment interference, both contrast and sequence effects. Since drivers had the opportunity to experience and compare both methods of speed control, one cannot confidently assume that program C will have the same beneficial effect when presented by itself because of possible contrast effects. One can only conclude that program C is effective when B has been presented. In addition, the effectiveness of C may have been due to the sequencing of B and C. By the time C has been presented, drivers have twice had experience with some type of speed control method (two presentations of B). This experience may have resulted in drivers being more practiced at reducing their speed by the time C was presented. These problems are not specific to the above study. Indeed, any investigator who uses this design or any design in which subjects are exposed to multiple treatments will be subject to the same limitations on external validity. As a result, no matter how many reversal phases are involved, an ABABACABACAB design is generally not recommended when answering comparison questions.

Using BCB Designs

The BCB variation of the reversal design also has been inappropriately used in comparing programs. In assessing the effects of monetary incentive systems on productivity, a BCB design (16C) was used (Dickinson and Gillette, 1993). First, piece-rate pay (B) was introduced, then base pay plus incentives (C), and finally the piece-rate pay system again (B). The authors wanted to know not only whether piece-rate pay and base pay with incentives each improved productivity, but also which improved productivity more.

Unfortunately, the authors could not answer the latter comparison question. Potential problems exist with contrast and sequence effects. If C had increased over B in this study, the authors still could not have correctly concluded that C is better than B, because the improvements might have been related to the order in which C was introduced. The only conclusion that could be safely drawn—if performance increased during C and then decreased during the reintroduction of B—was that C was responsible for the increases. The challenge is to make sure that the conclusions drawn are sound and do not overreach permissible boundaries given the design used.

Regrettably, workers in the Dickinson and Gillette (1993) study responded more or less the same regardless of whether B or C was used. This lack of differential responding coupled with the inappropriate design meant that none of the questions posed were answerable. Since knowledge consists of "knowledge of differences" (Runkel and McGrath, 1972, p. 51), the investigators are advised to use a between-group design to answer the comparison question. Other suggestions are to consider revising the questions and asking a facilitative question such as "does C improve performance when added to B," or to use an ABA or ACA reversal design to evaluate the effectiveness of the two systems on the productivity of the group.

The lack of differential responding in this study raises an interesting issue. Had a different design been used—ABA or ACA rather than BCB—would differences have been found? A study by McGonigle and colleagues (1987) suggests that multiple treatment interference can take the form of a lack of differential responding to various treatments. McGonigle et al. (1987) varied the time interval between the administration of one treatment and the next and found no differential responding to the second treatment when the interval was short. However, differential responding was found when the interval between the treatments was long. While the lack of differential responding may not always be a consequence of assessing multiple treatments within the same group, it would be wise to keep in mind McGonigle and colleague's (1987) findings as we seek to assess the "truth" and to avoid using variations of within-group designs in addressing comparison questions.

Objections to Counterbalanced Designs

The counterbalanced design is also sometimes used in addressing comparison questions. With this design, Group 1 receives the treatments in the order ABAC, while Group 2 experiences the treatments in the order ACAB. Or two teams receive treatments in the order ABC, with three teams receiving the treatments in the order ACB, as Fox and Sulzer-Azaroff (1989) did (17C). Although the counterbalancing addresses problems with the sequence effect, the same objections still hold for the contrast effect. If treatment B worked better regardless of its position, team members could still compare the two treatments, and their performance could still be a function of having experienced both. Also, Neale and Liebert (1986) point out, counterbalancing effectively rules out sequence effects only when "we are reasonably certain that the carryover effect from treatment A to treatment B is the same as the carryover effect from treatment B to treatment A" (p. 178). In short, although counterbalancing the order of treatments attempts to solve the sequence effect problem, it does not deal adequately with the contrast effect and with potential problems of carryover. As a result, the counterbalanced design is not recommended when comparing programs.

In short, the problems with sequence and contrast effects cannot be avoided when using variations of within-group designs because these designs require, by their very nature, comparisons within the group. Hence, we recommend the use of between-group designs with random assignment when answering comparison questions because of the potential problems with multiple-treatment interference when using ABC, ABCD, ABABACA, or BCB designs.

ASSESSING IMPACT OF MULTIPLE TREATMENTS: ALTERNATIVES TO ASKING COMPARISON QUESTIONS

Are questions involving more than one treatment off-limits if one cannot use a between-group design? Happily, the answer is no. Although problems exist addressing comparison questions using variations of within-group designs, other questions can still be addressed. Among the questions are those determining whether a program or a component of a treatment package is: (a) facilitative or (b) sufficient.

Determining if One Component Facilitates Another

One can ask whether one treatment *adds* to the effectiveness of another treatment (see Table 4.1). If one treatment or component has been shown to be effective, one can evaluate if adding a second would result in or facilitate an additional increase.

Using ABC, ABCD, or ABCDE Multiple Baseline

This facilitative question has been assessed by using an ABC or an ABCDE multiple-baseline design (18F) (Calpin, Edelstein and Redmon, 1988; Komaki, Collins, and Penn, 1982). What was the additional effect of consequences when antecedents were already in place? That was the the the question posed by Komaki, Collins, and Penn (1982). An ABC multiple-baseline design was used in which antecedents were first introduced in a staggered manner to four groups following the collection of baseline data on each group; and, after a time, consequences were added (once again, in a staggered fashion) to the antecedents. As shown in Figure 4.12, the following phases were implemented: baseline (A), antecedents (B), and consequences (C). The critical phase, for purposes of the discussion about facilitation, was phase C. During the C phase, performance significantly improved in all the groups over and above that of consequences, as confirmed by a time-series analysis appropriate for these data. Hence, the authors concluded that, despite the fact that in some groups significant changes had already occurred during the antecedent phase, consequences *added* to or facilitated the effectiveness of the antecedents.

Using ABCB Reversal Designs

Another facilitative question was addressed by Goltz and colleagues (1989). They wanted to assess whether one component—individual feedback—helped in enhancing the effects of another component—group feedback. To do this, they used a reversal (19F) design. As shown in Figure 4.13, a baseline phase was followed by group feedback (B), group feedback and individual feedback (C), and group feedback (B). If performance had increased during the C phase and decreased during the final B phase when individual feedback was withdrawn, then it could have been concluded that individual feedback facilitated group feedback. The ABCB design allowed the authors to draw conclusions about the facilitative impact of a single component. Because of the lack of a decrease during the reversal phase, however, the authors could not conclude that individual feedback was responsible for enhancing group feedback effects. It is important, however, to make a distinction between the design used and the results obtained. Similar to the earlier discussion of the Welsh, Luthans, and Sommer (1993) case, even though the results did not support the effectiveness of one of the components, the design was still appropriate to address the facilitative question.

FIGURE 4.12. Example of Using a Multiple-Baseline Design to Assess Whether a Component Adds to the Effectiveness of Another Component

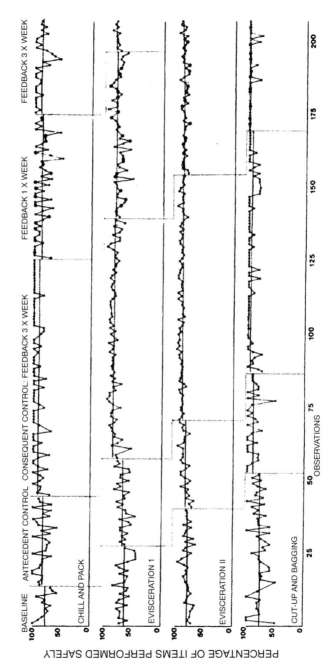

Note: Percentage of safe behaviors of workers in four departments of a poultry processing plant. The presentation of feedback with the presentation of rules and reminders (consequent control phase) increased performance significantly beyond that achieved with the presentation of rules and reminders alone (antecedent control phase). From Komaki, Collins, and Penn (1982). Copyright 1982 by the American Psychological Association, Inc. Reprinted by permission.

121

FIGURE 4.13. Example of Use of a Reversal Design to Assess Whether a Component Facilitates the Effectiveness of Another Component

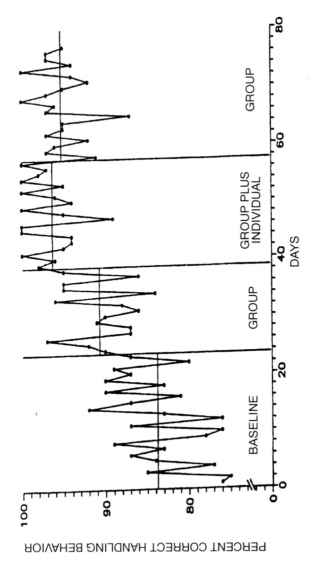

Note: Percentage of safe handling behaviors performed correctly by workers in a microelectronics plant. The addition of individual feedback resulted in performance improvements beyond that found with the presentation of group feedback only, but performance did not reverse when individual feedback was withdrawn. From Goltz et al. (1989). Copyright 1990 by The Haworth Press, Inc. Reprinted by permission.

Assessing If a Component Is Sufficient and Necessary

Using a Pair of Experiments

Another question that is sometimes raised is whether only one treatment or one component of a treatment package is adequate or sufficient.[2] This issue sometimes comes up when a treatment package that consists of two components—training and feedback—is successful, and questions arise as to whether only one of the components would result in the same findings.

As an illustration, let us look at a pair of experiments. In the first, an intervention was introduced consisting of a combination of training and feedback (Komaki, Barwick, and Scott, 1978). When management saw the dramatic rise in performance (Figure 4.14), they questioned whether the feedback was critical and posited that the training alone may have been responsible. Because both components had been introduced at the same time, however, it was difficult to address these issues. Hence, another experiment was done, using an ABC multiple-baseline design (18F) (Komaki, Heinzmann, and Lawson, 1980). The question raised was whether one component—in this case, training—would be sufficient. After baseline, as can be seen in Figure 4.15, training alone (B) was introduced in a staggered fashion to each of the four departments. When only slight but insignificant improvements occurred during the training only phase, as confirmed by an analysis appropriate for time-series data, the authors concluded that training alone was not *sufficient* to improve performance.

In summary, with the exception of comparison questions, within-group designs can be used to address a variety of questions in work settings. One can address program effectiveness and maintenance issues, as well as questions such as: Is one component effective alone? Does one component add to the effectiveness of other components?

WITHIN-GROUP DESIGNS IN PERSPECTIVE

Following our review of within-group designs, we have several concluding remarks. They differ from those of our colleagues in that they focus on the enhanced generalizability of the findings and the challenges of using within-subject designs to address more subtle questions concerning multiple treatments. In contrast, Luthans and Davis (1982) present how these designs lend themselves to a more idiographic approach; Wilson and Bornstein (1984) discuss the difficulties of comparing treatments for "clients who vary on particular dimensions of interest" (p. 201); and Cuvo (1979) the limitations of repeated testing.

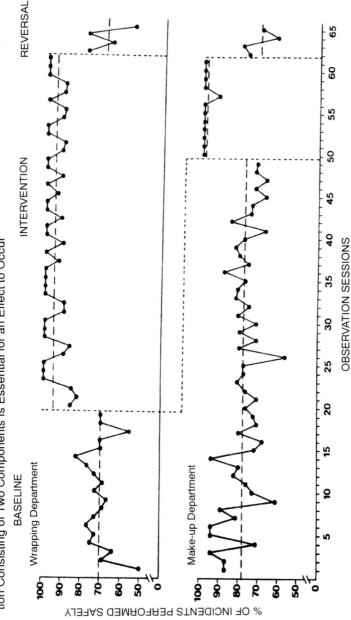

FIGURE 4.14. Illustration of Using a Multiple-Baseline Design with a Reversal Phase to Assess Whether an Intervention Consisting of Two Components Is Essential for an Effect to Occur

Note: Percentage of safe practices performed by workers in a bakery. Performance increased when the intervention, specification and feedback was applied; then decreased when one of the components, feedback, was withdrawn. From Komaki, Barwick, and Scott (1978). Copyright by the American Psychological Association, Inc. Reprinted by permission.

FIGURE 4.15. Example of Using a Second Study to Examine Whether a Component Is a Sufficient Condition for the Effectiveness of an Intervention

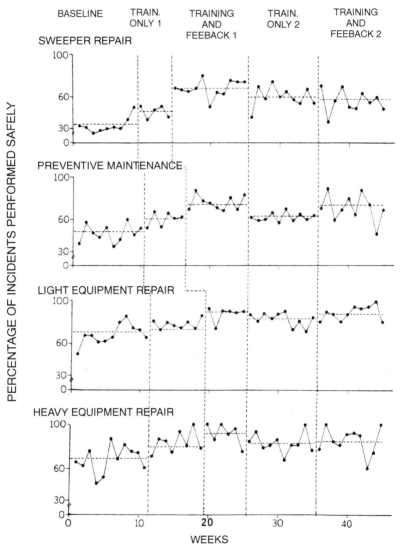

Note: Percentage of incidents performed safely by employees in four vehicle maintenance sections of a city's vehicle maintenance division. It was determined from this study that training alone had no significant effect on performance. From Komaki, Heinzman, and Lawson (1980). Copyright 1980 by the American Psychological Association, Inc. Reprinted by permission.

Expanding Subjects and Settings
to Which Findings Can Be Generalized

One of the advantages of within-group designs is that they do not require the random assignment of subjects to groups and hence enable the assessment of workers doing tasks in settings where they have rarely been evaluated. A single game room attendant (Komaki, Waddell, and Pearce, 1977) and as few as three workers in a small machine shop (Henry and Redmon, 1990) have been subjects. This flexibility to assess single individuals as well as large intact groups such as two mines (Fox, Hopkins, and Anger, 1987), three restaurants (George and Hopkins, 1989), and an entire package delivery company (Kortik and O'Brien, 1996), makes within-group designs uniquely suited to applied settings. Because the more divergent the groups studied, the better the generalizability, the external validity of findings is increased.

Tailoring Questions to Designs

Formidable constraints are imposed by applied settings. Adjustments often must be made to research plans. The traditional sequence used in planning research is to first select a research question and then work out the details—selecting the subjects, measures, and design. Field researchers have had to reexamine this sequence, tailoring their research plans to fit the boundaries of field situations. A study conducted by Goltz and colleagues (1989) in a department of a microelectronics plant illustrates this point. Initially, the authors were interested in comparing the effects of individual and group feedback. However, workers in one section were specially trained to assemble the product and were not interchangeable with employees in the quality control section. Hence, it was not possible to randomly assign subjects in the department to two or more groups, and a between-group design and a comparison question were ruled out. A multiple-baseline design across groups was also not workable since workers in the two sections were in close contact with each other. As a result, the authors decided to ask a facilitative question—"Individual feedback: Does it enhance effects of group feedback?" (p. 77). An ABC with reversal to B design (19F) was used. Data were collected during group feedback administered alone (B), individual feedback administered with group feedback (C), and finally during group feedback alone (B). As one can see, the authors adjusted their research question to fit a design that could reasonably be implemented within the constraints of the setting.

Distinguishing Between What Investigators Say and Do

Many discrepancies were found when reviewing studies to include in this chapter as well as in a review of the work motivation literature (Komaki et al., 2000). For instance, some investigators aimed to answer one research question, but ended up answering another question. Authors sometimes wanted to ask a comparison question but ultimately used a design that allowed them to address only a facilitative question. An example of this mismatch is the two-part study by Ducharme and Feldman (1992) titled "Comparison of Staff Training Strategies to Promote Generalized Teaching Skills." In the first study, they successfully answered the facilitative question: Does D add to B and C, and does E add to B, C, and D? Using an ABCDE multiple-baseline-across-groups design, the additional effect of common stimuli training (D) was assessed when training using written instructions (B) and single cases (C) were already in place. Later, the additional effect of general case training (E) was assessed after treatments B, C, and D were already in place.

It was found that performance significantly improved in both groups when treatment D was used over that which occurred during treatments B and C. Thus, it could be concluded that the common stimuli training did, in fact, *add* to the effectiveness of the other treatments. Furthermore, performance was found to significantly improve during treatment E, the general case training. Thus, the facilitative question could be and was addressed with not just one, but two separate treatments.

Still interested in pursuing the comparison question and in controlling for the possible sequence effects in the first study, the authors did a second experiment, this time using a multiple-baseline design evaluating only treatment E. When treatment E resulted in increased performance, the authors concluded, "general case training was more effective than other commonly used and recommended staff training strategies" (Ducharme and Feldman, 1992, p. 174), contrasting effects found in the first study with results of the second study. However, since subjects were not randomly assigned in the first and second experiments, alternative explanations such as selection, history, and maturation could not be ruled out. Hence, the designs the authors used and the results they obtained allowed them to answer the straightforward program evaluation question, the facilitative question, and possibly the question whether treatment E was sufficient, but not their original comparison question. To avoid mismatches such as these, authors should carefully consider whether what they say is consistent with what they do.

Addressing More Subtle Questions

As more subtle questions are asked and the results become less dramatic, adjustments need to be made in the way in which the results are evaluated. Traditionally, investigators scrutinize the graphs and do what is known as a visual inspection. Unfortunately, the potential exists for erroneous conclusions (Jones, Weinrott, and Vaught, 1978; Matyas and Greenwood, 1990). Particularly problematic is the high number of false alarm rates in which ever-optimistic authors conclude an effect exists when it does not (Matyas and Greenwood, 1990). On the other hand, data presentation methods can lead to underestimates of the importance of small reliable effects (Mawhinney, 1999). Another documented problem is poor interjudge reliability even with experienced judges (DeProsper and Cohen, 1979; Jones, Weinrott, and Vaught, 1978). In an attempt to make the criteria more clear, a new set of criteria, termed OCT, has been developed for studies using within-subject designs (Komaki et al., 2000). Using the OCT criteria, one assesses the overlap (O) in data points between phases, where the data in each phase stand with respect to the measure of central (C) tendency, and trends (T) in the direction of the subsequent phase. These criteria enable one to make judgements about the level of support for program effectiveness.

Statistical methods are recommended to supplement visual analyses (e.g., McCain and McCleary, 1979; Matyas and Greenwood, 1990). A handful of studies reporting the statistical significance of differences using t-tests or repeated measures of analysis of variance (e.g., Jones, Morris, and Barnard, 1986; Luthans, Paul, and Baker, 1981; Luthans, Paul, and Taylor, 1986; Hantula, Stillman, and Waranch, 1992). While the use of these statistics is to be commended in that they represent an improvement over simply relying on visual inspection, it has its limitations. The primary problem is the assumption that the data are independent and not correlated. Since the data collected in within-group designs are in the form of repeated measurements over time, the data points are not truly independent. In fact, the data points may be autocorrelated—that is, current and future values of each data point may be partially a function of the past values. (Note: Substantial disagreement currently exists as to the extent to which autocorrelation is found in behavioral data—e.g., Huitema, 1985, 1988; Matyas and Greenwood, 1991.)

Time-series analyses such as the nonlinear autoregressive integrated moving average analysis (ARIMA) or the linear autoregressive analysis are useful for analyzing repeated-measures data to both determine whether the data are autocorrelated and to take any autocorrelations into account. These analyses first assess the degree of autocorrelation, then calculate specialized t-tests that take it into account. To use these analyses, however, it is important to ensure that the data allow one to identify a model (see Huitema, 1986). (For more comprehensive discussions of time-series analyses, see Box and Jenkins, 1970; Glass, Willson, and Gottman, 1975; Gottman, 1981.)

Time-series analyses have been used to confirm that the changes in behavior that were visually apparent were also statistically significant (e.g., Chhokar and Wallin, 1984; Goltz, et al., 1989; Komaki, Collins, and Penn, 1982; Komaki, Heinzmann, and Lawson, 1980; Landau, 1993). For instance, in the Komaki, Collins, and Penn (1982) study, an ARIMA was used to see if performance consequences enhanced the effects of performance antecedents. A sizable number of data points per phase were obtained for all the groups: fourteen to fifty times during the baseline phase depending on the group, twenty-five to thirty during the antecedent phase in each group, and so on (as shown in Figure 4.12). Comparisons were made between baseline and antecedent, baseline and consequent, and antecedent and consequent conditions (see Table 4.4). Significant level or mean changes were found in all departments when comparing the consequent over baseline doncition *and* the consequent over the antecedent condition. The authors concluded that "the performance consequence, feedback, resulted in significant changes in all departments over baseline and antecedent conditions" (p. 339).

The importance of time-series analyses are shown in a study in which a visual analysis of the data might have led to an erroneous conclusion (Goltz, et al., 1989). As shown in Figure 4.13, this study involved the presentation of group feedback, the addition of individual feedback, and the removal of group feedback, in a reversal design. The analysis confirmed that the group feedback phase and the group plus individual feedback phase were different; however, it did not confirm that the drop in performance during the reversal phase was significant (see Table 4.5). Hence, the authors were not able to make a desired inference. These two studies illustrate the usefulness of time-series analyses in assessing more subtle changes.

In closing, within-group designs have been shown to be a valuable alternative to the traditional control group designs in answering questions about the effectiveness of programs. These designs can also be used to assess changes over time. Furthermore, these designs can be used to assess whether trends in performance exist over time and whether one component of a program facilitates another component. Because of problems of multiple treatment interference, however, these designs are not suitable for comparison questions.

TABLE 4.4. Results of the Time Series Analysis in Komaki and Colleagues (1982)

Departments

Comparison	Chill and Pack Level change	df	Evisceration 1 Level change	df	Evisceration 2 Level change	df	Cut-up and Bagging Level change	df
Baseline vs. antecedent	1.22	44	1.15	65	3.09**	70	5.09**	76
Baseline vs. consequent	5.28**	86	9.21**	88	11.49**	65	7.87**	78
Antecedent vs. consequent	6.62**	105	9.28**	79	5.12*	71	2.47*	62

Source: Table taken from Komaki, Collins, and Penn (1982). Copyright 1982 by the American Psychological Association, Inc. Reprinted by permission.

Note: Level change = probability of the observed change as determined by a *t*-test comparison.
*p < .01. **p < .001.

TABLE 4.5. Results of the Autoregressive Integrated Moving Averages Analysis[a] in Goltz and Colleagues (1989)

Comparison	Level Change[b]	Drift Change[c]	df
Baseline vs. Group Feedback	−4.58***	−.091	32
Group Feedback vs. Group and Individual Feedback	−8.88***	−.008	28
Group and Individual Feedback vs. Reversal to Group Feedback	.096	−.230	32

Source: Table taken from Goltz, Citera, Jensen, Favero, and Komaki (1989). Copyright 1990 by The Haworth Press, Inc. Reprinted by permission.

[a]A model of order one was used because of the limited number of data points.

[b]The observed level changed as determined by a t-text comparison.

[c]The observed trend change as determined by a t-text comparison.

*** $p < .001$.

In scientific research, the fit between the research question and design remains paramount. Hence, we have provided guidelines as to which designs are appropriate for which questions. When bringing the weight of scientific evidence to bear on issues, we hope that these guidelines will enable, in Oliver Wendell Holmes' words, "the best test of truth."

NOTES

1. Selection, another plausible explanation for performance effects (see Cook and Campbell, 1979), is not a threat to internal validity when reversal and multiple-baseline designs are used because comparisons are not made between groups, but within groups. Therefore, one need not be concerned with biases that can enter when individuals are selected for comparison groups. Similarly, testing as an alternative explanation can usually be ruled out because it primarily pertains to personality or paper-and-pencil tests, relatively rarely used in repeated-measures designs. Differential mortality can be difficult to rule out if subjects drop out of the intervention phases at a different rate than they do the baseline or reversal phases. In assessing the results of an intervention, one should be aware of this possible source of confounding.

2. Although components or treatments are sometimes referred to as both necessary and sufficient and sufficient but not necessary, our discussion concerns only the latter. Our rationale is based on the scientific method in which data are systematically collected to assess which explanation is most consistent with the evidence. One can test, for example, whether a component is sufficient, but not necessary, as we have shown. But one cannot readily test, given most social scientists "resources," whether a component is both necessary and sufficient. To do that, a component would have "to produce an effect and invariably do so" (Liebert and Liebert, 1995, p. 88). An example is the genetic anomaly causing Tay-Sachs disease. Each time the generic anomaly is present, Tay-Sachs disease occurs; when the genetic anomaly is not present, Tay-Sachs disease does not occur. The issue here is invariability. It is not possible to adequately test in a single or even a pair of experiments for this invariability. Given this requirement, we do not propose to provide evidence that a component is both necessary and sufficient. Another reason concerns the nature of causality. In the social sciences, many factors and conditions are responsible for a given effect. Liebert and Liebert (1995) conclude that: "in psychology, it is rare to find important causal relationships that are both necessary and sufficient" (p. 88). Hence, our discussion is limited to whether a given treatment or component is sufficient but not necessary.

REFERENCES

Abrams et al. v. United States, 250 U.S. 616, #360 (1919).

Allen, E. M. (1960). Why are research grant applications disapproved? *Science, 132,* 1532-1534.

Anderson, D. C., Crowell, C. R., Doman, M., and Howard, G. S. (1988). Performance posting, goal setting, and activity-contingent praise as applied to a university hockey team. *Journal of Applied Psychology, 73,* 87-95.

Arco, L. (1997). Improving program outcome with process-based performance feedback. *Journal of Organizational Behavior Management, 17*(1), 37-64.

Ashenfelter, O. (1987). The case for evaluating training programs with randomized trials. *Economics of Education Review, 6,* 333-338.

Barlow, D. H. and Hersen, M. (1992). *Single case experimental designs: Strategies for studying behavior change* (Second edition). Boston: Allyn and Bacon.

Boudreau, C. A., Christian, W. P., and Thibadeau, S. F. (1993). Reducing absenteeism in a human service setting: A low cost alternative. *Journal of Organizational Behavior Management, 13*(2), 37-50.

Box, G. E. P. and Jenkins, G. M. (1970). *Time-series analysis: Forecasting and control.* San Francisco: Holden-Day.

Brown, M. G. (1980). Evaluating training via multiple baseline designs. *Training and Development Journal,* October, pp. 11-16.

Brown, N. B. and Redmon, W. K. (1990). The effects of a group reinforcement contingency on staff use of unscheduled sick leave. *Journal of Organizational Behavior Management, 10*(2), 3-17.

Callahan, N. M. and Redmon, W. K. (1987). Effects of problem-based scheduling on patient waiting and staff utilization of time in a pediatric clinic. *Journal of Applied Behavior Analysis, 20,* 193-199.

Calpin, J. P., Edelstein, B., and Redmon, W. K. (1988). Performance feedback and goal setting to improve mental health center staff productivity. *Journal of Organizational Behavior Management, 9*(2), 35-58.

Campbell, D. T. and Stanley, J. C. (1966). *Experimental and quasi-experimental designs for research.* Chicago: Rand McNally.

Carter, N., Holmstrom, A., Simpanen, M., and Melin, L. (1988). Theft reduction in a grocery store through product identification and graphing of losses for employees. *Journal of Applied Behavior Analysis, 21,* 385-389.

Chhokar, J. S. and Wallin, J. A. (1984). A field study of the effect of feedback frequency on performance. *Journal of Applied Psychology, 69,* 524-530.

Christian, L. and Poling, A. (1997). Using self-management procedures to improve the productivity of adults with developmental disabilities in a competitive employment setting. *Journal of Applied Behavior Analysis, 30,* 169-172.

Cook, T. D. and Campbell, D. T. (1979). *Quasi-experimentation: Design and analysis issues for field settings.* Boston: Houghton-Mifflin Company.

Cuvo, A. J. (1979). Multiple-baseline design in instructional research: Pitfalls of measurement and procedural advantages. *American Journal of Mental Deficiency, 84*(3), 219-228.

DeProspero, A. and Cohen, S. (1979). Inconsistent visual analyses of intrasubject data. *Journal of Applied Behavior Analysis, 12,* 573-579.

Dickinson, A. M. and Gillette, K. L. (1993). A comparison of the effects of two individual monetary incentive systems on productivity: Piece-rate pay versus base pay plus incentives. *Journal of Organizational Behavior Management, 14*(1), 3-82.

Doan, T. Z. (1992). *RATS user's manual.* Evanston, IL: Estima.

Ducharme, J. M. and Feldman, M. A. (1992). Comparison of staff training strategies to promote generalized teaching skills. *Journal of Applied Behavior Analysis, 25,* 165-179.

Fox, D. K., Hopkins, B. L., and Anger, W. K. (1987). The long-term effects of a token economy on safety performance in open-pit mining. *Journal of Applied Behavior Analysis, 20,* 215-224.

Fox, D. K. and Sulzer-Azaroff, B. (1989). The effectiveness of two different sources of feedback on staff teaching of fire evacuation skills. *Journal of Organizational Behavior Management, 10*(2), 19-35.

George, J. T. and Hopkins, B. L. (1989). Multiple effects of performance-contingent pay for waitpersons. *Journal of Applied Behavior Analysis, 22,* 131-141.

Glass, G. V., Willson, V. L., and Gottman, J. M. (1975). *Design and analysis of time-series experiments.* Boulder, CO: Colorado University Associated Press.

Goltz, S. M., Citera, M., Jensen, M., Favero, J., and Komaki, J. L. (1989). Individual feedback: Does it enhance effects of group feedback? *Journal of Organizational Behavior Management, 10*(2), 77-92.

Gottman, J. M. (1981). *Time-series analysis: A comprehensive introduction for social scientists.* Cambridge, UK: Cambridge University Press.

Hantula, D. A., Stillman, F. A., and Waranch, H. R. (1992). Can a mass-media campaign modify tobacco smoking in a large organization? Evaluation of the Great American Smokeout in an urban hospital. *Journal of Organizational Behavior Management, 13*(1), 33-47.

Henry, G. O. and Redmon, W. K. (1990). The effects of performance feedback on the implementation of a statistical process control (SPC) program. *Journal of Organizational Behavior Management, 11*(2), 23-46.

Hermann, J. A., DeMontes, A. I., Dominquez, B., Montes, F., and Hopkins, B. L. (1973). Effects of bonuses for punctuality on the tardiness of industrial workers. *Journal of Applied Behavior Analysis, 6,* 563-570.

Hersen, M. and Barlow, D. H. (1976). *Single-case experimental design: Strategies for studying behavior change.* New York: Pergamon Press.

Hopkins, B. L., Conard, R. J., Dangel, R. F., Fitch, H. G., Smith, M. J., and Anger, W. K. (1986). Behavioral technology for reducing occupational exposure to styrene. *Journal of Applied Behavior Analysis, 19,* 3-11.

Huitema, B. (1985). Autocorrelation in applied behavior analysis: A myth. *Behavioral Assessment, 7,* 107-118.

Huitema, B. (1986). Statistical analysis and single-subject designs. In A. Poling and R. W. Fuqua (Eds.), *Research methods in applied behavior analysis: Issues and advances* (pp. 209-232). New York: Plenum Press.

Huitema, B. (1988). Autocorrelation: 10 years of confusions. *Behavioral Assessment, 10,* 253-294.

Johnson, C. M. and Masotti, R. M. (1990). Suggestive selling by waitstaff in family-style restaurants: An experiment and multi-setting observations. *Journal of Organizational Behavior Management, 11*(1), 35-54.

Johnson, M. D., and Fawcett, S. B. (1994). Courteous service: Its assessment and modification in a human service organizaiton. *Journal of Applied Behavior Analysis, 27,* 145-152.

Johnson, S. P., Welsh, T. M., Miller, L.K., and Altus, D.E. (1991). Participatory management: Maintaining staff performance in a university housing cooperative. *Journal of Applied Behavior Analysis, 24,* 119-127.

Jones, H. H., Morris, E. K., and Barnard, J. D. (1986). Increasing staff completion of civil commitment forms through instructions and graphed group performance feedback. *Journal of Organizational Behavior Management, 7*(3/4), 29-43.

Jones, R. R., Weinrott, M. R., and Vaught, R. S. (1978). Effects of serial dependency on the agreement between visual and statistical inference. *Journal of Applied Behavior Analysis, 11,* 277-283.

Kazdin, A. E. (1997). *Research design in clinical psychology* (Third edition). Boston: Allyn and Bacon.

Komaki, J. (1977). Alternative evaluation strategies in work settings: Reversal and multiple-baseline designs. *Journal of Organizational Behavior Management, 1,* 53-77.

Komaki, J. L. (1982). The case for the single case: Making judicious decisions about alternatives. In L. W. Frederiksen (Ed.), *Handbook of organizational behavior management* (pp. 145-176). New York: John Wiley and Sons, Inc.

Komaki, J. L., Barwick, K. D., and Scott, L. R. (1978). A behavioral approach to occupational safety: Pinpointing and reinforcing safe performance in a food manufacturing plant. *Journal of Applied Psychology, 63,* 434-445.

Komaki, J. L., Collins, R. L., and Penn, P. (1982). The role of performance antecedents and consequences in work motivation. *Journal of Applied Psychology, 67,* 334-340.

Komaki, J. L., Coombs, T., Redding, Jr., T. P., and Schepman, S. (2000). A rich and rigorous examination of applied behavior analysis reserach in the world of work. In C. L. Cooper and I. T. Robertson (Eds.), *International review of industrial and organizational psychology 2000.* Sussex, England: John Wiley.

Komaki, J. L., Heinzmann, A. T., and Lawson, L. (1980). Effect of training and feedback: Component analysis of a behavioral safety program. *Journal of Applied Psychology, 65,* 261-270.

Komaki, J. L. and Jensen, M. (1986). Within-group designs: An alternative to traditional control-group designs. In M. F. Cataldo and T. J. Coates (Eds.), *Health and industry: A behavioral medicine perspective* (86-138). New York: John Wiley.

Komaki, J. L., Waddell, L. M., and Pearce, M. G. (1977). The applied behavior analysis approach and individual employees: Improving performance in two small businesses. *Organizational Behavior and Human Performance, 19,* 337-352.

Kortick, S. A. and O'Brien, R. M. (1996). The world series of quality control: A case study in the package delivery industry. *Journal of Organizational Behavior Management, 16*(2), 77-93.

LaFleur, T. and Hyten, C. (1995). Improving the quality of hotel banquet staff performance. *Journal of Organizational Behavior Management, 15*(1/2), 69-93.

Lalonde, R. and Maynard, R. (1987). How precise are evaluations of employment and training programs: Evidence from a field experiment. *Evaluation Review, 11,* 428-451.

Landau, J. C. (1993). The impact of a change in an attendance control system on absenteeism and tardiness. *Journal of Organizational Behavior Management, 13,* 51-70.

Latham, G. P. and Baldes, J. J. (1975). The "practical significance" of Locke's theory of goal setting. *Journal of Applied Psychology, 60,* 122-124.

Lawler, E. E. and Hackman, J. R. (1969). The impact of employee participation on the development of pay incentive plans: A field experiment. *Journal of Applied Psychology, 53,* 464-471.

Liebert, R. M. and Liebert, L L. (1995). *Science and behavior: An introduction to methods of research* (Fourth edition). Englewood Cliffs, NJ: Prentice-Hall.

Luthans, F. and Davis, T. R. V. (1982). An idiographic approach to organizational behavior research: The use of single case experimental designs and direct measures. *Academy of Management Review, 7*(3), 380-391.

Luthans, F., Paul, R., and Baker, D. (1981). An experimental analysis of the impact of contingent reinforcement on salespersons' performance behavior. *Journal of Applied Psychology, 66,* 314-323.

Luthans, F., Paul, R., and Taylor, L. (1986). The impact of contingent reinforcement on retail salespersons' performance behavior. *Journal of Organizational Behavior Management, 7*(1/2), 25-35.

Matyas, T. A. and Greenwood, K. M. (1990). Visual analysis of single-case time series: Effects of variability, serial dependence, and magnitude of intervention effects. *Journal of Applied Behavior Analysis, 23,* 333-339.

Matyas, T. A. and Greenwood, K. M. (1991). Problems in the estimation of autocorrelation in brief time series and some implications for behavioral data. *Behavioral Assessment, 13,* 137-157.

Mawhinney, T. C. (1999). Cumulatively large benefits of incrementally small intervention effects: Costing metacontingencies of chronic absenteeism. *Journal of Organizational Behavior Management, 18*(4), 150-154.

McCain, L. J. and McCleary, R. (1979). The statistical analysis of the simple interrupted time-series quasi-experiment. In T. D. Cook and D. T. Campbell, *Quasi-experimentation: Design and analysis issues for field settings* (pp. 233-293). Boston: Houghton-Mifflin.

McGonigle, J. J., Rojahn, J., Dixon, J., and Strain, P. S. (1987). Multiple treatment interference in the alternating treatments design as a function of the intercomponent interval length. *Journal of Applied Behavior Analysis, 20,* 171-178.

Neale, J. M. and Liebert, R. M. (1986). *Science and behavior: An introduction to methods of research* (Third edition). Englewood Cliffs, NJ: Prentice-Hall.

Passell, P. (1993). Like a new drug. *The New York Times,* March 9, pp. C1, C12.

Pritchard, R. D., Jones, S. D., Roth, P. L., Stuebing, K. K., and Ekeberg, E. (1988). Effects of group feedback, goal setting, and incentives on organizational productivity. *Journal of Applied Psychology, 73,* 337-358.

Rogers, R. W., Rogers, J. S., Bailey, J. S., Runkle, W., and Moore, B. (1988). Promoting safety belt use among state employees: The effects of prompting and a stimulus-control intervention. *Journal of Applied Behavior Analysis, 21,* 263-269.

Runkel, P. J. and McGrath, J. E. (1972). *Research on human behavior.* New York: Holt, Rinehart, and Winston.

Siero, S., Boon, M., Kok, G., and Siero, F. (1989). Modification of driving behavior in a large transport organization: A field experiment. *Journal of Applied Psychology, 74,* 417-423.

Staw, B. M. (1977). The experimenting organization: Problems and prospects. In B. Staw (Ed.), *Psychological foundations of organizational behavior.* Santa Monica: Goodyear.

Van Houten, R. and Nau, P. A. (1981). A comparison of the effects of posted feedback and increased police surveillance on highway speeding. *Journal of Applied Behavior Analysis, 14,* 261-271.

Welsh, D. H. B., Luthans, F., and Sommer, S. M. (1993). Organizational behavior modification goes to Russia: Replicating an experimental analysis across cultures and tasks. *Journal of Organizational Behavior Management, 13*(2), 15-35.

Welsh, T. M., Miller, L. K., and Altus, D. E. (1994). Programming for survival: A meeting system that survives 8 years later. *Journal of Applied Behavior Analysis, 27,* 423-433.

Wilk, L. A. and Redmon, W. K. (1990). A daily-adjusted goal-setting and feedback procedure for improving productivity in a university admissions department. *Journal of Organizational Behavior Management, 11*(1), 55-75.

Wilson, G. L. and Bornstein, P. H. (1984). Paradoxical procedures and single-case methodology: review and recommendations. *Journal of Behavior Therapy and Experimental Psychiatry, 15,* 195-203.

Wittkop, C. J., Rowan, J. F., and Poling, A. (1990). Use of a feedback package to reduce machine set-up time in a manufacturing setting. *Journal of Organizational Behavior Management, 11*(2), 7-22.

Wyatt, E. (2000). Study finds higher test scores among blacks with vouchers. *The New York Times,* August 29, p. A14.

Chapter 5

Schedules of Reinforcement in Organizational Performance, 1971-1994: Application, Analysis, and Synthesis

Donald A. Hantula

The experimental analysis of behavior is concerned with identifying, to the extent it is possible, orderly relationships between the behavior of the intact individual and the environments within which the individual behaves, including organizational and social environments. Respondent behavior reflects effects of antecedent environmental stimuli on the individual's reflexive behavior. Operant behavior, on the other hand, is behavior of an individual that acts upon the environment, producing a consequent change in it or the individual's orientation to it (i.e., locomotion). Operant behavior typically exhibits sensitivity to its immediate, and sometimes delayed, consequences (Baum, 1973), and antecedent stimuli can evoke changes in operant behavior when they have reliably predicted its consequences. Relations among antecedents, operant behaviors, and their consequences (A-B-Cs) are described as three-term contingencies and contingencies of reinforcement by Poling and Braatz (Chapter 2, this book).

Operant behavior has captured the attention of applied researchers and behavior managers because changes this class of behavior produces on organizational environments can contribute to accomplishment of organizational objectives. And the effective management of behavior in organizations depends critically on its predictability and controllability. Thus, knowledge concerning the variables of which operant behavior is a function is essential to effective behavior management. One of the variables of which operant behavior is a function, and which has been thoroughly and systematically analyzed by basic behavior analytic researchers, is the relationship between a behavior and its consequence(s). These B-C contingencies or "if B then C" relationships are called *schedules of reinforcement* (Ferster and Skinner, 1957).

Schedules of reinforcement are environmental rules or E-rules (Baum, 1973). A full appreciation of their role in the orderly variation of behavior across environmental changes, e.g., changes in E-rules, is gained when their role in the description of operant behavior reinforcement, punishment, or extinction is understood. Zeiler (1977) succinctly presented this context for schedules of reinforcement as follows:

> The word reinforcement refers to the effect of an operation; it does not describe an independent variable but is the interaction of an independent variable with behavior. By reinforcement is meant an increase in responding as a function of a stimulus event following a response. The stimuli having these effects are reinforcing stimuli or reinforcers. Schedules of reinforcement are the rules used to present reinforcing stimuli. (p. 202)

Unlike reinforcement per se, a schedule of reinforcement can be an independent variable. Manipulating schedules of reinforcement can, under certain conditions, produce predictable effects on dimensions of operant behavior such as changes in its rate, maintenance of its rate, establishment and maintenance in patterns of rate variation (high at some times and low at others), and change in operant behavior topography. Although they may be subtle and sometimes difficult to identify, work environments include E-rules that function as schedules of reinforcement (hereafter referred to as schedules) and as such exert powerful control of behavior within the work setting.

THE BASIC IMPORTANCE OF SCHEDULES

All events occur in time. All behaviors and consequences transpire across a temporal plane. However, despite the seemingly basic and self-evident importance of behavior's temporal dimension, it has been largely minimized and most often ignored in organizational behavior research. In the few instances in which time is considered seriously in organizational behavior research, it is conceptualized as a moderating variable (e.g. Gersick, 1988, 1989, 1994), but not as an independent variable in its own right. However, because organizations are formal structures or administrations of people that exist in space through time and are *not* momentary gatherings of individuals (Scott, 1992), this ignorance of behavior's temporal dimension poses a serious challenge to understanding and managing behavior effectively. Indeed, the behavior analytic perspective explicitly recognizes the significance of temporality and has historically addressed time as both a moderating variable and as an independent variable in its own right. Thus, the accumulated knowledge of schedules of reinforcement is among the most important features of the distinctive and distinguished contribution that behavior analysis can make to understanding and managing behavior in organizations.

Since publication of *Schedules of Reinforcement* (Ferster and Skinner, 1957), basic research in schedules has flourished to the point that schedule research may be the most highly developed and theoretically fertile area in the experimental analysis of behavior (Zeiler, 1977, 1984). This research is characterized by orderly data, sophisticated mathematical models, complex questions, and theoretical advances that illustrate the vast and profound influences schedules exert on individual behavior. However, despite some early interest in the academic and professional management literatures concerning how to apply reinforcement schedules to address organizational challenges (e.g., Aldis, 1961; Jablonsky and DeVries, 1972; Nord, 1969; *Organizational Dynamics*, 1973), schedule applications in organizations and in simulated organizational settings have lagged behind developments in the basic science of behavior or behavior analysis by decades.

Reviews of schedule research in organizations and in simulated organizational settings (Ayllon and Kolko, 1982; Latham and Huber, 1992; Mawhinney, 1986) find that the majority of past research has been limited to investigations comparing different simple schedules and their effects on job performance. In contrast, the basic literature in schedules has abandoned this comparative and parametric research in favor of such investigations as: preference and choice between different schedules, drug effects, dynamics of schedule performance, and synthesis of complex schedules (see Davison and McCarthy, 1988; Honig and Staddon, 1977; Zeiler, 1984 for further elaboration).

The focus of early research into effects of reinforcement schedules on task performance and the dominant focus of organizational behavior management has been at the front line or shop floor level of employees within work organizations (Balcazar et al., 1989; Hantula, 1992; O'Hara, Johnson, and Beehr, 1985). More recently, however, researchers have employed simulated organizational settings to address more complex questions about performance in organizations including financial decision making (e.g., Goltz, 1992, 1993; Hantula and Crowell, 1994a, b) leader effectiveness (e.g., Rao and Mawhinney, 1991), and perplexing theoretical issues surrounding these phenomena.

Ayllon and Kolko (1982) supplied an earlier review of schedules of reinforcement in OBM research, and Latham and Huber (1992) provide a more recent review of application-focused schedule research. Rather than reiterate previous reviews, this chapter will focus on basic mechanisms of schedule performance, catalog past studies, and discuss recent advances and research in schedules of reinforcement in OBM. In this review, the research will be categorized as one of three levels of inquiry: application, analysis, and synthesis. *Application* studies are those in which schedules of reinforcement are used as tools to change important work performances. In *analysis* studies, ongoing work performances are examined to determine the schedules that may be exerting control. *Synthesis* studies are those in which known behavioral effects of schedules are used to create performances that resemble those occurring in organizations. This categorization scheme is a useful means to organize the research because schedules of reinforcement are not only applied tools that may be used judiciously by the OBM practitioner to manage important work performances, but are also important theoretical instruments that enable the OBM researcher to approach more complex and perplexing questions. Thus, other features of schedule research, such as subjects, settings, and performances addressed, should vary as a function of level of inquiry, as should the type of research questions addressed.

SCHEDULES OF REINFORCEMENT: THE BASICS

Schedules may be defined on the basis of responses, time, complexity, and periodicity (see Ferster and Skinner, 1957; Williams and Johnston, 1992; Zeiler, 1977, 1984). Although "schedules of reinforcement" implies a program or timetable for presenting reinforcement, in practice, the term has come to refer to not only the presentation of reinforcement, but also to the presentation of contingent punishing events and noncontingent events as well. Indeed, whether or not a consequent event will act as a reinforcer or punisher may change depending on the schedule under which it is delivered (see Morse and Kelleher, 1977). Schedules may have both direct-acting and indirect-acting effects on behavior. *Direct-acting effects* are generally those resulting from the response-reinforcer contingency of a particular schedule, such as the number of responses required to obtain reinforcement. *Indirect-acting effects* result from formal properties of a particular schedule, or often from the contextual impacts of a particular schedule or combination of schedules (Baum, 1973). For example, whether or not an individual will continue to invest resources in a venture that fails to return positive consequences is due both to the direct-acting effects of receiving repeated negative feedback during the venture's failure and the indirect effects of the pattern of positive consequences arranged by the schedule that was in effect prior to the venture's failure to continue delivering good returns (Goltz, 1992, 1993; Hantula and Crowell, 1994a).

Schedules may operate singly. When they do they are called *simple schedules*. When schedules occur in concert with other schedules, they are called *complex schedules*. A complete account of complex schedules is beyond the scope of this chapter (see Catania, 1992 for a review). Examples of complex schedules often found in organizational research are *concurrent schedules*, in which two or more schedules are available simultaneously, and *multiple schedules*, in which two or more schedules operate sequentially. The following sections describe basic schedules of reinforcement and provide examples of their use in organizational contexts.

Response-Based Schedules

Response-based or count-based schedules are called *ratio* schedules. They refer to rules of administering a reinforcement contingent upon the completion of a certain number (count) of responses. These schedules are similar to piece-rate pay systems. On ratio schedules, rate of response and rate of reinforcement are highly correlated; higher rates of response result in higher rates of reinforcement. Ratio schedules in which reinforcement is made available after every fixed number of responses (after the Nth response) are called *fixed-ratio schedules* (or FR-N, where N refers to ratio of responses to reinforcements received). Ratio schedules in which the ratio of response to reinforcements received (or N) varies about a mean of N responses per unit of reinforcement received are called variable (VR-N) schedules of reinforcement. A continuous reinforcement schedule (CRF), in which reinforcement is made available after each response, is analogous to an FR-N schedule for which N = 1, i.e., an FR-1 schedule of reinforcement. VR schedules generally support steady responding, while performance on FR schedules is generally characterized by "break and run" patterns in which rate of response increases as the behavior progresses from far from contact with the reinforcement to very near the completion of the ratio. For example, work rate on an FR-50 schedule might be somewhat slow up to completion of twenty or thirty responses and then increase rapidly up to the moment the reinforcement is received. Ultimate receipt of a reinforcer is often followed by the work rate break or a pause. The break in rate of response following a reinforcement is so reliable it is referred to as a *postreinforcement pause*.

Latham and Dossett (1978) compared the effects of CRF and VR schedules on the performance of rodent trappers. An FR-1 (or CRF) schedule in which trappers were paid $1 for each rodent trapped was later changed to a VR-4. Each time a trapper caught a rodent *and* correctly specified the color of one of four marbles before drawing it from a bag, he was paid $4. It was found that the VR-4 resulted in more rodents trapped than did the FR-1 for experienced trappers, but the reverse was found for inexperienced trappers. Saari and Latham (1982) studied the same group of trappers four years later and found that the VR-4 resulted in more rodents trapped than did the FR-1 for all trappers. It should be noted that in these studies, the two schedules were equivalent in terms of their cumulative value. The FR-1 paid $1 with a probability of 1.0; thus the overall expected value on this schedule is $1. The VR-4 paid $4 with a probability of .25; thus the overall expected value on this schedule is also $1. Because the expected value for each schedule was equivalent, the results obtained were not due to the magnitude or amount of reinforcement, but resulted from the scheduling of the reinforcers.

The issue of ratio "stretching effects" is of some interest to organizational researchers (Mawhinney, 1986). Ratio schedules of reinforcement (for example, piece rate pay systems) may be thinned or "stretched" by increasing the ratio requirement for reinforcement over time, so that additional work or response is necessary to maintain the same rate of reinforcement (Ferster and Skinner, 1957). Clearly, schedule stretching in regard to people's wages is abusive because the organization reaps the increased rewards of additional work while the employee must labor harder just to maintain a similar level of income under the stretched (higher value of N on the FR-N or VR-N) schedule. However, ratio stretching may also be employed to facilitate the maintenance and generalization of behavior using social reinforcers such as praise and recognition, as well as by gradually exposing the individual to larger periods of time in which reinforcement is delayed, but ultimately delivered. Stretching of this sort has the advantage of forestalling the known effects of satiation with respect to social reinforcements.

McNally and Abernathy (1989) used titrating or stretching schedules to promote initial adoption and use of ATMs (automatic teller machines) by bank customers. In this study, ATMs were programmed to play a "game" in which the customer was to enter a two-digit number. If the customer "won," a cash payoff of $5 to $100 was made. As individual customers used the ATM more frequently, the probability of "winning" decreased from a .50 probability for the first two uses, to .20 for the next eight uses, to .10 for the next ten uses, to .07 for the next twenty uses and finally to .05 for over forty uses. This titrating schedule arrangement resulted in increased use of ATMs, the goal of the project, as well as sustained use after these contingencies were withdrawn.

Time-Based Schedules

Using time-based schedules, reinforcement is delivered after a fixed period of time elapses (where FT refers to fixed time), or after a variable period of time elapses (where VT refers to variable time) whether or not any response has occurred. Consequences on FT and VT schedules are noncontingent with respect to specific operant responses. Although there is no correlation between rate of responding and reinforcement on FT or VT schedules, laboratory research indicates that these schedules do maintain low rates of response (Zeiler, 1977). While at first glance and VT schedules may not appear readily applicable to organizational settings, they may be useful in analyzing ongoing organizational activities such as pay delivery, performance reviews, inspections, and deadlines. Organizational events that occur regularly over time may evoke or facilitate behavior seemingly related to, but not maintained by these events. Called *adjunctive behaviors* (Falk, 1986; Thompson and Lubinski, 1986), these behaviors are not necessarily maintained by any reinforcing or punishing consequences delivered according to a schedule, but are evoked by the periodicity or pattern of the schedule itself.

Challenges in compensation administration may exemplify some of the differences between behavior maintained on time-based and response-based schedules. In most organizations employees are paid according to "standard" compensation plans in salaries or hourly wages and additional benefits, which may be fairly straightforward to administer, but may not be optimal in terms of motivating actual work performance. Such compensation plans provide money regularly but are largely noncontingent on job performance (Nord, 1969; Wallace and Fay, 1988), which is analogous to an FT or VT schedule. If any contingency is operating in this context, it is one of a compound schedule, in which fulfilling the requirements of one schedule (e.g., regular attendance) gives the employee access to the FT or VT salary schedule (see also, *Organizational Dynamics,* 1973).

George and Hopkins (1989) provide an interesting comparison of the effects of FT (hourly) pay vs. FR (performance-contingent) pay on the performance of waitpersons in three family-style restaurants. In this study, waitpersons' pay was changed from an hourly wage (FT) to an FR-type schedule that provided the individual with 7 percent of individual receipts (a generally accepted industry standard). Policies regarding tips and all other terms of employment remained constant. After instituting the FR schedule, mean pay increased 20 to 30 percent, mean sales increased 18 to 36 percent, mean customers served per hour increased 18 to 26 percent, and labor costs were unchanged. A similar study (Wagner, Rubin, and Callahan, 1988) examined long-term (114 months) effects of FR pay in a unionized iron foundry in which employees were switched from an FT (hourly) wage to an FR wage based on gains over standard production hours. Production showed a positively accelerating increase (resembling a learning curve) over a period of years. The FR wage based on gains system eventually produced performance rates twice those maintained by the FT wages. This provides prima facie evident that the direct correlation between response and reinforcement under this ratio schedule continued to exert long-term effects on performance. At the same time labor costs and grievances declined significantly, suggesting ancillary effects of the FR wage schedule.

Although the vast majority of research in schedules of reinforcement has been directed toward the behavior of individual subjects, similar schedule effects may also be seen at more macro levels. Baum (1974) observed that schedule-based analyses described choice behavior of populations as precisely as it had described choice in individuals. Staw (1991) argues that it should not be surprising that organizational action can be explained by individual-level principles and theories because, ultimately, organizations are collections of individuals. An example of schedule-induced organizational action is provided by Weisberg and Waldrop's (1972) analysis of some work habits of the United States Congress. In this study, cumulative numbers of bills passed were observed to increase slightly each month during the beginning of a legislative session, but increased rapidly as the session drew to a close, evidencing a scallop pattern of acceleration characteristic of FT or FI responding; a phenomenon whose existence in human affairs has been questioned by Hyten and Madden (1993). However, according to Sulzer-Azaroff and Mayer (1991), the schedule operating on the behavior of Congress is more properly characterized as a *limited-hold schedule* in which there is a restriction placed on an interval schedule requiring that, for reinforcement to occur, the response must occur within a particular time limit following the interval. Unless bills prepared during a given congressional session reach the floor prior to the regularly scheduled congressional recesses, reinforcement associated with their passage during the session is lost upon recess. The process recurs when the Congress reconvenes. Despite this terminological difference, the organization of Congress's work behavior around fixed intervals is striking and illustrates not only the powerful and pervasive effects schedules can exert over a period of years, but also the extent to which schedules may be determinants of cyclic or ritualistic behaviors in cultures and organizations (Falk, 1986).

Time and Response-Based Schedules

For combined time and response-based schedules, referred to as *interval* schedules, reinforcement is made available after a period of time elapses, but procurement of the reinforcer depends on occurrence of a response. Interval schedules may be either fixed (FI or fixed interval) or variable (VI or variable interval). The interval in fixed and variable interval schedules is a specified interval of elapsed time, t. Thus, FI and VI are typically designated FI-t and VI-t, where t refers to fixed elapsed time and average elapsed time respectively. Interval schedules maintain steady rates of response, with FI schedules sometimes evoking a positively accelerated "scallop" curve of response rate. Although only a single response is required for reinforcement on interval schedules, once the required time has elapsed, these schedules can engender many more responses than are necessary to obtain reinforcement. Because interval schedules maintain regular and steady rates of response, they have become popular as a means of establishing stable baseline response rates. Stable baseline response rates can serve as tools in basic behavior research for investigating the operation of many other variables and processes. Introducing these other variables in the context of the otherwise steady-state baseline behavior rate can reveal their effects as observed departures from the baseline behavior rates coincident with their introduction.

Alavosius and Sulzer-Azaroff (1990) compared the effectiveness of performance feedback delivered under CRF and FI schedules in the acquisition and maintenance of safely performed health care routines. Subjects were given feedback on either CRF or weekly FI schedules regarding the proportion of each patient health care routine performed safely. Both schedules led to better levels of performance than did written instructions. Although the performance reinforced under the CRF schedule reached mastery level in fewer work days than did the performance reinforced under the FI schedule, an equivalent number of feedback messages were needed to achieve mastery under each schedule.

The VI schedule is especially useful for studying the dynamics of behavior in probabilistic or equivocal environments. A properly programmed VI schedule (see Fleshler and Hoffman, 1962; Hantula, 1991) holds the probability of reinforcement constant over any given time horizon while keeping the occurrence of reinforcement at one time uncorrelated with the occurrence of reinforcement at any other time. Thus, a VI schedule allows a researcher to examine the effects of overall probability or density of reinforcement in a given situation or context, without the confounding of correlations between reinforcer deliveries.

For example, Hantula and Crowell (1994b) used multiple VI-VI schedules to study the effects of an alternative investment opportunity on financial decision making under conditions of equivocality and failure. Returns on investments were first provided on equal value multiple VI-VI schedules, and later one of the investments ceased to yield returns, while the other remained unchanged (a multiple VI-EXT schedule). (Recall that extinction [EXT] is termination or cessation of a previously operating schedule of reinforcement.) Previous research indicated that investment allocations escalated on an EXT schedule when EXT was preceded by experience with an intermittent schedule (Goltz 1992, 1993; Hantula and Crowell, 1994a). However, these studies did not include an alternative investment. McCain (1986) showed that presence of an alternative investment can attenuate escalation in a failing course of action (EXT context for one alternative) but did not document how funds might be reallocated to the alternative (if at all). In Hantula and Crowell (1994b), investing in the unchanged schedule alternative (i.e., the one that continued to deliver rewards) increased 1.5 times the original level while investing in the failing (changed to EXT schedule) alternative nearly ceased. This finding is consistent with basic research in behavioral contrast (Reynolds, 1961). But this finding was entirely unexpected and would not have been predicted based on the existing literature regarding decision-making behavior.

SCHEDULES OF REINFORCEMENT: THE RESEARCH

Table 5.1 summarizes past schedule research from 1971 to 1994 in organizations or under simulated organizational conditions. Included in this table are all empirical schedule-based experiments performed in actual organizations, schedule-based analyses of behavior in organizations, and laboratory studies that employed a schedule-based analysis of performance in a simulated organizational setting, or which addressed directly theoretical concerns in organizational research. In general, it may be concluded from these studies that (1) reinforcement schedules are an effective means for managing work performance; (2) reinforcement schedule effects on work performance in the field are generally similar to those found in organizational laboratory simulation research; (3) differences in schedule parameters have mixed effects, although the presence or absence of a schedule of contingent reinforcement accounts for the largest effects; (4) there is a good deal of promise in further application and investigation of reinforcement schedules in organizations and in simulated organizational settings; and (5) this promise of schedule research for organizational studies has gone largely unfulfilled.

TABLE 5.1. Summary of Schedule-Based Field, Simulation, and Analog Studies

Authors and Year	Outcome or Performance	Subjects and Method	Results	Level of Inquiry
		FIELD STUDIES		
Weisberg and Waldrop (1972)	Passing bills	Members of U.S. Congress; cumulative number of bills passed in each legislative session over fourteen-year period examined.	Negatively accelerating work habits (scallop curve) resembling FT performance.	Analysis
Ayllon and Carlson (1973)	Absenteeism	Employees of distributing company; FR schedule, gave tickets for weekly cash lottery to employees not tardy or absent for the entire week.	On-time attendance increased to over 80 percent; employee survey indicated employees liked lottery and attributed positive attitudinal changes in work environment to it.	Application
Everett, Hayward, and Meyers (1974)	Bus riding	Campus bus patrons; tokens given to bus riders under CRF and VR3 schedules.	27 percent increase in riders under CRF and 30 percent increase under VR3 over baseline.	Application
Pedalino and Gamboa (1974)	Absenteeism	Unionized manufacturing and distribution employees; FR schedule, weekly, then biweekly poker games.	18 percent decrease in absenteeism under baseline, no difference in weekly or biweekly games.	Application
Pierce and Risley (1974)	Task completion	Adolescent, minority recreation aides; hourly vs. CRF wages based on percentage of tasks completed.	Percentage tasks completed doubled under CRF wages; providing written job descriptions and termination threats ineffective under hourly wage.	Application
Yukl and Latham (1975)	Tree planting	Tree planters—"marginal workers" paid under hourly wage plus CRF or VR incentives. Reported schedule parameters innacurate.	Higher rate of planting under CRF and VR2 than no incentive; rate under CRF higher than VR2 (actually VR2000) and VR4 (actually VR4000).	Application

TABLE 5.1 *(continued)*

Yukl, Latham, and Pursell (1976)	Tree planting	Tree planters seasonal workers paid under hourly wage plus CRF or VR incentives. Reported schedule parameters inaccurate.	Higher rate of planting under CRF and VR2 than no incentive; rate under CRF higher than VR2 (actually VR2000) and VR4 (actually VR4000). Employees preferred CRF.	Application
Pritchard et al. (1976)	Performance on programmed training in basic electronics	Males in late teens; pay for tests passed on hourly, FR3, VR3, or VR3-variable amount schedules.	FR and VR schedules resulted in higher performance and earnings than hourly pay, subjects more satisfied with FR and VR pay than hourly with highest levels under FR.	Application
Latham and Dossett (1978)	Rodent trapping	Unionized beaver trappers; CRF vs. VR4 schedule.	Trapping rate higher under CRF than VR4 for inexperienced trappers, reverse for experienced trappers. Employees preferred VR4.	Application
Dickerson (1979)	Placing bets	Gamblers in U.K. betting offices, FI schedules.	Betting rate increases as a function of time to race; "scallop" curve for high-frequency gamblers, linear curve for low-frequency gamblers.	Analysis
Pritchard, Hollenbeck, and DeLeo (1980)	Performance on programmed training in basic electronics	Males and females in late teens; pay for tests passed on hourly, CRF, or VR-variable amount schedules.	Higher performace under CRF or VR than hourly, more effort exerted under CRF.	Application
Saari and Latham (1982)	Rodent trapping	Unionized mountain beaver trappers; CRF vs. VR4 schedules; replication of Latham and Dossett (1978).	CRF increased number of rodents trapped 50 percent over baseline, VR4 increased 108 percent over baseline, VR4 schedules perceived as including many motivating job enrichment variables.	Application

Gaetani, Hoxeng, and Austin (1985)	Machining metal parts	Machinists; hourly wage compared to CRF wage (standard wage plus 5 percent of dollar value exceeding standard).	CRF increased productivity 174 to 210 percent over hourly wage.	Application
Evans, Kienast, and Mitchell (1988)	Auto repair	Automobile service mechanics; hourly pay baseline compared with hourly pay plus 1 of 2 lotteries: (1) VR10 lottery for state lottery tickets plus weekly drawings for cash, (2) CRF lottery for state lottery tickets, both lotteries paid off in variable amounts.	Both lotteries increased output > 100 percent over baseline; lottery 2 more cost effective than lottery 1; employee acceptance of lotteries did not appear to be related to performance.	Application
Wagner, Rubin, and Callahan (1988)	Manufacturing iron castings	Unionized foundry employees; compared hourly (FT) wage to CRF based on standard production hours, divided among work groups according to the worth of individual jobs.	Production increased in positively accelerated curve over a period of years, mean increase 103.7 percent over FT wage. Labor costs decreased 33 percent, grievance rate decreased 64 percent 3 years into the CRF pay condition.	Application
George and Hopkins (1989)	Food sales	Waitpersons; compared hourly pay baseline to CRF pay (7 percent of sales), policies regarding tips unchanged.	Under CRF pay per hour increased; sales increased 37 to 61 percent over previous year, customers served/hour increased 18 to 26 percent over baseline; labor costs unchanged.	Application
McNally and Abernathy (1989)	Automatic teller machine (ATM) use	Bank customers; no incentive baseline, individually titrating cash payoff VR schedules for ATM use.	Number of cards used, number of uses per card and ATM transactions as percentage of teller transactions doubled during VR; no reversal when VR removed.	Application

TABLE 5.1 *(continued)*

Alavosius and Sulzer-Azaroff (1990)	Patient care	Direct-care medical service employees; concurrent CRF and FI feedback delivery.	Either CRF or FI more effective than written instructions in learning care routines; more rapid acquisition under CRF, maintenance equal under CRF or FI.	Application

SIMULATION AND ANALOG STUDIES

Cherrington, Reitz, and Scott (1971)	Clerical work	Junior business students; hourly pay plus contingent (FI) or noncontingent (FT) pay; "appropriate" (rewards for high performance and none for low performance) and "inappropriate" (reverse).	Output increase for all rewarded subjects, higher for "approximately" rewarded; positive correlations between satisfaction and performance for "appropriately" rewarded subjects.	Application
Yukl, Wexley, and Seymour (1972)	Clerical work	Female student employees; cash payment and schedules: baseline hourly pay, incentive .5 VR2, .25 VR2, or .25 CRF, plus hourly.	Higher output under any incentive schedule than baseline; .5 VR2 > .25 VR2 or CRF, no loss in quality when quantity increased.	Application
Berger, Cummings, and Heneman (1975)	Clerical work	Female student employees; cash payment and schedules: baseline hourly pay, .5 VR2, .25 VR2, or .25 CRF, plus hourly pay.	Higher output under any schedule (CRF or VR) than baseline; .5 VR2 > .25 VR2 or CRF.	Application
Farr (1976)	Clerical work	College students; compared hourly pay, individual and/or group (n = 3) CRF pay.	Output lowest with hourly pay; highest output with combined group and individual CRF pay; hourly subjects set goals below what was achieved by subjects on CRF pay.	Application
Mawhinney, Dickinson, and Taylor (1989)	Playing computer games or trigger pull task as indicator of "intrinsic motivation"	College students: VI schedule for trigger pulls throughout, no pay baseline for computer games, CRF pay for number	CRF pay increased number of preferred games played (quantity) and number of points earned per game (quality) for skill	Analysis

		of preferred games played for one session, reversal to no pay.	and chance-based games, decreased duration of chance-based games, and decreased number of other games played; baseline levels of game playing and points earned recovered when pay withdrawn, no "undermining" of "intrinsic motivation."	
Stoneman and Dickinson (1989)	Assembly	College students; base pay plus CRF individual or group (n = 2, 4, 5, or 9) incentive.	No difference in output between individual or group pay; greater variability in output as a function of group size.	Application
Frisch and Dickinson (1990)	Assembly	Freshman and sophomore college students; base pay or base pay plus incentives (10, 30, 60, or 100 percent) of base pay; total compensation held roughly equal for all subjects.	Earned incentive pay half of available; greater output under all incentive pay conditions than base pay alone, no difference between incentive pay conditions.	Application
Hantula (1990)	Investment decisions	Senior business and engineering students; investing in stock under mult VI-VI and VI-EXT schedules.	Equivalent investing under VI-VI, contrast effects (escalation in VI, decrease in EXT) under VI-EXT, effects reversed with schedule changes.	Synthesis
Rao and Mawhinney (1991)	Leadership	Male college students in "superior" and "subordinate" dyads; FT and reciprocal FR schedules for superior and subordinate.	Low rates of leader and subordinate response under FT, high rates under reciprocal FR.	Synthesis
Goltz (1992)	Investment decisions	College students' acquisition of stock investing on CRF, FR2, and VR2 schedules; schedule	Acquistion typical of schedule in effect, persistence, and escalation of investing during extinction	Synthesis

TABLE 5.1 *(continued)*

		effects examined in extinction.	for VR subjects; 2nd experiment showed subjects with no experience with task behaved as if under VR schedule.	
Oah and Dickinson (1992)	Check proofing	Freshman and sophomore college students; pay under either exponential or linear CRF schedule.	More money earned under exponential schedule, no difference in output between either schedule.	Application
Skaggs, Dickinson, and O'Connor (1992)	Playing video games as indicator of "intrinsic motivation"	College students; no pay baseline, CRF pay for number of preferred games played for 5 sessions, reversal to no pay; replication of Mawhinney, Dickinson and Taylor (1989).	CRF pay increased number of preferred games played (quantity), decreased number of points earned per game (quality) and decreased number of other games played; baseline levels of game playing and points earned recovered when pay withdrawn, no "undermining" of "intrinsic motivation."	Analysis
Goltz (1993)	Allocation of organizational resources	Freshman and sophomore business students; replication and extension of Goltz (1992); acquisition of resource allocation on CRF, FR2, and VR2 schedules; schedule effects examined in extinction.	Acquisition typical of schedule in effect, persistence, escalation of allocations during extinction for VR subjects, CRF and FR subjects did not persist or escalate allocations; schedule effects accounted for most of the variance, "responsibility" effects accounted for none.	Synthesis
Hantula and Crowell (1994a)	Investment decisions	Freshmen and sophomore college students; replication and extension of Goltz (1992); acquisition of resource allocation	Acquistion typical of schedule in effect, persistence, and escalation of investments during extinction for VR subjects	Synthesis

		on CRF and VR2 schedules; schedule effects examined in extinction.	only, 2-step escalation/de-escalation function found.	
Hantula and Crowell (1994b)	Investment decisions	Senior business and engineering students; stock investing on equal VI-VI schedules, then VI-EXT.	Equal investing under VI-VI; behavioral contrast effects evident, investing in EXT declined precipitiously, investing in VI stock escalated.	Synthesis

After experiencing a fallow period, research in organizational applications of schedules of reinforcement was the focus of renewed attention in the 1990s that promises to continue with vigor into the new millenium. The reasons for this resurgence are unclear. Latham and Huber (1992) attribute the revitalization of the research to an increased interest in performance-based compensation systems, which are de facto schedules of reinforcement; possibly this renewed interest is a reflection of an increased activity in schedule research and application in applied behavior analysis as a whole (e.g., Mace et al., 1994; Neef et al., 1992; Pierce and Epling, 1995), or perhaps interest in schedules may be schedule dependent, and is what Zeiler (1984) has alluded to as a sleeping giant that is waking again. Nevertheless, the rejuvenation of schedule-based application and research in organizational behavior management bodes well because it strengthens the ties between the basic science (the experimental analysis of behavior) and one of its applied branches. This trend should stimulate both theoretical progress and the development of more effective technologies (Mace, 1994).

APPLICATION, ANALYSIS, AND SYNTHESIS

Application studies are those in which schedule-based interventions have been designed to change organizationally important performance. This work is often experimental or preexperimental in nature. For example, Pedalino and Gamboa (1974) used a lottery system on an FR schedule to decrease absenteeism as did Evans, Kienast, and Mitchell (1988) on CRF and VR schedules to increase mechanics' productivity; and Gaetani, Hoxeng, and Austin (1985) employed a CRF (piece rate) pay system to increase productivity in a metal machine shop.

Application studies make up 72 percent of extant schedule research. That the majority of the research is application studies should be expected because the bulk of studies in the organizational behavior management tradition have been focused on application research, often with line-level or shop floor employees (Hantula, 1992; O'Hara, Johnson, and Beehr, 1985). Similarly, 70 percent of the application studies reviewed were conducted in field settings, and 30 percent in laboratory simulations or analog settings. Application studies have appeared regularly throughout the twenty-year period reviewed.

Analysis studies are those in which ongoing organizational activities, group and individual performances, and environmental events are examined for temporal regularities to determine the types of schedules that are controlling the performance of interest, such as the effects of regularly occurring deadlines on work rate. These studies are often correlational, but may also involve experimental research. For example, Weisberg and Waldrop (1972) and Dickerson (1979) observed and recorded the behavior of the U.S. Congress and British horse racing bettors respectively and determined that in both cases the subjects' behavior exhibited the temporal regularities expected on FT or FI schedules of reinforcement. In an example of an experimental laboratory study, Mawhinney, Dickinson, and Taylor (1989) arranged CRF and VI schedules for video game playing and trigger pulling to examine the alleged "undermining of intrinsic motivation" by "extrinsic" reinforcers and found typical schedule performance, but no "undermining of intrinsic motivation."

Analysis studies make up 12 percent of the research reviewed and were equally divided between field and laboratory settings. Half of the analysis studies appeared after 1989. Although not included in Table 5.1 as empirical studies, three important conceptual papers appeared that broached a schedule-based analysis of ongoing organizational activities. Two (Gowen, 1990; Mawhinney and Gowen, 1990) explored a schedule analysis of gain-sharing programs in organizations, a theme reiterated by Latham and Huber's (1992) review of schedule research, which interpreted schedule research in terms of compensation and incentive management. Redmon and Lockwood (1986) outlined a qualitative approach to analyzing both intra- and extra-organizational activities based on the matching law (Herrnstein, 1970; Baum, 1973).

Synthesis studies are those in which schedules are manipulated to model or build performances that are hypothesized to be controlled by those particular schedules in organizations so that the performances may be studied in the laboratory. This research is experimental and often highly theoretical. Examples of such research include Rao and Mawhinney's (1991) study of leadership as dyadic exchange, which found that interdependent FR-like exchanges of reinforcers in addition to FT pay increases both supervisor and subordinate performance, and noncontingent (FT) pay fails to support any appreciable level of supervisor/subordinate interaction and performance. Another line of research has investigated how investors will escalate resources expended in failing courses of action (i.e., "throwing good money after bad"). This phenomenon is the result of an interaction between an intermittent (VR) reinforcement history (Goltz, 1992, 1993; Hantula and Crowell, 1994a) and the onset of extinction (EXT). It can also be the result of behavioral contrast effects that occur when investment returns previously programmed as VI-VI schedules change to a VI-EXT arrangement (Hantula, 1990; Hantula and Crowell, 1994b).

Synthesis studies make up the remaining 16 percent of the research and are 100 percent laboratory based. All of the synthesis studies reviewed have appeared recently (since 1989), perhaps reflecting a growth and maturation of the OBM field as a whole as researchers address more complex and theoretical issues, while at the same time not abandoning the effective applications that are its stock-in-trade. Both application and synthesis studies share in common a truth criterion of pragmatism. In application studies, the focus is on superimposing a particular schedule or arrangement of schedules onto the present environment to achieve organizationally important outcomes. Issues of generalizability in application studies concern whether or not a particular schedule arrangement will have the same effects for a different performance or in a different organizational context.

Although synthesis also involves superimposing a schedule or arrangement of schedules onto a present environment, there are subtle but important differences between the two levels of inquiry. Unlike application studies, synthesis studies are concerned with constructing schedule arrangements that closely model or produce behavior found in organizations by first creating "reinforcement" histories for subjects, and then studying the effects of schedules or other variables while controlling for confounding variables that cannot be controlled in field settings. Issues of generality are concerned with whether a particular schedule arrangement effectively produces the behavior under examination, and then whether these effects can transfer into the organizational environment.

THEORETICAL ISSUES AND FUTURE DIRECTIONS

Schedules of reinforcement provide a theoretically rich basis from which behavior in organizations may be managed and analyzed. More successful applications to meet ongoing organizational challenges may be designed and built with deftly scheduled consequences. However, the real promise of schedule research in organizational performance lies in the more theoretical realm. Because any behavior or event of any real import in organizations occurs over time, schedule effects are paramount in making sense of activities in some context. Indeed, hypothetically constructed mechanisms can often become trivial when schedule and temporal matters are considered (Hantula, 1992).

Two recent examples are the research in "undermining intrinsic motivation" and escalation of commitment. Both of these phenomena were said to be contrary to a behavioral analysis of complex organizational behavior, and further, although both were said to influence behavior over time, they were hypothesized to result from hypothetical mechanisms measured at one point in time. In the case of "undermining intrinsic motivation," previous research employing one-shot measurement strategies found evidence that "extrinsic" rewards dilute one's "intrinsic motivation" to perform an activity (Deci and Ryan, 1985). Research using schedules of reinforcement showed that undermining effects, if they occur at all, are fleeting and unlikely if rewards are presented repetitively, rather than once (Mawhinney, Dickinson, and Taylor, 1989; Skaggs, Dickinson, and O'Connor, 1992). Similarly, escalating commitment to a failing course of action is purported to result from either self-justification/ego-defense mechanisms (Brockner, 1992), or cognitive framing effects (Whyte, 1993). Schedule research, on the other hand, indicates that escalation is yet another manifestation of the behavioral phenomenon called "extinction burst." The extinction burst is often observed when contingencies change from an intermittent reinforcement schedule to an extinction condition (Goltz, 1992; Hantula and Crowell, 1994a). Schedule research also suggests that if self-justification processes are operating within an experimental context, they do not operate past the first decision in a series of decisions (Goltz, 1993). Thus, in both of these examples, an imputed hypothetical causal mechanism may actually be an artifact of ill-considered temporal factors. That the operation of these hypothetical causal mechanisms may be artifacts is not evident unless and until a more contextually rich schedule-based analysis is brought to bear on the behavior in question.

In sum, schedules of reinforcement provide a ready source of method and theory to examine contextual determinants of behavior, and to design more effective interventions. This review has only scratched the surface of the promise and possibilities of schedules of reinforcement and their use in application, analysis, and synthesis of organizational performance. In the case of application, schedules are readily applicable to designing performance-based and incentive pay systems, which are becoming the focus of increasing concern (Wilson, 1995). However, beyond the readily apparent use of schedules in designing incentive systems, schedules may be applied creatively to many organizational challenges from managing consumer behavior to employee drug use.

In terms of managing consumer behavior, while Foxall (1990) broaches the subject of schedules in marketing, and McNally and Abernathy (1989) provide a compelling example of their use, the utility of schedules in this domain remains to be discovered. For example, sophisticated computerized point-of-sale technologies can be used to reinforce purchases with coupons or other discounts delivered according to appropriate schedules. Further, with the growth of "cybershopping" via the Internet and online services (Cronin, 1994), issues such as delay and probability of reinforcement, whether product delivery or system response, come to the forefront. These basic issues, which are essentially schedule properties, may well provide the impetus for further activity in schedule research in this context. Interestingly, just like the reawakened interest in schedules, interest in behavioral applications in marketing is on the rise (Foxall, 1992, 1994). Whether or not these events are causal is open to question, although their mutual resurgence is certainly cause for optimism.

Concerning the issue of employee drug use, schedules may provide an alternative to current drug testing practices, which are extremely controversial (Crant and Bateman, 1990). Presently, drug tests involve analyses of bodily fluids for metabolites correlated with specific drugs; however, such tests are viewed as invasive, and cannot determine whether an individual is impaired by drug use. In addition, the problem of false positives, even if extremely improbable, presents a serious ethical dilemma. Schedules have been widely utilized as baselines for studying drug effects (Dews, 1963). Schulz (1991) describes a computer game that is used to identify fatigued truck drivers; perhaps similar schedule-based games could be used to determine whether an employee may be under the influence of drugs. Because schedule performances are stable over time, significant deviations from an individual's "behavioral fingerprint" that resemble changes in schedule performance correlated with use of certain drugs could signal the need for a "for cause" drug test. Such a behavioral test would be both less invasive and objectionable than current drug tests, and it would also lower the probability of false positives dramatically because only individuals who show evidence of behavioral impairment would be tested. Perhaps a new specialty of organizational behavioral pharmacology may emerge from these types of applications.

In terms of analysis and synthesis, schedules may further bridge gaps between the fields of OBM and finance. Ferguson (1989) has presented a behavioral analysis of stock market crashes based on stimulus generalization and escape behavior that complements recent schedule research concerning determinants of continued investment under conditions of no return (Goltz, 1992; Hantula, 1990; Hantula and Crowell, 1994a, b; O'Flaherty and Komaki, 1992). Currently, the stock market is conceptualized as a white noise or random walk model in which today's stock price does not allow prediction of tomorrow's stock price (Malkiel, 1973). Interestingly, a properly programmed VI schedule provides a similar state of affairs in which the probability of each reinforcement delivery is uncorrelated with other deliveries (Fleshler and Hoffman, 1962; Hantula, 1991). Previous research has employed VI schedules to synthesize investment behaviors (Hantula, 1990; Hantula and Crowell, 1994b) and perhaps further schedule-based analyses of stock performance and investor behavior may lead to intriguing interdisciplinary investigations.

Advances in schedule research that have not been presented in detail, such as probability differential or "response deprivation" models (Podsakoff, 1982), and the matching law (Herrnstein, 1970), also hold a good deal of promise for future research and application. The latter provides a readily applicable quantitative tool for analyzing and managing behavior (Pierce and Epling, 1983, 1995; Redmon and Lockwood, 1986) and a solid link to economics (Hursh, 1980, 1984; Kagel, Battalio, and Green, 1995). Extensions of schedule research to other "organizational" disciplines including cultural analysis (Falk, 1986; Harris, 1980) and training (Pritchard et al., 1976) are promising, as are explorations of job satisfaction (Cherrington, Reitz, and Scott, 1971; Latham and Dossett, 1978; Mawhinney, 1989), and rational choice theory (Herrnstein, 1990a, b) await further research and application. The question to be addressed is not *whether* schedules are operating in a given context, but *which* schedules are operating. Indeed, Dews (1963) has suggested that just as osmosis is ubiquitous in its operation in physiology, schedules operate similarly in regard to behavior—wherever and whenever they can, they will.

REFERENCES

Alavosius, M. P. and Sulzer-Azaroff, B. (1990). Acquisition and maintenance of health care routines as a function of feedback density. *Journal of Applied Behavior Analysis, 23,* 151-162.

Aldis, O. (1961). Of pigeons and men. *Harvard Business Review,* July-August, 59-63.

Ayllon, T. R. and Carlson, R. (1973). Instilling responsibility through incentives. *World Trade Journal, 1,* 41-42.

Ayllon, T. and Kolko, D. J. (1982). Productivity and schedules of reinforcement in business and industry. In R. M. O'Brien, A. M. Dickinson, and M. P. Rosow (Eds.), *Industrial behavior modification: A management handbook* (pp. 35-50). New York: Pergamon Press.

Balcazar, F. E., Shupert, M. K., Daniels, A. C., Mawhinney, T. C., and Hopkins, B. L. (1989). An objective review and analysis of ten years of publication in the *Journal of Organizational Behavior Management. Journal of Organizational Behavior Management, 10*(1), 7-37.

Baum, W. M. (1973). The correlation based law of effect. *Journal of the Experimental Analysis of Behavior, 20,* 137-153.

Baum, W. M. (1974). Choice in free ranging pigeons. *Science, 185,* 78-79.

Berger, C. J., Cummings, L. L., and Heneman, H. G. (1975). Expectancy theory and operant conditioning predictions of performance under variable ratio and continuous schedules of reinforcement. *Organizational Behavior and Human Performance, 14,* 227-243.

Brockner, J. (1992). Escalation of commitment to a failing course of action: Toward theoretical progress. *Academy of Management Review, 17,* 39-61.

Catania, A. C. (1992). *Learning* (Third edition). Englewood Cliffs, NJ: Prentice-Hall.

Cherrington, D., Reitz, H., and Scott, W. (1971). Effects of contingent and non-contingent reward on the relationship between satisfaction and task performance. *Journal of Applied Psychology, 55,* 531-536.

Crant, J. M. and Bateman, T. S. (1990). An experimental test of the impact of drug testing programs on potential job applicants' attitudes and intentions. *Journal of Applied Psychology, 75,* 127-131.

Cronin, M. J. (1994). *Doing business on the Internet: How the electronic highway is transforming America's companies.* New York: Van Nostrand Reinhold.

Davison, M. and McCarthy, D. (1988). *The matching law: A research review.* NJ: Lawrence Erlbaum Associates.

Deci, E. L. and Ryan, R. M. (1985). *Intrinsic motivation and self-determination in human behavior.* New York: Plenum Press.

Dews, P. B. (1963). Behavioral effects of drugs. In S. M. Farber and H. L. Wilson (Eds.), *Conflict and creativity* (pp. 138-153). NY: McGraw-Hill.

Dickerson, M. G. (1979). FI schedules and persistence at gambling at the U.K. betting office. *Journal of Applied Behavior Analysis, 12,* 315-323.

Evans, K. M., Kienast, P., and Mitchell, T. R. (1988). The effects of lottery incentive programs on performance. *Journal of Organizational Behavior Management, 9*(2), 113-135.

Everett, P. B., Hayward, S. C., and Meyers, A. W. (1974). Effects of a token reinforcement procedure on bus ridership. *Journal of Applied Behavior Analysis, 7,* 1-9.

Falk, J. L. (1986). The formation and function of ritual behavior. In T. Thompson and M. D. Zeiler (Eds.), *Analysis and integration of behavioral units* (pp. 335-355). Hillsdale, NJ: Lawrence Erlbaum Associates.

Farr, J. (1976). Incentive schedules, productivity, and satisfaction in work groups: A laboratory study. *Organizational Behavior and Human Performance, 17,* 159-170.

Ferguson, R. (1989). On crashes. *Financial Analysts Journal,* March-April, 42-52.

Ferster, C. B. and Skinner, B. F. (1957). *Schedules of reinforcement.* New York: Appleton-Century-Crofts.

Fleshler, M. and Hoffman, H. S. (1962). A progression for generating variable-interval schedules. *Journal of the Experimental Analysis of Behavior, 5,* 529-530.

Foxall, G. S. (1990). *Consumer psychology in behavioural perspective.* London: Routledge.

Foxall, G. S. (1992). The consumer situation: An integrative model for research in marketing. *Journal of Marketing Management, 8,* 383-404.

Foxall, G. S. (1994). Behavior analysis and consumer psychology. *Journal of Economic Psychology, 15,* 5-91.

Frisch, C. J. and Dickinson, A. M. (1990). Work productivity as a function of monetary incentives to base pay. *Journal of Organizational Behavior Management, 11*(1), 13-33.

Gaetani, J. J., Hoxeng, D. D., and Austin, J. T. (1985). Engineering compensation systems: Effects of commissioned versus wage payment. *Journal of Organizational Behavior Management, 7*(1/2), 51-63.

George, J. T. and Hopkins, B. L. (1989). Multiple effects of performance-contingent pay for waitpersons. *Journal of Applied Behavior Analysis, 22,* 131-141.

Gersick, C. J. G. (1988). Time and transitions in work teams: Toward a new model of group development. *Academy of Management Journal, 31,* 9-41.

Gersick, C. J. G. (1989). Marking time: Predictable transitions in task groups. *Academy of Management Journal, 32,* 274-309.

Gersick, C. J. G. (1994). Pacing strategic change: The case of a new venture. *Academy of Management Journal, 37,* 9-45.

Goltz, S. M. (1992). A sequential learning analysis of decisions in organizations to escalate investments despite continuing costs or losses. *Journal of Applied Behavior Analysis, 25,* 561-574.

Goltz, S. M. (1993). Examining the joint role of responsibility and reinforcement history in commitment. *Decision Sciences, 24,* 977-994.

Gowen, C. R. (1990). Gainsharing programs: An overview of history and research. *Journal of Organizational Behavior Management, 11*(2), 77-99.

Hantula, D. A. (1990). The effects of an alternative course of action in sustaining and reversing escalation and persistence. Paper presented at the Meetings of the Academy of Management, August, San Francisco, CA.

Hantula, D. A. (1991). A BASIC program to generate values for variable-interval schedules of reinforcement. *Journal of Applied Behavior Analysis, 24,* 799-801.

Hantula, D. A. (1992). The basic importance of escalation. *Journal of Applied Behavior Analysis, 25,* 579-583.

Hantula, D. A. and Crowell, C. R. (1994a). Intermittent reinforcement and escalation processes in sequential decision making: A replication and theoretical analysis. *Journal of Organizational Behavior Management, 14*(2), 7-36.

Hantula, D. A. and Crowell, C. R. (1994b). Behavioral contrast in a two-option analogue task of financial decision making. *Journal of Applied Behavior Analysis, 27,* 607-617.

Harris, M. (1980). *Cultural materialism: The struggle for a science of culture.* New York: Random House.

Herrnstein, R. J. (1970). On the law of effect. *Journal of the Experimental Analysis of Behavior, 13,* 243-266.

Herrnstein, R. J. (1990a). Behavior, reinforcement, and utility. *Psychological Science, 1,* 217-223.

Herrnstein, R. J. (1990b). Rational choice theory: Necessary but not sufficient. *American Psychologist, 46,* 356-376.

Honig, W. K. and Staddon, J. E. R. (Eds.). (1977). *Handbook of operant behavior.* Englewood Cliffs, NJ: Prentice-Hall.

Hursh, S. R. (1980). Economic concepts for the analysis of behavior. *Journal of the Experimental Analysis of Behavior, 34,* 219-238.

Hursh, S. R. (1984). Behavioral economics. *Journal of the Experimental Analysis of Behavior, 42,* 435-452.

Hyten, C. and Madden, G. J. (1993). The scallop in human fixed-interval research: A review of problems with data description. *Psychological Record, 43,* 471-500.

Jablonsky, S. F. and DeVries, D. L. (1972). Operant conditioning principles extrapolated to the theory of management. *Organizational Behavior and Human Performance, 7,* 340-358.

Kagel, J. H., Battalio, R. C., and Green, L. (1995). *Economic choice theory: An experimental analysis of animal behavior.* New York: Cambridge University Press.

Latham, G. P. and Dossett, D. L. (1978). Designing incentive plans for unionized employees: A comparison of continuous and variable ratio schedules. *Personnel Psychology, 31,* 47-61.

Latham, G. P. and Huber, V. L. (1992). Schedules of reinforcement: Lessons from the past and issues for the future. *Journal of Organizational Behavior Management, 12*(1), 125-149.

Mace, F. C. (1994). Basic research needed for stimulating the development of behavioral technologies. *Journal of the Experimental Analysis of Behavior, 61,* 529-550.

Mace, F. C., Neef, N. A., Shade, D., and Mauro, B. C. (1994). Limited matching on concurrent-schedule reinforcement of academic behavior. *Journal of Applied Behavior Analysis, 27,* 585-596.

Malkiel, B. G. (1973). *A random walk down Wall Street.* New York: Norton.

Mawhinney, T. C. (1986). Reinforcement schedule stretching effects. In E. A. Locke (Ed.), *Generalizing from laboratory to field settings* (pp. 181-186). Lexington, MA: Lexington Books.

Mawhinney, T. C. (1989). Job satisfaction as a management tool and responsibility. *Journal of Organizational Behavior Management, 10*(1), 187-192.

Mawhinney, T. C., Dickinson, A. M., and Taylor, L. A., III. (1989). The use of concurrent schedules to evaluate the effects of extrinsic rewards on "intrinsic motivation." *Journal of Organizational Behavior Management, 10*(1), 109-129.

Mawhinney, T. C. and Gowen, C. R. (1990). Gainsharing and the Law of Effect as the matching law: A theoretical framework. *Journal of Organizational Behavior Management, 11*(2), 61-75.

McCain, B. E. (1986). Continuing investment under conditions of failure: A laboratory study on the limits to escalation. *Journal of Applied Psychology, 71,* 280-284.

McNally, K. A. and Abernathy, W. B. (1989). Effects of monetary incentives on customer behavior: Use of automatic teller machines (ATMs) by low frequency users. *Journal of Organizational Behavior Management, 10*(1), 79-91.

Morse, W. H. and Kelleher, R. T. (1977). Determinants of reinforcement and punishment. In W. K. Honig and J. E. R. Staddon (Eds.), *Handbook of operant behavior* (pp. 174-200). Englewood Cliffs, NJ: Prentice-Hall.

Neef, N. A., Mace, F. C., Shea, M. C., and Shade, D. (1992). Effects of reinforcer rate and reinforcer quality on time allocation: Extensions of matching theory to educational settings. *Journal of Applied Behavior Analysis, 25,* 691-699.

Nord, W. R. (1969). Beyond the teaching machine: The neglected area of operant conditioning in the theory and practice of management. *Organizational Behavior and Human Performance, 4,* 375-401.

Oah, S. and Dickinson, A. M. (1992). A comparison of the effects of a linear and exponential performance pay function on work productivity. *Journal of Organizational Behavior Management, 12*(1), 85-115.

O'Flaherty, B. and Komaki, J. L. (1992). Going beyond with Bayesian updating. *Journal of Applied Behavior Analysis, 25,* 585-598.

O'Hara, K., Johnson, C. M., and Beehr, T. A. (1985). Organizational behavior management in the private sector: A review of empirical research and recommendations for future investigation. *Academy of Management Review, 10,* 848-864.

Organizational Dynamics. (1973). Conversation with B. F. Skinner. *Organizational Dynamics,* Winter, 31-40.

Pedalino, E. and Gamboa, V. (1974). Behavior modification and absenteeism: Intervention in one industrial setting. *Journal of Applied Psychology, 59,* 694-698.

Pierce, C. and Risley, T. (1974). Improving job performance of neighborhood youth corps aides in an urban recreation program. *Journal of Applied Behavior Analysis, 7,* 207-215.

Pierce, W. D. and Epling, W. F. (1983). Choice, matching, and human behavior: A review of the literature. *The Behavior Analyst, 6,* 57-76.

Pierce, W. D. and Epling, W. F. (1995). The applied importance of research on the matching law. *Journal of Applied Behavior Analysis, 28,* 237-241.

Podsakoff, P. M. (1982). Effects of schedule changes on human performance: An empirical test of the contrasting predictions of the law of effect, the probability-differential model, and the response-deprivation approach. *Organizational Behavior and Human Performance, 29,* 322-351.

Pritchard, R. D., Hollenbeck, J., and DeLeo, P. J. (1980). The effects of partial and continuous schedules of reinforcement on effort, performance and satisfaction. *Organizational Behavior and Human Performance, 25,* 336-353.

Pritchard, R. D., Leonard, D. W., Von Bergen, C. W., and Kirk, R. J. (1976). The effects of varying schedules of reinforcement on human task performance. *Organizational Behavior and Human Performance, 16*, 205-230.

Rao, R. K. and Mawhinney, T. C. (1991). Superior-subordinate dyads: Dependence of leader effectiveness on mutual reinforcement contingencies. *Journal of the Experimental Analysis of Behavior, 56*, 105-118.

Redmon, W. K. and Lockwood, K. (1986). The matching law and organizational behavior. *Journal of Organizational Behavior Management, 8*(1), 57-72.

Reynolds, G. S. (1961). Behavioral contrast. *Journal of the Experimental Analysis of Behavior, 4*, 57-71.

Saari, L. M. and Latham, G. P. (1982). Employee reactions to continuous and variable reinforcement schedules involving a monetary incentive. *Journal of Applied Psychology, 67*, 506-509.

Schulz, J. D. (1991). Computer test flags tired truckers before they fall asleep at the wheel. *Traffic World*, April 1, 28-30.

Scott, W. R. (1992). *Organizations: Rational, natural, and open systems* (Third edition). Englewood Cliffs, NJ: Prentice-Hall.

Skaggs, K. J., Dickinson, A. M., and O'Connor, K. A. (1992). The use of concurrent schedules to evaluate the effects of extrinsic rewards on "intrinsic motivation": A replication. *Journal of Organizational Behavior Management, 12*(1), 45-83.

Staw, B. M. (1991). Dressing up like an organization: When psychological theories can explain organizational action. *Journal of Management, 17*, 805-819.

Stoneman, K. G. and Dickinson, A. M. (1989). Individual performance as a function of group contingencies and group size. *Journal of Organizational Behavior Management, 10*(1), 131-150.

Sulzer-Azaroff, B. and Mayer, R. G. (1991). *Behavior analysis for lasting change.* Orlando, FL: Holt, Rinehart, and Winston.

Thompson, T. and Lubinski, D. (1986). Units of analysis and kinetic structure of behavioral repertoires. *Journal of the Experimental Analysis of Behavior, 46*, 219-242.

Wagner, J. A., Rubin, P. A., and Callahan, T. J. (1988). Incentive payment and nonmanagerial productivity: An interrupted time series analysis of magnitude and trend. *Organizational Behavior and Human Decision Processes, 42*, 47-74.

Wallace, M. J. and Fay, C. H. (1988). *Compensation theory and practice* (Second edition). Boston: PWS-Kent.

Weisberg, P. and Waldrop, P. B. (1972). Fixed-interval work habits of Congress. *Journal of Applied Behavior Analysis, 5*, 93-97.

Whyte, G. (1993). Escalating commitment in individual and group decision making: A prospect theory approach. *Organizational Behavior and Human Decision Processes, 54*, 430-455.

Williams, D. C. and Johnston, J. M. (1992). Continuous versus discrete dimensions of reinforcement schedules: An integrative analysis. *Journal of the Experimental Analysis of Behavior, 58*, 205-228.

Wilson, T. B. (1995). *Innovative reward systems for the changing workplace.* New York: McGraw-Hill.

Yukl, G. A. and Latham, G. P. (1975). Consequences of reinforcement schedules and incentive magnitudes for employee performance: Problems encountered in an industrial setting. *Journal of Applied Psychology, 60,* 294-298.

Yukl, G. A., Latham, G. P., and Pursell, E. D. (1976). Effectiveness of performance incentives under continuous and variable ratio schedules of reinforcement. *Personnel Psychology, 29,* 221-231.

Yukl, G. A., Wexley, K. N., and Seymour, J. D. (1972). Effectiveness of pay incentives under variable ratio and continuous reinforcement schedules. *Journal of Applied Psychology, 56,* 19-23.

Zeiler, M. D. (1977). Schedules of reinforcement: The controlling variables. In W. K. Honig and J. E. R. Staddon (Eds.), *Handbook of operant behavior* (pp. 201-232). Englewood Cliffs, NJ: Prentice-Hall.

Zeiler, M. D. (1984). Reinforcement schedules: The sleeping giant. *Journal of the Experimental Analysis of Behavior, 42,* 485-493.

PART II:
APPLICATIONS
OF THE BEHAVIORAL MODEL

Chapter 6

Training and Development in Organizations: A Review of the Organizational Behavior Management Literature

Richard Perlow

There are several excellent literature reviews and other discussions on personnel training in organizations in the industrial and organizational (I/O) psychology literature (Campbell, 1971; Eden, 1987; Goldstein, 1980, 1991; Latham, 1988, 1989; Tannenbaum and Yukl, 1992; Wexley, 1984). These works have had an impact on the field of training and have contributed to the development and quality of training research. With few exceptions, however, these reviews have ignored organizational behavior management (OBM) training research. The present chapter attempts to fill that gap and extend earlier treatments of OBM training (Reid, Parsons, and Green, 1989; Ross, 1982). The chapter begins with a review of the OBM training literature followed by a critique and suggestions for future research.

Space constraints preclude treatment of the entire training literature from a behavior analytic perspective. Thus, I focus primarily on research investigating the process of instruction and skill acquisition of people employed in organizations. Research investigating transfer of training strategies is not emphasized because several excellent papers on generalization and maintenance already exist in the I/O (Baldwin and Ford, 1988), education (Royer, 1979), and behavior analysis (Stokes and Baer, 1977; Stokes and Osnes, 1989) literatures. Research where training was periph-

The author would like to express appreciation to Thomas S. Critchfield, Richard K. Fleming, and the editors for their comments on an earlier version of this chapter.

eral to other organizational interventions (e.g., Fox and Sulzer-Azaroff, 1989; Komaki, Blood, and Holder, 1980; Rowe, 1981; Streff, Kalsher, and Geller, 1993) is also excluded. Finally, research focusing primarily on trainee reactions to programs is not discussed (Reid and Parsons, 1995, 1996).

THE IMPORTANCE OF INSTRUCTION

Some suggest that training does not play as important a role in behavior change as consequences. In a discussion of organizational change, Murphy and Remnyi (1979) state that antecedent stimulus control techniques are not likely to yield long-term changes in behavior unless consequent stimuli are controlled. Similarly, Geller (1990) notes that workshops and training programs cannot maintain safe behavior or reduce work injuries because natural contingencies are not in place to support safe behavior. He stresses the importance of using operant conditioning principles to maintain safe behavior.

While reinforcement is certainly important in maintaining responses (Komaki, 1981/82; Kazdin, 1994), investigating how to structure material to be learned so that responses are acquired efficiently and in a cost-effective manner is worthy of study in and of itself. This is especially true for those behaviors that involve complex and interrelated sets of responses that jobs of the future are more likely to include (Howell and Cooke, 1989). Thus, training is viewed here as having a critical role in behavior change processes.

TRAINING RESEARCH

The purpose of studies described in this section was to evaluate effectiveness of training in terms of behavior change. This was generally accomplished by measuring behavior and evaluating performance before and after training.

Fawcett and Miller (1975) conducted a training study designed to improve public speaking. Topics included how to structure a talk (e.g., acknowledging the introduction, statement of appreciation to introducer, greeting the audience, topic introduction) and body movements such as hand movement and eye sweeps. The program included written instructions, role-playing, and performance feedback. Results showed the program effectively increased the frequency of target behavior and the speaker's performance ratings by members of the audience.

Maher (1981a) described a training project within which special educators were taught how to develop individualized educational programs (IEPs) for special education students. The program concentrated on discussing the essential roles of IEP components and skill development in developing educational goals and objectives. Training in group conflict management also was provided. Results indicated productivity with respect to developing IEPs improved among educators involved in the training project.

Hall and Hursch (1981/82) found that reading the training manual and holding meetings with a consultant increased the amount of time four university faculty spent on important tasks. Self-reports of efficiency and satisfaction also improved. One notable contribution of this study is that the authors presented information on ways to obtain accurate, reliable, nonreactive measures of time use. Some of the problems associated with those methods complemented other work on reactivity in behavioral observation (Haynes and Horn, 1982).

Maher (1982) also successfully implemented a time management program to increase the amount of time nine classroom teachers devoted to instructional behavior such as lecturing and holding discussions. Program components included diagnosing time management skills, analyzing time management problems, developing and implementing a plan for more productive use of time, and an evaluation phase in which trainees learned how to evaluate their progress in the use of time management. The program also included monthly social support meetings designed to facilitate generalization and maintenance.

Maher (1984) described and evaluated a training program designed to teach administrators OBM skills. Topics covered included problem identification, program design, implementation, behavior consequences, program evaluation, and staff involvement in the intervention. Results suggested the trainees were able to apply OBM techniques to improve organizational performance.

Bruwelheide and Duncan (1985) described a means by which an organization's labor relations course was evaluated. Supervisors received training and then scored a videotape on the degree to which the videotaped models adhered to the program principles. Results showed that subjects did better on the posttest than the pretest and that the trained group performed better on the test than a group that did not receive training. While scoring the participants' performance in role-playing sessions would have enhanced the meaningfulness of the learning measure, what was noteworthy in this study is that the authors attempted to assess the opportunities to engage in these behaviors both before and after training. This is important because practitioners can determine the percentage of opportunities on which responses were emitted and adjust absolute frequency accordingly.

Welsh et al. (1989) extended work on improving meeting effectiveness (Briscoe, Hoffman, and Bailey, 1975; Seekins, Mathews, and Fawcett, 1984) by developing a manual designed to improve the performance of meeting chairs. The manual required little facilitator time and resulted in improved performance on a skills generalization test.

Nordstrom, Lorenzi, and Hall (1990) instructed managers in city government on OBM techniques. Results from skill acquisition and performance measures showed that the managers learned the material and employee performance improved. Managers also were satisfied with the program.

Hopkins and colleagues (1986) conducted an intervention designed to reduce employee exposure to toxic chemicals. Training consisted of a description of behaviors that would reduce exposure, along with a rationale of why those behaviors would work. Modeling, answering trainee questions, daily feedback, and reinforcement were other intervention components. Results showed that the program worked.

Johnson and Fawcett (1994) trained three receptionists of a human service agency to increase their frequency of courteous behavior. They provided trainees with written instructions, practice, and feedback on performance. The authors also implemented a lottery system to enhance maintenance. While some of the target behaviors appear to be outside the boundaries of courteous service (e.g., asking closed-ended questions when requesting factual information), the research is interesting and results documented program effectiveness.

Wilson, Boni, and Hogg (1997) describe an intervention designed to enhance courteous behavior of two police officers and five public servants. The authors identified the target behaviors through on-the-job observation, a literature review, and a survey. Target behaviors included failing to smile or having a sullen expression, failing to give an appropriate greeting, keeping the customer waiting without acknowledgment, talking to a colleague while attending to the customer, having an abrupt or unfriendly tone of voice, failing to give the customer full attention, and ending the exchange abruptly. The training program included videos, discussions, and handouts describing the target behaviors. One video illustrated a discourteous interaction. The trainer played the video again while stopping the tape at various times to discuss the model's behavior. Trainees also viewed a modeling display of appropriate behavior. The trainees' supervisors also participated in a training session designed to teach them how to reinforce courteous behavior in subordinates and to correct instances of discourteous acts. Results showed that the frequency of courteous behavior increased and that there was greater uniformity among the public servants' percentages of courteous behavior following the workshop. However, performance decreased after a period of time.

Summary

A reasonable conclusion based on the ongoing research is that training is a useful technique for changing a variety of behaviors. What researchers need to ask and to investigate further is the question of why training is effective in changing behavior. Understanding why training works is important because it enables researchers to develop better programs for the target behaviors. For example, Maher (1982) described and evaluated a time management program that appeared to have been logically developed. Although we can conclude that the program was effective, we do not know whether the methods used were the most effective means by which people acquired skills such as analyzing time management problems. Incorporating the findings of the basic literature on learning theory into program development and validating those findings is one strategy that would increase our understanding of training and skill acquisition of employees.

COMPARISON RESEARCH

Comparison research typically involves determining which of two or more interventions is the most effective or efficient in changing behavior. Studies reviewed here compared different training techniques or compared training to other interventions.

Adams, Tallon, and Rimell (1980) compared the performance of trainees who received either a lecture on how to use positive reinforcement, or role-playing exercises supplemented with feedback. The performance of people who received the lecture improved initially after training, but declined thereafter. On the other hand, the performance of those who were involved in role-playing improved over time.

Brown and colleagues (1980) examined the effectiveness of training and feedback on customer service behaviors such as approaching customers, greeting them, and demonstrating courtesy. The four-hour program covered the company's courtesy standards, the relationship between customer service and performance appraisals, and listening skills and complaint handling. Training activities included viewing models, completing worksheets, and role-playing. Results showed that training had little effect on performance, but feedback improved performance dramatically. One feature of the investigation was the demonstration that the trained behaviors were associated with an important organizational outcome (customer satisfaction). One salesperson was told to perform alternately all of the target customer responses and then none of the behaviors for customer transactions. On average, customers who were recipients of the trained behaviors reported they were more satisfied than customers who were not exposed to the trained behaviors.

Maher (1981b) examined the differential effects of an active learning program (ALP) and an instructional learning program (ILP) in the development of educational programs. The author used social learning theory principles (Bandura, 1969) to develop the ALP. The ALP emphasized discussion, rehearsal, feedback, and social reinforcement. The ILP emphasized lectures, discussion, and formal didactic presentations. Trainee performance was evaluated in terms of quality and quantity of educational programs developed after training. Results showed that the active learning program was more effective than the ILP. However, we do not know what aspects of the ALP resulted in the program's superiority over the ILP. That is, we do not know the differential contributing effects of ALP components such as rehearsal or feedback. Moreover, the ALP program included homework assignments whereas the ILP did not. The impact of homework assignments on productivity, that is, above and beyond the ALP, remains undetermined.

Hanel, Martin, and Koop (1982) prepared a self-study time management guide and compared the effectiveness of that manual in developing and maintaining time management to that of a best-selling time management book. Participants in the self-instructional group were asked to work on the manual for one hour each day for eight days. People who used the popular-press book were asked to read it, which the researchers said could be accomplished within eight hours. Subjects in the self-study time management guide group also were given guidelines on how to use the manual; people in the best-seller group did not receive guidelines. The manual contained exercises, thereby enabling the participants to take a more active role in the learning process than subjects in the best-seller group. Results showed that the self-instructional group performed better than the best-seller group, although no rationale was offered as to why performance differences were expected. Moreover, although not assessed directly, guidelines on how to use the manual and supplemental exercises provided to the manual group may have enhanced subsequent performance.

Ford (1984) examined training in a health care facility. Specifically, he compared the relative effectiveness of a traditional training approach with a personalized system of instruction (PSI) approach. The traditional training methods included lectures, videotapes, films, and demonstrations. The personalized system of instruction in this study included features such as self-paced instruction, subject mastery before moving to new material, being able to work on multiple units simultaneously, and allowances for repeating performance evaluations. People trained with the PSI approach performed better on the training learning measures and received higher supervisory on-the-job performance ratings than those using the traditional approach. Training efficiency indices also were compared in this study. The percentage of people participating in the PSI approach who completed the program was greater than the percentage of people completing the alternative method (100 percent versus 73 percent). In addition, it took less time for the PSI participants to complete the program (47.32 hours versus 165 hours). Clearly, the PSI approach was more effective and efficient than the traditional learning approach.

Born, Gledhill, and Davis (1972) compared learning by subjects exposed to different instructional methods. One group received instruction via lectures; two other groups each received one of two types of PSI instruction; and a fourth group rotated among the three methods. Students in the PSI sessions performed better on tests than students who received lectures, especially on essay and fill-in-the-blank tests. Poor and average students appeared to obtain the most benefit from PSI.

Born and Davis (1974) also found that students scored slightly higher on knowledge tests after using the PSI approach than after the lecture method. The PSI approach also appears to have been the most cost-effective method, as the preparation time for the two instructional methods were equivalent.

Neef and colleagues (1991) conducted two studies that essentially examined the effectiveness of modeling and role-playing. Respite care providers viewed videotapes of models providing respite care alone, with one other person, or as part of a group. Overall training appeared effective as skills acquired during instruction generalized to the job and in many instances were maintained up to six months. The authors also reported that presentation format had no effect on performance. The experiment was replicated with subject participants from human service agencies. Results indicated that training improved performance, but presentation format (alone, dyad, and group) had no effect on behavior.

Karlsson and Chase (1996) examined effects of prompting procedures on college student acquisition of a computer spreadsheet program. Continuous prompting involves telling the learner what keys to punch during the entire learning process. Fading is a strategy involving a gradual transfer of stimulus control from the instructions to the computer interface (e.g., keyboard or mouse). One type of fading had students guess at which keys to punch. The time interval before being told the correct response increased on successive trials (i.e., prompt delay). The second fading strategy involved discrimination (i.e., additional choices). Students had to identify which keys to punch where the number of incorrect alternatives increased over successive trials. Results showed that the college students who had received continuous prompting made approximately twice as many errors on a posttest than students receiving either of the two fading strategies. Their theoretically-based research clearly documents the advantages of having trainees take an active role in the learning process.

Summary

The research reviewed here shows that training methods are differentially effective, although the quality and quantity of training such as the use of homework was not always controlled. What OBM researchers need to discover is why certain training techniques are better suited for developing target behavior than other methods. For example, Ford (1984) demonstrated the superiority of the PSI approach over the lecture method; however, we cannot determine from the research why the program was best suited for the target behaviors trained. An extension of the research reported here would (a) clearly specify the target behavior to be trained, and (b) identify the training methods best suited for development of the behavior through application of basic research on instructional design. A systematic program of research of this nature should lead to the development of guidelines that would enable trainers to match training methods with different classes of target behaviors.

TRAINING AND MOTIVATION

Training is best suited for developing skills; it is not a very efficient tool for resolving motivational problems unless the instructional experiences target self-management behavior (e.g., Frayne and Latham, 1987; Latham and Frayne, 1989). The OBM research reviewed in this section illustrates that training is not a panacea for all organizational problems.

Quilitch (1975) compared the effects of memos, a workshop, and publicly posted feedback on employee attendance. Results indicated that neither the attendance memos nor training were effective in improving attendance. Feedback was the only intervention that improved attendance. In this situation training was not warranted. The root of the problem was motivational. Trainees did not exhibit a skill deficit; they demonstrated the ability to come to work but did not do so on a consistent basis.

Geller and colleagues (1980) examined the relative effectiveness of a memo stressing the importance of practicing sanitation principles (hand washing), training, and feedback for improving cafeteria employees' sanitation behavior. After collecting baseline data, some employees received a one-paragraph memo about videotaping them as part of a project focusing on hand washing. Some of the employees received training a few days later. Training consisted of a thirty-minute lecture and slide presentation on the importance of sanitation, defining conditions that should be followed by hand washing, and proper hand washing procedures. Performance feedback commenced ten days following training. Results found the memo to be initially effective in increasing hand washing frequency, especially for conditions that should be followed by hand washing, such as after touching hair. Training effects also were weak. Feedback had the most pronounced effects on sanitation behavior for both the trained and untrained employees.

The Geller and colleagues (1980) study is another illustration of a motivational issue, not a training problem. Training did not appear necessary as the data showed that the no-training group performed as well as the subjects in the training group when both groups received performance feedback. While it is possible that the feedback checklist sheets that subjects received taught nontrainees when to wash their hands, no supporting evidence was presented.

Conrin (1982) compared the relative effects of training programs designed to improve the completion of projects versus setting a target date for completing projects. The investigation included four phases. The first part was a training phase in which trainees were given written instructions on how to complete behavioral data sheets and weekly behavioral reports on clients of a developmental center. The trainer (the employees' supervisor) stressed the importance of correctly completing the data sheets, explained the data system, reviewed sample reports, and answered questions during training. A psychologist gave the trainees blank data report forms requesting that they be completed by a predetermined date in the study's second phase. The psychologist gave the trainees blank data sheets with no completion deadline during the third phase of the investigation. The fourth phase was identical to the second phase in that a target date was assigned. Results indicated that trainees performed worst under the training-alone phase. Reports were on average twenty days late. Trainees performed best when given a deadline, where reports were on average two days late. Reports were submitted an average of nine days late during the third phase. The author concluded that the target date procedure was more effective than training in improving performance.

LaFleur and Hyten (1995) illustrate the importance of specifying work procedures and organizing the various job functions among hotel banquet staff. Hotel staff exhibited problems setting out all necessary equipment for banquet functions (e.g., napkins). Problems completing work as a unit also occurred because supervisors would assign staff identical tasks while leaving other tasks unassigned. The authors also noted that they could not identify deficiencies in the staff that precluded successful job performance. The treatment package included goal setting, feedback, a training manual, and a task checklist that were reviewed with the trainees as part of a training workshop. Results showed that the total intervention succeeded in changing staff behavior. However, it appears that training may have had little impact on performance. Employees who received the training prior to a second baseline data collection period did not have markedly different setup completion rates than the rates of recently hired employees who did not participate in training prior to the second baseline data collection period.

Summary

Successful training depends on several factors. As mentioned in the previous section, specifying the target behavior is critical. An analysis of whether the current behavior is a function of motivation or a skill deficit is equally important because, as each of the studies in this section show, training is not an effective tool for improving inadequate performance due to lack of effort. For example, the central issue in Conrin's (1982) research involved motivation, not skill deficits. Skills training is not appropriate in situations where people already possess skills needed to execute desired behavior. Self-management training (Kanfer, 1980; Marx, 1982) or the use of motivational strategies such as goal setting (Locke and Latham, 1990) and contingent reinforcement (Kazdin, 1994; Komaki, 1981/82) are more appropriate.

PROGRAM DEVELOPMENT

Several OBM papers have focused on, or have implications for, program development. Maher (1983) described a way to implement programs that included a framework from which implementation procedures can be derived. The implementation procedure was called DURABLE. The first step in this seven-step procedure, D (durable), is to meet with important people and/or groups in the organization to discuss the proposed intervention. U (understanding) refers to determining whether the organization is ready for program implementation (cf. Davis and Salasin, 1975). R (reinforcing) requires that management reinforce the behavior of those responsible for implementing the intervention. A (acquiring preconditions of successful implementation) includes ensuring that the goals of the program are clearly communicated and obtaining the budget necessary for successful implementation. B (building) reflects the importance of management exhibiting positive expectations about the program to the organization's staff. L (learning) includes providing activities to the implementors that enhance their ability to perform their assignments. Finally, E (evaluating) refers to assessing the extent to which the program was implemented, and the degree to which the program succeeded.

This article is important for two main reasons. First, it emphasized identification of organizational contextual factors to consider before implementing training (cf. Goldstein, 1991). The sample questions Maher provides are also noteworthy and should help practitioners gauge the likelihood of an intervention's success.

Behavior taught in training should have support in terms of whether emitting those behaviors actually leads to improved performance. Surprisingly, there has been little systematic OBM research on the identification of the most important behavior to train prior to program implementation. Clark and colleagues (1985) conducted research that is one notable exception. They surveyed subordinates regarding the type of supervisory skills they believed to be important in improving their satisfaction and productivity. Other individuals observed videotapes of supervisors and identified those behaviors likely to improve productivity and job satisfaction. The authors also conducted a literature search to identify good supervisory behavior. Clark et al. developed vignettes containing interactions based on the facilitative behaviors identified as well as interactions and behaviors that were believed to have negative and no effect on performance. Judges observed the vignettes and identified behaviors they felt would improve, maintain, or decrease performance. The authors developed a training program based on the principles identified as important in improving job performance. The program was found to be an effective means of improving supervisor behavior.

Alavosius and Sulzer-Azaroff (1986) studied the effects of feedback on safe lifting behavior. Although not a training study per se, the study is included here because it illustrates how to conduct a thorough task analysis. The authors based their analysis of the steps involved in safe lifting by reviewing training materials, consulting with a physical therapist, and reviewing the lifting literature.

Jones, Fremouw, and Carples (1977) conducted an interesting study examining the behavior of former trainees who became trainers. Three teachers were trained in classroom management. These three trainees then became trainers who instructed other teachers in classroom management. Results showed that the training worked. The frequency of student disruptive behavior decreased in the trainee-trainers' classrooms as well as in the other teachers' classrooms. One noteworthy feature of the project is the effects of becoming a trainer on classroom management performance. The two trainee-trainers who profited least from their original training improved their classroom management performance after training other teachers.

Van den Pol, Reid, and Fuqua (1983) extended our knowledge of peer training. They trained direct-care staff of a residential facility how to respond to fires, manage aggressive resident behavior, and aid residents experiencing convulsive seizures. Peer training was successful. What makes this study noteworthy is that the authors monitored the trainers' behavior after they provided instruction to others. The process of training others resulted in further development of the trainers' own skills in the topics they taught. Trainer performance in topics not taught declined over time. The van den Pol, Reid, and Fuqua (1983) and Jones, Fremouw, and Carples (1977) studies demonstrate the importance of spaced practice in learning. Using former trainees as trainers is one way of providing them with the opportunity to recall and practice previously acquired skills, which is important for generalization and maintenance of their own learned skills.

Summary

The research described here showed that the way programs are developed impacts training. Researchers should extend this body of literature by specifying the linkages among learning theory, instructional design, and target behavior. Knowledge of the linkages could be used to develop efficient and effective training programs. For example, incorporating spaced practice in the design of the program is one way to increase maintenance of the behaviors Jones, Fremouw, and Carples (1977) and van den Pol, Reid, and Fuqua (1983) investigated.

CRITIQUE AND FUTURE RESEARCH DIRECTIONS

Training and development of individuals in organizations has received a great deal of attention from OBM researchers. To date, investigations focusing on skill acquisition are in the minority relative to the number of studies examining the efficacy of reinforcement (Komaki, Blood, and Holder, 1980; Runion, Watson, and McWhorter, 1978). This is not surprising given radical behaviorism's emphasis on consequences in behavior repertoire development.

We can conclude from the OBM training research that training is an effective intervention. Organizational behavior management researchers and practitioners also know how to ensure generalization and maintenance of skills acquired in training. Illustrations in the OBM literature also describe how training fits into a broad range of techniques designed to bring about behavior change. On the other hand, we have not learned much about the generalizability of learning theory concepts in employment settings. There is a gap in the OBM training literature regarding knowledge of which instructional methods or combinations thereof are maximally effective in facilitating learning for classes of target behavior. Finally, we cannot conclude confidently that many of the programs were cost-effective.

Learning Principles

Little has been mentioned in the OBM training literature concerning how laboratory-based learning principles (see Bower and Hilgard, 1981; Catania, 1992; Honig and Staddon, 1977; Mazur, 1990) are incorporated into instructional techniques. It is almost as if readers have to accept at face value that developers designed training programs to facilitate and maximize acquisition and retention. One consequence is that little of the research reviewed here advanced our knowledge about the generalizability of basic learning principles to normal adults functioning in work settings. Although this assertion should not be construed as a criticism of OBM for overemphasizing technology (cf. Geller, 1991), more research needs to be done to increase understanding of human behavior in the laboratory and in applied settings.

Studying learning theory concepts is necessary to increase understanding of how people acquire skills. For example, induction, shaping, and fading are all important concepts in understanding how learning occurs; however, I could not find one OBM study that specifically addressed how these concepts can be used to train employees more efficiently.

Investigations are needed that improve our understanding of how strategies based on learning concepts such as induction, fading, and shaping enhance and/or detract from the acquisition of taxonomies of target work behaviors. Karlsson and Chase's (1996) work with college students' acquisition of a spreadsheet program is one excellent illustration of needed research. Another avenue of applied organizational research that is tied to basic learning theory is to conduct experiments that lead to development of a theoretically based set of rules indicating how to best shape the skills necessary to troubleshoot malfunctions in machinery.

Program Structure

In most of the articles reviewed here, researchers merely described the training without explaining why they chose the instructional methods. In some studies, authors described the training program in only one or two sentences (see Johnson and Fawcett, 1994, for an exception). Organizational behavior management researchers need to focus more attention on program design. Describing program design and why it is suited for development of the target behavior serves two purposes. It allows for empirical evaluation of instructional techniques and enables readers to judge the degree to which the training method adheres to sound instructional principles.

Organizational behavior management researchers and practitioners need to consider why certain training techniques are thought to be more effective and under what conditions they should be maximally effective (e.g., course content, purpose of training, etc.). Gagné's framework (Gagné, 1985; Gagné, Briggs, and Wager, 1988) is relevant here. He described different learning outcomes and the conditions needed to facilitate the learning of those outcomes. Applying Gagné's framework to training involves specifying the target behavior, classifying the target behavior in type of learning outcomes, and arranging instruction so that the relevant conditions for learning are present (see Resnick, Wang, and Kaplan [1973] for an illustration). Research of this kind is needed in OBM.

One method that has been used to evaluate different training strategies is comparative research. Researchers who wish to conduct comparative studies should review Van Houten (1987) and Johnston (1988). Van Houten (1987) claimed that one cannot indiscriminately compare training programs without ensuring that each program is optimally effective. To compare two programs (e.g., Programs A and B) where Program B is not optimally developed, and then conclude that Program A is superior to Program B is misleading because we do not know whether differences would have existed had Program B been developed adequately. While it is difficult to discern whether most interventions in the comparison research section of this chapter were optimally developed, Van Houten's article deserves attention because some comparative intervention research described previously did not appear to make fair comparisons.

Johnston (1988) questioned the value of comparison research for a variety of reasons, one of which being that the primary focus of comparison research is on understanding procedures rather than understanding behavior. He believes, like Van Houten (1987), that a full understanding of the behavior and the intervention is required before comparison studies are conducted. Doing otherwise leads to results that have poor generality. Johnston (1988) also adds that achieving full understanding is a highly unlikely event. In the event that complete understanding is achieved, it may be obvious which procedure is better, thereby obviating the need to conduct comparison research.

Van Houten (1987) and Johnston's (1988) papers have somewhat different implications for organizational behavior management researchers. While Van Houten (1987) suggests that comparison research is important provided that the programs compared are optimally developed, Johnston (1988) implies that comparison research may not be necessary in most instances.

One tactic that bridges the views of both authors is component analysis. Component analysis is used to understand the relative and/or additive contributions of a part, or several parts, of a strategy designed to predict and control a target behavior. It is accomplished by manipulating the exposure of trainees to features of the training program (e.g., role-playing exercises), and assessing the impact of the manipulation on behavior. In and of itself, a component analysis is not a research design. Rather, it is a tactic that can be employed in a variety of within- and between-subject research designs. Proper component analysis research requires specification of the task, identification of the desired learning outcome, and an explanation of the rationale behind the application of basic research on instructional methods to training program development. Describing the rationale behind the intervention involves some discussion of why we would expect the component alteration/inclusion to modify behavior. Research incorporating component analysis tactics integrates Van Houten's (1987) and Johnston's (1988) comments because it provides a justification for the intervention or any program alteration, thereby (a) avoiding the appearance of indiscriminately comparing methods, and (b) focusing attention where it should be, on the target behavior. When done properly, component analysis research results enable investigators to ascertain what components make the training intervention effective, and is useful in developing optimal training programs. Such research also increases understanding of how to change behavior efficiently.

Utility

The reporting of cost-benefit analysis is the exception rather than the norm. Although the demonstration of utility poses unique challenges and may have unanticipated effects (Latham and Whyte, 1994), organizational decision-maker requests to justify training necessitates the documentation of training value (Morrow, Jarrett, and Rupinski, 1997). Some approaches to cost-benefit analysis in the OBM literature include comparing the cost-benefit ratios of two programs (Brown et al., 1980) and logic (Alavosius and Sulzer-Azaroff, 1986). An alternative means by which the value of a program is determined is through a utility analysis, in which the cost of a program is examined relative to the gain in productivity. Excellent references on how to estimate training/intervention costs are found in the industrial and organizational psychology literature (Cascio, 1982; Goldstein, 1991).

More utility estimates should be reported in the OBM literature while concurrently being sensitive to the organization's need to remain competitive by keeping findings confidential (Balcazer et al., 1989). The recommendation to justify the costs of training is not new (Johnston et al., 1978; Mawhinney, 1975). Unfortunately, the call has not been heeded.

Perhaps one reason why there are few reports of utility in the OBM literature is that much of the training research occurred in mental retardation facilities. Programs designed to increase the effectiveness of people employed at mental retardation facilities are not likely to demonstrate economic utility. That is, the gain in dollars of improved client behavior as a result of staff training is not likely to outweigh the cost of the intervention. Evaluating these training programs in economic terms is inappropriate because decision makers may be tempted to conclude that such programs are not worthwhile.

Interventions aimed at helping direct-care workers better manage the behavior of developmentally disabled clients of residential facilities should be evaluated on other criteria. For example, Fleming, Oliver, and Bolton (1996) collected data on trainee subordinates to assess, in part, the effectiveness of a supervisory training program. Methot and colleagues (1996) examined the effects of their training intervention on two levels of supervision, frontline staff, and client behavior. Another alternative to computing utility estimates on a single training intervention is to evaluate the utility of different training programs. Allison, Silverstein, and Galante (1992) illustrate the approach in their work on monetary incentive systems.

CONCLUSION

Organizational behavior management research has focused on evaluating the efficacy of training in a variety of settings. The studies reviewed in this chapter indicate that while not a cure-all, training can be an effective technique for changing behavior. Training is essential to certain behavior changes. That is, against a context of high instrumentality and great reinforcement value for performing well, absence of knowledge or skill needed to produce reinforcers will preclude both performance and receipt of reinforcers contingent on it.

Much remains to be learned about how to train employees in the job-related knowledge and skills they need to perform effectively. Understanding how to best structure instructional sequences to maximize learning and behavior change for complex jobs is just one of the challenges facing researchers and practitioners. I look forward to reading original research addressing this and other substantive issues.

REFERENCES

Adams, G. L., Tallon, R. J., and Rimell, P. (1980). A comparison of lecture versus role-playing in training of the use of positive reinforcement. *Journal of Organizational Behavior Management, 2*(3), 205-212.

Alavosius, M. P. and Sulzer-Azaroff, B. (1986). The effects of performance feedback on the safety of client lifting and transfer. *Journal of Applied Behavior Analysis, 19*(3), 261-267.

Allison, D. B., Silverstein, J. M., and Galante, V. (1992). Relative effectiveness and cost-effectiveness of cooperative, competitive, and independent monetary incentive systems. *Journal of Applied Behavior Management, 13*(1), 85-112.

Balcazer, F. E., Shupert, M. K., Daniels, A. C., Mawhinney, T. C., and Hopkins, B. L. (1989). An objective review and analysis of ten years of publication in the *Journal of Organizational Behavior Management. Journal of Organizational Behavior Management, 10*(1), 7-37.

Baldwin, T. T. and Ford, J. K. (1988). Transfer of training: A review and directions for future research. *Personnel Psychology, 41*, 63-105.

Bandura, A. (1969). *Principles of behavior modification.* New York: Holt, Rinehart and Winston.

Born, D. G. and Davis, M. L. (1974). Amount and distribution of study in a personalized instruction course and in a lecture course. *Journal of Applied Behavior Analysis, 7*(3), 365-375.

Born, D. G., Gledhill, S., and Davis, M. (1972). Examination performance in lecture-discussion and personalized instruction courses. *Journal of Applied Behavior Analysis, 5,* 33-43.

Bower, G. H. and Hilgard, E. R. (1981). *Theories of learning* (Fifth edition). Englewood Cliffs, NJ: Prentice-Hall.

Briscoe, R. V., Hoffman, D. B., and Bailey, J. S. (1975). Behavioral community psychology: Training a community board to problem solve. *Journal of Applied Behavior Analysis, 8*(2), 157-168.

Brown, M. G., Malott, R. W., Dillon, M. J., and Keeps, E. J. (1980). Improving customer service in a large department store through the use of training and feedback. *Journal of Organizational Behavior Management, 2*(4), 251-264.

Bruwelheide, L. R. and Duncan, P. K. (1985). A method for evaluating corporation training seminars. *Journal of Organizational Behavior Management, 7*(1/2), 65-94.

Campbell, J. P. (1971). Personnel training and development. *Annual Review of Psychology, 22,* 565-602.

Cascio, W. F. (1982). *Costing human resources: The financial impact of behavior in organizations.* Belmont, CA: Wadsworth.

Catania, A. C. (1992). *Learning* (Third edition). Englewood Cliffs, NJ: Prentice-Hall.

Clark, H. B., Wood, R., Kuehnel, T., Flanagan, S., Mosk, M., and Northrup, J. T. (1985). Preliminary validation and training of supervisory interaction skills. *Journal of Organizational Behavior Management, 7*(1/2), 95-115.

Conrin, J. (1982). A comparison of two types of antecedent controls over supervisory behavior. *Journal of Organizational Behavior Management, 4*(3/4), 37-47.

Davis, H. R. and Salasin, S. E. (1975). The utilization of evaluation. In E. L. Struening and M. Guttentag (Eds.), *Handbook of evaluation research* (Vol. 1, pp. 621-666). Beverly Hills, CA: Sage.

Eden, D. (1987). Training. In B. M. Bass and P. J. D. Drench (Eds.), *Advances in organizational behavior: An international review* (pp. 99-113). Newbury Park, CA: Sage.

Fawcett, S. B. and Miller, L. K. (1975). Training public-speaking behavior: An experimental analysis and social validation. *Journal of Applied Behavior Analysis, 8*(2), 125-135.

Fleming, R. K., Oliver, J. R., and Bolton, D. N. (1996). Training supervisors to train staff: A case study in a human service organization. *Journal of Organizational Behavior Management, 16*(1), 3-25.

Ford, J. E. (1984). Application of a personalized system of instruction to a large, personnel training program. *Journal of Organizational Behavior Management, 5*(3/4), 57-65.

Fox, C. J. and Sulzer-Azaroff, B. (1989). The effectiveness of two different sources of feedback on staff teaching of fire evacuation skills. *Journal of Organizational Behavior Management, 10*(2), 19-35.

Frayne, C. A. and Latham, G. P. (1987). The application of social learning theory to employee self-management of attendance. *Journal of Applied Psychology, 72,* 387-392.

Gagné, R. M. (1985). *The conditions of learning* (Fourth edition). New York: Holt, Rinehart, and Winston.

Gagné, R. M., Briggs, L. J., and Wager, W. W. (1988). *Principles of instructional design* (Third edition). New York: Holt, Rinehart, and Winston.

Geller, E. S. (1990). Performance management and occupational safety: Start with a safety belt program. *Journal of Organizational Behavior Management, 11*(1), 149-174.

Geller, E. S. (Ed.). (1991). Science, theory, and technology: Varied perspectives. *Journal of Applied Behavior Analysis, 24*(3).

Geller, E. S., Eason, S. L., Phillips, J. A., and Pierson, M. D. (1980). Interventions to improve sanitation during food preparation. *Journal of Organizational Behavior Management, 2*(3), 229-240.

Goldstein, I. L. (1980). Training in work organizations. *Annual Review of Psychology, 31,* 229-272.

Goldstein, I. L. (1991). Training in work organizations. In M. D. Dunnette and L. M. Hough (Eds.), *Handbook of industrial and organizational psychology* (Vol. 2, pp. 507-619). Palo Alto, CA: Consulting Psychologists Press.

Hall, B. L. and Hursch, D. E. (1981/82). An evaluation of the effects of a time management training program on work efficiency. *Journal of Organizational Behavior Management, 3*(4), 73-96.

Hanel, F., Martin, G., and Koop, S. (1982). Field testing of a self-instructional time management manual with managerial staff in an institutional setting. *Journal of Organizational Behavior Management, 4*(3/4), 81-96.

Haynes, S. N. and Horn, W. F. (1982). Reactivity in behavioral observation: A review. *Behavioral Assessment, 4,* 369-385.

Honig, W. K. and Staddon, J. E. R. (1977). *Handbook of operant behavior.* Englewood Cliffs, NJ: Prentice-Hall.

Hopkins, B. L., Conard, R. J., Dangel, R. F., Fitch, H. G., Smith, M. J., and Anger, W. K. (1986). Behavioral technology for reducing occupational exposures to styrene. *Journal of Applied Behavior Analysis, 19,* 3-11.

Howell, W. C. and Cooke, N. J. (1989). Training the human information processor: A review of cognitive models. In I. L. Goldstein (Ed.), *Training and development in organizations* (pp. 121-182). San Francisco: Jossey-Bass.

Johnson, M. D. and Fawcett, S. B. (1994). Courteous service: Its assessment and modification in a human service organization. *Journal of Applied Behavior Analysis, 27,* 145-152.

Johnston, J. M. (1988). Strategic and tactical limits of comparison studies. *The Behavior Analyst, 11,* 1-9.

Johnston, J. M., Duncan, P. K., Monroe, C., Stephenson, H., and Stoerzinger, A. (1978). Tactics and benefits of behavioral measurement in business. *Journal of Organizational Behavior Management, 1*(3), 164-178.

Jones, F. H., Fremouw, W., and Carples, S. (1977). Pyramid training of elementary school teachers to use a classroom management "skill package." *Journal of Applied Behavior Analysis, 10*(2), 239-253.

Kanfer, F. (1980). Self-management methods. In F. H. Kanfer and A. P. Goldstein (Eds.), *Helping people change: A textbook of methods* (Second edition, pp. 334-389). New York: Pergamon.

Karlsson, T. and Chase, P. N. (1996). A comparison of three prompting methods for training software use. *Journal of Organizational Behavior Management, 16*(1), 27-44.

Kazdin, A. E. (1994). *Behavior modification in applied settings* (Fifth edition). Pacific Grove, CA: Brooks/Cole.

Komaki, J. L. (1981/82). Managerial effectiveness: Potential contributions of the behavioral approach. *Journal of Organizational Behavior Management, 3*(3), 71-83.

Komaki, J. L., Blood, M., and Holder, D. (1980). Fostering friendliness in a fast food franchise. *Journal of Organizational Behavior Management, 2*(3), 151-164.

LaFleur, T. and Hyten, C. (1995). Improving the quality of hotel banquet staff performance. *Journal of Organizational Behavior Management, 15*(1/2), 69-93.

Latham, G. P. (1988). Human resource training and development. *Annual Review of Psychology, 38*, 545-582.

Latham, G. P. (1989). Behavioral approaches to the training and learning process. In I. L. Goldstein (Ed.), *Training development in organizations* (pp. 256-295). San Francisco: Jossey-Bass.

Latham, G. P. and Frayne, C. A. (1989). Increasing job attendance through training in self-management: A review of two studies. *Journal of Applied Psychology, 74*, 411-416.

Latham, G. P. and Whyte, G. (1994). The futility of utility analysis. *Personnel Psychology, 47*, 31-46.

Locke, E. A. and Latham, G. P. (1990). *A theory of goal setting and task performance.* Englewood Cliffs, NJ: Prentice-Hall.

Maher, C. A. (1981a). Improving the delivery of special education related services in public schools. *Journal of Organizational Behavior Management, 3*(1), 29-44.

Maher, C. A. (1981b). Training of managers in program planning and evaluation: Comparison of 2 approaches. *Journal of Organizational Behavior Management, 3*(1), 45-68.

Maher, C. A. (1982). Improving teacher instructional behavior: Evaluation of a time management training program. *Journal of Organizational Behavior Management, 4*(3/4), 27-36.

Maher, C. A. (1983). Description and evaluation of an approach to implementing programs in organizational settings. *Journal of Organizational Behavior Management, 5*(3/4), 69-98.

Maher, C. A. (1984). Training educational administrators in organizational behavior management: Program description and evaluation. *Journal of Organizational Behavior Management, 6*(1), 79-97.

Marx, R. D. (1982). Relapse prevention for managerial training: A model for maintenance of behavior change. *Academy of Management Review, 7*, 433-441.

Mawhinney, T. C. (1975). Operant terms and description of individual work behavior: Some problems of interpretation, application, and evaluation. *Journal of Applied Psychology, 60*, 704-712.

Mazur, J. E. (1990). *Learning and behavior* (Second edition). Englewood Cliffs, NJ: Prentice-Hall.

Methot, L. L., Williams, W. L., Cummings, A., and Bradshaw, B. (1996). Measuring the effects of a manager-supervisor training program through the generalized performance of managers, supervisors, front-line staff and clients in a human service setting. *Journal of Organizational Behavior Management, 16*(2), 3-25.

Morrow, C. C., Jarrett, M. Q., and Rupinski, M. T. (1997). An investigation of the effect and economic utility of corporate-wide training. *Personnel Psychology, 50*, 91-109.

Murphy, G. C. and Remnyi, A. G. (1979). Behavior analysis and organizational reality: The need for a technology of program implementation. *Journal of Organizational Behavior Management, 2*(2), 121-131.

Neef, N. A., Trachtenberg, S., Loeb, J., and Sterner, K. (1991). Video-based training of respite care providers: An interactional analysis of presentation format. *Journal of Applied Behavior Analysis, 24*, 473-486.

Nordstrom, R. R., Lorenzi, P., and Hall, R. V. (1990). A behavioral training program for managers in city government. *Journal of Organizational Behavior Management, 11*(2), 189-211.

Quilitch, H. R. (1975). A comparison of three staff-management procedures. *Journal of Applied Behavior Analysis, 8*, 59-66.

Reid, D. H. and Parsons, M. B. (1995). Comparing choice and questionnaire measures of the acceptability of a staff training procedure. *Journal of Applied Behavior Analysis, 28*, 317-322.

Reid, D. H. and Parsons, M. B. (1996). A comparison of staff acceptability of immediate versus delayed verbal feedback in staff training. *Journal of Organizational Behavior Management, 16*(2), 35-47.

Reid, D. H., Parsons, M. B., and Green, C. W. (1989). *Staff management in human services: Behavioral research and applications.* Springfield, IL: Thomas.

Resnick, L., Wang, M., and Kaplan, J. (1973). Task analysis in curriculum design: A hierarchically sequenced introductory mathematics curriculum. *Journal of Applied Behavior Analysis, 6*, 679-710.

Ross, P. C. (1982). Training: Behavior change and the improvement of business performance. In L. W. Frederiksen (Ed.), *Handbook of organizational behavior management* (pp. 181-217). New York: Wiley.

Rowe, B. J. (1981). The use of feedback and reinforcement to increase the telephone reporting of independent automobile appraisers. *Journal of Organizational Behavior Management, 3*(2), 35-40.

Royer, J. M. (1979). Theories of the transfer of learning. *American Psychologist, 34*, 53-69.

Runion, A., Watson, J. O., and McWhorter, J. (1978). Energy savings in interstate transportation through feedback and reinforcement. *Journal of Organizational Behavior Management, 1*(3), 180-191.

Seekins, T., Mathews, M., and Fawcett, S. B. (1984). Enhancing leadership skills for community self-help organizations through behavioral instructions. *Journal of Community Psychology, 12*, 155-163.

Stokes, T. F. and Baer, D. M. (1977). An implicit technology of generalization. *Journal of Applied Behavior Analysis, 10*, 349-367.

Stokes, T. F. and Osnes, P. G. (1989). An operant pursuit of generalization. *Behavior Therapy, 20*, 337-355.

Streff, F. M., Kalsher, M. J., and Geller, E. S. (1993). Developing workplace safety programs: Observations of response covariation. *Journal of Organizational Behavior Management, 13*(2), 3-14.

Tannenbaum, S. E. and Yukl, G. (1992). Training and development in organizations. *Annual Review of Psychology, 43*, 399-441.

van den Pol, R. A., Reid, D. H., and Fuqua, R. W. (1983). Peer training of safety-related skills to institutional staff: Benefits for trainers and trainees. *Journal of Applied Behavior Analysis, 16*(2), 139-156.

Van Houten, R. V. (1987). Comparing treatment techniques: A cautionary note. *Journal of Applied Behavior Analysis, 20*(1), 109-110.

Welsh, T. M., Johnson, S. P., Miller, L. K., Merrill, M. H., and Altus, D. E. (1989). A practical procedure for training meeting chairpersons. *Journal of Organizational Behavior Management, 10*(1), 151-166.

Wexley, K. W. (1984). Personnel training. *Annual Review of Psychology, 35*, 519-551.

Wilson, C., Boni, N., and Hogg, A. (1997). The effectiveness of task clarification, positive reinforcement, and corrective feedback in changing courtesy among police staff. *Journal of Organizational Behavior Management, 17*(1), 65-99.

Chapter 7

Leadership:
Behavior, Context,
and Consequences

Thomas C. Mawhinney

In what is arguably the most comprehensive published review of the leadership literature, Bass (1990) noted that leadership "is one of the world's oldest preoccupations" with its origins in history that, from a early time, "has been the study of leaders—what they did and why they did it" (p. 3). From the vantage point of radical behaviorism and the related science called behavior analysis (Baum, 1994), what leaders do is no more nor less than what any other person does. Like every other normal person, leaders engage in a lifelong stream of interactions, or exchanges, that typically occur within an apparently seamless sequence of environmental stimuli comprising physical and social environments. They react to some stimuli with respondent behavior and they take action upon others via operant behavior, including verbal operant behavior (Chapter 2, this volume). This stream constitutes a life process with demarcation of its progress readily identified by a beginning and an end, birth and death. Behavior scientists seek to partition this stream with the aim of finding answers to questions such as: "Why do people do what they do within their life streams, and if they are likely to do something again, under what conditions and when will this happen?" Answers to questions of this sort suggest why leader behavior attracts so much attention and why the life stream must be partitioned to understand how events that occur within it evoke episodes of leader behavior and maintain frequencies of these episodes.

The fact that leaders engage in behavior that can and typically does have important consequences for followers in the cultural groups they lead (Bass, 1990) largely accounts for the intense and enduring interest in the question why and under what conditions leadership occurs. In addition, within formal organizational cultures, behavior among a leader and followers can have important consequences for the larger organizational culture in which the group is embedded. Post hoc life histories and psychohistories based on analyses of leaders' life streams of behavior can be both informative and entertaining. They may even provide limited anecdotal evidence regarding why leaders do what they do when they function effectively and ineffectively as leaders. However, histories of this sort do not necessarily yield the type of causal explanations of leader behavior from which one can extract more than vague guidelines for practical action aimed at improving leadership in the present. That is not to say historical variables are useless in developing such guidelines. On the contrary, behavior analytic explanations of effective leader behavior will describe effective and ineffective occasions of leadership in terms of current environmental contingencies, the leader's history with them, and other historical factors upon which leader behavior may depend. Because behavior analytic explanations of effective leadership arise from fairly detailed descriptions of the conditions in which leader behavior is likely to occur, they hold some promise of yielding guidelines for developing effective leadership (Mawhinney and Ford, 1977; Rao and Mawhinney, 1991).

Scott and Podsakoff (1982) asserted that leadership is behavior of one person that makes a difference in the behavior of others. They went on to develop convincing arguments in support of that proposition. I have adopted the position that their work obviates the need to present and defend that proposition again. Hopefully we have moved beyond the need to defend the idea that leadership, if it is anything, is behavior that makes a difference in the behavior of others. The analyses presented here do, nevertheless, depend on the validity of that assumption.

This chapter first presents the more traditional assumptions about the causes of leadership while avoiding a detailed review of theories related to them. The causal mode of selection by consequences upon which operant-based explanations of behavioral phenomena depend is examined in terms of the three levels at which it operates. A behavioral model that summarizes variables that determine operant behavior at some moment in time is presented within the context of selection by consequences. Versions of the law of effect reflecting the vantage points of molecular contiguity-based theory and molar or correlation-based theory are examined. Leadership is defined in terms compatible with both of these theoretical orientations, i.e., molecular-contiguity and molar-correlation. After identifying what are considered necessary conditions for the evolution of leadership, a controlled laboratory experiment in which these conditions produced leadership is described. Then a field case intervention study that represents a reasonable analog of the contingencies created in the lab experiment is described and related to the lab experiment. Developments with respect to the measurement of leadership as operant behavior in field settings are reviewed in terms of several field studies. Discussion is then focused on the implications of conceptualizing leadership and measuring it as a special class of operant behavior that obeys the law of effect.

A BEHAVIOR ANALYTIC VANTAGE POINT ON LEADERSHIP

Some dominant theories of leadership locate the causes of effective leadership within leaders per se. Effective leaders are said to possess innate or, at least, not very malleable characteristics. According to this genre of leadership theory it makes little sense to invest in training and development as means to improve leadership in organizational cultures. Rather, improving leadership among work groups depends primarily on selection and placement of leaders in situations that complement behavioral traits the leaders possess that are also correlated with effective leadership. A description of leadership from the behavior analytic vantage point, on the other hand, suggests that within reasonable limits a repertoire of effective leader behavior can be reliably developed through experiences known to result in development of this behavior. This can occur because the origin of a person's behavioral repertoire in a situation and across situations is a product of the causal mode of selection by consequences. Selection by consequences can be observed in the processes of respondent or classical and operant learning and conditioning (Skinner, 1981). The behavior analytic vantage point, therefore, holds some promise of providing more specific guidelines regarding how to develop effective leader behavior among people responsible for leading work group members. This is an important consideration for appointed leaders. Whether they possess the requisite behavior repertoire to effectively lead those they have been assigned to lead or not, "Persons appointed to leadership positions have always been held accountable for the behavior of their work groups" (Scott and Podsakoff, 1982, p. 39).

SELECTION BY CONSEQUENCES AS A CAUSAL MODE

Selection by consequences is the historic causal mode well recognized for the role it plays in the origin of species by natural selection (Skinner

1981). That is, living species that have a history of surviving because their behavioral repertoire has supported life of each generation and reproduction of successive generations that have themselves successfully reproduced generation upon generation through time remain members of the community of life on Earth at this time (Lovelock, 1988). Species that fail at these tasks upon which continued life of these species depend perish from the community of living things on Earth.

Operant conditioning is another kind of selection by consequences (Skinner, 1981). It can be directly observed within *three-term environmental contingencies* or the now familiar A-B-Cs (Chapter 2, this volume). *Operant behavior* is observed in the action(s), including verbal behavior, a person takes upon the array of three-term contingencies making up the person's physical and/or social environment. *Operant conditioning* selects for *effective behavior* (that which produces reinforcers and escape from or avoidance of aversive [punishing] stimulation) within environmental contingencies, while *ineffective behavior* (that which fails to produce reinforcement) perishes from or is extinguished within those contingencies (Chapter 2). Thus, operant conditioning is a causal mode of selection by consequences that explains the origins of behavioral repertoires typically observed within and across environmental settings that remain stable with respect to three-term contingencies. What people call their "daily ritual" and "habits" are products of the overlapping processes of operant and classical or respondent conditioning. The selection processes in action are revealed each time environmental contingencies shift dramatically enough to activate the operant and respondent conditioning process.

Selection by consequences, in conjunction with operant and respondent conditioning, accounts for the *function-altering effects* of experience on operant and respondent behavior that occurs when a person first encounters a three-term environmental contingency. This is evident when the contingencies in a setting are changed enough that behavior change occurs. For example, discrimination training begins with A in some A : B $\rightarrow$ C contingency (where C = S^{R+} functions as a positive primary reinforcer) exerting no stimulus control over B and culminates with A functioning as a discriminative stimulus (S^D) and exhibiting stimulus control of the behavior. When one refers to the origins of generalized conditional positive reinforcers and punishers, such as, respectively, money and praise, and loss of money and criticism, one is de facto referring to the function-altering effects of experience. These function-altering effects of experience are directly observed in the roles played by antecedents and consequences of behavior within "contingencies of reinforcement."

The important difference between a description of three-term environmental contingencies as *environmental rules* or *E-rules* (Baum, 1973) (i.e., A : B → C) and *contingencies of reinforcement* as the *causal context of behavior* observed within E-rules (S^D : B → C = S^{R+}) is that the latter reflect a particular history of reinforcement (Skinner, 1969). That particular history includes the function-altering effects of the causal mode of selection by consequences as the observable product of operant conditioning. To the extent that this history is recorded, it provides a tangible record of behavior-environment interactions that are located in time and space. In addition, contingencies of reinforcement will reflect another critical component of experience with the environment that is not evident in a description of three-term environmental contingencies or A-B-Cs per se. That is the individual's recent history with respect to deprivation/satiation for C, particularly when C is a primary reinforcer (punisher). Deprivation/satiation and other *establishing operations* or *EO*s (Michael, 1982) have function-altering effects on otherwise neutral A : B → C environmental contingencies or E-rules. (For an example of how establishing operations determine effectiveness of a consequence as a reinforcer see Vollmer and Iwata [1991].) The EO establishes conditions that alter the function of previously neutral A : B → C contingencies so that they then function as *behavioral contingencies of reinforcement*, i.e., A = S^D : B → C = S^{R+}.

The critical role played by historic behavioral interactions with the environment is probably nowhere more apparent than in those natural social phenomena characterized by a listener's dramatic behavior change in response to the verbal behavior of a speaker whose utterances qualify as advice, requests, directives, and commands. For example, suppose that at 7:00 a.m. the listener hears a weather announcer say: "It is virtually certain to be raining in Chicago by midday." The listener will be boarding a flight from New York City, where it is predicted to be sunny all day, to arrive in Chicago just before noon and returning that evening. The person's umbrella, which would normally exert no stimulus control over the person's behavior, does so on this occasion; i.e., the person picks it up and carries it along to the airport where most people in the terminal are not carrying umbrellas. At the check-in counter for the flight to Chicago, on the other hand, most of the boarding passengers are observed to be carrying their umbrellas. This scenario exemplifies the way in which verbal statements of advice and sheer informational utterances of a speaker can evoke rule statements and rule-following behavior on the part of a listener. *Rules* are contingency-specifying stimuli or statements (CSS), such as verbal behavior of a speaker (Skinner, 1957) who gives advice at one point in time, that have function-altering effects on otherwise neutral environmental contingencies, much like the EO described above (Agnew and Redmon, 1992). In some cases, however, the function-altering effects of the CSS may occur considerably later in time than when it was first uttered. An example for two people, one who experiences a CSS and another that does not, is depicted in the following diagram:

Listener A:

Speaker's CSS: . . .[A : B $\rightarrow$ C] No Response . . . [A : B $\rightarrow$ C]: A = S^D : B $\rightarrow$ C = S^{R+}

Listener B:

No Speaker: . . .[A : B $\rightarrow$ C] No Response . . . [A : B $\rightarrow$ C] No Response to A of A-B-C

Time-----------------$\rightarrow$ ----------------------$\rightarrow$ ----------------------$\rightarrow$

This phenomenon can account for stimulus control of behavior that appears to have no cause in the environment at the moment it is observed in that environment (Agnew and Redmon, 1992). For example, many people would explain the fact that so many more people in line for a flight to Chicago are carrying umbrellas by saying that those people "think it is going to be raining in Chicago." And this could be true since most of us know that we do in fact "think" (Skinner, 1974). But why do those people in that line seem to have had the same thought? The explanation is to be found in their common experiences that day: they had tickets to fly to Chicago and all either checked the weather report on TV, in the newspaper, or via an online network service. And the various CSSs they encountered had the same function-altering effects on their behavior.

The origins of rules that effect changes in behavior at a particular moment may well reside in the person's temporally more remote environmental history with respect to rule making, rule stating, rule following, and reliability of the rules others provide them in the form of advice or directions (Galizio, 1979). Nevertheless, the follower who arrives very early to work, to other workers, can appear to engage in unexplained behavior. Unless these other people are privy to the *operative environmental history*, which is not visible in the present situation, they will see no justification within the prevailing environmental contingencies for that behavior. That unobserved history, in this example, is that the day before the early arrival the follower and the follower's leader agreed to meet and make an important decision before work that morning. Motivation and leadership theorists are inclined to fill such temporal gaps with inner causes. The popularity of cognitive theories of work motivation and leadership probably arise from the temptation to locate causes and effects contiguously in time so they will resemble the powerful ahistoric laws of classical mechanics. Past experiences that matter in the present constitute the content of a person's environmental history regardless of when the events were experienced. The physical location of any piece of environmental history that matters at the moment, however, is some unspecified change that piece of experience has wrought within the person, which has some impact on the relationship between A and B in the present (Chance, 1979; Chapter 15, this volume). Behavior analysis is, however, focused on systematic interactions between the environment and behavior of the whole individual and not the inner workings of the nervous system (Baum, 1994). Although most useful when measured and used to predict or control behavior, reinforcement history is nevertheless a valid explanatory variable. That is why a documented history of reinforcement can be very useful when one seeks to interpret the origins of stimulus control phenomena, e.g., why a person follows the advice of one person and not that of another (Galizio, 1979; Mawhinney and Ford, 1977). Nevertheless, reliably measuring the unseen forces of reinforcement history supposedly located within the individual remains a daunting task (Cole and Hopkins, 1995).

A third kind of selection by consequences accounts for the evolution and survival of cultural practices in a cultural group. Cultural practices are the typical operant repertoires through which members of a cultural group deal with one another, outsiders, and problems related to the group's survival, i.e., production of survival-related resources and reproduction of successive generations capable of surviving and reproducing themselves. Individual members can invent new practices, which can be maintained by social reinforcement from other members of the group. That is, cultural practices are learned operant behaviors transmitted from one generation to another via effects on the reinforcement history of successive generations independent of their genetic histories or natural selection. Ultimately, however, cultural practices are selected by their consequences for the group as opposed to reinforcements for individual members of the group (Skinner, 1981). Cultural groups that fail to produce the resources required to support their continued life perish from the record of living cultures. And cultural groups that fail to reproduce successive generations, either via sexual reproduction or recruiting replacements for members who depart for whatever reason, eventually do perish.

This third form of selection by consequences is implicated in rates of formal organizational founding (and rates of culture creation by legislative bodies) and death by bankruptcy (and legislative fiat or budget cutting)

(Mawhinney, 1992a). It is probably implicated in the traditional practice of either electing or appointing leaders to head organizational cultures as well as the evolution of organizational cultures under the leadership of a protagonist in what are called "great man" theories of leadership (Bass, 1990). People probably join groups led by and follow "great men" who found cultures because followers enjoy increased access to reinforcements when they do compared to when they do not. Even among primate societies, groups with strong leaders have been observed to benefit from a larger feeding range. This is evident in the restrictions of feeding range of a primate group when the leader is removed (Bass, 1990). Thus, the cultural practice of following a leader and the ability of the leader to contribute to solving the group's survival-related problems is probably selected for its consequences relative to group survival in both animal and human societies that possess a repertoire of cultural practices.

Modern formal organizational cultures typically include a supreme leader or leadership group and a network of planned and emergent leader-follower relations. The supreme leader or leadership group is held responsible for inventing or adopting practices that enhance organizational survival and adapting practices to ensure survival and prosperity of a culture's members. When environmental change occurs, however, changing practices throughout the culture will depend on the network of leaders accomplishing change among followers. Leadership at the top involves the creation and adaptation of contingent relations between the organizational culture as a whole and the survival-related consequences of behavior within the culture.

Redmon and Mason (Chapter 17, this volume) suggest that a formal organizational culture can be defined by its dominant practices. A culture may include systems and procedures designed to transmit to or train new members with respect to the dominant practices that contribute to survival of the culture and prosperity of its members. However, erstwhile functional practices can become dysfunctional, or simply not as effective, when the culture's environment undergoes change. All surviving formal organizational cultures at some moment in time have, nevertheless, satisfied one overarching imperative of living things. That is, *adapt or die* (Rummler and Brache, 1991). Within competitive organizational ecologies the imperative is lead, adapt to environmental effects of other leading cultures, create or find and adapt to a niche in which survival is possible, or die (Hannan and Freeman, 1989; Mawhinney, 1992a).

Selection by consequences within the environments populated by multiple cultures that compete for resources operates at the level of *metacontingencies* (Glenn, 1988, 1991). "A metacontingency describes how classes of practices common to a group are related to molar consequences and refers to collective practices which determine the survival of a group as a whole" (Chapter 17, this volume). Supreme leaders or leadership groups in modern formal organizational cultures are held responsible for maintaining and changing dominant practices in the cultures they lead and their molar consequences. Molar consequences include financial results among for-profit organizations (Austin et al., 1996) and service quality delivered within budgets among service agencies that depend on legislative mandates or budgets that fund their activities (Clayton et al., 1997; Langeland, Johnson, and Mawhinney, 1998). Again, however, implementation of new and adaptive practices in terms of their adoption among other members of the culture depends on a network of leaders throughout the culture.

Formal organizational cultures can have many or very few layers of appointed leaders. Most, however, will include first-line leaders or supervisors who lead those members involved in production and/or service delivery activities, leaders of these frontline leaders called middle managers, and top-level or supreme leaders who lead the middle-level managers/ leaders and other appointed leaders.

The creation of leadership roles and appointment of people to fill them is a pervasive practice in modern formal organizational cultures. The numbers of these positions may rise and fall with changing environmental contingencies and vary across organizations engaged in different tasks (e.g., hospitals and schools versus chemical processors and auto manufacturers). Organizational histories suggest, however, that the creation and survival of organizational cultures depend on some number of leadership positions being created and filled by individuals who engage in "effective leadership." Leadership per se remains, nevertheless, a product of the laws of effect operating within environmental contingencies, and leadership can, therefore, be defined and analyzed in terms of the law of effect.

CONTIGUITY- AND MOLAR CORRELATION-BASED LAWS OF EFFECT

At least three versions of the law of effect are currently recognized in the operant literature. The one that reflects selection by consequences as a causal mode (Skinner, 1981), codified in what Baum (1973, p. 142) calls the *contiguity-based law of effect*, was first stated by Thorndike (1911):

Of several responses made to the same situation [A], those [B] that are accompanied or closely followed by satisfaction [C] to the animal will, other things being equal, be more firmly connected with the situation [A], so that, when it [A] recurs, they [B] will be more likely to recur. (p. 244)

Molar accounts of the law of effect arose from attempts to quantify the concepts of response strength and determinants of it. Response strength in a behavioral situation is measured by the relative rates of operant behaviors that occur during some interval of time. Determinants of response strength are captured by the concept of reinforcement value. *Reinforcement value* arises from dimensions of feedback produced by behavior or associated with a location through some time interval. The dimensions of this feedback can include amount, delay, and rate of reinforcement produced by a focal behavior (B_1) relative to amount, rate, and delay of reinforcement produced by all other behavior (B_0) that occurs during the same time interval. Histories of deprivation and satiation with respect to primary reinforcers were typically held constant in early experimental work concerning reinforcement value among animal subjects; i.e., part of the individual subject's environmental experience was fixed or held constant. Another element of history is typically held constant in work of this type: learning with respect to antecedent stimuli. This is held constant because the focus is on accounting for strength of behavior as a function of its consequences or the reinforcement value it produces relative to other behavior and value they produce. In a summary of work on response strength as a function of consequences, Herrnstein (1970) introduced the *law of relative effect:*

$$\frac{B_1}{B_1 + B_0} = \frac{r_1}{r_1 + r_0} \qquad \text{(Eq. 1)}$$

where B_1 = rate of a focal behavior, B_0 = rate of all other behavior that occurs in a setting, r_1 = rate of reinforcement generated by the focal behavior and r_0 = rate of reinforcement generated by B_0, with all rates measured over the same time interval. Equation 1 simply states that relative rate of a behavior in a behavioral situation will match its relative rate of reinforcement in that situation. It can be considered a quantitative summary of one aspect of reinforcement history. If total amount of behavior that can occur over a time interval is assumed to remain constant, then $B_1 + B_0 = K$, and multiplying both sides of equation 1 by K yields the *matching law* (Herrnstein, 1970):

$$B_1 = K \ \frac{r_1}{r_1 + r_0} \qquad \text{(Eq. 2)}$$

The left side of the equation can be expressed as time allocated to activities, and rates of reinforcements received can be expressed as value:

$$\frac{t_1}{t_1 + t_0} = \frac{v_1}{v_1 + v_0} \qquad \text{(Eq. 3)}$$

where values of consequences, v_i, can include a combination of amount, rate, and delay of reinforcement received for a given or a particular alternative while $v_1 + v_0$ measures the total reinforcement value of the situation wherein the behavior and reinforcement occur (Baum, 1973). The effect of delayed receipt of reinforcements based on responses or time at activity can reduce the reinforcement value of the delayed reinforcements if the person is "sensitive" to such delays. (For a thorough discussion see Rachlin [1989].) Limiting time available for all activities to $T = t_1 + t_0$, permits time on activities to be predicted from or described in terms of the following relation:

$$t_1 = T \ \frac{v_1}{v_1 + v_0} \qquad \text{(Eq. 4)}$$

After critically evaluating the contiguity-based law of effect, Baum (1973) restated the law of effect in terms of evidence supporting the law of relative effect and matching law. This restatement he called the *correlation-based law of effect:* "behavior increases in frequency if the increase is correlated with an increase in rate of reinforcement or a decrease in rate of aversive stimulation" (p. 145).

Baum contends that rate of events is a universal dimension shared by behavior, reinforcers, punishers, and discriminative stimuli. When a person's behavior interacts with three-term environmental contingencies for an extended period of time, this context will include a history with rates of discriminative stimuli, reinforcers, and punishers, and the latter two may follow an operant response immediately (i.e., contiguously) or with some delay. The correlation-based law of effect works as it does, i.e., results in reinforcement in the absence of contiguity, because the individual integrates all feedback from the environmental context over time (Baum, 1973).

Understanding Baum's notions about reinforcement requires an appreciation of what he calls value of an activity in a situation, i.e., consequences correlated with rate of a behavior. The value of an activity arises from the feedback it produces in a situation, i.e., *rate of reinforcements received.* Thus, *value of an activity* is directly proportional to the rate of reinforcement it produces and duration of access to reinforcements, and may be inversely proportional to delay of reinforcement (Baum, 1973, p. 149). Value is a *molar concept* that cannot be extracted from momentary events because " . . . value depends on integrated feedback, an activity has value and changes value only over extended periods of time, and behavior changes with value only over extended periods of time" (Baum, 1973, p. 150). Deprivation can have an impact on value. But it will be reflected in value measured over time. This is due to the fact that deprivation is typically momentary, lasting only until satiation results from access to consequences, if available. Value, on the other hand, is measured across conditions of both deprivation and satiation. Because periodic momentary fluctuations in value can be studied and related to molar value (Premack, 1965, 1971), however, the study of each is compatible with the other. Thus, EOs that precipitate abrupt momentary changes in behavior in conformity with the contiguity-based law of effect, nevertheless, enter a molar relation with behavior and its consequences if the EOs occur with some frequency through time. For example, if a leader prompts a follower with some frequency and that prompting momentarily raises the value of performance-related behavior each time it occurs, rate of prompting will be correlated with rate of the behaviors. To the extent that performance monitoring by a leader has this effect, it should be correlated with increased value and increased performance. There is some empirical evidence that this relationship between leader-follower relations occurs in field settings (Komaki, 1986).

Activities have value only under specified conditions that Baum (1973) calls *behavioral situations.* These are what I have been calling *context* or *behavioral context.* Behavioral situations are the equivalent of three-term environmental contingencies of reinforcement that arise from behavior interacting with three-term environmental contingencies through time as opposed to a priori descriptions of A-B-C relations at a moment in time. The value of feedback from a situation or behavioral context depends critically on relations between activity rates in the context and rates of reinforcements correlated with those activity rates in the context. For some reinforcement schedules a feedback function exists so that consequences of alternative rates of behavior can be related, a priori, to rates of reinforcement, i.e., feedback that these activity rates will produce (Baum,

1989). The *feedback function* for ratio schedules is simply the rate of B divided by the N parameter of the FR-N schedule. A ratio schedule feedback function appears in the following equation: $v = R = B/N$ where $v =$ value of activity in the context, and $R =$ rate of reinforcement that will occur in the context *if* behavior rate B occurs.

This notion of value should prove useful to applied behavior analysts and organizational behavior management theorists and practitioners. This is because it comprehends the fact that entering and staying in a location is controlled by reinforcements received therein. That is, entering a location where reinforcements are delivered on a fixed time (FT-t) schedule of reinforcement and remaining there rather than going somewhere else occurs because length of time spent there is correlated with rate of reinforcements received there. This will be recognized as a model of wages in a work organization (Chapter 5, this volume). In addition, such work settings may include other feedback functions, e.g., interesting work, social approval of task activities, or pay-for-performance schedules. And these other feedback functions provide sources of reinforcement that add value to the context, if the person engages in these activities in addition to simply spending time there. Discriminative stimuli in this conception of reinforcement signal a change in situations or contexts and their values. Thus, the entrances to alternative behavioral situations/contexts with which the person has had experience will typically be marked by discriminative stimuli. And among verbal humans, the decision regarding which context to enter can be the subject of contemplation or rule analysis and rule-governed behavior (Agnew and Redmon, 1992; Baum, 1994; Malott, 1992; Rachlin, 1989). It is also subject to stimulus control by tacts: "Go west young man" or "Remember. Plastics!" (Or, today, "Remember. Dot coms [*.coms], the Internet, and the Web.") *Reinforcement* per se is conceived as a transition from a lower valued to a higher valued situation, while *punishment* and *extinction* are transitions in the other direction in terms of value. If leaders make rules by uttering contingency-specifying statements or de facto operationalize situations by consistently rewarding followers contingent on their effective performances, these molar correlations between leader behavior and follower rewards should show up in verbal survey reports of follower satisfaction with leaders' reward administration. And they do (Podsakoff, Tudor, and Skov, 1982).

According to the correlation-based law of effect, leaders and followers can engage in interactions that result in exchanges of reinforcement value that extend through time longer than a moment-to-moment contiguity-based tit-for-tat basis. Matthews (1977) provides an important demonstration of this fact in a clever and revealing experiment concerning dyadic exchanges. Dyad members can respond to the values of reinforcements they receive that are correlated with their relationships. They may or may not formulate and follow rules during interactions. But dyadic interactions sometimes break down in the absence of rule specifications and rule following among members of dyads (Azrin and Lindsley, 1956).

Leadership As Overlapping Leader and Follower Behavior and Value Contexts

Context as used in the remainder of the chapter will refer to the right side of equations 1, 2, 3, or 4, or some combination I shall specify. For example, because the terms on the right side of equations 1 through 4 accrue through time, they can reasonably be considered a component of one's cumulative environmental history that is extant at the moment a behavioral response occurs or an action is taken upon the environment. Although leader behavior and follower behavior can be described relative to their respective *individual contexts,* by its very nature leadership must arise from a *social relationship* or *social context.* Social interactions that constitute leadership, however, may or may not be face-to-face interactions (Rao and Mawhinney, 1991). Nevertheless, it makes little sense to speak of a leader and leadership in the absence of followers and some difference in follower behavior that is effected by leader behavior. Both leader and follower behavior are "caused" by current and past experiences with the current context in which they interact. Thus, leadership must occur within a situation comprising an overlap between the *behavioral contexts* of leader behavior and follower behavior. This contextual vantage point on leader-follower relations serves as a foundation for and the definition of leadership used in this chapter.

For purposes of subsequent conceptualizations and interpretations in this chapter, *leadership* is defined as operant behavior of one person that effects a change in the context of the operant behavior of one or more other persons and thereby changes or maintains the other persons' operant behavior. This definition does not require that the leader be aware of the effects of leader behavior on follower behavior; i.e., the leader might not be able to tact or describe how the leader's behavior has changed follower behavior even when it has. All it requires is some overlap among elements of the leader's and the followers' behavioral histories and current three-term environmental contingencies that link their current behavior and thereby result in follower behavior changes attributable to changes in leader behavior. Thus, leaders might well engage in behavior that qualifies as leadership even though the changes in follower behavior resulting from it are unintended and unanticipated by the leader. When a leader intentionally or unintentionally models behavior and this modeling as a class of operant behavior is reinforced by a follower's imitation of it, the process qualifies as leadership. Given a thorough and reliable description of what leaders do when they engage in leadership, leaders might extract from such a description behavioral rules they can follow to produce the effects on follower behavior that they would like to achieve.

NECESSARY CONDITIONS FOR LEADERSHIP

Leadership cannot occur unless conditions exist in which consequences of leader and follower behavior involve *mutual reinforcement* arising from contingencies that link their behavior and consequences of it. This can occur in many ways. For example, better performance by a follower may result in the follower obtaining more reinforcement from effective task performance per se. Thus, leader behavior, in the form of advice or contingency-specifying statements (CSSs), that better specifies what constitutes effective task performance or how to achieve the specified task performance will result in more reinforcement value derived from task performance by a follower if the follower simply follows the leader's advice. A leader can engage in activities that do not directly deliver reinforcement value to a follower but that do empower the follower to more readily gain access to reinforcement value. Leaders can also produce this sort of reinforcement value for followers by assisting them in finding solutions to task-related problems the solution of which removes an obstacle to the followers' access to reinforcement value (Mawhinney, 1992b). The leader may or may not be directly reinforced by helping a follower gain access to reinforcement value.

However, in most situations where a leader has been appointed, the leader's leader makes the leader's access to reinforcement value depend on performance of the leader's followers. And according to the law of relative effect stated in terms of time allocations, the value of a work setting will increase and the value of remaining in it will increase when more positive reinforcements are obtained therein whether they are contingent on performance or not. Thus, activities that originally formed the basis of leader behavior measured by the Ohio State leadership scales (Fleishman, 1973), i.e., the LBDQ (Schriesheim and Kerr, 1977), referred to as initiating structure and consideration, should be correlated with sources of reinforcement value received by followers arising from leader behavior in a work setting. And followers' satisfaction with overall rewards in a setting can differ in subtle ways from satisfaction derived specifically from leaders' performance-contingent versus performance-noncontingent administration of rewards (cf. Podsakoff, Tudor, and Skov, 1982).

At higher levels of formal organizational cultures, leaders make strategic and tactical decisions regarding systems of work and reward in organizations (Chapter 17, this volume). These decisions have consequences for both leaders and followers lower in the organizational hierarchy. For example, pay-for-performance systems (Abernathy, 1996) at the level of line workers can *reduce* the need for supervisors to spend time monitoring and delivering performance-contingent reinforcements. In accordance with the law of relative effect, such practices can be expected to reduce the degree to which leader behavior is involved in strengthening follower work-related behavior and performance (Kerr and Jermier, 1978; Mawhinney and Ford, 1977). On the other hand, pay systems of this sort probably increase the reinforcement value of followers initiating requests for help from leaders to remove barriers to performance that cannot be changed without assistance from appointed leaders. These remarks are intended to suggest the myriad ways in which leaders and followers can behave that qualify as leadership by the appointed leader. They also suggest a problem with survey-based correlation research in the Ohio State leadership studies tradition.

The concepts of initiating structure and consideration are operationalized in ways that reflect de facto acceptance of the proposition that what is important about leader behavior is an average leadership style that occurs in varying degrees across all followers of a given leader. Mawhinney and Ford (1977) asserted that both leader behavior and follower behavior are regulated by objective reciprocal contingencies of reinforcement. This implicates the dyad as the appropriate unit of analysis in studies of leadership, whether Mawhinney and Ford (1977) made that point or not. Rao and Mawhinney (1991) manipulated objective reciprocal contingencies of reinforcement linking leader behavior with follower receipt of reinforcements, and follower behavior with leader receipt of reinforcement, and found they could produce and eliminate high rates of leader-follower interactions across all four dyads examined in their study. They clearly showed that high rates of leader-follower interactions were a function of mutual reinforcement within dyads. However, absolute rates of interaction did vary among dyads. This result suggests that individual differences that the leaders, followers, or both brought into the objective three-term contingencies were not eliminated by experience within those contingencies.

Thus, in field settings leader behavior might be reinforced by high rates of interaction with some followers while rates of interaction with other followers might extinguish as the other followers' performances are more and more controlled by effective task performance per se. According to this view, "substitutes for leadership" (Kerr and Jermier, 1978) arise simply from reinforcements followers receive for effective task performances or simply other activities that do not depend on interactions with their leader's behavior. Although survey research is greatly complicated when aimed at revealing differentiated patterns of leader behavior across leader-follower dyads, research in the tradition of what is called leader-member exchange (LMX) has developed data that suggests leaders can and do differentiate their behavior across leader-member dyads (Schriesheim, Neider, and Scandura, 1998). Whether this arises from the causal mode of selection by consequences as outlined in this chapter, however, remains to be confirmed by research that more directly examines the role of reinforcement in leader-follower behavior exchanges in field settings.

Initial Conditions of Leadership

After stating the environmental contingencies constituting contextual requirements that are the sine qua non of leadership in controlled laboratory experiments, the relationship of these requirements to leadership was demonstrated in a laboratory experiment designed to fulfill these requirements (Rao and Mawhinney, 1991). Initial conditions of leadership are the following:

- Members of a leader-follower dyad must decide to join the same organizational unit and remain in it for some time thereafter.
- The leader must engage in face-to-face contact with the follower and emit operant behavior during some period of contact or interact behaviorally via other media, e.g., phone conversations and written communications.
- The follower's behavior (rate) must change as a consequence of the leader's operant behavior.
- Changes in follower behavior rate must be correlated with a higher rate of reinforcement value received (and therefore increase in rate), and rate of the leader's acts of leadership must be positively correlated with rate of leader's reinforcement value received and correlated with follower behavior rate changes.

These four conditions must be established in either a lab or field setting if leadership is to be created in either setting.

Creating Leadership by Creating Overlapping Leader and Follower Behavior Value Contexts

Rao and Mawhinney (1991) conducted a laboratory experiment that permitted them to isolate contingencies of mutual reinforcement. The four elements essential to development of leadership listed previously were systematically designed into conditions of this experiment. In the experiment, dyad members never saw one another.

Each person sat alone in a room facing a response panel. Response panels appear in Figure 7.1. The person appointed leader or superior faced a response panel labeled A. On its face was a black button that could be pressed and feedback counters labeled according to the source of the points that appeared on the counters during experimental conditions. The other person sat alone in an adjacent room before response panel B, into which was plugged a double-sprung trigger (to increase resistance) on a flight joystick. For purposes of their experiment, Rao and Mawhinney (1991) defined "*effective leadership* [as] . . . the difference between the rates of subordinate responding under nonsocial bureaucratic contingencies [Condition 2] and under social contingencies administered by a superior [Condition 4]" (p. 105).

This experiment was designed to model into a controlled laboratory setting the essential features and contingencies that exist when a leader's behavior is one, but not the only, source of reinforcement value received by a follower within a work setting. In this case the reinforcer used was money paid to subjects solely on the basis of points that appeared on their respective response panel. Points were exchanged for cash between each of the numerous ten-minute sessions. Eight men worked in N = 4 dyads after volunteering to work as subjects for pay. The experiments were conducted in August 1977. Minimal instructions indicated that participants could press the button (squeeze the trigger) whenever they liked and at the end of each ten-minute session they would be paid in coin for any counter points that were indicated to be worth an amount of money. During all conditions the YOUR PAY counter advanced once every thirty seconds, so twenty points accrued each session. This modeled the molar value of the participants simply remaining in the work context, which they were free to leave at any time. This molar feedback function produced hourly pay of $3.60 and $2.40 per hour respectively for the superior and subordinate.

Condition 1 included the fixed time (YOUR PAY counter) pay and feedback on the leader's and the follower's YOUR BEHAVIOR counter, which advanced once for each button press or trigger squeeze. This condition was used to determine whether performance feedback per se or fol-

FIGURE 7.1. Superior and Subordinate Response Panels

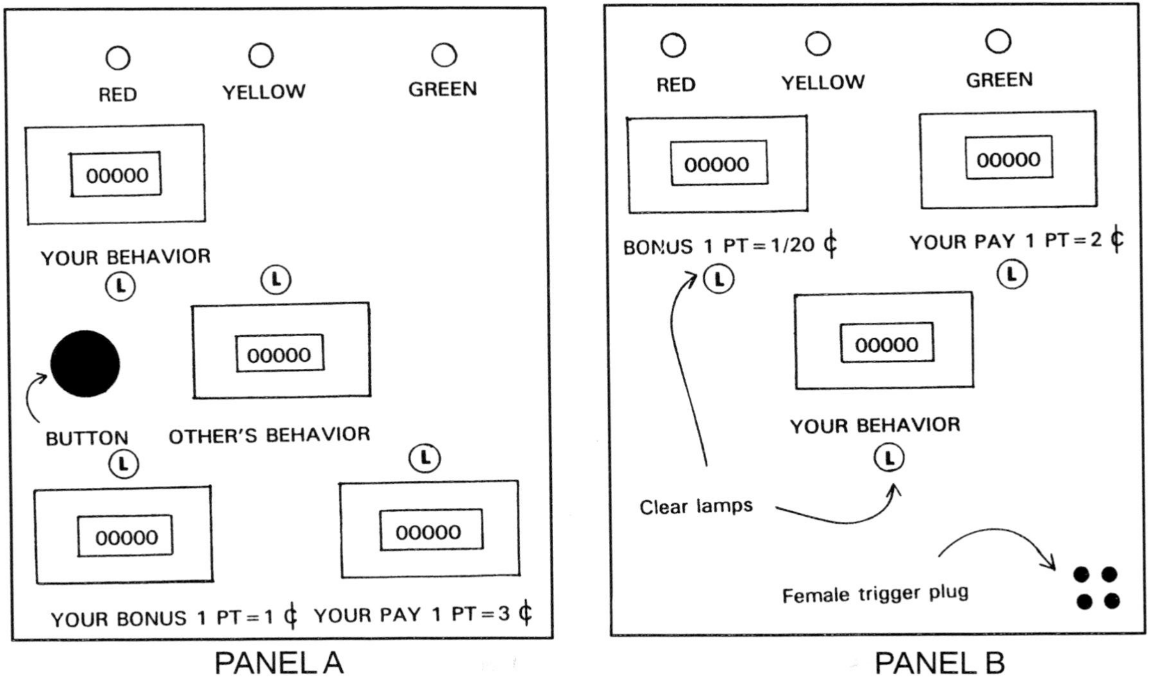

RED
YELLOW
GREEN
00000
YOUR BEHAVIOR
L
L
00000
BUTTON
OTHER'S BEHAVIOR
L
L
00000
00000
YOUR BONUS 1 PT = 1 ¢
YOUR PAY 1 PT = 3 ¢
PANEL A
RED
YELLOW
GREEN
00000
00000
BONUS 1 PT = 1/20 ¢
YOUR PAY 1 PT = 2 ¢
L
L
00000
YOUR BEHAVIOR
L
Clear lamps
Female trigger plug
PANEL B

Source: Rao and Mawhinney (1991, p. 107).

Note: The superior's panel is Panel A, and the subordinate's panel is Panel B.

lowing a self-stated rule such as "I must perform since I am earning money here" provided sources of reinforcement value associated with feedback generated by performance rates per se, i.e., rates of button pressing and trigger squeezing.

Condition 2 was identical to Condition 1 except that the superior's OTHER'S BEHAVIOR counter advanced every time the subordinate squeezed his trigger. This condition was used to determine whether this source of stimulation was associated with reinforcement value for button pressing by the superior. However, button presses by the leader would not provide stimulation of any kind to the subordinate; i.e., this was the *non-social bureaucratic contingency* referred to in the definition of effective leadership.

Condition 3 was identical to Condition 2 except that each button press by the superior advanced the subordinate's YOUR BONUS 1 PT = 1/20 cent counter by one point. This was an asymmetrical contingency in that the follower could experience an association between reinforcement value and trigger squeezing if the leader's button pressing occurred with sufficient frequency. The leader, on the other hand, could receive no monetary reinforcement value based on follower trigger squeezes.

Condition 4 was a model of what the authors called the *superior's leadership contingency*. It was identical to Condition 3 except that every nineteenth trigger squeeze by the subordinate advanced the superior's YOUR BONUS 1 PT = 1 cent counter by one count. This created a feedback function summarized by the following equation: $v = R = FB/19$, where v = value added to the work setting by reinforcement, R = rate of reinforcement delivered that depended on FB = rate of follower trigger squeezing divided by 19. Condition 4 was expected to present each dyad with a constellation of three-term environmental contingencies that would result in high superior-subordinate interaction rates if they succeeded in correlating their response rates and thereby created a condition of mutual reinforcement value exchanges through time. Mutual reinforcement would occur under these conditions if increases in follower behavior were empirically correlated with increases in leader behavior since this would ensure each person experienced a correlation between response rate and reinforcement value received from the work setting. If so, the correlation-based law of effect would select for high rates of leader and follower behavior (Herrnstein, 1970; Baum, 1973).

Conditions 5 and 6 respectively presented counts on the superior's and the subordinate's YOUR BONUS counter independent of what the other member of the dyad actually did in terms of button pressing or trigger squeezing. This "false feedback" was designed to mimic rate of feedback during the most recent session of Condition 4. The pace of interactions was "free" to vary in that it did not occur in discrete trials. Results of the experiment appear in Figure 7.2.

As the caption for Figure 7.2 indicates, one superior was subjected to a monetary response cost procedure because this superior (in Dyad D) responded at high rates across Conditions 1-4 for thirty consecutive ten-minute sessions. The correlation-based law of effect suggests that this behavior was maintained by the value of responding per se and any effect on it arising from receipt of fixed-time pay. During sessions following introduction of the response cost of 1 cent for every fifty of the superior's button presses, however, the superior-subordinate interactions in Dyad D became differentiated across conditions in much the same way as other dyads had from the start.

Data for Dyad B during the first two sessions of Condition 4 clearly indicate the consequence of a superior providing high rates of reinforcement to a subordinate uncorrelated with the subordinate's performance rate. Only when the superior slowed his responses and established a correlation between his rate of response and that of his subordinate did the subordinate's response rate begin to rise in Condition 4.

When subordinates' response rate data for Condition 2 are compared to data for Condition 4, the difference is monumental and obvious from visual inspection of Figure 7.2. Comparisons of follower response rates between Condition 2 (what we called bureaucratic contingencies) and Condition 4 (in which leadership was explicitly reinforced) make it abundantly clear that effective leadership occurred in this experiment. It was systematically produced by producing an overlap between the contexts of leader and follower behavior and access to reinforcement value. Leader and follower behavior obeyed the correlation-based law of effect (Baum, 1973).

Different feedback functions were created for the leaders in Condition 4 compared to Condition 3 by adding a contingency between the follower's behavior rate and rate of the leader's bonus reinforcements received. Each leader then established a correlation between his rate of button pressing and the rate of his followers' trigger squeezes. This molar relationship was anticipated from the logic of the correlation-based law of effect and law of relative effect (Mawhinney and Ford, 1977) and it occurred in all four dyads (Rao and Mawhinney, 1991).

Although the experimenters created these contingencies within this experiment, the experimenters' behavior could be viewed as a model of upper-level or supreme leadership in an actual organizational culture. For example, suppose that whatever dominant practices defining an organiza-

FIGURE 7.2. Rates of Superior and Subordinate Response for Each Dyad Across Conditions 1 Through 6

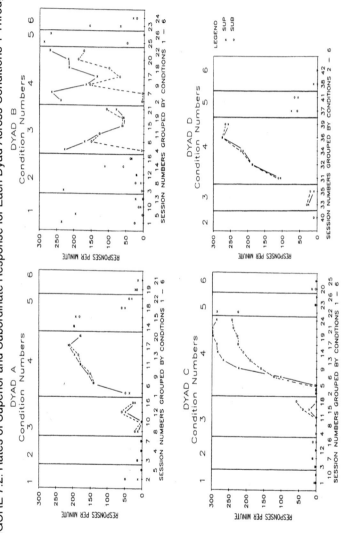

Source: Rao and Mawhinney (1991, p. 113).

Note: Condition numbers appear above the data panels within each graph. Vertical lines divide data panels. Session numbers within a condition appear under the abscissa. Condition 1 for Dyad D, and all data for this dyad are with response costs in effect for the superior. Data for the superiors are connected by solid lines and for followers by dashed lines in Conditions 3 and 4 only.

tional culture failed to support the level of efficiency or some other outcome of member behavior required to ensure survival of the culture. And suppose that an upper-level leadership decision was made to improve practices among lower-level leaders with the aim of "strengthening" the culture's metacontingencies by improving performance of these leaders' followers. What should the supreme leader do based on the theory and data presented so far in this chapter? Fortunately, an example of how these questions were answered exists in the OBM literature.

Creating Leadership by Creating Overlapping Leader-Follower Behavior Value Contexts in the Field

Organizational designers can and do arrange, sometimes in piecemeal fashion, for some of the four necessary conditions of leadership to be met in work settings. When they do not, appointed leaders may or may not be effective depending on the reinforcement history they bring with them to the work setting. Organizational designers can explicitly arrange for all four conditions to be met by making a leader's rate of reinforcement value received depend upon rate of specified follower behavior or work group accomplishments as defined by Gilbert (1978). For example, a leader's income can be made to depend on the output of his or her followers' behavior or accomplishments of the department for which the leader is the appointed head. Or over time evidence may accrue indicating that a correlation exists between those first-line leaders elevated to higher levels of leadership and histories of increased performance among their followers.

Sometime shortly before our first experiment was completed (Rao and Mawhinney, 1991; conducted during the summer of 1977), Bourdon (1977) conducted and published results of a field case study that well reflected the then-current values and traditions of OBM-based intervention research. The intervention in two manufacturing operations of a parent organization was precipitated by unsatisfactory performance as a result of ineffective management (or leadership) practices. Prior to the intervention, the work environment resembled that modeled by Contingencies 2 or 3 of the Rao and Mawhinney (1991) study. "Managers had not been significantly trained in any system of management and had developed management styles which were a function of their individual learning histories and which tended to be Theory 'X' oriented" (Bourdon, 1977, p. 23). The objective of the intervention was to train all management personnel "in the use of behavior management principles (Luthans and Kreitner, 1975; Miller, 1975) and thereby improve performance of both facilities. This was to be done using essentially positive procedures which would result in more positive and enjoyable work environments for all concerned (Bourdon, 1977, p. 23).

The theory of individual behavior developed here suggests this training would increase the similarity among management personnel with respect to their individual behavior histories and increase the likelihood these people would respond similarly to contingencies in their work environments. But the changes in their reinforcement histories arising from training would not necessarily result in use of what was learned so long as the work environment resembled Conditions 2 and 3 of the lab experiment. For their learned skills to be applied in the work environment, contingencies resembling those of Condition 4 of the Rao and Mawhinney (1991) lab experiment would be required.

Bourdon (1977) recognized the need to create a contingency that would link managers' reinforcement value received with follower performance across a variety of tasks. As he put it, "One of the major problems in applying behavior principles in a manufacturing environment with management personnel is how to equitably load positive consequences behind a myriad of complex and desired performances and performance outcomes which differ by job and by individual" (p. 23). The point system used in the intervention was, therefore, aimed at translating all performances into common values that were then administered in token system format and link them with reinforcement value received by managers. Although complexity of the intervention package meant effects of each component could not be isolated, the essential components required to produce effective leadership outlined in the four necessary conditions stated previously were included in Bourdon's intervention.

Components of his intervention appear in the following list:

- A thirty-week course in OBM methods among both line and staff personnel.
- Goal-setting sessions that included each manager, his or her immediate superior, and a training specialist.
- Goals were renegotiated with respect to improvements in efficiency, quality, attendance, and waste in each manager's area of responsibility.
- Negotiations took into account changes in time and conditions in the work setting " . . . in order to keep them equitable *and in line with current performance limitations not under the control of any individual manager* [emphasis added]" (Bourdon, 1977, p. 26).
- A point system was implemented in token economy format (Allyon and Azrin, 1968) in which points were weighted on more or less important target behaviors or accomplishments (Gilbert, 1978) among each manager's followers.

- A performance report was used to provide leaders with feedback on performance in their area of responsibility; points earned on each critical performance dimension, and their progress relative to their goals on a weekly basis. All individual reports were distributed to the plant manager, i.e., leader of leaders.
- At the tenth week of the thirty weeks of instruction in OBM methods, each manager initiated a behavior change project in his or her area; effective projects could have an impact on the performance report.
- "Reinforcers" were supposed to be points backed up by tangible items worth between $7.50 and $25.00 that could be selected from a catalog and purchased with points at prices ranging from 125 to 715 points per item.

Each of these elements of Bourdon's intervention can be associated with operant terms and concepts and contingencies created in the experiment by Rao and Mawhinney (1991). The thirty-week course in OBM methods was clearly aimed at creating a particular history of reinforcement or establishing operation (Agnew, 1998). That history should have had function-altering effects on the ways in which managers responded to their work settings as their training progressed. In particular, the ways in which they talked about work-related problems and statements they made regarding the causes of follower behavior in those settings should have changed as their training progressed. The goal-setting component in conjunction with the weekly performance report feedback seems to have satisfied several requirements Komaki and Reynard (Chapter 3, this volume) consider necessary to establish good performance criteria, which they elaborated using the SURF & C mneumonic.

As complex as they were in the field, the goal-setting procedures could be likened to telling subjects in the Rao and Mawhinney (1991) study that they could press the button and squeeze the trigger and these task activities would sometimes result in earning money. The point system, point exchange for tangible reinforcers, and weekly manager performance reporting systems are clearly analogs of the contingency that made leaders' pay depend on follower behavior in the lab study. That is because in this field study, accomplishment of some or many of each manager's goals and point earnings depended on the manager arranging conditions within which followers' activities contributed to goal accomplishments. (Also, the methods used to do this would have to be positive to avoid counter-controlling actions or aggression toward leaders by their followers [Mawhinney and Fellows-Kubert, 1999].) This is most evident in the attendance goal set by each manager; its achievement was measured in terms of followers' attendance behavior. The goals and performance reports targeted improvements in what Gilbert (1978) called accomplishments or what is of value to the organization that can be counted and remains when behavior has passed into history. Komaki and Reynard (Chapter 3) call this C, or how critical the component is to actual performance. Accomplishments are the *critical consequences* of dominant practices that strengthen survival-related metacontingencies.

Although this system was certain to produce a correlation between the managers' points earned and accomplishments, it would not produce improvements in levels of accomplishment unless the managers succeeded in changing follower behaviors that produced their accomplishment scores. These managers somehow had to, in a phenomenally more complicated setting than our lab, do what leaders in the lab study had done. They had to establish correlations among reinforcement value received by each of their followers and follower activities that had an impact on the managers' accomplishment scores.

Samples of results from this field experiment appear in Figures 7.3 and 7.4. Figure 7.3 reveals a strong correlation between points earned and attendance. This is to be expected since there is little room for ambiguity in the measurement of attendance and changes in that measure. To the eye, the correlation between points earned and efficiency is not as strong, but in neither instance was a correlation coefficient reported. Be that as it may, the more important consideration is what actually happened to measures of attendance and efficiency. In both cases measured performance improved six months into the intervention. Although it is not evident precisely how each manager was able to do it, it seems reasonable to infer that they somehow created and improved correlations between reinforcement value received among followers and followers' attendance behavior. Less clear is whether managers created greater reinforcement value or a stronger correlation between reinforcement value and follower contributions to efficiency. This is because there might have been more opportunities to change methods (Mawhinney, 1992b) to improve quality than to change follower behavior while attendance is behavior per se.

Observing and Recording Leader Behavior and Follower Performance

As a planned intervention aimed at improving leadership in a work organization, Bourdon's (1977) work provides an excellent model for others to imitate. However, it did not provide the fine-grained observations of leader-follower interactions that might shed light on which specific classes of leader operant behavior produced which effects. Studies in

FIGURE 7.3. Comparison of Point Earnings and Plantwide Performance
on Attendance

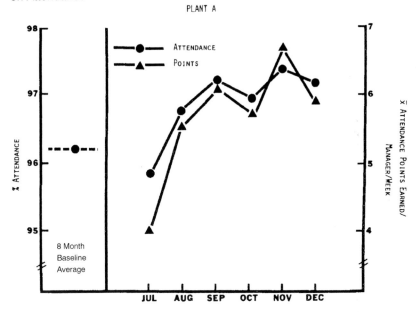

Source: Bourdon (1977, p. 31).

which Komaki's (Komaki, 1986; Komaki, Zlotnick, and Jensen, 1986)
Operant Supervisory Taxonomy Index (OSTI) are used to collect reliable
observations of leader behavior do this, but at considerable expense on the
part of researchers. The value of the taxonomy is that it permits development of reliable observations among multiple trained observers regarding
the time and frequency of a leader's operant behavior in a work setting.
Data collected with the OSTI and related protocols produce data that
might be related to the logic of the correlation-based law of effect and the
matching law.

For example, over time the matching law and correlation-based law of
effect suggest that behavior will be distributed in accordance with the
reinforcement value it generates. This would imply that managers who are
highly active in terms of interactions with followers receive more reinforcement value from those interactions. But a high rate of interactions
with followers alone should not be expected to result in a high rate of
follower performance. Merely interacting could actually reduce the time a
follower spends performing. This could be why Komaki (Komaki, 1986;

FIGURE 7.4. Comparison of Point Earnings and Plantwide Performance on Efficiency

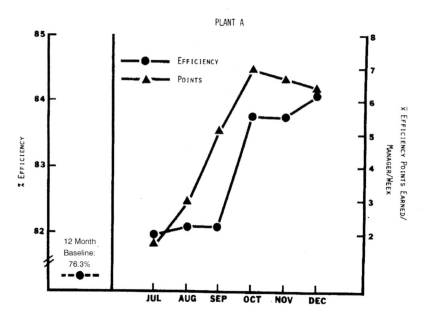

Source: Bourdon (1977, p. 31).

Komaki, Zlotnick and Jensen, 1986) found that effective managers more frequently monitored follower performance than did ineffective managers. Monitoring via personal contact can function as reinforcement per se (attention from a superior) and/or increase arousal levels, producing a type of social facilitation or audience effect (Zajonc, 1965) as a type of EO (Michael, 1982). However, attention from a manager may produce either positive reinforcement of what the follower was doing when contact was made or avoidance behavior manifest in an increased rate of performance-related behavior only so long as the leader is present (soldiering). Effectiveness of aversive consequences depend on the leader's visits occurring on a relatively unpredictable schedule (Schmitt, 1969).

The fact that Komaki, Desselles, and Bowman (1989) found correlations between order of finish among sailing crews and monitoring and feedback of consequences to crews by their captains suggests that some task settings are more likely than others to reveal relationships among the components of the OSTI and follower performance. We should also expect better relationships to occur when a leader is dealing with a new follower as opposed to a veteran group member. However, observation of this difference will depend on looking for correlations between time-series observations of leader behaviors and follower performances within dyads rather than across summaries of group data. In spite of the many contextual factors that should work against finding relations with the OSTI (e.g., those noted by Mawhinney and Ford, 1977), relationships have been found! We have not yet seen what can be made of the OSTI in the hands of behavior analysts working in the OBM traditions of data handling.

One of the most complex and revealing studies involving the OSTI was done by Methot and colleagues (1996) and published in the *Journal of Organizational Behavior Management* Special Series on Large Scale Interventions under the auspices of the series editor, Bill Hopkins (Methot et al., 1996). In this study, behavior among members of a leader-supervisor-staff-client hierarchy that included one manager, four supervisors, seven staff, and sixteen clients in a human services agency was examined within a multiple-baseline design. The intervention involved training the manager and supervisors to engage in goal setting with staff, objectively monitoring staff performance, and providing performance-contingent consequences to supervisors by the manager, to staff by the supervisors, and to clients by the staff. The OSTI was used to collect data regarding use of contingent performance consequences by the manager with supervisors, by the supervisors with their staff, and by the staff with their clients. The number of observed sessions in which supervisors and staff used performance-contingent consequences increased following training, as did manager use of performance-contingent consequences with supervisors. "Desired decreases in target behaviors occurred for 9 of 16 clients, and desired increases for 8 of 13 clients" (Methot et al., 1996, p. 4). This study suggests that the OSTI can be used not only to address questions concerning leadership, but to monitor effectiveness of training and support of training by monitoring and feeding back consequences based on observed performance. However, in this study, results of monitoring with OSTI were not fed back in order to avoid confounding this feedback with effects of the training interventions.

DISCUSSION AND CONCLUSION

Leadership in the traditions of behavior analysis and use of behavior principles by leaders, as shown in this chapter, can be integrated with respect to their roots in behavior analytic theory as well as their applied manifestations in OBM and performance management (Daniels, 1994;

Braksick, 2000). Our approach to leadership is reflected in relatively few of the 1,182 pages of the Bass (1990) compendium on the subject. Yet, operant based leadership theory and particularly its observational methodology represented by the OSTI are treated evenhandedly by Bass in 1990. The dearth of work in this tradition is no doubt due to the youth of this approach to leadership theory and research and the time-consuming observation and recording processes it requires.

The integrity of the relations between fine-grained laboratory analysis of leadership and field studies that support its generality, whether intended or not, bodes well for the field. The scope of our analyses of leadership and its context can and likely will be extended. Eventually it will encompass the higher level boundary-spanning roles involving leadership at the top and transmission of cultural change through the middle to the front lines of formal organizational life among levels roughly delineated by Redmon and Mason (Chapter 17, this volume). What will remain constant is the theory and facts about individual human behavior whether the focus is on leader, follower, or customer behavior. For example, a host of opinions exist concerning why Henry Ford resisted change in his system when confronted with the success of GM's introduction of paint color and other options to customers even though Ford lost market share. Undisputed, however, is the fact that Henry Ford had a very long history of variable and then fairly continuous and dense reinforcement for doing what he did from 1923 to 1928 while losing market share (Halberstam, 1986). An explanation in terms of reinforcement history seems worthy of consideration. It remains to be seen whether new areas of behavior analytic research such as the role that a history of partial reinforcement prior to extinction (Hantula and Crowell, 1994) and behavioral momentum (Nevin, Mandell, and Atak, 1983) might play in leader decision making (Rachlin, 1989). These phenomena have implications not only for leader decision making, but also for performance on the front line and might explain why some people perform in the absence of apparent reinforcement, at least in the short term (Chapter 5, this volume).

Methods of identifying dimensions of job performance that leaders should build into specifications of what they expect in terms of follower performance and how they evaluate it should become part of leadership training as should a focus on leadership research related to performance management (Chapter 3, this volume). What leaders turn their attention to is also important. In addition to the role of leadership in traditional topics such as follower performance, we should consider the leader's motivation as measured by one or another of equations 1 to 4. This might lead to some answers to the question of why some leaders do and others do not include organizational member health and safety among the dimensions of their organizational culture's performance. If effects on these elements of organizational performance produce no reinforcement value for a leader, the leader is unlikely to do anything that might have an impact on them. However, there is every reason to believe leaders will take responsibility for promoting these elements of culture development if their access to valued reinforcements depends on doing so (Austin et al., 1996; Chapters 8, 10, and 11, this volume).

In this chapter I have attempted to show the warp and woof of a basic laboratory analysis of leadership, the basic behavior analytic theory upon which it was founded, and how very closely the fundamental elements of the laboratory contingencies fit with and can be extended to applied field research. It has for years been my contention that maintaining relations among basic, basic applied, and fundamentally applied research in the behavior analytic, applied behavior analytic, OBM, PM, and I/O psychology traditions, represents good practice for these cultures. Hopefully, this chapter provides a modicum of support for that proposition.

REFERENCES

Abernathy, W. B. (1996). *The sin of wages.* Memphis, TN: PerfSys Press.

Agnew, J. L. (1998). The establishing operation in organizational behavior management. *Journal of Organizational Behavior Management, 18*(1), 7-19.

Agnew, J. L. and Redmon, W. K. (1992). Contingency specifying stimuli: The role of "rules" in organizational behavior management, *Journal of Organizational Behavior Management, 12*(2), 67-75.

Allyon, T. and Azrin, N. (1968). *The token economy: A motivational system for therapy and rehabilitation.* New York: Appleton-Century-Crofts.

Austin, J., Kessler, M. L., Riccobono, J. E., and Bailey, J. S. (1996). Using feedback and reinforcement to improve the performance and safety of a roofing crew. *Journal of Organizational Behavior Management, 16*(2), 49-75.

Azrin, N. H. and Lindsley, O. R. (1956). The reinforcement of cooperation between children. *Journal of Abnormal and Social Psychology, 52,* 100-102.

Bass, B. M. (1990). *Bass and Stogdill's handbook of leadership.* New York: The Free Press.

Baum, W. M. (1973). The correlation based law of effect. *Journal of the Experimental Analysis of Behavior, 20,* 137-153.

Baum, W. M. (1989). Quantitative prediction and molar description of the environment. *The Behavior Analyst, 12,* 167-176.

Baum, W. M. (1994). *Understanding behaviorism: Science, behavior, and culture.* New York: HarperCollins.

Bourdon, R. D. (1977). A token economy application to management performance improvement. *Journal of Organizational Behavior Management, 1*(1), 23-37.

Braksick, L. W. (2000). *Unlock behavior, unleash profits.* New York: The McGraw-Hill Companies.

Chance, P. (1979). *Learning and behavior.* Belmont, CA: Wadsworth Publishing.

Clayton, M. C., Mawhinney, T. C., Luke, D. E., and Cook, H. G. (1997). Improving the management of overtime costs through decentralized controls: Managing an organizational metacontingency. *Journal of Organizational Behavior Management, 17*(2), 77-98.

Cole, B. L. and Hopkins, B. L. (1995). Manipulations of the relationship between reported self-efficacy and performance. *Journal of Organizational Behavior Management, 15*(1/2), 95-135.

Daniels, A. C. (1994). *Bringing out the best in people.* New York: McGraw-Hill.

Fleishman, E. A. (1973). Twenty years of consideration and structure. In E. A. Fleishman and J. G. Hunt (Eds.), *Current developments in the study of leadership* (pp. 1-37). Carbondale: Southern Illinois University Press.

Galizio, M. (1979). Contingency-shaped and rule-governed behavior: Instructional control of human loss avoidance. *Journal of the Experimental Analysis of Behavior, 31,* 53-70.

Gilbert, T. F. (1978). *Human competence: Engineering worthy performance.* New York: McGraw-Hill.

Glenn, S. S. (1988). Contingencies and metacontingencies: Toward a synthesis of behavior analysis and cultural materialism. *The Behavior Analyst, 11,* 161-179.

Glenn, S. S. (1991). Contingencies and metacontingencies: Relations among behavioral, cultural, and biological evolution. In P. A. Lamal (Ed.), *Behavioral analysis of societies and cultural practices* (pp. 39-73). Washington, DC: Hemisphere.

Halberstam, D. (1986). *The reckoning.* New York: Avon Books.

Hannan, M. T. and Freeman, J. (1989). *Organizational ecology.* Cambridge, MA: Harvard University Press.

Hantula, D. A. and Crowell, C. R. (1994). Intermittent reinforcement and escalation processes in sequential decision making: A replication and theoretical analysis. *Journal of Organizational Behavior Management, 14,* 7-36.

Herrnstein, R. J. (1970). On the law of effect. *Journal of the Experimental Analysis of Behavior, 13,* 243-266.

Kerr, S. and Jermier, J. (1978). Substitutes for leadership: Their meaning and measurement. *Organizational Behavior and Human Performance, 22,* 374-403.

Komaki, J. L. (1986). Toward effective supervision: An operant analysis and comparison of managers at work. *Journal of Applied Psychology, 71,* 270-279.

Komaki, J. L., Desselles, M. L., and Bowman, E. D. (1989). Definitely not a breeze: Extending an operant model of effective supervision to teams. *Journal of Applied Psychology, 74,* 522-529.

Komaki, J. L., Zlotnick, S., and Jensen, M. (1986). Development of an operant-based taxonomy and observational index of supervisory behavior. *Journal of Applied Psychology, 71,* 260-269.

Langeland, K. L., Johnson, C. M., and Mawhinney, T. C. (1998). Improving staff performance in a community mental health setting: Job analysis, training, goal setting, feedback, and years of data. *Journal of Organizational Behavior Management, 18*(1), 21-43.

Lovelock, J. (1988). *The ages of Gaia: A biography of our living earth.* New York: W. W. Norton.

Luthans, F. and Kreitner, R. (1975). *Organizational behavior modification.* Glenview, IL: Scott-Foresman.

Malott, R. W. (1992). A theory of rule-governed behavior and organizational behavior management. *Journal of Organizational Behavior Management, 12*(2), 45-65.

Matthews, B. A. (1977). Magnitudes of score differences produced within sessions in a cooperative exchange procedure. *Journal of the Experimental Analysis of Behavior, 27,* 331-340.

Mawhinney, T. C. (1992a). Evolution of organizational cultures as selection by consequences: The Gaia hypothesis, metacontingencies, and organizational ecology. *Journal of Organizational Behavior Management, 12*(2), 1-26.

Mawhinney, T. C. (1992b). Total quality management and organizational behavior management: An integration for continual improvement. *Journal of Applied Behavior Analysis, 25,* 225-243.

Mawhinney, T. C. and Fellows-Kubert, C. (1999). Positive contingencies versus quotas: Telemarketers exert countercontrol. *Journal of Organizational Behavior Management, 19*(2), 35-57.

Mawhinney, T. C. and Ford, J. D. (1977). The path goal theory of leader effectiveness: An operant interpretation. *Academy of Management Review, 2,* 398-411.

Methot, L. L., Williams, W. L., Cummings, A., and Bradshaw, B. (1996). Measuring a manager-supervisor training program through generalized performance of managers, supervisors, front-line staff and clients in a human service setting. *Journal of Organizational Behavior Management, 16*(2), 3-34.

Michael, J. (1982). Distinguishing between discriminative and motivational functions of stimuli. *Journal of Experimental Analysis of Behavior, 37,* 149-155.

Miller, L. M. (1975). *Behavior management: New skills for business and industry.* Atlanta, GA: Behavioral Systems, Inc.

Nevin, J. A., Mandell, C., and Atak, J. R. (1983). The analysis of behavioral momentum. *Journal of the Experimental Analysis of Behavior, 39,* 25-47.

Podsakoff, P. M., Tudor, W. D., and Skov, R. (1982). Effect of leader contingent and noncontingent reward and punishment behaviors on subordinate performance and satisfaction. *Academy of Management Journal, 25,* 810-821.

Premack, D. (1965). Reinforcement theory. In D. Levine (Ed.), *Nebraska symposium on motivation* (pp. 123-180). Lincoln: University of Nebraska Press.

Premack, D. (1971). Catching up with common sense or two sides of a generalization: Reinforcement and punishment. In R. Glaser (Ed.), *The nature of reinforcement* (pp. 121-150) San Diego, CA: Academic Press.

Rachlin, H. (1989). *Judgement, decision, and choice.* New York: W. H. Freeman.

Rao, R. K. and Mawhinney, T. C. (1991). Superior-subordinate dyads: Dependence of leader effectiveness on mutual reinforcement contingencies. *Journal of Experimental Analysis of Behavior, 56,* 105-118.

Rummler, G. A. and Brache, A. P. (1991). *Improving performance: How to manage the white space on the organization chart.* San Francisco: Jossey-Bass.

Schmitt, D. R. (1969). Punitive supervision and productivity: An experimental analog. *Journal of Applied Psychology, 53*(3), 118-123.

Schriesheim, C. A. and Kerr, S. (1977). Theories and measures of leadership: A critical appraisal of current and future directions. In J. G. Hunt and L. L. Larson (Eds.), *Leadership: The cutting edge* (pp. 9-45). Carbondale, IL: Southern Illinois University Press.

Schriesheim, C. A., Neider, L. L., and Scandura, T. A. (1998). Delegation and leader-member exchange: Main effects, moderators, and measurement issues. *The Academy of Management Journal, 41,* 298-318.

Scott, W. E. and Podsakoff, P. M. (1982). Leadership, supervision, and behavioral control: Perspectives from an experimental analysis. In L. W. Frederiksen (Ed.), *Handbook of organizational behavior management* (pp. 39-69). New York: John Wiley and Sons.

Skinner, B. F. (1957). *Verbal behavior.* Englewood Cliffs, NJ: Prentice-Hall.

Skinner, B. F. (1969). *Contingencies of reinforcement.* New York: Meredith.

Skinner, B. F. (1974). *About behaviorism.* New York: Knopf.

Skinner, B. F. (1981). Selection by consequences. *Science, 213,* July 31, 501-504.

Thorndike, E. L. (1911). *Animal intelligence.* New York: The Macmillan Company.

Vollmer, T. R. and Iwata, B. A. (1991). Establishing operations and reinforcement effects. *Journal of Applied Behavior Analysis, 24,* 279-291.

Zajonc, R. B. (1965). Social facilitation. *Science, 149,* 264-269.

Chapter 8

The Management
of Occupational Stress

Terry A. Beehr
Steve M. Jex
Papia Ghosh

The practice of developing programs to help employees manage stress in the workplace has been on the increase over the past couple of decades, and there are currently no signs of abatement. As a research domain, however, job or occupational stress has been fraught with contradiction, confusion, and controversy. It is not always clear, for example, what occupational stress is, and terminologies often vary from one piece of literature to another (Beehr, 1991). In spite of this, most people agree that the topic is important. It is important enough to the field of organizational behavior management (OBM) that the *Journal of Organizational Behavior Management* devoted a special issue to it in 1986 (reprinted as a book; Ivancevich and Ganster, 1987).

However, a few commonalities exist among job stress researchers. In one way or another, stress is usually seen as a process in which some characteristics of work or a workplace produce harmful consequences or responses on the part of the employees. The confusion about what the term stress actually means may be a function of the wide variety of professions with interests in the topic. Each profession has tended to use its own language without much concern for consistency with other professions. Stress has commonly been defined in one of three ways: (1) as an environmental (workplace) stimulus, sometimes conceived as a force applied to the person; (2) as the person's psychological or physiological response to such stimuli; or (3) as the process in which these two events occur (e.g., Beehr and Franz, 1987; Ivancevich and Matteson, 1980; Mason, 1975). In this chapter, the third definition is used.

Furthermore, notwithstanding the somewhat philosophical "good stress-bad stress" dichotomy occasionally advocated, in practice and actual examples, the responses that are linked to work-related stressors are usually harmful or at least aversive to the person. The idea of "good" stress has two meanings in the literature. Sometimes it refers to the stressor, and in these cases it is sometimes termed "opportunity stress" (e.g., Beehr and Schuler, 1982), in which case it usually means that the work situation has presented the individual with a situation that would be judged by most people to be an opportunity for something good. Even these situations can potentially lead to stress-related illnesses, however. In other cases, the presumed causal situation might be judged either good or bad, but the reaction of the person is good (e.g., we can benefit in health and well-being from having experienced a bad situation). Selye's popular concept, "eustress," has been used to mean either of these, although it seems that he primarily meant the latter in his 1976 book. This seems to be another source of confusion. Is eustress a presumed good event that causes a bad response, or is it a bad environment that causes a good response? We will not try to resolve this confusion here, but will instead simply warn readers about it.

One consequence of defining stress as a situation in which environmental stimuli lead to deleterious individual responses is that stress refers to no single variable or even to a single class of variables. Instead, it refers to a process involving time and cumulative effects of environmental events that lead to poor individual health or welfare. Thus, occupational stress is a process in which stimuli in the work place cause employees to experience serious psychological discomfort or ill health.

The classes of variables must, of course, have labels in order to discuss them. Consistent with some past research and writing, the terms *stressor* and *strain* are used in this chapter. The job or organizational characteristics or stimuli that cause the problem are labeled stressors, and the individual's ill health or the response, be it physical, psychological, or behavioral, is labeled strain (Beehr, 1991). Thus, in the job stress process, stressors in the work environment lead to strain in the individual.

Job stressors that have commonly been studied in organizational psychology include role stressors (e.g., role overload, role conflict, role ambiguity), various forms of control (e.g., perceived control, lack of autonomy, machine pacing, lack of participation in decision making), constraints (e.g., lack of adequate supplies, equipment, or tools, and budget cuts) and shift work (Jex and Beehr, 1991). This list, however, is by no means exhaustive.

Individual strains that have been linked with these job stressors are often classified as psychological or emotional, physical or physiological, and behavioral. Psychological strains include increased depression, emotional exhaustion and "burnout," job alienation, frustration and anxiety, hostility, and turnover intentions. For measurement purposes people are nearly always asked directly about these states, usually in a self-report questionnaire, but sometimes in an interview.

Though not as frequently researched as psychological strains, the physical effects of job-related stress are considered very important. In fact, most assessments of the dollar cost of job-related stress (e.g., Ivancevich and Matteson, 1980) are based on the premise that many instances of employees' ill health are stress related. As with psychological strains, the physical effects of job-related stressors also have been assessed primarily by means of self-reports. Sometimes physicians' reports are used to assess physical symptoms, but it is not clear that the self-reports are empirically related to physician reports of the same symptoms (Costa and McCrae, 1987), although they have been shown to be related to visits to physicians and taking medication (e.g., Caplan et al., 1975; Spector, Dwyer, and Jex, 1988). It has even been argued that, since physicians' notes about patients' symptoms are likely to be related to what the patients report to them (e.g., "Doc, I have a headache and a sore back"; Frese, 1985), self-reported symptoms are just as valid as physician diagnoses. Typically, research participants in these field studies are asked whether they have experienced headaches, chest pains, or other symptoms that are thought to be stress related.

A somewhat less common method of assessing physical strain in studies of occupational stress is to measure stress-related physiological changes that are believed to be risk factors or precursors of more serious disease conditions. Common examples include cardiovascular disease symptoms (e.g., high blood pressure, elevated heart rate, and serum cholesterol levels) and more general biochemical symptoms (e.g., elevated catecholamine levels, lowered immune functioning). In contrast to the self-reported symptoms of strains, some of these effects can occur without the person realizing it. It would be hard to argue for the validity of self-reports of these. In some of his writings, Selye (1976) had considered certain hormonal responses, such as secretions of catecholamines, to be the common element of stress, although he also posited that there were biochemical "first mediators" that occurred before and led to these responses. These have never been clearly identified, however. Measures of these physical strains are usually correlated with job stressors to see whether job conditions might have affected people physiologically.

Work-related stress may also play a role in the etiology and expression of cardiovascular disease (both directly and through cigarette smoking), cancer, stroke, chronic lung disease, pneumonia, influenza, diabetes, and liver cirrhosis (e.g., Quick, Horn, and Quick, 1987). While it seems obvious at first blush that actual physiological measurement of physical strains should be superior, there are enough measurement problems to suggest that the obvious may not be true in this case. For example, Fried, Rowland, and Ferris (1984) noted that there is more than one way to measure many of the physiological responses, that both stable and transitory factors influence many physiological measures in addition to stressful stimuli in the workplace, and that the appropriate timing of measurement is very important if one is to have firm evidence that the response is related to a given workplace stimulus.

The behavioral strains or reactions to job-related stressors have been the least studied of all outcomes. Examples of these include behaviors that are deemed harmful to the individual (often an assumption made by the investigator), just as the psychological and physiological strains are deemed harmful to the individual. While harmfulness can be debated and is perhaps partially in the eye of the beholder, examples might include assumed self-destructive behaviors such as substance abuse, overeating, marital discord, and suicide.

JOB SATISFACTION

In the fields of organizational psychology and organizational behavior, one psychological response to the work environment probably has a longer history of research than any other—job satisfaction. This has not been the case in the field of OBM, however, and it is easy to discern the probable reason. The job satisfaction that is usually studied is an internal construct, which is outside the preferred bounds of OBM.

Low satisfaction, or job dissatisfaction, would seem to be an aversive psychological reaction to job stimuli, and many job stress studies have included it as a criterion variable. It is therefore important to understand what job satisfaction is and what its relationship to job stress might be.

Job satisfaction is most often defined as a pleasurable emotional state associated with one's job or job situation (Locke, 1976). For some, the construct of job satisfaction seems to be viewed as an end in itself, since positive emotional states are presumed pleasurable and reinforcing. Some studies, however, have also reported that pencil-and-paper measures of satisfaction might be related to measures of other attitudinal constructs such as life satisfaction, and to somewhat more observable outcomes such as physical health, longevity, mental health, turnover, and, to a lesser extent, absenteeism (Carsten and Spector, 1987; Hanisch and Hulin, 1991; Locke, 1976). Field research and theory indicate that job satisfaction is negatively associated with strains. Job satisfaction is, in turn, presumably at least partially caused by job characteristics (e.g., autonomy, variety, feedback, identity, and significance). It has been tempting, therefore, to call these job characteristics stressors, according to the current definition. Although filling in blanks on a survey about job satisfaction is a behavior, the construct people presume that what it measures is a far cry from an observable behavior. It is interesting, therefore, to note that some OBM-oriented researchers have called for the inclusion of job satisfaction in their OBM studies (e.g., Mawhinney, 1984).

Job satisfaction might represent antecedents to an employee's current situation, for example, the employee's past reinforcement history on the present or former jobs (Mawhinney, 1989). As such it might be a practical, shorthand way of estimating what the employee's behavior might be if it were not constrained by external forces currently in operation. A good example is provided by a study in which a snowstorm in Chicago provided a legitimate excuse (i.e., lifted the constraints on attendance or absenteeism) for people to be absent from work. A comparison, good-weather group in New York on the same day retained whatever normal constraints on absenteeism the organization's employees experience (Smith, 1977). For the Chicago group, the correlations between facets of job satisfaction and absenteeism were much stronger than they were for the New York group, whose constraints remained in place. Creative research on job satisfaction may yet show its value in predicting behaviors in the situations. It might show that job satisfaction is a practical substitute for knowledge about subjects' previous histories. It would then become a useful tool for OBM researchers. Occupational stress researchers from orientations other than OBM have been even more prone to include measures of job satisfaction in their studies, although not usually as the sole criterion measure. Examples can be drawn from our own research (e.g., Jex, Beehr, and Roberts, 1992; Spector, Dwyer, and Jex, 1988; Kaufmann and Beehr, 1986).

Is job dissatisfaction by itself truly a strain, however? The answer to this question is debatable, but we contend that, for conceptual clarity, it should not be considered a strain. According to the reasoning above, it might be an intervening variable in a process in which job stressors lead to employees' reports of job dissatisfaction, which then lead to strains. If job dissatisfaction were the only outcome associated with some job characteristics, job stress would not exist. Instead, we would only have job dissatisfaction, and we may or may not have any observable consequences that could indicate stress. Job satisfaction, while studied for decades before job stress became a popular issue, also differs from strains in an important way. Strains are more serious than job dissatisfaction alone. High levels of job-related anxiety or depression, for example, can be severe clinical disorders related to behavioral problems. It is unlikely that the same can be said for the construct of job dissatisfaction. Stress, by definition, leads to more serious problems than dissatisfaction, and dissatisfaction, by itself, cannot be taken as a good indicator that job stress exists.

We argue on the basis of the content of job stress theories that job satisfaction, while it might be an estimate of past experiences (Mawhinney, 1989), should not be considered a strain. We have no argument against including it as an additional variable in job stress studies, however. In fact, it might very well contribute useful information, just as it may make sense to include measures of job performance in job stress studies, even though performance is not a strain. A problem specific to job satisfaction, however, is measurement. A convincing sort of measure might start by observing what each individual would choose to spend his or her unconstrained time doing, that is, in a free operant situation. This would give insight into the person's ideal world, a world in which one could maximize one's values received. Then the discrepancy between this ideal and the actual value received would make sense as a measure of satisfaction (Mawhinney, 1984). The difficulty of doing this in an ongoing organization and on a large scale (i.e., over a large number of employees) is probably what has kept OBM research from adopting this approach very often.

THE MEASUREMENT OF JOB STRESSORS

Measurement has always been an important issue in organizational stress research. As in the general stress literature (i.e., the so-called life stress literature), there has been a great reliance on self-report measures. This reflects the fact that the majority of occupational stress theories focus heavily on the subjective experiences of the person under stress at nearly all points in the stress process. One of the best-known theories of stress (not necessarily *occupational* stress in particular, however) contends that individuals must appraise a stimulus or situation as threatening in order for it to be stressful (e.g., Lazarus, 1966). With cognitive appraisal as part of the definition, the person must necessarily be aware of the stressor. The focus of Lazarus's work, however, is coping with stressors. In coping, individuals take some overt action (e.g., removing the stressor, learning to live with the stressor) presumed to be aimed at alleviating the potential harm due to stressors. For coping to occur, a person would logically have to perceive some reason to do it—threat, for example. We would argue that, while conscious awareness is necessary for individuals to mobilize coping efforts, it may not really be necessary for stressors to have an impact. Thus, measurement through self-reports aimed at assessing cognitive awareness of potentially stressful work situations is not necessary in principle, in spite of its prevalence as a method of measurement in past occupational stress research.

Often, self-reports such as questionnaires and interviews are used to measure both stressors and strains in nonexperimental field studies. In studies of interventions or treatments of occupational stress, however, the treatment is usually some manipulation rather than a self-reported variable, and the research designs are experimental or at least quasi-experimental. Although many laboratory experiments treat bodily responses, studies that more clearly are related to occupational stress still usually measure strains subjectively by self-reports of the person. Although self-reports of responses to potentially stressful environmental stimuli have a long history in stress-related fields of psychology (e.g., they are deemed "necessary" but not sufficient by Poppen, 1988), they usually are not related strongly enough to behavioral or physiological measures to serve as a substitute for them.

APPROACHES TO THE TREATMENT
OF OCCUPATIONAL STRESS

At least four identifiable research and professional approaches to the study and treatment of occupational stress exist, which can be roughly classified by their field of origin: medical, clinical or counseling psychology, engineering psychology, and organizational psychology (Beehr and Franz, 1987). These four groups can be described in terms of whether the primary target of treatment is the individual or the individual's environment within the organization. Individually targeted treatments are those that attempt to change some characteristic or response of the individual directly (e.g., strains; Newman and Beehr, 1979). Organizationally targeted treatments, on the other hand, attempt to directly alter some aspect of the organization or the individual's work environment (e.g., stressors). The organizationally targeted stress treatments often are ultimately aimed at changing individuals' strain responses, but they do so by changing the individuals' environment. Each of the four approaches is described below.

The medical and clinical/counseling psychology approaches to treating occupational stress have typically focused on treating the individual directly. These approaches are similar in that they both implicitly adhere to a medical model of stress (Reynolds and Shapiro, 1991). That is, stressor stimuli are viewed as pathogenic agents which lead to disease responses (strains) in the individual. Like the physician, the aim of these treatments is to eliminate or manage the disease conditions rather than to eliminate the stressors. These approaches differ, however, in that the medical approach focuses on physical disease (e.g., cardiovascular disease) while the clinical/counseling psychology approach focuses on psychological disorders (e.g., depression).

The engineering psychology approach tends to focus on physical characteristics of the work or the workplace as stressors and on job performance as the primary outcome. This approach is often aimed at changing the physical design of the work and workplace as treatments. These physical characteristics would most often be physical stressors in the present terminology. A distinct feature of this approach is the concept of job performance as the primary outcome. But job performance does not fit the general definition of strain offered here, because it is not a psychological or physiological health-type outcome of primary importance to the individual. Instead, job performance is of primary importance to the organization (Beehr and Newman, 1978).

The organizational psychology approach aims to discover the psychological stressors associated with strains (in contrast to the engineering psychology approach, which emphasizes physical characteristics of the work or workplace as stressors). In the organizational psychology approach, treatments usually target workplace characteristics believed to be stressors, i.e., to produce strains. This approach is seldom used even though it is recommended more and more frequently (Ganster et al., 1982; Ilgen, 1990; Martin, 1992; Newman and Beehr, 1979). Among the few examples are (1) a quasi-experimental study by Jackson (1983, 1984) in which supervisors' leadership behaviors were altered and (2) a report that Johnson and Johnson's Live for Life program has at least the possibility of making available some kind of boss-subordinate relations training (Wilbur, Hartwell, and Piserchia, 1986). These treatments could alleviate occupational stress if the supervisors had been sources of stressors—for example, if they had provided ambiguous or conflicting directions. Regardless of the target, the aim is to remove the psychological stressors therein (and not the physical stressors; Beehr and Franz, 1987). Since the job stressors of interest here are psychological (e.g., pressure to perform) rather than physical (e.g., heat), their measurement has always been subject to debate. It should be noted that there is overlap among these four approaches to occupational stress; that is, some studies combine them.

The various approaches to occupational stress recall the biopsychosocial approach to behavioral medicine advocated by Schwartz (1982). Different disciplines might each be looking at different parts of a single, whole stress process. On the other hand, they might actually be studying quite different things but using the same term, "stress." For example, the engineering psychology approach includes no obvious reference to illness or medicine. Cross-disciplinary research is necessary to illuminate this issue. At any rate, in organizational psychology, the stressors are usually social-environmental, and the strains, as previously noted, are assumed to be behavioral, psychological, and physiological.

TREATMENTS FOR OCCUPATIONAL STRESS

Various strategies or treatments are available for handling job-related stress. The focus here will be on *behavioral* treatments. We define a behavioral treatment as one that either directly or indirectly uses some learning paradigm or principle (i.e., reinforcement, classical conditioning, systematic desensitization) to mitigate the effects of job-related stress. This definition is admittedly broad. We would prefer to add to the definition that (1) the outcomes studied should be observable behaviors or measurable physiological responses and (2) the stimulus originally eliciting those responses should be a stressor in the work environment. However, in doing so, we would be left with virtually no published empirical studies to discuss as examples. We focused primarily on behavioral principles on the intervention side, secondarily on evidence for environmental stressors, and, least of all on behavioral outcomes.

In practice, many occupational stress treatments that use learning principles in the implementation of the treatment are purportedly aimed at both behaviors and unseen constructs. We felt it desirable to be somewhat broad, since few stress management treatments are "purely" behavioral (i.e., both use learning principles and are aimed only at changing observable behavior). Locating studies that employ all three of our ideal criteria, i.e., using learning principles in implementing the treatment, using behaviors as outcomes, and having evidence that environmental stressors play a role, was almost impossible.

Elsewhere (Beehr and Newman, 1978), occupational stress management treatments, behaviorally based and otherwise, have been viewed from three different perspectives: (1) by whom the adaptive responses are made (by the person or stressee, by the person's work organization, or by some person or organization outside the organization); (2) by the nature and timing of the responses before or after stress occurs (preventive or curative); or (3) by the primary target of the adaptive responses (the individual or the organization) (Newman and Beehr, 1979). In this chapter one of these three is used to organize the following discussion of treatments: the primary target. This dichotomy, organizational versus individual targets, was chosen because it effectively emphasizes the nature of current practices and the apparent omission of some practices.

Individually Targeted Treatments

Individually targeted interventions have dominated the practice of occupational stress treatment (Martin, 1992; Murphy, 1987; Newman and Beehr, 1979). This is not surprising, since work by occupational stress professionals is typically guided by a medical model of stress. Like medical treatments, these occupational stress interventions are aimed directly at reducing individuals' symptoms that are commonly associated with work-related stressors. Johnson and Johnson's Live for Life (Wilbur, Hartwell, and Piserchia, 1986) and Control Data's Staywell (Naditch, 1986) programs, and countless other examples of wellness programs, corporate fitness programs, and employee assistance programs, focus almost entirely on changing the individual and leaving the presumably stress-producing stimuli in the working environment alone.

Incompatible Calming Responses

One group of treatments might be classified as attempts to calm the person by directly reducing the strength of physical or physiological responses that are strains or are thought to lead to strains. The idea of incompatible responses comes from social psychological research on aggression, which has shown that people are less likely to be aggressive when they are happy or in good moods (Baron, 1976). That is, the two responses (e.g., happiness and aggression) are incompatible. Jacobson (1938) long ago showed the potential for people to control their physiological tension responses, and Wolpe (1990) revived it and elaborated the theory for it.

Treatments of this type today include biofeedback training, relaxation training, and some meditation techniques. If job stress leads to potentially harmful, tension-related, physical strain responses, then calmness will be an incompatible response. This incompatible response is induced, and the person is reinforced by the feeling of calm. One can learn to bring about this calming response by oneself, and avoid some of the aversive tension-related effects of job stress.

Biofeedback training does this by giving a person almost instant feedback via electric instrument displays showing his or her bodily responses until they are brought under self-control. Relaxation training does this by teaching people to sense the feedback from their own bodies (e.g., muscle tension). By learned relaxation, reciprocal inhibition leads to the extinction of the connection between environmental stressor stimuli and tension responses. Meditation often has mystical trappings, but the essence of calming oneself remains; in this case the person often is taught to provide his or her own stimuli (e.g., focusing on a word or phrase) that serve to distract from the stress-producing stimuli in the environment.

Such calming techniques have been among the dominant stress treatments in practice. They would seem to work best if a person can learn to induce the response quickly and efficiently under stressful circumstances. If the private tension created by job stressors can become a discriminative stimulus signaling an appropriate time to respond with the incompatible calming response, and if this calming response alleviates the potentially harmful effects of the stress response, then the technique should be successful. Furthermore, the relief may become self-reinforcing relative to the tension produced by the job and strengthen behaviors involved in relaxation through negative reinforcement.

A survey of ninety-six research and practitioner experts in occupational stress management found that they rated relaxation training the most practical of six individually targeted treatments (Bellarosa and Chen, 1997). That is, for criteria such as cost, ease of implementation, and acceptance by employers and employees, it was judged very favorably. They also thought it ranked second overall on effectiveness criteria. Meditation was ranked fourth on practicality criteria and was especially low-rated on acceptance and popularity. It was also judged least effective of the individually targeted treatments.

Changing Voluntary Behaviors

A second set of treatments focuses on what are considered voluntary behaviors. A simple one, but one that is likely to be effective in limited circumstances, is withdrawal. If some aspects of the job situation are stressful, then the person can learn to escape or avoid those situations. This can work well only when the person can perform his or her job adequately without being in the stressful situation. Withdrawal might be maintained by the negative reinforcement of removing oneself from the stressful situation. Examples may include judicious use of vacation time and sick leave, or by an office worker simply maneuvering to obtain an office or desk away from most of the stressful action, or taking employment in relatively less stressful jobs.

Another set of voluntary behaviors includes changing one's lifestyle in various ways. One example, coming directly from the stress literature, is to change from Type A to Type B behaviors. The Type A behaviors of hurrying, aggressiveness, and especially hostility have been linked to coronary heart disease and therefore are considered a stressful behavioral style (e.g., Booth-Keweley and Friedman, 1987; Friedman and Rosenman, 1974). Changing to a calmer Type B behavioral style should therefore result in better health. This behavioral change would no doubt require teaching to acquire the new behaviors and reinforcement of these behaviors for maintenance. Very few studies have attempted to manipulate Type A behavior—and ultimately heart disease. A review of the few studies done so far provides encouraging evidence that Type A behavior can be altered, at least among white males and for durations up to several months (Thoresen and Powell, 1992). Furthermore, the effects of doing so on physiological measures are also encouraging. There is, however, a need for more research before a confident statement can be made about the viability of this approach to treating stress.

Still other behavioral changes that might help to reduce the harmful effects of job stress include alterations in diet and increased exercise. In spite of apparent national obsessions with dieting and exercise of all types, the difficulties of maintaining dieting behaviors and exercise are legendary (Dishman and Gettman, 1980; Dishman, Ickes, and Morgan, 1980). One might surmise that these treatments are not often self-reinforcing. At a minimum the naturally occurring reinforcements for dieting and exercise might be long-delayed, making them less powerful than the competing, more immediate reinforcers accompanying less desirable behaviors (e.g., binging or resting). Implementation of diet or exercise programs might therefore require the addition of some form of immediate extrinsic reinforcement for some people.

Imagery and Cognitive Behavior Modification

A number of treatments are aimed at changing or modifying individuals' cognitions through the combined use of behavioral principles and cognitive imagery. According to Beech, Burns, and Sheffield (1982), a number of cognitive distortions serve to exacerbate the effects of work-related stressors. For example, individuals may personalize the effects of stressors, or perhaps magnify the importance of stressful events. Treatments allowing for this are designed to replace these unhealthy cognitions with ones that will facilitate coping.

The best-known treatment of this type is Meichenbaum's (1977) stress inoculation training. This treatment consists of three distinct phases. First, an educational phase introduces the person to the concept of stress and provides a conceptual framework with which to understand the other phases of the treatment. Second, the individual learns and rehearses various coping strategies, which are usually taught in the form of self-statements one can use during episodes of stress. For example, when confronted with a stressor, one might say to oneself, "One step at a time; you can handle the situation" (Meichenbaum, 1977, p. 155). The final step in this treatment is referred to as application training. This simply involves applying the self-statements learned in the second phase in everyday situations. If this treatment is successful, an individual will learn, in the presence of stressful stimuli, to replace nonfunctional self-statements with those that facilitate coping.

Other similar forms of cognitive behavioral treatments include an approach developed by Goldfried (1971) in which individuals visualize stressful situations and are trained to "relax away" anxiety. Similarly, Langer, Janis, and Wolper (1975) trained individuals to use coping devices such as cognitive reappraisal of stressful events, calming self-talk, and cognitive control through selective attention. Finally, Suinn and Richardson (1971) have developed an approach similar to Goldfried's in which individuals learn to apply relaxation training to imagined stressful situations.

The occupational stress experts surveyed by Bellarosa and Chen (1997) ranked stress inoculation last (among six individually targeted treatments) on many practicality criteria, such as ease of implementation and acceptance, and fourth of six in effectiveness. They believed cognitive restructuring was the third most practical and also the third most effective.

Organizationally Targeted Treatments

Stress treatments oriented toward changing stressors in an organization have rarely been reported (e.g., Newman and Beehr, 1979; Ivancevich, 1987). Such treatments might include changing the organizational structure by decentralizing or by reducing levels of the hierarchy, changing the reward system, changing the distribution of resources, changing the personnel policies and programs, developing better communication systems, using temporary work groups, using participative decision making, redesigning individuals' jobs, and so on (Newman and Beehr, 1979). Unfortunately, little empirical research has documented the application of these strategies in organizational settings. Two exceptions, discussed here, are job redesign and participative decision making. Even when applied, however, these techniques are rarely, if ever, portrayed as means of stress management or evaluated in terms of stress outcomes.

Job Redesign

Job redesign is any systematic attempt to change the essential characteristics of a person's job. Most job redesign efforts today are guided by Hackman and Oldham's (1980) job characteristics theory, which states that jobs possessing high levels of autonomy, task variety, task identity, task significance, and feedback will lead to high levels of job satisfaction and motivation, quality work performance, and low levels of withdrawal. One of the job characteristics, autonomy, has been shown to correlate negatively with role ambiguity (meta-analysis by Jackson and Schuler, 1985). It is easy to suppose that jobs with more autonomy allow people to define or redefine their own jobs to some extent, which could reduce or prevent ambiguity. This is theoretically significant, because jobs characterized by role ambiguity have been consistently linked with employees' strain reactions (noted by Miller and Pfohl, 1982; and supported in meta-analyses by Fisher and Gitelson, 1983; Jackson and Schuler, 1985).

According to Hackman and Oldham (1980), a number of job redesign strategies can be used to increase levels of the previously mentioned job characteristics. Chief among these is *vertical loading,* which involves giving employees more control over how their jobs are performed. Other strategies include combining smaller tasks into a larger, more meaningful task, forming natural work units (e.g., a clerk handling all the accounts for a particular client), allowing employees to establish relationships with customers, and creating situations where employees can obtain immediate feedback on their performance (e.g., an employee performing his or her own quality control).

More recently, Campion and Thayer (1985) have developed an *interdisciplinary* approach to the redesign of work. Specifically, in addition to organizational psychology, they consider the perspectives of industrial engineering, ergonomics, and biology in the design and redesign of jobs. Their contention is that job redesign approaches such as Hackman and Oldham's (1980), with an emphasis on outcomes such as motivation and job satisfaction, ignore outcomes such as efficiency and the physical comfort of the job incumbent. It is only a short leap to argue that health, including strain or ill health, is also ignored as an outcome, but should not be.

Participative Decision Making

Participative decision making can be defined as an organizational mode of decision making whereby those who will be executing or carrying out decisions have a say in formulating those decisions (Lowin, 1968). One of the intended effects of increased participation in decision making is an increased perception of control on the part of employees. Increased perceptions of control have been negatively associated with a number of job-related strains (Spector, 1986).

A study by Jackson (1983, 1984) provides evidence that participative decision making can be used to ameliorate the effects of job-related stressors. In this study, participation was increased by having work groups increase the number of group meetings per month. In addition, work group supervisors were given training aimed at increasing the level of their skills required to facilitate high rates of participation among work group members. Employees reported lower levels of role stressors and emotional strain following these changes in meeting frequency and supervisory training.

Like job redesign, applications of participative decision making have rarely been portrayed as stress management treatments. Nevertheless, the effects of such applications could qualify them as such. Interestingly, this organizationally targeted approach meshes nicely with some behavioral principles in that it is an attempt to reduce or eliminate the stimuli presumed to cause strain responses. Yet, participative decision making is rarely implemented to achieve the objective of stress control and reduction.

Evaluation of Stress Management Treatments

In this section, selected studies that have evaluated stress management treatments are summarized. Although we touch on the issue of effectiveness, our major objective is to describe recent trends in the use of behavioral stress management treatments in organizations.

A summary of recent studies employing behavioral stress management treatments is presented in Table 8.1. They were identified through a search of the PsychLit database. Specifically, we cross-referenced the key words "stress management" and "occupational stress" to identify studies from the past ten years. Literature reviews and studies employing treatments that were either not aimed at changing behavior or did not use learning principles (e.g., systematic reinforcement, conditioning) were eliminated. For each study, the following information is included: authors and year, sample composition, stress management treatments utilized, criterion measures, whether or not stressors were measured, and the conclusions regarding the effectiveness of the treatments.

As can be seen in Table 8.1, the samples represent a variety of occupations. It is obvious, however, that nurses and especially teachers are more heavily represented than other occupations. This is not surprising, given that many studies of occupational stress have focused on these occupations (e.g., Motowidlow, Packard, and Manning, 1986). We suspect that it is also because (1) these occupations are assumed to be stressful, given

TABLE 8.1. Selected Reports of Occupational Stress Management Treatments

Authors and Year	Sample and Design	Intervention/ Independent Variable/ Treatment
Bertoch et al. (1989)	Thirty middle and high school teachers chosen based on their high "stress" levels Random assignment to one treatment and one control group Pre-post tests	1. "Twelve two-hour sessions including lecture-discussion, small-group sharing of progress and problems, audiovisual presentations, written test evaluation, and homework." In some of the sessions, relaxation and breathing, meditation exercises, concepts of nutrition, etc., were introduced 2. No treatment control group
Cecil and Forman (1990)	Fifty-four regular classroom teachers from elementary and middle schools Random assignment to two treatment and one control groups Pre-post tests plus four-week follow-up	1. Stress inoculation training 2. Co-worker support group
Cullen and Sandberg (1987)	Male technical staff of Irish telecom industry (N = unknown) Nonrandom assignment to three treatment and one control groups Pre-post tests	1. Redeployment 2. Training for new technology 3. Working with new technology 4. No treatment control group
Firth and Shapiro (1986)	Forty managerial professional workers seeking clinical help for severe "job-related distress" Random assignment to two treatment groups with switching treatments Tests before, between, and after treatments plus thirteen-week follow-up	1. "Prescriptive therapy" representing cognitive and multimodal behavioral therapies 2. "Exploratory therapy" representing psychodynamic and humanistic therapies

Criterion/ Dependent Variable/ Strains	Occupational Stressor (Measured or Assumed)	Findings
Structured clinical stress interview and self-report measures consisting of three inventories (Derogati's Stress Profile, Occupational Stress Inventory, and Teacher Stress Measure) "The subjects were assessed on environmental, personality, and emotional variables"	Assumed task-based stress and role conflict	Experimental group showed lower stress level than control.
Self-report of stress (four subscales of Teacher Stress Inventory and five subscales of job stress in school setting), coping skills as measured by written responses, and observational measure using Teacher Anxiety Observation Scale	Unnamed stressful teaching events, task-based stress, role overload	Stress inoculation training was effective in reducing teachers' self-reported stress, while the co-worker support group was not. Neither treatment was successful in changing motoric manifestation of anxiety.
Quality of work life, job satisfaction, level of boredom, mental and physical fatigue, overall psychological health status	Introduction of a program of computerization	The redeployed group had reduced level of job satisfaction, more mental and physical fatigue, felt left out, had worst level of overall psychological health, high job future ambiguity. The training group had highest level of job satisfaction and overall psychological health.
Structured interviews and self-ratings of psychological adjustment	Assumed problems related to self-concept, role, and colleagues	Prescriptive therapy was more potent in reducing the overall psychiatric symptoms than the exploratory therapy, but the two therapies were equal in relieving job-related problems.

TABLE 8.1 *(continued)*

Authors and Year	Sample and Design	Intervention/ Independent Variable/ Treatment
Friedman, Lehrer, and Stevens (1983)	Eighty-five schoolteachers Random assignment to two treatment and one control groups Pre-post tests	Two types of stress management training, both including cognitive coping skills and relaxation techniques 1. Lecture-discussion workshop 2. Self-directed training
Ganster et al. (1982)	Seventy-nine employees of a public service agency Random assignment to one treatment and one waitlist control group Pre-post tests	Cognitive restructuring of environmental perceptions and muscle relaxation with biofeedback demonstration
Higgins (1986)	Fifty-three working women in white collar jobs, working at least ten hours a week in paid jobs Random assignment to two treatment and one control groups Pre-post tests	1. Stress reduction program based on behavioral conditioning techniques, consisting of progressive relaxation and systematic desensitization 2. Stress reduction program involving instructions in cognitive coping skills consisting of instruction on time management, rational-emotive therapy, and assertiveness training
Keyes and Dean (1988)	One hundred direct contact staff working in medium-sized ICF/MR facilities Nonrandom assignment to one treatment and one attention-control group Pre-post tests of anger and post-three-week follow-up of workshop evaluation	1. Attention control procedure 2. Meichenbaum's stress inoculation

Criterion/ Dependent Variable/ Strains	Occupational Stressor (Measured or Assumed)	Findings
General state and trait anxiety, and subjective stress	Not mentioned	"Comprehensive stress reduction program using group or more individually oriented methods is effective in teaching individuals appropriate skills for coping with stress. . . . Locus of control is not an important factor in determining success in a stress reduction program."
State anxiety, depression, somatic complaints, urinary catecholamine levels	Assumed stressful work	Catecholamine levels were lower at posttest on experimental group, but effects did not persist at follow-up and effects did not replicate with waitlist control group.
Emotional exhaustion (burnout), personal strain, and absenteeism	Not mentioned	Both programs are equally effective.
Anger Inventory, workshop evaluation form, follow-up evaluation questionnaire, use of emergency restraints with clients	Conflicting situations arising out of working with agitated and disruptive clients	Stress inoculation training can be effective in reducing the intrapersonal aspect of stress of the subjects and also reduced anger.

TABLE 8.1 *(continued)*

Authors and Year	Sample and Design	Intervention/ Independent Variable/ Treatment
Long (1988)	Sixty-six schoolteachers Random assignment to two treatment groups Second group received treatments serially Tests before and after each treatment	1. Stress inoculation training with exercise 2. Exercise training only 3. Stress inoculation training following exercise only
Long and Haney (1988)	Sixty-one sedentary working women Random assignment to two treatment groups Pre-post tests plus eight-week follow-up	1. Progressive relaxation 2. Aerobic exercise (jogging)
Sharp and Forman (1985)	Sixty schoolteachers Nonrandom assignment to two treatment and one control groups Pre-post tests with four-week follow-up	1. Stress inoculation training 2. Classroom management training
Tunnecliffe, Leach, and Tunnecliffe (1986)	Twenty-one primary schoolteachers Random assignment to two treatment and one control groups Pre-post test with three-month follow-up	1. Collaborative behavioral consultation—consisting of (a) identification of stressors and their sources, (b) how to deal with personal-environmental stressors 2. Relaxation training
vonBaeyer and Krause (1983-84)	Fourteen registered nurses assigned to burn unit of a university medical center Nonrandom assignment to one treatment and one waitlist control group Pre-post tests	Training in cognitive-behavioral stress management skills

Criterion/ Dependent Variable/ Strains	Occupational Stressor (Measured or Assumed)	Findings
General trait and anxiety and teacher stress, self-reported coping activities, cardiovascular fitness, and self-report of physical activity	Not mentioned	Inoculation plus exercise more effective than exercise alone in reducing anxiety and teacher stress. Both equally effective for coping. Inoculation alone not effective in relation to anxiety, stress, or coping skills. No effects on cardiovascular fitness or physical activity.
General trait anxiety, general self-efficacy, and self-reported ways of coping	Subjects were asked to identify to work stressors	Both treatments reduced anxiety and increased self-efficacy, but coping strategies did not change.
Self-report of teaching anxiety, general state anxiety, and trait anxiety, observation of classroom anxiety behavior	Not mentioned	Both the treatments are effective in reducing school-related anxiety of the teachers.
Perceived teacher stress, measured by Teacher Occupational Stress Factor Questionnaire	Stressful events evaluated on questionnaire, which was the dependent variable	Collaborative behavioral consultation was effective even at follow-up. Relaxation training had no effect.
State and trait anxiety (weekly), stress record sheet (daily), stress management training evaluation questionnaire	Assumed stressful setting of burn unit	Training was effective in reducing work-related anxiety among inexperienced nurses, but not among experienced ones.

their emphasis on human service, and (2) the people in these occupations are more open to psychological treatments and research.

The interventions employed in these studies are also quite varied, although some trends are worth noting. First, virtually all these studies are targeted at the individual level, while none is aimed at changing stressful organizational conditions. Second, several studies utilized Meichenbaum's (1977) stress inoculation training or some variant. Thus, it appears that a widely held assumption is that the key to managing stress is for the individual to anticipate stressors and respond in a constructive manner.

A number of criterion measures were utilized, some of which appear to be more sound than others. The overwhelming majority of studies used self-report measures of psychological strain (e.g., anxiety, emotional exhaustion) or coping skills to assess the effects of the stress management treatment. Although such measures are certainly relevant to the evaluation of a stress management treatment, they are also problematic. A major problem with these measures is that they are easily distorted or biased in ways that inflate estimates of management program success or effectiveness.

In only one case (Cecil and Forman, 1990) was an observational measure of behavior used (the behavior of teachers was observed). In all other cases, program participants reported their own behavior. In addition, there was only one instance in which a physiological measure was used (Long and Haney, 1988). It is somewhat surprising that physiological measures were used so infrequently since many of the treatments were designed to induce calming responses. As a final comment, two studies used (personality) trait anxiety as a criterion measure (Long, 1988; Long and Haney, 1988). Given that trait anxiety is theoretically very stable over time and even appears to have a genetic component (cf. Eysenck, 1989), it is not likely to be responsive to any short-term stress management program. Thus, trait anxiety is probably not a reasonable criterion measure.

Since these studies are presented as evaluations of stress management treatments, it is interesting that very few of them clearly identified any specific stressor from which strains might result. In most of the studies, it is *assumed* that the strains which are the focus of these treatments are not only related to but caused by unexamined job-related stressors. It has been shown that self-reports of strains are affected by other factors such as personality, affective states, or nonwork stressors (Chen, Spector, and Jex, 1995; Greenhaus and Parasuraman, 1987; Jex and Spector, 1996). Similarly, physical illnesses can have many causes. Coronary heart disease is often attributed to family history, diet, exercise habits, and so forth, and is not by any means solely caused by job stress. Most studies we found that purport to be studies of job stress, and especially those not reported in the table, seem to have assumed that job stressors were involved based on one of two unstated reasons: because the study's subjects had jobs or because the treatments took place at the work site. Neither of these apparent reasons is based on *any* evidence!

Thus, most of the treatments in these studies focus on individuals' physical or psychological illnesses, which may or may not be due to job stressors. The studies can easily be classified as investigations of behavioral medicine that happen to occur in the workplace or with people who have jobs. There is usually no evidence at all, however, that stressors on the job are involved in any way. Although the treatments are often touted as occupational stress treatments, there seems little reason for them to carry this label. Just because someone who has a broken toe is employed does not mean that the toe was broken in the place of employment. Likewise, just because someone who has high blood pressure has a job does not mean that the job caused the high blood pressure. There is a focus on individual strain responses, sometimes *to the exclusion of* considering the job-related stressor stimuli. Kasl (1986) has described one version of this phenomenon as "inviting workers into a 'stress' management program solely on the basis of elevated scores on some symptom checklist" (p. 55). Although this may be useful in a medical model of treating illnesses, it is almost useless if one wants to study *job* stress and its treatment. There is no evidence that job stress played any role at all in the development of the illness.

Results of the studies in the table indicate that the treatments evaluated have some positive effects. Typically, results appear in the form of reductions in self-reported psychological strains following completion of the stress management treatment. Unfortunately, based on results of this type, it is very difficult to conclude that the stress management treatment was responsible for these changes (Beehr and O'Hara, 1987; Murphy, 1987). Therefore, one cannot be confident that the effects observed would not have occurred even in the absence of the treatment. Most of the studies evaluated employed no control groups—nor ABA, multiple baseline, or other designs that might help compensate for the lack of a control group. A second problem is that in most of these studies, employees self-selected the treatments. These employees may be different from other nonparticipating employees in ways that enhance their ability to profit from stress management treatments. Finally, all of the studies reviewed are short term. Therefore, it is unclear whether the effects observed persist over time. Considering these problems with validity and reliability of treatment effects, conclusions about the effectiveness of these treatments must be made with caution.

CONCLUSIONS AND RECOMMENDATIONS

This chapter has presented an overview of behaviorally based stress management treatments. A variety of potential techniques that could be used as stress management treatments were described, some of which directly target the individual and others the organization. In practice, however, only a fraction of the possible treatment types or modes of treatment have actually been utilized. Teaching calming responses and altering the way people process information appear to be the most popular approaches employed. Virtually all the studies reviewed were focused on treating individuals' symptoms rather than changing organizational conditions. Why is this? One possible reason is that organizations' decision makers believe their employees ultimately bear responsibility for job-related strains they experience. However, given the rise in stress-related workers' compensation claims and awards (National Council on Compensation Insurance Reports, 1985), clearly, this assumption is not shared by the members of the legal community. Another reason is that upper-level managers may believe it is much more difficult to change organizational systems than to change individuals one at a time.

A reasonable conclusion supported by material in this chapter is that very few organizations do any type of stress-related diagnosis before proceeding with stress management treatments. As previously noted, the vast majority of studies that have evaluated stress management treatments do not measure stressors. Thus, most organizations employing stress management treatments are, de facto, assuming that stressors in the work environment are causing strains. To the extent this assumption is wrong, organizations may be providing a useful service to employees, but this type of service does not clearly qualify as occupational stress management.

A final conclusion is that the effectiveness of stress management treatments is not easily assessed. As was noted earlier, flaws in experimental design make causal inferences about relations between the various stress management treatments and observed changes questionable. A related issue concerns the generalizability of findings that remain unknown. If a treatment is effective in one organizational setting, will it be effective in other organizational settings? To date, the extent to which a particular treatment *appeared* to work in a particular setting is all that is known. Ultimately, the extent to which treatment effects generalize to different settings with different types of employees must be identified.

Future Research

Undoubtedly the most pressing need in this area is for research that facilitates understanding the job stress process. Until the causes of job-related strain are understood, stress management treatments will achieve only limited success. For example, although little research on job-related stress has focused on cognitive appraisal, numerous treatments focus on changing cognitive processing of stressful stimuli. Unfortunately, progress in job stress research has been slow relative to other areas in organizational psychology (Jex, Beehr, and Roberts, 1992). Ultimately, stress management practices must be guided by sound theory and research if they are to be effective.

A second clear research need is for organizations employing stress management treatments to perform some type of stressor diagnosis before these programs begin. As indicated previously, without a diagnosis of situational stressors in the work environment, such treatments are more clearly in the behavioral medicine domain than in the job stress domain. Practically, it is difficult to justify the cost of stress management treatments if they are not fulfilling the intended organizational objective of stress reduction.

A final research need is for more rigorous research designs in the evaluation of stress management treatments. By using control groups, multiple baseline or other relatively sound quasi-experimental designs, sound measurement procedures, and longitudinal designs to check for long-term effects, it will become much more clear which stress management treatments are effective.

REFERENCES

Baron, R. A. (1976). The reduction of human aggression: A field study of incompatible responses. *Journal of Applied Social Psychology, 6*(3), 260-274.

Beech, H. R., Burns, L. E., and Sheffield, B. F. (1982). *A behavioral approach to the management of stress: A practical guide to techniques.* Chichester, England: John Wiley and Sons.

Beehr, T. A. (1991). Stress in the workplace: An overview. In J. W. Jones, B. D. Steffy, and D. W. Grant (Eds.), *Applying psychology in business: The handbook for managers and human resource professionals* (pp. 709-714). Lexington, MA: Lexington Books.

Beehr, T. A. and Franz, T. (1987). The current debate about the meaning of job stress. In J. M. Ivancevich and D. C. Ganster (Eds.), *Job stress: From theory to suggestion* (pp. 5-18). Binghamton, NY: The Haworth Press.

Beehr, T. A. and Newman, J. E. (1978). Job stress, employee health, and organizational effectiveness: A facet analysis, model, and literature review. *Personnel Psychology, 31*(4), 665-699.

Beehr, T. A. and O'Hara, K. (1987). Methodological designs for the evaluation of occupational stress interventions. In S. V. Kasl and C. L. Cooper (Eds.), *Stress and health: Issues in research and methodology* (pp. 79-111). Chichester, England: Wiley International.

Beehr, T. A. and Schuler, R. S. (1982). Stress in organizations. In K. M. Rowland and G. R. Ferris (Eds.), *Personnel management* (pp. 390-419). Boston: Allyn and Bacon.

Bellarosa, C. and Chen, P. Y. (1997). The effectiveness and practicality of occupational stress management interventions: A survey of subject matter experts. *Journal of Occupational Health Psychology, 2*(3), 247-262.

Bertoch, M. R., Nielsen, E. C., Curley, J. R., and Borg, W. R. (1989). Reducing teacher stress. *Journal of Experimental Education, 57*(2), 117-128.

Booth-Kewley, S. and Friedman, H. S. (1987). Psychological predictors of heart disease: A quantitative review. *Psychological Bulletin, 101*(3), 343-362.

Campion, M. A. and Thayer, P. W. (1985). Development and field evaluation of an interdisciplinary measure of job design. *Journal of Applied Psychology, 70*(1), 29-43.

Caplan, R. D., Cobb, S., French, J. R., Harrison, R. V., and Pinneau, S. R. (1975). *Job demands and worker health: Main effects and occupational differences.* Washington, DC: U.S. Government Printing Office.

Carsten, J. M. and Spector, P. E. (1987). Unemployment, job satisfaction, and employee turnover: A meta-analytic test of the Muchinsky model. *Journal of Applied Psychology, 72*(3), 374-381.

Cecil, M. A. and Forman, S. G. (1990). Effects of stress inoculation training and coworker support groups on teachers' stress. *Journal of School Psychology, 28*(2), 105-118.

Chen, P. Y., Spector, P. E., and Jex, S. M. (1995). Effects of manipulated job stressors and job attitude on perceived job conditions: A simulation. In S. L. Sauter and L. R. Murphy (Eds.), *Organizational risk factors for job stress* (pp. 341-356). Washington, DC: American Psychological Association.

Costa, P. T. and McCrae, R. R. (1987). Neuroticism, somatic complaints, and disease: Is the bark worse than the bite? *Journal of Personality, 55*(2), 299-316.

Cullen, J. and Sandberg, C. G. (1987). Wellness and stress management programs: A critical evaluation. *Ergonomics, 30*(2), 287-294.

Dishman, R. K. and Gettman, L. R. (1980). Psychobiologic influences on exercise adherence. *Journal of Sport Psychology, 2*(4), 295-310.

Dishman, R. K., Ickes, W., and Morgan, W. P. (1980). Self-motivation and adherence to habitual physical activity. *Journal of Applied Social Psychology, 10*(2), 115-132.

Eysenck, M. W. (1989). Personality, stress arousal, and cognitive processes in stress transactions. In R. W. Neufeld (Ed.), *Advances in the investigation of psychological stress* (pp. 133-160). New York: John Wiley and Sons.

Firth, J. and Shapiro, D. A. (1986). An evaluation of psychotherapy for job-related distress. *Journal of Occupational Psychology, 59*(2), 111-119.

Fisher, C. D. and Gitelson, R. (1983). A meta-analysis of the correlates of role conflict and ambiguity. *Journal of Applied Psychology, 68*, 320-333.

Frese, M. (1985). Stress at work and physical complaints: A causal interpretation. *Journal of Applied Psychology, 70,* 314-328.

Fried, Y., Rowland, K. M., and Ferris, G. R. (1984). The physiological measurement of work stress: A critique. *Personal Psychology, 37*(4), 583-615.

Friedman, G. H., Lehrer, B. E., and Stevens, J. P. (1983). The effectiveness of self-directed and lecture/discussion stress management approaches and the locus of control of teachers. *American Educational Research Journal, 20*(4), 563-580.

Friedman, M. and Rosenman, R. H. (1974). *Type A behavior and your heart.* New York: Alfred A. Knopf.

Ganster, D. C., Mayes, B. T., Sime, W. E., and Tharp, G. D. (1982). Managing organizational stress: A field experiment. *Journal of Applied Psychology, 67*(5), 533-542.

Goldfried, M. (1971). Systematic desensitization as training in self control. *Journal of Consulting and Clinical Psychology, 37*(2), 228-234.

Greenhaus, J. H. and Parasuraman, S. (1987). A work-nonwork interactive perspective of stress and its consequences. In J. M. Ivancevich and D. C. Ganster (Eds.), *Job stress: From theory to suggestion* (pp. 37-60). Binghamton, NY: The Haworth Press.

Hackman, J. R. and Oldham, G. R. (1980). *Work redesign.* Reading, MA: Addison-Wesley.

Hanisch, K. A. and Hulin, C. L. (1991). General attitudes and organizational withdrawal: An evaluation of a causal model. *Journal of Vocational Behavior, 39*(1), 110-128.

Higgins, N. C. (1986). Occupational stress and working women: The effectiveness of two stress reduction programs. *Journal of Vocational Behavior, 29*(1), 66-78.

Ilgen, D. R. (1990). Opportunities for industrial/organizational psychology. *American Psychologist, 45*(2), 273-283.

Ivancevich, J. M. (1987). Organizational level stress management interventions: A review and recommendations. In J. M. Ivancevich and D. C. Ganster (Eds.), *Job stress: From theory to suggestion* (pp. 229-248). Binghamton, NY: The Haworth Press.

Ivancevich, J. M. and Ganster, D. C. (Eds.). (1987). *Job stress: From theory to suggestion.* Binghamton, NY: The Haworth Press.

Ivancevich, J. M. and Matteson, M. T. (1980). *Stress and work.* Glenview, IL: Scott Foresman.

Jackson, S. E. (1983). Participation in decision making as a strategy for reducing job-related strain. *Journal of Applied Psychology, 68*(1), 3-19.

Jackson, S. E. (1984). Correction to "Participation in decision making as a strategy for reducing job-related strain." *Journal of Applied Psychology, 69*(3), 546-547.

Jackson, S. E. and Schuler, R. S. (1985). A meta-analysis and conceptual critique of research on role ambiguity and role conflict in work settings. *Organizational Behavior and Human Decision Process, 36*(1), 16-78.

Jacobson, E. (1938). *Progressive relaxation.* Chicago: University of Chicago Press.

Jex, S. M. and Beehr, T. A. (1991). Emerging theoretical and methodological issues in the study of work-related stress. In K. W. Rowland and G. R. Ferris (Eds.), *Research in personnel and human resources management* (pp. 311-365). Greenwich, CT: JAI Press.

Jex, S. M., Beehr, T. A., and Roberts, C. K. (1992). The meaning of occupational stress items to survey respondents. *Journal of Applied Psychology, 77*(5), 623-628.

Jex, S. M., and Spector, P. E. (1996). The impact of negative affectivity on stressor-strain relations: A replication and extension. *Work and Stress, 10*(1), 36-45.

Kasl, S. V. (1986). Stress and disease in the workplace. A methodological commentary on the accumulated evidence. In M. F. Cataldo and T. J. Coates (Eds.), *Health and industry: A behavioral medicine perspective* (pp. 52-85). New York: John Wiley and Sons.

Kaufmann, G. M., and Beehr, T. A. (1986). Interactions between job stressors and social support: Some counterintuitive results. *Journal of Applied Psychology, 71*(3), 522-526.

Keyes, J. B. and Dean, S. F. (1988). Stress inoculation training for direct contact staff working with mentally retarded persons. *Behavioral Residential Treatment, 3*(4), 315-323.

Langer, E., Janis, I., and Wolper, J. (1975). Reduction of stress in surgical patients. *Journal of Experimental Social Psychology, 11*(2), 155-165.

Lazarus, R. S. (1966). *Psychological stress and the coping process.* New York: McGraw-Hill.

Locke, E. A. (1976). The nature and causes of job satisfaction. In M. D. Dunnette (Ed.), *The handbook of industrial and organizational psychology* (pp. 1297-1349). Chicago: Rand McNally.

Long, B. C. (1988). Stress management for school personnel: Stress inoculation training and exercise. *Psychology in the Schools, 25*(3), 314-324.

Long, B. C. and Haney, C. J. (1988). Coping strategies for working women: Aerobic exercise and relaxation interventions. *Behavior Therapy, 19*(1), 75-83.

Lowin, A. (1968). Participative decision making: A model, literature critique, and prescriptions for research. *Organizational Behavior and Human Performance, 3*(1), 68-106.

Martin, E. V. (1992). Designing stress training. In J. C. Quick, L. R. Murphy, and J. J. Hurrell Jr. (Eds.), *Stress and well-being at work: Assessments and interventions for occupational mental health* (pp. 207-224). Washington, DC: American Psychological Association.

Mason, J. W. (1975). A historical view of the stress field: Part 1. *Journal of Human Stress, 1* (March), 6-12.

Mawhinney, T. C. (1984). Philosophical and ethical aspects of organizational behavior management: Some evaluative feedback. *Journal of Organizational Behavior Management, 6*(1), 5-31.

Mawhinney, T. C. (1989). Job satisfaction as a management tool and responsibility. *Journal of Organizational Behavior Management, 10*(1), 187-192.

Meichenbaum, D. (1977). *Cognitive-behavior modification: An integrated approach.* New York: Plenum Press.

Miller, R. and Pfohl, W. F., Jr. (1982). Management of job-related stress. In R. M. O'Brien, A. M. Dickinson, and M. P. Rosnow (Eds.), *Industrial behavior modification: A management handbook* (pp. 224-242). New York: Pergamon Press.

Motowidlow, S. J., Packard, J. S., and Manning, M. R. (1986). Occupational stress: Its causes and consequences for job performance. *Journal of Applied Psychology, 71*(4), 618-629.

Murphy, L. R. (1987). A review of organizational stress management research: Methodological considerations. In J. M. Ivancevich and D. C. Ganster (Eds.), *Job stress: From theory to suggestion* (pp. 214-228). Binghamton, NY: The Haworth Press.

Naditch, M. P. (1986). STAYWELL: Evolution of a behavioral medicine program in industry. In M. F. Cataldo and T. J. Coates (Eds.), *Health and industry: A behavioral medicine perspective* (pp. 323-337). New York: John Wiley and Sons.

National Council on Compensation Insurance (1985). *Emotional stress in the workplace—New legal rights in the eighties.* New York: National Council on Compensation Insurance.

Newman, J. E. and Beehr, T. A. (1979). Personnel and organizational strategies for handling job stress: A review of research and opinion. *Personnel Psychology, 32*(1), 1-43.

Poppen, R. (1988). *Behavioral relaxation training assessment.* New York: Pergamon Press.

Quick, J. D., Horn, R. S., and Quick, J. C. (1987). Health consequences of stress. In J. M. Ivancevich and D. C. Ganster (Eds.), *Job stress: From theory to suggestion* (pp. 19-36). Binghamton, NY: The Haworth Press.

Reynolds, S. and Shapiro, D. A. (1991). Stress reduction in transition: Conceptual problems in the design, implementation, and evaluation of worksite stress management interventions. *Human Relations, 44*(7), 717-733.

Schwartz, G. E. (1982). Testing the biopsychosocial model: The ultimate challenge facing behavioral medicine. *Journal of Consulting and Clinical Psychology, 50*(6), 1040-1053.

Selye, H. (1976). *The stress of life* (Second edition). New York: McGraw Hill.

Sharp, J. J. and Forman, S. G. (1985). A comparison of two approaches to anxiety management for teachers. *Behavior Therapy, 16*(4), 370-383.

Smith, P. C. (1977). Work attitudes as predictors of attendance on a specific day. *Journal of Applied Psychology, 62*(1), 16-19.

Spector, P. E. (1986). Perceived control by employees: A meta-analysis of studies concerning autonomy and participation at work. *Human Relations, 39*(11), 1005-1016.

Spector, P. E., Dwyer, D. J., and Jex, S. M. (1988). Relations of job stressors to affective, health, and performance outcomes: A comparison of multiple data sources. *Journal of Applied Psychology, 73*(1), 11-19.

Suinn, R. and Richardson, F. (1971). Anxiety management control: A nonspecific behavior therapy program for anxiety control. *Behavior Therapy, 2*(4), 498-510.

Thoresen, C. E. and Powell, L. H. (1992). Type A behavior pattern: New perspectives on theory, assessment, and intervention. *Journal of Consulting and Clinical Psychology, 60*(4), 595-604.

Tunnecliffe, M. R., Leach, D. J., and Tunnecliffe, L. P. (1986). Relative efficacy of using behavioral consultation as an approach to teacher stress management. *Journal of School Psychology, 24*(2), 123-131.

vonBaeyer, C. and Krause, L. (1983-84). Effectiveness of stress management training for nurses working in a burn treatment unit. *International Journal of Psychiatry in Medicine, 13*(2), 113-126.

Wilbur, C. S., Hartwell, T. D., and Piserchia, P. V. (1986). The Johnson and Johnson LIVE FOR LIFE program: Its organization and evaluation plan. In M. F. Cataldo and T. J. Coates (Eds.), *Health and industry: A behavioral medicine perspective* (pp. 338-350). New York: John Wiley and Sons.

Wolpe, J. (1990). *The practice of behavior therapy* (Fourth edition). New York: Pergamon Press.

Chapter 9

Pay for Performance

Phillip K. Duncan
Dee Tinley Smoot

Although readers of behavioral literature might conclude that interest in pay for performance issues is of recent origin, that conclusion would belie that fact that substantial investigations of performance pay have occupied researchers and practitioners for the better part of the nineteenth and twentieth centuries. For example, Mitchell, Lewin, and Lawler, writing in Blinder (1990), point out that Charles Babbage (1832) discussed a system whereby workers would be paid on the basis of their individual work, thus improving the profit of the individual and the firm, and eliminating the need to adjust wages periodically. Then they documented a variety of pay schemes proposed and implemented up to the present time.

Babbage (1832) was hardly the first to suggest that pay be based on performance. Peach and Wren (1992) cited the Code of Hammurabi as a source of incentive pay proposals. They also reviewed various pay philosophies and schemes proposed from the time of ancient Greece through the Middle Ages into the present century.

In this chapter, we will briefly describe several current performance pay systems, and then discuss research and applications of behaviorally-based pay systems. Readers interested in a historical treatment of performance pay systems should consult Peach and Wren (1992) or Blinder (1990).

VARIETY OF PLANS

The innumerable pay plans developed over the years have their basis in one or more of only a few basic pay strategies. These strategies are briefly discussed in the following sections.

Profit Sharing

Profit-sharing plans are designed to enhance productivity by linking worker pay to the profitability of the firm. Good worker performance may increase company profits, a percentage of which may then be paid to the workers. Typically, the "share" is paid annually as a cash addition to the base wage (Scott, Clothier, and Spriegel, 1961).

Mitchell, Lewin, and Lawler (1990) point out that profit sharing offers benefits to both management and labor. Management retains some flexibility in wages paid by means of the formula that determines the proportion of profits shared, and labor benefits by increases in pay related in part to its efforts.

The structure of profit-sharing plans may limit their effect on worker productivity. If the organization does not earn a sufficient profit, no profit-share pool will be formed, and so no shares will be paid. Market factors such as cost of materials and international political or economic conditions can create a poor profit picture. Thus, excellent individual performance may not lead to monetary gain. Second, because profit shares are usually computed and paid annually, the temporal gap between individual performance and profit share payment is large, reducing the effects of pay on performance.

Gainsharing

A second major method of linking performance with wages takes the form of gainsharing. Bullock and Lawler (1984) suggest that at its heart, gainsharing attempts ". . . to establish effective structures and processes of employee involvement and a fair means of rewarding systemwide performance improvements" (p. 24). Peach and Wren (1992) note that gainsharing plans focus on more circumscribed work units than do profit-sharing plans, thus creating a tighter link between worker and wages. Rather than focusing on organizational profits, gainshare plans focus on money saved by smaller units within the organization, such as work teams or departments. By finding ways to reduce costs, the work group creates a pool of money (the difference between the historical cost for some process and the new cost), a percentage of which is paid out to each worker. Because it fosters employee-based savings, Mitchell, Lewin, and Lawler (1990) suggest that gainsharing can create opportunities for union-management cooperation sorely needed in post-World War II U.S. industry. Detailed discussions of profit sharing and gainsharing plans appear in Bullock and Lawler (1984), Mitchell, Lewin, and Lawler (1990), Lawler (1992), and Gowen (1990).

Although they call for more research, Bullock and Lawler (1984) and Mitchell, Lewin, and Lawler (1990) agree that the existing literature supports the assertion that gainsharing programs are superior to profit-sharing plans. The gainsharing pool is more closely tied to individual worker performance, and because cost savings for a process can be computed relatively quickly, gainshare payments can occur more frequently than profit-share payments.

Two features of gainsharing plans may limit their influence on worker performance. First, gainshare payments may occur more often than profit-share payments, perhaps even monthly, but monthly payments are still temporally distant from worker performance. Second, the historical cost for a process against which the "gain" is computed will eventually cease to be considered the standard cost. The cost created by the revised process will become the standard, and the gainshare pool will evaporate until yet greater savings procedures are developed.

Abernathy (1990) makes the case that both profit sharing and gainsharing systems work because productivity is tied to monetary outcomes, but he proposes a model that tightens the link between individual work and monetary consequences. He advocates a performance pay strategy that begins with a gainsharing plan and, ideally, evolves into a program which freezes base salaries and puts scheduled, routine salary increases into an incentive pool. In addition to serving as a compensation plan, Abernathy argues that this plan serves as a general management strategy, because it requires clear definition and measurement of employee accomplishments and includes strategies by which performance improvements can be effected. Such strategies include the use of timely performance feedback and positive reinforcement, and discourage punishment. This marriage of clear performance requirements, feedback, and positive reinforcement has some historic precedent. Parsons (1974, 1992) in a fascinating reanalysis of the "Hawthorne Effect" (see Roethlisberger and Dickson, 1939), points out that data available from the Hawthorne studies showed clear and sustained increases in performance when monetary incentives and performance feedback were available for an individual's work.

BEHAVIORAL APPROACHES
TO PERFORMANCE-BASED PAY

Applications and Demonstrations

It is, arguably, the chapter by Abernathy, Duffy, and O'Brien (1982) that sparked the recent interest among behavioral practitioners and researchers in performance pay systems. They described the installation of performance pay systems in two banks, Virginia National Bank of Norfolk, Virginia, and Union National Bank of Little Rock, Arkansas. Although many features were important to these installations, four characteristics of the pay programs appear critical: the precise definition of performance, the precise and frequent measurement (not "assessment") of performance, clear and timely feedback to workers about their performance, and clear statements about the relation between performance and pay. For example, when proof operators at the Virginia bank were subjected to these four conditions they increased productivity from an average of 1,465 items processed per hour to an average of 2,250.

Abernathy's colleagues, Dierks and McNally (1987), reported proof operator data from Union National Bank similar to the data from the Virginia workers. Production increased from a baseline of just over 1,000 items per hour to over 2,000 processed checks per hour when feedback and praise were introduced. Following the introduction of bonus pay for daily output above standards, productivity increased to an average of 3,500 items per hour. Abernathy, Duffy, and O'Brien (1982) and Dierks and McNally (1987) described similar outcomes within several other areas of each bank.

Gaetani, Hoxeng, and Austin (1985) evaluated the effectiveness of performance feedback and pay incentives on auto mechanic performance, measured in terms of dollars billed to customers. Their data showed a clear increase in dollars billed over baseline when feedback was provided, a decrease when the feedback was removed, and highest performance when feedback was combined with an incentive system. In this case, the incentive system allowed workers to receive a commission of 5 percent of the value of work that exceeded the historical standard established during the previous six weeks.

George and Hopkins (1989) examined the performance of waitpersons in terms of dollars earned and sales per labor hour at several branches of a restaurant chain. The waitpersons were paid 7 percent of their gross sales, which permitted them to earn more than their flat rate wage. Performance across three restaurant locations was consistently higher during the performance pay conditions than during the same time period a year earlier, when the waitpersons were paid a standard hourly rate. Although sales per labor hour increased, other data showed that labor cost per gross sales dollar remained essentially unchanged. Thus, both sales and waitperson earnings increased, but labor costs for the owners did not.

Laboratory Analyses

Demonstrations of the utility of performance pay systems are convincing, yet the design of the systems varies. George and Hopkins (1989) defined their payoff at 7 percent of gross sales, Gaetani, Hoxeng, and Austin (1985) paid 5 percent commission above a historical standard, and Abernathy, Duffy, and O'Brien (1982) described a variety of pay procedures, the most prominent being one that paid workers incrementally more money as they produced more—described as a "shifting fixed ratio" schedule with no apparent upper limit. While successful performance pay systems were being implemented, interest began to emerge in determining the most efficient form of such systems.

Increased productivity and better efficiency notwithstanding, the workplace is not always conducive to experimental analyses of performance pay plans. Indeed, Gaetani, Hoxeng, and Austin (1985) report that the owner of the firm in that their study was conducted refused to continue a reversal phase that showed decreased performance. It is not surprising, then, that research directed at the analysis of components of performance pay systems occurred principally in laboratory settings.

Central to the laboratory research on performance pay systems has been the work of Dickinson and her research team. In addition, work done by Duncan and his team has provided useful replications and extensions of Dickinson's work. These teams have examined similar research questions, used different tasks, and employed various procedures and research designs in developing this body of literature.

Group Size and Individual/Group Contingencies

In the first in a series of studies, Stoneman and Dickinson (1989) examined individual performance as a function of group contingencies and group size. College student subjects assembled "widgets" from nuts, bolts, and washers, working in teams of two, four, five, or nine members. Research sessions were conducted three times per week for forty-five minutes per session. Group members were initially paid on an individual incentive system, in which a base salary of $1.50 per session was incremented by $0.02 for each correct widget constructed beyond an individual standard. A group incentive plan was then introduced, in which group members received the base pay and $0.02 for each widget produced beyond a group standard. Finally, the individual incentive condition was reintroduced. The research design was a combination of reversal (individual to group to individual contingencies) and between-group (fixed group size) designs. The mean number of correctly assembled widgets did not vary reliably with changes in either group size or incentive condition. One difference in widget assembly was observed: an inverse relation between group size and range of performance across individuals within the groups occurred where two-person groups showed higher variability than the nine-person group.

Johnstone and colleagues (1989) also used an assembly task to investigate the relation between group size and nature of contingency on productivity. In this research, groups of two, five, or ten college students assembled widgets from pop beads. Three sessions per week lasted fifteen minutes each. Subjects were paid a base salary of $1.00 during baseline. During the individual contingency condition, subjects received the base salary plus $0.05 for every widget assembled beyond the production standard. In the group pay plan, each person received the base salary plus $0.05 per widget for the mean number of widgets produced by the group over the standard. A combination of single subject and group design was employed. One of the incentive pay conditions was introduced first, followed by a base-rate-only condition, followed by the incentive-pay condition (one not yet presented to that group), thus constituting a counterbalanced reversal design. Subjects remained in their initial groups for the entire experiment, allowing for a between-groups comparison of productivity. Data reflecting number of correct widgets produced indicated clear increases during the two performance pay plans and no changes during base rate condition across all groups. However, as in Stoneman and Dickinson (1989), no differences appeared between the group and individual systems.

The results of these studies suggest that there is no important difference in the effect of individual or group performance pay contingencies on productivity. Although this interpretation may be justified, other considerations are important before a firm conclusion can be made. Both studies employed college students and relatively small amounts of money, so it is possible that subjects were not exposed to the more realistic conditions of having to use their earnings to pay for rent, food, or other necessities; thus, their behavior was not controlled by the money as the behavior of "real" workers would be. This difficulty is somewhat offset by casual observation of worker conversations during and after experimental sessions by Johnstone and colleagues (1989), who reported that subjects discussed saving the earnings for the purchase of clothing, doing laundry, and in one case, buying beer.

A second possible limitation of these studies is that there was no substantial difference in group size. That is, groups of two to ten persons are still quite small, especially compared to tens of thousands in corporate profit-sharing programs. Thus, group size differentials and pay plans may not have interacted because group size was not effectively manipulated. Further research utilizing larger groups must address this question.

Percentage of Incentive Pay

Several studies have investigated the relation between productivity and the amount of total pay available through incentives. As noted earlier, limits on incentive pay have been used in actual workplaces for pragmatic reasons, yet until recently no data were available that demonstrated the relation between the proportion of incentive pay and productivity. Frisch and Dickinson (1990) addressed this issue in a between-groups laboratory simulation similar to the one described by Stoneman and Dickinson (1989). The dependent variable was the assembly of widgets from nuts and bolts. The independent variable, percentage of incentive relative to base pay, took several values: 0 percent (no incentives), 10 percent, 30 percent, 60 percent, and 100 percent. The total amount of pay earned per forty-five-minute session was capped at $4.00. Thus, the 0 percent group earned $4.00 per session if their performance exceeded minimum standard (determined by pilot data), while the 100 percent incentive group earned $2.00 base pay and up to $2.00 incentive pay if their performance exceeded the standard. The production data showed significant differences between the 0 percent group and all other groups, but no differences among the incentive groups. Furthermore, data regarding dollars earned showed a clear separation among experimental groups, with earnings inversely proportional to the percentage of pay based on incentives. Frisch and Dickinson (1990) pointed out that their findings contradict the suggestion by Fein (1970) that incentives will not be effective if they are below 30 percent of base pay, because only one experimental group actually earned above 30 percent in incentives. Because there were no significant production differentials, it seems fair to conclude that the effective proportion of incentive to base pay may be well below the 30 percent figure commonly cited.

Leary and colleagues (1990) also examined the size of incentives relative to base pay. The laboratory assembly task was identical to that described by Johnstone and colleagues (1989). The independent variable, percentage of incentive pay available, was 0, 25, 50, 75, and 100 for each group. Thus, in the 0 group, no pay was available via incentives, and in the 100 group, all pay was via incentives (base pay was eliminated). Unlike the Frisch and Dickinson (1990) study, there was no cap on earnings. Production data suggested that there were significant differences between the 0 percent condition and the other incentive conditions, but revealed little difference among the remaining experimental conditions. This finding was consistent with that of Frisch and Dickinson (1990). In summarizing research that has examined the incentive pay ratio, Dickinson (1993) pointed out that results were quite consistent across a variety of experimental conditions—increased ratios of incentive to base pay do not produce commensurate increases in productivity, but all are better than standard hourly pay.

Linear versus Nonlinear Incentive Plans

Regardless of independent variables manipulated in studies cited thus far, as productivity increased, performance pay also increased by some fixed amount. However, such an arrangement is not the only possibility. Oah and Dickinson (1992) compared the effects of linear and exponential payoffs on productivity. The dependent variable was a simulation of a bank "proofing" task, similar to the task cited by Abernathy, Duffy, and O'Brien (1982) and Dierks and McNally (1987), in which information from simulated checks was entered via keyboard by college student subjects. The independent variable was the pay function, which was either linear (incremental increases in productivity produced fixed increments in pay) or exponential (incremental increases in productivity produced exponentially increasing pay). Although productivity data for the two groups did not differ statistically, the exponential group was never below the linear group. Furthermore, there was no difference in the rate at which productivity increased. Data reflecting dollars earned showed that the exponential group earned considerably more than the linear group, even though their productivity did not significantly exceed that of the linear group.

Smoot and colleagues (1991) examined the relationship between linear and nonlinear payoff systems and productivity (see Figure 9.1). The dependent variable was identical to that reported by Johnstone and colleagues (1989). The independent variable, the relation between productivity and payoff, took three forms: linear (each increment in productivity produced a fixed increment of payoff), positive acceleration (each increment in productivity produced an increasing payoff), and negative acceleration (each increment in productivity produced incrementally less payoff per unit of production). Productivity data showed increases for all experimental conditions over a baseline of base rate pay. The data also showed greatest proportional increases for the linear condition. In terms of cost per unit of production, the negative acceleration system was superior. It produced the least cost per unit; the positive system produced the next lowest cost per unit; and the linear system cost the most.

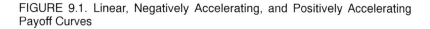

FIGURE 9.1. Linear, Negatively Accelerating, and Positively Accelerating Payoff Curves

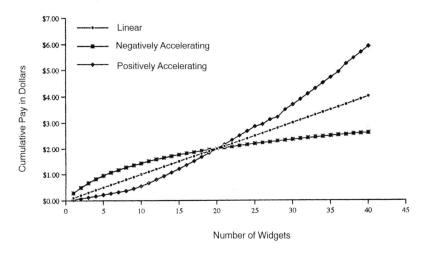

Smoot and colleagues (1992) examined linear, negative, and positive growth pay systems while subjects worked alone or in groups of four. In both alone and group conditions subjects were paid on the basis of their individual productivity. The results showed that there was no difference in productivity as a function of group versus alone conditions. As in the Smoot and colleagues (1991) study, the negative growth condition produced moderate increases in performance (36 percent) with only slight increases in cost (7 percent), whereas the other two conditions produced increases in productivity (41 percent for the positive and 19 percent for the linear), with much larger increases in cost (68 percent for positive and 62.5 percent for linear). (Smoot and Duncan [1997] provide a comprehensive presentation of the research results in this tradition, extant 1996.) (See Figures 9.2, 9.3, and 9.4.)

The laboratory-based studies provide some answers to questions about performance pay. First, it seems clear that pay procedures that are linked directly to performance lead to increased performance compared to procedures that are not strongly linked. Next, it appears that the actual amount of incentive pay as a proportion of base pay can be quite small and still be effective. Third, it appears that the size of the work group (when the number of subjects ranges from two to ten) is not an important factor influencing productivity when performance pay systems are in place. Finally, it appears that the slope of the payoff curve does not have a differen-

FIGURE 9.2. Individual and Group Performance Under Flat and Linear Pay Conditions

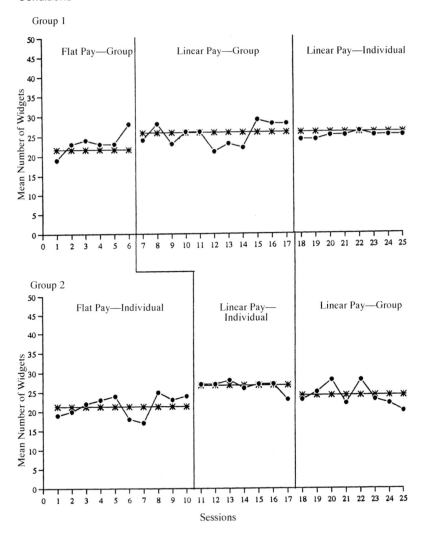

Source: Smoot et al., 1992.

Note: Closed circles represent the mean number of widgets produced per session by two groups that were exposed to the linear pay system while working in group and individual settings. Stars indicate condition means.

FIGURE 9.3. Individual and Group Performance Under Flat and Positively Accelerating Pay Conditions

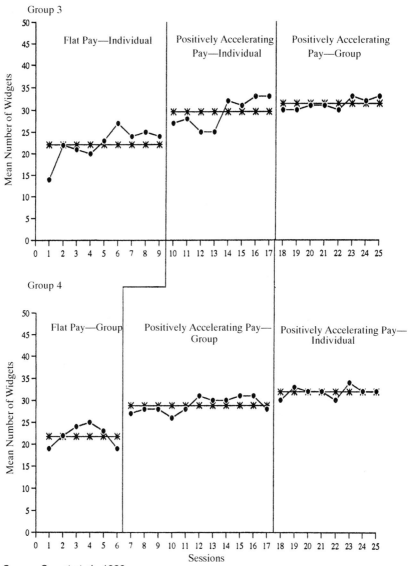

Source: Smoot et al., 1992.

Note: Closed circles represent the mean number of widgets produced per session by two groups that were exposed to the positively accelerating pay system while working in group and individual settings. Stars indicate condition means.

FIGURE 9.4. Individual and Group Performance Under Flat and Negatively Accelerating Pay Conditions

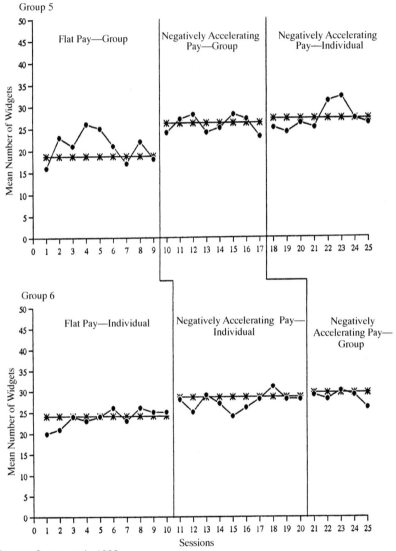

Source: Smoot et al., 1992.

Note: Closed circles represent the mean number of widgets produced per session by two groups that were exposed to the negatively accelerating pay system while working in group and individual settings. Stars indicate condition means.

tial effect on productivity, though a negatively accelerating curve may increase productivity and reduce cost per unit.

Limitations of Laboratory Research

A number of concerns about laboratory studies are valid and remain to be addressed (Oah and Dickinson, 1992). Typically, productivity has been the chief dependent variable, but other outcomes may be affected by performance pay systems, one of these being worker "satisfaction." Although satisfaction is not operationally defined in the literature in a consistent manner, determining what workers say about an incentive pay system may be useful in predicting important outcomes that do seem to be related to satisfaction, such as attendance and turnover.

Laboratory studies have utilized short sessions (fifteen to forty-five minutes) and have been conducted over relatively short time spans (weeks). Longer daily sessions (e.g., eight hours) and extended exposure (e.g., months) to the pay contingencies and general work settings may occasion different patterns of production behavior. Moreover, social behavior that may develop over time among workers and supervisors (see Parsons, 1974) may also affect productivity.

Although real money has been used in laboratory settings, the absolute amount of money involved has been relatively small. It is possible that performance pay systems cast on a larger scale of dollars may have different effects. Such a possibility could occur, in part, because payments in laboratories may constitute only discretionary funds for subjects, whereas earnings in the "real" world may be directed to basic necessities of life.

Another limitation of laboratory studies is that subjects are volunteers, whose participation can be withdrawn at any time, and therefore whose commitment to the work may be more tenuous than that of persons employed as a means of meeting necessities of living. Whereas workers may certainly quit at any time, the exigencies of paying bills make this option more difficult than for volunteer subjects. The necessity to remain in the workplace may affect productivity in ways not seen in the laboratory.

Generality of Research Findings

The very nature of laboratory studies, including those on performance pay, lead to questions of generality of the findings. Answers to such questions must come from research in the workplace, but such research is difficult because few organizations are willing or able, from a pragmatic view, to permit the periodic changes in payment schemes necessary to effectively ask experimental questions. LaMere and colleagues (1996) report one "real world" effort to experimentally evaluate performance pay. They measured jobs completed by truck drivers at a trash disposal service. After measuring baseline productivity, performance feedback was introduced, which led to an increase in jobs completed. For 135 weeks after the feedback condition, an incentive pay program was in effect. Whenever a worker's weekly performance exceeded average performance, that worker earned incentive pay. Incentive pay was either 3 percent, 6 percent, or 9 percent of total pay. Job performance increased compared to the feedback condition, but there were no differences in performance as a function of size of incentive. These findings are consistent with laboratory results reported by Frisch and Dickinson (1990) and Leary and colleagues (1990). Since the entire study lasted over three years in a work setting, many of the concerns about laboratory studies are eliminated.

Other studies have demonstrated the enduring effects of performance pay plans. For example, Wagner, Rubin, and Callahan (1988) examined the performance of foundry workers during base wage and incentive pay conditions. The incentive pay condition allowed workers to receive incentive pay for productivity that exceeded 80 percent of the standard. There were no base wages or other forms of compensation during the incentive pay condition. Upon introduction of the performance pay plan, productivity rose sharply above baseline and was sustained for approximately seventy months, until the study was terminated. Unfortunately, Wagner, Rubin, and Callahan (1988) do not report wages earned or cost per unit produced. Although their design utilized a simple comparison (A-B) format, the abrupt change after nearly four years of baseline data is persuasive. Similar, sustained effects have also been cited by Dierks and McNally (1987), Abernathy, Duffy, and O'Brien (1982), and Parsons (1992). Handlin (1992) suggests that decades of sustained success at the Lincoln Electric Company is based, in part, on a variety of incentive plans, including piece work and merit programs. Freund and Epstein (1984) also cite the many pay for performance plans used by Lincoln Electric to enhance productivity.

COMMON ELEMENTS

At this point, data from laboratory and workplace suggest that performance pay schemes of various sorts do increase productivity. This research also suggests that performance pay schemes can take many forms and still be effective. Still, it is useful to consider the differences between performance pay and traditional pay systems, because their effects are so remarkably different.

Unit of Measurement

Without exception, performance in successful performance pay systems has been measured by objective outcomes of the workers' efforts. These objective products take various forms, depending on the work setting, and range from "dollars sold" (Gaetani, Hoxeng, and Austin, 1985; George and Hopkins, 1989) to points earned for bank transactions (Abernathy, Duffy, and O'Brien, 1982) and effective trucking (LaMere et al., 1996). Objective measures of performance are quite different from the common supervisory ratings found in performance appraisals. Of the several advantages accompanying objective measures of performance, the one which perhaps aids the effectiveness of performance pay systems most is that there is minimal room for debate about whether or how well work was accomplished. Both employee and employer have the same data from which to compute performance pay.

When the index of performance is not an objective measure, such as in supervisory performance appraisals, the validity of the measure as a reflection of worker performance is in doubt. When worker pay is then tied to this dubious index, an occasion for unnecessary pay inequities is created. As Dickinson and O'Brien (1982) point out, it is virtually impossible to relate the traits and characteristics assessed by performance appraisals to job achievements, and " . . . as a consequence it is hard to justify or substantiate the evaluations" (p. 52).

Timely Consequences

A second characteristic of successful performance pay systems involves the delivery of consequences. Routinely, data about performance are made available to the workers soon after performance, that is, frequent and timely feedback. For example, George and Hopkins (1989) report providing productivity data daily for their subjects. Abernathy, Duffy, and O'Brien (1982) used automated systems to provide daily productivity data to bank workers. Parsons (1974, 1992) pointed out that workers in the famous Hawthorne studies obtained productivity data daily. The timely presentation of productivity data may serve as conditioned reinforcement, maintaining worker performance, with the delivery of money earned constituting generalized reinforcement for sustained high levels of productivity. In addition to these formally programmed consequences, it is possible that the actual completion of units of work serves as conditioned reinforcement for the workers. That is, completed work under a performance pay system is the occasion for monetary and possibly nonmonetary reinforcement (e.g., recognition, praise). Balcazar, Hopkins, and Suarez

(1986) observed that the reinforcer aggregate of performance data, recognition, and money has been particularly potent in affecting performance.

Closeness of Contingencies

Common in successful performance pay systems is a relationship between individuals' pay and work that can be described as a "closeness of contingencies." That is, whether workers are part of a group or working individually, the results of their work have a direct effect on their pay. This relationship is different than the contingencies under profit sharing and to some extent gainsharing plans, in which external factors, such as market conditions, may affect pay regardless of the quality or quantity of the workers' performance. There is a great body of literature which demonstrates that as significant consequences are separated, by time, from performance, the behavior becomes less controlled by those consequences (Skinner, 1969). Indeed, Abernathy (1990) suggests that designers of performance pay systems utilize nonmonetary contingencies to improve performance so that increased earnings or savings can become the basis of a gainsharing pool of money to fund performance pay.

No Losers

A final characteristic is that successful performance pay systems do not formally create losers—persons whose work is not reinforced because it was not as good as the work done by another. Performance pay systems operate on absolute rather than relative standards. Effective incentive pay systems are designed so that all workers can meet or exceed the work standard and earn the incentive. Use of relative standards, such as requiring the worker to exceed a group mean, automatically creates a subset of workers who fall below the mean. Regardless of any improvement in their work they fail to receive reinforcement.

FUTURE RESEARCH

Information from the laboratory and from applications in the work world suggest that performance pay systems are effective, yet additional research is necessary. Future research should include extensions of earlier research, and investigations of variables not yet addressed.

Extensions

Laboratory work (Stoneman and Dickinson, 1989; Johnstone et al., 1989) suggests that work group size is not a factor in performance pay systems. The upper level of work group sizes may have been too low, however, to reflect events in the work world. Therefore, additional research that includes work groups larger than ten workers both in the laboratory and in the work world would be useful.

There is no evidence from the laboratory that performance is differentially affected by payoffs given for individual versus group productivity. This result may be counterintuitive for those accustomed to working in a field where individual contingencies are advocated. Evaluation of the factors that maintain performance pay effects in groups would be helpful. Such evaluations might include analyses of contingencies involved in the phenomenon described as "social loafing" in the social psychology literature (Latane, Williams, and Harkins, 1979) where, among other factors, individual accountability seems to be an important factor in causing or preventing loafing.

Another laboratory finding that seems counterintuitive is the lack of correlation between productivity and size of the pay incentive (Frisch and Dickinson, 1990; Leary et al., 1990). Behavior analysts are familiar with research which indicates that size of the reinforcer affects the behavior it follows, at least to some limit. Such an effect would be diminished through satiation, but monetary reinforcement is unlikely to suffer this fate. It may be that merely establishing a reliable relation between work and its monetary effects, however modest, is sufficient to increase productivity. Investigations of this variable in the work world would be particularly informative, because the absolute value of monetary reinforcers as well as their relative values (percentage of base pay) has been limited in laboratory studies.

A final extension of laboratory work should address the shape of the incentive pay curve. Several forms of pay curve (linear, positive accelerating or growth, and negative growth) have produced increases in productivity in laboratory studies (Oah and Dickinson, 1992; Smoot et al., 1991; Smoot et al., 1992; Smoot and Duncan, 1997) when compared to flat-rate payoffs. These pay curves have generated different costs per unit of productivity, however, so that increases in units produced are offset by increased costs. Investigations in the work world might identify the most cost-effective pay curve.

Additional Questions

A number of areas related to the effectiveness of performance pay systems have yet to be examined. These include the nature of the work studied, demographics of the workers, and dependent variables other than the units produced.

Most research on performance pay has examined productivity units that are notable for their routinized character (widgets, data entered via a keyboard, dollars billed, etc.). Such indices are reasonable and have provided valuable data regarding the effects of pay systems. Future research should be directed at jobs that have heterogeneous, aperiodic tasks. Such jobs might include work done by managers and research and development staff. Such investigations would permit statements about performance pay effects on both blue-collar and white-collar work, and therefore add to the generality of the findings. It is unlikely that these apparently powerful contingencies would not work for managerial tasks.

One perspective posits no important difference between blue- and white-collar work. Gilbert (1978) has argued that any performance can be measured once the outcomes or accomplishments of that performance are clearly stated. It may simply be easier to state the accomplishments of a widget maker than those of a human resources manager. This viewpoint notwithstanding, empirical research demonstrating the efficacy of performance pay systems for a wide range of work would help establish the generality of these systems.

Worker demographics is an area largely unexamined in the performance pay literature. Of particular contemporary interest is the relation between membership in a protected class and performance pay systems. Although it is likely that members of various protected classes have participated in much of the laboratory and field research, the effects of the pay systems on these groups have not been evaluated.

A demographic variable of especial interest is age, because the workforce is getting older. In addition to the obvious question of generality between college-student subjects and "real world" workers, the question of differential effects of performance pay systems on the growing senior citizen work population is important. To some extent the return of senior citizens to the workforce may be due to financial considerations, but there also are arguments that social variables play an important role in this phenomenon (Machan, 1989). To the extent that social factors play a central role for this worker population, performance pay contingencies may have less effect than contingencies utilizing social relations.

An issue unaddressed in the behavioral literature is the effectiveness of compensation systems developed in the United States, but installed in U.S. companies overseas or in foreign-based companies. Harvey (1993) argues that a host of issues regarding the economic and cultural practices of foreign countries may alter compensation systems successfully implemented in the United States. McHale (1990) and Townsend, Scott, and

Markham (1990) also suggest that the culture of the country and company are major factors affecting the success of compensation systems.

Gaining attention recently are "skill-based" pay systems, which focus on "skill, knowledge, or competency development" (Lawler, 1992, p. 156). In such systems, the organization identifies needed tasks, the skills necessary to accomplish those tasks, and means to measure the tasks. Employees are then told what skills they are permitted to learn, and they are paid extra for acquiring the skills. Sets of skills may be "horizontal," such as sequential steps on an assembly line, or "vertical," cutting across hierarchy levels of the organization. The existence of skill-based pay does not necessarily imply performance-based pay, but the objective definition and measurement of the skills would be compatible with pay for performance schemes. Abernathy (1990) describes a compensation plan, "matrix gainsharing," which combines pay for performance and cross-training of workers (establishing workers with multiple skills) in order to allow the organization maximum flexibility.

A final set of factors worthy of investigation are non-production-dependent variables, such as turnover, absenteeism, and job satisfaction. The performance pay literature has been relatively quiet with respect to these, but their study could prove valuable. Oah and Dickinson (1992) and Mawhinney (1984) both refer to the notion that contingency systems, including performance pay systems, may have effects beyond worker productivity. To the extent that such effects involve behaviors such as coming to work regularly and on time, and/or behaving in ways beyond written work expectations, data about them are important.

A great deal of knowledge about performance pay systems has come from the laboratory, but much research advocated above must be done in the work world. Realistic group sizes, dollar values, work periods, etc. can only be simulated in the laboratory, but eventually generality must be demonstrated in the real world. This necessity poses a dilemma, however, since those in the work world who would most benefit from definitive findings about performance pay systems may be reluctant to support the research necessary to generate those findings. Although measurement of key performance and related variables may be initially intrusive, such intrusions can be defended easily by virtue of the valuable information they provide the organization in terms of productivity and worker views. Periodic manipulation of the pay system for research rather than business reasons may be seen as much more intrusive, and even though strong arguments can be made for the long-term good, the short-term contingencies (e.g., frequent revisions of compensation formulas, legal constraints, labor contracts) may effectively mitigate against such manipulation. Still, if behavior analysts are to move beyond laboratory studies and work world demonstrations of performance pay systems, persuasive arguments must be made.

REFERENCES

Abernathy, W. B. (1990). *Designing and managing an organization-wide incentive pay system.* Memphis, TN: W. B. Abernathy and Associates.

Abernathy, W. B., Duffy, E. M., and O'Brien, R. M. (1982). Multi-branch, multi-systems programs in banking: An organization-wide intervention. In R. M. O'Brien, A. M. Dickinson, and M. P. Rosow (Eds.), *Industrial behavior modification: A management handbook* (pp. 370-382). New York: Pergamon Press.

Babbage, C. (1832). *On the economy of machinery and manufacturers.* London: Charles Knight.

Balcazar, F., Hopkins, B. L., and Suarez, Y. (1986). A critical, objective review of performance feedback. *Journal of Organizational Behavior Management, 7*(3/4), 65-89.

Blinder, A. S. (Ed.). (1990). *Paying for productivity.* Washington, DC: The Brookings Institution.

Bullock, R. J. and Lawler, E. E. (1984). Gainsharing: A few questions, and fewer answers. *Human Resources Management, 23,* 23-40.

Dickinson, A. M. (1993). *Percentages, incentives, and productivity: A review of the results.* Paper presented at joint meeting of the Florida Association for Behavior Analysis/Organizational Behavior Management Network, St. Petersburg, FL, January.

Dickinson, A. M. and O'Brien, R. M. (1982). Performance measurement and evaluation. In R. M. O'Brien, A. M. Dickinson, and M. P. Rosow (Eds.), *Industrial behavior modification: A management handbook* (pp. 51-64). New York: Pergamon Press.

Dierks, W. and McNally, K. A. (1987). Incentives you can bank on. *Personnel Administrator, 32* (March), 61-65.

Fein, M. (1970). *Wage incentive plans.* Norcross, GA: American Institute of Industrial Engineers.

Freund, W. C. and Epstein, E. (1984). *People and productivity.* Homewood, IL: Dow Jones-Irwin.

Frisch, C. J. and Dickinson, A. M. (1990). Work productivity as a function of the percentage of monetary incentives to base pay. *Journal of Organizational Behavior Management, 11*(1), 13-33.

Gaetani, J. J., Hoxeng, D. D., and Austin, J. T. (1985). Engineering compensation systems: Effects of commissioned versus wage payment. *Journal of Organizational Behavior Management, 7*(1/2), 51-63.

George, J. T. and Hopkins, B. L. (1989). Multiple effects of performance-contingent pay for waitpersons. *Journal of Applied Behavior Analysis, 22,* 131-141.

Gilbert, T. F. (1978). *Human competence.* New York: McGraw-Hill.

Gowen, C. R. (1990). Gainsharing programs: An overview and history of research. *Journal of Organizational Behavior Management, 11*(2), 77-99.

Handlin, H. C. (1992). The company built upon the golden rule: Lincoln Electric. *Journal of Organizational Behavior Management, 12*(1), 151-163.

Harvey, M. (1993). Designing a global compensation system: The logic and a model. *Columbia Journal of World Business, 28*, 56-72.

Johnstone, J., Trefsgar, D., Berg, S., Kaufman, J., Jones, B., and Duncan, P. (1989). *Pay for performance.* Paper presented at the meeting of the Association for Behavior Analysis, Milwaukee, WI, May.

LaMere, J., Dickinson, A. M., Henry, M., Henry, G., and Poling, A. (1996). The effects of a multi-component monetary incentive program on the performance of truck drivers: A longitudinal study. *Behavior Modification, 20*, 385-406.

Latane, B., Williams, K., and Harkins, S. (1979). Many hands make light the work: The cases and consequences of social loafing. *Journal of Personality and Social Psychology, 37*, 822-832.

Lawler, E. E. (1992). *The ultimate advantage.* San Francisco: Jossey-Bass.

Leary, K., Roberts, S., Trefsgar, D., Jones, B., Jones, C., McKnight, J., and Duncan, P. (1990). *Affects of incentive pay on productivity.* Paper presented at the meeting of the Association for Behavior Analysis, Nashville, TN, May.

Machan, D. (1989). Cultivating the grays. *Forbes, 144* (September), 126-128.

Mawhinney, T. C. (1984). Philosophical and ethical aspects of organizational behavior management: Some evaluative feedback. *Journal of Organizational Behavior Management, 6*(1), 5-28.

McHale, P. (1990). Pay for performance or performance for pay? *Benefits and Compensation International, 20*, 12-18.

Mitchell, D. J. B., Lewin, D., and Lawler, E. E. (1990). Alternative pay systems, firm performance, and productivity. In Blinder, A. S. (Ed.), *Paying for performance* (pp. 15-94). Washington, DC: The Brookings Institute.

Oah, S. and Dickinson, A. M. (1992). A comparison of the effects of a linear and an exponential performance pay function on work productivity. *Journal of Organizational Behavior Management, 12*(1), 85-115.

Parsons, H. M. (1974). What happened at Hawthorne? *Science, 183*, 922-932.

Parsons, H. M. (1992). Hawthorne: An early OBM experiment. *Journal of Organizational Behavior Management, 12*(1), 27-43.

Peach, A. B. and Wren, D. A. (1992). Pay for performance from antiquity to the 1950s. *Journal of Organizational Behavior Management, 12*(1), 5-26.

Roethlisberger, F. J. and Dickson, W. J. (1939). *Management and the worker.* Cambridge, MA: Harvard University Press.

Scott, W. D., Clothier, R. C., and Spriegel, W. R. (1961). *Personnel management: Principles, practices and point of view.* New York: McGraw-Hill.

Skinner, B. F. (1969). *Contingencies of reinforcement.* Englewood Cliffs, NJ: Prentice-Hall, Inc.

Smoot, D. A. and Duncan, P. K. (1997). The search for optimum individual monetary incentive pay system: A comparison of the effects of flat pay and linear and non-linear incentive pay systems on worker performance. *Journal of Organizational Behavior Management, 17*(2), 5-75.

Smoot, D. A., Jones, B., Lynch, S., Bair, K., Carre, S., and Duncan, P. K. (1991). *Pay for performance in the laboratory: Linear versus non-linear incentive pay systems.* Paper presented at the meeting of the Association for Behavior Analysis, Atlanta, GA, May.

Smoot, D. A., Naylor, S., Carre, S., Gorelik, A., Greenberg, J., Johnson, P., Lubeach, S., and Duncan, P. K. (1992). *Affects of linear versus non-linear pay systems on productivity.* Paper presented at the meeting of the Association for Behavior Analysis, San Francisco, CA, May.

Stoneman, K. G. and Dickinson, A. M. (1989). Individual performance as a function of group contingencies and group size. *Journal of Organizational Behavior Management, 10*(1), 131-150.

Townsend, A., Scott, K., and Markham, S. (1990). An examination of country and culture-based differences in compensation practices. *Journal of International Business Studies, 21,* 667.

Wagner, J. A., Rubin, P. A., and Callahan, T. J. (1988). Incentive payment and nonmanagerial productivity: An interrupted time series analysis of magnitude and trend. *Organizational Behavior and Human Decision Processes, 42,* 47-74.

Chapter 10

The Safe Performance Approach to Preventing Job-Related Illness and Injury

Beth Sulzer-Azaroff
Kathleen Blake McCann
Todd C. Harris

Prevailing wisdom suggests that many job-related injuries are accidents and, therefore, not preventable, even as evidence to the contrary continues to mount. Death and injury rates remain high. For instance, in the United States alone, deaths from work-related injuries occur about every fifty minutes, and injuries occur every eighteen seconds (National Safety Council, 1991). The costs of these incidents in terms of human suffering are incalculable. Financial losses have been estimated to exceed $119.4 billion, including wage and productivity losses of almost $60 billion (National Safety Council, 1996). This chapter describes the unique contribution that management practices derived from the science and technology of behavior analysis can make toward reducing such injuries through promoting safe practices on the job.

CURRENT APPROACHES TO DEALING WITH SAFETY

Successful organizations tend to grant safety prime consideration in essentially all aspects of their operations, recognizing that widespread prevention of injuries at work depends on a multifaceted approach. Their efforts are aimed at simultaneously complying with governmental regulations and policies, encouraging collaboration between employees and their representatives within many professional specialties, including public health, occupational medicine, industrial hygiene, ergonomics, safety engineering, human resources, safety training, professional organizational management, and others. Together they design healthier, safer working environments, equipment, tools, job tasks, schedules, more effective training, and postinjury treatment methods and management techniques.

The Human Element

Despite the striking improvements these many efforts have generated, the risky behavior that results in occupational illness and injury persist. Technological experts remain frustrated by the fact that "although some gains in injury reduction may be achieved through engineering or regulatory approaches, individuals will adjust their behavior patterns to at least partially offset the gains from engineering 'solutions'" (Vilardo, 1988, p. 3). Experts are in agreement regarding the importance of the human element in processes that culminate in work-related illness, injury, and death (e.g., Chilton, Lombardo, and Pater, 1991; Geller, 1996; Heinrich, Peterson and Roos, 1980; McSween, 1995; Peters, 1991; and others). Even under optimal circumstances, people take unnecessary risks. Most people have witnessed others doing blatantly unsafe things at work, despite "knowing better." Indeed, all of us can probably recall an instance of our own risky behavior—such as standing on a chair to reach an object instead of using a sturdy stepladder. Frequently the issue is not one of not knowing or being incapable of choosing the safer alternative. More often than not we simply fail to do so. Why is this so?

REASONS FOR UNSAFE PERFORMANCE

Over the years, behavior analysts have begun to understand why people behave in ways detrimental to their health and safety on the job (Chhokar, 1987; Geller, 1996; Krause, 1984; McSween, 1995; Peterson, 1989; Smith, Anger, and Uslan, 1978; Sulzer-Azaroff, 1982, 1987; Sulzer-Azaroff, Harris, and McCann, 1994). According to this view, either they have not learned how to be safe consistently or the explanation lies in the contingencies (i.e., relations between the behavior and its consequences, antecedents and context). (For a complete discussion of environmental contingencies and contingencies of reinforcement see Chapter 2, this volume.) Until shaped otherwise by history or rules to act optimally under given circumstances, faulty performances tend to be repeated. Actually, such performances continue to strengthen when reinforcing events follow or are paired with the performance.

By contrast, if the typical reinforcement of performance-related behavior is not regularly forthcoming (extinction) or it is punished, the behavior will diminish. How slowly or rapidly these changes take place depends on performance fluency (the behavior's rate and consistency), and the arrangement of environmental contingencies. Unfortunately, ideal safe performance tends to remain unsupported in most natural work environments because being safe often requires extra steps, discomfort, or the additional effort entailed in changing habits.

Consider the natural consequences of working unsafely. In most cases, the act of working unsafely does not result in injury. Rather, the work is usually completed more rapidly and efficiently and the worker does not suffer injury. Additionally, the quality of the work product (the result of the performance) does not reflect whether or not the work was done safely. In actuality, compliance with many safety regulations (e.g., wearing personal protective equipment) is uncomfortable, hinders task performance, and may be awkward. As Heinrich, Peterson, and Roos (1980) pointed out, a person can act unsafely many times and never suffer injury as a consequence; however, we cannot wait until an injury occurs for this "natural lesson" to be learned.

Providing a safe environment and minimizing potential risk are both moral and legal responsibilities of the work organization. Therefore, along with other methods for ensuring employee safety, it is necessary to identify and alter deleterious contingencies if the dangerous circumstances are to be remedied. Training alone, even to mastery and fluency, is insufficient (Sulzer-Azaroff, Harris, and McCann, 1994). Beyond that, the work environment must program positive, immediate, and predictable consequences for practicing safe work habits and negative, immediate, and predictable consequences for unsafe ones. These, as will be demonstrated later, are the types of behavior consequences that strongly influence behavior and will tip the scales in favor of safe performance.

Although the steps just described are conceptually simple, in practice they are far more complicated. Identifying and treating risky practices can become a formidable task. First the organization must examine itself and select the performances most in need of attention. Then it must allocate human, organizational, and financial resources to the effort and establish assessment tools to implement and evaluate program efficacy. Covering all elements makes success more probable. The following model covers the most essential aspects of a systematic behavior management program.

THE SAFE PERFORMANCE MODEL

Some organizations are proactive. In these organizations, enhancement of job safety has always been accorded status as a key priority. Others are reactive. In these organizations the emphasis on safety is sporadic and occurs in response to specific untoward events. For instance, the decision to develop a safety program may derive from some unforeseen tragedy, an extraordinary increase in compensation costs, litigation, or an abrupt increase in incidence rates. More often than not, any effects of such sporadic efforts are short lived.

Whatever the catalyst, however, we advise against rushing into premature interventions. It is better to take the time to examine an array of factors to determine their influence on worker performance. Systematically identifying the detrimental and beneficial contingencies in effect and adjusting them favorably will generate a greater payoff in the long run. As in many choice situations, selecting for rapid payoff is not necessarily the most beneficial over time. Following an orderly sequence of actions typically is more advantageous. Toward this end, the steps characterizing successful safe job performance programs have been incorporated into an evolving model (see Sulzer-Azaroff, 1982, 1987) that focuses on enhancing safe performance of specific actions on the job. Figure 10.1 displays the most recent variation. Here we describe and illustrate the model in its present version and analyze each of the steps from the vantage point of organizational behavior management.

Ecobehavioral Analysis

Any program of behavior change occurs in a context that exerts a powerful influence on behavior in that context, including behavior targeted for change (Michael, 1982). Several years ago, the first author had occasion to visit a couple of industrial plants a few days apart. One produced airplane engines; the other paper products. Presumably both had the potential to be polluted, hazardous environments. Nevertheless, the first was immaculately clean; workers used protective equipment and had low rates of accidents. Incidentally, as often is the case with superior performers, quality and rate of production remained high. An inspection of the second plant revealed floors covered with debris, spills, obstructed aisles, teetering piles of materials, and inconsistent use of protective equipment among workers. Accident rates were comparatively higher. Safety officials in both locations were unable to explain the disparities between their own and the other's safety status beyond their spontaneous admission that "That's just the way we do it here," or casting blame on other people by asserting that "The workers just don't care; that is the safety climate around here."

A sensitive observer, on the other hand, would have been able to detect important differences in the dominant practices (see Chapter 17, this volume) in each setting. Unlike the second organizational setting, where the

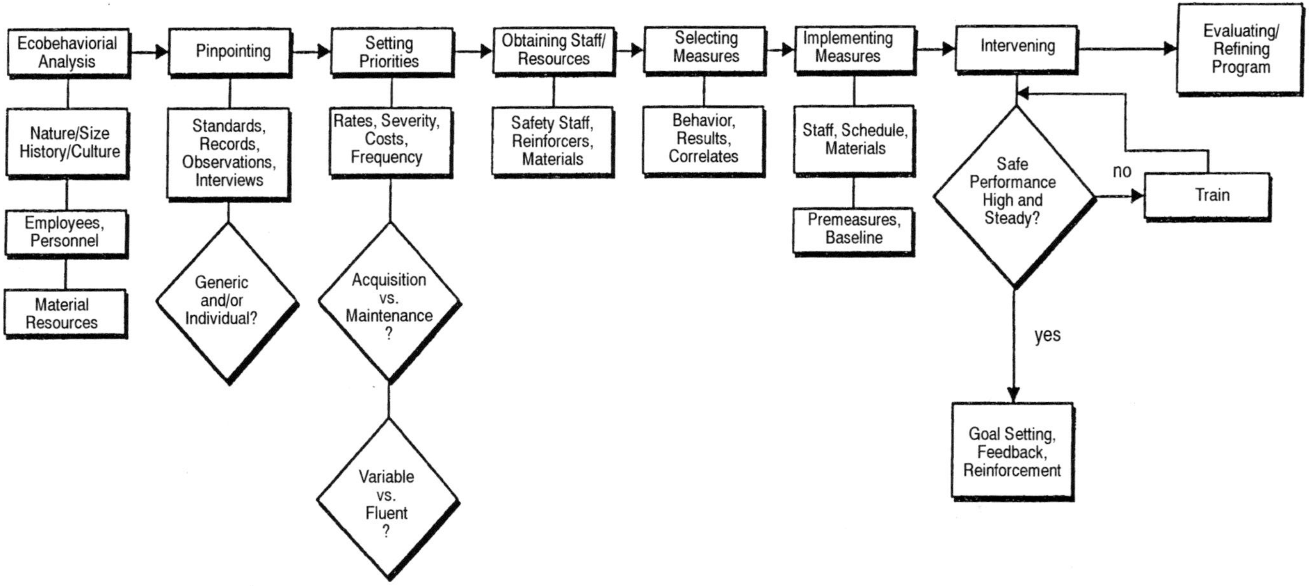

FIGURE 10.1. A Model for Improving Safety with Organizational Behavior Management

safety program was limited to doing only those things required to avoid fines and censure from regulatory agencies, the first setting gave safety top billing and carefully trained and supervised safe practices. Membership of safety and steering committees included hourly workers, professional staff, and union and managerial representatives, and they adhered to a regular schedule of meetings and safety-related activities. Other organizational structures, such as a system for consistently reviewing and recognizing continuous progress, were in place. Managers were visible and adhered to the same safety routines as line workers, thus serving as positive role models. Perhaps workers were asked to participate actively in the development and institutionalization of the safety program. In all likelihood, adhering to safe practices as well as other aspects of the job routine were reinforced positively. The corporate culture (see Chapters 7 and 17, this volume) embodied many of the features of successful performance management practices—the organizational environment supported safe behaviors.

Harshbarger and Rose (1991) emphasized the powerful influence of organizational culture. They found that when managers' and subordinates' roles were clarified and feedback and reinforcement became more positive, accident rates in a manufacturing plant began to diminish. Similarly, Pidgeon (1991) described a good safety culture as one in which workers were rewarded when they were attentive to safety issues; Turner (1991) advised that a positive safety culture can be developed through the allocation of praise, promotions, and cash to employees who behave safely.

Unfortunately, many organizational cultures lack those kinds of dominant practices. Ecobehavioral analysis is a tool that permits the situation to be improved as simply and nondisruptively as possible. The following is a recommended series of steps for tapping benefits of an ecobehavioral analysis.

Analyze the Organization's Mission and Ongoing Operation

This effort can (1) reveal conditions promoting or failing to temper problematic performances; (2) suggest promising levels or points of entry; and (3) permit a prediction about the potential for producing general and/or lasting change. If safety is not included explicitly in the company's mission, related policies and procedures may be absent or applied sporadically. Operational structures, such as safety committees composed of representatives of all relevant groups that encourage participative decision making, can influence the durability of any performance improvement efforts. Therefore, taking the time to examine the mission statement, written policies, and procedures, and to systematically observe the organization's safety efforts, is well advised.

Determine the Level of Enthusiasm of Organizational Leaders for Improving Safety

Ambivalence on the part of senior officers and popular worker representatives toward safety improvement is a threat to its long-term support. Obtaining advance evidence of probable cooperation is a sensible precaution (Hale et al., 1991). Keen scrutiny of reporting and data systems, talking confidentially to people at all levels, and being on-site regularly will suggest how closely safety issues are considered and where the process might be faulty. Questionnaires such as Zohar's (1980) Safety Climate Survey, Burke and Carder's HSE Survey (Carder, 1995), or Bailey's Minnesota Perception Survey (Bailey, 1993, 1997) also may yield information about contingencies possibly operating and even, as Bailey found, serve as a catalyst for change. A hospitable milieu is the best condition for initiating a program directed at both short and long-term accomplishments.*

Become Acquainted with the Current Safety Program

The current safety program is important because the present strengths can serve as the foundation for future activities. To illustrate, at a commercial bakery in Sweden, accident frequency and severity dropped substantially when two simple routines, (1) accident investigation and (2) follow-up procedures, were added to the ongoing activities of the safety department (Menkel, Carter, and Hellbom, 1993). Neither the organizational structure nor standard procedures required radical change and it was found that the company continued the modified routines over an eleven-year period. Similarly, Laitinen and Ruohomäki (1996) modified details of ongoing weekly inspections at two Finnish construction sites to include observing and recording of adherence to eight safety rules and publicly posting large graphs of the results.

Assess the Organization As a Whole Prior to Identifying Promising Points of Entry

Ecobehavioral assessments may suggest whether an organization-wide approach is essential or if the intervention needs to be focused more nar-

---

*What people report about their perceptions and what actually is happening may differ to varying degrees. We suggest formally sampling what people *do* before concluding it exactly matches what they *say*.

rowly (e.g., in a particular department or unit). Assessments also identify existing data systems that can be used or modified to pinpoint specific results or performances targeted for change. To illustrate, in an unpublished effort, the first and second authors used an approach similar to that conducted by Greenwood and colleagues (1984) to analyze staff injuries at a training school for the developmentally disabled. Safety incidents were recorded on a matrix form that included such information as time, place, personnel, and job routines. Findings indicated that the most frequent injuries involved assaults by clients in the hallway between day activities and dinner, thereby uncovering potential targets for intervention. This prompted staffing alterations during that time, leading in turn to a reduction in that class of injuries. This was seemingly simple, yet pinpointing, the next major step of the safe performance model, often is somewhat more complex.

Pinpoint

Identifying optimal performance objectives or *pinpoints* (behaviors and their direct results described as observable operations) is the most cost-efficient way to proceed (see Daniels, 1989, and Sulzer-Azaroff and Mayer, 1991, for technical aspects of pinpointing and Sulzer-Azaroff and Fellner, 1984, for specifics about safety pinpoints). Often objectives are selected arbitrarily, perhaps in reaction to an unusual incident. Only later is it discovered that accomplishing the objective is blocked by insufficient control over the reinforcement contingencies or that attaining it has been excessively costly while contributing little to the well-being of the workforce. As previously discussed, a better way is to invest time and effort initially to identify objectives that promise to impact most powerfully on employee fitness, cost reduction, and participant satisfaction.

Review Standards and Records

Much can be learned from reviewing accident records, incidence rates, and written governmental and organizational safety policies and standards particular to the job performances of concern. Most industrialized nations require accident reporting systems and studying those from the site involved can disclose useful information (see Fox and Sulzer-Azaroff, 1987, for strategies to improve accident reporting). Minutes of meetings of the safety committee (e.g., Menkel, Carter, and Hellbom, 1993), data collected by the safety department, suggestion box items, and other archival information can help identify the "hot spots" in the system—including near-accidents (Carter and Menkel, 1985), property damage (Bird and Germain, 1997), and the conditions under which accidents occurred most often.

Observe

Alone or with others (managers, union leaders, safety committee, or staff members), touring the work site several times can accomplish a number of purposes. Observers can learn about the nature of the operation of each work unit, meet personnel, and possibly speak informally with workers about safety issues. Additionally, during such tours, one may detect conditions that have escaped the recognition of regular staff more accustomed to their surroundings.

Interview

Beyond any informal conversations, systematic interviews with managers, safety personnel and committee members, and representatives from various work units can disclose information pertinent to selecting safety objectives. During such confidential meetings, respondents often bring applicable examples to the surface. Among others, these might include near misses, damaged property, "accidents waiting to happen," direct and indirect costs, strengths and weaknesses of the current system, workplace culture, and the informal contingencies currently influencing the probability of safe performance.

Generate Pool of Potential Pinpoints

Based on the preliminary activities just discussed, a pool of constructive safety practices (actions) and results (what remains right afterward) can be generated. When feasible, negative examples should be turned into positive ones (e.g., from "Don't store chemicals in unlabeled, breakable bottles" to "Store chemicals in unbreakable, clearly labeled containers") to clarify the appropriate performance and specify occasions for reinforcement. In large, diverse organizations, overly extensive lists of rules must be pared down. One tactic is to determine which items are general to the entire organization, such as "Exit immediately when the alarm rings," and which are more idiosyncratic, such as "Use hoists for lifting paper rolls." Next, the priority-setting phase will be discussed, during which the most crucial of these pinpoints may be chosen for inclusion in organization-wide and department-specific interventions.

Set Priorities

Assuming the array is extensive, pinpoints need to be sorted according to several dimensions: (1) how they relate to accident frequency and severity; (2) to whom they are relevant; (3) under what circumstances they occur; (4) whether they involve mastery and fluent performance of a new skill or consistent practice of a previously acquired one; and (5) associated cost. Analyzing variations in performance (i.e., through statistical process control, Mawhinney, 1992) will indicate whether a blanket approach throughout the organization or one focused on specific personnel and performances is more prudent.

Determining accident frequency requires tallying the number of times an incident has occurred when the objective was violated. Severity and costs can be assessed by counting number of deaths, permanent injuries, days involved in lost time injuries or occupational illnesses, amount of compensation paid, or by means of other formula developed by job safety experts (Heinrich, Peterson, and Roos, 1980; National Safety Council, 1996). Potential benefits also can be estimated (e.g., see Lopez-Mena et al., 1988). To initially focus on a receptive target population (Miller, 1991), pinpoints might be related to demographic variables, nature of the job, and supervisory particulars.

Discovering whether the workers involved actually have demonstrated mastery of the skill they are supposed to practice is essential. Expecting people to follow a routine with which they are not familiar is unreasonable. As discussed later, by assessing their ability to perform the task correctly *and* fluently (i.e., at high and steady rates), program developers can decide whether management or training-based approaches are indicated.

Consideration should be given to the difficulty and cost involved in assessing the desired performance; performance of some pinpoints is very simple to detect and reinforce, such as whether an aisle is unobstructed. Also, consider including a few important well-established performance objectives within the list of pinpoints so baselines are at moderate, not zero, levels. This primes the program by permitting some performances to qualify for reinforcement at the onset of the feedback/reinforcement program. Once the initial list of objectives has been established, it is time to take stock of available resources, so limitations of funds or personnel can be overcome.

Obtain Staff and Other Resources

As in any worthy endeavor, the success of performance-based job safety programs depends upon the availability of certain resources. People have to be permitted the time to be involved in overseeing the system, setting and finalizing pinpoints, developing measures and measurement systems, conducting audits, delivering feedback and reinforcement, and other activities. Often the very effectiveness and survival of a safety initiative depends in part on both employees and supervisors feeling that they are involved in it (e.g., Harris, 1997). Personnel qualified for these tasks may be selected from safety departments, committees, human resource departments, or elsewhere from within or outside an organization. In one case (Sulzer-Azaroff et al., 1990) a retired member of the safety department was hired on a part-time basis to conduct audits. Managers at all levels will need to commit time to the activity, as will participating employees (usually to provide and/or to receive feedback and reinforcement). The investment in personnel time is heavier initially and can be reduced once the program is operating steadily. Additionally, if the organization lacks a specialist in performance management, it is advisable for managers to obtain training in the basics or to seek external consultation to support the program.

Material resources include office supplies and perhaps funds for tangible reinforcers (e.g., awards, inexpensive items such as T-shirts, mugs, caps, etc.) and group celebrations. When contrasted with the enormous potential savings involved in injury prevention, costs for program resources constitute a minor investment.

At this point, investment of resources must be matched against the requirements of tentative objectives. The need to pare down the number of initial pinpoints, level of participant involvement, or auditing complexity may become apparent. Often the 80:20 rule (Pareto's Law) (Daniels, 1989) holds—that 80 percent of the gain can be achieved for 20 percent of the investment.

Select and Implement Measurement System

Select Measures

Specifying pinpoints precisely simplifies the selection of measures. In the case of ongoing behavior, all the elements of each behavior and/or result that constitute the safe performance objective are indicated, along with any elements that should not be present. Table 10.1 shows a task analysis for positioning multiply handicapped adults, upon which Alavosius and Sulzer-Azaroff (1990) based their observational recording form. Usually the process needs to be refined in order to obtain adequate levels of reliability (at least an 80 percent index of agreement between observers). Rating videotaped and on-site samples of distinctions, both obvious and subtle, between acceptable and unacceptable performance is a useful way of accomplishing this process of refinement.

Performances that may not be readily observed, such as throwing trash or spilling liquids on the floor, frequently leave a semipermanent result. Often these results can be tallied. When counting multiple results would be too time consuming, they can be sampled by using a "zone system."

TABLE 10.1. Task Analysis for Positioning Procedures

Step	Component

Seated in wheelchair

1	Inform resident what you are going to do.
2	Lock wheelchair brakes.
3	Position resident's buttocks squarely in the seat.
4	Stand behind and close to resident.
5	Grasp resident's arms and cross at chest; lift/pull resident to back of chair.
6	Lift with arms. Back remains straight.
7	Center resident's head and shoulders over hips.
8	Fasten seat belt across pelvis.
9	Place feet on footrests, if available.

Lying on side

1	Prepare and clean area; obtain materials to go beneath resident.
2	Check if person is dry (change if not).
3	Inform client what you are going to do.
4	Stand close to and in line with resident.
5	Locate head, shoulder, and pelvis against bolster.
6	Use pulling rather than pushing motions when moving client, when possible.
7	Set spine when bearing weight (no twists).
8	Place a pillow under client's head and between legs.
9	Place pillow at chest (hip to shoulder).

Supine

1	Prepare and clean area; obtain materials to go beneath client.
2	Check if client is dry (change if not).
3	Inform resident what you are going to do.
4	Stand close to and in line with resident.
5	Place a pillow beneath client's head.
6	Use pulling rather than pushing motions when moving client, when possible.
7	Set spine (no twists) when bearing weight.
8	Lift bed rails up, side supports in place.

Source: Alavosius and Sulzer-Azaroff (1990).

This method requires mapping out the work space and splitting it into a set of zones, perhaps the areas surrounding particular equipment, a quadrant, or given square footage of a room. Sulzer-Azaroff and colleagues (1990) used a factory blueprint to divide work areas into zones, each of which was individually audited. Zones free of hazardous conditions and those containing problems were tallied and any hazards were marked on the map with specific symbols indicating the types and placements of the dangers observed.

Other important measures related to the efficacy of safe performance programs include: accidents, injury rates, severity indices, direct and indirect costs, and satisfaction of people involved. Beyond the costs for resources listed previously, compensation payments, insurance premiums, medical charges, court settlements, equipment replacement and repair, personnel expenditures, down time, and other items need to be recorded if the cost/benefit ratio of the system is to be assessed fairly (see Heinrich, Peterson, and Roos, 1980; National Safety Council, 1996; Veltri, 1990).

Implement Measures

Personnel who collect the data need to be trained to the levels of reliability described previously and also to record in an unobtrusive, nonthreatening manner. Any concern by personnel about being observed rapidly begins to fade during the intervention, as the procedure becomes recognized as an antecedent to reinforcement. A formal system of support for safety auditors is warranted, because, like any person, they work best when they receive ongoing feedback and recognition for the quality of the job they are doing (Sulzer-Azaroff, 1995).

The schedule for conducting safety audits depends on the nature of the ongoing operations, personnel, pinpoints, resources, and other logistic factors. In a materials research laboratory where personnel work irregularly and accidents are very rare, monthly data collection has been adequate. Conversely, when dealing with repetitive motion, such as keyboard entry or grocery checkout, measures would need to be collected far more frequently to obtain representative samples of performance at steady state and while undergoing change. McCann and Sulzer-Azaroff (1996) recorded keyboard performance daily over a period of four months.

Prior to any OBM intervention, ongoing behavior and results need to be measured repeatedly to establish a representative baseline. Also, should any additional training or retraining of the pinpointed safety practices become necessary during measurement, the data collection needs to continue throughout and following training. Indeed, baseline data may reveal that some presumably problematic practices actually are very safe, illustrating the differences between perceived problems and objective information. Baseline data that do evidence of problematic performance then are used as a standard against which changes during the subsequent intervention may be assessed. Also, the distribution of data points within the baseline indicate steps (subgoals) toward which it is reasonable to strive initially.

Initially, personnel may react to the unaccustomed presence of observers by performing abnormally, thus invalidating the data. This reactivity can be diminished to some extent if participants are informed that the program is directed toward improving their own well-being and that, beyond ordinary policy, information obtained will not be used for negative personnel actions. However, the assessments can be assumed to be sufficiently representative when measures stabilize; that is, when graphed data reveal no new high or low points for at least three complete audits in a row.

Related measures also need to be assessed at this time including: previous years' accident rates, minor first aid and lost-time injuries, costs, and so on. These data can serve as premeasures against which the impact of any collateral changes promoted by the program can be contrasted.

Intervene

Train

Employers frequently react to worker deficiencies in job performance by providing additional training. As behavior analysts have discovered, however, lack of skill often is not the culprit. Rather, the presence of interference and the absence of supportive contingencies are at fault. Furthermore, additional training often produces only temporary modifications in long-established habitual practices (Berler, Gross, and Drabman, 1982; Fleming and Sulzer-Azaroff, 1992; McCann and Sulzer-Azaroff, 1996). In their book *Habit Control in a Day,* Azrin and Nunn (1977) discuss the importance of intervening intensively throughout all facets of a person's life in support of habit change.

Determine Training Requirements. If initial assessments suggest that given individuals consistently fail to execute each of the elements in a complicated routine smoothly, further training may indeed be indicated. To establish the necessity for taking this step, the worker could be asked to provide rationales for each critical performance, to describe the proper performance, and then demonstrate the skill several times. The results might indicate the necessity for instruction in the theory and/or knowledge of the skill. Halting or inconsistent performance points to the need for fluency training.

Conduct Training. Fortunately, people usually are preselected for their abilities to perform their jobs satisfactorily, and training skills tends to be relatively uncomplicated. Newly purchased equipment usually is accompanied by in-service instruction. However, sometimes employers incorrectly assume that the people they hire will be capable of doing their job safely or leave to others the responsibility to conduct the training on the job. We have seen inadequately prepared health care practitioners following routines improperly, thereby placing themselves at risk for injury. Often formal training segments have been developed to avoid those sorts of circumstances (Alavosius and Sulzer-Azaroff, 1990; Babcock et al., 1992; McCann and Sulzer-Azaroff, 1996; Fox, Hopkins, and Anger, 1987; and others).

Response fluency, or the rapid, steady practice of a skill, is a feature of job performance often overlooked. Research has shown that fluency tends to be paired with lower error rates, and enhanced endurance and generality of the skill (see Lindsley, 1992). Initially, fluency can be trained away from the place where the behavior is to be applied, as Blake (1991) did to teach safe posture and hand positions during keyboard entry tasks. Eventually, though, it needs to be transferred to the actual job site. Otherwise the stimuli distinctive to the natural setting may set the occasion for previously unsafe patterns. Health care providers' high consistent rates of safe lifting and transferring of adult patients were achieved by means of an "intensive feedback phase," during which almost every trial was treated with informational feedback and approval as merited (Alavosius and Sulzer-Azaroff, 1990).

When a complex skill is absent from the employee's repertoire or executed very poorly, more complete training, perhaps off and definitely on the job, is called for. Given space limitations, a thorough explanation of effective behavioral instruction is not feasible in this chapter. Suffice it to say that the recommended tactics are those involved in shaping, chaining, and promoting stimulus and verbal control of the type presented elsewhere in this volume (Chapter 2), in textbooks and papers on safety training (Goldstein, 1975), and in behavioral education literature in general (e.g., Alberto and Troutman, 1990; Maher and Forman, 1987; Tiemann and Markle, 1990; Sulzer-Azaroff and Mayer, 1986, 1991). Then, assuming adequate observational sampling has verified workers' mastery of the safe performances, the management aspect is activated. A good way to begin is with a kickoff event, during which all participants are assembled and informed about the rationale and methods of the program, and questions and comments received.

Provide Feedback

Thereafter, staff send or personally give specific detailed informational feedback to the people they have observed working and/or unit supervisors, team leaders, or other responsible individuals as soon as feasible after the observed act (see Alvero, Bucklin, and Austin, in press, and Balcazar, Hopkins, and Suarez, 1986). Table 10.2 lists a set of OBM safety programs that have included performance feedback as a key element. Written feedback often consists of a copy of the completed observation form accompanied by definitions and standards used to assess each performance. Overall performance scores, consisting of the number of safe performances and results divided by the total number observed, also are supplied, along with general comments. These scores then may be transferred to large wall-mounted graphs posted in the area to display change over time.

Set Goals

Goal-setting here refers to setting numerical performance levels to be achieved: terminal (e.g., 100 percent over three audits in a row) or subgoals to be met during the next phase of the change process (e.g., 10 percent higher than the last phase). Challenging, yet achievable, subgoals are selected on the basis of current performance (Chhokar and Wallin, 1984; Fellner and Sulzer-Azaroff, 1984; Komaki, Barwick, and Scott, 1978). Ideally, employees should become active participants in the program. For example, a supervisor might assemble the workers in the unit, indicate their performance levels over the past several audits, and ask that they suggest a new level to be achieved and sustained (or exceeded) for a set series of observations. Members should be asked to look to their recent best levels as a guide to selecting reasonably challenging but realistically achievable new goals.

Reinforce Safe Performance

Opportunities for reinforcement are now in place, because improvements from observation to observation provide the occasion for approval and recognition. (Of course, any dangerous acts observed are corrected instantly.) Sustained subgoal accomplishments may serve as a basis for what more substantial rewards. These may intermittently dispensing somewhat more substantial rewards. These may consist of items selected by participants from a "menu" or by observing to see what activities they tend to elect (e.g., an extra break).

TABLE 10.2. Summary of Percentage Reduction in Accident or Incident Rate Associated with OBM and Behavior-Based Safety Interventions

	Authors	Setting	% Reduction in Accident or Incident Rates (Unless reported in other form)
1.	Alavosius, M. (2000)	Fifty small companies	Lost work days per 100 workers: 184 pre to 111 during; 84 post 6 months and 58 post twelve months
2.	Calkins, M.D. (1971, August)	City refuse department	Vehicle accidents, bodily injuries, and lost man hours decreased
3.	Cooper, M.D., Phillips, R.A., Sutherland, V.J., and Makin, P.J. (1994)	Construction industry	From 6.33 prior to 3.88, at end; from 3.3 to .56 on checklisted items
4.	Fellner, D.J. and Sulzer-Azaroff, B. (1984)	Paper mill	Significant difference between pre- and during-feedback, from 6.9 to 4.9
5.	Fiedler, F. (1987)	Mine workers	Baseline = 226%; follow-up 2% over industry average
6.	Fox, D.K., Hopkins, B.L., and Anger, W.K. (1987)	Coal miners	Range 15% to 32%
7.	Harshbarger, D. and Rose, T. (1991)	Bedding; footwear	Lost-time accidents 95 and 87, respectively
8.	Haynes, R.S., Pine, R.C., and Fitch, H.G. (1982)	Urban transit	24.9%
9.	Karan, B.S. and Kopelman, R.E. (1987)	Vehicular and industrial	2.2% and 4%
10.	Komaki, J.L., Barwick, K.D., and Scott, L.R. (1978)	Food manufacturing plant	Injuries fell to " . . . less than ten lost-time accidents per million hours worked, a relatively low number" (p. 441)
11.	Komaki, J.L., Heinzmann, A.T., and Lawson, L. (1980)	Vehicle maintentance	Decline from 3.0 lost-time injury rate per month preceding to .4 during and 1.8 following program

TABLE 10.2 *(continued)*

	Authors	Setting	% Reduction in Accident or Incident Rates (Unless reported in other form)
12.	Krause, T.R. Seymour, K.J., and Sloat, K.C.M. (1999)	Seventy-three facilities participating for up to five years	Year 1: 26 Year 2: 42 Year 3: 50 Year 4: 60 Year 5: 69
13.	Larson, L.D. et al. (1980)	Police vehicles	Personal injury accidents from baseline of .40 to .13 per 100,000 miles
14.	Loafman, B. (1998)	Utility company	Reduction in treatment group and increase in control/comparison group
15.	Lopez-Mena, L. and Antidrian, J.V. (1990)	Two forestry and one cement factory	Reduction maintained for three years
16.	Lopez-Mena, L. and Bayes, R. (1988)	Electrical distribution system	Reduction in two work settings
17.	Lopez-Mena, L. et al. (1988)	Electrical energy distribution system	Reduction
18.	Mattila, M. and Hyödynmaa, M. (1988)	Building construction	Accident rate per 100 workers lower compared to rate among workers at a comparison site
19.	Mattila, M., Rantanen, E., and Hyttinen, M. (1994)	Construction	Statistically significant negative correlation ($p < .05$) between safety score and injury rates
20.	McSween, T.E. (1995)	Gas pipeline company	Reduction in lost-time accidents
21.	McSween, T.E.(1995)	Chemical company: union coordinated	Reduction from four to zero after eighteen months

	Authors	Setting	% Reduction in Accident or Incident Rates (Unless reported in other form)
22.	Montero, R. (1996)	Industry—general	"Rate dropped almost to zero"
23.	Naesaenan, M. and Saari, J. (1987)	Shipyard	Reduction
24.	Petersen, D. (1984)	Railroads	"Experimental groups had fewer injuries than controls"
25.	Reber, R.A., Wallin, J.A. and Chhokar, J. (1984)	Farm machinery manufacturing	Reduction
26.	Saarela, K.L. (1989)	Shipyard	Modest nonsignificant reduction in accident frequency (poster campaign—not full behavioral program but feedback to supervisors)
27.	Saarela, K.L. (1990)	Shipyard	Reduction during and after intervention
28.	Saarela, K., Saari, J., and Aaltonen, M. (1989)	Shipyards	No significant effect (poster campaign; general subject feedback)
29.	Saari, J. and Naesaenan, M. (1989)	Shipyard	Reduction in accidents and injuries
30.	Schwartz, R. (1989)	Grocery distribution workers	Reduction
31.	Smith, M., Anger, W., and Uslan, S. (1978)	Shipyard	Greater reduction in eye injuries per 100 workers compared to control/comparison group
32.	Sulzer-Azaroff, B. et al. (1986)	Paper mill	Reduction
33.	Sulzer-Azaroff, B. et al. (1990)	Telecommunications parts manufacturing plant	Reduction in OSHA recordables and lost time comparison

Accomplishing an end goal provides an opportunity for more powerful reinforcement—a celebration of some type known to appeal to all participants. In one program (Sulzer-Azaroff et al., 1990), workers in units achieving 100 percent safety scores for three audits in a row were treated to a special luncheon attended by plant officials. Many of the articles cited in Table 10.2 also combined social, tangible, and/or monetary rewards with feedback delivered following major improvements.

Evaluate and Revise the Program

Actually, program evaluation is continuous, because data are recorded regularly. This permits emerging trends in performance to be revealed. Therein lies the beauty of the OBM approach. Problems can be addressed as rapidly as they emerge, instead of waiting until statistics are analyzed at the end of the year or quarter. For instance, a leveling off in performance for several weeks might suggest that workers have become satiated with current reinforcing events. The obvious solution is to vary the reinforcers.

Although determining incident, injury, and cost figures along with other collateral measures may be delayed, these and other factors need to be analyzed and matched against program objectives. Often, once the system is ongoing, it can be streamlined by altering personnel functions and observation and reinforcement schedules, substituting pinpoints, and so on. At such times, though, it is especially important to continue to closely scrutinize the data. This facilitates the detection of any deterioration in performance, which might indicate the necessity for returning to the more rigorous program.

Support Lasting Change

Assuming the various organizational and managerial structures are in place, they should function to promote and sustain momentum. As mentioned earlier, these could include a system for information flow and feedback across and within all levels and functions, methods of reinforcing the safety efforts of all personnel, and a group or team to provide ongoing leadership (e.g., a steering committee) to do the following:

- Gather evidence that the system is functioning as designed ("treatment integrity")
- Review performance, injury, cost, safety climate, and other data
- Solicit input from all constituencies
- Suggest modifications such as adding new or deleting nonessential pinpoints, refining definitions, altering schedules, and reviewing and revising systems of recording, feedback, reinforcement, and goal setting

• Respond to new regulations, policies,
• Inform organizational members of progress by individuals and teams
• Showcase outstanding exemplars.

SUMMARY AND CONCLUSION

Organizational behavior management has demonstrated its value as an essential feature of a comprehensive approach to preventing illness and injuries on the job. A growing number of experimental analyses of procedures founded on behavior analytic principles and procedures are being reported. As time passes, program designs are becoming more sophisticated and results more valid, broad scale, and long lasting. Beyond modifying performance at risk for injury or illness, data during the past decade increasingly are showing reductions in injuries and their attendant costs.

Currently, it is recognized that if sustained improvement is to occur, the organizational context needs to be examined carefully and prepared to support subsequent interventions. Beyond that, numerous other aspects bear further investigation, including: analyzing the various elements of the model to determine what each contributes to the overall effort; interactions between pinpoints and types of interventions; methods for enhancing cost efficiency of systems; ideal observational schedules in general or for specific response classes; relations between actual behavior and assessed attitudes and perceptions; the value of and best composition and functioning of teams, and of employees' direct participation in designing and/or implementing the system; and methods for informing and transferring this technology to the larger organizational community, policymakers, related disciplines, and others. Refinements based on answers to questions of this nature should impact even more positively on the health and well-being of workers at large.

REFERENCES

Alavosius, M. (2000). Behavioral approaches to organizational safety. In J. Austin and J. E. Carr (Eds.), *The Handbook of Applied Behavior Analysis,* Context Press: Reno, NV: Caulkins.

Alavosius, M. P. and Sulzer-Azaroff, B. (1990). Acquisition and maintenance of health-care routines as a function of feedback density. *Journal of Applied Behavior Analysis, 23,* 151-162.

Alberto, P. A. and Troutman, A. C. (1990). *Applied behavior analysis for teachers* (Third edition). Columbus, OH: Merrill.

Alvero, A. M., Bucklin, B. R., and Austin, J. (in press). An Objective Review of the Effectiveness and Essential Characteristics of Performance Feedback in Organizational Settings (1985-1998). *Journal of Organizational Behavior Management.*

Azrin, N. H. and Nunn, R. G. (1977). *Habit control in a day.* New York: Simon and Schuster.

Babcock, R., Sulzer-Azaroff, B., Sanderson, M., and Scibek, J. (1992). Increasing nurses' use of feedback to promote infection control practices in a head injury treatment center. *Journal of Applied Behavior Analysis, 25,* 621-627.

Bailey, C. (1993). Improve safety program effectiveness with perception surveys. *Professional Safety,* October, 28-32.

Bailey, C. (1997). Managerial factors related to safety program effectiveness: An update on the Minnesota Perception Survey. *Professional Safety,* August, 33-35.

Balcazar, F., Hopkins, B. L., and Suarez, Y. (1986). A critical objective review of performance feedback. *Journal of Organizational Behavior Management,* 7(3/4), 65-89.

Berler, E. S., Gross, A. M., and Drabman, R. S. (1982). Social skills training with children. Proceed with caution. *Journal of Applied Behavior Analysis, 15,* 41-53.

Bird, F. E., Jr. and Germain, G. L. (1997). *The property damage accident: The neglected part of safety.* Loganville, GA: Institute Publishing, Inc.

Blake, K. E. (1991). *Toward the reduction of risk of carpal tunnel syndrome in video display terminal users through feedback.* Unpublished master's thesis, University of Massachusetts, Amherst.

Calkins, M. D. (1971). A municipal safety program that works. *The American City, 86,* 67-68.

Carder, B. (1995). How to develop leverage for safety improvement. Unpublished manuscript.

Carter, N. and Menkel, E. (1985). Near accident reporting: A review of Swedish research. *Journal of Occupational Accidents, 7,* 41-64.

Chhokar, J. S. (1987). Safety at the workplace: A behavioral approach. *International Labour Review,* March-April, 169-178.

Chhokar, J. S. and Wallin, J. A. (1984). Improving safety through applied behavior analysis. *Journal of Safety Research, 15,* 141-151.

Chilton, D. A., Lombardo, G. J., and Pater, R. F. (1991). Effective safety program design. *Proceedings of the First International Conference on Health, Safety and Environment in Oil and Gas Exploration and Production, 1,* 397-405.

Cooper, M. D., Phillips, R. A., Sutherland, V. J., and Makin, P. J. (1994). Reducing accidents using goal setting and feedback: A field study. *Journal of Occupational and Organizational Psychology, 67,* 219-240.

Daniels, A. (1989). *Performance management* (Third edition). Tucker, GA: Performance Management Publications.

Fellner, D. J and Sulzer-Azaroff, B. (1984). Increasing industrial safety practices and conditions through posted feedback. *Journal of Safety Research, 15,* 7-21.

Fielder, F. (1987). Structured management training in underground mining—five years later. Human Engineering and Human Resource Management in Mining; Proceedings Bureau of Mines Technology Transfer Seminar, Pittsburgh, PA, Bureau of Mines Information Circular 9145:149-153, 1987. Cited in Johnston, J. J., Cattledge, G. T. H. and Krause, T. R., Seymour, K. J. and Sloat, K. C. (1999). Long-term evaluation of a behavior-based method for improving safety performance: A meta-analysis of 73 interrupted time-series replications. *Safety Science, 32,* 1-18.

Fleming, R. and Sulzer-Azaroff, B. (1992). Reciprocal peer management: Increasing and maintaining beneficial staff-client interactions. *Journal of Applied Behavior Analysis, 25,* 611-620.

Fox, C. J. and Sulzer-Azaroff, B. (1987). Increasing the completion of accident reports. *Journal of Safety Research, 18,* 65-71.

Fox, D. K., Hopkins, B. L., and Anger, W. K. (1987). The long-term effects of a token economy on safety performance in open-pit mining. *Journal of Applied Behavior Analysis, 20,* 215-224.

Geller, E. S. (1996). *The psychology of safety.* Radnor, PA: Chilton Book Company.

Goldstein, I. L. (1975). Training. In B. L. Margolis and W. H. Kroes (Eds.), *The human side of accident prevention* (pp. 92-113). Springfield, IL: Charles C Thomas.

Greenwood, C. R., Dinwiddie, G., Terry, B., Wade, L., Stanley, S. O., Thibadeau, S., and Delquardi, J. C. (1984). Teacher- versus peer-mediated instruction: An ecobehavioral analysis of achievement outcomes. *Journal of Applied Behavior Analysis, 17,* 521-538.

Hale, A. R., Oortman Gerlings, P., Swuste, P., and Heimplaetzer, P. (1991). Assessing and improving safety management systems. *Proceedings of the First International Conference on Health, Safety and Environment in Oil and Gas Exploration and Production, 1,* 381-388.

Harris, T. C. (1997). *Predicting workplace safety outcomes through subordinate and supervisor involvement in safety issues.* Unpublished doctoral dissertation, University of Connecticut, Storrs.

Harshbarger, D. and Rose, T. (1991). New possibilities in safety performance and the control of worker's compensation costs. *Journal of Occupational Rehabilitation, 1,* 133-143.

Haynes, R., Pine, R. C., and Fitch, H. G. (1982). Reducing accident rates with organizational behavior modification. *Academy of Management Journal, 25,* 407-416.

Heinrich, H. W., Peterson, D., and Roos, N. (1980). *Industrial accident prevention.* New York: McGraw-Hill.

Karan, B. S. and Kopelman, R. E. (1987). The effects of objective feedback on vehicular and industrial accidents: A field experiment using outcome feedback. *Journal of Organizational Behavior Management, 8,* 45-56.

Komaki, J., Barwick, K., and Scott, L. (1978). A behavioral approach to occupational safety: Pinpointing and reinforcing safety performance in a food manufacturing plant. *Journal of Applied Psychology, 63,* 434-445.

Komaki, J. L., Heinzmann, A. T., and Lawson, L. (1980). Effect of training and feedback: Component analysis of a behavioral safety program. *Journal of Applied Psychology, 65,* 261-270.

Krause, R. T. (1984). Behavioral science applied to accident prevention. *Professional Safety Journal, 229,* 21-27.

Laitinen, H. and Ruohomäki, I. (1996). The effects of feedback and goal setting on safety performance at two construction sites. *Safety Science, 24,* 61-73.

Larson, L. D., Schnelle, J. F., Kirchner Jr., R., Carr, A., Domash, M., and Risley, T. R. (1980). Reduction of police vehicle accidents through mechanically aided supervision. *Journal of Applied Behavior Analysis, 13,* 571-581.

Lindsley, O. R. (1992). Precision teaching: Discoveries and effects. *Journal of Applied Behavior Analysis, 25,* 51-57.

Loafmann, B. (1998). Behavior-based safety: Power and pitfalls. *Professional Safety,* August, 20-23.

Lopez-Mena, L. and Antidrian, J. V. (1990). Applicaciones del refuerzo positivo a la reduccion de accidents en el trabajo. [Applications of positive reinforcement to reduction of work accidents.] *Revista Latinoamericana de Psicologia, 22,* 357-371.

Lopez-Mena, L. and Bayes, R. (1988). Prevencion de riesgos en el trabojo: Effectos de la retroalimentacion y la participacion. [Prevention of work accidents: Effects of feedback and participation.] *Avances en Psicologia Clinica Latinamericana, 6,* 53-65.

Lopez-Mena, L., Rodriguez-Moya, C., Soto-Elgueta, J. and Soto-Leconte, H. (1988). Beneficios económicos obtenidos con un programa conductual en seguridad del trabajo. [Economic benefits obtained with a behavioral work safety program.] *Psicologia del Trabajo y de Las Organizaciones, 4,* 74-86.

Maher, C. A. and Forman, S. G. (1987). *A behavioral approach to education of children and youth.* Hillsdale, NJ: Erlbaum.

Mattila, M. and Hyödynmaa, M. (1988). Promoting job safety on building: An experiment on the behavior analysis approach. *Journal of Occupational Accidents, 9,* 255-267.

Mattila, M., Rantanen, E., and Hyttinen, M. (1994). The quality of work environment, supervision and safety in building construction. *Safety Science, 17,* 257-268.

Mawhinney, T. C. (1992). Total quality management and organizational behavior management: An integration for continual improvement. *Journal of Applied Behavior Analysis, 25,* 525-543.

McCann, K. B. and Sulzer-Azaroff, B. (1996). Cumulative trauma disorders: Behavioral injury prevention at work. *Journal of Applied Behavioral Science, 32*(3), 277-291.

McSween, T. E. (1995). *The values-based safety process.* New York: Van Nostrand Reinhold.

Menkel, E., Carter, N., and Hellbom, M. (1993). The long-term effects of two group routines on accident prevention activities and accident statistics. *International Journal of Industrial Ergonomics, 12,* 301-309.

Michael, J. (1982). Distinguishing between discriminative and motivational functions of stimuli. *Journal of the Experimental Analysis of Behavior, 37,* 149-155.

Miller, L. K. (1991). Avoiding the counter control of applied behavior analysis. *Journal of Applied Behavior Analysis, 24,* 645-647.

Montero, R. (1996). How much "participation" does a behavior modification program need for improving safety? Paper presented at the International Conference on Occupational Health, September, Estocolmo, Suecia.

Naesaenan, M. and Saari, J. (1987). Effects of positive feedback on housekeeping and accidents at a shipyard. *Journal of Occupational Accidents, 8,* 237-250.

National Safety Council (1991). *Accident Facts.* Chicago: Author.

National Safety Council (1996). *Accident Facts.* Chicago: Author.

Peters, R. H. (1991). Strategies for encouraging self-protective employee behavior. *Journal of Safety Research, 22,* 53-70.

Peterson, D. (1984). An experiment in positive reinforcement. *Professional Safety,* May, 30-35.

Peterson, D. (1989). *Safe behavior reinforcement.* New York: Aloray, Inc.

Pidgeon, N. F. (1991). Safety culture and risk management in organizations. Special Issue: Risk and culture. *Journal of Cross-Cultural Psychology, 22(1),* 129-140.

Reber, R. A., Wallin, J. A., and Chhokar, J. (1984). Reducing industrial accidents: A behavioral experiment. *Employee Relations, 23,* 119-124.

Saarela, K. L. (1989). A poster campaign for improving safety on shipyard scaffolds. *Journal of Safety Research, 20,* 177-185.

Saarela, K. L. (1990). An intervention program utilizing small groups: A comparative study. *Journal of Safety Research, 21,* 149-156.

Saarela, K., Saari, J., and Aaltonen, M. (1989). The effects of an information safety campaign in the shipbuilding industry. *Journal of Occupational Accidents, 10,* 255-266.

Saari, J. and Naesaenan, M. (1989). The effect of positive feedback on industrial housekeeping and accidents: A long-term study at a shipyard. *International Journal of Industrial Ergonomics, 4,* 201-211.

Schwartz, R. (1989). Cognition and learning in industrial accident injury prevention: An occupational therapy perspective. *Health Promotion Prevention Programs, 6,* 67-85.

Smith, M. J., Anger, W. K., and Uslan, S. S. (1978). Behavioral modification applied to occupational safety. *Journal of Safety Research, 10,* 87-88.

Sulzer-Azaroff, B. (1982). Behavioral approaches to occupational health and safety. In L. Fredericksen (Ed.), *Handbook of Organizational Behavior Management* (pp. 505-538). New York: John Wiley and Sons.

Sulzer-Azaroff, B. (1987). The modification of occupational safety behavior. *Journal of Occupational Accidents, 9,* 177-197.

Sulzer-Azaroff, B. (1995). Lessons learned in enhancing safety performance in a paper mill. In T. E. McSween (Ed.), *The values based safety process: Improving your safety culture with a behavioral approach.* New York: Van Nostrand Reinhold.

Sulzer-Azaroff, B. and Fellner, D. (1984). Searching for performance targets in the behavioral analysis of occupational health and safety: An assessment strategy. *Journal of Organizational Behavior Management, 6*(2), 53-65.

Sulzer-Azaroff, B., Fox, C., Moss, S., and Davis, J. M. (1986). Feedback and safety: Involving workers. Final report to National Institute of Occupational Safety and Health. Grant #ROI-OHO-1928-01.

Sulzer-Azaroff, B., Harris, T. C., and McCann, K. (1994). Beyond training: Organizational performance management techniques. *Occupational Medicine: State of the Art Reviews, 9,* 321-339.

Sulzer-Azaroff, B., Loafman, B., Merante, R. J., and Hlavacek, A. C. (1990). Improving occupational safety in a large industrial plant: A systematic replication. *Journal of Organizational Behavior Management, 11*(1), 99-120.

Sulzer-Azaroff, B. and Mayer, G. R. (1986). *Achieving educational excellence using behavioral strategies.* Chicago: Holt, Rinehart and Winston.

Sulzer-Azaroff, B. and Mayer, G. R. (1991). *Behavior analysis for lasting change.* Chicago: Holt, Rinehart and Winston.

Tertinger, D. S., Greene, B. F. and Lutzker, J. R. (1984). Home safety: Development and validation of one component of an ecobehavioral treatment program for abused and neglected children. *Journal of Applied Behavior Analysis, 17,* 159-174.

Tiemann, P. W. and Markle, S. M. (1990). *Analyzing instructional design: A guide to instruction and evaluation.* Champaign, IL: Stipes.

Turner, B. A. (1991). The development of a safety culture. *Chemistry and Industry, 7,* 241-243.

Van Houten, R., Nau, P. A., and Marini, M. (1980). An analysis of public posting in Walters, H. A. (1998). Identifying and removing barriers to safe behaviors. *Professional Safety, 43*(1), 34-36.

Van Houten, R., Nau, P. and Zopito, M. (1980). An analysis of public posting in reducing speeding behavior on an urban highway. *Journal of Applied Behavior Analysis,* 383-395.

Veltri, A. (1990). Accident cost impact model: The direct cost component. *Journal of Safety Research, 21,* 67-73.

Vilardo, F. J. (1988). The role of the epidemiological model in injury control. *Journal of Safety Research, 19,* 1-4.

Zohar, D. (1980). Safety climate in industrial organizations: Theoretical and applied implications. *Journal of Applied Psychology, 65,* 96-101.

Chapter 11

Actively Caring for Occupational Safety: Extending the Performance Management Paradigm

E. Scott Geller

As illustrated throughout this volume, an arsenal of behavior change techniques is available (along with empirical validation) to increase desired work practices and decrease undesired work practices. Chapter 10 by Beth Sulzer-Azaroff, Kathleen Blake McCann, and Todd Harris, in particular, illustrates the wealth of behavior change technology available for the domain of occupational health and safety. Geller and colleagues (1990) introduced a system for categorizing behavior change interventions according to their relative cost-effectiveness (see also Geller, 1998). Interventions are categorized into multiple tiers or levels, each tier defined by its intrusiveness and cost-effectiveness. At the top of the "multiple intervention hierarchy" (i.e., Level 1), the interventions are least intrusive and target the maximum number of individuals for the least cost per individual. At this level, intervention techniques (e.g., behavioral prompting through signs, billboards, and public service announcements) are designed to have maximum large-scale appeal with minimal personal contact between target individuals and intervention agents. Geller and colleagues (1990) hypothesized

The author is grateful for numerous opportunities to learn occupational safety issues and challenges from the professionals at many Fortune 500 companies, including: Ford, ExxonMobil, Hoechst Celanese, Westvaco, Toyota, Georgia Pacific, American Standard, ARCO Chemical, AT&T, BHP Copper, Hercules, Coca-Cola, Chevron, Lockheed, Monsanto, 3M, Union Pacific Railroad, Walmart, Textron, Westinghouse, and Weyerhaeuser. Actively caring and constructive feedback on an earlier draft of this chapter was provided by Bill Redmon, Beth Sulzer-Azaroff, Tom Mawhinney, and Carl Johnson.

that those individuals uninfluenced by initial exposure to these types of interventions (i.e., Level 1) will be uninfluenced by repeated exposures to interventions at the same level of cost-effectiveness. These individuals require a more intrusive and costly (i.e., higher level) intervention.

Higher level (and more influential) intervention processes require increased costs in terms of materials and personnel (i.e., intervention agents). Compared to signs, lectures, and policy statements, for example, a feedback or incentive/reward process changes the behavior of more individuals, but such programs are much more costly to implement with regard to personnel, materials, and effort. These programs are in fact wasted on individuals who already emit the target behavior (perhaps as the result of a less intrusive intervention), but are necessary for "hard-core" problem individuals who are not influenced by behavior change techniques that are less intensive, less intrusive, and less costly.

Hypotheses and empirical support from problem behavior theory (e.g., Jessor, 1987; Melton, 1988; Wilson and Jonah, 1988) suggest that those persons most resistant to the less intensive and intrusive interventions are most likely to emit the most unsafe (or risky) behaviors. Thus, in the job setting, it is important to develop and implement higher order (more intrusive and costly) intervention processes for the more risky employees. These higher level intervention processes require the active assistance of other employees.

A key proposition in the multiple-intervention-level model proposed by Geller and colleagues (1990) and refined by Geller (1998) is that individuals influenced by an intervention program (at a particular level of cost-effectiveness and intrusiveness) should not be targeted for further intervention, but rather should be enrolled as intervention agents for the next (i.e., higher) level of behavior change intervention. In other words, "preaching to the choir" is not as beneficial as enlisting the "choir" to preach to others (cf. Katz and Lazarfeld, 1955). This chapter explores ways of identifying those employees most likely to become intervention agents for organizational behavior change, as well as ways to increase the probability that employees will become intervention agents. Although examples and illustrations refer to the domain of occupational health and safety (the author's intervention focus in organizations), the concepts and strategies are relevant for all areas of organizational performance management.

AN ACTIVELY CARING MODEL

In an editorial for a special issue of the *Journal of Applied Behavior Analysis,* I introduced an "actively caring model" that included constructs rarely used in performance management publications—self-esteem, empowerment, optimism, and belonging/ownership (Geller, 1991). The model developed from my discussions with leaders at Exxon Chemical Company who asked the question, "What does it take to get employees to care actively about the health and safety of their co-workers?" In this context, actively caring (AC) was operationally defined as employees acting to benefit the safety of other employees (e.g., implementing a particular intervention technique to benefit the safety or health of another employee). In more general terms, an AC employee is an intervention agent.

Our refined conceptualization of actively caring (Geller, Roberts, and Gilmore, 1992) defined three basic types of AC, depending upon the target of the intervention—environment, person, or behavior. Thus, when people intervene to reorganize or redistribute resources in an attempt to benefit others (e.g., cleaning another's work area, picking up litter, recycling, conducting an environmental safety audit), they are AC with an *environment* focus. Actively caring with a *person* focus is behaving in an attempt to make another person feel better (e.g., intervening in a crisis situation, actively listening in one-on-one communication, verbalizing unconditional positive regard for someone, sending a get-well card). Finally, *behavior*-focused AC is intervention attempting to influence another individual's behavior in desired directions (e.g., giving rewarding or correcting feedback, demonstrating or teaching desirable behavior, conducting a behavioral safety audit, or using a vehicle turn signal).

It is noteworthy that these three categories of AC represent the basic dimensions needing attention in a comprehensive occupational safety process (Geller, 1989b, 1990, 1996, in press). That is, occupational safety requires direct manipulation of the environment (e.g., equipment, tools, hazards, engineering) and ongoing work behaviors in ways that lead to increased safety and employee acceptance, commitment, and ownership (i.e., person factors). Although person factors (such as knowledge, intelligence, personality, motives, and attitudes) are not usually measured or managed directly by behavior analysts, these factors certainly influence acceptance of changes in the environment and in safe operating procedures, and they determine employees' resistance or commitment to improve the safety of the environment and behavior in their milieu. Indeed, Skinner (1971) himself wrote of the indirect person effects (i.e., perceptions of "freedom") resulting from different behavior change contingencies (i.e., positive versus negative reinforcement).

Differential perceptions of ownership, teamwork, commitment, and empowerment can result from objective manipulations of environments, behaviors, and environment-behavior contingencies. Likewise, although

AC intervention might focus on one particular factor (i.e., environment, person, or behavior), the intervention can certainly have indirect impact on other factors. For example, a direct attempt to increase safe behavior with a demonstration or feedback technique can increase perceptions of control, self-efficacy, and optimism in both the deliverers and recipients of the intervention, and in turn increase their propensity to participate in a subsequent environment-focused or behavior-focused intervention.

Figure 11.1 depicts our latest version of an AC model (from Geller, 1996) and represents the foundation of an assessment tool and training program we have used at more than 100 industrial complexes (i.e., for Exxon Chemical Company, Hoechst Celanese, and Sara Lee Knit Products) to help corporations achieve a "total safety culture." We teach employees that the individual difference (or person) factors represented in Figure 11.1 are states or expectancies (not traits) which influence one's propensity to get involved in a safety process to benefit other employees, and these person factors can be directly influenced by environmental and behavioral manipulations. Indeed, a critical group exercise involves the listing of specific situations and incidents in the employees' particular work setting that increase (or facilitate) and decrease (or inhibit) the person characteristics depicted in Figure 11.1 From a behavior analysis perspective these person factors (or expectancy states) represent establishing operations (Michael, 1982) that influence personal contingency-specifying statements and subsequent rule-governed behavior (Agnew and Redmon, 1992; Malott, 1992).

Variables consistently listed as influencers of self-esteem include communication strategies, reinforcement and punishment contingencies, and leadership styles. Our group discussions with employees have led to a number of suggestions for building self-esteem, including: (1) soliciting and following up employee suggestions, (2) providing opportunities for personal learning and peer mentoring, (3) increasing management and peer attention to the occurrence of *safe* as well as unsafe behaviors, and (4) increasing recognition of personal competence and accomplishments.

Common suggestions for increasing a sense of belonging among employees in a corporate culture have included decreasing the frequency of top-down directives and "quick-fix" programs obtained from other facilities, and increasing team-building discussions, group goal setting and feedback, group celebrations for both process and outcome achievements, and the use of self-managed (or self-directed) work teams.

By teaching employees that perceptions of personal control, self-efficacy, and optimism lead to employee empowerment, we are essentially distinguishing between a management and a psychological perspective of

FIGURE 11.1. The Active Caring Model for Occupational Safety

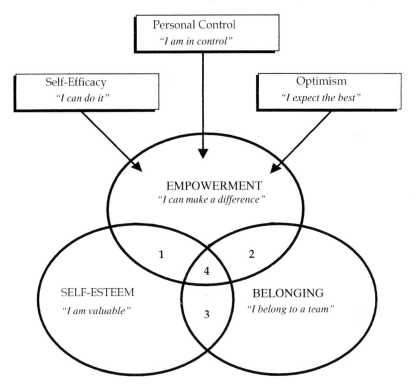

1. I can make *valuable* differences.
2. We can make a *difference.*
3. I am a *valuable team* member.
4. We can make *valuable differences.*

Source: Adapted from Geller (1996).

empowerment—one of the most popular constructs in contemporary industry. In the management literature, empowerment refers essentially to the delegation of authority or responsibility, or the sharing of decision making (Conger and Kanungo, 1988).

In contrast, the psychological (or person) perspective of empowerment considers the reaction of the employee or work group as a result of a delegation of power or responsibility. This person notion is clearly more subjective than the management view, but does explain variance in employee reactions to a top-management directive that implies more employee control. In other words, we presume that empowerment requires the personal perception that "I can make a difference," and this perception is enhanced by perceptions of personal control (e.g., Nowicki and Duke, 1974; Rotter, 1966), self-efficacy (Bandura, 1977), and optimism (Scheier and Carver, 1985, 1993; Seligman, 1991). Such empowerment perceptions are presumed to lead to increased motivation (or effort) to make a difference (e.g., to go beyond the call of duty in completing assignments), and there is significant empirical support for this intuitive supposition (e.g., Bandura, 1986; Barling and Beattie, 1983; Ozer and Bandura, 1990; Phares, 1976).

Employees in our corporate training groups have listed a number of operations to increase empowerment, including the following:

1. Break down overwhelming tasks into discrete smaller ones more easily managed (e.g., continuously monitored in terms of behaviors and/or outcomes).
2. Set short-term goals and track their accomplishment.
3. Offer frequent rewarding and correcting feedback for process activities (e.g., for practicing or coaching safe work behaviors) rather than only for outcomes (e.g., number of injuries or lost work days).
4. Provide opportunities for employees to set their own goals, teach co-workers, and chart "small wins" (Weick, 1984).
5. Teach employees how to define, observe, and record desired (e.g., safe) and undesired (e.g., at risk) environments and behaviors, and give them opportunities (i.e., time and resources) to conduct environmental and behavioral audits.
6. Teach employees basic behavior change intervention strategies (e.g., response feedback and recognition), and provide them time and resources to implement and evaluate the impact of their interventions.
7. Teach employees how to graph daily records of baseline, intervention, and follow-up data.
8. Post response feedback graphs of group performance (e.g., daily percentages of safe environmental conditions or work practices).

Our corporate training for occupational safety and health focuses on the establishment of resources, opportunities, and contingencies to increase the factors presumed to increase AC behavior. We do teach employees that certain person factors (e.g., as illustrated in Figure 11.1) influence their work behaviors, including their involvement in safety processes; and that work behaviors influence certain person factors (i.e., expectancy states or establishing operations). However, we emphasize that it is not cost-efficient to intervene directly with person factors in an industrial setting, partly because these variables are not easy to measure accurately and objectively on a large scale, and because effective person-focused intervention usually requires one-on-one or small group interaction, with assistance from a professional therapist or counselor. On the other hand, scientifically validated behavior-change interventions can be implemented and managed effectively by employees with minimum professional training and a willingness to become an intervention agent (e.g., to actively care for a co-worker's safety). In other words, it is much more cost-effective to "act" an employee into safety thinking than it is to "think" a person into safe acting.

EMPIRICAL SUPPORT
FOR THE ACTIVELY CARING MODEL

Many readers will recognize similarity between the AC concept and the psychological construct of altruism studied by personality and social psychologists for many years (e.g., Rushton, 1980). Altruism has been simply defined as unselfish behavior or acts intended to benefit others while resulting in no beneficial extrinsic material or interpersonal consequences to the perpetrator (e.g., Staub, 1978). Given roots in personality and social psychology, much of the research on altruism has attempted to define the dimensions of an altruistic personality, and to determine the extent that altruistic acts are actually unreinforced by extrinsic consequences (e.g., Batson et al., 1991; Batson et al., 1986). In contrast, actively caring is behavior presumably developed and maintained by extrinsic contingencies; and AC research will hopefully focus on the specification of establishing operations and response-consequence contingencies to increase the occurrence of AC behaviors.

An altruism and AC model might postulate the same intervening variables (e.g., self-esteem). However, for theorists and researchers studying altruism these variables define a personality construct, whereas for an applied behavior analyst (or performance manager) these intervening variables may suggest intervention techniques for increasing AC behavior. Given the AC model, for example, intervention strategies that increase perceptions of self-esteem, empowerment, and group belonging are preferred over intervention techniques that decrease such perceptions.

If the AC model is valid, social validity surveys (Schwartz and Baer, 1991; Wolf, 1978) should include questions to assess the impact of an intervention program on perceptions of self-esteem, empowerment (i.e., self-efficacy, personal control, and optimism), and belonging. In fact, a beneficial side effect of an intervention process might be an increase in one or more of the AC factors among the intervention recipients, and a resulting increase in the probability that these individuals will emit AC behaviors. Later in this chapter, I describe an AC survey we have been using to pinpoint work areas and people needing a particular intervention strategy, and to assess the social validity of corporate-based interventions to increase safe work practices. Also, the AC survey results often suggest the relevance of particular types of behavior change techniques.

I have found a number of empirical studies, mostly in the social psychology literature, that support the individual components of the AC model. Although these studies did not address more than one AC factor and did not implement rigorous behavior analysis methodology (e.g., no within-subject manipulations nor repeated measures), these studies did use objective experimental techniques and found robust differences. Thus, it seems the AC model warrants follow-up investigation with behavior analysis methodology.

The bystander intervention paradigm (Darley and Latane, 1968) has been the most common (and rigorous) laboratory paradigm used to study factors related to AC behaviors. With this paradigm, the factors presumed to affect AC behavior (i.e., self-esteem, perceived empowerment, and belonging) are measured or manipulated among a group of subjects, and subsequently these individuals are placed in a situation where they have an opportunity to help another individual who presumably encounters a personal crisis (e.g., falls off a ladder, drops personal belongings, or feigns a heart attack or illness). The latency in coming to a confederate's rescue is the dependent variable, studied as a function of a subject's social situation or personality state. It is noteworthy that the AC behaviors studied in these experiments were person focused (i.e., helping a person feel better) or environment focused (i.e., redistributing resources to benefit another person), but the AC behaviors were never behavior focused (i.e., attempting to change another person's behavior in beneficial directions).

Self-Esteem

According to Coopersmith (1967), self-esteem can be both relatively enduring *and* situational and transitory. In other words, self-esteem is generally considered a trait, but it can be affected by the environment. When situational changes return to normal, self-esteem returns to its chronic level. Self-esteem can vary across experience domains and across age, gender, and other role-defining conditions. For example, a person may regard himself or herself as a very worthy teacher but a completely unworthy musician or tennis player.

Michelini, Wilson, and Messe (1975) and Wilson (1976) measured subjects' self-esteem with a sentence completion test (described in Aronoff, 1967) and then measured whether subjects helped another individual in a bystander intervention paradigm. High self-esteem subjects were significantly more likely than low self-esteem subjects to help another person pick up dropped books (Michelini et al., 1975) and to leave an experimental room to assist a person in another room who screamed he had broken his foot following a mock explosion (Wilson, 1976). Similarly, subjects with higher self-esteem scores were more likely to help a stranger (i.e., a confederate) by taking his place in an experiment where they would presumably receive electric shocks (Batson et al., 1986).

In a study of AC behavior in a field setting, Bierhoff, Klein, and Kramp (1991) compared individual difference factors among people who helped or only observed at an accident scene. The people who stopped at the scene were identified by ambulance workers and were later given a questionnaire measuring certain personality constructs. Those who helped scored significantly higher on self-esteem, personal control, and social responsibility.

Personal Control

The personal control factor of AC is one of the most extensively researched individual difference variables, and refers to a general expectancy regarding the location of forces controlling a person's life—internal or external. Those with an *internal* locus of control believe they usually have direct personal control over significant life events as a result of their knowledge, skills, and abilities. In contrast, persons with an *external* locus of control believe that factors such as chance, luck, or fate play important roles in their lives (Rotter, 1966; Rushton, 1980). In other words, *internals* generally expect to have more personal control over the positive and negative reinforcers in their lives than do *externals*. Some studies have measured subjects' locus of control and then observed probability of AC behavior in a bystander intervention paradigm, whereas at least one study manipulated subjects' perception of personal control prior to a measurement of AC behavior.

The field study discussed in the previous section by Bierhoff, Klein, and Kramp (1991) found more AC behavior at an accident scene by bystanders with an internal locus of control. Also, those high self-esteem subjects who showed more AC behavior than low self-esteem behavior in Wilson's (1976) bystander intervention study (discussed previously) were also characterized as internals, in contrast to the lower self-esteem externals who were less apt to display AC behavior. In addition, Midlarsky (1971) found more internals than externals willing to help a confederate perform a motor coordination task that involved the reception of electric shocks.

Sherrod and Downs (1974) asked subjects to perform a task in the presence of loud, distracting noise, and manipulated subjects' perception of personal control by telling half the subjects they could terminate the noise (if necessary) by notifying them through an intercom. The subjects who could have terminated the noise (but did not) were significantly more likely to comply with a later request by a confederate to help solve math problems that required extra time and resulted in no extrinsic benefits.

Optimism

Optimism is the learned expectation that life events, including personal actions, will turn out well (Peterson, 2000; Scheier and Carver, 1985, 1993; Seligman, 1991). Other individual difference factors relate significantly to this construct, including self-esteem (Rosenberg, 1965), locus of control (Rotter, 1966), learned hopefulness (Zimmerman, 1990), and self-efficacy (Bandura, 1977). Zimmerman (1990), for example, defined empowering experiences as situations that provide opportunities to learn skills and develop a sense of personal control, and he presumed that empowerment is a product of learned hopefulness. In other words, as people gain control and mastery over their lives and learn to use their skills to affect life events and outcomes, they become empowered.

Researchers have manipulated optimistic states (or moods) among individuals by giving them unexpected rewards or positive feedback and then observing the occurrence versus nonoccurrence of AC behaviors. Isen and Levin (1972) observed that individuals who found a dime in the coin return slot of a public phone (placed there by researchers) were more likely to help a confederate who dropped a folder of papers than were individuals who did not find a dime. Similarly, students given a cookie while studying at the university library were more likely than those not given a cookie to agree to help another person by participating in a psychology experiment.

Isen, Clark, and Schwartz (1976) delivered free samples of stationery to peoples' homes and then called them later to request an AC behavior. Specifically, the caller said he had dialed a wrong number but since he used his last dime, he needed the subject to call a garage to tow his car. Subjects who had received the gifts of stationery were more likely to make the AC phone call than were subjects who had received no gift, even when the delay between gift receipt and the phone-call request was twenty minutes.

Carlson, Charlin, and Miller (1988) reviewed these and other studies that showed direct relationships between mood (or optimism) and AC behavior. They reported that the following pleasant experiences increased AC (i.e., helping) behavior, purportedly by inducing a positive mood (or optimistic outlook): finding a dime, receiving a packet of stationery, listening to soothing music, being on a winning football team, imagining a vacation in Hawaii, and being labeled a charitable person. The authors suggested that the state (or mood) caused by the pleasant experiences may have increased the perceived value of helping others as a positive reinforcer. From this author's perspective, the attempts to explain the relationship between an optimistic state and AC behavior have been circular or not convincing. However, the empirical findings are convincing and indicate that manipulations of mood states can influence the probability of AC behavior.

Berkowitz and Connor (1966) showed perceived success at a task to increase AC behavior in a different context. Subjects were instructed to complete certain puzzles in less than two and a half minutes. The task was manipulated to allow half of the subjects to succeed and half to fail. Subsequently, successful subjects made more boxes for a confederate than the unsuccessful subjects. In a series of analogous laboratory studies, Isen (1970) manipulated performance feedback on a perceptual motor task. Subjects told they had performed extremely well were more likely to emit AC behavior (e.g., by donating money to charity, picking up a dropped book, and holding a door open for a confederate) than those told they had performed very poorly.

These later studies illustrated potential overlap between optimism, self-efficacy, and personal control. That is, it is reasonable to assume positive feedback increases one's perception of self-efficacy and personal control in the situation, as well as one's optimism (i.e., expectation of good outcomes). Indeed, the first measure of optimism correlated significantly with locus of control (Scheier and Carver, 1985). Given that the AC model includes optimism, self-efficacy, and personal control as determinants of empowerment, these performance-outcome studies support the general hypothesis that the probability of AC behavior can be increased by increasing empowerment. Obviously, much follow-up research is needed to specify the discriminant validity and social validity of these three AC person factors.

Belonging

The social psychological construct most analogous to the AC concept of belonging or ownership is group cohesion—the sum of positive and negative forces attracting group members to one another (Wheeless, Wheeless, and Dickson-Markman, 1982). Satisfaction is considered a key determinant of group cohesiveness. The more cohesive a group, the more satisfied are members with belonging to the group; and the greater the member satisfaction with the group, the greater the group cohesiveness. The same authors identified two levels of satisfaction in interpersonal relationships: independence and involvement. Independence refers to an internal locus of control in group decision making, and group involvement reflects the level of interpersonal concern, respect, and warmth present in the group.

Ridgeway (1983) defined five beneficial consequences of group cohesiveness, including increased (1) quantity and quality of communication, (2) individual participation, (3) group loyalty and satisfaction, (4) ability to enforce group norms and focus energy toward goal attainment, and (5) elaboration of group culture, typified by special behavioral routines that increase the group's sense of togetherness. From this conceptualization, it follows that members of a cohesive group should demonstrate AC behavior for one another, but the AC model also predicts group cohesiveness will increase AC behavior for targets (i.e., persons, behaviors, and environments) outside the group.

Staub (1978) reviewed studies which showed that people are more likely to help victims who belong to their group, with "group" determined by race, nationality, or an arbitrary distinction defined by preference for an artist's paintings. Similarly, Batson and colleagues (1986) found subjects more likely to help a confederate if they rated her as similar to them. In a bystander intervention experiment, pairs of friends intervened faster to help a female experimenter who had fallen from a chair than did pairs of strangers. Thus, with friends, the bystander intervention effect (i.e., an inverse relationship between group size and victim-helping behavior) may not occur because group cohesiveness (or belonging) counteracts the diffusion of responsibility that presumably accounts for the bystander intervention effect (Latane and Nida, 1981).

By experimentally manipulating group cohesion in groups of two and four, Rutkowski, Gruder, and Romer (1983) tested whether group cohesion can reverse the usual bystander intervention effect. Cohesiveness was created by having the groups discuss topics and feelings they had in common related to college life. The dependent variables were the numbers of subjects (and the response latency of each) who left the experimental room to assist a "victim" (confederate) who had ostensibly fallen off a ladder. The findings indicated that group cohesiveness increased AC behaviors (perhaps because of reduced diffusion of responsibility), since both frequency and speed of helping was greater for the cohesive groups. The most AC behavior was found among subjects in the high-cohesion/ four-person group condition.

In a retrospective study, Blake (1978) examined real-world relationships between group cohesion and the ultimate in AC behavior—altruistic suicide. He gathered his data from official records of Medal of Honor awards given during World War II and the Vietnam War. The independent variable was the cohesiveness of combat units (estimated by group training and size), and the dependent variable was percentage of grenade acts—voluntarily using one's body to shield others from exploding devices. Results revealed that the smaller, more elite, specially trained combat units (e.g., the Marine Corps and Army airborne units) accounted for a substantially larger percentage of grenade acts than larger, less specialized units (e.g., Army nonairborne units), thus supporting the hypothesis that group cohesion increases AC behavior.

ASSESSMENT OF ACTIVELY CARING FACTORS

Surveys to measure the safety culture of industries are quite popular these days (Geller, 1992; Geller and Roberts, 1993; Simon and Simon, 1992), and proponents of these surveys often recommend their use to discriminate between "safe" and "unsafe" employees (Krause, 1992). To justify the use of these surveys, consultants often teach that individuals have stable personality traits which determine both their motivation level for particular tasks and their propensity to have an injury. This perspective on industrial safety seems to be increasing (as safety consultants peddle their quick-fix measurement devices), and can interfere with the more practical and cost-effective behavior-based approach to managing human resources, as illustrated in other chapters in this text.

At my industrial training workshops, I explain that valid individual differences scales are not available to reliably predict propensity to sustain a work injury, and even if approximations were available, more variance in injury risk is determined by environmental conditions, management systems, response contingencies, and peer pressure or support than any individual difference factor. I have found, however, that an assessment of individual differences (e.g., different lifestyles, personality factors, perceptions, cognitive strategies) can be useful in an employee training program to teach the concept of individual diversity and to increase employees' awareness of their own idiosyncrasies that potentially relate to injury proneness.

The Safety Climate Survey (SCS) that Steve Roberts, Mike Gilmore, and I developed for culture assessment and corporate training programs (Geller and Roberts, 1993; Geller, Roberts, and Gilmore, 1992, 1996) includes subscales to measure safety-related perceptions and risk propensity, including cognitive failures (Broadbent et al., 1982), sensation seeking (Zuckerman, 1979), psychological reactance (Tucker and Byers, 1987), and extroversion (Eysenck and Eysenck, 1985).

The most useful subscale of our SCS (from both a training and culture-change perspective) is an AC scale that includes adoptions from standard measures of self-esteem (Rosenberg, 1965), self-efficacy (Sherer et al., 1982), personal control (Nowicki and Duke, 1974), optimism (Scheier and Carver, 1985), and group cohesion (Wheeless, Wheeless, and Dickson-Markman, 1982). The SCS also includes measures of willingness to actively care with an environmental focus (e.g., "I am willing to pick up after another employee in order to maintain good housekeeping"), a person focus (e.g., "If an employee needs assistance with a task I am willing to help even if it causes me inconvenience"), and a behavior-change focus (e.g., "I am willing to observe the work practices of another employee in order to provide direct feedback to him or her"). The respondents' reactions to each item of the SCS are given on a five-point Likert-type scale ranging from "Highly Disagree" to "Highly Agree."

Our analyses from administrations of the SCS at three large industrial complexes showed remarkable support for the AC model (Geller and Roberts, 1993; Roberts and Geller, 1995). The stepwise regression analyses from these studies showed high levels of AC predictability from the individual difference factors deduced from the AC model. The personal control factor was consistently the most influential in predicting willingness to actively care; belonging predicted significant independent variance in AC propensity at two of the plants. Self-esteem and optimism always correlated highly with each other and with willingness to actively care, but only one or the other predicted independent variance in AC propensity. (For these administrations our SCS did not include a measure of self-efficacy.) The multiple regression coefficients and sample sizes were .54 (n = 262), .57 (n = 307), and .71 (n = 207) at the three plants, respectively (see Geller, Roberts, and Gilmore, 1996 for details).

These regression results were not of much interest to the plant managers, supervisors, and trainers at the target industries, but the more basic classification of AC-related items according to various work groups (e.g., managers, operators, secretaries, contractors, laboratory personnel, etc.)

did attract attention from industry leaders and had practical value. In one case, for example, relatively high levels of willingness to actively care convinced one plant manager to support an AC training and intervention process. At another plant, the extreme variability of AC propensity across work groups prompted the development of special AC intervention programs for certain work groups. These interventions are discussed in the next section.

ACTIVELY CARING IN ACTION

Of the numerous safety programs I have observed over the past two decades, the "Brothers/Sisters Keeper" process in effect at a Dupont plant I visited in Martinsville, Virginia, comes closest to an operational definition of actively caring. After volunteering to become a Brothers/Sisters Keeper, employees receive behavioral observation and communication training to qualify for a particular AC process. More specifically, the plant manager, safety personnel, and many supervisors and hourly workers at this plant recognize that safety requires ongoing monitoring and communicating between co-workers about safe work practice; and to achieve beneficial and continuous involvement for personnel safety, workers need to learn basic skills for observing and recording safe and at-risk work practices, and for communicating constructive feedback following the observations of their peers' safe or at-risk behavior.

Following this observation and communication training, the employees make a public commitment to look out for the safety of themselves and others, and then they begin working to meet the criteria necessary for becoming a certified Brothers/Sisters Keeper. When meeting these criteria, including twenty safety audits and forty personal safety contacts with a co-worker, employees participate in a formal ceremony and group celebration during which certificates and special Brothers/Sisters Keeper pins are distributed, and each employee's name and picture are added to the "Hall of Recognition."

Of course, the AC behavior of these employees does not end with this recognition; the ceremony promotes renewed commitment to actively care for others through behavioral observation and feedback communication. Some of these employees sign up for the "Disciple Program," whereby they become active teachers of new Brothers/Sisters Keepers and work to reach additional criteria of behavioral observation, corrective action, and instruction. Again, ceremonial recognition marks the achievement of "Disciple" status. Subsequently, Disciples can work toward the special status of "Apostle" in the Brothers/Sisters Keeper Program.

The Dupont Brothers/Sisters Keeper process incorporates a sound support system to maintain continual employee involvement, including (1) top management support and participation, (2) supportive leadership from all levels of the organization, (3) beneficial communication of all types (from employee newsletters, interdepartmental memos, and bulletin board announcements to one-on-one verbal interaction), and (4) motivating recognition processes for the AC activities of both individuals and groups. Recognition processes range from informal rewarding feedback in one-on-one communications to formal ceremonies for acknowledging specific accomplishments.

Recognition for Actively Caring

A few years ago Steve Roberts and I developed "Actively Caring Thank You Cards" for a particular work area of a large fiber-production plant of 2,000 employees. These cards were available to all hourly workers in the targeted work area (n = 33) as well as supervisors (n = 3), and were to be given to employees for demonstrating AC behavior. The cards listed examples of AC behaviors, such as warning a co-worker of a hazard, reminding a co-worker to follow certain safety procedures or to use certain safety equipment, demonstrating a safe operating procedure, or giving a co-worker feedback regarding safe or unsafe behavior. To recognize a co-worker for AC behavior, the particular AC behavior earning recognition needed to be defined in a space on the AC card. There was also space on the AC card for the giver and receiver of a card to record a personal code number which only they knew. The codes were used to match participants with codes on an AC survey taken by all employees in the work area. When turned in to the cashier in the company cafeteria, the AC card was worth $.55 toward a food purchase.

It was encouraging that those employees who distributed or received an AC card scored significantly higher on the AC survey (especially on belonging) than those who did not participate in the AC Thank You program, but it was quite discouraging that only twenty-three AC cards were distributed, involving only eight employees (Roberts and Geller, 1995). In a follow-up safety session with all employees in the work area, we solicited reasons for lack of participation in the AC Thank You Program and explored ways to increase participation. Two basic reasons were given for lack of participation, and they prompted particular program refinements. First, many workers expressed feelings of awkwardness or embarrassment at the thought of handing a co-worker a thank you card; and second, several employees indicated that the $.55 food coupon for the employee cafeteria was simply not a worthwhile reward. To eliminate the first concern, the employees could give an AC card to a supervisor, who in turn would deliver it to the appropriate employee. This concern also led to a decision by the plant manager and safety director that all employees in the plant needed training on the rationale and techniques of interpersonal behavioral feedback we subsequently developed and delivered an eight-hour AC coaching course for this purpose.

The concern that the $.55 food coupon was not a reinforcer was handled in an innovative way that is potentially beneficial in other situations. Instead of increasing the monetary value of the thank you card (which is the typical strategy for increasing the impact of a monetary reward), the employees agreed to pool the money and contribute it to homeless families in the community. Thus, the financial consequence for AC behavior was additional AC behavior. It is noteworthy that this method of increasing (or leveraging) the impact of small financial rewards is rare in the behavior analysis literature (cf. Geller, 1991; Jacobs, 1991), but in fact represents an approach that has several potential benefits. It is readily accepted (I have used it in several organizations where standard reward strategies were resisted), it generates goodwill between the local community and the industry, and it promotes the AC perspective useful for increasing employee involvement in industrial safety and health processes.

Several other plants have implemented an AC recognition process analogous to the AC Thank You Program, except these ongoing programs are larger scale and do not involve extrinsic rewards beyond the thank-you itself. More specifically, "Actively Caring Recognition Forms" introduced during training seminars have been distributed to the supervisory staff at each plant. The forms are printed on $5'' \times 7''$ notepads, and besides company logos, include space to write the name of the individual receiving recognition, the name of the person delivering the recognition, and the AC behavior warranting recognition. The recognition process is as simple as filling in this brief form, tearing it off the notepad, and delivering it to the target (e.g., by handing it to the person, placing it at the target's work station, or sending it through the mail). At one industrial site, this recognition process was implemented to target a certain work group (secretarial support staff) that scored significantly lower than the other work groups on certain AC factors (self-esteem, personal control, and optimism).

Flash Cards and Airline Life Savers

Several years ago, I developed a "Flash for Life" card to promote safety belt use. This intervention device was merely a brightly-colored $8\text{-}1/2'' \times 14''$ card with the message "Please Buckle Up—I Care" on one side and "Thank You for Buckling Up" on the other. If vehicle occupants were not using their safety belts, a "flasher" displayed the response-prompting side of the card; if the "flashee" buckled up or was already using a safety belt, the thank you consequence was flashed. This simple intervention technique was successful at increasing the use of vehicle safety belts when the flashers were (1) front-seat occupants of other vehicles (Geller, Bruff, and Nimmer, 1985), (2) young children standing at the entrance of a day care center (Geller, 1989a), or (3) university students standing at the entrance of a campus parking lot (Berry et al., 1992; Thyer et al., 1987).

To date, I have disseminated more than 3,000 of the Buckle-up flash cards nationwide. Several companies have used the flash card in their occupational safety programs. Ford Motor Company, for example, reproduced the flash cards in their company colors (blue and white) and distributed them to their employees, along with a score card and instructions for playing the "buckle-up flashing game." A behavior analyst would typically ask what behavioral impact this flash card intervention has on those receiving the buckle-up prompt. In the light of the concepts and research reviewed in this chapter, I suggest it is worthwhile to consider the effects of flashing on the flasher.

According to the AC concept, flashing a buckle-up card is the most desirable type of AC behavior (i.e., it has a direct behavior focus); and according to the AC model, certain person characteristics incase the probability that a person would flash for safety. Furthermore, flashing successfully could benefit certain person factors (especially self-efficacy, personal control, and optimism). Thus, AC behavior feeds AC person factors (including an AC attitude) which in turn increases the probability of further AC behaviors, followed by a greater AC attitude. This spiraling of AC behavior feeding AC person factors (including an AC attitude), feeding AC behavior, feeding AC attitudes, and so on can result in a truly committed and involved intervention agent for health and safety. And all of this started with one simple AC behavior—flashing a vehicle occupant to buckle up.

When I first proposed the Flash for Life intervention to my students, most of them laughed aloud. Holding a buckle-up flash card to a vehicle occupant seemed ridiculous (and perhaps risky) to most of them. Indeed, it was extremely difficult to find willing flashers among my students. Thus, our first flasher was my three-and-a-half-year-old daughter. After her "flashing success," showing potential for a research publication (including authorship contingencies), more flashers became available. This perhaps illustrates a greater impact on AC behavior of environmental factors (i.e., reinforcement) than person factors, but it is still possible that those who did eventually volunteer to be flashers had higher optimism and personal control regarding their AC efforts. And I definitely saw an increase in group cohesion among members of the research team after the AC experience.

The flashing experience seemed to have a marked effect on my daughter that has lasted to this day (Karly is now twenty years old). I can only speculate, of course, about effects of this AC experience on Karly's person factors, although her verbal behavior and excitement following a successful flashing could certainly be interpreted as enhancements of self-esteem, self-efficacy, personal control, and optimism. Certain subsequent behaviors from Karly provided more objective evidence of beneficial impact from her early reinforced AC behavior. Since that time she has always buckled her safety belt, and she often reminds others to do the same. And as a young teenager she often monitored my driving speed and asked me to slow down. I had never suggested such feedback behavior. In fourth grade, Karly gave an award-winning speech about her early flashing experiences.

On an airplane trip with my family, Karly (at the age of twelve) demonstrated further AC behavior, which illustrates the value of teaching intervention strategies to children (cf. Geller, 1989a). She asked me for an "Airline Lifesaver" card—a card that asks flight attendants to include a safety-belt use reminder in their end-of-the-flight message (Geller, 1989c). (Note that my rationale for this intervention strategy was based more on the impact it had on the AC card deliverer than on the passengers who hear the message.) I had given out my last Airline Lifesaver card at the safety conference we had just left (in Puerto Rico), and thus I could not honor my daughter's request. In a few minutes, Karly showed me a handwritten note with the following message, which she delivered personally to a flight attendant:

> I would really appreciate it if at the end of the plane trip you would say this. Thanks. Now that you have worn your safety belt throughout the plane trip maybe now you will consider wearing your safety belt when driving on the ground in your car.

When she returned to her seat, I asked Karly what the stewardess said about her note. To my surprise, my daughter informed me that she (Karly) would be able to read the announcement herself at the end of the flight. Of course, I did not believe this would happen. (After delivering Airline Lifesaver cards on more than 1,000 different flights over a fifteen-year period, I never received such an opportunity.) Thus, I expressed my lack of optimism with the statement, "I'll believe that when I see it." In this situation, Karly's self-esteem, personal control, and optimism were apparently not hampered by my verbal behavior, because she proceeded to write out a script for her debut as an airline announcer. Then, at the end of the flight, immediately after the bell sounded to signal permission for passengers to stand, the flight attendant called Karly from her seat; and as passengers waited for the exit door to open, Karly read the following message, slowly and clearly (more clearly, in fact, than most airline announcements I typically hear, particularly from pilots).

> Dear Passengers: Hello, my name is Karly Geller and I am twelve years old, and I have a very important message I would like to share with you. Now that you have worn your safety belt for this plane trip, hopefully now you will consider wearing your safety belt in your own vehicle, even on short trips. Thank you.

After her announcement many passengers clapped their hands, and you can guess who clapped the loudest. Perhaps such social reinforcement for this AC behavior increased the probability that Karly emitted future AC behavior. I might even surmise that certain person factors (i.e., hypothetical constructs) were strengthened by this AC behavior and social reinforcement, and that the support of these factors increased the propensity for future AC behavior, particularly the best kind of AC behavior—that which is behavior focused.

Some readers will object to the subjectivity of this supposition; others will claim nonpracticality or a lack of functional utility for such a conceptualization. I hope some readers will at least entertain the possibility that increasing an understanding of person factors that accompany AC behavior might facilitate the development of conditions and contingencies for increasing AC behavior. Obviously, much research is needed to operationalize the validity and utility of these notions. Surely no reader can deny, however, the urgent need for increased levels of AC behavior in every domain of human life, especially at the workplace where most of us spend most of our productive hours.

REFERENCES

Agnew, J. L. and Redmon, W. K. (1992). Contingency specifying stimuli: The role of "rules" in organizational behavior management. *Journal of Organizational Behavior Management, 12*(2), 67-76.

Aronoff, J. (1967). *Psychological needs and cultural systems.* NY: Van Nonbrand.

Bandura, A. (1977). Self-efficacy: Toward a unifying theory of behavioral change. *Psychological Review, 84,* 191-215.

Bandura, A. (1986). *Social foundations of thought and action.* Englewood Cliffs, NJ: Prentice-Hall.

Barling, J. and Beattie, R. (1983). Self-efficacy beliefs and sales performance. *Journal of Organizational Behavior Management, 5,* 41-51.

Batson, C. D., Batson, J. G., Slings, J. K., Harry, K. L., Peeking, H. M., and Tod, R. M. (1991). Empathic joy and the empathy-altruism hypothesis. *Journal of Personality and Social Psychology, 61,* 413-426.

Batson, C. D., Pollen, M. H., Cross, J. A., and Enuring-Benefic, H. E. (1986). Where is altruism in the altruistic personality? *Journal of Personality and Social Psychology, 1,* 212-220.

Berkowitz, L. and Connor, W. H. (1966). Success, failure, and social responsibility. *Journal of Personality and Social Psychology, 4,* 664-669.

Berry, T. D., Geller, E. S., Calef, R. S., and Calef, R. A. (1992). Moderating effects of social assistance on verbal interventions to promote safety belt use: An analysis of weak plys. *Environment and Behavior, 24,* 653-669.

Bierhoff, H. W., Klein, R., and Kramp, P. (1991). Evidence for altruistic personality from data on accident research. *Journal of Personality, 59*(2), 263-279.

Blake, J. A. (1978). Death by hand grenade: Altruistic suicide in combat. *Suicide and Life-Threatening Behavior, 8,* 46-59.

Broadbent, D., Cooper, P. F., Fitzgerald, P., and Parker, K. (1982). The cognitive failures questionnaire (CFQ) and its correlates. *British Journal of Clinical Psychology, 21,* 1-16.

Carlson, M., Charlin, V., and Miller, N. (1988). Positive mood and helping behavior: A test of six hypotheses. *Journal of Personality and Social Psychology, 55,* 211-229.

Conger, J. A. and Kanungo, R. N. (1988). The empowerment process: Integrating theory and practice. *Academy of Management Review, 13,* 471-482.

Coopersmith, S. (1967). *The antecedents of self-esteem.* San Francisco, CA: W. H. Freeman.

Darley, J. M. and Latane, B. (1968). Bystander intervention in emergencies: Diffusion of responsibility. *Journal of Personality and Social Psychology, 8,* 377-383.

Eysenck, H. J. and Eysenck, M. W. (1985). *Personality and individual differences: A natural science approach.* New York: Plenum.

Geller, E. S. (1989a). Intervening to increase children's use of safety belts. *Alcohol, Drugs and Driving, 5,* 37-59.

Geller, E. S. (1989b). Managing occupational safety in the auto industry. *Journal of Organizational Behavior Management, 10*(1), 181-185.

Geller, E. S. (1989c). The Airline Lifesaver: In pursuit of small wins. *Journal of Applied Behavior Analysis, 22,* 333-335.

Geller, E. S. (1990). Performance management and occupational safety: Start with a safety belt program. *Journal of Organizational Behavior Management, 11*(1), 149-174.

Geller, E. S. (1991). If only more would actively care. *Journal of Applied Behavior Analysis, 24,* 607-612.

Geller, E. S. (1992). *A critical review of human dimension sessions at the 1992 National Safety Council Congress and Exposition.* Technical Report for Exxon Chemical Company.

Geller, E. S. (1996). *The psychology of safety: How to improve behaviors and attitudes on the job.* Rednor, PA: Chilton Book Company.

Geller, E. S. (1998). *Applications of behavior analysis to prevent injury from vehicle crashes* (Second edition). Monograph. Cambridge, MA: Cambridge Center for Behavioral Sciences.

Geller, E. S. (in press). The psychology of safety handbook. Boca Raton, FL: CRC Press.

Geller, E. S., Berry, T. D., Ludwig, T. D., Evans, R. E., Gilmore, M. R., and Clarke, S. W. (1990). A conceptual framework for developing and evaluating behavior change interventions for injury control. *Health Education Research: Theory and Practice, 5,* 125-137.

Geller, E. S., Bruff, C. D., and Nimmer, J. G. (1985). "Flash for Life": Community-based prompting for safety-belt promotion. *Journal of Applied Behavior Analysis, 18,* 145-149.

Geller, E. S., Lehman, G. R., and Kalsher, M. J. (1989). *Behavior analysis training for occupational safety.* Newport, VA: Make-A-Difference, Inc.

Geller, E. S. and Roberts, D. S. (1993). *Beyond behavior modification for continuous improvement in occupational safety.* Paper presented at the FABA/OBM Network Conference, St. Petersburg, FL, January.

Geller, E. S., Roberts, D. S., and Gilmore, M. R. (1992). *Achieving a total safety culture through employee involvement.* Newport, VA: Make-A-Difference, Inc.

Geller, E. S., Roberts, D. S., and Gilmore, M. R. (1996). Predicting propensity to actively care for occupational safety. *Journal of Safety Research, 27,* 1-8.

Isen, A. M. (1970). Success, failure, attention, and reaction to others: The warm glow of success. *Journal of Personality and Social Psychology, 15,* 294-301.

Isen, A. M., Clark, M., and Schwartz, M. (1976). Duration of the effect of good mood on helping: "Footprints in the sands of time." *Journal of Personality and Social Psychology, 34,* 385-393.

Isen, A. M. and Levin, P. F. (1972). Effect of feeling good on helping: Cookies and kindness. *Journal of Personality and Social Psychology, 21,* 384-388.

Jacobs, J. J. (1991). The recycling solution: How I increased recycling on Dilworth Road. *Journal of Applied Behavior Analysis, 24,* 617-619.

Jessor, R. (1987). Risky driving and adolescent problem behavior: An extension of problem behavior theory. *Alcohol, Drugs and Driving, 3*(3-4), 1-11.

Katz, E. and Lazarfeld, P. E. (1955). *Personal influence: The part played by people in the flow of mass communication.* Glencoe, IL: Free Press.

Krause, T. R. (1992). *Behavior science methods for accident prevention.* Presentation at the National Safety Council Congress and Exposition, Orlando, FL, October.

Latane, B. and Nida, S. (1981). Ten years of research on group size and helping. *Psychological Bulletin, 89*(2), 308-324.

Malott, R. W. (1992). A theory of rule-governed behavior and organizational behavior management. *Journal of Organizational Behavior Management, 12* (2), 67-76.

Melton, G. B. (1988). Adolescents and prevention of AIDS. *Professional Psychology: Research and Application, 19*(4), 403-408.

Michael, J. (1982). Distinguishing between discriminative and motivational functions of stimuli. *Journal of the Experimental Analysis of Behavior, 37*, 149-155.

Michelini, R. L., Wilson, J. P., and Messe, L. A. (1975). The influence of psychological needs on helping behavior. *The Journal of Psychology, 91*, 253-258.

Midlarsky, E. (1971). Aiding under stress: The effects of competence, dependency, visibility, and fatalism. *Journal of Personality, 39*, 132-149.

Nowicki, S. and Duke, M. P. (1974). A locus of control scale for college as well as noncollege adults. *Journal of Personality Assessment, 38*, 136-137.

Ozer, E. M. and Bandura, A. (1990). Mechanisms governing empowerment effects: A self-efficacy analysis. *Journal of Personality and Social Psychology, 58*, 472-486.

Peterson, C. (2000). The future of optimism. *American Psychologist, 55*, 44-55.

Phares, E. J. (1976). *Locus of control in personality*. Morristown, NJ: General Learning Press.

Ridgeway, C. L. (1983). *The dynamics of small groups*. New York: St. Martin's Press.

Roberts, D. S. and Geller, E. S. (1995). An actively caring model for occupational safety: A field test. *Applied and Preventative Psychology, 1*, 53-59.

Rosenberg, M. (1965). *Society and the adolescent self-image*. Princeton, NJ: Princeton University Press.

Rotter, J. B. (1966). Generalized expectancies for internal versus external control of reinforcement. *Psychological Monographs, 80*(1), No. 1.

Rushton, J. P. (1980). *Altruism, socialization, and society*. Englewood Cliffs, NJ: Prentice-Hall, Inc.

Rutkowski, G. K., Gruder, C. L., and Romer, D. (1983). Group cohesiveness, social norms, and bystander intervention. *Journal of Personality and Social Psychology, 44*, 545-552.

Scheier, M. F. and Carver, C. S. (1985). Optimism, coping and health: Assessment and implications of generalized outcome expectancies. *Health Psychology, 4*, 219-247.

Scheier, M. F. and Carver, C. S. (1993). On the power of positive thinking: The benefits of being optimistic. *Current Directions in Psychological Sciences, 2*, 26-30.

Schwartz, I. S. and Baer, D. M. (1991). Social validity measurements: Is current practice state of the art? *Journal of Applied Behavior Analysis, 24*, 189-204.

Seligman, M. E. P. (1991). *Learned optimism*. New York: Alfred A. Knopf.

Sherer, M., Maddox, J. E., Mercandante, B., Prentice-Dunn, S., Jacobs, B., and Rogers, R. W. (1982). The self-efficacy scale: Construction and validation. *Psychological Reports, 51*, 663-671.

Sherrod, D. R. and Downs, R. (1974). Environmental determinants of altruism: The effects of stimulus overload and perceived control on helping. *Journal of Experimental Social Psychology, 10,* 468-479.

Simon, S. and Simon, R. (1992). *Improving safety through innovative behavioral and cultural approaches.* Presentation at the National Safety Council Congress and Exposition, Orlando, FL, October.

Skinner, B. F. (1971). *Beyond freedom and dignity.* New York: Alfred A. Knopf.

Staub, E. (1978). *Positive social behaviors and morality: Social and personal influence.* New York: Academic Press.

Thyer, B. A., Geller, E. S., Williams, M., and Purcell, S. (1987). Community-based "flashing" to increase safety-belt use. *The Journal of Experimental Education, 53,* 155-159.

Tucker, R. K. and Byers, P. Y. (1987). Factorial validity of Mertz's psychological reactance scale. *Psychological Reports, 61,* 811-815.

Weick, K. E. (1984). Small wins: Redefining the scale of social problems. *American Psychologist, 39,* 40-49.

Wheeless, L. R., Wheeless, V. E., and Dickson-Markman, F. (1982). The relations among social and task perceptions in small groups. *Small Group Behavior, 13,* 373-384.

Wilson, J. P. (1976). Motivation, modeling, and altruism: A person x situation analysis. *Journal of Personality and Social Psychology, 34,* 1078-1086.

Wilson, R. J. and Jonah, B. A. (1988). The application of problem behavior theory to the understanding of risky driving. *Alcohol, Drugs and Driving, 4*(3-4), 193-204.

Wolf, M. M. (1978). Social validity: The case for subjective measurement or how behavior analysis is finding its heart. *Journal of Applied Behavior Analysis, 11,* 203-214.

Zimmerman, M. A. (1990). Toward a theory of learned hopefulness: A structural model analysis of participation and empowerment. *Journal of Research in Personality, 24,* 71-86.

Zuckerman, M. (1979). *Sensation seeking: Beyond the optimal level of arousal.* Hillsdale, NJ: Lawrence Erlbaum Associates.

Chapter 12

A Behavioral Approach
to Sales Management

Mark J. Martinko
William W. Casey
Paul Fadil

Sales improvement is one path to profitability. Often, through the straightforward application of behavioral principles, tremendous gains are possible. Successful applications of behavioral principles have been achieved in a variety of settings such as retail (Mirman, 1982; Dickinson and O'Brien, 1982), department stores (Brown et al., 1980; Luthans, Paul, and Baker, 1981), airlines (Feeney et al., 1982), grocery stores (Greene et al., 1984), clubs and lounges (Martinko, 1986a; Ralis and O'Brien, 1986), fast-food restaurants (Martinko, White, and Hassel, 1989), and newspapers (Johnson, 1985).

The literature includes several helpful reviews of the sales literature (Casey, 1989; Mirman, 1982) as well as some useful theoretical discussions of this issue (Nord and Peter, 1980; Peter and Nord, 1982; Rothschild and Gaidis, 1981). Our purpose is not to cover old ground. Rather, it is to offer concrete guidance that can help sales managers, sales personnel, consultants, and students of behavior management by describing a sequence of steps that can lead to sales improvements.

BACKGROUND

Several authors have proposed or discussed models for applying behavior management principles (e.g., Brethower, 1972; Gilbert, 1978; Luthans and Martinko, 1978; Luthans and Kreitner, 1985; Luthans and Martinko, 1987; Miller, 1978). In addition, some chapters in this book discuss such models.

Since each model was founded on similar theoretical assumptions, the models are essentially identical or, at most, variations on a common theme. All the models include the same basic steps: assess the general needs of the organization; identify key behaviors or accomplishments; develop measures of these key behaviors; analyze the behavioral environment by identifying the cues and consequences of the behavior; modify the behavior by changing the cues and consequences; and evaluate outcomes (Brethower, 1972; Gilbert, 1978; Luthans and Kreitner, 1975, 1985; Luthans and Martinko, 1978).

The behavior sales management (BSM) model, which we propose, differs from earlier behavior management models in that it specifically addresses sales applications and draws upon the sales literature mentioned earlier. Additionally, it has been validated in sales applications (Luthans, Paul, and Taylor, 1985; Martinko, 1986a; Martinko, White, and Hassell, 1989) and offers a helpful level of detail for practitioners.

THE BEHAVIORAL SALES MANAGEMENT MODEL (BSM): AN OVERVIEW

Figure 12.1 summarizes the BSM model. Behavior sales management begins by identifying the key sales-related behaviors or key organizational outcomes, such as sales volume, which have significant impact on sales performance. The identification of these behaviors or outcomes should allow the sales or performance manager to successfully isolate the key variables and proceed with analysis and modification. From among many factors contributing to sales performance, managers should attempt to narrow the selection process to focus on the behaviors most likely to influence sales performance. The goal of this step is to identify the key variables that are targeted for modification.

The second stage of the model is to measure key sales-related behaviors. A baseline of individual sales-related behaviors will establish their importance to sales volume.

The third step is to perform a functional analysis of the critical, measured sales-related behaviors. To analyze the key behaviors, one must know the antecedent cues and the consequences of the behaviors. Only when the sales manager has gained this functional understanding of how the cues and consequences control the frequencies of current behaviors can he or she move toward designing the intervention.

The objective of the fourth step is to design and develop an intervention strategy to increase the frequency of critical sales-related behaviors and reduce the frequency of nonproductive behaviors. Based on the analysis of

FIGURE 12.1. The Behavioral Sales Management Model

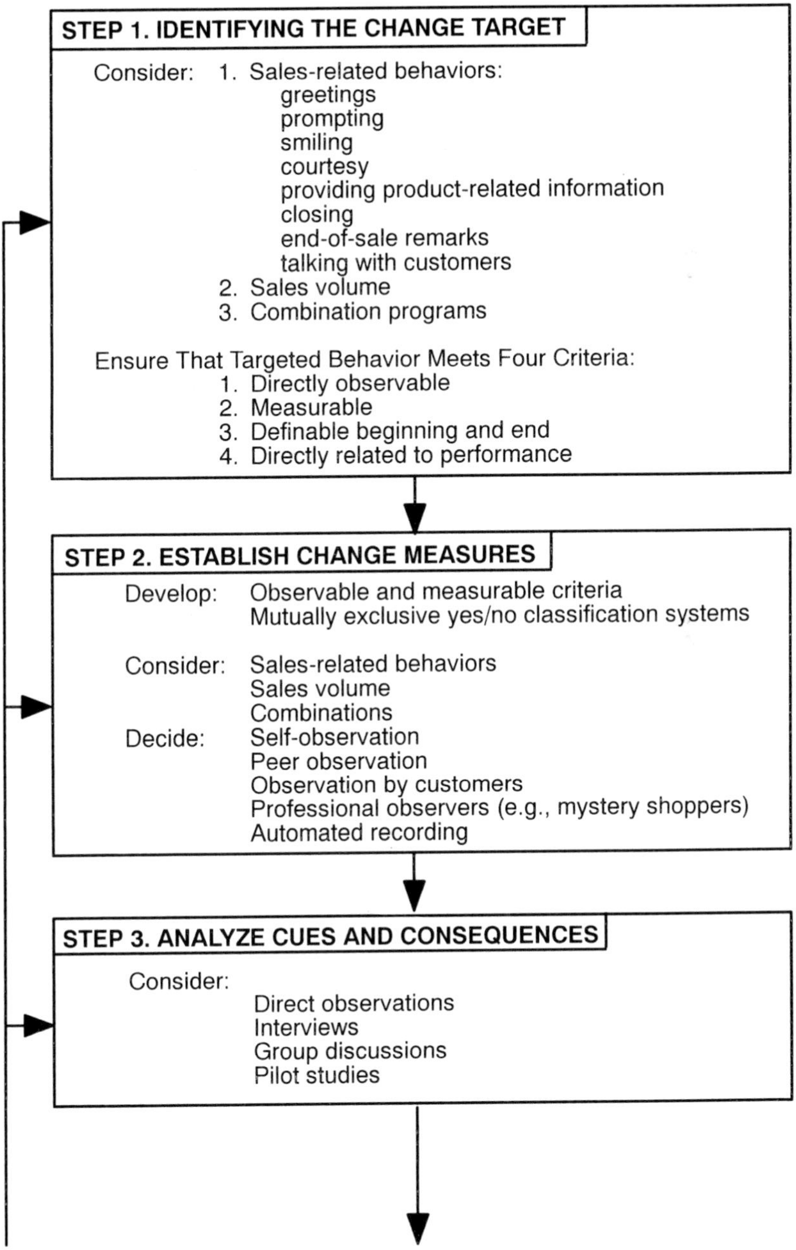

STEP 1. IDENTIFYING THE CHANGE TARGET

Consider: 1. Sales-related behaviors:
- greetings
- prompting
- smiling
- courtesy
- providing product-related information
- closing
- end-of-sale remarks
- talking with customers

2. Sales volume
3. Combination programs

Ensure That Targeted Behavior Meets Four Criteria:
1. Directly observable
2. Measurable
3. Definable beginning and end
4. Directly related to performance

STEP 2. ESTABLISH CHANGE MEASURES

Develop: Observable and measurable criteria
Mutually exclusive yes/no classification systems

Consider: Sales-related behaviors
Sales volume
Combinations
Decide: Self-observation
Peer observation
Observation by customers
Professional observers (e.g., mystery shoppers)
Automated recording

STEP 3. ANALYZE CUES AND CONSEQUENCES

Consider:
Direct observations
Interviews
Group discussions
Pilot studies

FIGURE 12.1 *(continued)*

STEP 4. DESIGNING THE INTERVENTION

Consider:
- Target:
  - salesperson
  - customer
- Program design:
  - training/coaching
  - modeling
  - rehearsal
  - task clarification
- Potential antecedents:
  - goals
  - awareness of any consequence
  - job/role clarification
  - training/practice
  - obtrusive cues in the work environment
- Potential consequences:
  - salesperson feedback
    - direct observations
    - measurement data
      - sales-related behaviors
      - sales volume
  - customer feedback
  - commissions
  - reporting to home office
  - public posting
    - group
    - individual
  - incentive programs
  - competitive contests
  - public praise
  - self-recording
  - plaques and awards
- Schedules of reinforcement

STEP 5. IMPLEMENTING THE INTERVENTION

Consider:
- Reversal designs
- Multiple baseline designs
- Training

STEP 6. EVALUATION

Consider:
- Bottom-line results
- Ratio of rewards to costs
- Need for continual renewal and recycling

the antecedents and consequences of critical sales-related behaviors, the sales manager develops programs to augment the cues and reinforcers and to reduce potential punishers for desirable behaviors. Concurrently, decreasing the cues and reinforcers for undesirable behaviors is intended to decrease the frequency of dysfunctional behaviors. In this step the manager selects a target audience such as a subgroup of sales representatives, defines an appropriate method for presenting the strategy, provides realistic antecedent cues that will produce the desired responses, and develops consequences that will maintain the desired sales-related behaviors.

The fifth step of the model is to implement the intervention strategy. Commonly, the target audience for the intervention is the sales staff. When the intervention is aimed at customers, the availability of the new incentives may be cued through a series of advertisements or sales promotions. Regardless of the vehicle used, managers should consider phased implementation of programs. Initially, the program should be implemented on a temporary "pilot" basis using a reversal, multiple baseline, or a combined design that allows managers to determine whether the program actually produces the results desired. Only when the program passes such tests of effectiveness should it be implemented on a large scale.

The final stage of the model is evaluation. Evaluation of the results and use of the BSM model is not a one-time event. Both the application of the model and evaluation are ongoing; sales managers continuously monitor the intervention to improve the intervention technique and achieve optimal results.

A more detailed description of the BSM model's components follows.

Identify the Change Target

Key sales-related behaviors are behavioral events related to performance. A high frequency of these behaviors is desirable when it leads to the accomplishment of organizational goals; or undesirable when it blocks the attainment of those goals. Identification of these key sales-related behaviors and subsequent interventions are needed to positively reinforce desirable behaviors or to extinguish undesirable behaviors.

According to Luthans and Kreitner (1975), key sales-related behaviors must satisfy four major criteria before they become targets for change. The behaviors must be directly observable. This allows the practitioner to manipulate antecedent cues and consequences. Behaviors must be measurable: the behavioral events must be countable so that their frequency over time can be recorded. Third, the key behaviors have to be definable. Events must have a distinct beginning and end. The manager of the BSM model must understand what an employee must do before a response can be recorded. Finally, the key behaviors must be directly related to performance. If a specific behavior is targeted for change, the manager should be able to demonstrate a direct relationship between that behavior and bottom-line performance. The manager should look for organizational consequences that would occur if the employees do not emit the desired behavior. For example, a manager might ask, "How much will sales volume decrease if the employees are not courteous?" One way to answer this question is to compare the sales volume of representatives who have the highest frequencies of courteous behaviors to that of those who have lower frequencies. If no differences in sales are found, courteous behaviors may not be productive targets for change. A manager may wish to target behaviors resulting in sales of specific products. If two products sell at nearly the same frequency, but one has a higher profit margin, the one with the higher profit margin should be targeted.

Throughout the sales literature (Casey, 1989; Martinko, 1986a; Mirman, 1982; Martinko, White, and Hassell, 1989; Ralis and O'Brien, 1986) numerous key sales behaviors have been identified and described. In all cases, these behaviors are observable, measurable, definable, and related to sales performance. Key sales behaviors include: greeting, prompting, smiling, courtesy, providing product-related information, end-of-sale remarks, and talking with customers. Some controversy exists concerning whether specific behaviors or summary statistics such as sales volume are more appropriate as targets of change (Casey, 1989).

Casey (1989) reviewed the literature on operant approaches to sales improvement. He assigned these studies to three categories, based on what the researchers targeted for change. A summary of the major findings for each of these categories is presented below.

Sales-Related Behavior Programs

Sales-related behavior (SRB) programs focus on behaviors which, if performed better or more often, should improve sales. Interventions might focus on smiling at customers, suggesting additional merchandise, or greeting customers. These programs take either of two forms. They either develop new behaviors or reinforce existing behaviors.

The SRB approach has advantages in each case. Training programs help salespeople learn new skills to help them make sales. Frequently these are skills they might never have learned on their own, or would have learned only through costly trial and error.

Some programs promote the use of existing skills to help salespeople improve sales. The behaviors are often unpleasant or so far removed from the actual sale that salespeople tend to avoid them. The "cold call" is one example.

Sales Volume Programs

Sales volume (SV) programs focus exclusively on outcomes such as monthly sales, average number of items sold per transaction, gross margins, and so on. An intervention in this category might reinforce a department store's sales staff for increased sales per hour.

In effect, the SV approach says to the salesperson, "We'll leave it up to you. Use your own skills, experiment, and take advantage of opportunities we could never have imagined or codified. All we're asking for is results."

Combination Programs

Some programs combine the other two approaches, targeting both the means (SRB) and ends (SV) of sales improvement. For example, a delicatessen staff might receive cash bonuses for suggesting additional food items to customers, but only if their sales per hour exceed the hourly goal, which fluctuates based on time of day.

Which approach works best? Casey (1989) and other researchers (Kim, 1984; Neider, 1980) found that while all three approaches may be effective, the evidence favors combination programs. As practitioners select which targets to change, there seems little point in choosing between SV and SRB if both can be included. But there are caveats for both elements of the combination.

The SRB component appears to work best only when targeted behaviors fit the guidelines suggested previously. Programs with ill-defined targets such as "friendliness," "enthusiasm," and "fire in the belly" will be difficult for managers to evaluate and difficult for salespeople to achieve. The SRB component will be likely to succeed when the targeted behaviors are sales and performance related. A program that ensures a robotlike greeting will probably improve sales less than one that ensures the employees offer genuine help to customers who look lost.

The SV approach also has pitfalls. If factors beyond the salesperson's control affect the SV target, then one would do better to select a different target, or abandon the SV approach altogether. Such targets frustrate and annoy salespeople and do little to increase sales. Imagine if the salespeople in a chain of specialty clothing stores were offered incentives for each store's profitability. But imagine also that each store's profit formula included allocated costs such as advertising and staff functions (often unwanted) that can cut into profits. Such programs reflect the efforts of salespeople poorly and do little to improve sales. It would be better to substitute sales per hour, or a gross margin formulation that does not include uncontrollable costs.

Establish Change Measures

To measure the strength of behavioral events, we observe their frequency over time and their relationship to specific, targeted organizational outcomes. These measures are necessary (1) to determine the relative frequency and importance of the target behavior as compared to other behaviors; (2) to determine whether the behavior is related to the targeted outcomes; and (3) as a baseline of data to assess the effectiveness of the change effort.

Performance managers take baseline measures to show how often potential target behaviors occur in their current sales environments. If a manager believes that a salesperson's lack of courtesy is the reason for his or her poor performance and then records the employee's use of courteous behavior, the manager may discover that the employee is courteous 95 percent of the time. The data demonstrate that courtesy does not appear to be a problem or a legitimate target behavior. The manager should then develop other measures and collect data to further identify and eliminate inconsequential behaviors. In this way key target behaviors are gradually identified before applying BSM.

A common way of recording frequencies of behavioral events is to directly observe and count all or a sample of the desired responses. Time constraints will dictate selection of an empirical recording method. Two rules should be followed when recording these data (Luthans and Kreitner, 1975). First, observable and measurable characteristics should be described. For example, if courtesy is the behavior being observed, the manager must know its defining features. Opening the door, offering assistance, and smiling may define courtesy. Each behavior will be defined by a different set of characteristics. The manager must determine what actions must take place for the key behavior to occur.

Second, behavioral data must fit specific categories. Did the employee emit the desired response or not? Was the employee courteous or not? This simplification of the observation process reduces the chance of subjectivity entering into the observations.

Referring again to Casey's (1989) sales-related behavior and sales volume dichotomy, one can compare and contrast the ease and accuracy of measuring these two factors. For sales-related behavior, someone must actually observe and record the data needed to determine the frequency of the behavior over time. Data on sales volume may already be on hand in the form of financial statements, inventory records, etc. Another problem that may occur in recording sales-related behaviors is the unpredictability of the human element. Both the observer and the employee are human. Either one can inaccurately record a behavior or instantaneously change a behavior due to the awareness that measurement is taking place. Inaccuracy is intrinsic to the recording process. On the other hand, sales volume data are generally considered less subject to biased recording. Accurate recording of sales-related behaviors is difficult compared to measuring sales volume, but if these behaviors are not observed and changed, the effect of the intervention on sales outcomes may not be as great (Kim, 1984; Neider, 1980).

If a manager elects to use sales-related behaviors as a primary target for intervention, the manager must determine whether and how often or how well they occur. Assume that a hardware store manager wants salespeople to ask customers questions about their needs and then to suggest appropriate merchandise: "What are you going to use those nails for? You're using them outside? Well then, you might want to use these galvanized ones over here so you don't have any rust problems."

The manager may believe this approach will produce more sales and happier customers, but it will be difficult to evaluate how often salespeople ask this sort of question. One can only know from observation, and there are only a few ways to do that. Options include self-observation (by the salesperson), peer observation, observation by the supervisor, and by customers, or by professional observers pretending to be customers (usually termed "mystery shoppers"), or automated recording such as hidden cameras. A comprehensive discussion of these various processes as well as their respective advantages and disadvantages is provided by Martinko (1986b). Regardless of which alternative recording method is selected, the process must focus on behaviors that are clearly defined; the occurrence or nonoccurrence of the behavior must be accurately classified. Adherence to these guidelines should significantly reduce recording biases, particularly if self-recording is the strategy selected.

Typically, managers gravitate toward SV-based programs for the very good reason that their companies already collect such data. Total sales by hour, by person, and by department are easy to determine wherever employees use electronic cash registers. Other sales environments offer similar advantages. For example, managers of industrial sales (e.g., chemicals or equipment) collect every manner of sales data so they can fill orders, pay commissions, and plan inventories. In other words, establishing useful

SV change measures is easy, since SV measurement is probably already under way, or easy to establish.

Analyze Cues and Consequences

The next major step involves analyzing the antecedent cues and consequences that influence the targeted sales behaviors. The functional analysis must clarify two questions: (1) What cues the onset of the behaviors (identify the antecedents)? and (2) What are the immediate consequences of the targeted behaviors? This process assumes that the target behavior is being maintained at its current frequency by the consequences provided by the environment (Luthans and Kreitner, 1975). In addition, it assumes that the behavior is not only a function of its consequences, but also is influenced by antecedent cues (Luthans and Martinko, 1976). It is through these two factors that the frequencies of the target behavior can be changed.

Suppose courtesy is the behavior being analyzed, and a supervisor has found that a particular employee's discourteous and abrupt attitude has caused decreased sales. The manager then decides to functionally analyze the situation to determine what is causing the discourteous behaviors. During the analysis, the supervisor discovers that discourteous behavior consistently occurs fifteen minutes before break, lunch, and quitting time. Thus, the manager can conclude that specific times are antecedents for the key behavioral events associated with courtesy.

According to Luthans and Martinko (1976), antecedent cues control behavior because they are associated with particular consequences. In the previous example, informal consequences may be punishing courteous behavior because the employee's manager does not extend break periods or pay for the workday to compensate for time spent with customers during break. The threat of the loss of break time and pay could lead to short, abrupt, and discourteous interactions with customers prior to the break and at the end of the day.

Several methods are used to determine the antecedents and consequences of an employee's key sales behaviors. The first and most reliable method is direct observation. Other techniques include interviews (Komaki, Heinzmann, and Lawson, 1980), group discussions, and pilot studies. Analysis of antecedents and consequences, or diagnosis of the environmental conditions reinforcing or punishing the key behavior, is an integral part of the sales behavior modification process.

During this step, it is essential that the cues and consequences relate to the target behavior of the person whose behavior is to be modified. More specifically, although upselling (increasing the volume of existing accounts) may have positive consequences for an organization, it may have negative consequences for the sales staff if they do not receive commissions for existing accounts or if the additional sales result in more punishing paperwork. Thus, the cues and consequences identified must be directly experienced by those whose behaviors are the targets for change. Although long-range organizational consequences are perceived as important by management, they are frequently perceived as irrelevant and as having no direct or immediate impact by the people on the front line.

Designing the Intervention Strategy

The fourth stage of the process is development of the intervention strategy. An effective intervention strategy should: (1) target the people who have a direct effect on the desired behavior (such as the salesperson or the customer); (2) be designed so that the program clearly identifies both desirable and undesirable behaviors for the targets of the intervention; (3) identify and provide additional antecedents that stimulate the desired behaviors while eliminating cues for undesirable behaviors; and (4) identify and provide reinforcing consequences and remove punishing consequences for desired behaviors and also apply punishing consequences and remove reinforcers for undesired behaviors. If an intervention strategy consists of these four components, it should modify sales-related behaviors.

The first step is to identify the program's target. Even though the logical targets may appear to be the salesperson or the sales manager, the ultimate target of any change is the customer, with the sales personnel acting as mediators. If the major goal of the model is to develop a strategy to control the frequency of key sales-related behaviors, anyone who provides cues or consequences for these behaviors should be considered a potential recipient of the intervention.

The second step in designing an intervention strategy involves communicating the design of the intervention to the recipients. An important part of this step is developing techniques to make the recipients aware of both desirable and undesirable behaviors as well as their cues and consequences. Typically, this is done through training programs (Brown et al., 1980). During training, the trainers make clear what behaviors are desirable and emphasize their importance to the target group as well as the corporation. A second method is modeling, which involves the imitation of skilled models. Through modeling, organizational participants learn the following: how to behave, relevant behavior/consequence contingencies, and when it is appropriate to respond in given ways (Luthans and Kreitner, 1975). A third technique is rehearsal, which allows employees to practice key behaviors until their performance is satisfactory. For example, in a study done by Komaki, Blood, and Holder (1980), rehearsal involved "smiling practice," so the employee would know exactly how and when to smile. The final technique, task clarification, involves clearly defining the target person's job in terms of cues, desirable and undesirable behaviors, and the likely reinforcing and punishing consequences for both desirable and undesirable behaviors. These techniques are frequently used to communicate program designs and to inform target employees of key behaviors, cues, and consequences in the workplace.

To identify and develop cues for the target behaviors, one method frequently used is to publish well-defined goals. Goals that are related to directly observable and measurable behaviors or outcomes clarify the consequences for the recipients. Another option is to make the recipients aware of the consequences of both desirable and undesirable key sales behaviors. Consequences of desirable behaviors must benefit the target directly, especially if the desired behavior will require more effort. By clarifying the salesperson's job, the practitioner can emphasize the necessary information regarding the key sales behaviors within the employee's job description. A solid intervention strategy sets the stage with tangible antecedents that provide the targets with clear information about the nature, timing, frequency, and magnitude of both reinforcing and punishing consequences.

The most critical stage in the design of the intervention is to determine the behavioral contingencies tied to the desirable and undesirable behaviors. Numerous consequences can reinforce key sales behaviors. Feedback based on direct observations (e.g., frequencies of desirable sales-related behaviors observed), company data (e.g., the increases in sales volume), and customer reactions are often viewed as significant consequences by salespeople.

In most situations, sales commissions may serve as potent reinforcers. Incentive programs, which include consequences such as extra pay, time off, or allowing the employees to schedule their own working hours, can serve as effective positive reinforcers. Public posting of group or individual accomplishments has also been shown to reward individuals.

Reporting major achievements to the home office or public praise for these achievements provides recognition and acknowledgement for desirable behavior and illustrates the key sales performance that the organization seeks. Finally, contests and awards are two other types of consequences that can be used to reward target behaviors. The types of consequences described previously may be used to maintain as well as increase desired behaviors.

The final stage of the intervention design is to determine appropriate schedules of reinforcement for the contingencies identified. Since thorough discussions of reinforcement schedules can be found in the literature (Luthans and Kreitner, 1975; Luthans and Martinko, 1976) and in Chapter 5, only the key components of reinforcement scheduling are discussed here.

Continuous schedules are most appropriate during training or in the earlier stages of a program. The major exception is a commission sales program that rewards employees with a specified amount as a consequence of each sale. These programs are extremely successful and appropriate if the organization has the technology and resources to manage the program effectively. Their major disadvantage is that there are almost always strong reactions if the commission schedule is changed. Such schedules build loyalty to the schedule rather than the company.

In most situations, intermittent schedules that space out reinforcers over time or frequencies of behavior are more appropriate. Fixed-interval schedules in which a reward occurs after the first response following a specific amount of time may be appropriate to reinforce some behaviors such as loyalty and tenure with the organization. Thus, faculty members often receive sabbatical opportunities after a specific number of years of service. Variable-interval schedules in which rewards are varied over time are generally more effective and produce higher rates of response than fixed-interval schedules. Thus, for example, spot checks of sales logbooks or daily receipts may be effective in establishing consequences for sales behaviors. Fixed-ratio schedules program reinforcement after specific frequencies of behaviors are achieved. They are common and extremely effective. Examples are sales incentive programs offering bonuses for specific levels of sales and piece rate programs that reward specific levels of sales.

Finally, variable-ratio schedules distribute rewards for performance over variable frequencies of behavior. Variable and random-ratio schedules appear to be extremely effective, as demonstrated by the success of Las Vegas casinos. When such schedules are used, the recipients cannot predict exactly when rewards will be administered, so they continue to perform. Despite the strength of these variable and random-ratio schedules, the human desire for a stable and predictable income raises questions about the ethics and practicality of such schedules. But the benefits of variable and random-ratio schedules can be realized through combinations with other schedules. Thus, many salespeople receive base wages combined with sales incentives and contests that may be administered according to the principles of variable ratio, fixed ratio, and interval schedules. On any given day or in any given week, an unusually desirable reward may be obtained for normal productive behavior, and additional sales increase the probabilities of rewards.

Two additional considerations are relevant in designing effective programs. A common error in the design of many programs is to concentrate all of the resources on rewards. It is also critical to remove anything such as unnecessary paperwork that may be punishing target behaviors. Another common problem is organizational commitment over time. As the feedback loops in the model indicate, the intervention should be constantly changed and modified depending on the results. The entire process should be viewed as developmental, with continuous fine-tuning and modification.

Implementing the Intervention

The fifth stage of the BSM model involves implementing the intervention strategy. The objective is not only to decide on a strategy, but to implement it in such a way that its effectiveness can be evaluated and assessed. Successful implementation should allow the manager to accurately determine the value and potency of the program's consequences.

The reversal design is the simplest of the research designs, but it has two critical limitations. First, many practitioners are reluctant to go back to baseline conditions, especially if the increases in sales during the intervention are significant. Second, the intervention often contaminates the return to baseline period and the behavior will not reverse. The latter problem is often caused by natural reinforcers from the environment that are activated by the desirable behaviors and continue to influence behavior even after the reversal. For example, even though an incentive may be the primary causal reason for a salesperson's increase in sales, the salesperson may have also experienced more positive interactions with customers and with his or her boss during an intervention. The reinforcing properties of these satisfying interactions may continue to reinforce and maintain increases in sales even if other incentives are suspended during a reversal.

Multiple-baseline designs are often viewed as relatively more efficacious than reversal designs. They overcome most of the problems associated with contamination and return to baseline conditions, although contamination across behaviors, settings, or subjects may be a problem in this design.

When implementing any program, research design must be an integral part of its enactment. By measuring the impact of the intervention on sales-related behaviors and sales performance, the practitioner can determine if the program has achieved its objectives, or if minor changes are needed to optimize results. Research designs are vital to any implementation strategy, because they allow constant and effective evaluation of the program and provide a useful method for its measurement.

Evaluation

The use of the research designs explained in stage five of the BSM model pave the way for the final step: evaluation. In this stage, the bottom-line results of the intervention are identified. All intervention programs must be constantly fine-tuned and their consequences evaluated, so they can consistently achieve their targeted increase in sales performance. Evaluation is an ongoing critical component of the model and provides an effective base for future interventions. Although program evaluation has traditionally been the domain of academicians, the competitive environments which typify today's organizations demand that practitioners become more systematic and effective in assessing the merits of their sales programs.

According to Luthans and Kreitner (1975), to test the effectiveness of an intervention, an objective evaluation of the impact on performance and organizational consequences must be given. Did the program's modification of desired behavior frequency meet the targeted objectives? What was the bottom-line performance effect? Was it the intervention that produced the change, or was it something else? Was the change practically significant? The BSM model must not manipulate employee behavior just for the sake of change. It must be able to modify the frequency of key behavioral events to improve performance, thus effectuating tangible, positive, and measurable gains.

One method of assessing effectiveness is to calculate the reward/cost ratio of the intervention. Included in the costs of the intervention are the expenses of any incentives, any consulting fees or instructional fees associated with the intervention, and the dollar value of managerial and employee time devoted to the intervention. The rewards are determined by calculating or estimating the increases in sales realized during the intervention periods. Obviously, if rewards are proportionally greater than costs, the intervention is profitable. A general rule of thumb is that the rewards should outweigh the costs by a ratio of five to one. If the bottom-line results are not acceptable, as suggested by the feedback loops in the model, the manager should return to an earlier stage in the model. It may be, for example, that the initial behavior identified was not performance related. Similarly, it is possible that the functional analysis was not thorough and that significant punishers for the desirable behavior continued to exist during the intervention. Whatever the problem, the model suggests that through systematic iterations, effective interventions can be developed and implemented.

FINAL THOUGHTS

In many respects the BSM model is a common sense approach to sales management. As Benjamin Franklin reportedly commented, "Nothing is quite so uncommon as common sense." From a common sense standpoint, almost all effective sales managers follow the BSM model: they know and are able to discern which behaviors are important and which are unimportant; they constantly observe and monitor (i.e., measure) performance to make sure their people are doing the right things; when they see problems they constantly analyze the situation to try to determine the source of the problem (i.e., search for the factors reinforcing or punishing the behaviors); they continually design programs (interventions) to improve performance; they implement their programs; and they evaluate the success of their programs. The process we have described is a formal version of the natural process that all effective managers probably follow.

The major advantage of the current description is that it clarifies this normally effective process, allowing for improved communication of the program methods and stronger analysis. It also provides additional potential for improvement compared to more informal methods. It is a good diagnostic tool for analysis when the more informal processes fail. In almost all cases of failure, some step of the BSM model has been omitted inadvertently.

The challenge for sales managers is to create the increments in sales that make the difference between average and high performance. The BSM model offers a specific and systematic approach to achieving high performance. It is not a magic elixir or formula for success. Quite literally, the BSM model is the job description for effective sales management.

REFERENCES

Brethower, D. M. (1972). *Behavioral analyses in business and industry: A total performance system.* Kalamazoo, MI: Behaviordelia.

Brown, M. G., Malott, R. W., Dillon, M. J., and Keeps, E. J. (1980). Improving customer service in a large department store through the use of training and feedback, *Journal of Organizational Behavior Management, 2*(4), 251-266.

Casey, W. (1989). Review of applied behavior analytic research on sales performance improvement. *Journal of Organizational Behavior Management, 10*(2), 53-76.

Dickinson, A. M. and O' Brien, R. M. (1982). Performance measurement and evaluation. In R. M. O'Brien, A. M. Dickinson, and M. P. Rosow (Eds.), *Industrial behavior modification: A management handbook* (pp. 51-64). Elmsford, NY: Pergamon Press.

Feeney, E. J., Staelin, J. R., O'Brien, R.M., and Dickinson, A. M. (1982). Increasing sales performance among airline reservation personnel. In R. M. O'Brien, A. M. Dickinson, and M. P. Rosow (Eds.), *Industrial behavior modification: A management handbook* (pp. 141-158). Elmsford, NY: Pergamon Press.

Gilbert, T. F. (1978). *Human competence: Engineering worthy performance.* New York: McGraw-Hill.

Greene, B. F., Rouse, M., Green, R. B., and Clay, C. (1984). Behavior analysis in consumer affairs: Retail and consumer response to publicizing food price information. *Journal of Applied Behavior Analysis, 17,* 3-21.

Johnson, C. M. (1985). Customer feedback to the main office: Selling newspapers plot, stock and bare shelf. *Journal of Organizational Behavior Management, 7*(1/2), 37-49.

Kim, J. S. (1984). Effect of behavior plus outcome goal setting and feedback on employee satisfaction and performance. *Academy of Management Journal, 27,* 139-149.

Komaki, J., Blood, M. R., and Holder, D. (1980). Fostering friendliness in a fast food franchise. *Journal of Organizational Behavior Management, 2*(3), 151-164.

Komaki, J., Heinzmann, A. T., and Lawson, L. (1980). Effects of training and feedback: Component analyses of behavioral safety programs. *Journal of Applied Psychology, 65,* 261-270.

Luthans F. and Kreitner, R. (1975). *Organizational behavior modification.* Glenview, IL: Scott, Foresman and Co.

Luthans, F. and Kreitner, R. (1985). *Organizational behavior modification and beyond: An operant and social learning approach.* Glenview, IL: Scott, Foresman and Co.

Luthans, F. and Martinko, M. J. (1976). An organizational behavior modification analysis of absenteeism. *Human Resource Management, 15,* 11-18.

Luthans, F. and Martinko, M. J. (1978). *The power of positive reinforcement: A workshop on organizational behavior modification.* New York: McGraw-Hill.

Luthans, F. and Martinko, M. J. (1987). Behavioral approaches to organizations. In C. L. Cooper and I. T. Robertson (Eds.), *International review of industrial and organizational psychology* (pp. 35-60) New York: Prentice-Hall.

Luthans, F., Paul, R., and Baker, D. (1981). An experimental analysis of the impact of contingent reinforcement on salespersons' performance behavior. *Journal of Applied Psychology, 66,* 314-323.

Luthans, F., Paul, R., and Taylor, L. (1985). The impact of contingent reinforcement on retail salespersons' performance behavior: A replicated field experiment. *Journal of Organizational Behavior Management, 7*(1/2), 25-35.

Martinko, M. J. (1986a). An O.B. mod analysis of consumer behavior. *Journal of Organizational Behavior Management, 8*(1), 19-43.

Martinko, M. J. (1986b). Observation methods. In S. Gael (Ed.), *Job analysis handbook for business, industry, and government* (pp. 419-431). New York: Wiley and Sons.

Martinko, M. J., White, J. D., and Hassell, B. (1989). An operant analysis of prompting in a sales environment. *Journal of Organizational Behavior Management, 10*(1), 93-107.

Miller, L. M. (1978). *Behavior management: The new science of managing people at work.* New York: John Wiley and Sons.

Mirman, R. (1982). Performance management in sales organizations. In L. W. Frederiksen (Ed.), *Handbook of organizational behavior management* (pp. 427-475). New York: Wiley.

Neider, L. L. (1980). An experimental field investigation utilizing an expectancy theory view of participation. *Organizational Behavior and Human Performance, 26*, 425-442.

Nord, W. R. and Peter, P. J. (1980). A behavior modification perspective on marketing. *Journal of Marketing, 44*, 36-37.

Peter, P. J. and Nord, W. R. (1982). A clarification and extension of operant conditioning principles in marketing. *Journal of Marketing, 46*, 102-107.

Ralis, M. T. and O'Brien, R. M. (1986). Prompts, goal setting and feedback to increase suggestive selling. *Journal of Organizational Behavior Management, 8*(1), 5-18.

Rothschild, M. L. and Gaidis, W. C. (1981). Behavioral learning theory: Its relevance to marketing and promotions. *Journal of Marketing, 45*, 70-78.

PART III:
PROFESSIONAL
AND THEORETICAL ISSUES

Chapter 13

Marketing Behaviorally Based Solutions

Leslie Wilk Braksick
Julie M. Smith

When you have experienced the effectiveness of behavioral interventions—when you have replicated results and delighted clients—when you yourself believe in the science of human behavior, it is difficult to imagine anyone *not* "buying" it. The reality of the situation for organizational behavior analysts, however, is that few businesses and organizations have a history of reinforcement for choosing behavioral strategies to improve work-related behaviors. This poses a unique challenge for practitioners who have the tools and strategies to produce a measurable impact on organizations. Organizational behavior analysts may be able to create positive, lasting change, but unless they can communicate this to potential clients, their skills will achieve good for no one.

There are many ways to market your services. When people think of marketing, they often think of the traveling salesman who drags along all of his wares door to door. Such face-to-face contact with a single potential client is only one approach. We present several different marketing strategies in this chapter as well as ways of locating your services in a competitive position in the marketplace.

This chapter is organized to provide framework for developing a marketing strategy and covers the following main topics: defining your product/service, promotion and advertising, sales strategies, and market research.

DEFINING CORE PRODUCTS/SERVICES

Deciding who you are and what you have to offer is a first and necessary step in marketing organizational behavior management (OBM) or performance management (PM) services and products. After spending years, and perhaps decades, testing and refining performance improvement models and strategies, it may seem like a step backward to describe such features in common terms; however, this is a critical first step.

Connor and Davidson (1985) described a comprehensive approach to marketing consultation services and recommended (1) use of a "client-centered orientation," which defines critical services and products in terms of what clients want and need; and (2) systematic description of strengths and the market opportunities they permit one to address. They recommend that a client-centered services analysis be done to clearly identify what you can do to help clients improve or protect something they value (i.e., their market share) and what kinds of unwanted conditions your service reduces or eliminates. The client-centered method guides thinking toward the client's point of view and focuses attention on the value added by your services and not on technical descriptions or jargon peculiar to training, management development, or some other professional area.

When you describe what you have to offer, it is also important to consider three levels of benefits: core, augmented, and enhanced. Core benefits refer to the primary problem addressed or need served by your service. For example, if you educate workers to use safe practices on the job to comply with government regulations, a core benefit would be evidence of compliance with requirements across work areas. This outcome has immediate value for the client because it reduces the chances of fines or other sanctions by government inspectors. Safety education may also produce additional benefits (augmented) such as decreased accident rates or fewer lost work hours, which in the long run pay off for a client in terms of decreased health care or worker compensation costs. Finally, a safer workplace may have many indirect effects that do not translate readily into economic value (enhanced) but are easily identified; for example, a safer workplace may result in increased worker satisfaction.

Whatever the specific benefits of your services, it is important to carefully examine what value they add for clients and to describe what you do using phrasing and terms that clearly communicate these benefits. OBM consultants have an advantage over others in this regard because the outcomes of behavioral interventions are, in most cases, measurable and observable, making benefits quantifiable. Additionally, OBM interventions focus on performance change and not just lectures and attitude change; thus, behavior changes and their resulting effects can be identified as outcomes of your consultation. Such tangible effects can be justified more readily by clients than "train and hope" strategies used by many who use less direct intervention methods (e.g., motivational lectures, general communication skills, worker morale).

ADVERTISING AND PROMOTION

Marketing Materials

Once a core description has been constructed, this information must be communicated through effective marketing materials. Printed marketing materials are frequently the first source a prospective client will encounter. Key decision makers will want to see in writing the services or products they will receive if they commit their company's resources. Additionally, marketing materials make it possible for people who are not in decision-making positions to describe and perhaps recommend your services to others. In fact, one measure of success of your marketing strategy is the extent to which written materials are circulated beyond your initial contact. In keeping with the client-centered approach, it is important to demonstrate knowledge of factors that are likely to be of interest to clients. Many industry buzzwords convey current knowledge such as total quality management (TQM), ISO 9000 registration, OSHA STAR, price of nonconformance (PONC), and others.

A clear marketing message and effective materials require that you know who your competitors are and your position in the marketplace relative to them. Take it as a given that dozens of other consultants and practitioners are purporting to do what you do. For OBM consultants, competitors often include seasoned business professionals, counseling psychologists, communication specialists, and industrial engineers. The most frequently observed difference between behavioral approaches and other more eclectic ones is that nonbehavioral interventions typically lack precision in implementation or, in lay terms, tactics for getting others to carry out the plans. Behavioral technologies for reinforcement and punishment can be extremely effective in arranging an environment that promotes follow-through. Nonbehavioral strategies also place little emphasis on measurement, especially at the individual-behavior level. Your specific skills and training may create other advantages over your competition and define a market niche for you or your consulting firm; it is up to you to complete the research that permits development of a comparative profile with competitors and a clear message that describes the relative advantage of doing business with you or your firm.

One other reason for packaging your services in a written brochure or other presentation document is that it forces you to think through logically the system of intervention you use. You should be able to answer basic questions such as:

- "What steps or phases does a typical project include?"
- "What will be the project outcomes or deliverables?"
- "What sets you apart from the competition?"
- "How will you get started with the project?"
- "When can an organization expect to be doing this without your services?"
- "At what level of the organization will you work?"
- "What project results have you been able to produce elsewhere?"
- "Whom can I talk to about your previous projects and performance?"

If you are just getting started you might not have enough of your own "war stories" or project results to include in your materials. As an alternative, you can illustrate the power of behavior analysis by using published results from studies that have applied similar technology (after receiving releases from the journals or publishers).

Your promotional materials can be packaged in many different ways, ranging from threefold pamphlets on standard paper to color-coordinated glossy folders with multiple inserts. Choice of packaging depends largely upon your budget and the target audience. The appearance and content of materials is less critical if a prior relationship exists with a client organization. For example, if you were given entrée into an organization by a personal referral from a close friend of the key decision maker, your materials will be less important than if you are meeting someone for the first time on a cold call.

In summary, your marketing materials should contain, at a minimum, a description of your core services, an explanation of who you are, your approach to solving organizational problems, and your specialty areas (e.g., safety, quality, instructional design, compensation, etc.). Additionally, you should provide a clear means for differentiating your services and products from those of competitors who are likely to have contacted your prospects. Finally, any information on your history of success and client references, which attest to your effectiveness, is helpful in creating confidence on the part of prospects.

Exposure in the Marketplace

Once the message is defined and packaged in promotional materials, you must arrange for frequent exposure of this information to those who are likely to be good prospects. Several promotional strategies are described in the following sections.

Seminars

Most have seen seminar brochures that cross every manager's desk daily. Seminars are a popular marketing tool for a number of reasons. First, they offer potential clients a chance to better understand you and your approaches before buying a bigger contract. Second, they offer you the opportunity to showcase materials, past successes, and unique applications. Finally, they allow you to cover marketing costs through seminar fees, rather than as additional overhead. You might want to consider working out an arrangement with a university to offer your seminars as part of its continuing education program. Many professionals need to complete a certain number of continuing or professional education courses each year, and this provides a good way to attract participants and potential future clients to your sessions.

If you are interested in offering seminars, attend one or two taught by the competitors to assess their weaknesses, and develop a seminar outline and materials that overcome these weaknesses. We have found that most seminars do not build significant skills; this is where behavior analysts can make a difference. People should leave a seminar with at least one or two new skills that can be applied immediately. Also, remember that adult learners like to be entertained while learning something useful; games or active learning exercises provide an effective approach to teaching and permit you to display your information in a stimulating way.

Professional Writing

Another effective marketing technique is professional writing. Authors of magazine articles, management texts, and popular books can reach larger, more diverse audiences than any individual on a one-to-one basis. Many of us come from academic backgrounds and are tempted to write only for students and other faculty. Although these books are necessary for the growth of behavior analysis, they will not have a broad-scale impact on your client base. More potential clients can be contacted and informed when we write books with mass appeal. Read the business books on *The New York Times* Bestseller List. Try to figure out what it is that attracts people to these books. Look at books such as *Unlock Behavior, Unleash Profits* (Braksick, 2000), *Bringing out the Best in People* (Daniels, 2000), the *One Minute Manager* series (e.g., Blanchard and Johnson, 1982), and

In Search of Excellence (Peters and Waterman, 1982) to identify the critical features that made them successful, such as readability, case studies based on common examples, and prescriptions for problem solving. The authors of these books are sought after by their clients.

Even if you do not have time to write a book, it is worthwhile to spend time producing other written materials that can be presented to clients to demonstrate your ability to organize ideas and training materials in a visually pleasing manner. Develop training materials, quick reference guides, and manuscripts for publication in trade journals and periodicals as a way of getting your expertise and success before the public.

Conference Presentations and Speeches

Conference presentations and association memberships provide additional opportunities to network with potential clients and showcase your materials and services. Participating in local community groups and statewide organizations provides networking opportunities and additional exposure for your talents and products.

Adjunct faculty appointments with teaching opportunities in the evening or on weekends offer a good means for connecting with business community members who are likely to need your services. University courses, particularly those offered to adult learners and working professionals, provide an excellent opportunity for practitioners to market their services and receive positive and constructive feedback on the content and delivery of the instruction. If you do not have much experience in presenting to adult learners, this is an excellent way to gain experience in a relatively nonpunitive environment. Contact your local college to see if you might be able to teach courses. If you are asked to teach a course that is nonbehavioral, such as personnel management or organizational development, do not reject this option. A behavioral approach can be applied to most subject matter and nonbehavioral approaches provide good opportunities to demonstrate the comparative effectiveness of different methods to learners.

Front-End Assessments

Many organizational systems require audits or formal measurement of achievements or problem conditions. Supplier quality certification (e.g., International Standards Organization [ISO] registration), safety audits, and customer satisfaction audits are but a few of the internal audits that many organizations are required to do. Offering to assist or execute such audits provides a useful way to aid an organization with an immediate need and demonstrate the services and strategies you have to offer. Organizational climate surveys, training needs assessments, employee satisfaction surveys, and leadership development needs assessments are additional popular and useful assessments. Some consultants offer one- to two-day audits at little or no cost in the hope of gaining a larger project. The information you will obtain during the audit will help identify project opportunities and provide invaluable time on-site to begin to build relationships.

Regardless of the approach taken, the marketing activities above offer opportunities to demonstrate your capabilities and strategies and display past client successes. Furthermore, you can convey to potential clients the range of services you offer and the uniqueness of your approach relative to competitors. Conducting seminars or audits allows potential clients to sample your services and increase the chances of further business based on outcomes rather than on promises.

SALES AND MARKET RESEARCH

Identifying Potential Clients

Once you have developed materials and selected marketing activities, your next task is to identify who might benefit from your offerings. Several factors are important: potential for securing a contract, lowest marketing cost, and lowest effort up front. Undoubtedly the best way to obtain useful marketing contacts is via referral from past clients. Past clients can offer objective data on approach, style, intervention strategies, and outcomes achieved. Furthermore, if that client is still working with, or has maintained a continued relationship with you, commitment and satisfaction with services can be conveyed to the potential client.

Reference books such as manufacturing or health care directories for your state provide information on businesses, including the services and products they produce, the number of employees, organizational contact names and numbers, and brief descriptions of the organizations. Researching the background of targeted industries and businesses allows you to further customize your materials and approaches as well as target your potential client list. It is wise to target specific industries (e.g., chemical products, health care) so the experience in one firm transfers quickly to the next and materials development is made easier.

Getting Your Foot in the Door

Once you have decided to whom you wish to market, the challenge is getting your foot in the door. When following up a referral or client-initiated contact, this step may involve nothing more than a simple phone call. If you initiate through a cold call, this can be a make-or-break contact for you. Be sure to include the following activities before and during your initial phone contact.

Write Out a Script

You may be nervous and forget to include important information about yourself and your services. Avoid this pressure by writing out what you wish to say, and a brief checklist of information you wish to convey.

Identify the Right Person

Knowing the person to whom you should speak is important. Just as you dislike being disturbed at home by phone calls from solicitors, potential clients will fail to appreciate being taken away from business unless it is for something worthwhile. If you do not have the name of the person you need to speak with, call the organization's main phone number and ask for his or her name by title (e.g., manager of quality, human resources manager, etc.).

Get a Referral/Name Drop

Even during an initial cold call, having a referral can be extremely helpful. If a past client or contact has already mentioned your name or services to the prospective client, much of the initial formality of introduction and description can be dispelled. Drop the names of organizations with which you have worked (if you have already received the organization's permission to do this) and describe results you have achieved. This can help sway individuals to meet with you to learn more.

Schedule Initial Meeting

Your goal during the initial phone discussion is to arrange for a future meeting with the contact (and/or additional persons) to further describe how you might assist their organization. In doing so, you will need to describe what you have to offer, how you think it could be of assistance them, and how much of their time you will need (e.g., one hour) in the future meeting.

Use High-Impact Words

The initial discussion is a prime opportunity to use high-impact words that might affect the organization's willingness to meet. Through minor, preliminary research, you can quickly learn about issues with which an organization or industry is struggling (e.g., quality, safety, recruitment, communications, union relations) and use these issues to increase confidence that you know not only the science of behavior, but also the current concerns of organizations.

Get Directions

Be sure to get directions to the organization including parking and security clearance information. Most facilities have multiple entrances and designated parking for visitors. Be sure to get specific instructions so confusion and complications are minimized on the day of your arrival.

Send a Confirmation Letter and Something to Read

Follow up your discussion with a confirmation letter and an article, brochure, one-page summary, or similar description of you and your services. This serves as a reminder, as well as an opportunity to further specify how you might be helpful.

Find Out How Many People Will Be Present

Be certain you learn how many people you will be meeting with so you may bring one to two extra sets of materials and business cards. It is important to be prepared for the meeting; additional participants provide an opportunity to increase the number of internal sales agents for your services. Prepare for more than the number you are told, just to be safe.

Preparing for the First Visit

Prior to your first visit to a site, study the industry and the organization. The *U.S. Industrial Handbook* is a reference manual that contains a summary of all industries according to classification codes. If you are marketing to a medical supply manufacturer, you can look up information about that industry's viability, growth strategies, competition, trends, and pay rates. In three or four short pages you can become very familiar with the concerns of the organization you are about to visit, and use this information in targeting your presentation to address critical issues. The handbook also includes the names and phone numbers of government employees who are responsible for answering more detailed questions. The Internet offers unlimited options for researching companies. For example, information found on the Internet becomes more extensive and detailed every day.

Search engines such as Yahoo, Infoseek, AltaVista, Hotbot, Dogpile, and Metacrawler offer users the opportunity to search the Internet with keywords. The complexity of a generic Internet search can be overwhelming because most search engines are designed to search an entire Web site for a keyword. Marketing research has become more refined with the addition of sites such as eLibrary.com, Northernlight, and Hoover's Online. eLibrary and Northernlight are large database sites that include magazine articles, books, reports, newspaper, and newswire, as well as radio, TV, and government transcripts. In addition to these sites, many of these sources also have Web sites with archived information from publications such as the *Journal of Behavior Management, New York Times, Wall Street Journal, Forbes, Business Week, Harvard Business Review,* and *Sloan Management Review.*

Hoover's features links to news, lists, stock quotes, and profiles such as Hoover's Industry Snapshots (global industry overviews). Hoover's offers approximately 14,000 company capsules (brief company descriptions and financials) for free and approximately 4,000 company profiles (company histories, strategies, market positions, major events, and other information) available through an online subscription. The profiles cover U.S. and foreign public and nonpublic companies and are written for executives, investors, job seekers, salespeople, consumers, and scholars—anyone who needs company information written in an informed and engaging style. Other notable online research tools available are Harvard Business School Publishing, Amazon, and Barnes and Noble where users can purchase books, reference materials, and videos quickly.

Many of today's companies have Web sites, and users can obtain mission and vision statements, annual reports, press releases, executive profiles, contact information, human resources, company policy, and community projects. The Internet is not only a good resource for establishing and recognizing a potential client's culture, but also your competitor's culture.

Another way to gather information about your prospective client is to speak with people who are experts in the topic area. For example, if you are going to focus on safety, then talk to someone who is outstanding in the field or read materials on safety issues. Ask the experts how they conduct their work, what types of outcome measures they apply, and what is happening in the area of safety for the particular industry you will be visiting. Spend time talking to people in organizations similar to the client organization. Ask them how their organization is structured. Query them about their competitors. Ask what they know about the organization you will be visiting (be sure to maintain the confidentiality of the potential client's name through this process). Ask them to describe typical pressures facing the industry and current threats and opportunities. Find out if industry organizations are amenable to change.

Finally, you should read journals and trade magazines in the potential client's industry. These trade journals will help you to quickly learn the language of the industry. You should be familiar with common acronyms within the industry. For example, DRG became an important acronym for hospitals in the 1980s because the basis for payment for services rendered was switched to Diagnostic Related Groups instead of individual cases. A consultant who did not know this faced a significant disadvantage when marketing consulting services to health care organizations, even if DRGs were not involved directly in the proposed activity.

The Marketing Visit

Once you have invested the time and energy to secure a meeting, be sure to take the steps described here to heighten the probability of success during that face-to-face interaction.

Arrive Early and Read Lobby Information

You can learn important things about an organization by perusing what is posted in the lobby. Often organizations will display their mission or vision statements, quality awards they have received, certifications or other recognition from customers, publications or brochures in which they are featured, and other pieces of information that may help direct your questions and presentation to your prospective client.

Dress Appropriately

Because it is important to dress appropriately, you are advised to consult, where possible, with internal people on how they define "appropriate." Consider the activities in which you might participate while you are there, and target your dress accordingly. For example, for a presentation at a manufacturing plant, it would be impractical and unsafe for a woman to wear a skirt or high-heeled shoes because this would likely rule out the possibility of a plant tour (which is a rich source of data collection when visiting with a prospective client). The same may be true of a tie or other loose clothing for men, especially in manufacturing plants where clothing may become caught in machinery.

Briefly Introduce Yourself

Do not run down your litany of accomplishments, but ensure that the individuals with whom you are meeting understand your preferred pronunciation of your name and can confidently introduce you to others. You will have time during your meeting and through the written materials you leave with the client to describe your many experiences and accomplishments in a more humble fashion.

Get Them Talking—General to Specific

It is important to get the prospect talking in general about how things are going at the company, the initiatives they have underway, problems they are facing, etc. This provides an excellent data-gathering opportunity for you, as well as a chance to learn the company's terminology and organizational structure.

Listen for Strengths and Weaknesses

While you are setting the stage with a more free-flowing discussion about the client organization, you should listen closely for what it perceives to be its strengths and areas in need of improvement. This will allow you to target your presentation and describe the ways in which you can specifically add value to the organization.

Past and Current Efforts

Accept as a given that your proposed system will be evaluated against current or past programs. It is important that you fully understand the organization's history with OBM or PM interventions, the systems it has tried and maintained, and those which have "failed" in their opinion. This will allow you to learn the ways in which you can better assist them, or modify your proposal if necessary.

OBM/PM Goals

It is important to have the potential client identify its goals with respect to OBM or PM interventions. This will allow you to understand the company's expectations and measurable performance improvements it is looking for from your intervention.

Decision Processes/Makers

Depending on the level at which you enter the organization, the person with whom you are speaking may not have the budget or positional authority to hire you as a consultant. Furthermore, in the numerous team-based organizations of today, there are often several decision makers or teams that will need to endorse your proposed intervention before a decision is made. Be sure to fully review this process and to get the names and positions of those involved. Furthermore, identify the time frame for decision making so you may plan accordingly.

Commitment to Next Step

Before leaving your meeting, identify a clear next step for both the prospective client and yourself. Set a target date and time to get back together either in person or by phone to discuss the follow-up steps and what has changed since you last met. Do not leave the next steps undefined by speaking in generalities about getting back in touch.

Overcoming Objections

In most cases, objections will arise during your meeting. Sometimes these objectives will center on the intervention steps, whereas other times they will revolve around the proposed costs, and they could even involve the project scope or you. Sample objections include the following: "We're already doing this." "We do not have the budget or time." "How does this fit in with our other programs?" "This is manipulation." "This is too simplified." "We're working on problem solving and team building." When these points are raised, ask clarifying questions, and use paraphrasing to ensure that you fully understand the objections. Provide simple, direct, nonblaming replies to their objections. Use examples and case studies to provide additional data that they can base their opinion on.

Avoid Letting Them Take the Next Step

You want to determine the next steps, so you can be sure they occur. Whether it be a follow-up phone call or a visit, writing a letter, or mailing a proposal, offer a specific suggestion—one which you have control over—for the next step in developing a working relationship.

History with Respect to Consultants

Although we would like to think otherwise, consultants are common. They are everywhere. And, as downsizing in large companies continues to occur at a high frequency, more and more individuals will be entering the job market with the nondescript title of "consultant." Because the field is full and the skills and experiences of these individuals vary so much, the probability that a company has had a bad previous experience with consultants is high. Be prepared for this, and be ready to describe how you are different. Cite a track record that contradicts assumptions that you are "just another consultant." Share the risks of the project with your client by using a pay-at-risk model tied to the achievement of agreed-upon business results.

Preparing the Proposal

A good proposal tells a client exactly what you will be doing for them, how long it will take, and what it will cost. The proposal should be written concisely and should get to the heart of the matter quickly. Most proposals are about five to ten pages and contain the following components.

Cover Letter

Each proposal should go out with a cover letter that has your company's letterhead across the top. Oftentimes, proposals will get circulated around the organization, and it helps to let the reader know who is sending the proposal and to whom it was sent. By attaching a cover letter, you increase the probability that this information will be routed with the proposal. Also, proposals are often not accepted for a year or more, and the cover letter serves as the one document to help the client organization piece together the background on why the proposal was developed and who requested it.

Proposal Cover Page

On the proposal's cover page, include a title for the project (which becomes your official descriptor for your project files) and the client's name and city, along with the date, and your company name, address, and phone number. Anyone who reads the proposal should be able to determine quickly which company submitted it and how to contact that company.

Project Background

The project background section describes your understanding of the organization and the particular problems you plan to address. It is designed to clearly show the clients that you listened carefully to their issues during the initial marketing discussion, and you understand the way their organization is structured. Use their terms and acronyms. Use specific titles and names of people you talked to in order to personalize this section.

Project Description

The project description is the meat of the proposal. It lays out clearly what you will do for the organization (e.g., conduct training, complete an audit, coach senior managers, facilitate teams) and what will be the project deliverables (e.g., interim reports, training modules, audit results). Structure this section using sequential steps if possible. Indicate who will be affected in the organization and how much time will be required of each person.

Project Budget

Determining a project budget is the most difficult part of developing a proposal. First, budget development requires experience with estimating the time required for each step (usually in number of days). Avoid quoting one overall price without estimating the number of days each major portion of the project will require. As a consultant, you will need to keep detailed records of how you spend your time, so you can justify it to the client and determine the actual costs of conducting future projects. If you do not have such records in place yet, ask others who have conducted similar types of projects to help you with the estimate. Do not lose contact with the needs of the customer during the estimation process. They might tell you that another consultant proposed the same project with a budget of $50,000. If this was too expensive for them, they might not accept your $75,000 proposal even though you have calculated that as your true cost. In such cases, it is better to find ways to cut the scope of your work rather than trying to justify a larger budget. Also, find out how many days per week they would like to see you on-site. Find out whether they would like you to attend their regularly scheduled meetings or whether they want you in for special events only. This type of information will give you an idea of how extensive they want your involvement to be. Often you can gain acceptance for a smaller project and once you have gained a foothold, use your newfound information about the organization to obtain additional work. Whatever you do, avoid submitting an artificially low budget estimate just to get in the door, only to later find that you cannot complete what you proposed because of a shortfall.

Project Timelines

Use a Gantt Chart or other graphic display to show the client what activities will occur and when (see Kerzner, 1989, for a description of planning and management tools). This is a very important component because it will help the organization determine how much time needs to be freed up for its staff to participate in the project and when to expect important milestones to be reached. You will need to be considerate of the client's vacation schedules and production peaks in planning the time frame.

Project Staffing

If a team of consultants is involved in conducting the project, you will need to briefly describe their expertise. Emphasize their experience in solving similar problems and describe the types of clients with whom they have worked. Also include a description of everyone's role on the project (e.g., who will discuss the invoices with the client, who will oversee the project team, who will interview employees, who will analyze the data, who will be responsible for the quality of the consulting services, who will deliver the training, etc.). Some clients will want to know the daily rates of each project staff member, and this also should be inserted with the list of staff.

Proposal Delivery

It is important to deliver the proposal in person. That way you can better gauge which parts of the proposal the client likes and which parts need to be changed. One strategy is to show the client the most extensive version of what can be done, and, if they find it overwhelming, work with them to determine which pieces of the larger picture they want to implement first. In such cases, you should rewrite the proposal and recalculate budget estimates; do not rely on informal notes or understandings as a basis for a business relationship. Oftentimes the relationship will have developed to the point that you can discuss the second draft over the phone.

Proposal development has two golden rules. First, ensure the elapsed time between the initial marketing trip and the proposal presentation is no more than ten working days. Second, try to make sure all the key decision makers are available for your presentation of the proposal. If this is not possible, ask to speak with them individually. Never rely on someone else to sell your proposal up the chain of command. OBM is hard enough for a behavior analyst to sell, let alone an untrained manager.

If your proposal is not accepted immediately, do not give up. Look at it as a success that you were asked to present a proposal. The organization is now familiar with your approach and your pricing strategies. In such cases, an organization will be more likely to think of you in the future if other projects come up. We have experienced situations in which three or four years of relationship building were required before a client accepted a proposal. Consider any interaction you have with the potential client as a relationship builder, not as a sales job for a particular project. Develop a tickler file to call them periodically to see how they are doing. You will often obtain useful information to help you approach the same client again more effectively. Do not give up even if they accepted another consultant over you. Many consultants cannot produce the results that behavior analysts can, and many companies come back because they remembered the original presentation.

Do not be shy about sharing the results of other projects on which you are working. Oftentimes, we have developed relationships with current clients to the point that they will meet with prospective clients to discuss PM and OBM. Exposure to others helps reinforce a current client's use of behavioral principles by prompting them to prepare for a guest tour and showcases expertise to the prospective client.

Closing the Sale

Once you have presented your proposal and obtained feedback, prospective clients may ask that adjustments in the proposed intervention be made to better fit their needs. Also, the proposed budget may have to be adjusted to fit within client guidelines or projections. It is important that any adjustments requested be done very quickly and that follow-up meetings with key contacts be scheduled to complete the sale. It is a good idea to provide a project agreement letter or contract along with the revisions so the client can indicate formal acceptance of the proposal and budget at the first opportunity. A request for a formal commitment provides a clear indication of whether the client is willing to go forward. The project acceptance form or letter should include a synopsis of the project, the names of consultants and staff who will be working on the project, and the budget total to which you have agreed. It should contain the signature of key participants and decision makers for the consulting firm and the client.

It is important to limit the number of revisions and meetings you are willing to arrange after the formal proposal has been presented. During this phase, clients are receiving valuable information concerning their current problems and needs and the exact procedures required to address them. If they obtain your expertise and ideas without cost, they are likely to try to extend this interaction as long as possible. It is reasonable to ask that a short-term assessment contract be developed to pay your expenses and fees if the proposal process extends too long or if the client seems unwilling to make a financial commitment; if the client is unwilling to provide these resources, it is unwise to continue regular contact at your own expense.

Building Relationships

Although your expertise and advice should not be provided to a prospective client without cost, it is important to build relationships with past and potential clients over the long run. Thus, even if a proposal is not accepted by a client, occasional contact should be made to obtain information on current needs and the possibility of activating the proposed interaction at some later time. A client might choose not to go forward with a proposed project for many reasons including budget limitations, change in leadership, indecision by leaders, disagreement among leaders, etc. These factors are subject to change, possibly causing a shift in receptiveness to your proposal; in such cases, it is important to have an open line of communication so the proposal can be updated quickly and resubmitted. If a formal presentation already has occurred and the needs are unchanged, your proposed intervention could be activated without delay and could lead to immediate work for you or your firm.

Ongoing relationships are also important in a general sense. Even if a proposed intervention is never accepted, the proposal process makes it possible for you to showcase your skills, products, and services and to encourage a client organization to review what you can do and how well you do it. This general knowledge may lead a decision maker to ask for your help when a problem arises rather than seek out a completely new consultant and initiate a new relationship. This holds true, however, only if you maintain contact and keep your communication lines open. This can be done through an occasional telephone call to a key person for a quick chat about recent events (e.g., newspaper stories about the company) or by sending clippings, articles, and other items of interest to key people with a personal note.

CONCLUSION

The brief treatment of marketing strategies presented in this chapter outlines several critical factors in successful prospecting and sales. Because of space limitations, many details have been omitted; however, sufficient information to provide context for beginning a marketing effort was presented. To achieve maximum effects, it is recommended that a written marketing plan be developed by an internal cross-functional team so all concerned become familiar with your organization's products and services, position in the marketplace, and client relationship-building strategies.

REFERENCES

Blanchard, Kenneth H. and Spencer Johnson (1982). *The One Minute Manager.* New York: Morrow, William & Co.

Braksick, L. W. (2000). *Unlock behavior, unleash profits.* New York: McGraw-Hill.

Connor, Richard A. and Jeffrey P. Davidson (1985). *Marketing Your Consulting and Professional Services.* New York: John Wiley & Sons.

Daniels, A. C. (2000). *Bringing out the best in people* (Second edition). New York: McGraw-Hill.

Kerzner, Harold. (1989). *Project Management: A Systems Approach to Planning, Scheduling, and Controlling* (Third edition). New York: Van Nostrand-Reinhold.

Peters, Thomas and Robert H. Waterman Jr. (1982). *In Search of Excellence: Lessons from America's Best-Run Companies.* New York: Warner.

Chapter 14

Organizational Behavior Management and Organization Development: Potential Paths to Reciprocation

James L. Eubanks

The origins of applied behavioral science can be traced back more than fifty years. While Skinner was pioneering efforts in the experimental analysis of behavior, and the grand theorists, Tolman, Hull, and Guthrie were battling for supremacy in the behavioral science arena, Kurt Lewin and Rensis Likert, prominent social psychologists of the era, began emphasizing the importance of connecting research and theory with practice. Their work strongly influenced the field of organizational behavior (OB), and spawned the field we will consider in detail in the present chapter: organization development (OD).

Neither OB nor OD share many of the features commonly identified with organizational behavior management (OBM): direct and frequent recording of behavior, targeting outcomes that workers can influence, and focusing on performance consequences. Indeed, current OD texts (e.g., Burke, 1982; French and Bell, 1990; Cummings and Worley, 1993) pay very little attention, if any, to Skinner's work and neglect to acknowledge OBM altogether. The OB field, on the other hand, has had fruitful interaction with behavior analysis (Komaki, 1986a). Virtually all OB texts (e.g., Luthans, 1992) include OBM as part of the OB field, although it is more often referred to as organizational behavior modification, or O.B. Mod.

The purpose of this chapter is to explore the potential for reciprocation between OD and OBM. The field of OD has matured considerably during the past two decades, with calls for systematic evaluation and research designed to determine what works and to begin assembling a theoretical basis for the field (Dunn and Swierczek, 1977; Eubanks and Marshall, 1990; Eubanks, Marshall, and O'Driscoll, 1990; Eubanks et al., 1990;

Golembiewski, Proehl, and Sink, 1982; Nicholas, 1982; O'Driscoll and Eubanks, 1992, 1993, 1994). Clients have also become more sophisticated and are requiring OD practitioners to show performance gains in exchange for the considerable effort and cost involved in systemwide interventions (Beer and Walton, 1987, 1990). The OD field is briefly described in the following section as a basis for contrasting it with OBM.

DEFINITION AND COMPARISON OF OD WITH OBM

Numerous definitions of OD exist. According to one of the more comprehensive descriptions of the field, OD is:

> a top-management-supported, long-range effort to improve an organization's problem solving and renewal processes, particularly through a more effective and collaborative diagnosis and management of organization culture—with special emphasis on formal work team, temporary team, and inter-group culture—with the assistance of a consultant-facilitator and the use of the theory and technology of applied behavioral science, including action research. (French and Bell, 1990, p. 17)

This definition encompasses a number of dimensions that require elaboration. Table 14.1 lists these dimensions and provides a basis for comparing and contrasting OD and OBM. These dimensions will be used later as a basis for evaluating possible areas of interaction and reciprocation among the two fields.

Client

Within the OD approach to organizational change, support is required by the organization's chief executive, and the client is typically one or more members of the top management group. Recent writings have emphasized the importance of active involvement and ongoing approval by this power structure in order for change to occur in an organization (Burke, 1982; French and Bell, 1990). In contrast, OBM efforts typically occur in response to somewhat more focused problems identified by line managers (Balcazar et al., 1989, p. 20).

Time Frame

Although there are certainly exceptions in each case, successful OD efforts typically are either ongoing or are framed in terms of one or more

TABLE 14.1. Comparison of OD and OBM As Technologies of Organizational Change

Dimension	OD	OBM
Client	Top management	Line managers
Time Frame	Long-range/ongoing	Limited/months
Change Goals	Problem-solving/ "renewal processes"	Frequency of targeted behavior(s)
Technology Base	Applied behavioral science	Behavior analysis
Unit of Analysis	Groups/teams and intergroup culture	Individual worker behavior
Intervention Strategy	Collaborative diagnosis, action research, culture management	Performance audit, single-subject design, contingency management
Change Agent	Consultant-facilitator	Behavioral consultant

years (French and Bell, 1990; Huse and Cummings, 1989), while OBM interventions are frequently completed in less than a year (Balcazar et al., 1989).

Change Goals

OD interventions emphasize *how* an organization makes decisions, whether it typically involves a select few individuals or uses the resources of all its members. Closely related to organizational decision making is the notion of "renewal processes" (Argyris, 1970). It is not enough to enhance the effectiveness of an organization's decisions. Within the OD perspective, ongoing realignment is required between the organization's purpose and its direction in response to a constantly changing *external* environment. This process perspective is a hallmark of OD efforts, and intervention strategies such as process consultation (Schein, 1988) emphasize it. Environmental change is also a focus of OBM. Such change, however, is systematically arranged *within* the organization in order to change the frequency of carefully targeted and pinpointed behaviors (cf. Brown, 1982; Daniels, 1989).

Technology Base

The history of OD is aligned with the development of applied behavioral science, with contributions from fields such as social psychology, cultural anthropology, psychiatry, management/administrative sciences, economics, sociology, and political science. An underlying theme running through the interdisciplinary OD field is that of humanism and existentialism (French and Bell, 1990), ranging from the early writers on the Hawthorne studies (Roethlisberger and Dickson, 1939) to more widespread "person-centered" approaches (e.g., Schein and Bennis, 1965). OBM draws its change technology from applied behavior analysis, with more recent pleas to incorporate basic research data and theory from the experimental analysis of behavior.

Unit of Analysis

The primary focus in OD efforts is the work group, or team, including both superiors and subordinates. Dependent variables within an OD effort tend to emphasize team or work group measures reflecting intergroup relations, decision making, trust, and communication. However, individual behavioral measures are sometimes included, along with organization-wide measures and variables related to leader behavior (Porras and Berg, 1978, pp. 252-253). For the most part, OD addresses rather stable work teams, but attention is also directed at temporary work teams, such as committees, boards of directors, task forces, and "cross-functional teams." In contrast, OBM efforts have traditionally focused on targeting behavior and accomplishments (e.g., Gilbert, 1978) of individual workers for change.

Intervention Strategy

The main focus of the OD process is data collection concerning the current functioning of the organization to detect gaps between the status quo and desired mission or goal statements. This activity is commonly referred to as organizational diagnosis (Weisbord, 1987). The data are usually based on interviews, observations, questionnaires, and archival information, with a heavy reliance on verbal self-report by clients and organizational members.

The results of the organizational diagnosis are important, but, consistent with OD's process approach, *how* the information is collected and what is done with that information are also of prime concern. This process is usually imbedded within what has come to be known as action research

(French and Bell, 1990). Action research essentially involves a cyclical process in which a problem is collaboratively defined by the persons affected (client group) in concert with an OD consultant, followed by data collection, action (interventions undertaken to establish new behavior), data collection, and feedback to the client group. This cycle is repeated until the problem has been solved or a previously established criterion is met.

Collaborative diagnosis and action research are usually applied within an OD intervention in the context of what is known as culture management (cf. Deal and Kennedy, 1982; Schein, 1990). Organizational culture is a relatively new concept that is being embraced by the management and OD communities. Recently, it was introduced in the OBM literature as well (Eubanks and Lloyd, 1992; Lamal, 1991; Mawhinney, 1992; Chapter 17, this volume). From the vantage point of management and OD, this approach involves a shared examination of how work is done in an organization (by managers, subordinates, and consultants) and assessing the values, technology, and behavior of its members in terms of how functional these elements are in meeting both short- and long-range goals of the organization and its members. The OBM approach presents a common process, selection by consequences, which underlies all behavior in organizations. For example, Glenn (1986, 1988, 1991a) advanced the concept of metacontingencies that control large segments of societal practice, though she did not specify organizations as specific subunits for analysis. Such analyses have been recently applied from an OBM vantage point to both private and public sector organizations (Redmon and Wilk, 1991; Redmon and Agnew, 1991).

A hallmark of OD has been its values-based approach to organizational change. Encompassed within this approach is a concern for increasing individual as well as organizational effectiveness. Related to this concern for individual development is the basic assumption that people want to, and are capable of, making sustained, high-level contributions to the goals and mission of the organization (see Gellerman, 1984, 1985, for a treatment of OD values and ethics).

Change Agent

An external facilitator-consultant has been a consistently distinguishing element of OD efforts, and continues to be preferred over do-it-yourself programs (cf. French and Bell, 1990, p. 20). Although internal OD consultants (staff persons usually residing in the human resources department) may be employed, particularly in collaboration with an external consultant, external persons are believed to be more effective because they are relatively free of the cultural constraints of the organization, more independent of local politics than the internal person, and less dependent on the long-range reinforcement afforded by salary and career advancement within the firm. No data exist, however, directly comparing the effectiveness of internal and external consultants. In fact, Beer and Walton (1990) note the transition of OD from a set of skills held by an external consultant to requisite skills held by all effective managers in an organization. This trend, if it continues, would make the distinction between external and internal consultants obsolete, since OD would become acculturated into the daily management practices of the firm. It is not clear, however, that the consequences of OD practices are sufficiently effective to be selected into the mainstream culture of most organizations.

DOES OD WORK?

Anecdotal reports of successful OD interventions abound in the literature (cf., Beer and Walton, 1987, 1990). However, several recent literature reviews have reported mixed results (cf. Golembiewski, Proehl, and Sink, 1982; Hantula et al., 1991; Mirvis and Berg, 1977). To date the data suggest that positive effects are obtained in 50 to 87 percent of the studies reviewed. A meta-analysis by Guzzo, Jette, and Katzell (1985) evaluated 207 field studies and found that the OD programs reviewed increased worker productivity, on the average, about one-half a standard deviation. With respect to worker satisfaction and job-related attitudes, a similar meta-analysis procedure was conducted (Neuman, Edwards, and Raju, 1989) and the authors concluded that comprehensive, multifaceted OD interventions were more effective in enhancing attitudinal measures than were those that focused on a more specific technique, such as team building or laboratory training. The majority of the studies included in these reviews, however, relied primarily on verbal self-report measures of productivity (see Nicholas, 1982, for an exception to this). It is not clear to what extent the positive effects of OD interventions would hold using actual production data (e.g., number of defects, scrap rate, etc.).

The rigor of available research on OD effectiveness is cause for caution. One review article drew the following conclusion: "Stated kindly, the quality of research in OD is not always spectacular; indeed, some of it is shoddy" (Woodman, 1989, p. 223). Several analyses of OD research have found an inverse relationship between the degree of methodological rigor and the reported outcome success of OD (Terpstra, 1981; Woodman and Wayne, 1985; Hantula et al., 1991).

In short, data concerning efficacy of OD as a systemwide approach to organizational change are equivocal. Anecdotal observations indicate that

OD rarely diffuses throughout the entire organization and that it is too limited (Strauss, 1973; Walton, 1975). It has also been suggested that all current human resource management and behaviorally oriented techniques, not just OD, have come up short in terms of providing the "strategic integration" required for a positive impact on organizational performance (Guest, 1990, p. 388).

OBM AND OD:
POTENTIAL FOR RECIPROCATION

As discussed above, and as Hantula et al. (1991) have noted, OD and OBM exhibit similarities and differences in their approach to organizational change. Critical elements of OD and recent work accomplished within the OBM field that might provide the basis of active reciprocation between the two fields is now considered. The comparison begins with the ways in which OBM might enhance the goals of OD.

What OBM Can Offer OD

Balanced Process and Outcome Emphasis

A consistent theme of OD has been a process-based approach to organizational change. This is evident in process consultation (Schein, 1988) and in definitions of OD (e.g., Burke, 1982; French and Bell, 1990), as well as in recent calls for OD to be more relevant to leaner, flatter, strategically oriented organizations proposed to meet the demands of the present and future global marketplace (Beer and Walton, 1990). Few empirical data are available, however, to support one single organizational structure as most effective for all combinations of environment, task, technology, and people. In short, although new OD interventions are said to be required, the focus of this approach is still within the humanistically based context of *how* people work, not the outcomes of their work per se. Although OD is primarily process-oriented in approach, numerous attempts have been made, as discussed previously, at linking OD to overall outcome measures, such as productivity.

OBM, on the other hand, focuses on outcomes that workers can influence as primary strategy for intervening in organizations (Komaki, 1986a). Only after a thorough analysis of prevailing contingencies operating within the organization, or at least the organizational subunit of interest, does the performance manager begin prescribing intervention strategies to accomplish changes in the target performance. This approach to change that emphasizes outcomes directly under the control of worker behavior is proposed as a first contribution that OBM can offer OD. The technology of targeting and pinpointing behavior (Daniels, 1989), coupled with an analysis of the relationship between individual accomplishments and organizational mission (Gilbert, 1978), can help balance a sometimes excessive emphasis of OD on organizational processes and place them in a more goal-oriented context.

Functional Analysis of OD Consultant Behavior

As previously noted, the existence of an external facilitator/consultant is often listed as a critical element of systematic OD efforts. On the other hand, Beer and Walton (1987) present cogent arguments that OD research has been preoccupied with consultant-centered intervention methods and that there is a need for expansion in the scope of OD consultation as a set of skills possessed by managers, rather than these skills being the sole domain of the external consultant. Given the pervasiveness of change programs that entail extensive consultant involvement, from both internal and external vantage points, there is a need for more systematic investigation of consultant behaviors. Consequently, a second area wherein OBM may significantly impact OD is in determining the critical skills that differentiate effective from ineffective organizational interventions.

Previous work was undertaken by the author and his associates (Eubanks, Marshall, and O'Driscoll, 1990; Eubanks, O'Driscoll, Hayward, Daniels, and Connor, 1990; O'Driscoll and Eubanks, 1992, 1993, 1994) in an attempt to determine specific consultant behaviors that are likely to lead to desired organizational outcomes. The results of our work yielded six competency categories that represent the range of OD performance in which practitioners engage: contracting, using data, implementation, interpersonal skills, group process, and client relations. Details regarding the process for extracting these categories may be found in Eubanks and colleagues (1990, pp. 83-84). The specific labels for each of the competency categories are based on the judgments of a panel of OD experts. Regardless of whether identification of these categories represents cutting-edge OD related to strategic management, for example, we are concerned with the specific behavioral skills within each category.

To date, we have used our behavioral observation scale, called the Consultant Competency Inventory (CCI), to collect data from forty-five organizations in the United States and New Zealand that had recently completed OD interventions. As a result of various analyses of our data, we have discovered a limited set of critical practitioner behaviors that seem to reliably predict successful OD intervention outcomes. These behaviors are listed in Table 14.2 according to the original category scheme we developed. Our ultimate objective is to refine this critical consultant behavior set in the manner that Komaki and her colleagues refined their supervisory behavior inventory (Komaki, 1986b; Komaki, Zlotnick, and Jensen, 1986). Similar to the previously mentioned potential of OBM for providing OD with a framework for functional analyses of organizational behavior, clear specification of OD consulting competencies, as they functionally relate to intervention outcomes, should provide a platform for training future practitioners as well as a set of criteria for evaluating existing consultation practices by clients and practitioners alike.

TABLE 14.2. Critical Consultant Behaviors by Competency Category

Contracting
- States clearly what can and cannot be done for the organization
- Demonstrates verbal and social behavior consistent with the organization's culture
- Provides options from which the client can choose

Using Data
- Interprets data quickly and effectively
- Shows clients how their behavior affects the organization
- Breaks problems down into smaller parts and deals with each in turn

Implementation
- Brings organization members together to discuss the intervention
- Gives management responsibility by working with their ideas
- Models desired behavior for clients
- Brings top-level management together to collaborate
- Checks regularly with clients to ensure their needs are being met
- Modifies the intervention to meet changing client requirements

Interpersonal
- Listens carefully by accurately paraphrasing client statements
- Uses questions effectively with clients

Group Process
- Keeps groups focused on positive aspects of the intervention
- Summarizes the ideas and feelings of individuals who are impeding group work

Client Relations
- Confronts the organization to bring out crucial issues
- Represents accurately his or her skills and training
- Follows up after the intervention by maintaining close contact

Rigorous Measurement and Evaluation

Numerous strategies for analyzing or diagnosing an organization's functioning exist within the OD literature (e.g., Weisbord, 1987). While these strategies are helpful in suggesting a range of potential dependent variables, the outcomes of these procedures often yield lists of problems generated by interviews, surveys, or questionnaires that tap organizational members' verbal responses to a standard set of questions. Sometimes results based on these verbal behaviors are coordinated with other data, such as attendance data, employee turnover, or productivity measures, but often they are not.

Although verbal-based measures will continue to be used, managers require results expressed in terms of a common metric, such as dollars (Carnevale and Schulz, 1990; Cascio, 1991; Cascio and Ramos, 1986; Davidove and Schroeder, 1992; Schneider, Monetta, and Wright, 1992). By combining measures such as dollars returned on training investment (Schneider et al., 1992), marginal utility of training investment (Cascio, 1991), or other similar measures from the human resource accounting literature (e.g., Fitz-Enz, 1980, 1984; Flamholtz, 1985; Steffy and Maurer, 1988) with basic discriminations of what can and cannot be influenced directly by worker behavior, the OD practitioner will produce a powerful new repertoire of analytic tools. Quantitative tools and techniques such as ROI (return on investment) analyses should help to shift the preoccupation of OD with work processes per se to a greater balance of process and outcome-based interventions (see Church and Burke, 1993, for a discussion of changing directions in OD).

It would appear that OBM has unprecedented potential for providing crucial data for evaluating the dollar impact of organizational interventions (Eubanks and Hayward, 1992). As a data-based approach to organizational change, evaluation is built in from the beginning of the intervention (Komaki, 1986a). Deciding what performances to target, however, and providing data that managers understand remains a problem. That is, the OBM convention of focusing on narrow definitions of small units of performance often stands in stark contrast to the prevailing verbal community of managers emphasizing "dynamic cultural change," which is believed to be requisite to making organizations more responsive to rapidly changing environments (cf. Eubanks and Lloyd, 1992). As mentioned previously, however, Gilbert (1978; see also Rummler and Brache, 1995) has made significant inroads in this area with his concept of vantage points, which include policy and culture, as well as his notion of potential for improved performance (PIP), which can be readily converted to dollar estimates of return on investment (cf. Schneider, Monetta, and Wright,

1992). Behavioral approaches to the study of culture represent a fourth and final area we will consider wherein OBM may significantly enhance OD's approach to increasing organizational effectiveness.

Organizational Culture Perspectives

Interest in culture within behavior analysis has been stimulated by cultural anthropologist Marvin Harris (1977, 1979, 1986, 1987). Reviews of his publications have appeared in behavioral journals (Lloyd, 1985; Lloyd and Eubanks, 1989; Vargas, 1985) and he has presented papers at meetings of the Association for Behavior Analysis (Glenn, 1991b; Harris, 1986; Penny-packer, 1987). Extensions of behavior analytic principles to cultural phenomena have emphasized contingency analysis (Glenn, 1988; Lamal, 1991), rule-governed behavior (Malott, 1988, 1992), and cultural design to address global issues (Malagodi, 1986; Malagodi and Jackson, 1989).

Changes in organizational culture represent a recurrent theme in OD interventions. Within the management and OD communities, the interest in organizational culture derives largely from its presumed impact on effectiveness (e.g., Deal and Kennedy, 1982; Ouchi, 1979; Ott, 1989; Peters and Waterman, 1982; Saffold, 1988; Uttal, 1983; Wiener, 1988; Wilkins and Dyer, 1988). Although reports linking culture to organizational success have received widespread attention (cf. Peters and Waterman, 1982), the underlying evidence is weak (Wilkins, 1983). Peters and Waterman (1982) examined cultural characteristics of successful companies but failed to examine unsuccessful firms to determine if the cultural attributes were absent. It seems that the opposite and more desirable design of looking first at cultural characteristics and then at their success was not used.

In spite of the assertion by organizational culture perspective advocates of the unique suitability of their approach to organizational change, this literature remains ambivalent about its prospects for successful cultural change (Eubanks and Lloyd, 1992). Conflicting views range from whether a manager should even attempt to change organizational culture because of potential harmful effects (Schein, 1990), to arguments about which strategy to use. Some propose changing organizational culture by changing behavioral norms (Allen and Kraft, 1982), while others postulate that chief executive officers are the gatekeepers of organizational culture (Davis, 1984). Equivocation over the ethics of change and strategies for change are attributed to the relative infancy of the organizational culture perspective (Ott, 1989, p. 6) and the lack of grounding in systematic theory and research in the OD literature (Sathe, 1985, p. 1).

A ten-year review of the *Journal of Organizational Behavior Management* concluded that, while the journal has produced an archive of behavioral change data in organizations, ". . . we have yet to investigate very large scale interventions in which behavioral principles are employed to change the 'cultural foundations' of an organization" (Balcazar et al., 1989, p. 36). More recently, however, interest in organizational culture from a behavioral point of view has gained momentum, including a special issue of the *Journal of Organizational Behavior Management* devoted exclusively to behavioral approaches to organizational culture. In-depth coverage of the potential of OBM for the study of organizational culture is beyond the scope of the present chapter (see Eubanks and Lloyd, 1992, for an overview of possibilities in this area).

Within the context of OBM contributions to OD goals discussed thus far, the issue of how to maintain and reinforce behavior in organizations leading to enhanced quality in products and services seems most cogent. Total quality management (TQM) emphasizes the improvement of organizational performance and work life quality (Deming 1982; Mawhinney, 1992). A primary emphasis of TQM is on employee participation (Redmon, 1992), which places it squarely within the class of OD interventions known as employee involvement (Cummings and Worley, 1993). The implementation of TQM, however, is not without its problems, and it is becoming clear that it is not a panacea for enhancing the productivity of either America or Japan ("Is the Baldrige Overblown," 1991; "The Quality Imperative," 1991). The importance of OBM in this context is that it provides a way of determining the set of contingencies required for implementing TQM or related employee involvement interventions. Performance feedback, for example, has been shown to be effective in enhancing the implementation of TQM in a small metal-part processing company (Henry and Redmon, 1990).

Organizational culture represents a crossover point wherein OBM and OD significantly overlap in their influence. OBM is new to the cultural analysis scene, while OD interventions have been concerned with culture change issues for well over a decade. OBM, as we have noted, has potential for enhancing the implementation of OD-related interventions such as TQM. Much of the OD literature related to organizational culture, however, is concerned with large-scale system change, an area that has not been well represented in OBM literature (Balcazar et al., 1989). However, both the volume on behavioral perspectives of culture (Lamal, 1991), and the current *Handbook of Organizational Performance* with repeated references to organizational culture attest to the changing interest within OBM related to large-scale system change issues. At this point of crossover between the two fields, we consider what OD may suggest about the question of how to broaden the scope of OBM.

What OD Can Offer OBM

As we have seen, OD has a history of beginning and executing large, systemwide change programs in a plethora of both public and private sector organizations since the 1950s. But what can a traditionally nonempirical, humanistically oriented discipline offer the empirically-based field of OBM? Can we still learn something from a discipline, though traditionally much different from our own, that has nearly a generation of seniority? We now examine four ways in which OD might enhance current OBM technology.

Large-Scale System Change Emphasis

A systems view of organizations clearly plays an important role in organization development efforts (French and Bell, 1990, pp. 52-59). Although systems concepts are not new to OBM, wide-scale, system-level interventions are still the exception (Balcazar et al., 1989; but see Brethower, 1982, and Parsons, Cash, and Reid, 1989, for variations on this exception).

Goal setting, for example, has been a primary strategy in many OBM interventions, but generally at the individual rather than the organization-wide level. We might begin thinking about goals in terms of descending levels of abstraction, e.g., end-result, strategic, tactical, and program goals (see French and Bell, 1990, p. 59; Gilbert, 1978, p. 118; Rummler and Brache, 1995). Viewed in this manner, goals and the goal-setting process, including the development of mission statements and strategic planning, become part of the larger organizational system (cf. Locke and Latham, 1990). Another view is that these processes are an integral part of organizational culture (Mawhinney, 1992; Redmon and Agnew, 1991; Redmon and Wilk, 1991).

Focus on Work Team Performance

An integral part of systemwide interventions is the examination of an organization's component subsystems (Weisbord, 1987). Work units, or teams, often constitute an intermediate level of analysis between system-level and individual worker behavior change. As we have seen, a primary emphasis in OD activities is the ongoing work team, including both superiors and subordinates.

A great deal of the current emphasis on work teams can be attributed to the attention, sometimes to the point of obsession, directed at the competitive threat of Japan and other Asian countries. A key element in the TQM approach advocated by Japanese management style and quality gurus such as Deming, Juran, and Crosby is the coordination of work team output to reduce defects. An entire issue of the *Journal of Organizational Behavior Management* (Mawhinney, 1987) was devoted to reviewing advances in statistical process control (SPC), a prevalent technique within the TQM movement, and its relevance to current OBM technology. Data and guidelines are now increasingly available on how OBM can be used to enhance implementation of SPC programs (Brown, 1989; Henry and Redmon, 1990; Mawhinney, 1987; Redmon, 1992).

Facilitating Organizational Entry

Many organizations have undertaken a wide variety of OD efforts, from large corporations to schools, communities, and local, state, and federal governments, as well as increasingly international efforts (Cummings and Worley, 1993; French and Bell, 1990). Although numerous reasons have been put forth for OD's widespread popularity, no data are available to empirically address this question. Based on the author's experience, two aspects of OD seem to facilitate entry into organizations and acceptance of its interventions: (1) compatibility among the verbal communities of OD and business/administrative clientele (OD practitioners often receive their training in business schools), and (2) client participation and involvement inherent in the action research approach.

Action research underlies most organization development activities (French and Bell, 1990, p. 98) and essentially involves data collection, feedback of the data to clients, and action planning based on the data (Lewin, 1946). The key element in action research is participation by the client in all phases of the process. Participative management and team building can be important in implementing interventions (Fawcett, 1991) and may reduce countercontrol attempts and resistance to change by organizational members (Miller, 1991; Redmon, 1992).

Perspectives on Social Validity

Participation and involvement by clients relates directly to the notion of social validity (Schwartz and Baer, 1991; Wolf, 1978). Social validation assessments are aimed at evaluating the acceptability or viability of an intervention. Such assessments are usually accomplished by asking consumers to complete a satisfaction questionnaire in order for the program planners or experimenters to be able to anticipate rejection of the program and take steps to prevent or ameliorate problem areas. Surprisingly few interventions reported in the OBM literature address or include social validation processes (Balcazar et al., 1989).

As we have noted with the action research paradigm employed in OD interventions, choices can be made interactively with clients. The concept of collaboration has served the OD community well in involving clients as partners and owners of the process of research and action. Community psychology, a close companion of OD, has a long tradition of client-researcher collaboration (Kelly, 1986), and calls have been registered for establishing this collaborative process as a value for future applications of behavior analysis in communities (Fawcett, 1991, pp. 622-624). A similar approach is suggested by Mawhinney (1989, p. 190) wherein operant measures of job satisfaction are routinely employed as dependent variables in OBM interventions.

PATHS TO RECONCILIATION

Both commonalities and differences among OBM and OD approaches to organizational change have been noted, along with suggestions whereby each field may learn from examining the other's history. We now examine some issues that require consideration in order to enhance the likelihood of behavior change by practitioners in both fields.

Humble Behaviorism Issues

Neuringer (1991) outlined a concept he named "humble behaviorism," wherein he called upon behavior analysts to be more tentative in their methodological and theoretical positions, to consider alternatives, and to realize that all knowledge is subject to change. Chase (1991) suggested in response to Neuringer's humble behaviorist position, "An I'm right/ You're wrong perspective is disheartening, damaging to the image of behavior analysis held by other scientists, and probably as responsible for the misinterpretations of behavior analysis as any single variable" (p. 15). This call for greater acceptance of diversity by behavior analysts constitutes a critical issue both for evaluating the feasibility of interaction among OD and OBM and for gaining widespread acceptance of OBM.

The issue is not so simple as greater tolerance by behavior analysts, nor does Neuringer imply that it is. As McDowell (1991) suggests, there may be fundamental, and perhaps irreconcilable differences between behavior analysis and other competing behavioral science approaches. The difference that McDowell emphasized was ontological: behavior analysis and other behavioral sciences disagree about what constitutes reality. Behavior analysts advocate a materialist ontology, i.e., the world consists of material objects and events, while other approaches, such as OD, include nonmaterial phenomena, as well as spiritual underpinnings.

OD in Transition

As a field, OD is in a state of flux (cf. Church and Burke, 1993). Many forces evoking behavior in organizations will require new OD techniques. These forces include a shift from traditional hierarchical organizations to flexible networks, empowerment of employees for decision making, and transitions to global thinking as a consequence of ever-increasing competition. Such changes have recently called into question whether the old OD techniques are now appropriate. Alternatives to the traditional top-down, single-organization OD interventions are now being proposed. One approach, for example, might involve interventions with the organization's board of directors, taking a bottom-up rather than top-down approach, and focusing the OD effort at an interorganizational level.

Regardless of the anticipated changes in organizations and concomitant OD techniques required to meet the challenge of these changes, it is clear that OD has never been a panacea for all of management's problems (cf. Mirvis and Berg, 1977). Perhaps OD can respond more effectively to these challenges by adopting some of the contributions that OBM has to offer.

Reconciling Different Verbal Communities

OBM and OD have developed concomitantly but are a part of very different verbal communities. The OD approach has been grounded in humanistic philosophy and applied social psychology/management theory, while OBM relies on behavior analysis for its technical and theoretical foundations (however, see Newman, 1992, for a view of behavior analysis as an extension of humanistic philosophy). Consistent with a behavioral perspective, the effectiveness of the two approaches may be left to empirical evaluation and the data that emerge from their application.

But an empirical evaluation is not a criterion for the acceptance of such a descriptive approach in the marketplace. Often description (without empirical evaluation) in the social sciences is accepted by consumers as equivalent to explanation. Management fads come and go and neither OD nor OBM can claim the current spotlight in this arena. Although organizational culture received a great deal of attention in the 1980s, the shift is now toward organizational learning and continuous improvement and related efforts. A metacontingency that encompasses all of these trends or fads is the globalization of the marketplace under conditions of diminished worldwide resources and overpopulation. Clearly, these are challenging times and we need to constantly reexamine the extent to which our technology is serving to enhance the human condition. An overriding implication is that marketability of an organizational change technology cannot be considered as a benchmark of success for either OBM or OD.

SUMMARY AND CONCLUSION

The points made here describe important ways in which OBM and OD may reciprocate in developing change technologies that address the challenges of these crucial times for organizations. Behavior analysts are rapidly adopting many of these suggestions and are improving the acceptance by management of behavioral methods (cf. Redmon, 1992). OBM is truly expanding its focus to wide-scale system change. Witness the recent issue of *Journal of Organizational Behavior Management* (Mawhinney, 1992) devoted to organizational culture and rule-governed behavior. The edited book on behavioral analyses of culture by Lamal (1991) is also an important contribution to this expanded focus by behavior analysts.

In spite of an expanding focus, however, OBM can still benefit from making contact with the OD literature. A rich source of research ideas can be gleaned from the effort. For example, Kurt Lewin's work was not cited by Skinner, perhaps due to Lewin's incompatibility with the Baconian orientation that drove Skinner's work (Smith, 1992). Yet it is clear that many of the ideas behind Lewin's action research paradigm are proving beneficial to the advancement of behavioral approaches to community development (cf. Fawcett, 1991). Action research is a basic paradigm for the OD field and it is not incompatible with a rigorous, empirical approach.

Many of the research ideas that emerge from a perusal of the OD literature by OBM practitioners will probably be centered on pinpointing the complex social and verbal contingencies that prevail in organizations, contingencies that are currently lumped together under the generic notion of organizational culture (cf. Agnew and Redmon, 1992; Eubanks and Lloyd, 1992; Malott, 1992; Malott, Shimamune, and Malott, 1992). It is not clear at this juncture, however, under what metacontingencies either OBM or OD are effective. As Mawhinney (1992) suggests, even the best-developed organizations may not survive under conditions of chaotic change or a punctuation in some critical aspect of the environment. As contingency theorists, OBM practitioners have much opportunity awaiting them in determining the metacontingencies of organizational survival and in continuing to demonstrate the utility of behavior analysis in solving crucial problems for organizations. There is much work to be done and behavior analysts are well equipped to do it.

REFERENCES

Agnew, J. and Redmon, W. K. (1992). Contingency specifying stimuli: The role of "rules" in organizational behavior management. *Journal of Organizational Behavior Management, 12*(2), 67-76.

Allen, R. and Kraft, C. (1982). *The organizational unconscious: How to create the corporate culture you want and need.* Englewood Cliffs, NJ: Prentice-Hall.

Argyris, C. (1970). *Intervention theory and method: A behavioral science view.* Reading, MA: Addison-Wesley.

Balcazar, F. E., Shupert, M. K., Daniels, A. C., Mawhinney, T. C., and Hopkins, B. L. (1989). An objective review and analysis of ten years of publication in the *Journal of Organizational Behavior Management. Journal of Organizational Behavior Management, 10*(1), 7-37.

Beer, M. and Walton, A. E. (1987). Organization change and development. *Annual Review of Psychology, 38,* 339-367.

Beer, M. and Walton, A. E. (1990). Developing the competitive organization: Interventions and strategies. *American Psychologist, 45,* 154-161.

Brethower, D. (1982). Total performance systems. In R. O'Brien, A. Dickinson, and M. Rosow (Eds.), *Industrial behavior modification* (pp. 350-369). New York: Pergamon.

Brown, P. L. (1982). *Managing behavior on the job.* New York: Wiley.

Brown, P. L. (1989). Quality improvement through activity analysis. *Journal of Organizational Behavior Management, 10*(1), 169-179.

Burke, W. W. (1982). *Organization development.* Boston: Little, Brown.

Carnevale, A. P. and Schulz, E. (1990). Return on investment: Accounting for training. *Training and Development Journal, 44*(1), 41-75.

Cascio, W. F. (1991). *Costing human resources: The financial impact of behavior in organizations* (Third edition). Boston: PWS-Kent.

Cascio, W. F. and Ramos, R. A. (1986). Development and application of a new method for assessing job performance in behavioral/economic terms. *Journal of Applied Psychology, 71,* 20-28.

Chase, P. N. (1991). Humble behaviorism or equal doses of skepticism? *The Behavior Analyst, 14,* 15-18.

Church, A. H. and Burke, W. W. (1993). What are the basic values of OD? *Academy of Management ODC Newsletter,* Winter, 1-10.

Cummings, T. G. and Worley, C. G. (1993). *Organization development and change* (Fifth edition). San Francisco: West Publishing Company.

Daniels, A. C. (1989). *Performance management: Improving quality productivity through positive reinforcement* (Third edition). Tucker, GA: Performance Management Publications, Inc.

Davidove, E. A. and Schroeder, P. A. (1992). Demonstrating ROI of training. *Training and Development Journal, 46*(8), 70-71.

Davis, S. (1984). *Managing corporate culture.* Reading, MA: Addison-Wesley.

Deal, T. E. and Kennedy, A. A. (1982). *Corporate cultures: The rites and rituals of corporate life.* Reading, MA: Addison-Wesley.

Deming, W. E. (1982). *Quality, productivity, and competitive position.* Cambridge, MA: Massachusetts Institute of Technology, Center for Advanced Engineering Study.

Dunn, W. N. and Swierczek, F. W. (1977). Planned organizational change: Toward grounded theory. *Journal of Applied Behavioral Science, 13,* 135-157.

Eubanks, J. L. and Hayward, G. B. (1992). *Cost-benefit approaches to training evaluation.* Paper presented at the 18th Annual Convention of the Association for Behavior Analysis: International, San Francisco, CA, May.

Eubanks, J. L. and Lloyd, K. E. (1992). Relating behavior analysis to the organizational culture concept and perspective. *Journal of Organizational Behavior Management, 12*(2), 27-44.

Eubanks, J. L. and Marshall, J. M. (1990). Training requirements and future roles for consultants to organizations. In K. Noro and O. Brown Jr. (Eds.), *Human factors in organizational design and management—III: Proceedings of the Third International Symposium on Human Factors in Organizational Design and Management held in Kyoto, Japan, 18-21 July, 1990* (pp. 457-460). Amsterdam: Elsevier Science Publishers.

Eubanks, J. L., Marshall, J. M., and O'Driscoll, M. (1990). A competency model for OD practitioners. *Training and Development Journal, 44*(11), 85-90.

Eubanks, J. L., O'Driscoll, M., Hayward, G., Daniels, J., and Connor, S. (1990). Behavioral competency requirements for organization development consultants. *Journal of Organizational Behavior Management, 11*(1), 77-97.

Fawcett, S. B. (1991). Some values guiding community research and action. *Journal of Applied Behavior Analysis, 24,* 621-636.

Fitz-Enz, J. (1980). Quantifying the human resources function. *Personnel, 57*(3), 41-52.

Fitz-Enz, J. (1984). *How to measure human resources management.* New York: McGraw-Hill.

Flamholtz, E. G. (1985). *Human resource accounting.* San Francisco: Jossey-Bass.

French, W. and Bell, C. H. (1990). *Organization development* (Fourth edition). Englewood Cliffs, NJ: Prentice-Hall.

Gellerman, W. (1984). Issues in developing a statement of values and ethics for organization development professionals. *Organization Development Journal, 2,* 39-47.

Gellerman, W. (1985). Values and ethical issues in the organization and human system development profession. In R. Tannenbaum, N. Marguiles, and F. Massarik (Eds.), *Human systems development: New perspectives on people and organizations* (pp. 351-378). San Francisco: Jossey-Bass.

Gilbert, T. F. (1978). *Human competence: Engineering worthy performance.* New York: McGraw-Hill.

Glenn, S. S. (1986). Meta contingencies in *Walden Two. Behavior Analysis and Social Action, 5*(1), 2-8.

Glenn, S. S. (1988). Contingencies and metacontingencies: Toward a synthesis of behavior analysis and cultural materialism. *The Behavior Analyst, 11,* 161-179.

Glenn, S. S. (1991a). Contingencies and metacontingencies: Relations among behavioral, cultural, and biological evolution. In P. A. Lamal (Ed.), *Behavioral analysis of societies and cultural practices.* New York: Hemisphere Publishing Corporation.

Glenn, S. S. (1991b). *The integration of cultural materialism and behavior analysis.* Symposium conducted at the meeting of the Association for Behavior Analysis: International, Atlanta, GA, May.

Golembiewski, R. T., Proehl, C. W., Jr., and Sink, D. (1982). Estimating the success of OD applications. *Training and Development Journal, 36,* 86-95.

Guest, D. E. (1990). Human resource management and the American Dream. *Journal of Management Studies 24*(1), July, 388-393.

Guzzo, R. A., Jette, R. D., and Katzell, R. A. (1985). The effects of psychologically based intervention programs on worker productivity: A meta-analysis. *Personnel Psychology, 38,* 275-291.

Hantula, D. A., Riley, A. W., Rudd, J. R., Wagner, B. D., and Frederiksen, L. W. (1991). *A quantitative analysis of the relationship between methodological rigor and outcome success in OBM and OD programs.* Paper presented at the 17th Annual Convention of the Association for Behavior Analysis: International, Atlanta, GA, May.

Harris, M. (1977). *Cannibals and kings: The origins of culture.* New York: Random House.

Harris, M. (1979). *Cultural materialism: The struggle for a science of culture.* New York: Random House.

Harris, M. (1986). *Cultural materialism and behavior analysis: Common problems and radical solutions.* Invited address presented at the meeting for the Association for Behavior Analysis: International, Milwaukee, WI, May.

Harris, M. (1987). Discussant. In H. S. Pennypacker (Chair), *Behavior analysis and cultural materialism.* Symposium conducted at the meetings of the Association for Behavior Analysis: International, Nashville, TN, May.

Henry, G. O. and Redmon, W. K. (1990). The effects of performance feedback on the implementation of a statistical process control (SPC) program. *Journal of Organizational Behavior Management, 11*(2), 23-46.

Huse, E. F. and Cummings, T. G. (1989). *Organization development and change* (Fourth edition). St. Paul, MN: West Publishing.

Is the Baldridge overblown? (1991). *Fortune,* July 1, 62-65.

Kelly, J. G. (1986). An ecological paradigm: Defining mental health consultation as a preventative service. In J. G. Kelly and R. E. Hess (Eds.), *The ecology of prevention: Illustrating mental health consultation.* Binghamton, NY: The Haworth Press, pp. 1-36.

Komaki, J. L. (1986a). Applied behavior analysis and organizational behavior: Reciprocal influence of the two fields. In L. L. Cummings and B. M. Staw (Eds.), *Research in organizational behavior: An annual series of analytical essays and critical reviews, 8.* Greenwich, CT: JAI Press, pp. 297-334.

Komaki, J. L. (1986b). Toward effective supervision: An operant analysis and comparison of managers at work. *Journal of Applied Psychology, 71,* 270-279.

Komaki, J. L., Zlotnick, S., and Jensen, M. (1986). Development of an operant-based taxonomy and observational index of supervisory behavior. *Journal of Applied Psychology, 71,* 260-269.

Lamal, P. A. (1991). *Behavioral analysis of societies and cultural practices.* New York: Hemisphere Publishing Corporation.

Lewin, K. (1946). Action research and minority problems. *Journal of Social Issues, 2*(4), 34-46.

Lloyd, K. E. (1985). Behavioral anthropology: A review of Marvin Harris' cultural materialism. *Journal of the Experimental Analysis of Behavior, 43,* 279-287.

Lloyd, K. E. and Eubanks, J. L. (1989). Why nothing works in America now: A review of two books by Marvin Harris. *Journal of Organizational Behavior Management, 10*(2), 212-218.

Locke, E. and Latham, G. (1990). *A theory of goal-setting and task performance.* Englewood Cliffs, NJ: Prentice-Hall.

Luthans, F. (1992). *Organizational behavior* (Sixth edition). New York: McGraw-Hill.

Malagodi, E. (1986). On radicalizing behaviorism: A call for cultural analysis. *The Behavior Analyst, 9,* 1-17.

Malagodi, E. and Jackson, K. (1989). Behavior analysts and cultural analysis: Troubles and issues. *The Behavior Analyst, 12,* 17-34.

Malott, R. W. (1988). Rule governed behavior and behavioral anthropology. *The Behavior Analyst, 11,* 181-204.

Malott, R. W. (1992). A theory of rule-governed behavior and organizational behavior management. *Journal of Organizational Behavior Management, 12*(2), 45-65.

Malott, R. W., Shimamune, S., and Malott, M. E. (1992). Rule-governed behavior and organizational behavior management: An analysis of interventions. *Journal of Organizational Behavior Management, 12*(2), 103-116.

Mawhinney, T. C. (Ed.). (1987). Organizational behavior management and statistical process control: Theory, technology, and research [Special Issue]. *Journal of Organizational Behavior Management, 9*(1).

Mawhinney, T. C. (1989). Job satisfaction as a management tool and responsibility. *Journal of Organizational Behavior Management, 10*(1), 187-192.

Mawhinney, T. C. (1992). Evolution of organizational cultures as selection by consequences: The Gaia hypothesis, metacontingencies, and organizational ecology. *Journal of Organizational Behavior Management, 12*(2), 1-26.

McDowell, J. J. (1991). Irreconcilable differences and political reality in these dark ages. *The Behavior Analyst, 14,* 29-34.

Miller, L. K. (1991). Avoiding the countercontrol of applied behavior analysis. *Journal of Applied Behavior Analysis, 24,* 645-647.

Mirvis, P. H. and Berg, D. N. (1977). *Failures in organization development and change.* New York: Wiley.

Neuman, G. A., Edwards, J. E., and Raju, N. S. (1989). Organizational development interventions: A meta-analysis of their effects on satisfaction and other attitudes. *Personnel Psychology, 42,* 461-483.

Neuringer, A. (1991). Humble behaviorism. *The Behavior Analyst, 14,* 1-14.

Newman, B. (1992). *The reluctant alliance: Behaviorism and humanism.* New York: Prometheus Books.

Nicholas, J. M. (1982). The comparative impact of organization development interventions on hard criteria measures. *Academy of Management Review, 7,* 531-541.

O'Driscoll, M. and Eubanks, J. L. (1992). Consultant and client perceptions of consultant competencies: Implications for OD consulting. *Organization Development Journal, 10*(4), 53-59.

O'Driscoll, M. and Eubanks, J. L. (1993). Behavioral competencies, goal setting and OD practitioner effectiveness. *Group and Organizational Management, 18*(3), 308-327.

O'Driscoll, M. and Eubanks, J. L. (1994). Consultant behavioral competencies and effectiveness: A cross-national perspective. *Organization Development Journal, 12*(1), 41-47.

Ott, J. (1989). *The organizational culture perspective.* Pacific Grove, CA: Brooks/ Cole.

Ouchi, W. G. (1979). *Theory Z: How American business can meet the Japanese challenge.* Reading, MA: Addison-Wesley.

Parsons, M. B., Cash, V. B., and Reid, D. H. (1989). Improving residential treatment services: Implementation and norm-referenced evaluation of a comprehensive management system. *Journal of Applied Behavior Analysis, 22,* 143-156.

Pennypacker, H. S. (1987). *Behavior analysis and cultural materialism.* Symposium conducted at the meeting of the Association for Behavior Analysis: International, Nashville, TN, May.

Peters, T. and Waterman, R. H. (1982). *In search of excellence: Lessons from America's best-run companies.* New York: Harper and Row.

Porras, J. I. and Berg, P. O. (1978). The impact of organization development. *The Academy of Management Review, 3,* 249-266.

Redmon, W. K. (1992). Opportunities for applied behavior analysis in the total quality movement. *Journal of Applied Behavior Analysis, 25,* 545-550.

Redmon, W. K. and Agnew, J. L. (1991). Organizational behavioral analysis in the United States: A view from the private sector. In P. A. Lamal (Ed.), *Behavioral analysis of societies and cultural practices* (pp. 125-139). New York: Hemisphere Publishing Corporation.

Redmon, W. K. and Wilk, L. A. (1991). Organizational behavioral analysis in the United States: Public sector organizations. In P. A. Lamal (Ed.), *Behavioral analysis of societies and cultural practices* (pp. 107-123). New York: Hemisphere Publishing Corporation.

Roethlisberger, F. J. and Dickson, W. J. (1939). *Management and the worker.* Cambridge, MA: Harvard University Press.

Rummler, G. and Brache, A. (1995). *Improving performance: How to manage the white space on the organizaitonal chart, 2E.* San Francisco: Jossey-Bass.

Saffold, G. S., III. (1988). Culture traits, strength, and organizational performance: Moving beyond "strong" culture. *Academy of Management Review, 13,* 546-558.

Sathe, V. (1985). *Culture and related corporate realities: Text, cases, and readings on organizational entry, establishment, and change.* Homewood, IL: Irwin.

Schein, E. H. (1988). *Process consultation: Its role in organization development.* Reading, MA: Addison-Wesley.

Schein, E. H. (1990). Organizational culture. *American Psychologist, 45,* 109-119.

Schein, E. H. and Bennis, W. G. (1965). *Personal and organizational change through group methods.* New York: Wiley.

Schneider, H., Monetta, D. J., and Wright, C. C. (1992). Training function accountability: How to really measure return on investment. *Performance and Instruction, 31*(3), March, 12-17.

Schwartz, I. S. and Baer, D. M. (1991). Social validity assessments: Is current practice state of the art? *Journal of Applied Behavior Analysis, 24,* 189-204.

Smith, L. D. (1992). On prediction and control: B. F. Skinner and the technological ideal of science. *American Psychologist, 47,* 216-223.

Steffy, B. D. and Maurer, S. D. (1988). Conceptualizing and measuring the economic effectiveness of human resource activities. *Academy of Management Review, 13,* 271-286.

Strauss, G. (1973). Organizational development: Credits and debits. *Organizational Dynamics 2*(3), Winter, 2-19.

Terpstra, D. (1981). Relationship between methodological rigor and reported outcomes in organizational development evaluation research. *Journal of Applied Psychology, 66,* 541-542.

The quality imperative. (1991). *BusinessWeek.* October 25, p. 34.

Uttal, B. (1983). The corporate culture vultures. *Fortune, 17,* 66-72.

Vargas, E. A. (1985). Cultural contingencies: A review of Marvin Harris's "Cannibals and Kings." *Journal of the Experimental Analysis of Behavior, 43,* 419-428.

Walton, R. (1975). The diffusion of new work structures: Explaining why success didn't take. *Organizational Dynamics 4*(3), Winter, 3-22.

Weisbord, M. R. (1987). *Organizational diagnosis: A workbook of theory and practice.* Reading, MA: Addison-Wesley.

Wiener, Y. (1988). Forms of value systems: A focus on organizational effectiveness and cultural change and maintenance. *Academy of Management Review, 13*, 534-545.

Wilkins, A. L. (1983). Organizational stories as symbols which control the organization. In L. R. Pondy, P. J. Frost, G. Morgan, and T. C. Dandridge (Eds.), *Organizational symbolism.* Greenwich, CT: JAI Press.

Wilkins, A. L. and Dyer, W. G., Jr. (1988). Toward culturally sensitive theories of cultural change. *Academy of Management Review, 13*, 522-533.

Wolf, M. M. (1978). Social validity: The case for subjective measurement, or how behavior analysis is finding its heart. *Journal of Applied Behavior Analysis, 11*, 203-214.

Woodman, R. W. (1989). Organizational change and development: New arenas for inquiry and action. *Journal of Management, 15*, 205-228.

Woodman, R. W. and Wayne, S. J. (1985). An investigation of positive-findings bias in evaluation of organization development interventions. *Academy of Management Journal, 28*, 889-913.

Chapter 15

Social Learning Analysis of Behavioral Management

Robert Waldersee
Fred Luthans

The recognized goals of the scientific study and application of organizational behavior management are understanding/explanation, prediction, and control. Our position is that the cognitive approach leads to relatively better understanding, but the behavioral approach is clearly superior in terms of prediction and control (Luthans, 1992). The work of cognitively oriented behavioral scientists such as Vroom (1964), Porter and Lawler (1968), and Locke (1978) identified systems of needs that motivate employees and laid out the complex cognitive processes employees use to decide which behaviors to perform, how much effort to put forth, and what impact this has on their satisfaction and performance. This cognitively based approach generated considerable research, but has produced few techniques that can be applied to the more effective management of human resources. In particular, such complex cognitive models provide an understanding of why employees act as they do, but do not provide the prediction and control today's managers want and need to manage their people more effectively.

The alternative to cognitive approaches is to examine how employee performance is related to the environment in which the employee is behaving. The behavioral approach focuses on the controlling effects of the environment in terms of the stimuli that evoke performance-related behaviors as well as the reinforcers and punishers that follow the behaviors and maintain their rates of occurrence (Luthans and Kreitner, 1985). Under this approach, managers who control the antecedent and consequent environment effectively control the performance of employees. Such an approach has, like the cognitive approach, generated considerable research over the years. Importantly, however, unlike the cognitive approach, the behavioral approach yielded many practical applications for the management of human performance in organizations (Andrasik, 1989; Luthans and Kreitner, 1985; Merwin, Thompson, and Sanford, 1989; O'Hara, Johnson, and Beehr, 1985).

391

Achieving the three objectives of understanding/explanation, prediction, and control involves an integration of cognitive and behavioral approaches. This chapter presents social learning theory (SLT) as such an integrative approach. SLT incorporates reciprocal interactions among cognitive factors, environmental factors, and the behavior itself (Bandura, 1977). SLT provides the prediction and control offered by the behavioral approach and the understanding/explanation offered by the cognitive approach. Before presenting SLT, it is necessary to first briefly summarize the behavioral and cognitive theories upon which SLT is based.

BEHAVIORAL THEORIES

Operant theory is the predominant behavioral theory and underlies much of social learning theory. Operant theory holds that behavior is a function of its contingent environmental consequences, which distinguishes it from classical or respondent (S-R) theory of reflexive behaviors (Skinner, 1953, 1969). According to operant theory, environmental antecedents set the occasion for behaviors that in the past have been reinforced or decrease the probability of behaviors that in the past have been followed by punishers. For example, the presence of a pleasant customer may increase the probability of a smile by a customer service employee, while an angry customer may occasion a different facial expression. That is, the type of customer may be an environmental cue as to the type of consequence that will follow different types of employee behaviors. The environmental consequences that follow a behavior are the central mechanisms by which the frequency of occurrence of a behavior is determined on future occasions. Behavior will become more frequent on future occasions when followed by a positive consequence (reinforcer), and will become less frequent when followed by no consequence (extinction) or an undesirable consequence (punisher).

In an unmodified environment, individuals' behaviors occur in an ongoing stream of events that make up the natural consequences which increase, maintain, or reduce the frequency of behaviors. Natural consequences generally follow all behaviors a person emits. In ongoing interactions with others, a behavior by one party can be both a consequence for the other party's previous behavior and a behavior for which the other party subsequently provides reinforcers. Thus, polite comments by an employee (behavior) may be followed by a pleasant response from a customer (customer behavior as well as positive reinforcer for the employee's behavior), which may be followed by helpful service from the employee (both an employee behavior and positive reinforcer for the customer's behavior) and so on. If the customer is not pleasant or ignores the employee (extinction), the frequency of polite behavior may quickly be reduced in subsequent iterations.

Organizational behavior modification (O.B. Mod.) is the application of operant theory to human resources management (Luthans and Kreitner, 1975, 1985). By understanding and modifying antecedents and consequences, managers are able to increase, maintain, or reduce the frequency of employee behaviors. That O.B. Mod. can be applied to improve effectiveness of performance management (PM) efforts is supported by a growing body of empirical research. For example, even difficult-to-manage quality service behaviors among drug store clerks (Newby and Robinson, 1983), bank tellers (Dierks and McNally, 1987; Luthans, Fox, and Davis, 1991), real estate agents (Anderson et al., 1982), and retail employees (Brown et al., 1980; Luthans, Paul, and Baker, 1981) have been increased with O.B. Mod. types of interventions. O.B. Mod. was even applied cross-culturally and had a positive impact on performance among Russian factory workers (Welsh, Luthans, and Sommer, 1993). A recent meta-analysis of nineteen studies that used the O.B. Mod. model found a 17 percent average improvement in performance (Stajkovic and Luthans, 1997).

COGNITIVE THEORIES

Although many cognitively based theories have implications for performance management, goal setting, expectancy, and equity theories are the most widely recognized. Goal setting as a management technique can be traced back as far as Frederick Taylor's principles of scientific management at the turn of the twentieth century, but the contemporary approach is most closely associated with the theory and research findings of Locke and his associates. In particular, his theoretical premise is that goals are the immediate regulators of human action (Locke and Latham, 1990) and are the mechanism by which human actions become purposeful (Locke, 1978). Although other theorists acknowledge that there are more basic sources of motivation such as the various needs, Locke states that goal setting is "the most directly useful motivational approach in a managerial context, since goals are the most immediate regulators of human action and are more easily modified than the values of subconscious premises" (Locke, 1978, p. 559).

Research on the effectiveness of goal setting as a performance-enhancing method has shown the importance of the difficulty and specificity of the goals being set. Meta-analyses of a large number of goal-setting studies of specific, difficult goals have demonstrated effect sizes ranging from .43 to .80 (Locke and Latham, 1990). However, setting specific, difficult goals is of no use if they are rejected by employees. Therefore, a second crucial component of goal setting is obtaining employee acceptance and commitment to the goals. Subordinates must perceive the goals as fair and reasonable, and they must trust management (Latham and Locke, 1979). A number of studies by other researchers have supported the relationship between goal commitment and performance (e.g., Erez and Arad, 1986; Klein, 1989).

Despite the impressive research results by Locke and others, goal setting is not without criticism. Particularly problematic for goal setting is the lack of a comprehensive theoretical account of the mechanisms by which goals relate to behavior (Shapira, 1989). Theoretical understanding depends critically on descriptions of the mechanisms through which goals have their effects on behavior. Attempts made to fill this gap (e.g., Campion and Lord, 1982; Garland, 1985) have not been widely accepted.

In addition to goal setting, expectancy theory has received considerable attention as a cognitively based approach to the management of human performance. Although a number of different expectancy models have been proposed, the general expectancy model of Vroom (1964) is best known. This model has three major components: expectancies, instrumentalities, and valences. Valence is the perceived or anticipated positive or negative value (attractiveness) of outcomes that are expected to follow from a behavior. Initially operationalized as a perceived correlation, instrumentality is now defined as the perceived probability that the first-level outcome will lead to the desired end outcome, and expectancy is the perceived probability that the level of effort will actually produce the first-level outcome. Thus, employees may ask themselves how likely (expectancy) it is that they will finish a project by the end of the week (first-level outcome), and if so, how likely (instrumentality) it is that a valued (valance) bonus will be received (second-level outcome).

Although expectancy theory is widely accepted in the organizational behavior field, research has been only moderately supportive and there has been very little linkage to the actual practice of human performance management. For example, a review by Landy and Trumbo (1980) concluded that expectancy models are unnecessarily complex, and that the valence of the second-level outcome is the primary motivational component in the theory. They also concluded that the relationship between effort and the components of the theory are significant but not overly strong, typically ranging from .25 to .40.

A third major cognitive approach is equity theory. According to equity theory a person will view the ratio of his or her work outcomes to inputs in comparison to relevant others and will be motivated to attain equity with the others (Adams, 1965). In the workplace, inputs include anything a person brings to a job that is considered to have value. This may be experience, training, seniority, effort, and/or ability. Outcomes may include such factors as pay, promotions, working conditions, tasks assigned, job security, and treatment by superiors. A "comparison other" may be someone else in a similar position within the organization or a similar organization, the self in a previous position, or system referents such as an implicit employment agreement (Goodman, 1974).

Most research on equity theory has been conducted with pay inequalities. Studies generally support the theory, although evidence for the overpayment hypothesis has been more questionable than for the underpayment hypothesis (Mowday, 1991). Problems also exist in the understanding of the choice of comparison others. Although crucial to the theory, there has been relatively little study of how comparison others are selected, or how composite comparison others are constructed by the person calculating the equity ratio (Summers and DeNisi, 1990). Finally, Leventhal (1976) argues that equity of reward distributions is only one of three possible reward distribution rules. He suggests that people move between the distribution rules based on variations in circumstances. Equitable distribution is appropriate in situations in which individual performance is clear; equal distribution is appropriate when individual input is hard to determine; and need-based distribution is appropriate when persons have needs arising from factors beyond their control.

CONVERGENCE AND DIVERGENCE
OF THE BEHAVIORAL AND COGNITIVE MODELS

Both the behavioral and cognitive approaches have important areas of commonality, but also significant differences. For example, O.B. Mod. and goal setting can be viewed as complementary techniques that originated from different perspectives. Locke and Latham (1990) suggest that O.B. Mod. studies often have implicit goals in the form of performance standards, and Fedor and Ferris (1981) point out that goal-setting studies often have incentive rewards associated with the goals. Others, such as Fellner and Sulzer-Azaroff (1984), argue that goals may be viewed as discriminative stimuli that cue goal-seeking behavior. If goal attainment is paired with a positive consequence or removal of a negative one, then the discriminative stimuli can also take on the properties of conditioned reinforcers.

The same analysis can be made of expectancy and operant theories. Although the expectancy models are generally viewed as being very different from the operant model, in many ways the two are complementary (Organ and Bateman, 1986; Naylor, Pritchard, and Ilgen, 1980). They may even be viewed as alternative conceptualizations of the same phenomena. Expectancy models describe a cognitive process that is anticipatory or future oriented. Yet, these judgments in the expectancy model are based on past experiences or observations. Operant theory is based on individual reinforcement histories, yet is future oriented to the extent that observations of contingent relationships produce "rules." Under the expectancy interpretation, a valued reward that follows a behavior regularly will increase the instrumentality of the behavior, and the probability that the behavior will occur again. Operant theory makes the same prediction, although instrumentality would be described in terms of rule-governed behavior. However, in predictions of performance levels under different schedules of reinforcement, operant theory and expectancy theory would differ.

Expectancy theory predicts that a continuous reinforcement schedule maximizes performance as it maximizes instrumentality, while operant theory holds that ratio schedules maximize performance (Berger, Cummings, and Heneman, 1975; Organ and Bateman, 1986). However, it should be noted that although laboratory studies have found that the ratio (or variable) schedules led to better performance (Yukl, Wexley, and Seymore, 1972), some field studies have found that continuous schedules of reinforcement actually led to better performance (Yukl and Latham, 1975; Yukl, Latham, and Pursell, 1976; Latham and Dossett, 1978). There are methodological problems in these studies on schedules of reinforcement and the results should probably not be generalized for monetary schedules in performance management (Mawhinney, 1986).

SOCIAL LEARNING THEORY

Despite some attempts to integrate behavioral and cognitive theories, there has been, and continues to be, an either/or mentality. Social learning theory provides one approach to integrating behavioral and cognitive theories. SLT and its comprehensive expansion as social cognitive theory (Bandura, 1986) transcends the traditional dichotomy. SLT views environmental factors, cognitive factors, and the behavior itself as existing in a state of reciprocal interaction or determination. Thus, behavior influences, and is influenced by, cognitive and environmental factors; cognitive factors influence, and are influenced by, behaviors and the environment; and the environment influences, and is influenced by, cognitive factors and behaviors. Importantly, SLT presents a complex series of mechanisms by which individuals learn and then exhibit behavior. These include the environmental antecedents and consequences of behavior as in operant theory, but also modeling or vicarious learning, self-efficacy levels, self-set goals, and self-regulatory or self-evaluative processes.

The Role of Antecedents and Consequences

As in operant theory, SLT views environmental antecedents and consequences as very important in the learning process, particularly those consequences that are observed being applied to others. However, SLT distinguishes between learning and performance. SLT views antecedent and consequent environmental events as playing a very important role in the acquisition of cognitive representations of how to perform, rather than in the actual effort and performance of a behavior. Unlike operant theory, SLT proposes that actual performance is generally under the control of cognitive self-regulatory processes. For example, Bandura notes that people "achieve a close approximation of the new behavior by modeling, and they refine it through self-corrective adjustments on the basis of informative feedback" (Bandura, 1977, p. 28).

The Role of Modeling

SLT emphasizes learning that takes place by observing or modeling other persons in the social environment. By observing how another person acts, the observer forms a mental picture of the act and its consequences. With repeated exposure, modeling stimuli produce images of modeled performances that can later be summoned to guide performance (Bandura, 1977). However most observed behavior is coded verbally (Bandura, 1977), and in this regard, SLT modeling closely resembles the "rule-governed" concept in operant theory.

Rule-governed behavior is based on rules people derive from their understanding of the contingencies in the environment. Skinner (1969) specifically states that a rule is a verbal description of a behavioral contingency. He notes that such rules can be derived from a study of the reinforcing system or from large samples of behavior reinforced by such a system. Such rule-governed behavior from operant theory can be used to explain modeling. For example, Mawhinney (1975) noted that a person who has experience with the environment may be able to verbalize the contingencies in it and therefore instruct another on how to behave in order to be reinforced. Recently, operant theorists have used such rule-governed behavior to explain not only modeling and self-management, but also organizational culture (Malott, 1992) and performance feedback (Agnew and Redmon, 1992).

In SLT, modeling relies on four subprocesses: attentional processes, representational processes, behavioral production processes, and motivational processes. To learn a behavior, a person must pay attention to what the model is doing and the consequences that are applied to the model's behavior. What the model does and the consequences that follow are cognitively represented, according to SLT. This cognitive representation is then retained as rules and conceptions. The nature of cognitive retention gives the person the capability to convey generalized rules. This, in turn, allows judgments to be made about consequences that may occur in subsequent environmental variations and thus permits generation of innovative behavior. The ability to be innovative and to use general rules is what sets modeling apart from simple copying or imitation.

By observing and cognitively coding the consequences that follow the model's behavior, people are able to evaluate and then decide whether to perform the behavior they have learned. The modeled behavior then becomes part of the SLT self-regulatory system. If people do perform the learned behavior, the adequacy of their actions is compared against their cognitive conceptual models (Carroll and Bandura, 1987). As with all self-regulatory processes in SLT, the behavior and/or the conceptual model are modified to minimize any discrepancy perceived between the desired and actual performance levels.

The Role of Self-Efficacy

Self-efficacy has recently emerged as one of the most important components of the self-regulatory process in SLT. Self-efficacy is a judgment about how well people feel they could perform at their best rather than a self-judgment about how much effort they will choose to apply to a particular task. A person's self-efficacy, or belief about their ability to perform a task, plays a major role in the performance standards a person sets for a task, and their perseverance on the task. Self-efficacy perceptions are derived from sources of information such as: previous performance accomplishments, vicarious experience, verbal persuasion, and physiological states (Bandura, 1977). That is, prior success or failure experiences (Bandura and Jourden, 1991), the success of strategies used by others with similar ability, encouragement from others, and the emotional state at the time all affect people's judgment of how well they could perform the task.

The role of self-efficacy tends to be particularly important in the absence of externally set performance standards (goals) or other task-relevant modeled or learned behaviors. Self-efficacy judgments play a crucial role in the setting of performance goals, and therefore play a central role in self-regulatory and self-control mechanisms. Research by Early and Lituchy (1991) suggest that self-efficacy may shift from effect to cause (of personal goals) as an individual gains task experience. In summary, Bandura (1986) notes that self-efficacy judgments influence human performance through their impact on choice behavior, on effort expenditure and perseverance, on self-hindering or self-aiding thought patterns, and on affective and neuropsychological reactions to environmental demands.

The Role of Self-Regulation

As discussed under The Role of Modeling, what people have learned through experience and modeling, their beliefs about their abilities, and their goal systems all come together in the SLT self-regulatory system. The basis of the self-regulatory process in SLT is the cybernetic or negative feedback loop found in theories such as control theory (Carver, 1979) and the closed-loop model of self-regulation (Kanfer, 1971). In the negative feedback loop, an input such as behavior feedback is perceived by the sensor, which sends a signal to a comparator, where it is tested against a standard such as a performance goal (Powers, 1973). If there is a discrepancy, an error message causes the cybernetic or self-regulation system to adjust its behavior. Feedback on the adjusted behavior provides new input and the system continues until the input matches the standard (Klein, 1989).

Bandura (1988) elaborates on this self-regulation loop, proposing a discrepancy production mechanism (proactive control) in addition to discrepancy reduction mechanisms. Proactive control consists of self-set performance standards that are partially a function of a person's self-efficacy levels. By setting higher standards a person creates a performance-standard discrepancy that the negative feedback loop addresses by increasing performance. This forms the basis of the self-control or self-management system.

In summary, SLT transcends the traditional environmental versus cognitive debate that has sidetracked the study of human behavior for so long. It blends the need for understanding the cognitive complexities of human behavior with the pragmatism of the prediction and control of operant theory.

BASIC RESEARCH ON SLT

A recent meta-analysis of 114 studies found an average weighted correlation between self-efficacy and work-related performance of .38, which transforms to a 28 percent gain in performance (Stajkovic and Luthans, 1998). In addition, other meta-analytic studies have shown self-efficacy to be significantly related to health-related outcomes (Holden, 1991), academic outcomes

(Multon, Brown and Lent, 1991), and the behavior of children (Holden et al., 1990). Outside the domain of human performance in organizations, self-efficacy has been shown to play a role in chronic pain coping (Jensen, Turner, and Romano, 1991), exertion on a bicycling task (Bandura and Cervone, 1983, 1986), finding uses for common objects (Locke et al., 1984), physical fitness behaviors, and many other behaviors. In addition, reviews of the literature have also concluded that the relationship between self-efficacy and a variety of other behaviors is strong (e.g., Bandura, 1984; Betz and Hackett, 1986; Maddux and Stanley, 1986).

The effect of task outcome on subsequent self-efficacy levels also has been demonstrated. For example, in the exercise bicycling task Bandura and Cervone (1986) showed feedback of very large failures lowered motivation by lowering self-efficacy. Feedback of small successes had little impact on performance. Feedback indicating a dramatic surpassing of the standard had a mixed effect, raising some subjects' self-efficacy and self-set goals while not affecting others.

Another major component of SLT, the role of the negative feedback loop, has also been subjected to considerable basic research. For example, Grimm (1983) and Matsui, Okada, and Inoshita (1983) have found dissatisfaction with performance and increased effort on future trials followed information indicating failure to achieve a standard or goal. The Bandura and Cervone (1986) study also showed that feedback of medium failures was motivating because it was dissatisfying. The importance of goals in the operation of this feedback loop has been supported by other research. Cervone, Jiwani, and Wood (1991) showed that the specificity of the goals affected self-efficacy judgments and the self-evaluative process. Stock and Cervone (1990) showed that setting a subgoal boosted initial self-efficacy, and attainment of the subgoal increased satisfaction with performance, self-efficacy perceptions, and subsequent task persistence.

The modeling component of SLT also has received strong basic research support in a very broad range of situations and behaviors. For example, research has linked modeling to alcohol and cigarette use in high school students (Graham, Marks, and Hansen, 1991), the harshness of parental child-rearing practices (Simons et al., 1991), and the tendency of persons to ride with drinking drivers (DiBlasio, 1988). Modeling as a training technique has been used in very diverse contexts such as antidrug programs (Parcel et al., 1989), programs designed to increase levels of blood donations in high schools (Sarason, Sarason, and Pierce, 1991), drinking driver prevention programs in high schools (Yates and Dowrick, 1991), and programs to promote improved agricultural techniques in third-world villages (Kunkel, 1986). Findings also suggest modeling begins very early in life, and may even be innate. Legerstee (1991) showed that modeling of facial expressions such as mouth openings and tongue protrusions began as early as five to eight weeks of age. Poulson et al. (1991) demonstrated modeling of vocalizations occurred in nine- to thirteen-month-old infants, but only when followed by contingent social reinforcement.

Overall, the basic research briefly outlined provides strong support for the components of SLT. Particularly notable is the extreme range of tests of the theory components, which touch on almost all aspects of human endeavor, behavior, and thought, regardless of culture or age. The theoretical components and this basic research support can serve as a foundation and point of departure for the application of SLT to behavioral management.

AN SLT MODEL AND FRAMEWORK
FOR BEHAVIORAL MANAGEMENT

SLT offers a comprehensive theory that incorporates the interactive nature of the behavior itself, the environment (especially other organizational participants and the job design, goals, and even organizational culture), and the organizational participant (including cognitions) (Bandura, 1977; Davis and Luthans, 1980). An SLT model for behavioral management is shown in Figure 15.1. This model is an adaptation of Bandura's original model to organizational behavior. Organizational behavior is viewed as affecting and being affected by the participants' cognitions, the environment, and the person-situation interactions. Although highly abstract and probably oversimplified, the reciprocal interaction between organizational behavior and the person's cognitions can be represented by symbolic processes; the interaction between organizational behavior and the environment can be represented by vicarious learning; and the interaction between the person's cognitions and the environment can be depicted as self-control.

Application of a social learning model requires a framework for functional analysis. The S-O-B-C framework presented in Figure 15.2 represents the functional relationships that portray the interactive, reciprocal nature of the environment, behavior, and the person. The S-O-B-C framework expands on the antecedent stimulus-behavior-consequence (S-B-C) framework of O.B. Mod. (Kreitner and Luthans, 1984) by including the cognitive mediating processes that are occurring within the person or organism (O). The cognitive mediating processes come from goal setting, expectancy, and equity components, as well as self-efficacy and self-regulatory

FIGURE 15.1. A Social Learning Theory Model for Behavioral Management

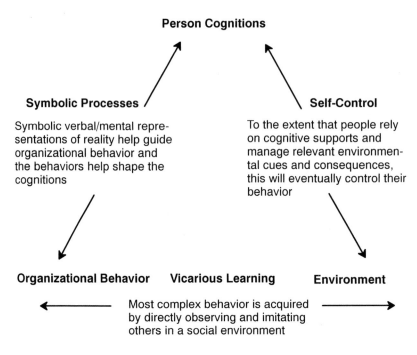

Person Cognitions

Symbolic Processes

Symbolic verbal/mental representations of reality help guide organizational behavior and the behaviors help shape the cognitions

Self-Control

To the extent that people rely on cognitive supports and manage relevant environmental cues and consequences, this will eventually control their behavior

Organizational Behavior   Vicarious Learning   Environment

Most complex behavior is acquired by directly observing and imitating others in a social environment

Source: Adapted from Kreitner, R. and Luthans, F. (1984). A social learning approach to behavioral management: Radical behaviorists "mellowing out." *Organization Dynamics, 13*(2), 55.

mechanisms. Each of these cognitive mediating processes can be thought of as a highly personalized gatekeeper that determines which environmental cues and consequences will prompt which particular behavior.

APPLIED SLT RESEARCH RELEVANT TO BEHAVIORAL MANAGEMENT

Although SLT has been applied to complex managerial strategic decision making (e.g., Wood and Bandura, 1989), the primary application of the theory has been to managing behavior of operating employees. In this latter application, self-management, training and development, and perfor-

FIGURE 15.2. A Functional Analysis Framework for SLT Behavioral Analysis

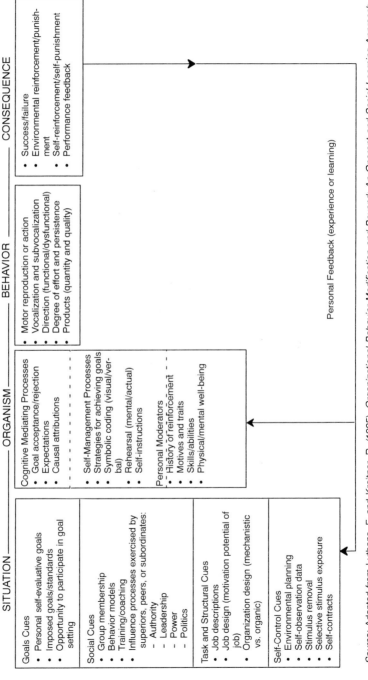

S SITUATION	O ORGANISM	B BEHAVIOR	C CONSEQUENCE

Goals Cues
• Personal self-evaluative goals
• Imposed goals/standards
• Opportunity to participate in goal setting
 	
Social Cues
• Group membership
• Behavior models
• Training/coaching
• Influence processes exercised by superiors, peers, or subordinates:
  – Authority
  – Leadership
  – Power
  – Politics
 	
Task and Structural Cues
• Job descriptions
• Job design (motivation potential of job)
• Organization design (mechanistic vs. organic)
 	
Self-Control Cues
• Environmental planning
• Self-observation data
• Stimulus removal
• Selective stimulus exposure
• Self-contracts
	Cognitive Mediating Processes
	• Goal acceptance/rejection
	• Expectations
	• Causal attributions
	
	Self-Management Processes
	• Strategies for achieving goals
	• Symbolic coding (visual/verbal)
	• Rehearsal (mental/actual)
	• Self-instructions
	
	Personal Moderators
	• History of reinforcement
	• Motives and traits
	• Skills/abilities
	• Physical/mental well-being
		• Motor reproduction or action
		• Vocalization and subvocalization
		• Direction (functional/dysfunctional)
		• Degree of effort and persistence
		• Products (quantity and quality)
			• Success/failure
			• Environmental reinforcement/punishment
			• Self-reinforcement/self-punishment
			• Performance feedback

Personal Feedback (experience or learning)

Source: Adapted from Luthans, F. and Kreitner, R. (1985). *Organizational Behavior Modification and Beyond: An Operant and Social Learning Approach.* Glenview, IL: Scott, Foresman and Co..

403

mance management techniques have benefitted significantly from the use of SLT as a guide to intervention. Examples of such applications are described in the following sections.

Self-Management Applications

Managing has traditionally been conceptualized as something a superior does to a subordinate, a group, or an organization. The traditional approach to leadership, even that advocating participative management, took a top-down perspective that required constant monitoring of subordinate performance through either direct observation or through the quantity and/or quality of some sort of output. In many jobs such control is difficult if not impossible because the supervisor is incapable of watching the subordinate perform and there are no tangible outputs. The quality service interaction is a prime example of an employee behavior that cannot be easily monitored, yet is central to organizational success. By their very nature such jobs require employees to self-manage their own performance.

The well-developed system of mechanisms that constitute the self-regulatory system of SLT provides an important focus for the application of self-management techniques. The S-O-B-C model helps identify the cues, cognitive processes, and consequences that can be used by organizational participants to manage their own behavior (Luthans and Davis, 1978, 1981). Managers or even operating-level employees can be trained to monitor and record their own behavior and to control the cues that trigger those behaviors. This may involve simple steps such as limiting the hours an open-door policy is maintained in order to minimize disruptions, or may involve more complex behavioral self-contracts with goals and self-administered reinforcers. Although operant theory explains self-management through the mechanism of rule-generated behavior (Malott, 1992), operant theory provides less direction for intervention than the social learning approach. That is, the complex system of constructs in SLT directs attention toward specific aspects of the person, behavior, and the environment which may be targeted.

Despite some problems with areas such as self-appraisal, research has tended to support the effectiveness of behavioral self-management. Luthans and Davis (1978) targeted a variety of managers with a variety of problem behaviors. These behaviors included getting to work on time, following plans, completing paperwork, and so on. Behavioral self-management plans were developed that involved manipulation of cues and consequences surrounding the problem behaviors. The reversal design allowed the effectiveness of the approach to be clearly attributed to the behavioral self-management approach. Manz (1983), Manz and Sims (1989, 1993), and Sims and

Lorenzi (1992) have developed a comprehensive approach to leadership and management based on behavioral self-management principles.

More recent research has continued to support behavioral self-management, and the importance of self-efficacy in the effectiveness of behavioral self-management applications is becoming clear. For example, Frayne and Latham (1987) gave self-management training to twenty government workers to increase their attendance record. The employees were trained to manage personal and social obstacles to their job attendance. Self-efficacy and job attendance were significantly improved. A six month follow-up study (Latham and Frayne, 1989) showed that self-efficacy and job attendance improvements were maintained over time, and perceived self-efficacy at the end of training predicted subsequent job attendance. Similar results were obtained by Gintner and Poret (1988). Thirty-five community professionals were given a thirty-hour self-management training program, which included a self-modification project. A ten-week follow-up indicated that end-of-class self-efficacy correctly classified over 80 percent of those who maintained gains versus those who relapsed.

In summary, behavioral self-management based on SLT appears to be an effective approach to performance management. The increasing levels of autonomy and empowerment that are found in flatter organizational structures and in the service industries makes behavioral self-management highly relevant to today's quality-conscious organizations. As supervisor control of contingencies becomes less possible with expanding spans of control, the responsibility for behavioral control must shift to the individual. Self-efficacy in particular appears to influence the effectiveness of self-management, possibly by affecting the levels of self-set goals that occur in the self-regulatory process. In addition, both stimulus and consequence management of self-behaviors can be employed. For example, on the stimulus side, self-management may involve exposure to or removal of stimuli that evoke behaviors, and on the consequence side, there may be self-reinforcement/ punishment. In other words, operant principles still hold under an SLT approach. However, it appears current methods of self-management training may be somewhat simplistic, failing to fully incorporate all the self-regulatory mechanisms identified by SLT, particularly the intertwined effects of self-monitoring, self-set goals and their specificity, and the role of self-efficacy.

Training Applications

Training programs based on vicarious learning processes must address the four component processes coming from SLT: Attentional, representational, behavioral production, and motivational processes. The attention process must be addressed by using a model that is respected by the trainee, but is perceived as similar and relevant to the trainee. Use of models similar in status to trainees, particularly at the mastery level, also has a greater impact on trainees' self-efficacy perceptions (Bandura, 1986). The second process, cognitive representation, can be assisted by cognitive rehearsal (Wood and Bandura, 1989), which should be built into the training process. Effective modeling teaches general rules and strategies for dealing with different situations rather than specific responses. Training should address the behavior production process portion of learning by including participative modeling, such as guided role plays. Finally, the motivational processes involved in learning are crucial to the performance of observationally learned behaviors. Trainees need to be reinforced, and they need to see the model being reinforced, preferably within the actual workplace.

Effectiveness of modeling-based training has been demonstrated in achieving a variety of organizational training goals: enhancing supervisor interpersonal skills (Porras and Singh, 1986), improving supervisory handling of poor performers (Mitchell and Wood, 1980), handling discipline and complaints (Birkenbach, Kamfer, and ter-Morshuizen, 1985), improving idea generation among managers (Gist, 1989), raising general managerial skills (Hall and Cockburn, 1990), and improving social work skills of social work practitioners (LeCroy, 1982). Hall and Cockburn (1990) also demonstrated that the 10 to 70 percent gains made from modeling-based training were maintained at six-month and one-year follow-ups.

Performance Management Applications

The S-O-B-C model provides a practical framework for performance management. This SLT approach builds on the O.B. Mod. approach (Luthans and Kreitner, 1975, 1985) by recognizing that the person or organism (O) itself affects the relationship between the stimuli (S), consequences (C), and the behaviors (B). The effect of the cognitions of the person on the behavior-stimulus-consequence relationship is viewed as a function of the mechanisms proposed by SLT as well as the processes included in the cognitive theories described earlier.

The S-O-B-C framework recognizes the following:

1. People learn vicariously through the observation of others.
2. They learn through covert processes in which the individual cognitively processes information about behavior and environmental contingencies.
3. They purposefully control their own behavior by managing environmental contingencies.

4. Beliefs about their own performance ability affect the goals they set for themselves.
5. Beliefs about the ultimate consequences of a behavior affect performance of a behavior.
6. Specific goals affect self-regulation of performance.
7. Value judgments such as fairness affect the self-set goals in the regulatory process.

The S-O-B-C model provides a comprehensive approach to behavioral management by providing an understanding of the relevant cognitive constructs, thus providing direction to the diagnosis and intervention steps of O.B. Mod. Goal setting, explicitly tying behavior to goals and consequences, being sensitive to the effect of consequence changes on self-efficacy, ensuring that consequence changes are fair, providing models of the desired behavior, and teaching employees to manipulate the environment to self-reinforce are all techniques that are not only explained but specifically suggested by the S-O-B-C model.

CONCLUSIONS AND IMPLICATIONS

Over the years those studying human behavior in organizations and human performance management have argued about the relative merits of cognitive versus behavioral theories, leaving practicing managers with conflicting messages and little practical assistance. O.B. Mod. has been demonstrated to have a positive impact on human performance in organizations (Luthans and Kreitner, 1975; Stajkovic and Luthans, 1997), but the time now seems right to expand the model to incorporate SLT (Luthans and Kreitner, 1985). The extension of O.B. Mod. through the application of SLT and the development of the S-O-B-C framework allows the debate of cognitive versus behavioral approaches to be transcended, and a more utilitarian stance to be adopted (Kreitner and Luthans, 1984). The theoretical departures represented by the inclusion of goal setting, expectancy, and equity theories in the S-O-B-C model also provide additional bases for strengthening and building upon a strictly operant foundation of behavioral management. Although both operant theory and SLT are capable of explaining all the phenomena covered in this chapter, SLT has a usefulness that stems from a series of constructs and proposed mechanisms which provide useful direction to diagnoses and interventions.

The integration of the modeling approach into training and development opens up a variety of empirically validated techniques for training as well as bringing the necessary emphasis into training with actual performance of the behavior in situ (Davis and Luthans, 1980). In addition to training, the self-regulatory processes identified by SLT have made a significant contribution to the area of behavioral self-management. In particular, incorporation of concepts such as the role of the feedback loop, self-efficacy, and self-set goals has added to the comprehensiveness of the behavioral self-management approach. The effectiveness of behavioral self-management has been demonstrated by research and has wide application to a variety of behaviors and situations including the customer-employee service interaction. The intent is not to suggest that SLT should replace operant theory, but rather that SLT can extend both the theory and practice of behavioral performance management.

REFERENCES

Adams, J. (1965). Inequity in social exchange. In L. Berkowitz (Ed.), *Advances in experimental social psychology* (pp. 267-299). New York: Academic Press.

Agnew, J. L. and Redmon, W. K. (1992). Contingency specifying stimuli: The role of "rules" in organizational behavior management. *Journal of Organizational Behavior Management, 12*(2), 67-76.

Anderson, D. C., Crowell, C. R., Sucec, J., Gilligan, K. D., and Wikoff, M. (1982). Behavior management of client contacts in a real estate brokerage: Getting agents to sell more. *Journal of Organizational Behavior Management, 4*(1), 67-95.

Andrasik, F. (1989). Organizational behavior modification in business settings: A methodological and content review. *Journal of Organizational Behavior Management, 10*(1), 59-77.

Bandura, A. (1977). *Social learning theory.* Englewood Cliffs, NJ: Prentice-Hall.

Bandura, A. (1984). Recycling misconceptions of self-efficacy. *Cognitive Therapy and Research, 8,* 231-255.

Bandura, A. (1986). *Social foundations of thought and action: A social cognitive theory.* Englewood Cliffs, NJ: Prentice-Hall.

Bandura, A. (1988). Self-regulation of motivation and action through goal systems. In V. Hamilton, G. Bower, and N. Frijda (Eds.), *Cognitive perspectives on motivation and emotion* (pp. 37-61). Dordrecht: Kluwer Academic Publishers.

Bandura, A. and Cervone, D. (1983). Self-evaluative and self-efficacy mechanisms governing the motivational effects of goal systems. *Journal of Personality and Social Psychology, 45,* 1017-1028.

Bandura, A. and Cervone, D. (1986). Differential engagement of self-reactive influences in cognitive motivation. *Organizational Behavior and Human Decision Processes, 32,* 92-113.

Bandura, A. and Jourden, F. (1991). Self-regulatory mechanisms governing the impact of social comparison on complex decision making. *Journal of Personality and Social Psychology, 60,* 941-951.

Berger, C. J., Cummings, L. L., and Heneman, H. G., III. (1975). Expectancy theory and operant conditioning predictions of performance under variable ratio and continuous schedules of reinforcement. *Organizational Behavior and Human Performance, 14,* 227-243.

Betz, N. and Hackett, G. (1986). Applications of self-efficacy theory to understanding career choice behavior. *Journal of Social and Clinical Psychology, 4,* 279-289.

Birkenbach, X., Kamfer, L., and ter-Morshuizen, J. (1985). The development and evaluation of a behavior modelling training program for supervisors. *South African Journal of Psychology, 15,* 11-19.

Brown, M. G., Malott, R. W., Dillon, M. J., and Keeps, E. J. (1980). Improving customer service in a large department store through the use of training and feedback. *Journal of Organizational Behavior Management, 2*(4), 251-264.

Campion, M. and Lord, R. (1982). A control system conceptualization of the goal setting and changing process. *Organizational Behavior and Human Performance, 30,* 265-287.

Carroll, W. and Bandura, A. (1987). Translating cognition into action: The role of visual guidance in observational learning. *Journal of Motor Behavior, 19,* 385-398.

Carver, C. (1979). A cybernetic model of self-attention processes. *Journal of Personality and Social Psychology, 37,* 1251-1281.

Cervone, D., Jiwani, N., and Wood, R. (1991). Goal setting and the differential influence of self-regulatory processes on complex decision making performance. *Journal of Personality and Social Psychology, 61,* 257-266.

Davis, T. and Luthans, F. (1980). A social learning approach to organizational behavior. *Academy of Management Review, 5,* 281-290.

DiBlasio, F. (1988). Pre-driving riders and drinking drivers. *Journal of Studies on Alcohol, 49,* 11-15.

Dierks, W. and McNally, K. A. (1987). Incentives you can bank on. *Personnel Administrator,* March, 60-65.

Early, C. and Lituchy, T. (1991). Delineating goal and efficacy effects: A test of three models. *Journal of Applied Psychology, 76,* 81-98.

Erez, M. and Arad, R. (1986). Participative goal setting: Social, motivational and cognitive factors. *Journal of Applied Psychology, 71,* 591-597.

Fedor, D. and Ferris, G. (1981). Integrating O.B. Mod with cognitive approaches to motivation. *Academy of Management Review, 6,* 115-125.

Fellner, D. and Sulzer-Azaroff, B. (1984). A behavioral analysis of goal setting. *Journal of Organizational Behavior Management, 6*(1), 33-51.

Frayne, C. and Latham, G. (1987). Application of social learning theory to employee self-management of attendance. *Journal of Applied Psychology, 72,* 387-392.

Garland, H. (1985). A cognitive mediation theory of task goals and human performance. *Motivation and Emotion, 9,* 345-367.

Gintner, G. and Poret, M. (1988). Factors associated with maintenance and relapse following self-management training. *Journal of Psychology, 122,* 79-87.

Gist, M. (1989). The influence of training method on self-efficacy and idea generation among managers. *Personnel Psychology, 42,* 787-805.

Goodman, P. (1974). An examination of referents used in the evaluation of pay. *Organizational Behavior and Human Performance, 12,* 170-195.

Graham, J., Marks, G., and Hansen, W. (1991). Social influence processes affecting adolescent substance abuse. *Journal of Applied Psychology, 76,* 291-298.

Grimm, L. (1983). The relation between self-evaluation and self-reward: A test of Kanfer's self-regulation model. *Cognitive Therapy and Research, 7,* 245-250.

Hall, D. and Cockburn, E. (1990). Developing management skills. *Management Education and Development, 21,* 41-50.

Holden, G. (1991). The relationship of self-efficacy appraisals to subsequent health related outcomes: A meta-analysis. (Special issue). *Applied Social Work Research in Health and Social Work, 16*(1), 53-93.

Holden, G., Moncher, M., Schinke, S., and Barker, K. (1990). Self-efficacy of children and adolescents: A meta-analysis. *Psychological Reports, 66,* 1044-1046.

Jensen, M., Turner, J., and Romano, J. (1991). Self-efficacy and outcome expectancies: Relationship to chronic pain coping strategies and adjustment. *Pain, 44,* 263-269.

Kanfer, F. (1971). The maintenance of behavior by self-generated stimuli and reinforcement. In A. Jacobs and L. Sachs (Eds.), *The psychology of private events* (pp. 39-59). New York: Academic Press.

Klein, H. (1989). An integrated control theory model of work motivation. *Academy of Management Review, 14,* 150-172.

Kreitner, R. and Luthans, F. (1984). A social learning approach to behavioral management: Radical behaviorists mellowing out. *Organizational Dynamics, 13*(2), 47-65.

Kunkel, J. (1986). The Vicos project: A cross cultural test of psychological propositions. *Psychological Record, 36,* 451-466.

Landy, F. and Trumbo, D. (1980). *Psychology of work behavior.* Homewood, IL: The Dorsey Press.

Latham, G. P. and Dossett, D. L. (1978). Designing incentive plans for unionized employees: A comparison of continuous and variable ratio reinforcement schedules. *Personnel Psychology, 31,* 47-61.

Latham, G. P. and Frayne, C. (1989). Self-management training for increasing job attendance: A follow-up and replication. *Journal of Applied Psychology, 74,* 411-416.

Latham, G. P. and Locke, E. (1979). Goal setting—A motivational technique that works. *Organizational Dynamics, 8,* 68-80.

LeCroy, C. (1982). Practitioner competence in social work: Training and evaluation. *Journal of Social Service Research, 5,* 71-83.

Legerstee, M. (1991). The role of person and object in eliciting early imitation. *Journal of Experimental Child Psychology, 51,* 423-433.

Leventhal, G. (1976). Fairness in social relationships. In J. Thibaut, J. Spence, and R. Carson (Eds.), *Contemporary topics in social psychology* (pp. 211-239). NJ: General Learning Press.

Locke, E. (1978). The ubiquity of the technique of goal setting in theories of and approaches to employee motivation. *Academy of Management Review, 3,* 594-601.

Locke, E., Frederick, E., Bobko, P., and Lee, C. (1984). Effect of self-efficacy, goals, and task strategies on task performance. *Journal of Applied Psychology, 69,* 241-251.

Locke, E. and Latham, G. (1990). *A theory of goal setting and task performance.* Englewood Cliffs, NJ: Prentice-Hall.

Luthans, F. (1992). *Organizational behavior.* New York: McGraw-Hill.

Luthans, F. and Davis, T. R. V. (1978). Behavioral self-management: The missing link in managerial effectiveness. *Organizational Dynamics,* Summer, 42-60.

Luthans, F. and Davis, T. (1981). Beyond modeling: Managing social learning processes in human resource training and development. *Human Resource Management,* Summer, 19-27.

Luthans, F., Fox, M. L., and Davis, E. (1991). Improving the delivery of quality service: Behavioral management techniques. *Leadership and Organization Development Journal, 12,* 3-6.

Luthans, F. and Kreitner, R. (1975). *Organizational behavior modification.* Glenview, IL: Scott, Foresman and Co.

Luthans, F. and Kreitner, R. (1985). *Organizational behavior modification and beyond.* Glenview, IL: Scott, Foresman and Co.

Luthans, F., Paul, R., and Baker, D. (1981). An experimental analysis of the impact of contingent reinforcement on salespersons' performance behavior. *Journal of Applied Psychology, 66*(3), 314-323.

Maddux, J. and Stanley, M. (1986). Self-efficacy theory in contemporary psychology: An overview. *Journal of Consulting and Clinical Psychology, 4,* 249-255.

Malott, R. W. (1992). A theory of rule-governed behavior and organizational behavior management. *Journal of Organizational Behavior Management, 12*(2), 45-65.

Manz, C. C. (1983). *The art of self-leadership.* Englewood Cliffs, NJ: Prentice-Hall.

Manz, C. C. and Sims, H. P. (1989). *Superleadership: Leading others to lead themselves.* Englewood Cliffs, NJ: Prentice-Hall.

Manz, C. C. and Sims, H. P. (1993). *Business without bosses.* New York: Wiley.

Matsui, T., Okada, A., and Inoshita, O. (1983). Mechanisms of feedback affecting performance. *Organizational Behavior and Human Performance, 31,* 114-122.

Mawhinney, T. C. (1975). Operant terms and concepts in the description of individual work behavior: Some problems of interpretation, application, and evaluation. *Journal of Applied Psychology, 60,* 704-712.

Mawhinney, T. C. (1986). Reinforcement schedule stretching effects. In E. A. Locke (Ed.), *Generalizing from laboratory to field settings* (pp. 181-186). Lexington, MA: Lexington Books.

Merwin, G. A., Thompson, J. A., and Sanford, E. E. (1989). A methodology and content review of organizational behavior management in the private sector 1978-1986. *Journal of Organizational Behavior Management, 10*(1), 39-57.

Mitchell, T. R. and Wood, R. E. (1980). Supervisors' responses to subordinate poor performance: A test of an attribution model. *Organizational Behavior and Human Performance, 25,* 123-138.

Mowday, R. (1991). Equity theory predictions of behavior in organizations (Fifth edition). In R. Steers and L. Porter (Eds.), *Motivation and work behavior.* New York: McGraw-Hill.

Multon, K., Brown, S., and Lent, R. (1991). Relation of self-efficacy beliefs to academic outcomes: A meta-analytic investigation. *Journal of Counseling Psychology, 38*(1), 30-38.

Naylor, J., Pritchard, R., and Ilgen, D. (1980). *A theory of behavior in organizations.* New York: Academic Press.

Newby, T. J. and Robinson, P. W. (1983). Effects of group and individual feedback on retail employees' performances. *Journal of Organizational Behavior Management, 5*(2), 51-68.

O'Hara, K., Johnson, C. M., and Beehr, T. A. (1985). Organizational behavior management in the private sector: A review of empirical research and recommendations for further investigation. *Academy of Management Review, 10,* 848-864.

Organ, D. W. and Bateman, T. (1986). *Organizational behavior.* Plano, TX: Business Publications, Inc.

Parcel, G., Taylor, W., Brink, S., and Gottlieb, N. (1989). Translating theory into practice: Intervention strategies for the diffusion of health promotion innovation. *Family and Community Health, 12,* 1-13.

Porras, J. and Singh, J. (1986). Alpha, beta and gamma change in modelling based organization development. *Journal of Occupational Behavior, 7,* 9-24.

Porter, L. and Lawler, E. (1968). *Managerial attitudes and performance.* Homewood, IL: Irwin.

Poulson, C., Kyissmis, E., Reeve, K., and Andreatos, M. (1991). Generalized vocal imitation in infants. *Journal of Experimental Child Psychology, 51,* 267-279.

Powers, W. (1973). *Behavior: The control of perception.* Chicago: Aldine.

Sarason, I., Sarason, B., and Pierce, G. (1991). A social learning approach to increasing blood donations. *Journal of Applied Social Psychology, 21,* 896-918.

Shapira, Z. (1989). Task choice and assigned goals as determinants of task motivation and performance. *Organizational Behavior and Human Decision Processes, 44,* 141-165.

Simons, R., Whitbeck, L., Conger, R., and Wu, C. (1991). Intergenerational transmission of harsh parenting. *Developmental Psychology, 27,* 159-171.

Sims, H. P. and Lorenzi, P. (1992). *The new leadership paradigm.* Newbury Park, CA: Sage.

Skinner, B. F. (1953). *Science and human behavior.* New York: Free Press.

Skinner, B. F. (1969). *Contingencies and reinforcement: A theoretical analysis.* New York: Appleton-Century-Crofts.

Stajkovic, A. D. and Luthans, F. (1997). A meta-analysis of the effects of organizational behavior modification on task performance, 1975-95. *Academy of Management Journal, 40,* 1122-1149.

Stajkovic, A. D. and Luthans, F. (1998). Self-efficacy and work-related performance: A meta-analysis. *Psychological Bulletin, 24,* 240-261.

Stock, J. and Cervone, D. (1990). Proximal goal setting and self-regulatory processes. *Cognitive Therapy and Research, 14,* 483-498.

Summers, T. and DeNisi, A. (1990). In search of Adams' other: Reexamination of referents used in the evaluation of pay. *Human Relations, 43,* 497-511.

Vroom, V. (1964). *Work and motivation.* New York: Wiley.

Welsh, D. H. B., Luthans, F., and Sommer, S. M. (1993). Managing Russian factory workers: The impact of U.S.-based behavioral and participative techniques. *Academy of Management Journal, 36,* 58-79.

Welsh, D. H. B., Luthans, F. and Sommer, S. M. (in press). Organizational behavior modification goes to Russia: Replicating an experimental analysis across cultures and tasks. *Journal of Organizational Behavior Management 13*(2), 15-35.

Wood, R. and Bandura, A. (1989). Social cognitive theory of organization management. *Academy of Management Review, 14,* 361-384.

Yates, B. and Dowrick, P. (1991). Stop the drinking driver: A behavioral school based prevention program. *Journal of Alcohol and Drug Education, 36,* 12-19.

Yukl, G. A. and Latham, G. P. (1975). Consequences of reinforcement schedules and incentive magnitudes for employee performance: Problems encountered in an industrial setting. *Journal of Applied Psychology, 60,* 294-298.

Yukl, G. A., Latham, G. P., and Pursell, E. D. (1976). The effectiveness of performance incentives under continuous and variable ratio schedules of reinforcement. *Personnel Psychology, 29,* 221-231.

Yukl, G. A., Wexley, K. N., and Seymore, J. D. (1972). Effectiveness of pay incentives under variable ratio and continuous reinforcement schedules. *Journal of Applied Psychology, 56,* 19-23.

Chapter 16

Ethics and Behavior Analysis in Management

Howard C. Berthold Jr.

Ethical issues seem to dominate the news these days, and they extend to all areas of human endeavor including, of course, business and psychology. This chapter explores the topic of ethical issues when behavioral methods are applied to industrial/organizational (I/O) settings. The goal is not to create ethical guidelines. Rather, it is to provide an overview of the types of ethical guidelines already available as well as the nature, relevance, and importance of ethical issues that underlie such guidelines.

WHAT ARE ETHICAL PRINCIPLES?

Philosophers have long debated ethical issues. Numerous competing schools each adhere to tenets that not only are different, but sometimes opposite (Macklin, 1982). Part of this debate concerns the basic issue of how to define an ethical principle.

Philosophers sometimes quibble over whether our perceptions are reliable indicators of reality, but this issue seems to be of less concern to scientists. Scientists start with the observable, or what can be defined in terms of the observable (operational definitions). In most cases, there is a strong consensus about what is really "out there," a consensus that is in large part based upon the consistency among observations. Scientists then attempt to find relationships between these observable entities or events, an activity that produces factual statements called laws. Factual statements deal with what might be called objective reality, descriptions about how things *are*.

In addition to factual statements, there are statements of value. Value statements are assertions about what is "good," "right," or "wrong," and how entities and events in the world should be, not the way they necessarily are. Value statements are a cornerstone of ethics. Ethical principles look beyond what is, and ask what should be.

Other chapters in this book describe principles that can be used in organizational settings to modify behavior. In effect, the authors are presenting laws describing relationships between antecedent conditions, behaviors, and consequences. The process of discovering and describing these laws is identical to the process of discovering and describing laws in all other sciences, and as such, is grounded in objective reality and statements of fact. This chapter goes beyond such objective considerations and deals with ethical issues associated with the discovery and use of such laws.

WHY WOULD ORGANIZATIONAL BEHAVIOR MANAGEMENT RAISE ETHICAL CONCERNS?

Organizational behavior management (OBM) utilizes information derived from the field of behavior analysis (Mawhinney, 1984). Behavior analysis attempts to find universal laws of behavior. As a scientist, the behavior analyst believes that human behavior is lawful in the same sense that the behavior of physical objects is lawful. This concept of behavioral determinism is upsetting to many people, and has led to considerable criticism, some sophisticated, some not. For some, the mere concept of behavioral determinism is upsetting in the same way that it was upsetting for people of another century to be confronted with the fact that the earth was not the center of the universe. For others, the fear relates more to how such knowledge might be used.

Similar fears surround other sciences. For example, some people object to current work in genetics because such research might lead to discoveries that could be used to alter plants, animals, people, or society in ways that some people would not like.

Deceased U.S. Supreme Court Justice Thurgood Marshall is purported to have said, "Our whole constitutional heritage rebels at the thought of giving government the power to control men's minds." The sentiment he expressed goes beyond "minds" and government. People rebel at the concept of control in general, even though, as Skinner (1971) noted in a discussion of control and countercontrol, control is always present no matter how vehemently one argues for free will or independence from genetic influences. The discovery of laws of behavior increases the possibility of effective control. Management is one of many areas in which control of people's behavior is an explicit goal. Combining the two, therefore, is alarming to some and raises issues pertaining to what should be controlled and who would decide. Decisions pertaining to the appropriateness of applying these laws move us from the field of objective scientific inquiry into the domain of ethical practice.

How do we differentiate between ethical and unethical applications of laws of behavior? We shall look at some writings that pertain to this issue in the fields of philosophy, psychology, business, behavior analysis, and OBM.

Ethics and Philosophy

The study of ethical issues most clearly lies within the domain of philosophy, and there is a vast literature one could read on the topic. On the other hand, if one is looking for answers, then a better strategy would be to read a single source, because picking up a second will almost certainly demonstrate the lack of any fundamental agreement.

Despite the number and complexity of positions, the ends of the spectrum are easily described. At one end is the position that fundamental ethical principles exist, and the duty of philosophers is to find them. This position is sometimes referred to as ethical objectivism (Klemke, Kline, and Hollinger, 1986). At the other extreme is the position that there are no universal or absolute ethical principles. This is not to say that people do not classify objects or events as good or bad. Rather, these statements are opinions held by the people themselves and not objective properties of whatever has been observed.

Many eloquent arguments support each position. Moreover, there are many fascinating variations of these positions, some of which draw the two closer together. And each position has spawned hundreds, perhaps thousands, of interesting subquestions and ramifications. For example, assuming absolute values exist, are they the same for every culture and time? If values are completely relative, then why even talk about good and bad—throw this chapter out of the book!

If philosophers cannot agree on even the most basic issue of whether or not fundamental ethical principles exist, what help are they to those of us struggling with the very practical issue of ethics in OBM? If nothing else, philosophers offer us the assurance that we have not missed something. If philosophers had discovered a set of incontrovertible ethical principles, then the principles should be incorporated into our literature. Knowing that these experts have not reached agreement is, in a perverse way, reassuring because it means that those who have devised ethical guidelines in our own fields have not naively overlooked some obvious, absolute ethical standards.

Ethics and Psychology

There are many formal documents on ethical practices in psychology. At the national level, the American Psychological Association (APA) published its first statement on ethical standards of psychologists in 1953 and its most recent statement in 1992. The comprehensive nature of the American Psychological Association (1992) report is evident from its table of contents, shown in Table 16.1.

State psychological associations have their own guidelines and committees that attempt to promote and regulate activities of psychologists in accordance with ethical standards. If psychologists violate the ethical standards of national or state psychological associations, they may be censured or expelled from the association.

These guidelines provide fairly inclusive ethical standards for psychologists. Nevertheless, they only scratch the surface. There are also federal and state laws. These laws are value judgments (and therefore ethical guidelines) devised by groups that have the power to levy penalties on those who do not obey them. Licensing of individuals, groups, and facilities is part of this legal system, which details standards and constraints on training, techniques, and environmental conditions. The most restrictive rules controlling psychologists' efforts to influence behaviors tend to be state rather than federal laws; therefore practices can vary widely from state to state. A compilation of the laws governing psychologists in all fifty states would result in a truly enormous set of general and specific ethical principles.

In addition to the formal ethical guidelines by psychological associations and governmental agencies, various types of discourse are found in journal articles and books. On occasion, a psychologist has attempted to identify a single overriding principle to serve as the standard for all specific ethical decisions. For example, in writing about the types of constraints that might be appropriate in psychologists' acquisition and development of knowledge, Sarason (1984) suggested that the ultimate question should be how psychologists' activities improve the psychological sense of community. Skinner (1971) suggested that the ultimate ethical imperative is the preservation of human culture and society. In writing about workplace ethics from a behavioral standpoint, Clark and Lattal (1993) argued that the ultimate goal should be trying to achieve an appropriate balance between concern for others and respect for oneself (e.g., respecting the autonomy and intrinsic worth of every human being).

TABLE 16.1. Contents of APA Ethical Principles of Psychologists and Code of Conduct

CONTENTS

INTRODUCTION
PREAMBLE

GENERAL PRINCIPLES
Principle A: Competence
Principle B: Integrity
Principle C: Professional & Scientific Responsibility
Principle D: Respect for People's Rights & Dignity
Principle E: Concern for Others' Welfare
Principle F: Social Responsibility

ETHICAL STANDARDS

1.   General Standards
1.01 Applicability of the Ethics Code
1.02 Relationship of Ethics and Law
1.03 Professional & Scientific Relationship
1.04 Boundaries of Competence
1.05 Maintaining Expertise
1.06 Basis for Scientific & Professional Judgments
1.07 Describing the Nature & Results of Psychological Services
1.08 Human Differences
1.09 Respecting Others
1.10 Nondiscrimination
1.11 Sexual Harassment
1.12 Other Harassment
1.13 Personal Problems & Conflicts
1.14 Avoiding Harm
1.15 Misuse of Psychologists' Influence
1.16 Misuse of Psychologists' Work
1.17 Multiple Relationships
1.18 Barter (With Patients or Clients)
1.19 Exploitative Relationships

1.20 Consultations & Referrals
1.21 Third-Party Requests for Services
1.22 Delegation to & Supervision of Subordinates
1.23 Documentation of Professional & Scientific Work
1.24 Records and Data
1.25 Fees & Financial Arrangements
1.26 Accuracy in Reports to Payors & Funding Sources
1.27 Referrals and Fees

2.   Evaluation, Assessment, or Intervention
2.01 Evaluation, Diagnosis, & Interventions in Professional Context
2.02 Competence & Appropriate Use of Assessments Intervention
2.03 Test Construction
2.04 Use of Assessment in General & With Special Populations
2.05 Interpreting Assessment Results
2.06 Unqualified Persons
2.07 Obsolete Tests & Outdated Test Results
2.08 Test Scoring & Interpretation Services
2.09 Explaining Assessment Results
2.10 Maintaining Test Security

3.   Advertising and Other Public Statements
3.01 Definition of Public Statements
3.02 Statements by Others
3.03 Avoidance of False or Deceptive Statements
3.04 Media Presentations
3.05 Testimonials
3.06 In-Person Solicitation

4.   Therapy

TABLE 16.1 *(continued)*

5. Privacy and Confidentiality	**6. Teaching, Training Supervision, Research, and Publishing**
5.01 Discussing the Limits of Confidentiality	**7. Forensic Activities**
5.02 Maintaining Confidentiality	**8. Resolving Ethical Issues**
5.03 Minimizing Intrusions on Privacy	8.01 Familiarity with Ethics Code
5.04 Maintenance of Records	8.02 Confronting Ethical Issues
5.05 Disclosures	8.03 Conflicting Between Ethics & Organizational Demands
5.06 Consultations	
5.07 Confidential Information in Databases	8.04 Informal Resolution of Ethical Violations
5.08 Use of Confidential Information for Didactic or Other Purposes	8.05 Reporting Ethical Violations
5.09 Preserving Records & Data	8.06 Cooperating with Ethics Committees
5.10 Ownership of Records & Data	8.07 Improper Complaints
5.11 Withholding Records for Nonpayment	

Source: From American Psychological Association. (1992). Ethical Principles of Psychologists and Code of Conduct. *American Psychologist, 47,* p. 1597. Copyright 1992 by the American Psychological Association, Inc. Adapted by permission.

More often, however, writers direct their efforts toward less encompassing issues related to narrower areas of work. For example, ethical issues are discussed in relation to socially sensitive research (Sieber and Stanley, 1988), counseling (Stein, 1990), and teaching (Strike and Soltis, 1985). In addition to journal articles, textbooks are available (e.g., Carroll, Schneider, and Wesley, 1985; Corey, Corey, and Callanan, 1988; Keith-Spiegel and Koocher, 1985; Steininger, Newell, and Garcia, 1984). The books appear to be particularly useful for courses designed to meet APA's certification requirement that ethics be taught in applied programs.

Ethics and Behavior Analysis

Having considered some of the approaches to ethics in philosophy and psychology in general, I now narrow the focus to writings by and about people in the field of behavior analysis. The types of information on ethical approaches to behavior analysis are similar to those for psychology in general. Specifically, there are formal guidelines, legal guidelines, general proclamations about overriding issues, and individual articles dealing with more narrowly defined ethical problems.

Two sets of formal guidelines were published in the late 1970s and appear to have withstood the test of time quite well. The first was titled "Ethical Issues for Human Services" and was adopted on May 22, 1977, by the board of directors of the Association for Advancement of Behavior Therapy and published in *Behavior Therapy*. The statement consists of eight major questions with two to five subquestions under each (for a total of thirty-three questions), which anyone planning to implement a behavioral program should be able to answer in the affirmative. The second set of guidelines arose from a commission appointed by the American Psychological Association to delineate ethical issues in behavior modification (Stolz and associates, 1978). Eight major issues were discussed in the report.

More recently, Van Houten and colleagues (1988) published results of work by a task force appointed by the Executive Council of the Association for Behavior Analysis to "consider treatment-related issues, with particular focus on clients' rights" (Iwata, 1988, p. 110). Six basic rights of clients subject to programs designed to change behavior were identified and discussed.

Considerable overlap exists between these three sets of guidelines, although each has some unique components and cuts a little deeper into certain areas than the others. Taken together, they provide a set of ethical principles that are fairly inclusive for anyone using behavioral methods, including those working in I/O environments.

It has been noted that public laws are related to ethical issues in that they define what is and is not appropriate behavior. Cataloguing federal and state laws that are relevant in any way to behavioral interventions would require volumes, and will not be attempted here. Worth noting, however, is an increasing interest by psychologists in becoming involved in the formation of public policy. This is evident in general writings in psychology (e.g., Brown, 1992; DeWall, 1992; Sneed and Chavis, 1992) and in the behavioral literature (Fawcett et al., 1988). The Fawcett et al. (1988) report was the result of work by the Task Force on Behavior Analysis and Public Policy, sponsored by the Association for Behavior Analysis. The report is extremely important, not because it contains any recommendations regarding what should become public policy, but because it recognizes the importance of behavior analysts becoming involved in the creation of public policy, which in a sense is equivalent to the creation of legally binding ethical standards.

The principles identified in the preceding documents represent the efforts of carefully selected individuals appointed by organizations representing large numbers of people who work in the field of behavior analysis. In addition to these documents, countless other journal articles and portions of books relate to ethical conduct in the practice of behavior analysis.

Ethics and Business

The history of distrust toward business practices extends into antiquity. By the 1950s and 1960s, the old horror stories about sweatshops and child labor were replaced by fear and anger toward the "military-industrial complex." In the 1980s people such as Marvin Harris (1987) argued that business practices that spawned oligopolies, increased bureaucracy, and a shift to a service-and-information economy were the root causes of most of our social and personal problems. In the 1990s, we were bombarded by tales of insider trading, savings and loans scandals, illicit deals with foreign governments, and so on. One might think that little or no consideration has been given to the issue of ethics by business. Indeed, pollster Louis Harris (1986) found that 70 percent of the public answered "no" to the question, "Does business see to it that its executives behave legally and ethically?" (p. 236). Despite such reports, ethical guidelines do exist in the business world. For example, Dreilinger and Rice (1991) cited a study showing that between 1984 and 1987, 75 to 87 percent of Fortune 1000 companies claimed to have a formal code of ethics and 14 to 32 percent had corporate ethics committees. The most far-reaching guidelines are those issued by the federal government. It issued revised ethics rules on August 6, 1992, applying to some 2.1 million federal civilian employees in the executive branch (but not Congress or the courts) and officers (but not enlisted personnel) in the armed forces. The rules, which originated with the U.S. Office of Government Ethics, were intended to replace and unify separate rules governing different agencies.

Although it appears that less space tends to be devoted to ethical issues in the typical management text than the typical behavior modification text, courses on ethics in business are now commonplace in undergraduate and graduate school curricula, and numerous books are devoted to the topic (e.g., Beauchamp and Bowie, 1993; Blanchard and Peale, 1988; Iannone, 1989; Liebig, 1990; Madsen and Shafritz, 1990).

One of the more telling indicators of the amount of scholarly interest in ethics and business comes from a study by Randall and Gibson (1990). They utilized three computerized databases: Management Contents, which indexes 500 U.S. and international journals from 1974 onward, the Social Sciences Citation Index, which contains over one million citations from 1972 onward, and the Business Periodicals Index, which indexes 304 periodicals from 1982 onward. In addition, they conducted manual searches of

The Reader's Guide to Periodical Literature from 1960 onward, which indexes around 175 U.S. periodicals, and the *Business Periodicals Index* from 1958 to present. Finally, they studied the reference sections of the articles they found through the preceding sources for any additional studies. The result was over 700 citations on ethical beliefs and behavior in organizations. This is not an overwhelming number considering the fact that it represents everything that could be found in hundreds of journals over a thirty-year period. Nevertheless, a significant literature does exist. Together with the books, a review of articles in the *Journal of Business Ethics* would provide the interested reader with a good representative sample of the writing and research on business ethics. The literature encompasses both ethical knowledge and practice (behavior), including the oftentimes imperfect correlation between the two.

Ethics and I/O Psychology

As they are a subset of all psychologists, the majority of guidelines already discussed in this chapter apply to I/O psychologists as well. Other guidelines speak specifically to activities undertaken by I/O psychologists. Most noteworthy, perhaps, is "Specialty Guidelines for the Delivery of Services by Industrial/Organizational Psychologists" (American Psychological Association, 1981), which extended APA's *Standards for Providers of Psychological Services* (American Psychological Association, 1977) to I/O psychology. The document (1) discusses the importance to I/O psychology of supplementing and clarifying the more general APA standards upon which it is based; (2) defines the education and experience required of an I/O psychologist, including a doctoral degree from a regionally accredited university in a primarily psychological program committed to the scientist-professional model; (3) defines the types of services I/O psychologists provide, including selection and placement, organizational development, training and development, personnel research, improving motivation, and optimization of work environments; and (4) provides specific guidelines for I/O psychological services. The guidelines are summarized in Table 16.2. In the document, each of these guidelines is followed by one or more paragraphs of "interpretation."

The Society for Industrial and Organizational Psychology helped in the formulation of these standards. The society holds high standards of ethics and conduct as a primary goal (Society for Industrial and Organizational Psychology, Inc., 1983), and has issued other reports dealing with ethical issues. For example, *Principles for the Validation and Use of Personnel Selection Procedures* (Society for Industrial and Organizational Psychology, 1987) sets guidelines for "validation research, personnel selection, and

TABLE 16.2. Summary of Specialty Guidelines for the Delivery of Services by Industrial/Organizational Psychologists

---

Guideline 1
PROVIDERS

Staffing and Qualifications of Staff

1.1 Professional I/O psychologists maintain current knowledge of scientific and professional developments that are related to the services they render.

1.2 Professional I/O psychologists limit their practice to their demonstrated areas of professional competence.

1.3 Professional psychologists who wish to change their specialty to I/O areas meet the same requirements with respect to subject matter and professional skills that apply to doctoral training in the new specialty.

1.4 Professional I/O psychologists are encouraged to develop innovative procedures and theory.

Guideline 2
PROFESSIONAL CONSIDERATIONS

Protecting the User

2.1 I/O psychological practice supports the legal and civil rights of the user.

2.2 All providers of I/O psychological services abide by policies of the American Psychological Association that are relevant to I/O psychologists.

2.3 All providers within an I/O psychological service unit are familiar with relevant statutes, regulations, and legal precedents established by federal, state, and local governmental groups.

Planning Organizational Goals

2.4 Providers of I/O psychological services state explicitly what can and cannot reasonably be expected from the services.

2.5 Providers of I/O psychological services do not seek to gain competitive advantage through the use of privileged information.

2.6 Providers of I/O psychological services who purchase the services of another psychologist provide a clear statement of the role of the purchaser.

2.7 Providers of I/O psychological services establish a system to protect confidentiality of their records.

Guideline 3
ACCOUNTABILITY

Evaluating I/O Psychological Services

3.1 The professional activities of providers of I/O psychological services are guided primarily by the principle of promoting human welfare.

3.2 There are periodic, systematic, and effective evaluations of psychological services.

Source: From American Psychological Association (1981). Specialty Guidelines for the Delivery of Services by Industrial/Organizational Psychologists. *American Psychologist, 36,* pp. 666-668. Copyright 1981 by the American Psychological Association, Inc. Adapted by permission.

promotion" (p. 1). In the area of assessment and personnel, documents on standards and ethical principles abound. Many of these were developed by professional organizations, and many have the status of federal and state laws. London and Bray (1980) provide a somewhat dated but informative overview of this area.

In addition to the ethical guidelines provided by professional organizations, the numerous legal statutes, and the organizations within which I/O psychologists work, numerous individuals have published ideas and research relating to ethics in the I/O environment (Saal and Knight, 1988). It was surprising, therefore, to find that the 1990 special issue of the *American Psychologist* which focused on organizational psychology contained no articles about ethics, standards, or legal issues (Offermann and Gowing, 1990).

Ethics and Organizational Behavior Management

With roots in philosophy, psychology, business, behavior analysis, and I/O psychology, OBM psychologists have a vast array of ethical principles to draw upon. It is tempting at this point to try to identify a small set of principles that could serve as guideposts for OBM practitioners. There are many ways to approach this task. For example, Berthold (1982) used a type of critical incident technique to generate six principles OBM practitioners could follow to avoid some of the difficulties that arose when behavioral methods were applied to other areas. Clark and Lattal (1993) opted instead for a process approach based on moral pluralism. They identified four basic values that should be weighed and balanced in arriving at ethical decisions in the workplace. The values were (1) rights: All people deserve equal rights because all people are equally valuable; (2) justice: Those in greatest need should receive the greatest help; (3) the common good: The good of all human kind should take precedence over the good of the few; and (4) self-interest: Each person must try to meet his or her own needs. Rather than debating the relative merits of these and other approaches, I will use the remaining space to discuss a far more serious issue pertaining to ethics and OBM.

Professor Fisher, a management professor at Franklin and Marshall College, had a habit of endlessly repeating principles he considered important. He uttered one more than all the others combined. It went something like this (with the expletives deleted): "It doesn't matter what the truth is; it only matters what people think the truth is!" Bypassing the issue of the ethicality of the statement itself, most would agree that even if OBM practitioners followed impeccable ethical standards, if people involved in the decision to adopt or use OBM principles viewed them as unethical, then the likelihood of adoption would be greatly reduced.

In the absence of universally agreed-upon ethical principles, such factors as culture (the aggregate of learned principles in a society), individual learning histories, and current contingencies are likely to govern what is considered ethically correct and what will be used. Homme and Tosti (1971) brought this point home in a powerful fashion. They noted how Skinner was laughed out of the room by a group of military strategists after demonstrating a pigeon's ability to guide a rocket to an intended target. They also described two cases in which management was horrified that someone would suggest using pigeons in quality control, even though the pigeons did demonstrably better than humans. Goddard had all the knowledge necessary to send a rocket into space, but his ideas were rejected and overlooked until the Russians put the first satellite into orbit. It was not the scientific knowledge or technology that was lacking; it was the absence of positive consequences accruing to the acceptance and use of what was known.

OBM would appear to be in a similar situation. Although this book contains numerous examples of situations where OBM has been used, the question remains: With successes such as these, why isn't OBM used more often? No doubt, there are numerous answers, but one answer has to be the way behavioral methods are viewed by people outside the field. These views reflect people's cultural history, just as they did when people laughed at Skinner and ignored Goddard. An OB textbook illustrates the persistence of the problem. After citing several OBM successes, Robbins (1993) ends the section with a series of questions relating to whether OBM techniques are ethical. He concludes, "There are no easy answers to questions like these" (p. 254).

In discussing such matters, behavior analysts often utilize the term "acceptability," because "acceptability" is more easily operationally defined than terms such as "image," or phrases such as "what people think is true." If one were to take an extreme relativistic stance, then acceptability might be considered an operational definition of ethics as well. At the very least, acceptability is related to ethics and the issue of the way that behavioral methods are viewed by potential users.

Turco and Elliott (1986) credit Wolf (1978) with first discussing intervention (treatment) acceptability in terms of social validity of applied behavior analysis. Providing a theoretical base such as social validity for work in an area such as treatment acceptability has enormous heuristic value because it ties together areas and prompts research hypotheses. Earlier writers had studied the issue, but in a more isolated context. For example, Frey (1974), Musgrove (1974), and Throll and Ryan (1976) measured schoolteachers' knowledge and attitudes toward behavior modification. Woolfolk, Woolfolk, and Wilson (1977) studied students who rated behavior modification procedures less acceptable than procedures described as "humanistic" or "affective education."

Kazdin (1980) provided excellent statements on the importance of the acceptability issue, and developed two scales for measuring treatment acceptability. One utilized a Likert-type format and the other used the semantic differential by Osgood, Suci, and Tannenbaum (1957). Kazdin's scales have been used in numerous studies on acceptability (e.g., Kazdin, 1981, 1984; Kazdin and Cole, 1981; Singh and Katz, 1985; Singh, Watson, and Winton, 1987). These studies have focused primarily upon the use of behavioral techniques in the treatment of children with behavioral problems, most often in institutional or clinic settings.

Stephen Elliott and Joseph Witt developed an instrument which they used to measure intervention acceptability, primarily in classroom and educational settings (Turco and Elliott, 1986; Witt and Elliott, 1985). Elliott (1988) provided an informative review of the treatment acceptability literature, including a table that summarizes important aspects of the cited studies. Elliott (1986) is a good source of information about Kazdin's Treatment Evaluation Inventory and Witt and Elliott's Children's Intervention Rating Profile.

The information provided by the acceptability/social validity literature is valuable as a model for research that should be done in OBM. Some evidence exists that these results may generalize to the I/O setting. Dubno et al. (1978) developed a scale to assess attitudes toward behavior modification utilizing a hypothetical management situation that was psychometrically tested on a sample of 252 graduate business students. More work needs to be done at this level of sophistication. Berthold (1983) reported a series of less formal studies which also suggest that findings involving educational and clinical settings might generalize to I/O settings. Disturbed by animosity from colleagues toward his adherence to the behavioral approach and reports such as those by Turkat and Feuerstein (1978) documenting the negative image of behavior modification in articles in *The New York Times,* Berthold (1983) and several of his students studied attitudes toward OBM. Their techniques varied. Chris Ivanoff asked students which of two lists of terms seemed more ethical. A list of words from the glossary of the book *Organizational Behavior Modification* by Luthans and Kreitner (1975) and a list from a more traditional management text by Elbing (1978) were used. Bill Vadinsky performed a similar study with paired titles from readings in the Elbing (1978) text and titles from readings in the OBM text by O'Brien, Dickinson, and Rosow (1982). These and other studies showed that undergraduates consistently rated behavioral words, techniques, and readings as less ethical, interesting, and desirable than nonbehavioral words, techniques, and readings.

Two other studies refined and extended the initial research (Berthold, 1983). In a five-part experiment, Debbie Cardinale questioned approximately equal numbers of managers and workers in a large fabric dyeing plant and others in small retail establishments in Lewisburg, Pennsylvania. In addition to confirming the results from college students, Cardinale found that the businesspeople were confused about what behavioral terminology meant, and were not very interested in finding out. She found no statistically significant differences between managers and workers or between factory and retail environments. Daniel Murray pursued the relationship between familiarity and acceptability of behavioral terms and methods. He found a statistically significant relationship between the two, a finding that was consistent with an earlier study by Young and Patterson (1981) on college students and faculty.

The aforementioned studies suggest a challenge for those involved in OBM. The challenge is not new. In an article for *Newsday* back in 1978, B. F. Skinner asked, "Why aren't we using science to change behavior?" Wolpe expressed a similar concern in a 1981 article in the *American Psychologist*. Like the businesspeople in Cardinale's study, he found that despite its demonstrated superiority over the traditional technique (psychoanalysis in this case), only 25 percent of the psychiatrists at an American Psychiatric Association meeting claimed to know anything about behavior modification.

Is there a way to help ensure that OBM programs not only are ethical, but appear to be ethical as well? The research points to two causal elements that could be used to solve the problem. One has to do with level of knowledge about OBM and the other with behavioral terminology per se.

Level of Knowledge

Woolfolk and Woolfolk (1979) reported one of the first attempts to improve acceptability through enhanced knowledge by documenting behavior modification's efficacy and popularity. They met with little success. Likewise, Kazdin (1981) found that the effectiveness of treatments in altering behavior did not influence acceptability ratings.

On the other hand, Kazdin (1984) found that aversive procedures and medication were rated more acceptable when they had more marked effects than when they had weaker effects. Moreover, Kreitner (1981) found that managers did not react negatively toward behavioral terms provided the techniques worked. The mixed results suggest that telling people how well behavioral techniques work may or may not improve acceptability. The effectiveness of this approach may depend upon interacting variables such as actually witnessing a successful application or increasing the importance of using effective techniques. Just as the Russian space program advanced Goddard's standing, so too might global economic competition advance OBM.

Rather than presenting information on efficacy, another strategy is to teach the behavioral techniques themselves. Singh and Katz (1985) obtained acceptability ratings for several behavioral and humanistic techniques involving treatment of children and then presented lectures on the behavioral techniques to the undergraduate subjects. A posttest showed significant increases in ratings for the behavioral approaches and decreases in ratings for the humanistic techniques even though the humanistic techniques were not discussed.

Although the results are somewhat mixed, direct tests of the hypothesis that increased knowledge about OBM would improve acceptability are clearly warranted. If the relationship is found to hold, then OBM psychologists would have an important tool for not only improving people's evaluations of OBM's ethical standards, but also increasing the likelihood of OBM being used in I/O settings.

Behavioral Terminology

In addition to educating people about behavioral *methods,* particularly the reinforcement techniques advocated by OBM proponents, the studies cited in this chapter also demonstrate a need to give serious consideration to reactions to behavioral *terminology.* Spiegler (1983) suggested that behaviorists simply use operational definitions when talking with clients, telling them in concrete terms what will be done without reference to theoretical principles and the accompanying jargon. Kazdin and Cole (1981) showed that operationalizing terminology might not be enough. They separated out the impact of the label (behavior modification), content of the procedure, and jargon used to describe the procedures. Results showed that the label did not produce large negative evaluations; rather, undergraduates found the procedure itself unacceptable. Moreover, the behavioral jargon actually improved the negative evaluations somewhat.

More important than the language used when we apply behavior modification may be the language used when we talk *about* behavior modification. Krasner (1976) noted that behaviorists had allowed writers to establish a dichotomy between behaviorism and humanism which conveyed the impression that behaviorists are not as concerned about people per se as humanists. Bevan (1982) stated ". . . I believe that if we are to achieve a balanced national life, we must somehow reconcile our needs for a technology based on science with those for a humanely inspired culture" (p. 1304). According to Offerman and Gowing (1990), I/O psychologists need more than scientific expertise and publications describing successful programs to persuade organizations to adopt their methods. "In garnering support for our activities, I/O psychologists need to be able to speak the language of business" (p. 104).

In business, that language will often be bottom-line dollars and cents, with little emotional content. At other times, however, even in the business world, the emotional correlates of language produced through higher order conditioning become important. Nonbehaviorists have made effective use of terms that have acquired positive associations through everyday usage; Behaviorists have not in many instances. But behaviorists can use the same language as the nonbehaviorists in describing their concern for people and their ideals. Utilizing this language might prompt people to learn and use behavioristic language more effectively.

Laws governing human behavior continue to operate whether or not they are known or accurately stated. Parsons (1992) convincingly demonstrated that the classic Hawthorne studies followed an OBM paradigm, but the research was not originally conceived or interpreted in this manner. Indeed, so many different explanations were used to account for the results that Parsons (1978) dubbed the Hawthorne studies ". . . the biggest Rorschach blot in the history of behavioral and social science" (p. 261).

Laws may be objective statements of reality, but people's reactions to their disclosure may not be at all objective, as Galileo and numerous other scientists could testify. Politicians employ "spin doctors" to rephrase policies, programs, and actions (behaviors) into a language that may be very different from how they were conceived so as to evoke a positive reaction from the general public.

Money is a powerful reinforcer. Nevertheless, behaviorists who have used money in educational, institutional, and private settings have sometimes been criticized for giving "bribes." This would be less of a concern in business, where money has always been viewed as an appropriate motivator. But other concerns can emerge. Money may seem an entitlement to people accustomed to a noncontingent relationship between pay and work. Changing a system so that money becomes contingent on performance can lead to protests and grievances. Careful analysis would show that the primary issue is not whether pay-for-performance contingencies are ethical, but whether changing the system of payment is ethical, no matter how superior the new system. As a start, employees must be convinced that the performance goals are realistic and that they will have the necessary resources to succeed. But there will be an important language component as well. The reinforcing value of a monetary contingency might differ if it is introduced as "an exciting new way to earn some extra cash" rather than as a "reinforcer." However helpful our language and knowledge is in designing an OBM program, we must realize that if we introduce that language into the implementation stage, it becomes one of the factors that will affect the outcome of the program.

CONCLUSION: OBM AND ETHICS

A limited number of attempts have been made to identify specific ethical principles for OBM (e.g. Berthold, 1982; Clark and Lattal, 1993). Perhaps it is time for members of a national or international organization interested in OBM to attempt to devise a set of ethical standards. On the other hand, there is little ambiguity in the way guidelines from associated fields generalize to the OBM environment, and there seems to be little evidence of unethical behavior by OBM psychologists. Positive reinforcement, praise, feedback, etc. would seem preferable to the aversive control procedures commonly used in I/O settings. As Clark and Lattal (1993) note, OBM provides the best method for improving the current ethical climate in business.

Of greater immediate concern is an apparent discrepancy between actual ethics and perceived ethics (acceptability). Many researchers have recognized the importance of acceptability. Kazdin (1980), for example, stated: "Improving the overall acceptability may increase the likelihood that treatment is sought, initiated, and adhered to once it is initiated" (p. 330). A similar situation may well pertain to OBM programs. If so, we need to increase our efforts to educate businesspeople, and indeed all people, about principles of behavior analysis. While assumptions of external rather than internal control and unfamiliar terminology present obstacles to acceptance, other aspects of OBM work in its favor. Positive reinforcement, after all, is something people find desirable. Finding and providing contingent positive reinforcers has great potential for being interpreted as an ethical activity. In evaluating OBM programs, it is important to measure not only productivity, but such factors as job satisfaction and job involvement as well. Finally, OBM psychologists need to increase their usage of not only the language of business, but language that conveys the concern we most certainly share with practitioners of other approaches for doing the best and most ethical job we can toward the ultimate goal of ensuring the most productive and, yes, we should be willing to say it, the most humane, fair, and personally enriching work environment possible.

REFERENCES

American Psychological Association. (1953). *Ethical standards of psychologists.* Washington, DC: Author.

American Psychological Association. (1977). *Standards for providers of psychological services* (Revised edition). Washington, DC: Author.

American Psychological Association. (1981). Specialty guidelines for the delivery of services by industrial/organizational psychologists. *American Psychologist, 36,* 664-669.

American Psychological Association. (1992). Ethical principles of psychologists and code of conduct. *American Psychologist, 47,* 1597-1611.

Association for Advancement of Behavior Therapy. (1977). Ethical issues for human services. *Behavior Therapy, 8,* v-vi.

Beauchamp, T. L. and Bowie, N. E. (1993). *Ethical theory and business* (Fourth edition). Englewood Cliffs, NJ: Prentice-Hall.

Berthold, H. C. (1982). Behavior modification in the industrial/organizational environment: Assumptions and ethics. In R. M. O'Brien, A. M. Dickinson, and M. P. Rosow (Eds.), *Industrial behavior modification: A management handbook* (pp. 405-427). New York: Pergamon Press.

Berthold, H. C. (1983). *Behavioranalysisphobia: The current image of behavior analysis.* Paper presented at the meeting of the Association for Behavior Analysis, Milwaukee, WI, May.

Bevan, W. (1982). A sermon of sorts in three plus parts. *American Psychologist, 37,* 1303-1322.

Blanchard, K. and Peale, N. V. (1988). *The power of ethical management.* New York: William Morrow and Company.

Brown, A. B. (1992). Politics and psychology: A personal journey. *The Pennsylvania Psychologist Quarterly, 52*(5), 2, 20.

Carroll, M. A., Schneider, H. G., and Wesley, G. R. (1985). *Ethics in the practice of psychology.* Englewood Cliffs, NJ: Prentice-Hall.

Clark, R. W. and Lattal, A. D. (1993). *Workplace ethics: Winning the integrity revolution.* Lanham, MD: Rowman and Littlefield.

Corey, G., Corey, M. S., and Callanan, P. (1988). *Issues and ethics in the helping professions* (Third edition). Pacific Grove, CA: Brooks/Cole.

DeWall, T. H. (1992). Sausages and laws. *The Pennsylvania Psychologist Quarterly, 52*(5), 3, 9.

Dreilinger, C. and Rice, D. (1991). Office ethics: Five common ethical dilemmas and how to resolve them. *Working Woman,* December, 35-39.

Dubno, P., Hillburn, D., Robinson, G., Sandler, D., Trani, J., and Weingarten, E. (1978). An attitude toward behavior modification scale. *Behavior Therapy, 9,* 99-108.

Elbing, A. O. (1978). *Behavioral decisions in organizations* (Second edition). Glenview, IL: Scott, Foresman and Co.

Elliott, S. N. (1986). Children's ratings of the acceptability of classroom interventions for misbehavior: Findings and methodological considerations. *Journal of School Psychology, 24,* 23-35.

Elliott, S. N. (1988). Acceptability of behavioral treatments: Review of variables that influence treatment selection. *Professional Psychology: Research and Practice, 19,* 68-80.

Fawcett, S. B., Bernstein, G. S., Czyzewski, M. J., Greene, B. F., Hannah, G. T., Iwata, B. A., Jason, L. A., Mathews, R. M., Morris, E. K., Otis-Wilborn, A., Seekins, T., and Winett, R. A. (1988). Behavior analysis and public policy. *The Behavior Analyst, 11,* 11-25.

Frey, S. H. (1974). Teachers and behavior modification. *Phi Delta Kappan, 55,* 634-635.

Harris, L. (1986). *Inside America.* New York: Vintage Books.

Harris, M. (1987). *Why nothing works: The anthropology of daily life.* New York: Simon and Schuster.

Homme, L. and Tosti, D. (1971). *Behavior technology: Motivation and contingency management.* San Rafael, CA: Individual Learning Systems, 1971.

Iannone, P. (1989). *Contemporary moral controversies in business.* New York: Oxford University Press.

Iwata, B. A. (1988). Task force on the right to effective behavioral treatment: Executive council liaison commentary. *The Behavior Analyst, 11,* 110.

Kazdin, A. E. (1980). Acceptability of time out from reinforcement procedures for disruptive child behavior. *Behavior Therapy, 11,* 329-344.

Kazdin, A. E. (1981). Acceptability of child treatment techniques: The influence of treatment efficacy and adverse side effects. *Behavior Therapy, 12,* 493-506.

Kazdin, A. E. (1984). Acceptability of aversive procedures and medication as treatment alternatives for deviant child behavior. *Journal of Abnormal Child Psychology, 2,* 289-302.

Kazdin, A. E. and Cole, P. M. (1981). Attitudes and labeling biases toward behavior modification: The effects of labels, content, and jargon. *Behavior Therapy, 12,* 56-68.

Keith-Spiegel, P. and Koocher, G. P. (1985). *Ethics in psychology: Professional standards and cases.* Hillsdale, NJ: Lawrence Erlbaum Associates, Inc.

Klemke, E. E., Kline, A. D., and Hollinger, R. (Eds.). (1986). *Philosophy: The basic issues* (Second edition). New York: St. Martin's Press.

Krasner, L. (1976). Behavior modification: Ethical issues and future trends. In H. Leitenberg (Ed.), *Handbook of behavior modification and behavior therapy* (pp. 627-649). Englewood Cliffs, NJ: Prentice-Hall.

Kreitner, R. (1981). Managerial reaction to the term behavior modification. *Journal of Organizational Behavior Management, 3,* 53-58.

Liebig, J. (1990). *Business ethics: Profiles in civic virtue.* Golden, CO: Fulcrum Publishing.

London, M. and Bray, D. W. (1980). Ethical issues in testing and evaluation for personnel decisions. *American Psychologist, 35,* 890-901.

Luthans, R. and Kreitner, R. (1975). *Organizational behavior modification.* Glenview, IL: Scott, Foresman and Co.

Macklin, R. (1982). *Man, mind, and morality: The ethics of behavior control.* Englewood Cliffs, NJ: Prentice-Hall.

Madsen, P. and Shafritz, J. M. (1990). *Essentials of business ethics.* New York: Meridian Books.

Mawhinney, T. C. (1984). Philosophical and ethical aspects of organizational behavior management: Some evaluative feedback. *Journal of Organizational Behavior Management, 6*(1), 5-31.

Musgrove, W. J. (1974). A scale to measure attitudes toward behavior modification. *Psychology in the Schools, 11,* 392-396.

O'Brien, R. M., Dickinson, A. M., and Rosow, M. P. (Eds.). (1982). *Industrial behavior modification: A management handbook.* New York: Pergamon Press.

Offermann, L. R. and Gowing, M. K. (Eds.). (1990). Organizational psychology (Special issue). *American Psychologist, 45*(2).

Osgood, C. E., Suci, G. J., and Tannenbaum, P. H. (1957). *Measurement of meaning.* Urbana, IL: University of Illinois Press.

Parsons, H. M. (1978). What caused the Hawthorne effect?: A scientific detective story. *Administration and Society, 10,* 259-283.

Parsons, H. M. (1992). Hawthorne: An early OBM experiment. *Journal of Organizational Behavior Management, 12*(1), 27-43.

Randall, D. M. and Gibson, A. M. (1990). Methodology in business ethics research: A review and critical assessment. *Journal of Business Ethics, 9,* 457-471.

Robbins, S. P. (1993). *Organizational behavior* (Sixth edition). Englewood Cliffs, NJ: Prentice-Hall.

Saal, F. E. and Knight, P. A. (1988). *Industrial/organizational psychology: Science and practice.* Belmont, CA: Wadsworth.

Sarason, S. B. (1984). If it can be studied or developed, should it be? *American Psychologist, 39,* 477-485.

Sieber, J. E. and Stanley, B. (1988). Ethical and professional dimensions of socially sensitive research. *American Psychologist, 43,* 49-55.

Singh, N. N. and Katz, R. C. (1985). On the modification of acceptability ratings for alternative child treatments. *Behavior Modification, 9,* 375-386.

Singh, N. N., Watson, J. E., and Winton, A. S. W. (1987). Parents' acceptability ratings of alternative treatments for use with mentally retarded children. *Behavior Modification, 11,* 17-26.

Skinner, B. F. (1971). *Beyond freedom and dignity.* New York: Knopf.

Skinner, B. F. (1978). Why aren't we using science to change behavior? *Newsday,* April 16, Ideas Section, pp. 5, 12.

Sneed, R. J. and Chavis, P. (1992). Working with legislators: Beyond the mystique. *The Pennsylvania Psychologist Quarterly, 52*(5), 10.

Society for Industrial and Organizational Psychology, Inc. (1983). Bylaws. *The Industrial-Organizational Psychologist, 20*(2), 67-77.

Society for Industrial and Organizational Psychology, Inc. (1987). *Principles for the validation and use of personnel selection procedures* (Third edition). College Park, MD: Author.

Spiegler, M. D. (1983). *Contemporary behavioral therapy.* Palo Alto, CA: Mayfield.

Stein, R. H. (1990). *Ethical issues in counseling.* Buffalo, NY: Prometheus Books.

Steininger, M., Newell, J. D., and Garcia, L. T. (1984). *Ethical issues in psychology.* Homewood, IL: Dorsey.

Stolz, S. B. and associates. (1978). *Ethical issues in behavior modification.* San Francisco: Jossey-Bass.

Strike, A. K. and Soltis, F. J. (1985). *The ethics of teaching.* New York: Teachers College Press.

Throll, D. and Ryan, B. A. (1976). Research note: Teacher attitudes toward behavior modification. *New Zealand Journal of Educational Studies, 11,* 68-71.

Turco, T. L. and Elliott, S. N. (1986). Students' acceptability ratings of interventions for classroom misbehaviors: A study of well-behaving and misbehaving youth. *Journal of Psychoeducational Assessment, 4,* 281-289.

Turkat, I. D. and Feuerstein, M. (1978). Behavior modification and the public misconception. *American Psychologist, 33,* 194.

Van Houten, R., Axelrod, S., Bailey, J. S., Favell, J. E., Foxx, R. M., Iwata, B. A., and Lovaas, O. I. (1988). The right to effective behavioral treatment. *The Behavior Analyst, 11,* 111-114.

Witt, J. C. and Elliott, S. N. (1985). Acceptability of classroom management strategies. In T. R. Kratochwill (Ed.), *Advances in school psychology* (Vol. 4, pp. 251-288). Hillsdale, NJ: Lawrence Erlbaum.

Wolf, M. M. (1978). Social validity: The case for subjective measurement or how applied behavior analysis is finding its heart. *Journal of Applied Behavior Analysis, 11,* 203-214.

Wolpe, J. (1981). Behavior therapy versus psychoanalysis: Therapeutic and social implications. *American Psychologist, 36,* 159-164.

Woolfolk, A. E., Woolfolk, R. L., and Wilson, T. (1977). A rose by any other name . . . : Labeling bias and attitudes toward behavior modification. *Journal of Consulting and Clinical Psychology, 45,* 184-191.

Woolfolk, R. L. and Woolfolk, A. E. (1979). Modifying the effect of the behavior modification label. *Behavior Therapy, 10,* 575-578.

Young, L. D. and Patterson, J. N. (1981). Information and opinions about behavior modification. *Journal of Behavior Therapy and Experimental Psychiatry, 12,* 189-196.

Chapter 17

Organizational Culture
and Behavioral Systems Analysis

William K. Redmon
Matthew A. Mason

OVERVIEW

Management gurus forecast dramatic changes in the goals and structures of private and public organizations in the United States (Block, 1993; Drucker, 1991; Hammer and Champy, 1993; Peters, 1992). In the private sector, changes are predicted as a result of increased competition in the global marketplace. These changes are likely to focus more attention on customer needs and, in turn, lead to changes in organizational structure and practices (Peters, 1992). In the public sector, tighter budgets and a deteriorating infrastructure promise to increase pressure on government to be more responsive to citizen needs and more efficient in spending tax dollars (Osborne and Gaebler, 1992). As a result of these trends, more effective methodologies for organizational culture change will be needed to permit alteration of large-scale practices and to facilitate rapid response to threats to survival.

This chapter presents a methodology for analysis of organizational cultures. It is the purpose of this chapter to (1) describe how organizational cultures can be defined in functional terms; (2) provide a model for describing, analyzing, and changing cultural practices; and (3) describe methods of strengthening and supporting effective practices when desirable outcomes are known and a technology of performance management has been mastered.

THEORETICAL MODELS
OF ORGANIZATIONAL CULTURE

An organization's culture can be characterized in terms of the dominant practices of its members and a description of the causes of these practices.

437

Thus, a model of cultural change should include methods of observing and describing what is done and techniques for identifying variables that influence what is done. Two contrasting theoretical models have been described in the literature: the cultural materialist view (Harris, 1979) and the cognitive view (Huse and Cummings, 1990). The materialist view focuses on the effects of cultural practices on the environment (e.g., production, reproduction): practices that are effective in gaining resources or offsetting threats are repeated, whereas those which are ineffective in producing survival-related outcomes occur less often and eventually disappear. According to Harris (1979), cultural practices are learned behaviors that can be transmitted from one group to another or one generation to another independent of genetics. Within this framework, similar environmental demands should lead to development of similar practices. The materialist view is compatible with a natural science view of culture (Pierce, 1991; Skinner, 1953). At the individual level, the natural science view holds that changes in consequences (i.e., reinforcement and punishment) must occur to change practices and ultimately to shift the probability of survival of a group.

The cognitive view holds that culture stems from beliefs, values, expectations, and other constructs which influence the organization's practices. Thus, change in cultures requires change in cognitive constructs that mediate environmental influences on practices. This view is well illustrated by Schein (1990), who maintains that the feelings, values, and behaviors which make up cultural practices are ultimately determined by perceptions, language, and thought processes that a group comes to share. Accordingly, recent cognitive studies have focused on descriptions of the content of culture (Schneider, Wheeler, and Cox, 1992), and correlations between changes in beliefs, values, and other constructs and the practices of culture members (Burke, Borucki, and Hurley, 1992).

Probably the most well-known of the cognitive definitions is that of Deal and Kennedy (1982), which says that culture is a function of shared values and beliefs of the organization's members. Thus, members work to achieve valued end states and engage in practices that they believe will be most likely to achieve such end states. The principle sources of beliefs are statements by individual organizational members (especially top management), and beliefs and values are selected based on their effects on organizational success (e.g., solving problems, reaching major objectives) (Reidenbach and Robin, 1991).

At present, neither the materialist nor the cognitive model has led to a systematic methodology for change, and science is lagging behind the needs of organizations (Eubanks and Lloyd, 1992). As a result, many have entered into change programs with little guidance and, in some cases, damaging effects. A practical change model is needed to provide guidance for management in identifying changes in the marketplace and facilitating adaptive responses when a change in market factors is discerned. Certainly, a change in the stated mission of an organization is important in changing strategies and practices, but this is not enough. Pervasive change in individual performance patterns is required to instill a new culture throughout a transformed organization. Only when critical practices are shifted to the point that adaptive outcomes are more likely can a culture be said to have been changed successfully.

ORGANIZATIONAL CULTURES:
A BEHAVIORAL VIEW

In the past decade, operant scientists have begun to devise ways of studying cultures (e.g., Lamal, 1991a; Malagodi and Jackson, 1989) and have considered how societal practices might be analyzed (Lamal, 1991b). This work has focused on strategies that combine methods from anthropology and behavior analysis and suggests methods of analyzing and explaining how cultures change and how cultural practices are selected over time (Glenn, 1988, 1991; Malott, 1988; Mawhinney, 1992a). Methods also have been suggested for the study of relatively limited organizational cultures (Eubanks and Lloyd, 1992; Mawhinney, 1992b; Sulzer-Azaroff, Pollack, and Fleming, 1992).

At the most general level, an organization's culture can be analyzed in terms of three components: outcomes important to survival, practices of organizational members, and linkages between outcomes and practices. Outcomes refer to accomplishments necessary to succeed given the demands of the external environment. Practices refer to behaviors emitted by organizational members on a recurring basis. Linkages refer to methods of management which, under ideal conditions, ensure that practices are correlated with desirable outcomes. Ineffective cultures include practices which, in large proportion, interfere with or fail to contribute to important outcomes, whereas effective cultures are dominated by practices that contribute to adaptive outcomes (i.e., those which satisfy or alter the demands of the external environment).

One responsibility of management involves monitoring external demands and setting conditions within an organization to produce and support adaptive practices. According to this view, organizations are more likely to survive when external demands are monitored closely and when adaptive responses to environmental changes by decision makers are rewarded (Mawhinney, 1992a). Traditionally, it has been the role of middle management to communicate changing demands from the outside to organizational members inside and design incentive systems that reward effective practices and weaken ineffective ones. In this sense, managers can be characterized as cultural designers or planners who ensure that relatively remote influences (e.g., competition from abroad) are transformed into immediate influences that increase the adaptive nature of responses (Malott, 1988). In many organizations, this middle management function has been assumed by cross-functional teams that react to customer needs and collaborate with top management to solve problems (Scholtes, 1988).

It should also be noted here that management may act to change external demands through a variety of strategies. For example, organizations might alter consumer choices by developing new products or services or influence government regulations (e.g., safety requirements) by lobbying Congress. This approach, however, does not eliminate the need to adapt to the requirements of the consumer or the government by arranging for appropriate performance by organization members. The fact that the demands of consumers were initiated by an organization may make it more likely that the organization will survive in an immediate sense, but once the standards are set (by whatever means), responsiveness within the organization is critical to continuing success. It is important to understand that management is capable of setting expectations which cannot be met by its own workers. This is especially true if linkages among levels within an organization are weak or communication is confusing or absent; in such cases, what management does may have little effect on the routine performances of individual organizational members.

Adaptation to changing environments across organizations can be analyzed in terms of metacontingencies (Glenn, 1988, 1991). A metacontingency describes how classes of practices common to a group are related to molar consequences and refers to collective practices that determine the survival of a group as a whole. Metacontingencies operate concurrently with local contingencies that affect the practices of individuals or subgroups and may be compatible with or in conflict with local contingencies. In the case of a metacontingency, if the practices of large numbers of members of a culture lead to adaptation to the environment and survival, then the practices that succeeded are likely to be passed on to other members and perpetuated. Thus, for example, in cultures where a drought results in crop failure, those who discover other ways of obtaining food quickly ensure their own survival and live to tell others about their strategies. The same may be said for organizations in general. When the demands of the marketplace change, practices must shift. If they do not, failed practices are not likely to be remembered nor repeated. For example, few would hold up the practices of the now defunct American Motors as exemplary; instead, strategies used by Ford or Chrysler are studied and written about as successful and potentially useful for others who want to survive difficult times.

BEHAVIORAL SYSTEMS MODELS

Existing operant models of culture are general, theoretical, and concerned with selection patterns that cut across organizations more than practices within a single organization (Glenn, 1991). Although the metacontingency concept has been applied to explain the survival of a single organization (Redmon and Agnew, 1991; Redmon and Wilk, 1991), it has more often been used to explain how people or organizations in general survive in a competitive environment. A more detailed analysis is needed to occasion the design of effective organizational practices and to provide a method of solving organizational problems to increase adaptive responses in the short run. Selection is not sufficient to guide a single organization's strategy; direct action must be arranged on a short-term basis to achieve outcomes assumed to be correlated with ultimate survival.

Behavioral systems models supplement metacontingency analyses by offering a means of analyzing events that make up existing organizational cultures and suggesting strategies for change within a single organization (Brethower, 1982; Krapfl and Gasparotto, 1982; Redmon and Wilk, 1991; Rummler and Brache, 1995). According to Malott and Garcia (1987),

> . . . behavioral systems analysis is an effort to use a systems analysis approach to analyze the ultimate objectives of an organization; then to determine the manner in which the various components of the organization contribute or fail to contribute to the accomplishments of that organization—its ultimate objectives; and finally behavioral systems analysis involves the use of behavior analysis in the design of improved organizational environments to help the individuals and groups in the organization perform in such a manner that their components of the organization will contribute more effectively to the ultimate objectives of that organization (cf. Malott, 1974). (pp. 134-135)

Several behavioral systems models have been used in practice, including the performance engineering matrix (PEM) (Gilbert, 1978), the total performance system (TPS) (Brethower, 1982), and the adaptive systems model (Rummler and Brache, 1995). All of these models describe organizations in terms of (1) survival-related outcomes, (2) practices of organizational members (which may or may not be correlated with survival), (3) linkages between outcomes and practices, and (4) factors that strengthen or weaken individual practices in an immediate sense. Behavioral systems models, however, go beyond description; they provide rules for determining whether practices should be changed and suggest methods for controlling environmental conditions to alter practices. The major steps in a systems analysis are described in the following sections.

Step 1: Adaptive System Description

The first step in applying a systems analysis involves description of the functional elements of an organization including the following:

1. Inputs (e.g., raw materials)
2. A process that converts inputs into outputs (e.g., products, services)
3. A receiving system that consumes the outputs (e.g. customers in a store)
4. Internal feedback that guides the process prior to output (e.g., quality control data)
5. Feedback from the receiving system to calibrate internal criteria and communicate changing market needs (e.g., sales data)
6. Factors external to the system (i.e., in the environment) that influence the effectiveness and efficiency of system elements (e.g., competition, government regulations)

Figure 17.1 depicts these components and the relationships among them.

Description of a system prompts identification of important environmental factors that affect an organization's survival and the major components of an organization's structure. This step is completed by collecting information in interviews or group meetings with organization members of all levels and reviewing policies and other written documents (e.g., annual reports). System description is complete when an adaptive systems diagram (see Figure 17.1) has been filled in to the satisfaction of systems analysts and key organization personnel. A guide for questioning in this initial step has been suggested by Smith and Chase (1990) in the form of the Vantage Analysis Chart, which provides sample questions at all levels from philosophy to day-to-day logistics.

Step 2: Internal Analysis

The second step of a systems analysis focuses on internal resources and strategies and requires a description of organizational goals, processes, and

FIGURE 17.1. Diagram of the General Adaptive Systems Model

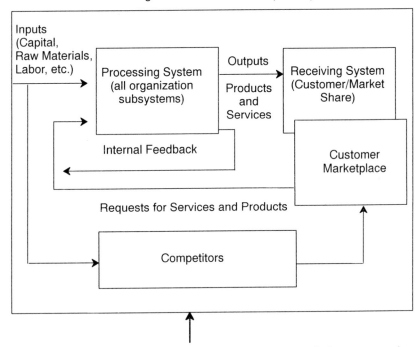

Other influences from the environment (government regulations, economic conditions, social and cultural requirements, etc.)

Source: Based on Rummler and Brache (1995).

jobs (Rummler and Brache, 1995). This information is contained in the processing system of the adaptive systems model depicted in Figure 17.1. Step 2 begins with statement of the organization's mission (i.e., the single most critical goal), which specifies outcomes designed to satisfy marketplace criteria. The mission is then translated into subgoals or strategy objectives that often are associated with working groups such as departments, units, or teams of employees (e.g., marketing, finance, etc.). Finally, individual performance outcomes needed to achieve subgoals (e.g., job descriptions) are stated. This three-level framework arranges the important elements of an organization such that the performances of individuals are linked to subgoals at the strategy level, and subgoals are linked to the mission.

Several different tools have been proposed for analysis of internal system elements. In a recent treatment of this topic, Rummler and Brache (1995) used a three-level analysis that integrates organization, work processes, and jobs/performers. This approach is based on a nine-cell matrix that lists three performance levels on one dimension (i.e., organization, processes, job/performer) and three types of performance needs for each level on a second dimension (i.e., goals, design, and management). The result is a matrix like that depicted in Figure 17.2, Panel A. *Goals* at each level state standards that ultimately reflect customer expectations; *design* involves specification of a structure which ensures that goals will be met; and *management* ensures that goals are relevant, sufficient resources are allocated, and progress toward goals is maintained.

Rummler and Brache (1995) recommend the use of specific design tools for analyzing activities at the upper two levels. At the organization level, a *relationship map* is completed to depict the customer-supplier relationships within an organization and to show how inputs move through a complete process to become services or products delivered to the customer. At the process level, a *process map* is completed to show how each set of work steps transforms inputs to outputs. The process map elaborates each of the functions depicted in the relationship map. For example, in a relationship map, the connections among major departments or units might be depicted (e.g., sales submits order to finance, which arranges for products from manufacturing), whereas at the process level, each of the elements of the relationship map would be further elaborated into detailed procedural steps (e.g., within sales, a field representative contacts a customer and writes up the order, the order is submitted to computer entry, computer clerks type in all relevant information and alert billing, and billing clerks check the order for completeness and submit it to finance for a credit check). At the job/performer level, job requirements are specified to ensure that all critical process steps are assigned and that task-level goals are set properly. This is typically accomplished by writing realistic and relevant job descriptions and setting individual performance goals.

Rummler and Brache (1995) believe that intense focus on processes will maximize the chances of finding and changing factors critical to the success of an organization. In this regard, they stated:

> In our experience, *the greatest opportunities for performance improvement often lie in the functional interfaces—those points at which the baton (for example, "production specs") is being passed from one department to another.* Examples of key interfaces include the passing of new product ideas from Marketing to Research and Development, the handoff of a new product from Research and Development to Manufacturing, and the transfer of customer billing information from sales to finance. (p. 9)

FIGURE 17.2. Matrices That Depict Internal Systems Factors According to the Adaptive Systems Model (Panel A), the Performance Engineering Matrix (Panel B), and a Depiction of the Behavior Engineering Matrix (Panel C)

Panel A: Nine-Celled Table (Rummler and Brache, 1995)

Performance Needs

Performance Levels	Goals	Design	Management
Organization Level			
Process Level			
Job/Performer Level			

Panel B: Performance Engineering Matrix (Gilbert, 1978)

Stages of Analysis

Vantage Levels	Models	Measures	Methods
Policy			
Strategy			
Tactics			

Panel C: Behavior Engineering Matrix (Gilbert, 1978)

	Information	**Instrumentation**	**Motivation**
Environmental Supports	Data	Instruments (tools)	Incentives
Person's Repertoire	Knowledge	Capacity	Motives

Step 3: Individual Performance Analysis

At the job/performer level, the performances of individuals on a day-to-day and moment-to-moment basis are described and conditions are arranged to support individual and small-group performance. Great care must be taken to be sure that job standards are linked to subgoals and, ultimately, to customer criteria. At this level, Rummler and Brache recommend that attention be given to outputs (clear and attainable performance standards), input (adequacy of resources, job procedures, clarity of onset of input), consequences (timeliness, effectiveness, support for appropriate performances), feedback (information received by performers about their performances), knowledge/skill (previous learning and experience, knowledge of importance of required performance), and capacities of the worker (physical, mental, and emotional factors that affect performance). Thus, if desired performance is not occurring, one should examine supporting and interfering conditions to identify factors to be changed. If a new set of tasks is to be added to existing jobs, one should examine the environment for supporting and interfering conditions in advance of implementation and make adjustments as necessary.

Other systems models have been described, most notably the performance engineering matrix (Gilbert, 1978). The full PEM includes six levels of vantage including philosophy, culture, policy, strategy, tactics, and logistics. The top two levels (philosophy and culture) refer to events outside the organization and within the marketplace and greater community; the last four levels refer to events within the organization and directed by management. In practice, Gilbert recommends use of a "simplified" PEM that includes only policy, strategy, and tactics. Gilbert's approach utilizes two dimensions; thus, for each of three levels from top to bottom, three stages of analysis are specified including models, measures, and methods. The resulting matrix consists of nine cells—three stages of analysis for each of three levels of vantage (see Figure 17.2, Panel B).

Gilbert suggests that a definition of the mission (policy models cell) be constructed first. After the mission is clear, subgoals should be specified to translate the mission into differentiated strategies (strategy models cell). Subsequently, specific tasks and duties included in individual jobs should be stated for each subgoal (tactics models cell). For each vantage level, measures of accomplishments also should be devised (measures column), and methods of managing progress toward objectives at each level should be developed (methods column).

At the tactics level in the methods cell, Gilbert considers methods for producing individual performances to support the organization's subgoals and mission. Here he recommends use of the behavior engineering matrix

(BEM) (see Figure 17.2, Panel C), which specifies conditions in the work environment and the history of the worker that should be examined to identify supporting and interfering conditions for desired performance. The BEM includes three general categories of factors (information, instrumentation, and motivation) for both the work environment and the person. Factors present in the environment are typically influenced by management or teams directly, whereas factors related to the worker's history can be influenced less directly through selection and placement methods or training of new skills. According to Gilbert, each cell of the BEM defines an important set of conditions for supporting worthy performance (i.e., performance that is valuable in terms of outputs which contribute to survival of the organization). For example, in the information environment cell, a manager or team members might provide clearer job standards and/or provide feedback to communicate the results of work already done. In the information person cell, personnel specialists might select a worker who has been trained in important job tasks or provide training to develop the repertoire of the person to better suit organization needs.

Step 4: Analytical Sequence

Both the adaptive systems and PEM models specify a sequence of steps involved in analyzing organization effectiveness. According to Rummler and Brache (1995), the following steps are critical: (1) description of overall goals, structure, and management at the organization level; (2) describing, prioritizing, and managing processes needed to achieve overall goals; and (3) setting job goals, designing jobs, and managing performance to support key processes. Gilbert (1978) recommends a troubleshooting sequence that begins with a review of accomplishments at the policy level and moves down through strategy-level outcomes to tactics, until individual behaviors correlated with higher level outcomes can be pinpointed. Once contributing behaviors are identified, the BEM can be used as a framework to guide changes in controlling conditions to affect individual performance.

The systems analysis models described above can be used as an analytical tool to examine and redesign existing systems (Jewell and Jewell, 1992), or as a guide for the design of future systems. In the first case, members of an organization can be interviewed and/or performance observed to describe controlling conditions and practices within the current culture. In such cases, missing elements can be identified and new components added to improve the chances of the organization's success. In other cases, organizational structures and functions can be designed before implementation (e.g., a small business startup). If outcomes are known or can be projected, strategies and supporting performances needed to achieve them can be described as part of a hypothetical situation.

Linking Levels for Maximum Benefit

Linkages among levels from top to bottom are critical to a successful system and to organizational culture design or change (Powers, 1992; Stolovitch and Keeps, 1992). The extent to which the performances of individuals will in fact be supportive of an adaptive outcome at the mission level is determined by the extent to which strong connections are arranged between practices and processes and between processes and the mission. Unfortunately, there is no sure method for determining if strategic goals are sufficient to achieve a mission or if a set of individual jobs or performances is sufficient to ensure achievement of strategic outcomes. Furthermore, it is difficult to determine if goals of a sufficient number and type have been set to ensure that all critical tasks are covered. Although many have written about the importance of linkages across organization levels, specific mechanisms for evaluating the adequacy of such linkages are scarce. Rummler and Brache (1995) suggest that the role responsibility matrix be used to identify specific responsibilities for each role required in supporting a strategic objective. Brethower (1982) recommends use of a job model in which outputs relevant to the marketplace are identified and correlated with specific job functions. In both cases, individual performance requirements are reviewed to determine if they add up to produce strategic outcomes, and job responsibilities are prioritized based on their value in achieving adaptive outcomes for the organization as a whole.

Mediation of the Effects of Delayed Events

System factors that influence performance across the three levels of organization, process, and performer can be characterized as remote, intermediate, and immediate; furthermore, at each point, both antecedents and consequences are relevant. This results in six categories of controlling variables: remote antecedents and consequences, intermediate antecedents and consequences, and immediate antecedents and consequences. At the remote point, the mission statement or statement of the philosophy of the organization serves as an antecedent controlling stimulus for the practices of an individual worker; annual or semiannual performance reviews or pay raises are typical remote consequences. At the intermediate point, typical antecedent stimuli involve descriptions of work processes or work flow, and consequences include the usual paycheck (delivered weekly or biweekly) along with recognition of effective performance that occurs infrequently but regularly (e.g., employee of the week). At the immediate point, directions and prompts given by a supervisor or peer, daily work assignments, and other similar events often serve as antecedent controlling stimuli, whereas performance feedback provided by a supervisor or peer or daily data on work quantity or quality might serve as consequences.

The linkages among these controlling conditions can be established to strengthen the relevance of individual practices for organization outcomes. For example, directions given by a supervisor or peer (immediate antecedent stimulus) might be based on a job description that is derived from a work process (intermediate antecedent stimulus) that contributes to quality of production and consumer satisfaction (mission-related outcomes). For consequences, the linkages can be established by arranging for immediate events to be correlated with intermediate outcomes and intermediate outcomes to be correlated with remote events. For example, incentive pay for sales personnel might be paid as a percentage of total sales volume, or team members might identify monthly quality goals on the way to quarterly and annual goals and track their success in achieving milestones along the way by plotting progress on a publicly posted graph.

It is likely that responses to remote events (e.g., reaction by an individual employee to the mission of the organization) are strengthened considerably through rule-governed behavior (Agnew and Redmon, 1992; Malott, 1992). Rules in such cases state the relationship between individual performance and organizational success and describe the conditions under which performance should occur along with the likely consequences of performing well. Rule statements probably serve as a discriminative stimuli that increase the probability of effective individual actions even in the absence of direct influences from customers or upper management. In fact, one could argue that correspondence among actions at all levels of a system can best be achieved by statement of clear rules about what is acceptable and what is unacceptable and the relationship and provision of rewards for individuals who follow the rules well. In this case, adaptive rules are those which specify performance that has a high probability of supporting an outcome essential to long-term survival, and faulty rules are those which produce damaging outcomes (e.g., result in poor product quality).

The approach presented here assumes organizations increase their chances of survival when they change dominant practices (i.e., the culture) in response to changes in the external environment. This appears to be especially true in recent times when the focus has been on the needs and preferences of consumers, a relatively changeable criterion relative to historical benchmarks such as industry standards, government regulations, or internal strategies (Du Gay and Salaman, 1992; Walton, 1986). Implicit within this approach is the assumption that cultures underlie ultimate effectiveness in that they consist of the events which affect individual performance on a day-to-day basis. Thus, much like an individual organism, an organization must be changeable; and the faster the change can occur in response to a threat, the greater the chances of survival. If the dominant practices within a culture can be described and their causes identified, then adaptation is possible. If this cannot be done, the lag time may be too long, and survival may be threatened.

EXAMPLES OF CULTURAL CHANGE VIA SYSTEMS ANALYSIS

An organization, like an individual, survives by adapting to the demands of its environment. This requires that cultural practices change when the external environment changes. Of course, the speed of change and extensiveness of shifts in practices are critical to adaptation. This point has been emphasized in recent strategy shifts by large corporations that have downsized or subdivided to create several smaller businesses, each with its own outcomes and independent strategic response capability.

An example of organizational adaptation is provided by a cultural intervention undertaken by Thorn EMI of Great Britain, a conglomerate that, at one time, included more than 100 business entities under a single corporate umbrella (Kennedy, 1989). A major portion of the business was in television and VCR rentals, including repair services. The company was designed to provide an inexpensive means of getting entertainment technology to residential consumers. When the company first offered these services, video technology was expensive and subject to frequent failures; thus, consumers found rentals to be an effective means of access equipment. In the 1980s, however, corporate executives noted that financial losses were mounting and began to identify contributing factors in the marketplace. They discovered that over the years: (1) video equipment had become easier and cheaper to manufacture, making it less expensive and more affordable to consumers; (2) electronics had become more reliable, thus reducing breakdowns and the need for repair service; and (3) lifestyles had changed, making service visits less convenient during the day. Executives realized that extensive changes were needed to save the company and instituted the following steps:

1. Workshops were held to clarify the goals of the business and to condense the statement of business objectives into a few sentences that were easily understood.

2. Other companies in the industry were studied as role models (benchmarking).
3. The mission was changed to emphasize flexible service and new product lines appropriate to current lifestyles (i.e., offer a level of service better than all others including twenty-four-hour, on-the-spot teams and new convenience products for rent).
4. The main office was reduced in size and the company was divided into six semiautonomous businesses.
5. Many basic practices were changed (e.g., the statistics department was eliminated and much of the routine paperwork was eliminated to speed service delivery and to free up time for employees).
6. The reward system was altered to support new practices.

The Thorn EMI approach represents a comprehensive change in mission, strategy, and practices brought about by declining market demand for existing products and services. Management discerned changes in demand and the resulting threat to the company and altered conditions at all levels of the system to create a coordinated response.

Other examples illustrate this comprehensive systems-based approach. Albrecht and Zemke (1985) reported one such case involving Scandinavian Airlines System (SAS). In the early 1980s SAS was struggling and reported severe losses. The president resigned and was replaced by Jan Carlzon, who immediately set about establishing a service culture in the company. Carlzon focused on customer satisfaction rather than the more mechanical aspects of air transportation and turned the company around in less than two years. Carlzon emphasized customer service as a mission and took steps to orient every person and every job toward that end. He implemented this new approach across all levels of the company simultaneously, including 20,000 employees in more than three countries in the transformation. Changes were implemented initially by a team of consultants and top managers who traveled from site to site teaching employees about the new approach and identifying new mission-level outcomes for the entire company.

Carlzon also used the following implementation methods in getting the comprehensive changes in place:

1. All employees and middle managers were trained in two-day workshops.
2. Top executives and union representatives were trained in a three-week intensive workshop on the philosophy and strategy of the service mission.

3. An internal consulting group was formed to help others overcome problems in getting the new program implemented.
4. Emphasis was changed from the average traveler to business flyers (i.e., a new business class was given top priority and special services were developed for this market segment).
5. A detailed plan was developed to make SAS the most punctual airline in Europe.

Carlzon and SAS developed a model that defined the important factors in creating a service culture from top to bottom in terms of a *service triangle*, which includes strategy, system, and people as major factors. *Strategy* includes the mission statement and the service package (output); the *system* includes all of the processes needed to create and deliver the service package; the *people* provide the behavior needed to operate the system. Also important in this model is motivation of individual performers; thus, feedback and rewards were arranged to strengthen practices that were in line with the service mission and consistent with strategic objectives underlying the mission (e.g., leaving and arriving on time and faster check-in for business class travelers). In Carlzon's terms, a series of repeated events that affect service (cycles of service) and individual interactions between organization members and customers (moments of truth) are at the base of a successful service culture. To reinforce the view that every performance is a critical performance, he was reported to monitor flight arrival and department times (via a monitor on his desk) and call pilots when they walked off their planes to ask why they were late. The information he obtained through these reports permitted him to identify many contributors to late arrivals and to address these in the overall design.

The SAS triangle of service is an excellent example of application of an adaptive systems model. Management monitored the success of the company in its marketplace and determined that a serious threat to survival existed. Subsequent action was taken to (1) alter the mission to appeal to other market segments and increase effectiveness with current segments, (2) establish new strategies that stated the revised mission in terms of achievable goals, (3) identify specific practices that would contribute to the new goals, and (4) provide support in the form of performance management methods (e.g., rewards, training, instructions) for individual practices. Like the systems models of Rummler and Brache (1995) and Gilbert (1978), the managed-service model incorporated organization, process, and performer levels and identified supporting and interfering events at the level of the individual along with general statements (rules) about what should be done overall. In everyday practice, a moment of truth supports a cycle of service that strengthens the service triangle and, hopefully, increases satisfaction in the marketplace.

MAINTENANCE OF EFFECTIVE CULTURAL PRACTICES

The focus of this chapter is change. Practices can produce cumulative outcomes, however, only if they are maintained. Thus, effective cultures must include continuing management of system processes. To accomplish this, relevant goals must be continuously set, adaptive practices rewarded, and resources allocated to support desired practices and outcomes (Rummler and Brache, 1995). Probably the least contaminated way of assessing maintenance involves the use of naturalistic observations on a regular basis (via probe measures at random) during which individual practices are observed at all levels. In particular, it is important to discern which practices appear to be encouraged and which appear to be discouraged by the actions of management and to assess the extent to which appropriate goals are set for departments and individuals. In such a system, one could determine whether dominant practices are consistent with or deviate from preferred practices and summarize the implications for the organization's survival.

SUMMARY

The methods described in this chapter show how a behavioral systems model can be used to describe, analyze, and change organizational cultures. As noted, the following general steps are important:

1. Description of the current culture in terms of an adaptive systems model.
2. Analysis of internal functions linked to important outcomes through at least three levels (organization, process, and performer).
3. Description of informal practices through naturalistic observation and their likely effects on important goals.
4. Pinpointing individual or small group practices that contribute to or detract from an organization's survival.
5. Systematic change in antecedents and consequences to strengthen adaptive practices and weaken ineffective or damaging practices.
6. Integration and maintenance of new practices and processes into organization structure.

REFERENCES

Agnew, J. L. and Redmon, W. K. (1992). Contingency specifying stimuli: The role of "rules" in organizational behavior management. *Journal of Organizational Behavior Management, 12*(2), 67-75.

Albrecht, K. and Zemke, R. (1985). *Service America!* New York: Warner.

Block, P. (1993). *Stewardship: Choosing service over self-interest.* San Francisco: Berrett-Koehler.

Brethower, D. (1982). The total performance system. In R. O'Brien, A. Dickinson, and M. Rosow (Eds.), *Industrial behavior modification* (pp. 350-369). New York: Pergamon.

Burke, M. J., Borucki, C. C., and Hurley, A. E. (1992). Reconceptualizing psychological climate in a retail service environment: A multiple-stakeholder perspective. *Journal of Applied Psychology, 77,* 717-729.

Deal, T. E. and Kennedy, A. A. (1982). *Corporate cultures: The rites and rituals of corporate life.* Reading, MA: Addison-Wesley.

Drucker, P. F. (1991). Choose your company's size. *Fortune,* December, 58-59.

Du Gay, P. and Salaman, G. (1992). The cult[ure] of the customer. *Journal of Management, 29*(5), 615-633.

Eubanks, J. L. and Lloyd, K. E. (1992). Relating behavior analysis to the organizational culture concept and perspective. *Journal of Organizational Behavior Management, 12*(2), 27-44.

Gilbert, T. F. (1978). *Human competence: Engineering worthy performance.* New York: McGraw-Hill.

Glenn, S. S. (1988). Contingencies and metacontingencies: Toward a synthesis of behavior analysis and cultural materialism. *The Behavior Analyst, 11,* 161-179.

Glenn, S. S. (1991). Relations among behavioral, cultural, and biological evolution. In P. A. Lamal (Ed.), *Behavioral analysis of societies and cultural practices* (pp. 39-73). Washington, DC: Hemisphere.

Hammer, M. and Champy, J. (1993). *Reengineering the corporation: A manifesto for business revolution.* New York: HarperCollins.

Harris, M. (1979). *Cultural materialism.* New York: Random House.

Huse, E. F. and Cummings, T. G. (1990). *Organizational development and change* (Fourth edition). Los Angeles: West.

Jewell, S. F. and Jewell, D. O. (1992). Organization design. In H. D. Stolovitch and E. J. Keeps (Eds.), *Handbook of human performance technology: A comprehensive guide for analyzing and solving performance problems in organizations* (pp. 211-232). San Francisco: Jossey-Bass.

Kennedy, C. (1989). Culture club: Companies with a mission to change. *Director,* December, 40-44.

Krapfl, J. E. and Gasparotto, G. (1982). Behavioral systems analysis. In L. W. Frederiksen (Ed.), *Organizational behavior management* (pp. 21-38). New York: Wiley.

Lamal, P. A. (Ed.). (1991a). *Behavioral analysis of societies and cultural practices.* Washington, DC: Hemisphere.

Lamal, P. A. (1991b). Aspects of some contingencies and metacontingencies in the Soviet Union. In P. A. Lamal (Ed.), *Behavioral analysis of societies and cultural practices* (pp. 77-85). Washington, DC: Hemisphere.

Malagodi, E. F., and Jackson, K. (1989). Behavior analysts and cultural analysis: Troubles and issues. *The Behavior Analyst, 12,* 17-33.

Malott, R. W. (1974). A behavioral-systems approach to the design of human services. In D. Harshbarger and R. Maley (Eds.), *Behavior analysis and systems analysis: An integrative approach to mental health programs.* Kalamazoo, MI: Behaviordelia.

Malott, R. W. (1988). Rule-governed behavior and behavioral anthropology. *The Behavior Analyst, 11,* 181-203.

Malott, R. W. (1992). A theory of rule-governed behavior and organizational behavior management. *Journal of Organizational Behavior Management, 12*(2), 45-65.

Malott, R. W. and Garcia, M. E. (1987). A goal-directed model for the design of human performance systems. *Journal of Organizational Behavior Management, 9(*1), 125-159.

Mawhinney, T. C. (1992a). Evolution of organizational cultures as selection by consequences: The Gaia hypothesis, metacontingencies, and organizational ecology. *Journal of Organizational Behavior Management, 12*(2), 1-26.

Mawhinney, T. C. (Ed.). (1992b). Organizational culture, rule-governed behavior and organizational behavior management [Special issue]. *Journal of Organizational Behavior Management, 12*(2).

Osborne, D. and Gaebler, T. (1992). *Reinventing government: How the entrepreneurial spirit is transforming the public sector.* Reading, MA: Addison-Wesley.

Peters, T. (1992). *Liberation management: Necessary disorganization for the nanosecond nineties.* New York: Alfred A. Knopf.

Pierce, W. D. (1991). Culture and society: The role of behavioral analysis. In P. A. Lamal (Ed.), *Behavioral analysis of societies and cultural practices* (pp. 13-37). Washington, DC: Hemisphere.

Powers, B. (1992). Strategic alignment. In H. D. Stolovitch and E. J. Keeps (Eds.), *Handbook of human performance technology: A comprehensive guide for analyzing and solving performance problems in organizations* (pp. 247-258). San Francisco: Jossey-Bass.

Redmon, W. K. and Agnew, J. L. (1991). Organizational behavioral analysis in the United States: A view from the private sector. In P. A. Lamal (Ed.), *Behavior analysis of societies and cultural practices* (pp. 125-139). Washington, DC: Hemisphere.

Redmon, W. K. and Wilk, L. A. (1991). Organizational behavioral analysis in the United States: Public sector organizations. In P. A. Lamal (Ed.), *Behavior analysis of societies and cultural practices* (pp. 107-123). Washington, DC: Hemisphere.

Reidenbach, R. E. and Robin, D. P. (1991). A conceptual model of corporate moral development. *Journal of Business Ethics, 10,* 273-284.

Rummler, G. A. and Brache, A. P. (1995). *Improving performance: How to manage the white space on the organization chart* (Second edition). San Francisco: Jossey-Bass.

Schein, E. H. (1990). Organizational culture. *American Psychologist, 45,* 109-119.

Schneider, B., Wheeler, J. K., and Cox, J. F. (1992). A passion for service: Using the content analysis to explicate service climate themes. *Journal of Applied Psychology, 77,* 705-716.

Scholtes, P. R. (1988). *The team handbook: How to use teams to improve quality.* Madison, WI: Joiner and Associates.

Skinner, B. F. (1953). *Science and human behavior.* New York: Macmillan.

Smith, J. M. and Chase, P. N. (1990). Using the vantage analysis chart to solve organization-wide problems. *Journal of Organizational Behavior Management, 11*(1), 127-148.

Stolovitch, H. D. and Keeps, E. J. (Eds.). (1992). *Handbook of human performance technology: A comprehensive guide for analyzing and solving performance problems in organizations.* San Francisco: Jossey-Bass.

Sulzer-Azaroff, B., Pollack, M. J., and Fleming, R. K. (1992). Organizational behavior management within structural and cultural constraints: An example from the human service sector. *Journal of Organizational Behavior Management, 12*(2), 117-137.

Walton, M. (1986). *The Deming management method.* New York: Perigee.

Epilogue

C. Merle Johnson
Thomas C. Mawhinney
William K. Redmon

You can observe a lot by watching.

Yogi Berra

We have been observing the field of organizational behavior management now for over twenty-five years. We have watched it move from its infancy in the 1970s to the stage of adulthood in the 1990s. As we begin the twenty-first century, behavior analysis and management shows continued promise as a field that produces reliable data regarding linkages among behavior of individuals and groups, their environmental contexts, and organizational performance.

Observing a lot by watching also validates the SURF & C methodology of performance appraisal described by Komaki and Reynard in Chapter 3. Too often managers assess performance in organizations without really watching. Decades of indirect measures of performance in organizational behavior may have utility in the global assessment of some dimensions of an individual or members of a work team. Nevertheless, measuring work behavior directly in the organizational setting is an essential step in learning how it is related to desired organizational performances. And far too often this critical step is skipped in favor of less reliable methods of "observation."

The promise of behavior analysis has been demonstrated in the various chapters of this text. Work safety, sales and marketing, training and development, occupational stress, pay for performance and reinforcement schedule effects, leadership, and systems analysis are all provinces that readily employ behavioral approaches. These chapters provide but a brief introduction to the many domains where behavioral approaches have been employed or have shown their promise in improving organizational performance.

The strength of organizational behavior management derives partly from its scientific grounding and empirical validation of techniques, and

457

partly from its implicit preference for humane prescriptions for managing individuals in diverse organizational settings. As Berthold noted in Chapter 16, the question whether behavioral principles used in various organizational settings conform to ethical standards of conduct has been the locus of controversy. We contend that the haphazard and sometimes inappropriate use of behavioral approaches is the problem. Aversive control is pervasive; unfortunately owners and managers frequently punish employee behavior and think nothing of it. Without the moniker behavioral principle attached to them, all sorts of aversive practices are uncritically accepted as standard operating procedures. Lack of knowledge regarding the side effects and ignorance in applying contingencies of reinforcement, both direct and indirect, is a major shortcoming in managing employee behavior.

Replacing aversive control with contingencies of positive reinforcement is one of the hallmarks of organizational behavior management. Slowly this transition is occurring in many organizational settings, sometimes through organizational culture change via training and education, sometimes through market influences such as employee turnover and reductions in market share for poorly managed companies, and sometimes through government regulation or accreditation standards. Although we believe these changes are reassuring, the pace of change is often slow and some of the regulatory or "watchdog" organizations would benefit as much from embracing organizational behavior management methods as the organizations they oversee. For example, when is the last time you received a letter of thanks from the Internal Revenue Service?

The changes in work behavior and the boom in information technology also have led to organizational change. People are more aware of aversive control in many organizations as well as the positive contingencies of reinforcement in others. For example, public awareness of the best companies for which to work draws applicants in such great numbers that these companies have little difficulty attracting and keeping the best employees. Moreover, stock options for established corporations and entrepreneurs in many start-up companies demonstrate the power of rule-governed behavior in both direct and indirect contingencies of reinforcement. These examples give us an optimistic view of the future. We strongly believe that these cleverly designed contingency-specifying stimuli have fueled the ongoing economic boom in the United States and in other market-driven countries in the global economy. Positive contingencies of reinforcement, rather than aversive control, are better ways to manage people and produce organizational change that is more humane and effective. Concerning the

Epilogue   459

question of how a culture should arrange contingencies to achieve enthusiastic participation and support among its members, Skinner said:

> ... the answer depends on how people are induced to work for the good of their culture. If they do so under the threat of punishment, then freedom (from such a threat) is sacrificed, but if they are induced to do so through positive reinforcement, their sense of freedom is enhanced. (1978, pp. 197-198)

We hope to see behavior analysis and management continue to expand its theoretical, technical, humane, and organizational horizons in the new century. The promise is great and the reinforcement for carrying this out is rich. We hope you will be among those who help us promote it.

REFERENCE

Skinner, B. F. (1978). *Reflections on behaviorism and society*. Englewood Cliffs, NJ: Prentice-Hall.

Index

Page numbers followed by the letter "i" indicate illustrations; those followed by the letter "n" indicate notes; those followed by the letter "t" indicate tables.

461

Order Your Own Copy of
This Important Book for Your Personal Library!

HANDBOOK OF ORGANIZATIONAL PERFORMANCE
Behavior Analysis and Management

_____ in hardbound at $92.95 (ISBN: 0-7890-1086-0)

_____ in softbound at $49.95 (ISBN: 0-7890-1087-9)

COST OF BOOKS_____

OUTSIDE USA/CANADA/
MEXICO: ADD 20%_____

POSTAGE & HANDLING_____
(US: $4.00 for first book & $1.50
for each additional book
Outside US: $5.00 for first book
& $2.00 for each additional book)

SUBTOTAL_____

IN CANADA: ADD 7% GST_____

STATE TAX_____
(NY, OH & MN residents, please
add appropriate local sales tax)

FINAL TOTAL_____
(If paying in Canadian funds,
convert using the current
exchange rate. UNESCO
coupons welcome.)

☐ **BILL ME LATER:** ($5 service charge will be added)
(Bill-me option is good on US/Canada/Mexico orders only;
not good to jobbers, wholesalers, or subscription agencies.)

☐ Check here if billing address is different from
shipping address and attach purchase order and
billing address information.

Signature_____

☐ **PAYMENT ENCLOSED: $**_____

☐ **PLEASE CHARGE TO MY CREDIT CARD.**

☐ Visa   ☐ MasterCard   ☐ AmEx   ☐ Discover
☐ Diner's Club   ☐ Eurocard   ☐ JCB

Account # _____

Exp. Date _____

Signature _____

Prices in US dollars and subject to change without notice.

NAME _____

INSTITUTION _____

ADDRESS _____

CITY _____

STATE/ZIP _____

COUNTRY _____ COUNTY (NY residents only) _____

TEL _____ FAX _____

E-MAIL_____

May we use your e-mail address for confirmations and other types of information? ☐ Yes   ☐ No
We appreciate receiving your e-mail address and fax number. Haworth would like to e-mail or fax special
discount offers to you, as a preferred customer. **We will never share, rent, or exchange your e-mail
address or fax number.** We regard such actions as an invasion of your privacy.

Order From Your Local Bookstore or Directly From
The Haworth Press, Inc.
10 Alice Street, Binghamton, New York 13904-1580 • USA
TELEPHONE: 1-800-HAWORTH (1-800-429-6784) / Outside US/Canada: (607) 722-5857
FAX: 1-800-895-0582 / Outside US/Canada: (607) 772-6362
E-mail: getinfo@haworthpressinc.com
PLEASE PHOTOCOPY THIS FORM FOR YOUR PERSONAL USE.
www.HaworthPress.com

BOF00